Foundation Learning Guide
Designing Cisco Network Service Architectures (ARCH)
Third Edition

John Tiso

Cisco Press

800 East 96th Street

Indianapolis, IN 46240

Foundation Learning Guide

Designing Cisco Network Service Architectures (ARCH)

Third Edition

John Tiso

Copyright © 2012 Cisco Systems, Inc.

Published by:
Cisco Press
800 East 96th Street
Indianapolis, IN 46240 USA

Printed in the United States of America

Fifth Printing: February 2015

Library of Congress Cataloging-in-Publication Data

Tiso, John.
    Authorized self-study guide designing Cisco network service architectures (arch) / John Tiso. -- 3rd ed.
        p. cm.
    Rev. ed. of: Authorized self-study guide / Hutton, Keith. 2009. 2nd ed.
    ISBN 978-1-58714-288-8 (hardcover)
    1.   Computer network architectures--Examinations--Study guides.   2.   Computer networks--Design--Examinations--Study guides.   3.   Internetworking (Telecommunication)--Examinations--Study guides.   I. Hutton, Keith. Authorized self-study guide. II. Title.
    TK5105.52.H98 2012
    004.6'5--dc23

                                                                          2011036250

ISBN-13: 978-1-58714-288-8

ISBN-10: 1-58714-288-0

Warning and Disclaimer

Trademark Acknowledgments

Corporate and Government Sales

The publisher offers excellent discounts on this book when ordered in quantity for bulk purchases or special sales, which may include electronic versions and/or custom covers and content particular to your business, training goals, marketing focus, and branding interests. For more information, please contact:

U.S. Corporate and Government Sales
1-800-382-3419
corpsales@pearsontechgroup.com

For sales outside the United States, please contact:
International Sales
international@pearsoned.com

Feedback Information

At Cisco Press, our goal is to create in-depth technical books of the highest quality and value. Each book is crafted with care and precision, undergoing rigorous development that involves the unique expertise of members from the professional technical community.

Readers' feedback is a natural continuation of this process. If you have any comments regarding how we could improve the quality of this book, or otherwise alter it to better suit your needs, you can contact us through e-mail at feedback@ciscopress.com. Please make sure to include the book title and ISBN in your message.

We greatly appreciate your assistance.

Publisher: Paul Boger	**Cisco Press Program Manager:** Jeff Brady
Associate Publisher: Dave Dusthimer	**Technical Editors:** Diane Teare; Dr. Peter J. Welcher
Executive Editor: Brett Bartow	**Development Editor:** Marianne Bartow
Managing Editor: Sandra Schroeder	**Copy Editor:** Keith Cline
Project Editor: Mandie Frank	**Proofreader:** Sheri Cain
Editorial Assistant: Vanessa Evans	**Indexer:** Tim Wright
Designer: Gary Adair	**Composition:** Mark Shirar

About the Author

John Tiso, CCIE #5162, CCDP is a Product Manager at Cisco Systems. His current responsibilities include the product management of Cisco's training and certification programs around design and architecture. Before working with Cisco, John held various engineering and architecture roles in the Cisco partner channel. In addition to his CCIE and CCDP certifications, he holds multiple industry certifications from Cisco, Microsoft, CompTIA, and Sun Microsystems. He holds a Graduate Citation in strategic management from Harvard University and a Bachelor of Science degree in computer science and mathematics from Adelphi University. John is a published author and has served as a technical editor for both McGraw-Hill and Cisco Press. He has spoken multiple times at the Cisco Live! (Networkers) conference and the national CIPTUG conference. He has served as an expert on Cisco's NetPro Forum "Ask the Expert" online events. John currently resides in Amherst, New Hampshire, with his wife, three children, and his running partner, Molly (who never complains, but sometimes barks). He is a nine-time marathon finisher, including five Boston Marathons. He can be reached at johnt@jtiso.com.

Contributing Author

Ed Caswell is a Systems Engineering Manager at Cisco Systems. Ed has spoken several times at the CIPTUG national convergence event and many times at regional architectural conferences. He has served as a Subject Matter Expert (SME) on many industry panels. Ed has also edited several collaboration books for Cisco Press. Prior to Cisco, Ed held positions in system management and other individual contributor roles. He is considered a trusted collaboration expert in the industry. Ed is a military veteran and an active member of his community.

About the Technical Reviewers

Diane Teare, P.Eng, CCNP, CCDP, PMP, is a professional in the networking, training, project management, and e-learning fields. She has more than 25 years of experience in designing, implementing, and troubleshooting network hardware and software, and has been involved in teaching, course design, and project management. She has extensive knowledge of network design and routing technologies, and is an instructor with one of the largest authorized Cisco Learning Partners. She was the director of e-learning for the same company, where she was responsible for planning and supporting all the company's e-learning offerings in Canada, including Cisco courses. Diane has a Bachelor's degree in applied science in electrical engineering and a Master's degree in applied science in management science. She authored or co-authored the Cisco Press titles *Implementing Cisco IP Routing (ROUTE) Foundation Learning Guide*; the previous (second) edition of *Designing Cisco Network Service Architectures (ARCH)*; *Campus Network Design Fundamentals*; the three editions of *Authorized Self-Study Guide Building Scalable Cisco Internetworks (BSCI)*; and *Building Scalable Cisco Networks*. Diane edited the *Authorized Self-Study Guide Designing for Cisco Internetwork Solutions (DESGN)* (the first two editions) and the *Designing Cisco Networks*.

Dr. Peter J. Welcher, CCIE #1773, works for Chesapeake NetCraftsmen, a small but highly skilled Cisco Gold Partner with a stellar reputation in the industry. Pete has developed numerous design and other courses for Cisco while teaching and consulting. His consulting includes campus and data center design and migration to N x 10-Gbps technology and 6500 VSS plus NAC for a fairly large federal agency, data center assessment, and other design-related work with a large international hotel chain, design review for two universities, redesign for a internationally known university and research hospital, WAN/QoS for a federal agency with more than 250,000 employees, WLAN pilot design that may impact another large federal agency, work for two New York stock market quotation firms, and so on. He has reviewed a number of book proposals and done tech edits in the past for Cisco Press and is well known in the industry. Pete is currently focusing on data center technology and enjoys teaching the Nexus class one week a month. He has also written more than 170 blog posts (a number that might be significantly larger by the time these words see print).

Acknowledgments

I want to acknowledge and thank the following persons.

The team at Cisco Press, especially Brett Bartow, for pulling everything together and listening to my rants. Marianne Bartow for tolerating my poor formatting, whining, and general mistakes. Marianne, you made it all happen. Thank you!

The technical editors: Dr. Peter Welcher and Diane Teare. Your feedback kept me honest.

Ed Caswell for his contributions to the book.

All the friends and co-workers who have been supportive of me over the past few years.

My wife, Lauren, and my children, Danny, Nick and Katie, for tolerating me and just for being a great family!

Finally, you, the reader and certification candidate. Without you, I would have neither the opportunity to work on this nor a job. Good luck in what you seek.

Contents at a Glance

Contents

Icons Used in This Book

 Access Point

 Cisco Unified Communications Manager

 Router

 Bridge

 Hub

 DSU/CSU

 Cisco IP Phone

 H.323 Device

 PBX

 Catalyst Switch

 Multilayer Switch

 ATM Switch

 ISDN/Frame Relay Switch

 Content Switch

 Voice-Enabled Router

 Router with Firewall

 Communication Server

 Gateway

 Access Server

 Phone

 Netflow Router

 VPN Concentrator

 Network Management Appliance

 DSLAM

 Wide Area Application Engine

 WiSM

 Optical Services Router

 Lightweight Double Radio Access Point

 WLAN Controller

 PC with Software

 Terminal

 File Server

 Web Server

 Cisco Works Workstation

 Modem

 PC

 Printer

 Laptop

 Cisco Security MARS

 NAC Appliance

 PIX Security Appliance

 Network Cloud

 Cisco SN 5428-2 iSCSI Storage Router

 Optical Transport

 NAS

 InfiniBand

 WAFS

 IDS

 Token Ring

 FDDI

 Line: Ethernet

Line: Serial

Line: Switched Serial

 Wireless Connection

Command Syntax Conventions

The conventions used to present command syntax in this book are the same conventions used in the IOS Command Reference. The Command Reference describes these conventions as follows:

- **Boldface** indicates commands and keywords that are entered literally as shown. In actual configuration examples and output (not general command syntax), boldface indicates commands that are manually input by the user (such as a **show** command).

- *Italic* indicates arguments for which you supply actual values.

- Vertical bars (|) separate alternative, mutually exclusive elements.

- Square brackets ([ ]) indicate an optional element.

- Braces ({ }) indicate a required choice.

- Braces within brackets ([{ }]) indicate a required choice within an optional element.

Foreword

With emerging IT trends such as virtualization, data center, collaboration, and mobility, the demands placed on network professionals have become more varied and sophisticated. Knowledge of networking fundamentals is no longer sufficient. Network professionals must understand networking systems with integrated security, wireless, and voice capabilities.

The technology evolution is creating a global IT skills gap, as corporations, regardless of size, industry, or geography, seek professionals who have more than product and technology skills. Instead, the focus on today's IT professional is their ability to fulfill real-world job role requirements. In fact, new careers in IT are being established that are based more on complex services and architectures than systems.

In support of the industry's demand for "the right resources, at the right place, at the right time," Cisco remains dedicated to the development of the next-generation IT workforce. Assessment of an individual's knowledge and ability to perform the required job tasks of a particular role is measured by the Cisco Career and Specialist Certifications, which are recognized worldwide.

Cisco Press, an industry leader in networking education content, offers the only self-study books authorized by Cisco. The Cisco Press exam certification guides and preparation materials offer exceptional and flexible access to the knowledge and information required to stay current in one's field of expertise or to gain new skills. Whether used to increase internetworking skills or as a supplement to a formal certification preparation course, these materials offer networking professionals the information and knowledge required to perform on-the-job tasks proficiently.

Additional authorized Cisco instructor-led courses are available exclusively through our Authorized Cisco Learning Partners worldwide. Other self-study materials including e-learning, practice exams, labs, and simulations are available from the Cisco Learning Network, our Web 2.0 social learning community. To learn more, visit https://learningnetwork.cisco.com. I hope that you find this material to be an essential part of your education, exam preparation, and professional development and that it becomes a valuable addition to your personal library.

Tejas R. Vashi
Director, Product Management
Cisco Technical Services

August 2011

Authors Note

This self-study work has received GOLD certification as an IPv6 certified course from the IPv6 forum for the content of this book. The related certification—CCDP—has received GOLD certification as an IPv6 certified certification as well. As a networking design professional, please keep IPv6 in the forefront of your designs:

Introduction

Designing Cisco Network Service Architectures (ARCH), Third Edition, covers how to perform the conceptual, intermediate, and detailed design of a network infrastructure. This design supports network solutions over intelligent network services to achieve effective performance, scalability, and availability of the network. This book enables readers, applying solid Cisco network solution models and best design practices, to provide viable and stable enterprise internetworking solutions. In addition, the book has been written to help candidates prepare for the Designing Cisco Network Service Architectures Exam (642-874 ARCH). This exam is one of the requirements for the Cisco Certified Design Professional (CCDP) certification. This exam tests a candidate's knowledge of the latest development in network design and technologies, including network infrastructure, intelligent network services, and converged network solutions.

Since the first edition was published in 2004, the Designing Cisco Network Services Architectures (ARCH) authorized training course has been updated to keep pace with the industry. Therefore, the exam was consequently updated to match these changes. This led to the immediate need for an update to this examination preparation text. Readers of the previous edition of this work can use this text to update their knowledge and skill sets.

In certain cases, parts of this book may discuss obsolete, end-of-life, or suboptimal configurations. This ensures that the book aligns with the ARCH exam. Whenever possible, this is noted.

Goals of This Book

Upon completing this book, you will be able to meet these objectives:

■ Introduce the Cisco Borderless Networks architectural framework and explain how it addresses enterprise network needs for performance, scalability, security, unified communications, and availability.

■ Describe how the Cisco enterprise architectures are used in the Borderless Networks framework for designing enterprise networks.

■ Create intermediate and detailed enterprise campus network, enterprise edge, and remote infrastructure designs that offer effective functionality, performance, scalability, and availability.

■ Create conceptual, intermediate, and detailed intelligent network service designs for network management, high availability, security, quality of service (QoS), and IP multicast.

■ Create conceptual, intermediate, and detailed virtual private network (VPN) designs.

Prerequisite Knowledge

Although enthusiastic readers will tackle less-familiar topics with some energy, a sound grounding in networking is advised. To gain the most from this book, you should be familiar with internetworking technologies, Cisco products, and Cisco IOS Software features. Although exams for the CCDP (or Cisco Certified Network Professional [CCNP]) do not require you to pass them in order, I strongly advise you to consider passing them in order because the program builds on itself. This book is also an excellent resource to learn about Borderless Networks (perhaps even in preparation for the Cisco Systems Borderless Networks Specialization certification).

Note Many Cisco specialist certifications are aligned to Channel Partner specialization requirements. Channel Partner employees should access the Partner Education Connection (Cisco.com partner level access) to find the latest roadmaps and information as it pertains to Channel Partner certifications and requirements. Specialization certifications are open to all members of the public and are not limited to Channel Partner employees.

This book covers the following topics to aid your journey toward CCDP certification:

- How to design the necessary services to extend IP addresses using variable-length subnet masking (VLSM), Network Address Translation (NAT), and route summarization

- How to implement appropriate networking routing protocols, such as Open Shortest Path First (OSPF), Enhanced Interior Gateway Routing Protocol (EIGRP), and Border Gateway Protocol (BGP) on an existing internetwork

- How to redistribute routes between different routing protocols

- The required Cisco products and services that enable connectivity and traffic transport for a multilayer campus network

- Design of data center services

- The necessary services at each layer of the network to enable all users to obtain membership in multicast groups in a working enterprise network

- How to control network traffic by implementing the necessary admission policy at each layer of the network topology

- How to identify the appropriate hardware and software solutions for a given set of WAN technology requirements, including access between a central campus, branch offices, and telecommuters

- The Cisco equipment to establish appropriate WAN connections

- How to use protocols and technologies that enable traffic flow between multiple sites while minimizing the amount of overhead traffic on each connection

- QoS capabilities to ensure that mission-critical applications receive the required bandwidth within a given WAN topology

- How to implement Cisco Unified Communications

- How to implement Cisco wireless solutions

- How to implement basic security steps and mitigation techniques

How This Book Is Organized

Of course, you can read the chapters in this book sequentially, but the organization of this book also allows you to focus your reading on specific topics of interest. For example, if you want to focus on advanced routing design, you can skim Chapters 1 and 2 (which cover Borderless Networks and the elements of the enterprise campus network design), and then focus on the advanced IP addressing and routing topics in Chapter 3. Each chapter examines topics around a specific set of design issues. Specifically, the chapters in this book cover the following topics:

- Chapter 1, "The Cisco Enterprise Architecture," introduces the methodology configured for network engineers to design scalable, robust infrastructures to support today's complicated business applications. This includes the Cisco Borderless Networks architecture.

- Chapter 2, "Enterprise Campus Network Design," reviews high-availability designs and how to implement optimal redundancy. An in-depth look at recommended practices for Layer 2 and Layer 3 design elements follows. A discussion of the Layer 2 to Layer 3 boundary designs and issues concludes with a number of considerations for supporting infrastructure services.

- Chapter 3, "Developing an Optimum Design for Layer 3," begins by reviewing the importance of IP address planning, and then covers advanced routing elements. Discussions focus on scalable EIGRP, OSPF, and BGP designs.

- Chapter 4, "Advanced WAN Services Design Considerations," covers advanced WAN service layers. This overview goes into more detail about the common WAN optical technologies of Synchronous Optical Network (SONET), Synchronous Digital Hierarchy (SDH), dense wave-division multiplexing (DWDM), and Resilient Packet Ring. A discussion about Metro Ethernet, Virtual Private Line Service (VPLS), and Multiprotocol Label Switching virtual private network (MPLS VPN) technologies follows (and includes an examination of a number of design considerations). The discussion then turns to implementing advanced WAN services.

- Chapter 5, "Enterprise Data Center Design," focuses on the enterprise data center, and covers the data center architecture model and design consideration in the data center core, aggregation, and access layers. The discussion then turns to scaling, with a look at how to scale a three-layer data center architecture.

- Chapter 6, "SAN Design Considerations," covers storage-area networks, from components and topologies to SAN technologies. SAN design factors center on port density and topology, with some discussion about extending the SAN with various protocols.

- Chapter 7, "E-Commerce Module Design," begins with an e-commerce overview and a look at the components of high availability in this module. The chapter covers common e-commerce design components, designing an integrated e-commerce architecture, and how to fine-tune e-commerce designs.

- Chapter 8, "Security Services Design," delves into designing firewall services in various scenarios. The chapter also covers network admission control services, with a review of Cisco Network Admission Control (NAC) appliance fundamentals and NAC Appliance Server (NAS) deployment options and designs. The discussion then turns to intrusion-detection and -prevention design.

- Chapter 9, "IPsec and SSL VPN Design," examines remote-access VPN design. Site-to-site VPN designs are covered, too. This chapter also covers IPsec VPN technologies, including Cisco Easy VPN, generic routing encapsulation (GRE) over IPsec, and Dynamic Multipoint VPN (DMVPN). Recommendations for managing VPNs and considerations for scaling VPNs conclude the chapter.

- Chapter 10, "IP Multicast Design," covers IP multicast and multicast routing. Topics covered in this chapter include Protocol Independent Multicast (PIM), rendezvous points, and securing IP multicast.

- Chapter 11, "Network Management Capabilities Within Cisco IOS Software," examines Cisco network management capabilities embedded in Cisco IOS Software. This chapter also covers the syslog process, NetFlow, and Network-Based Application Recognition (NBAR), with a focus on the Cisco technologies themselves and how they enable other discovery tools, including Cisco AutoQoS. The chapter concludes with an overview of IP service-level agreement (SLA) measurements.

This book also contains an appendix and an acronym list:

- Appendix A, "Answers to Review Questions," provides the answers to all the chapter-ending review questions.

- Appendix B, "Acronyms and Abbreviations," identifies abbreviations, acronyms, and initialisms used in this book.

- Appendix C, "VoWLAN Design," introduces the Cisco Unified Wireless Network and examines requirements for voice over WLAN in the enterprise network. This appendix, which was Chapter 11 in the previous edition, also discusses VoWLAN coverage considerations and the site-survey process. It has been moved here because the matter within is not part of the ARCH exam in this version.

Note   The website references in this book were accurate at the time of this writing. However, some might have changed since then. If a URL is unavailable, you can always search using the title as keywords in your favorite search engine.

Chapter 1

The Cisco Enterprise Architecture

Upon completing this chapter, you will be able to

■ Explain the Cisco enterprise architecture

■ Describe how the Cisco enterprise architecture is used to design enterprise networks

■ Explain the Cisco six-phase network lifecycle methodology: prepare, plan, design, implement, operate, and optimize

The Cisco enterprise architecture is a methodology configured for network engineers to design scalable robust infrastructures to support today's complicated business applications. When implemented correctly, the design methodology provides a foundation that is easily scalable with both tactical and strategic support for business applications. This architecture includes not only design and implementation guidelines but also measurement and documentation principles. When used properly, this methodology provides a complete systematic approach to design and implementation.

Reviewing Cisco Enterprise Architecture

The rich variety of application-level business solutions available today, and the need to integrate these applications, has driven the establishment of a new network architecture. This chapter reviews the hierarchical network model. It also discusses how Cisco network architectures for the enterprise take into account new developments in the enterprise environment, such as worker mobility, collaboration across the enterprise, and the use of data and desktop virtualization. The chapter describes how network services can be leveraged to deliver consistent application performance and user experience across the enterprise network Borderless Network. It also identifies and describes modularity in the enterprise architecture.

The Hierarchical Model

The foundation of the Cisco network architecture is the hierarchical network model. Historically used in the design of enterprise LAN and WAN data networks, a hierarchical model also applies to the infrastructure modules of Borderless Networks and the Cisco enterprise architecture. Figure 1-1 shows the layers in the hierarchical model.

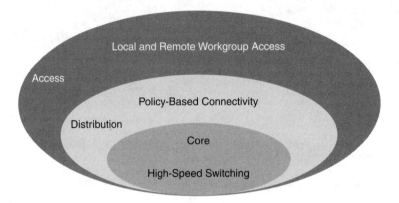

Figure 1-1 *Layers in the Hierarchical Model*

The hierarchical network model provides a modular view of a network, making it easier to design and build a deterministic scalable infrastructure. The hierarchical network structure is composed of the access, distribution, and core layers. Each layer has its own functions, which are used to develop a hierarchical design.

The model provides a modular framework that enables flexibility in design and facilitates ease of implementation and troubleshooting. The hierarchical network model divides networks into the access, distribution, and core layers, with these features:

- **Access layer:** Grants user access to network devices. In a network campus, the access layer generally incorporates switched LAN devices with ports that provide connectivity to workstations (including virtualized desktops), IP phones, servers, and wireless access points. In the WAN environment, the access layer for teleworkers or remote sites may provide entry to the corporate network across WAN technology.

- **Distribution layer:** Aggregates the wiring closets, using switches to segment workgroups and isolate network problems in a campus environment. Similarly, the distribution layer aggregates WAN connections at the edge of the campus and provides policy-based connectivity.

- **Core layer (also referred to as the backbone):** A high-speed backbone, designed to switch packets as fast as possible. Because the core is critical for connectivity, it must provide a high level of availability and adapt quickly to changes. It also provides scalability and fast convergence and an integration point for data center virtualization.

Example Hierarchical Network

Figure 1-2 shows a network mapped to the hierarchical model.

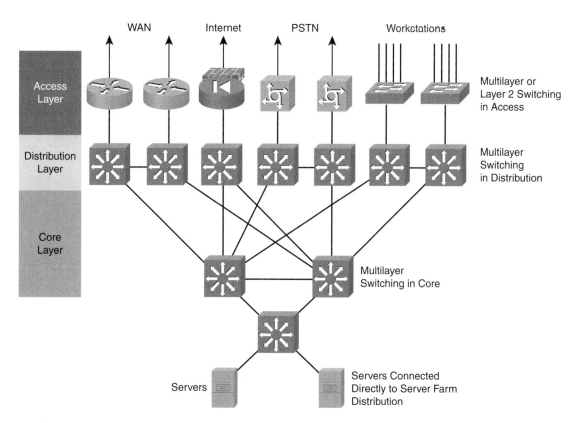

Figure 1-2   *A Hierarchical Network*

The enterprise hierarchical layer model contains the following components:

- **Access layer:** Access layer devices control traffic by localizing service requests to the access media. Access layer devices must also provide connectivity without compromising network integrity. For example, the devices at the access layer must detect whether a user workstation is legitimate, with minimal authentication steps.

- **Distribution layer:** Distribution layer devices control access to resources that are available at the core layer and must, therefore, make efficient use of bandwidth. In addition, a distribution layer device must address the quality of service (QoS) needs for different protocols by implementing policy-based traffic control to isolate backbone and local environments. Policy-based traffic control enables you to prioritize traffic to ensure the best performance for the most time-critical and time-dependent applications.

■   **Core layer:** Core layer devices provide services that optimize communication transport within the network. In addition, core layer devices are expected to provide maximum availability and reliability with minimum packet processing. Core layer devices
should be able to maintain connectivity when the circuits that connect them fail. A
fault-tolerant network design ensures that failures do not have a major impact on network connectivity.

Enterprise Network Design for Cisco Architectures

Cisco developed three overlapping architectures for the enterprise as part of a network
architecture and design, as shown in Figure 1-3: Borderless Networks, collaboration, and
virtualization (data center and desktop). This section describes these architectures and
the developments in the enterprise network they represent.

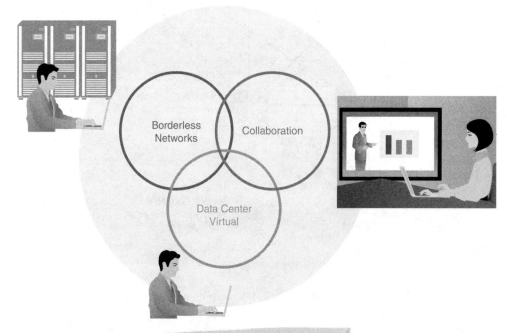

Figure 1-3   *Enterprise Network Design for Cisco Architectures*

Enterprise network design is about ensuring a consistent user experience and meeting
business objectives. Enterprises depend on different applications for productivity. With
few exceptions, most applications today are network enabled. To perform their daily
tasks, workers require access to network tools and applications. Therefore, users expect
and need to have access to networks and resources any time of day and from any location. These factors affect the network design and architecture.

Traditionally, the network support organizations of large enterprises have been segmented by technology domain or location. For example, an enterprise would have a server support team, storage support team, campus LAN support team, and a WAN and branch office support team. Although this segmentation may be sensible from a support standpoint, it often leads to segmented network design. Each individual team designs and implements new solutions to meet its specific challenges. The risk of this approach is that application accessibility and performance may vary, depending on the location of the users and how they access their applications.

Therefore, Cisco has taken a more holistic approach to network architectures for the enterprise. Instead of dividing the network by location or technology, three different overlapping domains are identified. Each domain centers on a specific development in the enterprise environment. By focusing on these three domains (Borderless Networks, collaboration, and data center virtualization), architectures can be developed to support current and future application and user requirements and to ensure a consistent high-quality user experience on the network.

Network designs should be able to adapt to new developments and trends in the enterprise environment. Cisco has identified three major trends and created architectures around them:

- **Borderless Networks:** Increasingly, workers are more mobile. More workers are working from different locations: the office, home, even the road. Also, working hours are shifting. Instead of the traditional 9 to 5 workday, working hours have become more flexible. The traditional boundaries between work and private lives are becoming blurred. Users are bringing a new mix of devices to the network, such as personal digital assistants (PDA), tablets, smart phones, and cameras. The Borderless Network architecture was specifically created to manage these new developments and deliver a consistent user experience to all users—anywhere, anytime, and from any device.

- **Collaboration:** Communication methods are constantly changing (for example, instant messaging, video conferencing, IP telephony, and social networking). Workers use these communication methods as a way to communicate with co-workers, partners, and customers and switch between these methods based on their needs. The collaboration architecture aims at building a network that integrates all these different means of communication and an infrastructure that is ready to support this mix of multimedia applications.

- **Data center virtualization:** The Borderless Networks and collaboration architectures focus on the changes in communication and work styles. In contrast, the data center virtualization architecture does not focus on the user, but on the provisioning of applications and services available to the user. Data centers contain the back-end services and data that enable the applications that are used in the enterprise. To ensure that applications can be scaled as demand changes, it is important that data centers be built in a cost-effective, energy-efficient, resilient and scalable manner. This is what the data center virtualization architecture was designed to provide.

A point that all three architectures have in common is that they begin with the business benefits that are delivered by the applications they enable. They provide a complete architecture that ensures a consistent user experience for all of these applications.

Each of the three architectures leverages a different set of technologies to achieve its design objectives. On the other hand, there is no strict separation; a certain amount of overlap exists between the three domains. They work together to deliver the desired user experience and associated benefits. For example, security technologies play a key role in the Borderless Networks architecture because of its focus on connectivity from anywhere using any device. However, security is also a design consideration in the collaboration and data center virtualization architectures.

As shown in Figure 1-4, each of the architectures leverages a different set of supporting technologies. The technologies in the Borderless Networks architecture focus on providing high-performance secure mobile connectivity. The technologies that are used in the collaboration architecture focus on integrating many different types of communication methods and devices. The technologies in the data center virtualization architecture focus on provisioning data storage and computing resources to applications in a highly scalable and resilient manner by leveraging virtualization technology.

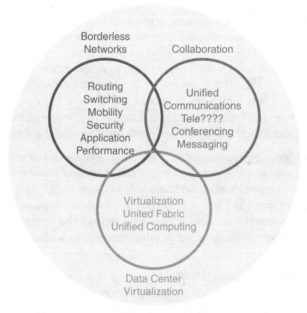

Figure 1-4   *Enterprise Network Design for Cisco Architectures (Continued)*

Service and Application Integration

All three architectures in the Cisco network architectures for the enterprise have in common a focus on application delivery. In addition to providing connectivity, the network should deliver various applications and services to ensure a consistently high-quality user experience.

Ultimately, all enterprise networks are built to enable the applications that are needed to support the enterprise's primary business processes. The applications deliver the tangible business benefits. User experience is central in realizing the potential of an application. If consistent application performance cannot be guaranteed, business benefits that are associated with that application are lost.

Therefore, network design should not focus just on providing connectivity and bandwidth; ensuring a high-quality user experience by optimizing application performance should also be a major consideration.

This is why the Cisco network architectures for the enterprise incorporate common network services in the frameworks. For example, the Borderless Networks and collaboration architectures are built on a medianet network foundation. A medianet is an intelligent network (IN) that is optimized for rich media, such as voice and video.

When these services are built in to the network foundation, many different multimedia applications can use the same set of services, which simplifies the overall design and increases interoperability between the different applications. Allowing applications to share common services, instead of providing separate services for each application, leads to more rapid and efficient application deployment.

Therefore, network service design is an essential part of any network design.

Network Services

This section describes the network services that are provided by the medianet architecture. The main purpose of this architecture is to move these specific services into the network, providing the services and resources required to support advanced media-based technologies.

Figure 1-5 illustrates an example of typical network services.

The Cisco medianet architecture includes network services such as the following:

■ **Network management:** Includes LAN management for advanced management of multilayer switches; routed WAN management for monitoring, traffic management, and access control to administer the routed infrastructure of multiservice networks; service management for managing and monitoring service-level agreements (SLA); and virtual private network (VPN) and security management for optimizing VPN performance and security administration.

■ **High availability:** Ensures end-to-end availability for services, clients, and sessions. Implementation includes reliable, fault-tolerant network devices (to automatically identify and overcome failures) and resilient network technologies.

■ **QoS:** Manages the delay, delay-variation (jitter), bandwidth-availability, and packet-loss parameters on a network to meet the diverse needs of voice, video, and data applications. QoS features provide value-added functionality such as Network-Based Application Recognition (NBAR) for classifying traffic on an application basis, a Service Assurance Agent (SAA) for end-to-end QoS measurements, Resource Reservation Protocol (RSVP) signaling for admission control and reservation of resources, and various configurable queue-insertion and -servicing disciplines.

■ **IP multicasting:** Provides bandwidth-conserving technology that reduces network traffic by delivering a single stream of information that is intended for many corporate recipients and homes throughout the transport network. Multicasting enables distribution of video conferencing, corporate communications, distance learning, distribution of software, and other applications. Multicast packets are replicated only as necessary in the network by Cisco routers that are enabled with Protocol Independent Multicast (PIM) and other supporting multicast protocols, resulting in the most efficient delivery of data to multiple receivers

■ **Transcoding:** Digital signal processors (DSP) that are embedded in routers, such as the Cisco Integrated Services Routers Generation 2 (ISR G2), can be used to transcode or transrate voice and video streams to adapt the media stream to match the client device and bandwidth limitations. By providing transcoding and transrating services, multimedia applications can be optimized to ensure a consistent high-quality user experience across the entire Borderless Network.

■ **Authentication and encryption:** IP Security (IPsec) and Cisco IOS Secure Sockets Layer VPN (SSL VPN) capabilities that are embedded in network devices provide authentication and encryption services to ensure data integrity and confidentiality on the network.

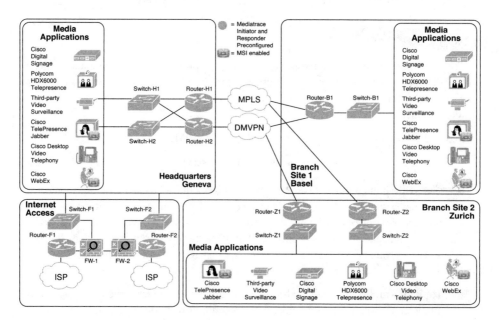

Figure 1-5 *Network Services Example*

Network Applications

This section defines the applications that can be supported using the services provided by medianet. The end game for medianet is to provide the services at the network level to support the applications required by the user community.

Collaborative applications that leverage the services provided by the medianet architecture include the following:

- **Cisco Unified Communications:** Includes voice, video, and web conferencing solutions. Desktop video conferencing solutions that are integrated into multimedia collaboration tools can enable higher productivity through more effective meetings. This type of application is interactive in nature, and as such, it is sensitive to network delay, jitter, and packet loss.

- **Cisco Digital Media Systems:** Includes applications such as Cisco Digital Signage, which delivers video and application content to many large display monitors that are placed throughout the organization. It also includes Cisco Enterprise TV, which allows end users to select and receive live and prerecorded video on large screens, and Cisco Desktop Video, which allows users to receive live and prerecorded video on desktop PCs. These applications are all forms of streaming media and are not interactive in nature.

- **Cisco IP Video Surveillance:** Provides real-time monitoring of the environment, people, and assets and provides recording for investigative purposes. Video surveillance is a key component of the safety and security procedures of many organizations. Reliability of the solution and security and privacy of the information are key considerations for this type of video application.

- **Cisco TelePresence:** Provides a deeply immersive video experience. This application is key to the new generation of communication experience and is becoming pervasive in many enterprises. Consistent network behavior, to deliver a consistent experience, is critical.

Modularity in Cisco Network Architectures for the Enterprise

To optimize user experience and application performance, network services should be designed end to end across the entire Borderless Network. The detailed design can be modularized to facilitate gradual implementation and address the specific requirements of each individual part of the network.

A common way to divide the network into separate modules is by place in the network:

- **Campus:** The campus network is the regional or headquarters operating center of a business. This module is where most users access the network. The campus combines a core infrastructure of intelligent switching and routing with tightly integrated productivity-enhancing technologies, including Cisco Unified Communications, mobility, and advanced security. The hierarchical architecture of the Cisco enterprise campus architecture provides the enterprise with high availability through a resilient multilayer design, redundant hardware and software features, and automatic procedures for reconfiguring network paths when failures occur. Multicast provides optimized bandwidth consumption, and QoS prevents oversubscription to ensure that real-time traffic, such as voice and video, or critical data is not dropped or delayed. Integrated security protects against and mitigates the impact of worms, viruses, and other attacks on the network (even at the switch-port level). The architecture extends authentication support using standards such as IEEE 802.1X and Extensible Authentication Protocol (EAP). It also provides the flexibility to add IPsec and Multiprotocol Label Switching virtual private networks (MPLS VPN), identity and access management, and VLANs to compartmentalize access. These additions help improve performance and security while also decreasing costs.

- **Data Center:** A cohesive, adaptive network architecture that supports the requirements for consolidation, business continuance, and security, while enabling emerging service-oriented architectures, virtualization, and on-demand computing. IT staff can easily provide departmental staff, suppliers, or customers with secure access to applications and resources. This ability simplifies and streamlines management, significantly reducing overhead. Redundant data centers provide backup using synchronous and asynchronous data and application replication. The network and devices offer server and application load balancing to maximize performance. This solution allows the enterprise to scale without major changes to the infrastructure. The data center can be located either at the campus as a server farm or at a remote facility.

- **WAN and MAN:** This module offers the convergence of voice, video, and data services over a single Cisco Unified Communications network. This convergence enables the enterprise to cost-effectively span large geographic areas. QoS, granular service levels, and comprehensive encryption options help ensure the secure delivery of high-quality corporate voice, video, and data resources to all corporate sites, enabling staff to work productively and efficiently wherever they are located. Security is provided with multiservice VPNs (IPsec and MPLS) over Layer 2 or Layer 3 WANs, hub-and-spoke, or full-mesh topologies.

- **Branch:** The branch module allows enterprises to extend head-office applications and services such as security, Cisco Unified Communications, and advanced application performance to thousands of remote locations and users or to a small group of branches. Cisco integrates security, switching, network analysis, caching, and converged voice and video services into a series of ISRs in the branch so that enterprises can deploy new services when they are ready, without buying new equipment. This solution provides secure access to voice, mission-critical data, and video applications anywhere and anytime. Advanced network routing, VPNs, redundant WAN links, application content caching, and local IP telephony call processing provide a robust architecture with high levels of resilience for all the branch offices. An optimized network leverages the WAN and LAN to reduce traffic and save bandwidth and operational expenses. The enterprise can easily

support branch offices with the ability to centrally configure, monitor, and manage
devices that are located at remote sites. This ability includes tools such as Cisco
AutoQoS, which proactively resolves congestion and bandwidth issues before they
affect network performance.

■ **Teleworker:** The teleworker module allows enterprises to securely deliver voice and
data services to a remote small office/home office (SOHO) over a standard broadband access service, providing a business-resiliency solution for the enterprise and
a flexible work environment for employees. Centralized management minimizes
the IT support costs, and robust integrated security mitigates the unique security
challenges of this environment. Integrated security- and identity-based networking
services enable the enterprise to help extend campus security policies to the teleworker. Staff can securely log in to the network over an "always-on" VPN and gain
access to authorized applications and services from a single cost-effective platform.
The productivity can be further enhanced by adding a Cisco IP phone, providing
cost-effective access to a centralized IP communications system with voice and
unified messaging services.

Figure 1-6 illustrates typical criteria for modular design.

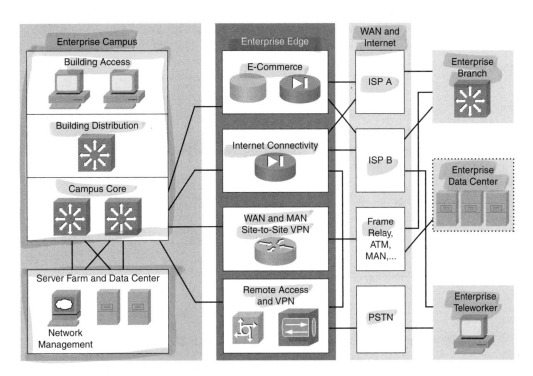

Figure 1-6 *Modular Network Design*

The previous section covered the Cisco enterprise architecture as it is intended to be designed. The following section briefly reviews the main subjects of this section.

The hierarchical network model provides a modular view of a network, making it easier to design and build a deterministic scalable network. The hierarchical network structure consists of the access, distribution, and core layers.

Cisco has developed three overlapping network architectures for the enterprise as part of a holistic approach to network architecture and design; together, these architectures make up the Cisco network architectures for the enterprise. These architectures focus on three recent developments in the enterprise environment:

- The Borderless Networks architecture addresses increasing worker mobility and focuses on connecting anyone from anywhere, using any device, to any resource (securely, reliably, and seamlessly).

- The collaboration architecture addresses the increased need for interaction among companies, including partners and suppliers. Cisco collaboration solutions are built on a modular architecture that integrates with your existing environment while introducing new communication and collaboration capabilities.

- The virtualization architecture addresses three major business challenges: business alignment, cost and power efficiency, and risk management and compliance. Virtualization technology enables more rapid application deployment and more-efficient use of resources, allowing you to do more with the same resources. Virtualization also offers better protection against disasters and outages.

- Infrastructure services add intelligence to the network infrastructure, supporting application awareness within the network. Network applications are enabled by critical network services that support networkwide requirements for the application. Integrated network services provide a common set of capabilities that many different applications can leverage.

Although network applications and services should be designed from end to end, the network itself can be broken down into separate components. This modularization allows addressing of the specific requirements of each part of the network and a gradual implementation of the end-to-end services.

Each component has a distinct network infrastructure and services and has network applications that extend between the components.

Reviewing the Cisco PPDIOO Approach

To design a network that meets customer needs, the organizational goals, organizational constraints, technical goals, and technical constraints must be identified. Cisco has formalized the lifecycle of a network into six phases: prepare, plan, design, implement, operate, and optimize (PPDIOO).

The section begins with a review of PPDIOO, and then discusses the design methodology under PPDIOO.

PPDIOO Network Lifecycle Approach

This section reviews the PPDIOO approach for the network lifecycle, as shown in Figure 1-7.

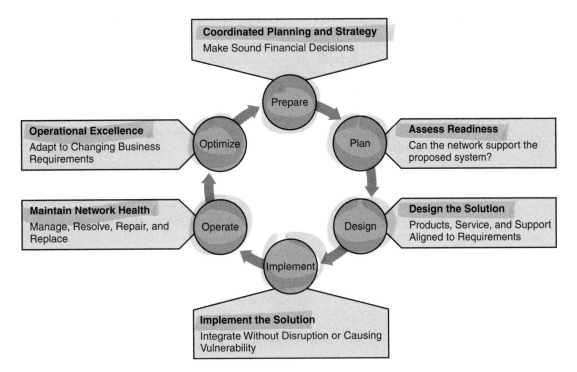

Figure 1-7   *PPDIOO Network Lifecycle Approach*

The PPDIOO network lifecycle approach reflects the lifecycle phases of a standard network. The PPDIOO phases are as follows:

■ **Prepare:** The prepare phase involves establishing the organizational requirements, developing a network strategy, proposing a high-level conceptual architecture, and identifying technologies that can best support the architecture. The prepare phase can establish financial justification for network strategy by assessing the business case for the proposed architecture.

■ **Plan:** The plan phase involves identifying initial network requirements based on goals, facilities, user needs, and so on. The plan phase involves characterizing sites, assessing any existing networks, and performing a gap analysis to determine whether the existing system infrastructure, sites, and operational environment can support the proposed system. A project plan facilitates management of the tasks, responsibilities, critical milestones, and resources required to implement changes to the network. The project plan should align with the scope, cost, and resource parameters established in the original business requirements.

■ **Design:** The initial requirements that were derived in the plan phase drive the activities of the network design specialists. The network design specification is a comprehensive, detailed design that meets current business and technical requirements and incorporates specifications to support availability, reliability, security, scalability, and performance. The design specification is the basis for the implementation activities.

■ **Implement:** After the design has been approved, implementation (and verification) begins. The network or additional components are built according to the design specifications, with the goal of integrating devices without disrupting the existing network or creating points of vulnerability.

■ **Operate:** The final test of the appropriateness of a design is whether it operates. The operate phase involves maintaining network health through day-to-day operations, including maintaining high availability and reducing expenses. The fault detection, correction, and performance monitoring that occur in daily operations provide initial data for the optimize phase.

■ **Optimize:** The optimize phase involves proactive management of the network. The goal of proactive management is to identify and resolve issues before they affect the organization. Reactive fault detection and correction (troubleshooting) is needed when proactive management cannot predict and mitigate failures. In the PPDIOO process, the optimize phase may prompt a network redesign if too many network problems and errors arise, if performance does not meet expectations, or if new applications are identified to support organizational and technical requirements.

Note   Although design is listed as one of the six PPDIOO phases, some design elements may be present in all the other phases.

Benefits of the Lifecycle Approach

The network lifecycle approach provides four main benefits: It lowers the total cost of network ownership, increases network availability, improves business agility, and speeds access to applications and services. By following this methodology, designers and engineers can deliver a consistent user experience to the enterprise user community. This section breaks these concepts out into detailed strategies.

The total cost of network ownership is lowered via these strategies:

■ Identifying and validating technology requirements

■ Planning for infrastructure changes and resource requirements

- Developing a sound network design aligned with technical requirements and business goals

- Accelerating successful implementation

- Improving the efficiency of your network and of the staff supporting it

- Reducing operating expenses by improving the efficiency of operation processes and tools

Network availability is increased via these strategies:

- Assessing the network's security state and its capability to support the proposed design

- Specifying the correct set of hardware and software releases and keeping them operational and current

- Producing a sound operations design and validating network operation.

- Staging and testing the proposed system before deployment

- Improving staff skills.

- Proactively monitoring the system and assessing availability trends and alerts

- Proactively identifying security breaches and defining remediation plans

Business agility is improved via these strategies:

- Establishing business requirements and technology strategies

- Readying sites to support the system you want to implement.

- Integrating technical requirements and business goals into a detailed design and demonstrating that the network is functioning as specified

- Expertly installing, configuring, and integrating system components

- Continually enhancing performance

Access to applications and services is accelerated through these strategies:

- Assessing and improving operational preparedness to support current and planned network technologies and services

- Improving service-delivery efficiency and effectiveness by increasing availability, resource capacity, and performance

- Improving the availability, reliability, and stability of the network and the applications running on it

- Managing and resolving problems affecting your system and keeping software applications current

Using the Design Methodology Under PPDIOO

The design methodology under PPDIOO consists of three basic steps, as follows:

Step 1.   Identify customer requirements. In this step, key decision makers identify the initial requirements. Based on these requirements, a high-level conceptual architecture is proposed. This step is typically done during the PPDIOO prepare phase.

Step 2.   Characterize the existing network and sites. The plan phase involves characterizing sites, assessing any existing networks, and performing a gap analysis to determine whether the existing system infrastructure, sites, and operational environment can support the proposed system. Characterization of the existing network and sites includes a site and network audit and network analysis. During the network audit, the existing network is thoroughly checked for integrity and quality. During the network analysis, network behavior (traffic, congestion, and so on) is analyzed. This is typically done within the PPDIOO plan phase.

Step 3.   Design the network topology and solutions. In this step, a detailed design is developed. Decisions about network infrastructure, intelligent network services, and network solutions (VoIP, content networking, and so on) are made. A pilot or prototype network to verify the design may be built and a detailed design document compiled.

Identifying Customer Requirements

This section reviews the logical flow of the process for gathering customer requirements for the enterprise network design discussed in the Cisco Press design book, as shown in Figure 1-8.

The process of gathering the design requirements from the customer consists of five steps that serve as goals for the designer. These steps involve discussions with customer staff members, during which you gather the information and documentation that is necessary to begin the design process.

The process of identifying required information is not unidirectional. You might return to a step and make additional inquiries about issues as they arise during the design process. The steps for data gathering are as follows:

Step 1.   Identify planned network applications and network services.

Step 2.   Define organizational goals.

Step 3.   Define and check all possible organizational constraints.

Step 4.   Define technical goals.

Step 5.   Define and check all possible technical constraints.

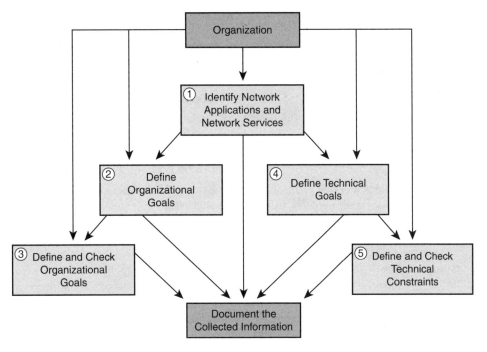

Figure 1-8 *Identifying Customer Requirements*

After completing the data-gathering process, users are ready to interpret and analyze the data and develop a design proposal.

Characterizing the Existing Network and Sites

This section describes the steps necessary to characterize the existing network infrastructure and all sites. This process requires three steps:

Step 1.   Gather existing documentation about the network, and query the organization to discover additional information. Organization input, a network audit, and traffic analysis provide the key information you need. (Note that existing documentation may be inaccurate.)

Step 2.   Perform a network audit that adds detail to the description of the network. If possible, use traffic-analysis information to augment organizational input when you are describing the applications and protocols used in the network.

Step 3.   Based on your network characterization, write a summary report that describes the health of the network. With this information, you can propose hardware and software upgrades to support the network requirements and the organizational requirements.

Designing the Topology and Network Solutions

Designing an enterprise network is a complex project. Top-down design facilitates the process by dividing it into smaller, more-manageable steps. Top-down design clarifies the design goals and initiates the design from the perspective of the required applications and network solutions.

In assessing the scope of a network design, you must determine whether the design is for a new network or is a modification of the entire network, a single segment or component, a set of LANs, a WAN, or a remote-access network. The design scope may address a single function or all of the Open Systems Interconnection (OSI) model layers.

Structured top-down design practices focus on dividing the design task into related, less-complex components or modules, using the following steps:

Step 1.   Identify the applications that will be needed to support the customer's requirements.

Step 2.   Identify the logical connectivity requirements of the applications, with a focus on the necessary network solutions and the supporting network services. Examples of infrastructure services include voice, content networking, and storage networking, availability, management, security, QoS, and IP multicast. Split the network functionally to develop the network infrastructure and hierarchy requirements. In this course, the Cisco enterprise architecture provides a consistent infrastructure.

Step 3.   Split the network functionally to develop the network infrastructure and hierarchy requirements. The Cisco enterprise architecture provides a consistent infrastructure.

Step 4.   Design each structured element separately in relation to other elements. Network infrastructure and infrastructure services design are tightly connected, because both are bound to the same logical, physical, and layered models.

When the design is completed in the PPDIOO process, the next step is to develop the implementation and migration plan in as much detail as possible. The more detailed the implementation plan documentation, the less knowledgeable the network engineer needs to be to implement the design.

After a design is complete, it is often appropriate to verify the design. You can test the design in an existing or live network (pilot), or in an isolated test network (prototype) that will not affect the existing network.

Dividing the Network into Areas

This section describes how to divide a network into areas, which is an important step in the process of designing the network.

Figure 1-9 illustrates the division of the network.

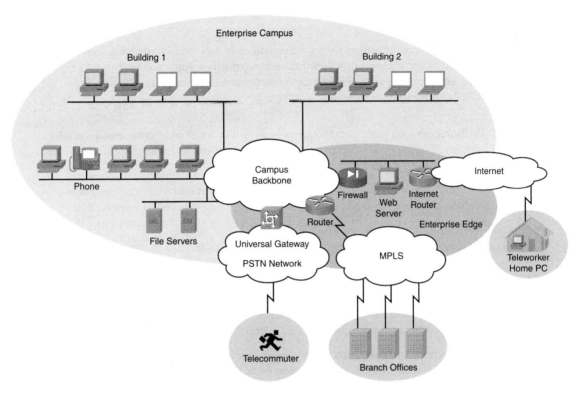

Figure 1-9   *Dividing the Network into Areas*

Dividing the network into areas requires the following:

- Divide the network into areas, with the enterprise campus module including all devices and connections within the main campus. Ensure that the enterprise edge module covers all communications with remote locations from the perspective of the enterprise campus. Finally, make certain that the remote module includes the remote branches, teleworkers, and the remote data center.

- Define clear boundaries between the enterprise campus, the enterprise edge, and the remote module.

Summary

The Cisco network architectures for the enterprise consist of three overlapping architectures that enable rapid application deployment and consistent application performance across the enterprise network. Each of the three domains addresses a specific development in the enterprise environment:

- The Borderless Networks architecture provides solutions to address increased worker mobility. It focuses on connecting anyone from anywhere, using any device, to any resource (securely, reliably, and seamlessly).

- The collaboration architecture provides a framework that enables new communication and collaboration applications to address the increased need to communicate and collaborate across corporate boundaries, companies, and continents.

- The data center virtualization architecture consolidates network, storage, and computing resources by leveraging virtualization technologies. This architecture enables rapid deployment of new applications and services, scaling of existing services, and optimization of applications through flexible assignment of resources.

The design methodology under the PPDIOO network lifecycle consists of three basic steps:

Step 1. Identify customer requirements. In this step, key decision makers identify the initial requirements. Based on these requirements, a high-level conceptual architecture is proposed. This step is typically done during the PPDIOO prepare phase.

Step 2. Characterize the existing network and sites. The plan phase involves characterizing sites, assessing any existing networks, and performing a gap analysis to determine whether the existing system infrastructure, sites, and operational environment can support the proposed system. Characterization of the existing network and sites includes a site and network audit and network analysis. During the network audit, the existing network is thoroughly checked for integrity and quality. During the network analysis, network behavior (traffic, congestion, and so on) is analyzed. This is typically done within the PPDIOO plan phase.

Step 3. Design the network topology and solutions. In this step, you develop the detailed design. Decisions about network infrastructure, intelligent network services, and network solutions (VoIP, content networking, and so on) are made. You may also build a pilot or prototype network to verify the design. You also write a detailed design document.

References

For additional information, refer to the following:

Cisco Systems, Inc. Cisco network architectures for the enterprise documentation at http://www.cisco.com/en/US/netsol/ns517/networking_solutions_market_segment_solutions_home.html

Cisco Systems, Inc. *Cisco Borderless Networks Solutions* at http://www.cisco.com/en/US/partner/netsol/ns1015/index.html (Cisco.com login required)

Cisco Systems, Inc. *Cisco Collaboration* Solutions at http://www.cisco.com/en/US/partner/netsol/ns1007/index.html (Cisco.com login required)

Cisco Systems, Inc. *Overview of a Medianet Architecture* at http://www.cisco.com/en/US/docs/solutions/Enterprise/Video/vrn.html

Cisco Systems, Inc. *Design Zone for Data Centers* at http://www.cisco.com/en/US/netsol/ns743/networking_solutions_program_home.html

Cisco Systems, Inc. *Lifecycle Services Portfolio* at http://www.cisco.com/en/US/products/ps6890/serv_category_home.html

Oppenheimer, P. *Top-Down Network Design, Third Edition*. Indianapolis, Indiana: Cisco Press; 2010.

Cisco Systems, Inc. "Internetworking Design Basics" chapter of *Cisco Internetwork Design Guide* at http://www.cisco.com/en/US/docs/internet

Cisco Systems, Inc. *Design Zone for Borderless Networks* at http://www.cisco.com/en/US/netsol/ns1063/networking_solutions_program_home.html

Cisco Systems, Inc. *Borderless Networks Architecture* at http://www.cisco.com/en/US/netsol/ns1015/architecture.html

Cisco Systems, Inc. *Cisco Validated Design Program* at http://www.cisco.com/en/US/netsol/ns741/networking_solutions_program_home.html

Review Questions

Answer the following questions, and then refer to Appendix A, "Answers to Review Questions," for the answers.

1. Which three architectures are in the Cisco network architectures for the enterprise?

    a. Service-oriented networks

    b. Borderless Networks

    c. Collaboration

    d. Composite networking

    e. Unified networks

    f. Virtualization

2. Which three are roles of the core layer in a LAN design?

    a. Provides high-speed data transport

    b. Performs packet filtering

    c. Serves as a fast convergent infrastructure with a high level of redundancy

    d. Avoids data manipulation

    e. Performs mainly policy-based decisions

    f. Provides access to the network

3. Which three sections provide network infrastructure and services for remote enterprise users?

    a. Remote database section

    b. Teleworker section

    c. Remote branch section

    d. Enterprise branch section

    e. Data center section

4. Which three are basic steps of the design methodology under PPDIOO?

    a. Characterize the existing network and sites.

    b. Examine conceptual architecture.

    c. Design the network topology and solutions.

    d. Identify customer requirements.

    e. Validate the design.

5. Which three tasks are involved in characterizing an existing network?

    a. Collecting information using the existing documentation and direct organizational input

    b. Using tools to analyze network traffic

    c. Using design tools to create a framework for the design

    d. Using tools for automated auditing of the network

    e. Identifying the business objectives of the organization

Chapter 2

Enterprise Campus Network Design

After completing this chapter, you will be able to

- Design enterprise campus network infrastructures

- Review high-availability campus design features and make recommendations

- Describe Layer 2 campus design options and make recommendations

- Describe Layer 3 campus design options and make recommendations

- Discuss options for Layer 2 to Layer 3 boundary placement in the campus

- Describe infrastructure service considerations, including IP telephony, QoS, and Cisco Catalyst Integrated Security features

Note This chapter discusses the Catalyst line of Cisco switching only. There is both feature parity and enhancement in the Nexus switching platform for both high-performance and data center applications. However, because of its tight integration with the data center, the Nexus and NX-OS are discussed in Chapter 5, "Enterprise Data Center Design." Currently, the Nexus product line targets and has features supportive of data center and service provider environments. However, the Nexus products may also fit other campus locations fairly well. This chapter presents design principles that can prove useful regardless of the actual hardware choices that are made.

The complexity inherent in today's campus networks necessitates a design process capable of separating solutions into basic elements. The Cisco hierarchical network model achieves this goal by dividing the network infrastructure into modular components. Each module is used to represent a functional service layer within the campus hierarchy.

Designing High Availability in the Enterprise Campus

The Cisco hierarchical network model enables the design of high-availability modular topologies. Through the use of scalable building blocks, the network can support evolving business needs. The modular approach makes the network easier to scale, troubleshoot, and understand. It also promotes the deterministic traffic patterns.

This section reviews design models, recommended practices, and methodologies for high availability in the Cisco enterprise campus architecture infrastructure.

Enterprise Campus Infrastructure Review

The building blocks of the enterprise campus infrastructure are the access layer, the distribution layer, and the core layer. The principal features associated with each layer are hierarchal design and modularity. A hierarchical design avoids the need for a fully meshed network in which all nodes are interconnected. A modular design enables a component to be placed in service or taken out of service with little or no impact on the rest of the network. This methodology also facilitates troubleshooting, problem isolation, and network management.

Access Layer

The access layer is the point of entry into the network for end devices, as illustrated in Figure 2-1.

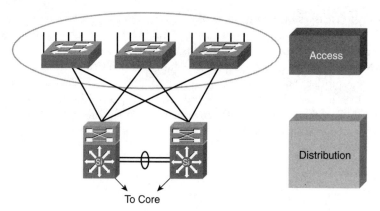

Figure 2-1 *Access Layer*

The campus access layer aggregates end users and provides uplinks to the distribution layer. The access layer can support multiple features:

■ **High availability:** At the access layer, high availability is supported through various hardware and software attributes. With hardware, system-level redundancy can be provided using redundant supervisor engines and redundant power supplies. It can also be provided by default gateway redundancy using dual connections from access switches to redundant distribution layer switches. With software, high availability is supported through the use of first-hop routing protocols (FHRP), such as the Hot Standby Router Protocol (HSRP), Virtual Router Redundancy Protocol (VRRP), and Gateway Load Balancing Protocol (GLBP).

Note   Cisco offers a unique high-availability feature with its 3750 Workgroup Switch and Etherswitch Services Module called StackWise. StackWise technology enables switches to be interconnected to create a single logical unit through the use of special stack cables. The cables create a bidirectional path that behaves as a switch fabric for all the interconnected switches. The stack is managed as a single unit, eliminating the need for spanning tree and streamlining the interface to a single management session for all devices. For more information about StackWise, see www.cisco.com/en/US/prod/collateral/switches/ps5718/ps5023/prod_white_paper09186a00801b096a.html.

Note   StackWise switches also support StackPower, which allows common management of the Power over Ethernet (PoE) in the stack. For more information, see www.cisco.com/en/US/prod/collateral/switches/ps5718/ps6406/white_paper_c11-578931.pdf.

■ **Convergence:** The access layer supports inline PoE for IP telephony and wireless access points, allowing customers to converge voice onto their data network and providing roaming wireless LAN (WLAN) access for users.

■ **Security:** The access layer provides services for additional security against unauthorized access to the network through the use of tools such as IEEE 802.1X, port security, DHCP snooping, dynamic ARP inspection (DAI), and IP source guard.

- **Quality of service (QoS):** The access layer allows prioritization of mission-critical network traffic using traffic classification and queuing as close to the ingress of the network as possible. It supports the use of the QoS trust boundary.

- **IP multicast:** The access layer supports efficient network and bandwidth management using software features such as Internet Group Management Protocol (IGMP) snooping.

Distribution Layer

The distribution layer aggregates traffic from all nodes and uplinks from the access layer and provides policy-based connectivity, as illustrated in Figure 2-2.

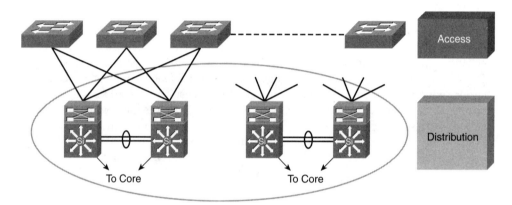

Figure 2-2 *Distribution Layer*

Availability, load balancing, QoS, and provisioning are the important considerations at this layer. High availability is typically provided through dual paths from the distribution layer to the core and from the access layer to the distribution layer. Layer 3 equal-cost load sharing allows both uplinks from the distribution to the core layer to be used.

The distribution layer is the place where routing and packet manipulation are performed and can be a routing boundary between the access and core layers. The distribution layer represents a redistribution point between routing domains or the demarcation between static and dynamic routing protocols. The distribution layer performs tasks such as controlled routing and filtering to implement policy-based connectivity and QoS. To further improve routing protocol performance, the distribution layer summarizes routes from the access layer. For some networks, the distribution layer offers a default route to access layer routers and runs dynamic routing protocols when communicating with core routers.

The distribution layer uses a combination of Layer 2 and multilayer switching to segment workgroups and isolate network problems, preventing them from impacting the core layer. The distribution layer may be used to terminate VLANs from access layer switches. The distribution layer connects network services to the access layer and implements QoS, security, traffic loading, and routing policies. The distribution layer provides default gateway redundancy using an FHRP, such as HSRP, GLBP, or VRRP, to allow for the failure or removal of one of the distribution nodes without affecting endpoint connectivity to the default gateway.

Note   Cisco has introduced the Virtual Switching System (VSS), which can reduce or eliminate the need for FHRPs at the distribution layer. For more information about VSS, visit www.cisco.com/go/vss.

Core Layer

The core layer provides scalability, high availability, and fast convergence to the network, as illustrated in Figure 2-3. The core layer is the backbone for campus connectivity, and is the aggregation point for the other layers and modules in the Cisco enterprise campus architecture. The core provides a high level of redundancy and can adapt to changes quickly. Core devices are most reliable when they can accommodate failures by rerouting traffic and can respond quickly to changes in the network topology. The core devices implement scalable protocols and technologies, alternate paths, and load balancing. The core layer helps in scalability during future growth.

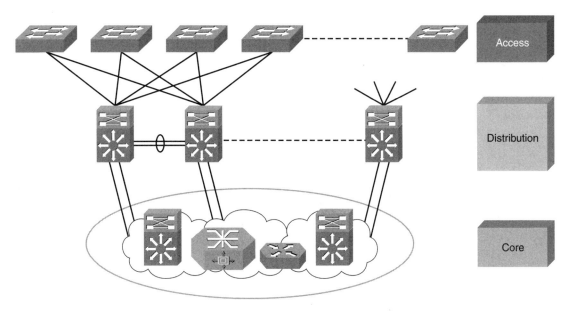

Figure 2-3   *Core Layer*

The core is a high-speed, Layer 3 switching environment that should use hardware-accelerated services if possible. The core's redundant point-to-point Layer 3 interconnections make fast convergence around a link or node failure possible, with this design yielding the fastest and most deterministic convergence results. The core layer is designed to avoid any packet manipulation, such as checking access lists and filtering, which could slow down the switching of packets.

Not all campus implementations require a campus core. The core and distribution layer functions can be combined at the distribution layer for a smaller campus.

Without a core layer, the distribution layer switches need to be fully meshed, as illustrated in Figure 2-4. This design can be difficult to scale, and increases the cabling requirements, because each new building distribution switch needs full-mesh connectivity to all the distribution switches. The routing complexity of a full-mesh design increases as new neighbors are added.

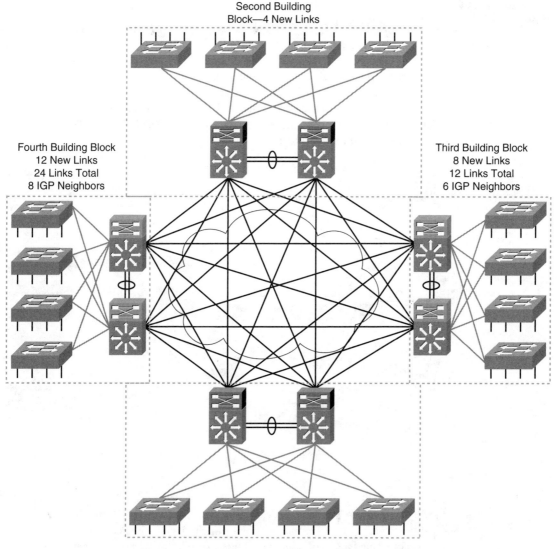

Figure 2-4 *Is a Core Layer Needed?*

Note   Combining distribution and core layer functionality (collapsed core) requires a great deal of port density on the distribution layer switches. An alternative solution is a Layer 2 core with discrete VLANs on each core switch. This scenario requires only two ports per distribution layer switch—regardless of the number of buildings (switch blocks)—so you can avoid the expense of multilayer core switches.

In Figure 2-4, a distribution module in the second building of two interconnected switches requires four additional links for full-mesh connectivity to the first module. A third distribution module to support the third building would require 8 additional links to support connections to all the distribution switches, or a total of 12 links. A fourth module supporting the fourth building would require 12 new links, for a total of 24 links between the distribution switches. Four distribution modules impose eight Interior Gateway Protocol (IGP) neighbors on each distribution switch.

As a recommended practice, deploy a dedicated campus core layer to connect three or more buildings in the enterprise campus, or four or more pairs of building distribution switches in a very large campus. The campus core helps make scaling the network easier by addressing the requirements for the following:

■   Gigabit density

■   Data and voice integration

■   LAN, WAN, and MAN convergence

Collapsed-Core Model

In smaller networks, the core and the distribution layer eliminates the need for extra switching hardware and simplifies the network implementation. This, however, eliminates the advantages of the multilayer architecture, specifically fault isolation.

Figure 2-5 displays a collapsed-core deployment. In a collapsed-core design, changes in the campus distribution layer automatically result in changes to the network core devices. Therefore, changes on the distribution layer may also affect the traffic in other parts of the network. For example, in the network that is shown in Figure 2-5, a software upgrade that is necessary to introduce certain distribution layer features could potentially affect the traffic flow between the data center and the WAN modules. By using separate core and distribution layers, you can maintain better fault isolation between the network core and the access and distribution layers of the network.

Note   On the Cisco Nexus 7000 series switches, you can use virtual device contexts (VDC) to combine the core and distribution layer on a single physical device, while still maintaining a functional and administrative separation between the layers. However, although the hardware is partitioned and each VDC operates as a separate unit, there is no physical isolation.

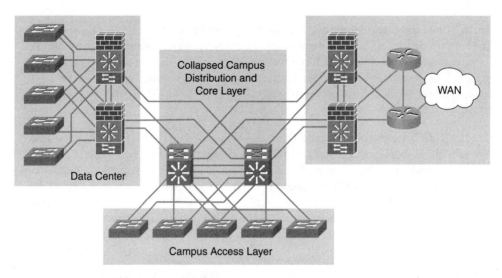

Figure 2-5 *Collapsed-Core Topology*

High-Availability Considerations

In the campus, high availability is concerned with minimizing link and node failures and optimizing recovery times to minimize convergence and downtime.

Implement Optimal Redundancy

The recommended design is redundant distribution layer switches and redundant connections to the core with a Layer 3 link between the distribution switches. Access switches should have redundant connections to redundant distribution switches, as illustrated in Figure 2-6.

As stated previously, it is a recommended practice to have the core and distribution layers built with redundant switches and fully meshed links to provide maximum redundancy and optimal convergence. In addition, access switches should have redundant connections to redundant distribution switches. The network bandwidth and capacity is engineered to withstand a switch or link failure, supporting 120 ms to 200 ms to converge around most events. Open Shortest Path First (OSPF) Protocol and Enhanced Interior Gateway Routing Protocol (EIGRP) timer manipulation attempts to quickly redirect the flow of traffic away from a router that has experienced a failure toward an alternate path.

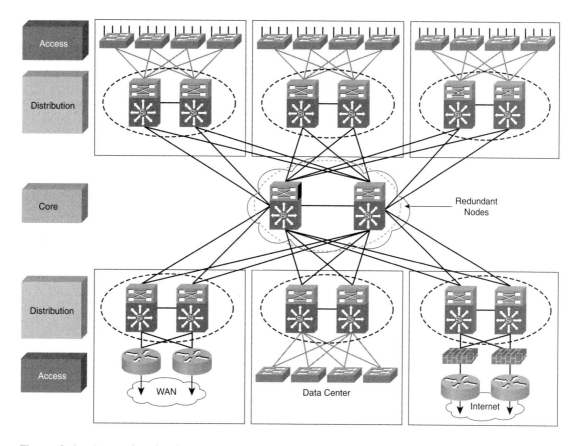

Figure 2-6 *Optimal Redundancy*

In a fully redundant topology with tuned IGP timers, adding redundant supervisors with Cisco nonstop forwarding (NSF) and stateful switchover (SSO) may cause longer convergence times than single supervisors with tuned IGP timers. NSF attempts to maintain the flow of traffic through a router that has experienced a failure. NSF with SSO is designed to maintain a link-up Layer 3 up state during a routing convergence event. However, because an interaction occurs between the IGP timers and the NSF timers, the tuned IGP timers can cause NSF-aware neighbors to reset the neighbor relationships.

Note   Combining OSPF and EIGRP timer manipulation with Cisco NSF might not be the most common deployment environment. OSPF and EIGRP timer manipulation is designed to improve convergence time in a multiaccess network (where several IGP routing peers share a common broadcast media, such as Ethernet). The primary deployment scenario for Cisco NSF with SSO is in the enterprise network edge. Here, the data link layer generally consists of point-to-point links either to service providers or redundant Gigabit Ethernet point-to-point links to the campus infrastructure.

In nonredundant topologies, using Cisco NSF with SSO and redundant supervisors can result in significant resiliency improvements.

Provide Alternate Paths

The recommended distribution layer design is redundant distribution layer switches and redundant connections to the core with a Layer 3 link between the distribution switches, as illustrated in Figure 2-7.

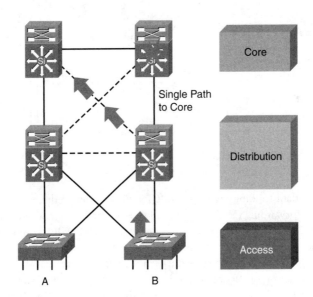

Figure 2-7   *Provide Alternate Paths*

Although dual-distribution switches connected individually to separate core switches reduce peer relationships and port counts in the core layer, this design does not provide sufficient redundancy. In the event of a link or core switch failure, traffic is dropped.

An additional link providing an alternate path to a second core switch from each distribution switch offers redundancy to support a single link or node failure. A link between the two distribution switches is needed to support summarization of routing information from the distribution layer to the core.

Avoid Single Points of Failure

Cisco NSF with SSO and redundant supervisors has the most impact in the campus in the access layer. An access switch failure is a single point of failure that causes outage for the end devices connected to it. You can reduce the outage to one to three seconds in this access layer, as shown in Figure 2-8, by using SSO in a Layer 2 environment or Cisco NSF with SSO in a Layer 3 environment.

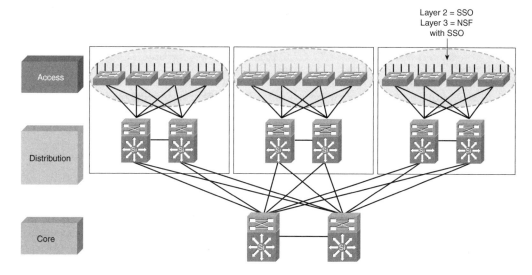

Figure 2-8 *Avoid Single Points of Failure*

Note The SSO feature is available on the Catalyst 4500 and 6500/7600 switches and the Aggregation Services Routers (ASR) series of routers.

Cisco NSF with SSO

Cisco NSF with SSO is a supervisor redundancy mechanism in Cisco IOS Software that allows extremely fast supervisor switchover at Layers 2 to 4.

SSO allows the standby route processor (RP) to take control of the device after a hardware or software fault on the active RP. SSO synchronizes startup configuration, startup variables, and running configuration; and dynamic runtime data, including Layer 2 protocol states for trunks and ports, hardware Layer 2 and Layer 3 tables (MAC, Forwarding Information Base [FIB], and adjacency tables) and access control lists (ACL) and QoS tables.

Cisco NSF is a Layer 3 function that works with SSO to minimize the amount of time a network is unavailable to its users following a switchover. The main objective of Cisco NSF is to continue forwarding IP packets following an RP switchover. Cisco NSF is supported by EIGRP, OSPF, Intermediate System-to-Intermediate System (IS-IS), and Border

Gateway Protocol (BGP) for routing. A router running these protocols can detect an internal switchover and take the necessary actions to continue forwarding network traffic using Cisco Express Forwarding (CEF) while recovering route information from the peer devices. With Cisco NSF, peer networking devices continue to forward packets while route convergence completes and do not experience routing flaps.

Routing Protocol Requirements for Cisco NSF

Usually, when a router restarts, all its routing peers detect that routing adjacency went down and then came back up. This transition is called a routing flap, and the protocol state is not maintained. Routing flaps create routing instabilities, which are detrimental to overall network performance. Cisco NSF helps to suppress routing flaps.

Cisco NSF allows for the continued forwarding of data packets along known routes while the routing protocol information is being restored following a switchover. To meet the requirements for Cisco NSF, a graceful restart mechanism is necessary. With graceful restart, peer devices do not experience routing flaps because the interfaces remain up during a switchover and adjacencies are not reset. Data traffic is forwarded while the standby RP assumes control from the failed active RP during a switchover. User sessions that are established before the switchover are maintained.

The ability of the intelligent line cards to remain up through a switchover and to be kept current with the FIB on the active RP is crucial to Cisco NSF operation. While the control plane builds a new routing protocol database and restarts peering agreements, the data plane relies on pre-switchover forwarding-table synchronization to continue forwarding traffic. After the routing protocols have converged, CEF updates the FIB table and removes stale route entries, and then it updates the line cards with the refreshed FIB information.

Note   Transient routing loops or black holes may be introduced if the network topology changes before the FIB is updated.

The switchover must be completed before the Cisco graceful restart dead and hold timers expire; otherwise, the peers reset the adjacency and reroute the traffic.

Cisco NSF protocol enhancements enable a Cisco NSF-capable router to signal neighboring Cisco NSF-aware devices during switchover.

Note   A device is said to be graceful restart aware if it runs graceful restart-compatible software. A device is said to be graceful restart capable if it has been configured to support graceful restart. A graceful restart-capable device rebuilds routing information from grace-ful restart-aware or graceful restart-capable neighbors.

A graceful restart-aware neighbor is required so that graceful restart -capable systems can rebuild their databases and maintain their neighbor adjacencies across a switchover.

Following a switchover, the graceful restart-capable device requests that the graceful restart neighbor devices send state information to help rebuild the routing tables as a graceful restart.

The graceful restart protocol enhancements allow a graceful restart-capable router to sig-nal neighboring graceful restart-aware devices. The signal asks that the neighbor relation-ship not be reset. As the graceful restart router receives and communicates with other routers on the network, it can begin to rebuild its neighbor list. After neighbor relation-ships are reestablished, the graceful restart-capable router begins to resynchronize its database with all the graceful restart-aware neighbors.

Based on platform and Cisco IOS Software release, graceful restart with SSO support is available for many routing protocols:

- EIGRP
- OSPF
- BGP
- IS-IS

Cisco IOS Software Modularity Architecture

The Cisco Catalyst 6500 series with Cisco IOS Software Modularity supports high avail-ability in the enterprise. Figure 2-9 illustrates the key elements and components of the Cisco Software Modularity architecture.

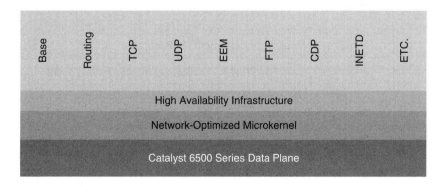

Figure 2-9 *Cisco IOS Software Modularity Architecture*

When Cisco IOS Software patches are needed on systems without Cisco IOS Software Modularity, the new image must be loaded on the active and redundant supervisors, and the supervisor must be reloaded or the switchover to the standby completed to load the patch.

The control plane functions (that manage routing protocol updates and management traffic) on the Catalyst 6500 series run on dedicated CPUs on the multilayer switch forwarding card complex (MSFC). A completely separate data plane is responsible for traffic forwarding. When the hardware is programmed for nonstop operation, the data plane continues forwarding traffic even if a disruption occurs in the control plane. The Catalyst 6500 series switches benefit from the more resilient control plane offered by Cisco IOS Software Modularity.

Note   Catalyst switch forwarding fabrics are broken down into three planes or functional areas, as follows:

Control plane: The control plane is a logical interface that connects physical chassis components and software functions into a unified logical unit. The control plane connects the system controller functionality on the RP to the service processor (SP) module used to control each card and module in the chassis.

Data plane: The data plane is where packet forwarding takes place. It is the path that packets take through the routing system from the physical layer interface module (PLIM) to the modular services card (MSC) to the switch fabric. On the 6500 series platforms, this would include the policy feature card (PFC) used for high-performance packet processing, and the distributed forwarding card (DFC), which provides local packet forwarding on select line cards.

Management plane: The management plane is where control/configuration of the platform takes place.

The Cisco Catalyst 6500 series with Cisco IOS Software Modularity enables several Cisco IOS control plane subsystems to run in independent processes. Cisco IOS Software Modularity boosts operational efficiency and minimizes downtime:

- It minimizes unplanned downtime through fault containment and stateful process restarts, raising the availability of converged applications.

- It simplifies software changes through subsystem in-service software upgrades (ISSU), significantly reducing code certification and deployment times and decreasing business risks.

- It enables process-level, automated policy control by integrating Cisco IOS Embedded Event Manager (EEM), offloading time-consuming tasks to the network and accelerating the resolution of network issues. EEM is a combination of processes designed to monitor key system parameters, such as CPU utilization, interface counters, Simple Network Management Protocol (SNMP), and syslog events. It acts on specific events or threshold counters that are exceeded.

Note   EEM is discussed in more detail in Chapter 11, "Network Management Capabilities Within Cisco IOS Software."

Example: Software Modularity Benefits

Cisco IOS Software Modularity on the Cisco Catalyst 6500 series provides these benefits:

■ **Operational consistency:** Cisco IOS Software Modularity does not change the operational point of view. Command-line interfaces (CLI) and management interfaces such as SNMP or syslog are the same as before. New commands to EXEC and configuration mode and new **show** commands have been added to support the new functionality.

■ **Protected memory:** Cisco IOS Software Modularity enables a memory architecture where processes make use of a protected address space. Each process and its associated subsystems live in an individual memory space. Using this model, memory corruption across process boundaries becomes nearly impossible.

■ **Fault containment:** The benefit of protected memory space is increased availability, because problems occurring in one process cannot affect other parts of the system. For example, if a less-critical system process fails or is not operating as expected, critical functions required to maintain packet forwarding are not affected.

■ **Process restartability:** Building on the protected memory space and fault containment, the modular processes are now individually restartable. For test purposes or nonresponding processes, the **process restart** *process-name* command is provided to manually restart processes. Restarting a process allows fast recovery from transient errors without the need to disrupt forwarding. Integrated high-availability infrastructure constantly checks the state of processes and keeps track of how many times a process restarted in a defined time interval. If a process restart does not restore the system, the high-availability infrastructure takes more drastic actions, such as initiating a supervisor engine switchover or a system restart.

Note   Although a process restart can be initiated by the user, it should be done with caution.

■ **Modularized processes:** Several control plane functions have been modularized to cover the most commonly used features. Examples of modular processes include but are not limited to these:

    ■ Routing process

    ■ Internet daemon

    ■ Raw IP processing

    ■ TCP process

- User Datagram Protocol (UDP) process

- Cisco Discovery Protocol process

- Syslog daemon

- Any EEM components

- File systems

- Media drivers

- Install manager

- **Subsystem ISSU:** Cisco IOS Software Modularity allows selective system maintenance during runtime through individual patches. By providing versioning and patch-management capabilities, Cisco IOS Software Modularity allows patches to be downloaded, verified, installed, and activated without the need to restart the system. Because data plane packet forwarding is not affected during the patch process, the network operator now has the flexibility to introduce software changes at any time through ISSU. A patch affects only the software components associated with the update.

Designing an Optimum Design for Layer 2

Layer 2 architectures rely on the following technologies to create a highly available, deterministic topology: Spanning Tree Protocol (STP), trunking (ISL/802.1Q), Unidirectional Link Detection (UDLD), and EtherChannel.

The following section reviews design models and recommended practices for Layer 2 high availability and optimum convergence of the Cisco enterprise campus infrastructure.

Recommended Practices for Spanning-Tree Configuration

For the most deterministic and highly available network topology, the requirement to support STP convergence should be avoided by design, as shown in Figure 2-10.

You may need to implement STP for several reasons:

- When a VLAN spans access layer switches to support business applications.

- To protect against user-side loops. Even if the recommended design does not depend on STP to resolve link or node failure events, STP is required to protect against user-side loops. Loops can be introduced on the user-facing access layer ports in many ways. Wiring mistakes, misconfigured end stations, or malicious users can create a loop. STP is required to ensure a loop-free topology and to protect the rest of the network from problems created in the access layer.

- To support data center applications on a server farm.

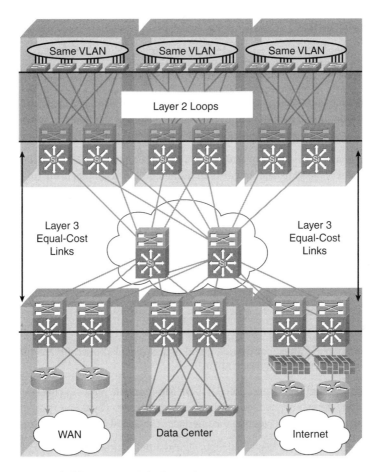

Figure 2-10   *Deterministic Design*

Note   Some security personnel have recommended disabling STP at the network edge. This practice is not recommended because the risk of lost connectivity without STP is much greater than any STP information that might be revealed. A bridging loop can be caused by this practice and could potentially create a loss of connectivity and loss of device management.

If you need to implement STP, use Rapid Per-VLAN Spanning-Tree Plus (RPVST+). You should also take advantage of the Cisco enhancements to STP known as the Cisco STP Toolkit.

Cisco STP Toolkit

The Cisco enhancements to STP include the following. (Note that the enhancements marked with an * are also supported with RPVST+.)

- **PortFast***: Causes a Layer 2 LAN interface configured as an access port to enter the forwarding state immediately, bypassing the listening and learning states. Use PortFast only when connecting a single end station to a Layer 2 access port.

- **UplinkFast:** Provides from three to five seconds convergence after a direct link failure and achieves load balancing between redundant Layer 2 links using uplink groups.

- **BackboneFast:** Cuts convergence time by **max_age** for indirect failure. BackboneFast is initiated when a root port or blocked port on a network device receives inferior bridge protocol data units (BPDU) from its designated bridge.

- **Loop guard***: Prevents an alternate or root port from becoming designated in the absence of BPDUs. Loop guard helps prevent bridging loops that could occur because of a unidirectional link failure on a point-to-point link.

- **Root guard***: Secures the root on a specific switch by preventing external switches from becoming roots.

- **BPDU guard***: When configured on a PortFast-enabled port, BPDU guard shuts down the port that receives a BPDU.

- **UniDirectional Link Detection (UDLD):** Monitors the physical configuration of fiber-optic and copper connections and detects when a one-way connection exists. When a unidirectional link is detected, the interface is shut down and the system alerted.

- **Bridge assurance:** When enabled, bridge assurance alters the spanning behavior to send BPDUs on all ports, as opposed to the normal behavior, where BPDUs are sent only on designated ports. When a port that has been enabled for bridge assurance stops receiving BPDUs from its neighbor, it moves to the BA Inconsistent state, so that it prevents a potential bridging loop.

Note   The STP Toolkit also supports the BPDU filter option, which prevents PortFast-enabled ports from sending or receiving BPDUs. This feature effectively disables STP at the edge and can lead to STP loops. It is not recommended.

STP Standards and Features

STP enables the network to deterministically block interfaces and provide a loop-free topology in a network with redundant links. There are several varieties of STP:

- STP is the original IEEE 802.1D version (802.1D-1998) that provides a loop-free topology in a network with redundant links.

- Common Spanning Tree (CST) assumes one spanning-tree instance for the entire bridged network, regardless of the number of VLANs.

- Per VLAN Spanning Tree Plus (PVST+) is a Cisco enhancement of STP that provides a separate 802.1D spanning-tree instance for each VLAN configured in the network.

  The separate instance supports PortFast, UplinkFast, BackboneFast, BPDU guard, BPDU filter, root guard, and loop guard.

- Multiple Spanning Tree (MST) is an IEEE standard inspired from the earlier Cisco proprietary Multi-Instance Spanning Tree Protocol (MISTP) implementation. MST maps multiple VLANs into the same spanning-tree instance. The Cisco implementation of MSTP is MST, which provides up to 16 instances of Rapid Spanning Tree Protocol (RSTP, 802.1W) and combines many VLANs with the same physical and logical topology into a common RSTP instance. Each instance supports PortFast, UplinkFast, BackboneFast, BPDU guard, BPDU filter, root guard, and loop guard.

Note   Some software releases support up to 65 MST instances per MST domain. Refer to the documentation of the software release in use to determine the maximum number for the version in use.

- RSTP, or IEEE 802.1W, is an evolution of STP that provides faster convergence of STP.

- RPVST+ is a Cisco enhancement of RSTP that uses PVST+. It provides a separate instance of 802.1W per VLAN. The separate instance supports PortFast, UplinkFast, BackboneFast, BPDU guard, BPDU filter, root guard, and loop guard.

Note   When Cisco documentation and this book refer to implementing RSTP, they are referring to the Cisco RSTP implementation, or PVRST+.

Note   The Cisco RSTP implementation is far superior to the 802.1D STP and even PSVT+ in convergence and greatly improves the restoration time for any VLAN that needs to reconverge as a result of a topology change.

Note   In a multivendor switch environment, MST should be used for maximum compatibility or isolate the various STP domains at Layer 3 to avoid compatibility issues.

Recommended Practices for STP Hardening

To configure a VLAN instance to become the root bridge, enter the **spanning-tree vlan** *vlan_ID* root primary command to modify the bridge priority from the default value (32768) to a significantly lower value. The bridge priority for the specified VLAN is set to 8192 if this value will cause the switch to become the root for the VLAN. If any bridge for the VLAN has a priority lower than 8192, the switch sets the priority to one less than the lowest bridge priority Manually placing the primary and secondary bridges along with enabling STP Toolkit options enables you to support a deterministic configuration where you know which ports should be forwarding and which ports should be blocking. A bridge with priority 0 always becomes the root bridge unless a bridge with priority 0 and a lower MAC address joins the topology. Changing the bridge priority can be done with the **spantree priority** command.

Setting a deterministic root bridge selection increases network stability and convergence time. A root bridge (priority of 0) and an alternate root bridge (priority of 1) should be set.

Note   Defining the root bridge under MST is done using the **spanning-tree mst** *instance_id* **root primary** command. When you use this command, the switch reviews all bridge ID values it receives from other root bridges. If any root bridge has a bridge ID equal to or less than 24576, it sets its own bridge priority to 4096 less than the lowest bridge priority. To ensure that it retains its position as the root bridge, you must also enable root guard.

Figure 2-11 illustrates recommended placements for STP Toolkit features:

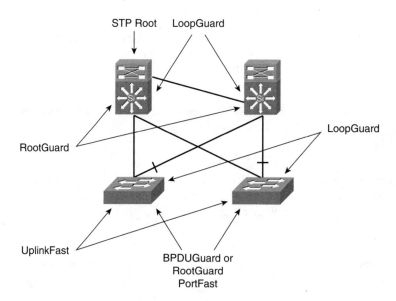

Figure 2-11   *Layer 2 Hardening*

- Loop guard is implemented on the Layer 2 ports between distribution switches, and on the uplink ports from the access switches to the distribution switches.

- Root guard is configured on the distribution switch ports facing the access switches.

■ UplinkFast is implemented on the uplink ports from the access switches to the distribution switches.

Note When you are configuring MST, UplinkFast is not required as a feature on dual-homed switches. Rapid root port failover occurs as part of the default MST protocol implementation.

■ BPDU guard or root guard is configured on ports from the access switches to the end devices, as is PortFast.

■ The UDLD protocol allows devices to monitor the physical configuration of the cables and detect when a unidirectional link exists. When a unidirectional link is detected, UDLD shuts down the affected LAN port. UDLD is often configured on ports linking switches.

■ Depending on the security requirements of an organization, the port security feature can be used to restrict a port's ingress traffic by limiting the MAC addresses allowed to send traffic into the port.

Recommended Practices for Trunk Configuration and VLAN Trunking Protocol

A trunk is a point-to-point link between two networking devices that carry the traffic of multiple VLANs. Trunks are typically deployed on the interconnection between the access and distribution layers. The current recommended practice is to use IEEE 802.1Q trunks. Cisco extensions to 802.1Q avoid security concerns related to the 802.1Q non-tagged, native VLAN. The native VLAN is assigned to an unused ID, or the tagged, native VLAN option is used to avoid VLAN hopping. Cisco originally developed a proprietary mechanism, Inter-Switch Link (ISL), which has structural differences in the protocol, but theoretically achieves the same results. ISL is rarely seen; it's usually only in legacy devices.

Note VLAN hopping is an attack using a double 802.1Q-encapsulated packet. If the attacker has specific knowledge of the 802.1Q native VLAN, a packet could be crafted that when processed, the first or outermost tag is removed when the packet is switched onto the untagged, native VLAN. When the packet reaches the target switch, the inner or second tag is then processed, and the potentially malicious packet is switched to the target VLAN. The traffic in this attack scenario is in a single direction, and no return traffic can be switched by this mechanism. In addition, this attack cannot work unless the attacker knows the native VLAN identity.

VLAN Trunking Protocol (VTP) is a protocol that enables network managers to centrally manage the VLAN database. VTP Transparent mode is now a recommended practice because it decreases the potential for operational error.

By default, Cisco switches are configured as a VTP server with no VTP domain name specified.

Therefore, it is also recommended when configuring switches, along with setting the mode to Transparent, to set the VTP domain name. This is important if you are connecting your switch to other domains, such as a service provider switch. Misconfiguration of the switch as a server or client with no VTP domain name causes it to accept the domain name of an adjacent VTP server and overwrite the local VLAN database.

As a recommended practice, when configuring switch-to-switch interconnections to carry multiple VLANs, set Dynamic Trunking Protocol (DTP) to Desirable and Desirable with Encapsulation Negotiate to support DTP negotiation.

Note   Turning DTP to On and On with Nonnegotiate could save seconds of outage when restoring a failed link or node. However, with this configuration, DTP is not actively monitoring the state of the trunk, and a misconfigured trunk is not easily identified.

One instance where you would use On with Nonnegotiate is if you are trunking between two different VTP domains. DTP includes the VTP domain name in its messages; and if the names do not match, the trunk does not come up if set to Desirable.

Another recommended practice is to manually prune unused VLANs from trunked interfaces to avoid broadcast propagation. You should avoid automatic VLAN pruning.

The final recommendation for trunk configuration is to disable trunks on host ports, because host devices do not need to negotiate trunk status. This practice speeds up PortFast and is a VLAN-hopping security measure.

VTP version 3 supports centralized VLAN administration in a switched network. VTP runs only on trunks and provides the following four modes:

■   **Server:** Updates clients and servers. The VTP server switch propagates the VTP database to VTP client switches.

■   **Client:** Receives updates but cannot make changes.

■   **Transparent:** Does not participate in the VTP domain. Lets updates pass through.

■   **Off:** Ignores VTP updates.

With VTP, when you configure a new VLAN on a switch in VTP Server mode, the VLAN is distributed through all switches in the VTP domain. This redistribution reduces the need to configure the same VLAN everywhere.

With hierarchical networks that do not span VLANs across the distribution layer, there is little need for a shared common VLAN database. In the recommended campus design, the same VLAN should not appear in two access layer switches. Adding and removing VLANs is generally not a common network management practice. In most cases, VLANs are defined once during switch setup, with few, if any, additional modifications to the

VLAN database in an access layer switch. The benefits of dynamic propagation of VLAN information across the network are not worth the potential for unexpected behavior that might result from operational error. For these reasons, VTP Transparent mode is the recommended configuration option.

Dynamic Trunking Protocol

DTP provides switch ports to negotiate the trunking method with another device and to automatically allow a link to become a trunk.

With Cisco devices, there are five Layer 2 port modes:

- **Trunk:** Puts the port into permanent trunking mode and negotiates to convert the link into a trunk link. The port becomes a trunk port even if the neighboring port does not agree to the change.

- **Desirable:** Actively attempts to form a trunk, subject to neighbor agreement. The port becomes a trunk port if the neighboring port is set to On, Desirable, or Auto mode.

- **Auto:** Makes the port willing to convert the link to a trunk link. The port becomes a trunk port if the neighboring port is set to On or Desirable mode.

- **Access:** This is the access mode in Cisco IOS Software that specifies that the port never become a trunk, even if the neighbor tries. This mode puts the LAN port into permanent nontrunking mode and negotiates to convert the link into a nontrunking link.

- **Nonnegotiate:** Prevents the port from generating DTP frames. You must configure the neighboring port manually as a trunk port to establish a trunk link.

With Cisco devices, there are three Ethernet trunk encapsulation types:

- **ISL:** Uses Inter-Switch Link (ISL) encapsulation on the trunk link

- **Dot1q:** Uses 802.1Q encapsulation on the trunk link.

- **Negotiate:** Specifies that the LAN port negotiate with the neighboring LAN port to become an ISL or 802.1Q trunk, depending on the configuration and capabilities of the neighboring LAN port. ISL is now considered a legacy protocol and is not supported on many new platforms.

The trunking mode, the trunk encapsulation type, and the hardware capabilities of the two connected LAN ports determine whether a link becomes an ISL or 802.1Q trunk.

A common practice is to configure both ends of the trunk to desirable. This has the operational benefit of providing a clear indication of a functional trunking connection with **show** commands and is the general recommendation for DTP trunking.

An alternative practice is to set one side of the link (typically the access layer) to Auto and the other end (typically the distribution layer) to Desirable. This setting allows for automatic trunk formation, with DTP running on the interconnection to protect against some rare hardware failure scenarios and software misconfigurations.

For fastest convergence, a third configuration turns DTP to On and On with Nonnegotiate to save a few seconds of outage when restoring a failed link or node. However, DTP is not actively monitoring the state of the trunk with this configuration, and a misconfigured trunk is not easily identified. The Nonnegotiate setting can also cause loss of connectivity if the process is not performed in the correct order and there is no out-of-band connectivity to the farthest switch from where the in-band modifications are being made.

As a recommended practice, when configuring switch-to-switch interconnections to carry multiple VLANs, set DTP to Desirable and Desirable with Encapsulation Negotiate to support DTP negotiation.

Note   Turning DTP to On and On with Nonnegotiate could save seconds of outage when restoring a failed link or node. However, with this configuration, DTP is not actively monitoring the state of the trunk, and a misconfigured trunk is not easily identified.

One instance where you would use On with Nonnegotiate is if you are trunking between two different VTP domains. DTP includes the VTP domain name in its messages; and if the names do not match, the trunk does not come up if set to Desirable.

Recommended Practices for UDLD Configuration

UDLD enables devices to monitor the physical configuration of the cables and detect when a unidirectional link exists where bidirectional communication has not been established.

As Figure 2-12 shows, UDLD is typically deployed on fiber topologies where physical misconnections can occur that enable a link to appear to be up/up when there is a mismatched set of transmit/receive pairs. UDLD supports both fiber-optic and copper Ethernet cables connected to LAN ports.

Each switch port configured for UDLD will send UDLD protocol hello packets at Layer 2 containing the device and port identifications of the port and the device and port identifications of the neighbor as seen by UDLD on that port. Neighboring ports should see their own device and port identifications in the packets received from the other side. If the port does not see its own device and port identifications in the incoming UDLD packets for a specific duration of time, the link is considered unidirectional and is shut down. The default 15-second hello timers are the same for normal and aggressive UDLD. In Normal mode, UDLD error-disables only the end where the UDLD is detected; Aggressive mode error-disables both ends of a connection after aging on a previously bidirectional link in eight seconds.

A recommended practice is to enable UDLD Aggressive mode in all environments where fiber-optic interconnections are used. UDLD is enabled globally on all fiber-optic LAN ports with the Cisco IOS Software **udld** {**enable** | **aggressive**} command. UDLD is enabled on individual LAN ports with the **udld port** [**aggressive**] **interface** command.

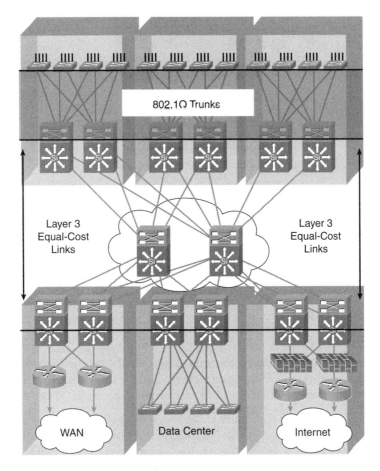

Figure 2-12 *Topology for UDLD*

Note You should enable UDLD in Global mode so that you do not have to enable it on every individual fiber-optic interface.

Recommended Practices for EtherChannel

An EtherChannel bundles individual Ethernet links into a single logical link that provides the aggregate bandwidth of up to eight physical links.

As shown in Figure 2-13, EtherChannels are usually deployed between the distribution-to-core and core-to-core interconnections where increased availability and scaled bandwidth are required. EtherChannel link aggregation is used to provide link redundancy and prevent a single point of failure, and to reduce peering complexity because the single logical entity reduces the number of Layer 3 neighbor relationships as compared to multiple parallel links.

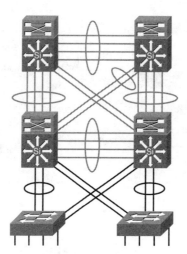

Figure 2-13   *EtherChannels*

> **Note**   EtherChannel also provides an optimization to STP by enabling all member ports to be placed in Forwarding mode. STP views the EtherChannel as a single logical link.

EtherChannels create channels containing up to eight parallel links between switches. If the channels are on interfaces that are on different physical line cards, there is increased availability because the failure of a single line card does not cause a complete loss of connectivity.

There are two variants for the control mechanism for EtherChannel: the prestandard Cisco implementation that uses Port Aggregation Protocol (PAgP) and the IEEE 802.3ad standards-based implementation that uses Link Aggregation Control Protocol (LACP). PAgP and LACP do not interoperate. You can manually configure a switch with PAgP on one side and LACP on the other side in the On/On mode. When this is done, ports configured in the On mode do not negotiate, and therefore there is no negotiation traffic between the ports. This configuration results in the EtherChannel being hard-coded.

When connecting a Cisco IOS Software device to a Catalyst operating system device, make sure that the PAgP settings used for establishing EtherChannels are coordinated. The defaults are different for a Cisco IOS Software device and a Catalyst operating system device. As a recommended practice, Catalyst operating system devices should have PAgP set to Off when connecting to a Cisco IOS Software device if EtherChannels are not configured. If EtherChannel PAgP is used, set both sides of the interconnection to Desirable.

Port aggregation should be disabled when not needed. Port aggregation can most effectively be controlled by disabling it on interfaces facing end users with the Set Port Host macro on the Catalyst operating system or the Switchport Host macro on Cisco ISO Software. These macros disable both trunking and EtherChannel while enabling STP PortFast.

Port Aggregation Protocol

PAgP is one of the control mechanisms for EtherChannel. PAgP has four modes related to the automatic formation of bundled, redundant switch-to-switch interconnections:

- **On:** Mode that forces the LAN port to channel unconditionally. In the On mode, a usable EtherChannel exists only when a LAN port group in the On mode is connected to another LAN port group in the On mode. Because ports configured in the On mode do not negotiate, no negotiation traffic occurs between the ports. You cannot configure the On mode with an EtherChannel protocol. If one end uses the On mode, the other end must also use the On mode.

- **Desirable:** Places a port into an active negotiating state, in which the port starts negotiations with other ports by sending PAgP packets. This mode is not supported when the EtherChannel members are from different switches in the switch stack (cross-stack EtherChannel).

- **Auto:** Places a port into a passive negotiating state, in which the port responds to PAgP packets it receives but does not start PAgP packet negotiation. This setting minimizes the transmission of PAgP packets. This mode is not supported when the EtherChannel members are from different switches in the switch stack (cross-stack EtherChannel).

- **Off:** Do not become a member.

As with DTP, the long-standing practice for EtherChannel/PAgP has been to set one side of the interconnection (typically the access switch) to Auto and the other side (typically the distribution switch) to Desirable, or both sides to Desirable. In these configurations, an EtherChannel is established when configuration is complete, and connectivity to the remote switch is always available, even when the EtherChannel is not completely established.

Note   For Layer 2 EtherChannels, a desirable/desirable PAgP configuration is recommended so that PAgP is running across all members of the bundle, ensuring that an individual link failure will not result in a STP failure.

Link Aggregation Control Protocol

LACP is another control mechanism for EtherChannel. LACP has four modes related to the automatic formation of bundled, redundant switch-to-switch interconnections:

- **On:** Mode that forces the LAN port to channel unconditionally. In the On mode, a usable EtherChannel exists only when a LAN port group in the On mode is connected to another LAN port group in the On mode. Because ports configured in the On mode do not negotiate, no negotiation traffic occurs between the ports. You cannot configure the On mode with an EtherChannel protocol. If one end uses the On mode, the other end must also use the On mode.

- **Active:** LACP mode that places a port into an active negotiating state, in which the port initiates negotiations with other ports by sending LACP packets.

- **Passive:** LACP mode that places a port into a passive negotiating state, in which the port responds to LACP packets it receives but does not initiate LACP negotiation.

- **Off:** Do not become a member.

Note   The recommended practice for EtherChannel LACP is to set one side of the interconnection (typically the access switch) to Active and the other side (typically the distribution switch) to Passive, or both sides to Active. In these configurations, a channel is established when configuration is complete, and connectivity to the remote switch is always available, even when the channel is not completely established.

Supporting Virtual Switching Systems Designs

As shown in Figure 2-14, VSS is a network virtualization technology that combines two Cisco Catalyst 6500 switches into a single logical entity. The two switches form a single virtual switch, with a single integrated control and management plane. From a network design perspective, the VSS can appear as a single switch with dual redundant supervisors, even if these supervisors are located in two separate physical chassis.

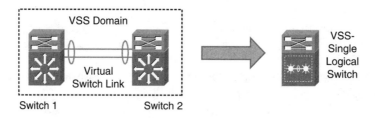

Figure 2-14   *VSS Logical Versus Physical Topology*

A special EtherChannel link, the virtual switch link (VSL), extends the backplane between the two switches. This extension allows the supervisor module in one switch to control the hardware in the other chassis. Also, the extension carries system control information such as hot-standby supervisor programming, line card status, distributed forwarding card (DFC) programming, system management, diagnostics, and more. In addition, the VSL carries user data when necessary. The VSL EtherChannel should consist of at least two 10-Gbps links, which should be terminated on different line cards in the chassis for maximum availability.

From a control and management plane standpoint, only one of the two supervisors is active and controls all the line cards in both chassis. The RP on the second supervisor in the other chassis runs as a hot standby, and is ready to take over when the active RP fails. However, all data plane components, such as switch fabrics, PFCs, and DFCs, and even those data plane components that are on the standby supervisor, are active and are used to forward traffic. As a result, the VSS has access to the complete forwarding capacity of the combined chassis.

To attain high availability, the VSS uses existing SSO and NSF mechanisms to ensure rapid stateful failover. The RP on the secondary supervisor is kept in a hot standby state. State information is synchronized between the supervisors through the VSL. When the control plane on the primary supervisor fails, the secondary supervisor assumes the active role by using similar mechanisms to those mechanisms that are used in a single chassis SSO or Cisco NSF failover.

From a design perspective, the most important benefit of a VSS is that it now becomes possible to build an EtherChannel bundle that each link is physically terminated on two separate Catalyst 6500 chassis. This is also referred to as a Multichassis EtherChannel (MEC). Because the two chassis form a single logical entity, the devices on the other end of the EtherChannel link use standard EtherChannel technology to connect to the VSS. As a result, the VSS solution is entirely transparent to EtherChannel peer devices such as access switches or servers.

Common Access-Distribution Block Designs

Figure 2-15 shows the most common access-distribution block designs: Layer 2 loop free, Layer 2 looped, and Layer 3 routed.

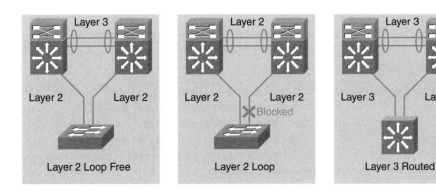

Figure 2-15 *Access-Distribution Block Designs*

Three design models for the access-distribution block are commonly deployed:

■   **Layer 2 loop-free design:** In this design, the access switches use Layer 2 switching. The links between the access and distribution layers are configured as Layer 2 trunks. The link between the distribution switches is configured as a Layer 3 routed link. An EtherChannel is typically used for this link to increase availability. In this design, there are no Layer 2 loops in the access-distribution block, which means that the Spanning Tree Protocol is not involved in network convergence and load balancing.

All the ports are in the spanning-tree Forwarding state. Load balancing of the traffic from the access to the distribution layer is based on the First Hop Router Protocol (FHRP) that is used in this design. Reconvergence time in the case of failure is driven primarily by FHRP reconvergence. A limitation of this solution is that it is optimal for networks where each access layer VLAN can be constrained to a single access switch. Stretching VLANs across multiple access switches is not recommended in this design.

Note   The Layer 2 loop-free design is a current best-practice design. However, it is often not feasible to use it because of the restriction that VLANs should not be stretched across multiple access switches. For various legacy reasons, many existing networks are using VLANs that are stretched across multiple access switches, and it is impossible to migrate to a Layer 2 loop-free design in these scenarios.

- Layer 2 looped design: The Layer 2 looped design also uses Layer 2 switching on the access layer, and the links between the access and distribution switches are also configured as Layer 2 trunks. However, unlike the Layer 2 loop-free design, the link between the distribution switches is configured here as a Layer 2 trunk. This configuration introduces a Layer 2 loop between the distribution switches and the access switches. To eliminate this loop from the topology, the Spanning Tree Protocol blocks one of the uplinks from the access switch to the distribution switches. This design is recommended for networks that require an extension of VLANs across multiple access switches. A drawback is that network convergence in the case of failure is now dependent on spanning-tree convergence that is combined with FHRP convergence. Another downside is limited load balancing. PVST root election tuning can be used to balance traffic on a VLAN-by-VLAN basis. However, within each VLAN, spanning tree always blocks one of the access switch uplinks.

- **Layer 3 routed design:** The Layer 3 routed design uses Layer 3 routing on the access switches. All links between switches are configured as Layer 3 routed links. The advantage of this design is that it eliminates the Spanning Tree Protocol from the inter-switch links. It is still enabled on edge ports to protect against user-induced loops, but it does not play a role in the network reconvergence in the access-distribution block. FHRPs are also eliminated from the design, because the default gateway for the end hosts now resides on the access switch instead of on the distribution switch. Network reconvergence behavior is determined solely by the routing protocol being used. Like the Layer 2 loop-free design, the Layer 3 routed design constrains VLANs to a single access switch. Also, this design does not allow VLANs to be extended across multiple access switches, and it requires more sophisticated hardware for the access switches.

Multichassis EtherChannels and VSS

VSS enables designs that are based on MECs. Figure 2-16 illustrates the differences.

As discussed, the VSS enables new design options for the access-distribution block. Because the VSS is a single logical switch, EtherChannel technology can now be used to bundle two uplinks from each access switch into a single logical channel, even if they are terminated on two separate physical Catalyst 6500 chassis.

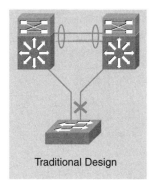 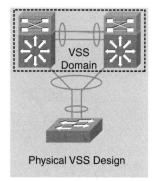 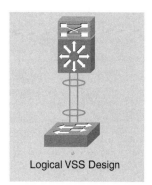

Traditional Design   Physical VSS Design   Logical VSS Design

Figure 2-16   *VSS and MEC*

Because the Spanning Tree Protocol recognizes the EtherChannel link as a single logical link, spanning tree is effectively removed from the network topology. Like the Layer 2 loop-free design, spanning tree is still enabled to guard against loops that are caused by miswiring or other human errors. It no longer plays a role in network convergence, however. A primary advantage of designs that are based on the MEC is that all links between the access and distribution layers are used in forwarding. Traffic is load balanced across the links through the EtherChannel hashing mechanisms.

Another advantage is that this design allows VLANs to extend across multiple access switches if necessary, without introducing Layer 2 loops into the topology.

VSS Design Considerations

VSS enables loop-free logical star designs that retain full physical redundancy.

As shown in Figure 2-17, with the other common campus access-distribution block designs, VSS and the MEC deliver a robust and highly available design without sacrificing design flexibility. They also do not impose restrictions on the hardware to be used at the access layer.

The VSS and the MEC can be used to create logical star topologies while retaining complete redundancy in the underlying physical topology. The MEC links can be configured as Layer 2 trunks toward the Layer 2 access switches or as routed links toward the core. They can even be configured as routed links toward the access layer in a routed access layer design.

The most common point to deploy the VSS in the campus is in the distribution layer. However, it can be deployed also in the core of the network or even in the access layer of a server farm or data center to connect dual-homed servers to a VSS by using MECs.

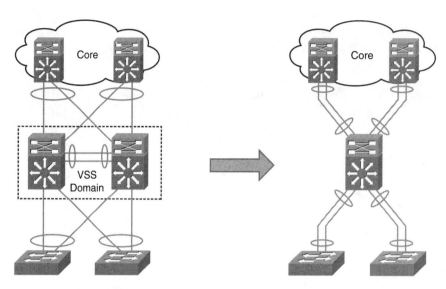

Figure 2-17 *VSS Logical Topology*

Dual Active Detection and Recovery

The VSL is a vital component of the VSS, and the design should carefully ensure its availability and its ability to recover from VSL failures.

A key point to consider when using the VSS in a network design is sufficient redundancy for the VSL between the two chassis. The VSL is used by the hot-standby supervisor to monitor the state of the active supervisor. If the VSL fails, the standby supervisor assumes that the other supervisor has been lost and it takes on the active role. However, only the VSL has actually failed, not the active switch itself. As a result, two separate switches run as the active switch. Because both switches are using the same configuration, various failures can occur, depending on the protocols being used:

■ **Layer 2 MEC:** Both switches start sending BPDUs on the MEC toward the neighboring switches. Because they use separate source MAC addresses for the BPDUs, the neighboring switch sees the separate MAC addresses as an EtherChannel inconsistency and moves the EtherChannel to the error-disabled state.

■ **OSPF:** Both supervisors start using the same OSPF router ID. Depending on whether a Layer 3 MEC or separate links are used, failing SPF adjacencies or OSPF flood wars result. Access layer subnets become unreachable.

■ **EIGRP:** Adjacencies may be lost, depending on how EIGRP traffic is hashed when using Layer 3 MEC. In the case of separate links, EIGRP remains functional because the router ID has less significance in EIGRP than it has in OSPF.

The best way to prevent any of these failures is to make the VSL itself as resilient as possible. At a minimum, two links are required for the VSL EtherChannel, but using additional links increases the availability of the VSL.

Note   The only interfaces that can be used for the VSLs are the 10-Gbps ports on the VS-S720-10G-3C/XL supervisor engine, the WS-X6708-10G-3C/XL line card, and (as of Cisco IOS Release 12.2(33)SXI) the WS-X6716-10G-3C/XL line card.

VSS Design Best Practices

When designing and deploying the VSS, follow the best-practice recommendations for optimal results:

- Always use star topologies that are based on MEC with the VSS. Then, you can be sure that the topology remains loop free and yields the best possible convergence times.

- Use unique VSS domain numbers for each VSS pair in your network, even if the pairs are not directly connected to each other.

- As with any EtherChannel, always use a number of links that is a power of 2 (2, 4, 8) to optimize the load balancing of traffic across the VSLs.

- Do not configure switch preemption. Switch preemption ensures that the same supervisor is always active when both switches are up. However, switch preemption can cause unnecessary switch reboots in some scenarios, and there are no tangible benefits in always having one specific supervisor that takes on the active role.

- Tuning the Link Management Protocol (LMP), LACP, and PAgP timers in an aggressive manner may adversely affect the system performance. When you use star topologies that are based on VSS and MEC, the Spanning Tree Protocol is not actively involved in maintaining the network topology. However, it should not be and spanning-tree PortFast and BPDU guard should be used in the access layer to protect against loops at the network edge.

- Enable a dual-active detection mechanism to guard against VSL failures. Use the PAgP method where possible. If that method is not available, use fast hellos. If the fast hellos method also cannot be used, use Bidirectional Forwarding Detection (BFD) instead.

Developing an Optimum Design for Layer 3

To achieve high availability and fast convergence in the Cisco enterprise campus network, the designer needs to manage multiple objectives, including the following:

- Managing oversubscription and bandwidth

- Supporting link load balancing

- Routing protocol design

- FHRPs

This section reviews design models and recommended practices for high availability and fast convergence in Layer 3 of the Cisco enterprise campus network.

Managing Oversubscription and Bandwidth

Typical campus networks are designed with oversubscription, as illustrated in Figure 2-18. The rule-of-thumb recommendation for data oversubscription is 20:1 for access ports on the access-to-distribution uplink. The recommendation is 4:1 for the distribution-to-core links. When you use these oversubscription ratios, you may make congestion on the uplinks an infrequent occurrence. QoS is needed for these occasions. If congestion is occurring frequently, the design does not have sufficient uplink bandwidth.

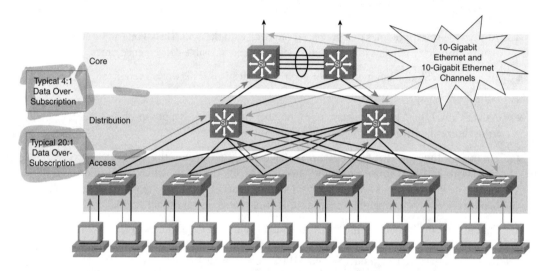

Figure 2-18   *Managing Oversubscription and Bandwidth*

As access layer bandwidth capacity increases to 1 Gbps, multiples of 1 Gbps, and even 10 Gbps, the bandwidth aggregation on the distribution-to-core uplinks might be supported on many Gigabit Ethernet EtherChannels, on 10 Gigabit Ethernet links, and on 10 Gigabit EtherChannels.

Bandwidth Management with EtherChannel

As bandwidth from the distribution layer to the core increases, oversubscription to the access layer must be managed, and some design decisions must be made.

Just adding more uplinks between the distribution and core layers leads to more peer relationships, with an increase in associated overhead.

EtherChannels can reduce the number of peers by creating single logical interface. However, you must consider some issues about how routing protocols react to single link failure:

■   OSPF running on a Cisco IOS Software-based switch notices a failed link and increases the link cost. Traffic is rerouted, and this design leads to a convergence event.

■ EIGRP might not change link cost, because the protocol looks at the end-to-end cost. This design might also overload remaining links.

The EtherChannel Min-Links feature is supported on LACP EtherChannels. This feature allows you to configure the minimum number of member ports that must be in the link-up state and bundled in the EtherChannel for the port channel interface to transition to the link-up state. You can use the EtherChannel Min-Links feature to prevent low-bandwidth LACP EtherChannels from becoming active.

Bandwidth Management with 10 Gigabit Interfaces

Upgrading the uplinks between the distribution and core layers to 10 Gigabit Ethernet links is an alternative design for managing bandwidth. The 10 Gigabit Ethernet links can also support the increased bandwidth requirements.

This is a recommended design:

■ Unlike the multiple link solution, 10 Gigabit Ethernet links do not increase routing complexity. The number of routing peers is not increased.

■ Unlike the EtherChannel solution, the routing protocols can deterministically select the best path between the distribution and core layer.

Link Load Balancing

In Figure 2-19, many equal-cost, redundant paths are provided in the recommended network topology from one access switch to the other across the distribution and core switches. From the perspective of the access layer, there are at least three sets of equal-cost, redundant links to cross to reach another building block, such as the data center.

Cisco Express Forwarding (CEF) is a deterministic algorithm. As shown in Figure 2-19, when packets traverse the network that all use the same input value to the CEF hash, a "go to the right" or "go to the left" decision is made for each redundant path. When this results in some redundant links that are ignored or underutilized, the network is said to be experiencing CEF polarization.

To avoid CEF polarization, you can tune the input into the CEF algorithm across the layers in the network. The default input hash value is Layer 3 for source and destination. If you change this input value to Layer 3 plus Layer 4, the output hash value also changes.

As a recommendation, use alternating hashes in the core and distribution layer switches:

■ In the core layer, continue to use the default, which is based on only Layer 3 information.

■ In the distribution layer, use the Layer 3 plus Layer 4 information as input into the CEF hashing algorithm with the command Dist2-6500 (config)#**mls ip cef load-sharing full**.

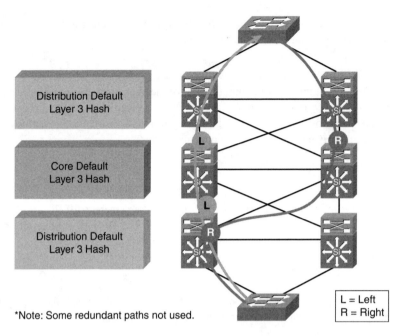

Figure 2-19 *CEF Load Balancing (Default Behavior)*

This alternating approach helps eliminate the always-right or always-left biased decisions and helps balance the traffic over equal-cost, redundant links in the network.

Link Load Balancing with EtherChannel

EtherChannel allows load sharing of traffic among the links in the channel and redundancy in the event that one or more links in the channel fail.

You can tune the hashing algorithm used to select the specific EtherChannel link on which a packet is transmitted. You can use the default Layer 3 source and destination information, or you can add a level of load balancing to the process by adding the Layer 4 TCP/IP port information as an input to the algorithm.

Figure 2-20 illustrates some results from experiments at Cisco in a test environment using a typical IP addressing scheme of one subnet per VLAN, two VLANs per access switch, and the RFC 1918 private address space. The default Layer 3 hash algorithm provided about one-third to two-thirds utilization. When the algorithm was changed to include Layer 4 information, nearly full utilization was achieved with the same topology and traffic pattern.

The recommended practice is to use Layer 3 plus Layer 4 load balancing to provide as much information as possible for input to the EtherChannel algorithm to achieve the best or most uniform utilization of EtherChannel members. The command **port-channel load-balance** is used to present the more unique values to the hashing algorithm. This can be achieved using the command dist1-6500(config)#**port-channel load-balance src-dst-port**.

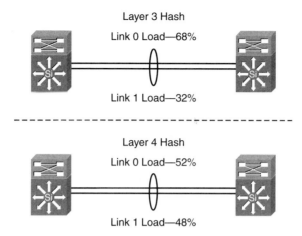

Figure 2-20   *EtherChannel Load Balancing*

To achieve the best load balancing, use two, four, or eight ports in the port channel. Older Cisco switches required that bundles needed to be on the same ASIC.

One drawback of EtherChannel load balancing is that it does not support per-packet load balancing. If there is one large data transfer in an application using the same information up to Layer 4, the transfer traverses just one link.

EtherChannel Design Versus Equal-Cost Multipathing

In some network designs, you may have the option to use either EtherChannel or routing protocol Equal Cost Multipath (ECMP) to balance the load between two Layer 3 switches.

The best method depends on the specific design requirements, but the following includes some general considerations:

- The load-balancing hashing options for EtherChannel and ECMP differ, and the specific options that are available are platform dependent. The hashing method and traffic mix determine how well the traffic will be balanced across the links.

- With EtherChannel, the links between the switches are treated as a single logical link by the routing protocol. Only a single routing adjacency is established between the two Layer 3 switches. With ECMP, a neighbor relationship is established for each of the links, which increases routing protocol overhead.

- ECMP uses routing protocol mechanics to select links, add or remove paths, and balance traffic across the links. EtherChannel uses LACP for link control. Routing protocols generally allow more granular control of path-selection, convergence, and load-balancing characteristics.

- With ECMP, only the routing protocol is involved in directing traffic across the links. EtherChannel uses both the routing protocol and LACP. In this regard, ECMP is easier to set up and maintain.

- The combination of better control and visibility makes ECMP easier to troubleshoot than EtherChannel.

Routing Protocol Design

This section reviews design recommendations for routing protocols in the enterprise campus.

Routing protocols are usually deployed across the distribution-to-core and core-to-core interconnections.

Layer 3 routing design can be used in the access layer, too, but this design is currently not as common.

Layer 3 routing protocols are used to quickly reroute around failed nodes or links while providing load balancing over redundant paths.

Build Redundant Triangles

For optimum distribution-to-core layer convergence, build redundant triangles, not squares, to take advantage of equal-cost, redundant paths for the best deterministic convergence.

The topology connecting the distribution and core switches should be built using triangles, with equal-cost paths to all redundant nodes. The triangle design is shown in Figure 2-21 Model A, and uses dual equal-cost paths to avoid timer-based, nondeterministic convergence. Instead of indirect neighbor or route-loss detection using hellos and dead timers, the triangle design failover is hardware based and relies on physical link loss to mark a path as unusable and reroute all traffic to the alternate equal-cost path. There is no need for OSPF or EIGRP to recalculate a new path.

In contrast, the square topology shown in Figure 2-21 Model B requires routing protocol convergence to fail over to an alternate path in the event of a link or node failure. It is possible to build a topology that does not rely on equal-cost, redundant paths to compensate for limited physical fiber connectivity or to reduce cost. However, with this design, it is not possible to achieve the same deterministic convergence in the event of a link or node failure, and for this reason the design will not be optimized for high availability.

Peer Only on Transit Links

Another recommended practice is to limit unnecessary peering across the access layer by peering only on transit links.

By default, the distribution layer switches send routing updates and attempt to peer across the uplinks from the access switches to the remote distribution switches on every VLAN. This is unnecessary and wastes CPU processing time.

Triangles: Link or box failure does *not* require routing protocol convergence.

Squares: Link or box failure requires routing protocol convergence.

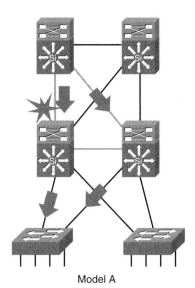
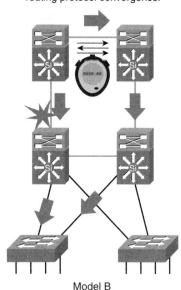

Model A   Model B

Figure 2-21   *Build Redundant Triangles*

Figure 2-22 shows an example network where with 4 VLANs per access switch and 3 access switches, 12 unnecessary adjacencies are formed. Only the adjacency on the link between the distribution switches is needed. This redundant Layer 3 peering has no benefit from a high-availability perspective, and only adds load in terms of memory, routing protocol update overhead, and complexity. In addition, in the event of a link failure, it is possible for traffic to transit through a neighboring access layer switch, which is not desirable.

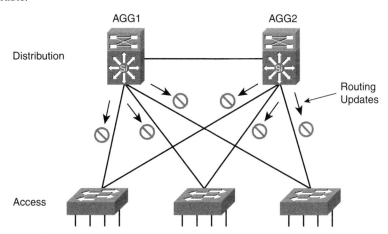

Figure 2-22   *Use Passive Interfaces at the Access Layer Triangles*

As a recommended practice, limit unnecessary routing peer adjacencies by configuring the ports toward Layer 2 access switches as passive and thus suppress the advertising of routing updates. If a distribution switch does not receive routing updates from a potential peer on a specific interface, it does not need to process these updates, and it does not form a neighbor adjacency with the potential peer across that interface.

There are two approaches to configuring passive interfaces for the access switches:

■   Use the **passive-interface** default command, and selectively use the **no passive-interface** command to enable a neighboring relationship where peering is desired.

■   Use the **passive-interface** command to selectively make specific interfaces passive.

A passive interface configuration example for OSPF is shown here:

```
AGG1(config)#router ospf 1
AGG1(config-router)#passive-interface Vlan 99
! Or
AGG1(config)#router ospf 1
AGG1(config-router)#passive-interface default
AGG1(config-router)#no passive-interface Vlan 99
```

A passive interface configuration example for EIGRP is shown here:

```
AGG1(config)#router EIGRP 1
AGG1(config-router)#passive-interface Vlan 99
! Or
AGG1(config)#router EIGRP 1
AGG1(config-router)#passive-interface default
AGG1(config-router)#no passive-interface Vlan 99
```

Use whichever technique requires the fewest lines of configuration or is the easiest for you to manage.

Summarize at the Distribution Layer

A hierarchical routing design reduces routing update traffic and avoids unnecessary routing computations. Such a hierarchy is achieved through allocating IP networks in contiguous blocks that can be easily summarized by a dynamic routing protocol.

It is a recommended practice to configure route summarization at the distribution layer to advertise a single summary route to represent multiple IP networks within the building (switch block). As a result, fewer routes are advertised through the core layer and subsequently to the distribution layer switches in other buildings (switch blocks). If the routing information is not summarized toward the core, EIGRP and OSPF require interaction with a potentially large number of peers to converge around a failed node.

Summarization at the distribution layer optimizes the rerouting process. If a link to an access layer device goes down, return traffic at the distribution layer to that device is dropped until the IGP converges. When summarization is used and the distribution nodes send summarized information toward the core, an individual distribution node does not advertise loss of connectivity to a single VLAN or subnet. This means that the core does not know that it cannot send traffic to the distribution switch where the access link has failed. Summaries limit the number of peers that an EIGRP router must query or the number of link-state advertisements (LSA) that OSPF must process, and thereby speeds the rerouting process.

Summarization should be performed at the boundary where the distribution layer of each building connects to the core. The method for configuring route summarization varies, depending on the IGP being used. Route summarization is covered in detail in Chapter 3, "Developing an Optimum Design for Layer 3." These designs require a Layer 3 link between the distribution switches, as shown in Figure 2-23, to allow the distribution node that loses connectivity to a given VLAN or subnet the ability to reroute traffic across the distribution-to-distribution link. To be effective, the address space selected for the distribution-to-distribution link must be within the address space being summarized.

Summarization relies on a solid network addressing design.

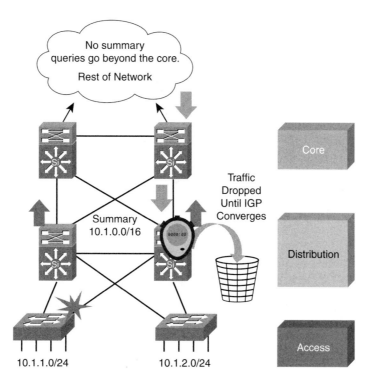

Figure 2-23 *Summarize at the Distribution Layer Triangles*

First-Hop Redundancy

First-hop redundancy or default-gateway redundancy is an important component in convergence in a highly available hierarchical network design.

First-hop redundancy allows a network to recover from the failure of the device acting as the default gateway for end nodes on a physical segment. When the access layer is Layer 2, the distribution layer switches act as the default gateway for the entire Layer 2 domain that they support, as illustrated in Figure 2-24.

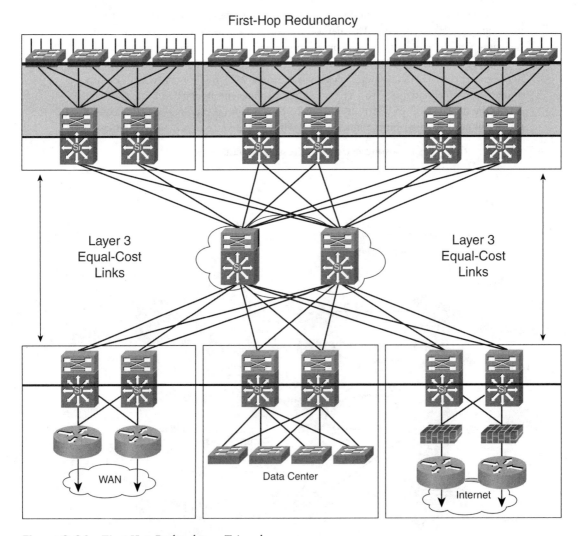

Figure 2-24 *First-Hop Redundancy Triangles*

A first-hop redundancy protocol is needed only if the design implements Layer 2 between the access switch and the distribution switch. If Layer 3 is supported to the access switch, the default gateway for end devices is at the access level.

In Cisco deployments, HSRP, developed by Cisco, is typically used as the FHRP. VRRP is an Internet Engineering Task Force (IETF) standards-based method of providing default-gateway redundancy. More deployments are starting to use GLBP, which can more easily achieve load balancing on the uplinks from the access layer to the distribution layer, and first-hop redundancy and failure protection.

HSRP and VRRP with Cisco enhancements both provide a robust method of backing up the default gateway and can provide subsecond failover to the redundant distribution switch when tuned properly. HSRP is the recommended protocol over VRRP because it is a Cisco-owned standard, which allows for the rapid development of new features and functionality before VRRP. VRRP is the logical choice over HSRP when interoperability with other vendor devices is required.

HSRP or GLBP timers can be reliably tuned to achieve 800-ms convergence for link or node failure in the Layer 2 and Layer 3 boundary in the building distribution layer. The following configuration snippet shows how HSRP can be tuned down from its default 3-second hello timer and 10-second hold timer in a campus environment to achieve subsecond convergence on aggregation switches:

```
interface Vlan5
ip address 10.1.5.3 255.255.255.0
ip helper-address 10.5.10.20
standby 1 ip 10.1.5.1
standby 1 timers msec 200 msec 750
standby 1 priority 150
standby 1 preempt delay minimum 180
```

Preempt Delay Tuning

One important factor to take into account when tuning default gateway redundancy using HSRP or another protocol is its preemptive behavior.

Preemption causes the primary HSRP peer to reassume the primary role when it comes back online after a failure or maintenance event. Preemption is the desired behavior because the RSTP root should be the same device as the HSRP primary for a given subnet or VLAN. However, if HSRP and RSTP are not synchronized after failure recovery, the interconnection between the distribution switches can become a transit link, and traffic takes a multihop Layer 2 path to its default gateway.

HSRP preemption needs to be aware of switch boot time and connectivity to the rest of the network. Preempt delay must be longer than the switch boot time:

- Layer 1 traffic, when the switch is able to start forwarding on line cards

- Layer 2, STP convergence and all ports are in the correct state

■ Layer 3 IGP convergence, all neighbor states for link state protocols or all updates from distance vector protocols are processed and correct routes are in the routing table

It is possible for HSRP neighbor relationships to form and preemption to occur before the primary switch has Layer 3 connectivity to the core. If this happens, traffic from the access layer can be dropped until full connectivity is established to the core.

The recommended practice is to measure the system boot time and set the HSRP preempt delay with the standby **preempt delay minimum** command to 50 percent greater than this value. This ensures that the HSRP primary distribution node has established full connectivity to all parts of the network before HSRP preemption is allowed to occur.

Figure 2-25 demonstrates the positive impact that proper HSRP tuning can have on network convergence.

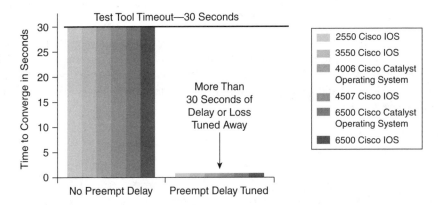

Figure 2-25   *HSRP Preempt Delay Tuning Triangles*

Elimination of FHRP in VSS Designs

The VSS combines two physical switches into a single logical entity, eliminating the FHRP on the distribution layer.

In traditional Layer 2-based access-distribution block designs, an FHRP is deployed at the distribution layer to ensure that the default gateway of the end hosts remains available even when one of the two redundant distribution switches fails. To achieve optimal convergence times in the case of failures, you need to tune the FHRP, STP, and IGP to ensure that these protocols converge in a coordinated manner.

The VSS deployed at the distribution layer collapses the two distribution switches into a single logical switch. As a result, an FHRP is no longer required. The default gateway redundancy is now taken care of by the failover mechanisms that are inherent to VSS and MEC.

If one of the two distribution switches fails, this failure now equates to losing half of the line cards and a supervisor in the virtual switch. On the data plane, the failure translates into losing one of the two links in the EtherChannel. Traffic continues to be forwarded on the remaining link. On the control plane, the hot-standby supervisor assumes the active role. Because this switchover uses Cisco NSF with SSO, it assumes all control plane responsibilities of the failed switch supervisor, including the role of the default gateway.

The elimination of the FHRP from the design is another benefit of VSS in the access-distribution block.

Overview of Gateway Load Balancing Protocol

GLBP is a first-hop redundancy protocol designed by Cisco that allows packet load sharing among groups of redundant routers.

When HSRP or VRRP is used to provide default-gateway redundancy, the backup members of the peer relationship are idle, waiting for a failure event to occur before they take over and actively forward traffic. Methods to use backup uplinks with HSRP or VRRP are difficult to implement and manage. In one technique, the HSRP and STP or RSTP roots alternate between distribution node peers, with the even VLANs homed on one peer and the odd VLANs homed on the alternate. Another technique uses multiple HSRP groups on a single interface and uses DHCP to alternate between the multiple default gateways. These techniques work but are not optimal from a configuration, maintenance, or management perspective.

GLBP provides all the benefits of HSRP and includes load balancing, too. For HSRP, a single virtual MAC address is given to the endpoints when the endpoints use Address Resolution Protocol (ARP) to learn the physical MAC address of their default gateways. GLBP allows a group of routers to function as one virtual router by sharing one virtual IP address while using multiple virtual MAC addresses for traffic forwarding. Figure 2-26 shows a sample configuration supporting GLBP and its roles.

When an endpoint uses ARP for its default gateway, by default the virtual MACs are provided by the GLBP active virtual gateway (AVG) on a round-robin basis. These gateways that assume responsibility for forwarding packets sent to the virtual MAC address are known as active virtual forwarders (AVF) for their virtual MAC address. Because the traffic from a single common subnet goes through multiple redundant gateways, all the uplinks can be used.

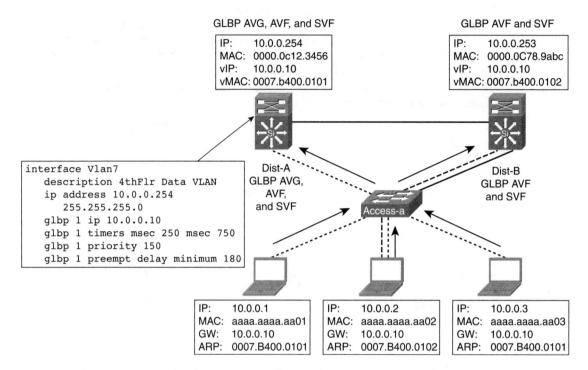

Figure 2-26   *Gateway Load Balancing Protocol Triangles*

Failover and convergence in GLBP work in a similar fashion as HSRP. A secondary virtual forwarder (SVF) takes over for traffic destined to a virtual MAC impacted by the failure and begins forwarding traffic for its failed peer. The end result is that a more equal utilization of the uplinks is achieved with minimal configuration. As a side effect, a convergence event on the uplink or on the primary distribution node affects only half as many hosts with a pair of GLBP switches, giving a convergence event an average of 50 percent less impact.

Note that using GLBP in topologies where STP has blocked one of the access layer uplinks may result in a two-hop path at Layer 2 for upstream traffic, as illustrated in Figure 2-27.

In environments where VLANs span across the distribution switches, HSRP is the preferred FHRP implementation.

In some cases, the STP environment can be tuned so that the Layer 2 link between the distribution switches is the blocking link while the uplinks from the access layer switches are in a forwarding state.

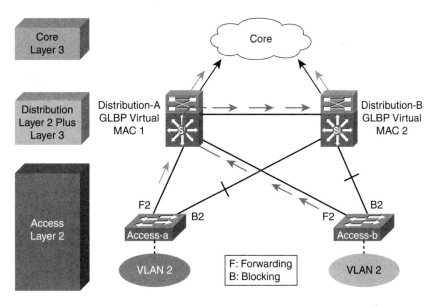

Figure 2-27   *GLBP VLAN Spanning Triangles*

You can tune STP by using the **spanning-tree cost interface configuration** command to change the port cost on the interface between the distribution layer switches on the STP secondary root switch. This option works if no VLANs span access switches.

However, as shown in Figure 2-28, if the same VLAN is on multiple access switches, you will have a looped figure-8 topology where one access layer uplink is still blocking. The preferred design is to not span VLANs across access switches.

Optimizing FHRP Convergence

HSRP can be reliably tuned to achieve 800-ms convergence for link or node failure. With HSRP, all flows from one subnet go through the active HSRP router; so the longest, shortest, and average convergence times are the same and less than a second.

VRRP can be tuned with subsecond timers, although the results of this timer tuning deterministic. With VRRP, all flows from one subnet go through the same VRRP master router; so the longest, shortest, and average convergence times are the same and about a second.

GLBP can also be reliably tuned to achieve 800-ms convergence for link or node failure. With GLBP, a convergence event on an uplink or on the primary distribution node affects only half as many hosts, so a convergence event has an average of 50 percent less impact than with HSRP or VRRP if the default round-robin load-balancing algorithm is used.

GLBP is currently supported on the Cisco Catalyst 6500 series switches and the Cisco Catalyst 4500 series switches.

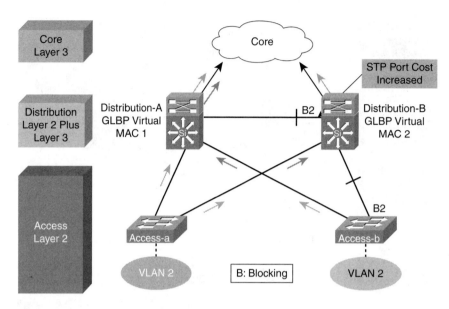

Figure 2-28 *GLBP and STP Tuning Triangles*

Figure 2-29 illustrates the difference in convergence times between each of the respective FHRP when deployed on a distribution to access link in a server farm.

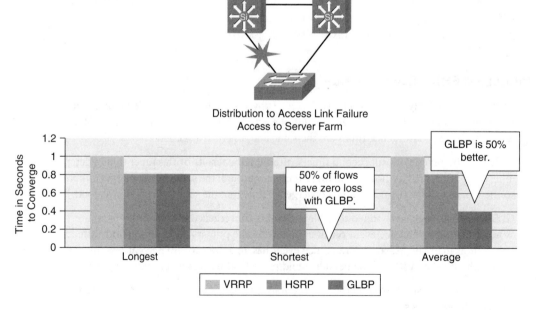

Figure 2-29 *Optimizing FHRP Convergence Triangles*

Supporting a Layer 2 to Layer 3 Boundary Design

This section reviews design models and recommended practices for supporting the Layer 2 to Layer 3 boundary in highly available enterprise campus networks.

Layer 2 to Layer 3 Boundary Design Models

There are several design models for placement of the Layer 2 to Layer 3 boundary in the enterprise campus.

Layer 2 Distribution Switch Interconnection

If the enterprise campus requirements must support VLANs spanning multiple access layer switches, the design model uses a Layer 2 link for interconnecting the distribution switches.

The design, illustrated in Figure 2-30, is more complex than the Layer 3 interconnection of the distribution switches. The STP convergence process is initiated for uplink failures and recoveries.

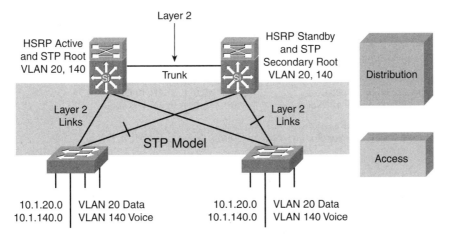

Figure 2-30 *Layer 2 Distribution Switch Interconnection*

You can improve this suboptimal design as follows:

■ Use RSTP as the version of STP.

Note RPVST+ is a Cisco enhancement of RSTP that uses PVST+. It provides a separate instance of 802.1W per VLAN. The separate instance supports PortFast, UplinkFast, BackboneFast, BPDU guard, BPDU filter, root guard, and loop guard. (RPVST+ is also known as PVRST+.)

- Provide a Layer 2 trunk between the two distribution switches to avoid unexpected traffic paths and multiple convergence events.

- If you choose to load balance VLANs across uplinks, be sure to place the HSRP primary and the STP primary root bridge candidates on the same distribution layer switch. The HSRP and RSTP root should be collocated on the same distribution switches to avoid using the interdistribution link for transit.

Layer 3 Distribution Switch Interconnection (with HSRP)

Figure 2-31 shows a model that supports a Layer 3 interconnection between distribution switches using HSRP as the FHRP.

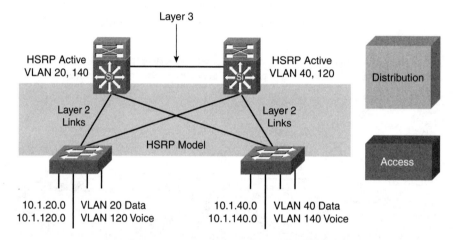

Figure 2-31   *Layer 3 Distribution Switch Interconnection Triangles*

In this time-proven topology, no VLANs span between access layer switches across the distribution switches. A subnet equals a VLAN, which equals an access switch. The root for each VLAN is aligned with the active HSRP instance. From a STP perspective, both access layer uplinks are forwarding, so the only convergence dependencies are the default gateway and return-path route selection across the distribution-to-distribution link.

This recommended design provides the highest availability.

With this design, a distribution-to-distribution link is required for route summarization. A recommended practice is to map the Layer 2 VLAN number to the Layer 3 subnet for ease of use and management.

Layer 3 Distribution Switch Interconnection (with GLBP)

GLBP can also be used as the FHRP with the Layer 3 distribution layer interconnection model, as shown in Figure 2-32.

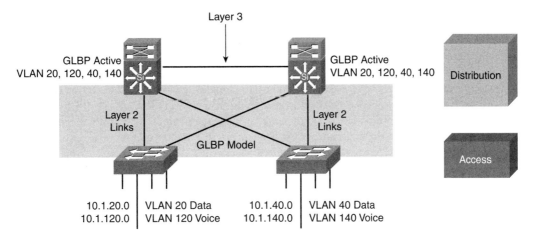

Figure 2-32 *Layer 3 Distribution Switch Interconnection with GLBP*

GLBP allows full utilization of the uplinks from the access layer. However, because the distribution of ARP responses is random, it is less deterministic than the design with HSRP. The distribution-to-distribution link is still required for route summarization. Because the VLANs do not span access switches, STP convergence is not required for uplink failure and recovery.

Layer 3 Distribution Switch with VSS Interconnection

A virtual switching system (VSS) can be used to create a logical star topology for the access distribution block, while maintaining complete physical redundancy, as illustrated in Figure 2-33.

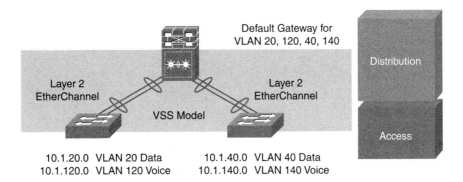

Figure 2-33 *VSS Layer 3 Interconnect*

Deploying VSS in the distribution layer greatly simplifies the access-distribution block design. VSS reduces the block topology to a logical star, creating a loop-free topology.

From an STP perspective, all the links are now forwarding, and STP is no longer involved in the network reconvergence. If one of the distribution switches fails, or if an access-to-distribution link fails, only the MECs are affected and lose one of the links in the bundle. Traffic continues to be forwarded on the remaining link.

VSS reduces the Layer 3 to Layer 2 boundary to a single logical device. This action eliminates the need for an FHRP. Only one router transmits between the access layer VLANs in the access-distribution block and the core layer. High availability of this single router is guaranteed through the high-availability mechanisms that are inherent to VSS.

In this design, load balancing between the access layer and the distribution layer is not based on FHRP load balancing. Rather, this load balance is on the EtherChannel load-balancing method that the Layer 2 MECs use between the access layer and the distribution layer. This method allows all access-to-distribution uplinks to be fully utilized.

This design allows VLANs to span across multiple access switches without any impact on convergence. Because the logical topology is loop free, spanning tree is not involved in network reconvergence when a link or node fails.

> **Note**   A limitation applies to VSS designs. VSS switches are always deployed in pairs. It is not possible to add a third switch to a VSS to increase availability.

Layer 3 Access to Distribution Interconnection

The design extending Layer 3 to the access layer, shown in Figure 2-34, provides the fastest network convergence.

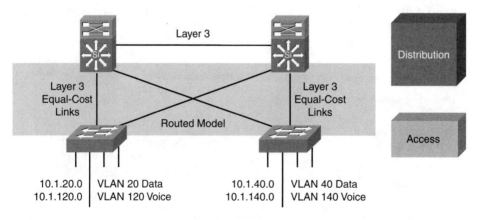

Figure 2-34   *Layer 3 Access to Distribution Interconnection*

A routing protocol such as EIGRP, when properly tuned, can achieve better convergence results than designs that rely on STP to resolve convergence events. A routing protocol can even achieve better convergence results than the time-tested design placing the Layer

2 to Layer 3 boundary at the distribution layer. The design is easier to implement than configuring Layer 2 in the distribution layer because you do not need to align STP with HSRP or GLBP.

This design supports equal-cost Layer 3 load balancing on all links between the network switches. No HSRP or GLBP configuration is needed, because the access switch is routing at Layer 3. So, because this switch is a multilayer switch, it serves as the default gateway for the end users. VLANs cannot span access switches in this design.

The convergence time required to reroute around a failed access-to-distribution layer uplink is reliably under 200 ms as compared to 900 ms for the design placing the Layer 2 and Layer 3 boundary at the distribution layer. Return-path traffic is also in the sub-200 ms of convergence time for an EIGRP reroute, again compared to 900 ms for the traditional Layer 2 to Layer 3 distribution layer model.

Because both EIGRP and OSPF loads share over equal-cost paths, this design provides a convergence benefit similar to GLBP. Approximately 50 percent of the hosts are not affected by a convergence event because their traffic is not flowing over the link or through the failed node.

However, some additional complexity associated with uplink IP addressing and subnetting and the loss of flexibility is associated with this design alternative.

Routing in the access layer is not as widely deployed in the enterprise environment as the Layer 2 and Layer 3 distribution layer boundary model.

Note Deploying a Layer 3 access layer may be prohibited because of conformance with the existing architecture, price of multilayer switches, and application or service requirements.

EIGRP Access Design Recommendations

When EIGRP is used as the routing protocol for a fully routed or routed access layer solution, with tuning it can achieve sub-200-ms convergence.

EIGRP to the distribution layer is similar to EIGRP in the branch, but it is optimized for fast convergence using these design rules:

- Limit scope of queries to a single neighbor:

    - Summarize at the distribution layer to the core as is done in the traditional Layer 2 to Layer 3 border at the distribution layer. This confines impact of an individual access link failure to the distribution pair by stopping EIGRP queries from propagating beyond the core of the network. When the distribution layer summarizes toward the core, queries are limited to one hop from the distribution switches, which optimizes EIGRP convergence.

    - Configure all access switches to use EIGRP stub nodes so that the access devices are not queried by the distribution switches for routes. EIGRP stub nodes cannot act as transit nodes and do not participate in EIGRP query processing. When the distribution node learns through the EIGRP hello packets that it is talking to a stub node, it does not flood queries to that node.

- Control route propagation to access switches using distribution lists. The access switches need only a default route to the distribution switches. An outbound distribution list applied to all interfaces facing the access layer from the distribution switch will conserve memory and optimize performance at the access layer.

- Set hello and dead timers to 1 and 3 as a secondary mechanism to speed up convergence. The link failure or node failure should trigger convergence events. Tune EIGRP hello and dead timers to 1 and 3, respectively, to protect against a soft failure in which the physical links remain active but hello and route processing has stopped.

An EIGRP optimized configuration example is shown here.

```
interface GigabitEthernet1/1 ip hello-interval eigrp 100 2 ip hold-time
eigrp 100 6
router eigrp 100 eigrp stub connected
```

Note An EIGRP stub is included in the base image of all Cisco multilayer Catalyst switches.

OSPF Access Design Recommendations

When OSPF is used as the routing protocol for a fully routed or routed access layer solution with tuning, it can also achieve sub-200-ms convergence.

OSPF to the distribution layer is similar to OSPF in the branch, but it is optimized for fast convergence. With OSPF, summarization and limits to the diameter of OSPF LSA propagation is provided through implementation of Layer 2 to Layer 3 boundaries or Area Border Routers (ABR). It follows this design rule, to control the number of routes and routers in each area:

- Configure each distribution block as a separate, totally stubby OSPF area. The distribution switches become ABRs with their core-facing interfaces in area 0, and the access layer interfaces in unique, totally stubby areas for each access layer switch. Do not extend area 0 to the access switch because the access layer is not used as a transit area in a campus environment. Each access layer switch is configured into its own unique, totally stubby area. In this configuration, LSAs are isolated to each access layer switch so that a link flap for one access layer switch is not communicated beyond the distribution pairs.

- Tune OSPF millisecond hello, dead-interval, SPF, and LSA throttle timers as a secondary mechanism to improve convergence. Because CPU resources are not as scarce in a campus environment as they might be in a WAN environment, and the media types common in the access layer are not susceptible to the same half-up or rapid transitions as are those commonly found in the WAN, OSPF timers can safely be tuned, as shown in the configuration snippet here:

```
interface GigabitEthernet1/1 ip ospf dead-interval minimal
   hello-multiplier 4
router ospf 100 area 120 stub no-summary timers throttle spf 10 100 5000
timers throttle lsa all 10 100 5000 timers lsa arrival 80
```

Note   OSPF support is not included in the base image of all Cisco multilayer Catalyst switches, but it is available with the IP Services upgrade.

Potential Design Issues

The following sections discuss potential design issues for placement of the Layer 2 to Layer 3 boundary in the enterprise campus.

Daisy Chaining Access Layer Switches

If multiple fixed-configuration switches are daisy chained in the access layer of the network, you risk black holes occurring in the event of a link or node failure.

In the topology in Figure 2-35 before failures, no links are blocking from a STP or RSTP perspective, so both uplinks are available to actively forward and receive traffic. Both distribution nodes can forward return-path traffic from the rest of the network toward the access layer for devices attached to all members of the stack or chain.

Two scenarios can occur if a link or node in the middle of the chain or stack fails. In the first case, the standby HSRP peer can go active as it loses connectivity to its primary peer, forwarding traffic outbound for the devices that still have connectivity to it. The primary HSRP peer remains active and also forwards outbound traffic for its half of the stack. Although this is not optimum, it is not detrimental from the perspective of outbound traffic.

The second scenario is the issue. Return-path traffic has a 50 percent chance of arriving on a distribution switch that does not have physical connectivity to the half of the stack where the traffic is destined. The traffic that arrives on the wrong distribution switch is dropped.

The solution to this issue with this design is to provide alternate connectivity across the stack in the form of a loopback cable running from the top to the bottom of the stack. This link needs to be carefully deployed so that the appropriate STP behavior will occur in the access layer.

An alternate design uses a Layer 2 link between the distribution switches.

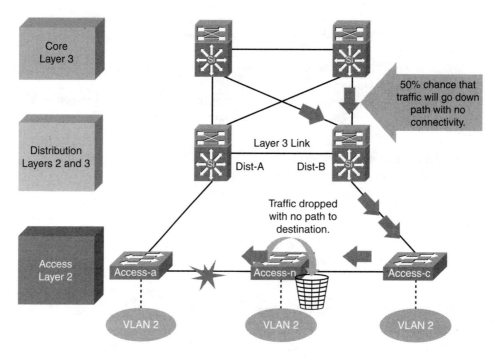

Figure 2-35   *Daisy Chaining Access Layer Switches*

Cisco StackWise Technology in the Access Layer

Cisco StackWise technology can eliminate the danger that black holes occur in the access layer in the event of a link or node failure. It can eliminate the need for loop-back cables in the access layer or Layer 2 links between distribution nodes.

StackWise technology, shown in the access layer in Figure 2-36, supports the recommended practice of using a Layer 3 connection between the distribution switches without having to use a loop-back cable or perform extra configuration.

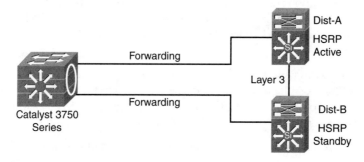

Figure 2-36   *StackWise Technology*

The true stack creation provided by the Cisco Catalyst 3750 series switches makes using stacks in the access layer much less complex than chains or stacks of other models. A stack of 3750 switches appears as one node from the network topology perspective.

If you use a modular chassis switch to support ports in the aggregation layer, such as the Cisco Catalyst 4500 or Catalyst 6500 family of switches, these design considerations are not required.

Too Much Redundancy

Be aware that even if some redundancy is good, more redundancy is not necessarily better.

In Figure 2-37, a third switch is added to the distribution switches in the center.

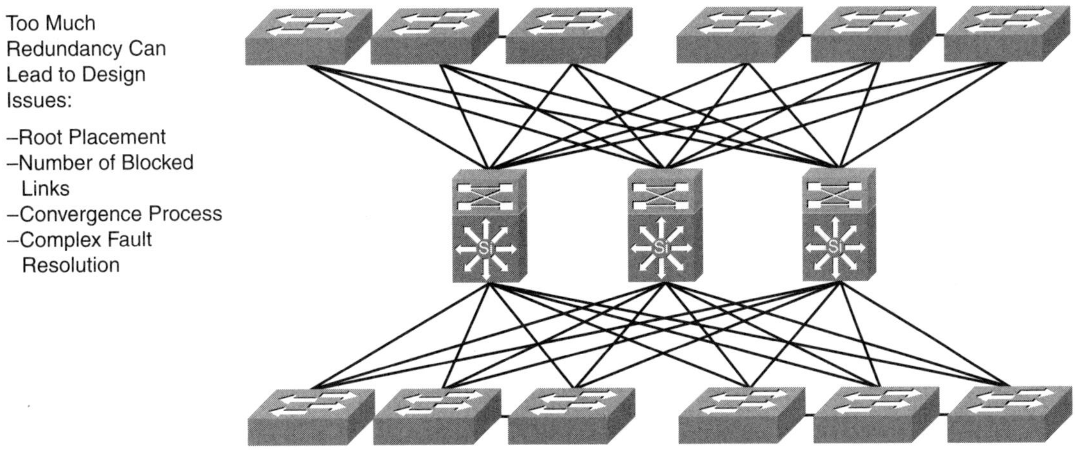

Too Much
Redundancy Can
Lead to Design
Issues:

–Root Placement
–Number of Blocked
 Links
–Convergence Process
–Complex Fault
 Resolution

Figure 2-37   *Too Much Redundancy*

This extra switch adds unneeded complexity to the design and leads to these design questions:

■   Where should the root switch be placed? With this design, it is not easy to determine where the root switch is located.

■   What links should be in a blocking state? It is very hard to determine how many ports will be in a blocking state.

■   What are the implications of STP and RSTP convergence? The network convergence is definitely not deterministic.

■   When something goes wrong, how do you find the source of the problem? The design is much harder to troubleshoot.

Too Little Redundancy

For most designs, a link between the distribution layer switches is required for redundancy.

Figure 2-38 shows a less-than-optimal design where VLANs span multiple access layer switches. Without a Layer 2 link between the distribution switches, the design is a looped figure-eight topology. One access layer uplink will be blocking. HSRP hellos are exchanged by transiting the access switches.

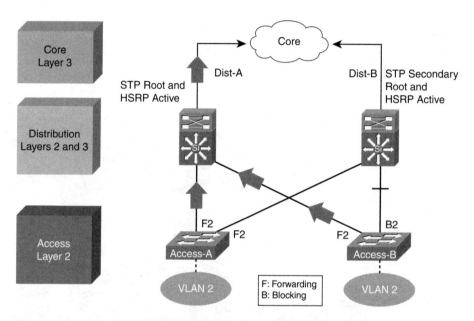

Figure 2-38   *Too Little Redundancy*

Initially, traffic is forwarded from both access switches to the Distribution A switch that supports the STP root and the primary or active HSRP peer for VLAN 2. However, this design will black-hole traffic and be affected by multiple convergence events with a single network failure.

Example: Impact of an Uplink Failure

Figure 2-39 examines at the impact of an uplink failure on the design when there is no link between the distribution layer switches.

In Figure 2-39, when the uplink from Access A to Distribution A fails, three convergence events occur:

1. Access A sends traffic across its active uplink to Distribution B to get to its default gateway. The traffic is black-holed at Distribution B because Distribution B does not initially have a path to the primary or active HSRP peer on Distribution A because of

the STP blocking. The traffic is dropped until the standby HSRP peer takes over as the default gateway after not receiving HSRP hellos from Distribution A.

Note   With aggressive HSRP timers, you can minimize this period of traffic loss to approximately 900 ms.

2.   The indirect link failure is eventually detected by Access B after the maximum-age (**max_age**) timer expires, and Access B removes blocking on the uplink to Distribution B. With standard STP, transitioning to forwarding can take as long as 50 seconds. If BackboneFast is enabled with PVST+, this time can be reduced to 30 seconds, and RSTP can reduce this interval to as little as 1 second.

3.   After STP and RSTP converge, the distribution nodes reestablish their HSRP relationships and Distribution A (the primary HSRP peer) preempts. This causes yet another convergence event when Access A endpoints start forwarding traffic to the primary HSRP peer. The unexpected side effect is that Access A traffic goes through Access B to reach its default gateway. The Access B uplink to Distribution B is now a transit link for Access A traffic, and the Access B uplink to Distribution A must now carry traffic for both the originally intended Access B and for Access A.

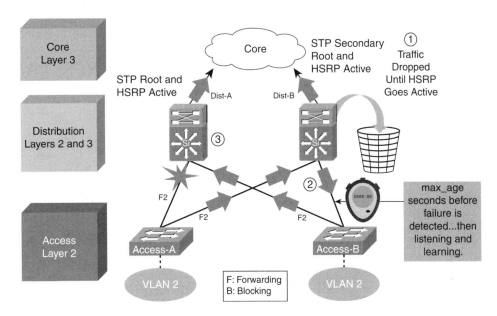

Figure 2-39   *Impact of an Uplink Failure*

Example: Impact on Return-Path Traffic

Because the distribution layer in Figure 2-40 is routing with equal-cost load balancing, up to 50 percent of the return-path traffic arrives at Distribution A and is forwarded to Access B. Access B drops this traffic until the uplink to Distribution B is forwarding. This indirect link-failure convergence can take as long as 50 seconds. PVST+ with UplinkFast reduces the time to 3 to 5 seconds, and RSTP further reduces the outage to one second. After the STP and RSTP convergence, the Access B uplink to Distribution B is used as a transit link for Access A return-path traffic.

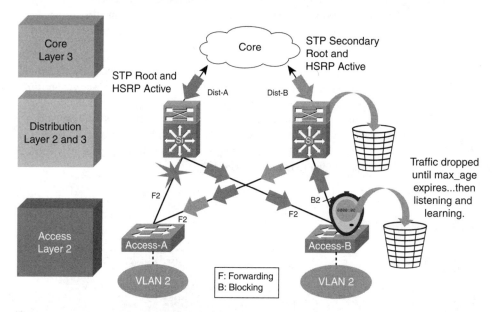

Figure 2-40   *Impact on Return-Path Traffic*

These significant outages could affect the performance of mission-critical applications, such as voice or video. Traffic engineering or link-capacity planning for both outbound and return-path traffic is difficult and complex and must support the traffic for at least one additional access layer switch.

The conclusion is that if VLANs must span the access switches, a Layer 2 link is needed either between the distribution layer switches or the access switches.

Asymmetric Routing (Unicast Flooding)

When VLANs span access switches, an asymmetric routing situation can result because of equal-cost load balancing between the distribution and core layers.

Up to 50 percent of the return-path traffic with equal-cost routing arrives at the standby HSRP, VRRP, or alternate, nonforwarding GLBP peer. If the content-addressable memory

(CAM) table entry ages out before the ARP entry for the end node, the peer may need to flood the traffic to all access layer switches and endpoints in the VLAN.

In Figure 2-41, the CAM table entry ages out on the standby HSRP router because the default ARP timers are four hours and the CAM aging timers are five minutes. The CAM timer expires because no traffic is sent upstream by the endpoint toward the standby HSRP peer after the endpoint initially uses ARP to determine its default gateway. When the CAM entry ages out and is removed from the CAM table, the standby HSRP peer must forward the return-path traffic to all ports in the common VLAN. The majority of the access layer switches do not have a CAM entry for the target MAC, and they broadcast the return traffic on all ports in the common VLAN. This unicast traffic flooding can have a significant performance impact on the connected end stations because they may receive a large amount of traffic that is not intended for them.

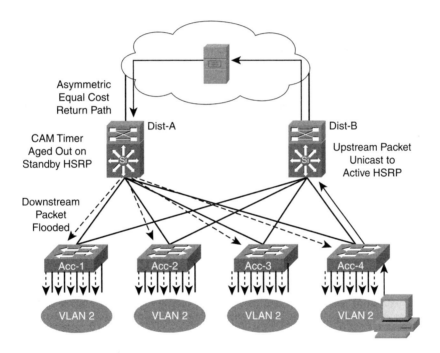

Figure 2-41   *Asymmetric Routing*

Unicast Flooding Prevention

The unicast flooding situation can be easily avoided by not spanning VLANs across access layer switches.

Unicast flooding is not an issue when VLANs are not present across multiple access layer switches because the flooding occurs only to switches supporting the VLAN where the traffic would have normally been switched. If the VLANs are local to individual access layer switches, asymmetric routing traffic is flooded on only the one VLAN interface on the distribution switch. Traffic is flooded out the same interface that would be used normally to forward to the appropriate access switch. In addition, the access layer switch receiving the flooded traffic has a CAM table entry for the host because the host is directly attached, so traffic is switched only to the intended host. As a result, no additional end stations are affected by the flooded traffic.

If you must implement a topology where VLANs span more than one access layer switch, the recommended workaround is to tune the ARP timer so that it is equal to or less than the CAM aging timer. A shorter ARP cache timer causes the standby HSRP peer to use ARP for the target IP address before the CAM entry timer expires and the MAC entry is removed. The subsequent ARP response repopulates the CAM table before the CAM entry is aged out and removed. This removes the possibility of flooding asymmetrically routed return-path traffic to all ports. You can also consider biasing the routing metrics to remove the equal cost routes.

Supporting Infrastructure Services

This section reviews considerations for supporting infrastructure services in highly available enterprise campus networks. Considerations for building a converged network to support IP telephony are discussed. QoS attributes and aspects of the Cisco Catalyst Integrated Security features are also described.

IP Telephony Considerations

IP telephony services are supported at each layer of the campus network.

High availability, redundancy, and fast convergence needed by IP telephony services are supported throughout the enterprise campus network. QoS features are implemented throughout the network. The distribution layer typically supports policy enforcement.

However, because implementing IP telephony services extends the network edge, IP telephony has the most impact at the access layer of the network. The access layer supports device attachment and phone detection, inline power for devices, and QoS features, including classification, scheduling, and the trust boundary.

IP Telephony Extends the Network Edge

Because the IP phone is a three-port switch, IP telephony services actually extend the network edge, as shown in Figure 2-42.

The IP phone shown in Figure 2-42 contains a three-port switch that is configured in conjunction with the access switch and Cisco Unified Communications Manager (CUCM):

- Power negotiation

- VLAN configuration

- 802.1X interoperation

- QoS configuration

- DHCP and CUCM registration

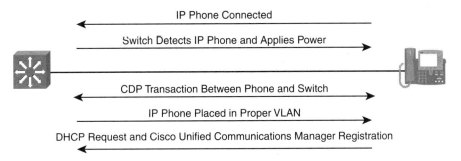

IP Phone Connected

Switch Detects IP Phone and Applies Power

CDP Transaction Between Phone and Switch

IP Phone Placed in Proper VLAN

DHCP Request and Cisco Unified Communications Manager Registration

Figure 2-42   *IP Telephony Extends the Network Edge*

When a Cisco IP phone is connected to the network, Cisco Catalyst multiservice switches detect and integrate the phone with the network. The switches can deliver Power over Ethernet (PoE) using existing copper cabling to power the IP phones. The switches place the IP phones and attached devices in the appropriate VLAN, often using 802.1X services. The switch supports the QoS configuration needed for the IP phones, and provides connection to DHCP servers and CUCM systems for registration.

PoE is the ability for the LAN switching infrastructure to provide power over a copper Ethernet cable to an endpoint or powered device. This capability is also referred to as inline power and was originally developed by Cisco Systems in 2000 to support the emerging IP telephony deployments.

To support PoE delivery to power capable devices, a number of issues need to be resolved: phone detection, power delivery, power management, and cable and bandwidth management.

PoE Requirements

There are two PoE implementations available, and two ways to provide power to the IP phones:

- Cisco line cards support prestandard PoE, IEEE 802.3af, and a mix of devices. IEEE 802.3af-only devices will not negotiate or receive power from an original Cisco PoE-only line card.

- Cisco devices use a bidirectional Cisco Discovery Protocol (CDP) exchange to negotiate the exact power requirements. Power negotiation optimizes power consumption by allowing the switch to reserve only the power needed for the device.

The earlier Cisco prestandard PoE devices initially receive 6.3 watts (W) and then optionally negotiate their power requirements using CDP. Cisco prestandard devices use a relay in the powered device to reflect a special FastLink pulse for device detection.

The devices based on the IEEE 802.3af (also known as 802.3at type 1) initial power standard initially receive 12.95 W of power and 802.3at type 2 devices receive 25.5 W of power, unless a power-sourcing equipment (PSE) device can detect a specific powered device classification. An 802.3af PSE device applies a voltage in the range of −2.8 to −10 volts on the cable and then looks for a 25K ohm signature resistor in the powered device.

IEEE 802.3af power may be delivered using a PoE-capable Ethernet port, which is referred to as an endpoint PSE, or by a midspan PSE that can be used to deliver PoE in the event an existing non-PoE-capable Ethernet switch is used. An endpoint PSE, such as a PoE-capable Ethernet switch, can use either active data wires of an Ethernet port or spare wires to a powered device. Some midspan PSEs can only implement power over spare pairs of copper cabling and cannot be used to deliver PoE over 1000BASE-T connections.

The IEEE 802.3 at power standard-class specification are shown in Table 2-1.

Table 2-1   *802.3 at Power Specification*

Property	802.3af (802.3 at Type 1)	802.3 at Type 2
Power available at PD	12.95 W	25.50 W per mode
Maximum power delivered by PSE	15.40 W	34.20 W per mode
Voltage range (at PSE)	44.0 V to 57.0 V	50.0–57.0 V
Voltage range (at PD)	37.0 V to 57.0 V	42.5–57.0 V
Maximum current	350 mA	600 mA per mode
Maximum cable resistance	20Ω (Category 3)	12.5Ω (Category 5)
Power Management	Three power class levels negotiated at initial connection	Four power class levels negotiated at initial connection or 0.1 W steps negotiated continuously
Derating of maximum cable ambient operating temperature	None	5°C with one mode (two pairs) active, 10°C with two modes (four pairs) simultaneously active
Supported cabling	Category 3 and Category 5	Category 5
Supported modes	Mode A (endspan) Mode B (midspan)	Mode A, Mode B, Mode a and B operating simultaneously

Note   A midspan PSE takes up rack space and adds a patch point to every PoE cable, increasing cabling costs and complexity.

Power Budget and Management

Power budget planning is necessary to determine what devices can be supported today and in the future.

The switches manage power by what is allocated, not by what is currently used. However, the device power consumption is not constant:

- Cisco Unified IP Phone 7960G requires 7 W when the phone is ringing at maximum volume.

- Cisco Unified IP Phone 7960G requires 5 W when it is on or off hook.

Delivery of PoE using the IEEE 802.3af default classification may significantly increase the power requirements on both the PSE switch and the power infrastructure. To provide PoE in a cost-effective and efficient manner, Cisco Catalyst switches support Cisco Intelligent Power Management (Cisco IPM) in addition to IEEE 802.3af classification. This enables a powered device and PSE to negotiate their respective capabilities to explicitly manage how much power is required to power the device and also how the PSE-capable switch manages the allocation of power to individual powered devices. These Cisco IPM capabilities enable a network and facilities manager to effectively and economically manage the power resources within a wiring closet and help PSE-capable switches meet the objectives of the network.

Power management is complex. Power management can have significant ramifications with respect to the power supply required to drive all the powered devices and line cards, how power is delivered within the switch, how the switch manages power allocation, and finally, for the power-delivery requirements of the wiring closet. You need to plan for maximum theoretical draw that so that sufficient power is available to be allocated to end devices and the line cards in the switch. Even if the PSE and powered device support power classification, the classification ranges are fairly broad and can lead to wasted power budget allocation. When there is insufficient power in a chassis, the power management system deactivates line cards.

You can use the Cisco Power Calculator at http://tools.cisco.com/cpc/launch.jsp to estimate power requirements.

The Cisco Power Calculator enables you to estimate the power supply requirements for a specific PoE and line card configuration.

The Cisco Power Calculator requires a username and password. The tool allows a series of selections for the configurable products and provides results showing the output current, output power, and system heat dissipation for a specific configuration.

The calculator is an educational resource and a starting point in planning power requirements; it does not provide a final power recommendation from Cisco.

The Cisco Power Calculator supports the following Cisco product series: Cisco Catalyst 6500, Catalyst 4500, Catalyst 3750, and Catalyst 3560 series switches, and the Cisco 7600 series router.

Note To see the current devices supported in the power calculator, see http://tools.cisco.com/cpc/ (Cisco.com login required).

The Power Consumption Summary screen shown in Figure 2-43 displays the minimum power supply required for the selected configuration and percentage of power usage. The table displays output current (amperes), output power (watts), and heat dissipation (BTUs per hour).

Power Consumption/Heat Dissipation Summary			
Slot	Line Card	Optional DFC	Power over Ethernet Capabilities
1	WS-SUP32-GE-3B	---	---
2	WS-SUP32-GE-3B	---	---
3	-- EMPTY-SLOT --	---	---
4	-- EMPTY-SLOT --	---	---
Minimum Power Supply		Percentage of Power Used	
Single/Redundant PWR-2700-DC/4 with one input		28.05%	
First Alternative Power Supply		Percentage of Power Used	
Combined PWR-2700-DC/4 with one input		16.80%	
Total Output Current	Total Output Power		Total Heat Dissipation
8.81 Amps	370.02 Watts		1706.10 BTU/Hr

Figure 2-43 *Power-Consumption Summary*

The Cisco Power Calculator recommends the smallest power supply that meets the requirements of the configuration. The tool reports single and redundant power-supply options, and also the combined power configuration mode as appropriate.

The power supply details area shown in Figure 2-44 displays power utilization with various-sized power supplies.

Minimum Power Supply	Percentage of Power used	Total Output Current for this PSU (A)	Total Output Current Used (A)	Total Output Current Remaining (A)
Combined WS-CAC-2500W	68.92%	45.77	31.55	14.22
Other Power Supply Options	Percentage of Power used	Total Output Current for this PSU (A)	Total Output Current Used (A)	Total Output Current Remaining (A)
Combined WS-CAC-3000W	67.87%	46.48	31.55	14.93
Single/Redundant WS-CAC-6000W with Dual 110V inputs	49.59%	63.62	31.55	32.07
Combined WS-CAC-6000W with Dual 110V inputs	35.05%	90.00	31.55	58.45

[Top]

Configuration Details				
Slot	Line Card	Output Current (A)	Output Power (W)	Heat Dissipation (BTU/Hr)
FAN2	WS-C6K-9SLOT-FAN2	0.00	0.00	546.00

Figure 2-44 *Power Supply Details*

The Configuration Details section of the Cisco Power Calculator output shown in Figure 2-45 displays the current, power, and heat dissipation for each component.

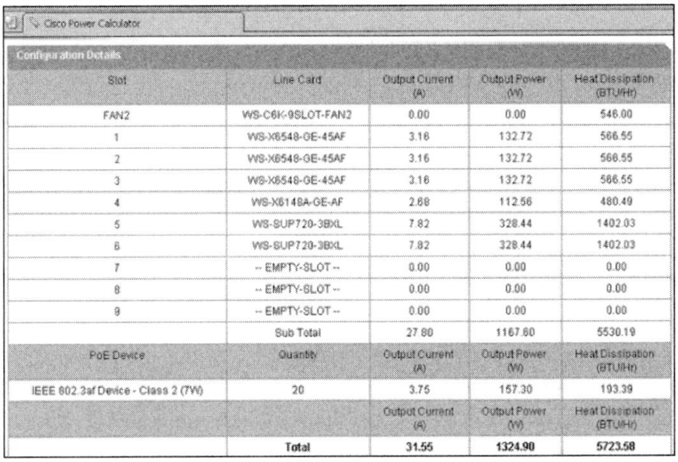

Slot	Line Card	Output Current (A)	Output Power (W)	Heat Dissipation (BTU/Hr)
FAN2	WS-C6K-9SLOT-FAN2	0.00	0.00	546.00
1	WS-X6548-GE-45AF	3.16	132.72	566.55
2	WS-X6548-GE-45AF	3.16	132.72	566.55
3	WS-X6548-GE-45AF	3.16	132.72	566.55
4	WS-X6148A-GE-AF	2.68	112.56	480.49
5	WS-SUP720-3BXL	7.82	328.44	1402.03
6	WS-SUP720-3BXL	7.82	328.44	1402.03
7	-- EMPTY-SLOT --	0.00	0.00	0.00
8	-- EMPTY-SLOT --	0.00	0.00	0.00
9	-- EMPTY-SLOT --	0.00	0.00	0.00
	Sub Total	27.80	1167.60	5530.19
PoE Device	Quantity	Output Current (A)	Output Power (W)	Heat Dissipation (BTU/Hr)
IEEE 802.3af Device - Class 2 (7W)	20	3.75	157.30	193.39
		Output Current (A)	Output Power (W)	Heat Dissipation (BTU/Hr)
	Total	31.55	1324.90	5723.58

Figure 2-45   *Configuration Details*

Multi-VLAN Access Port

The concept of an access port has been extended to a multi-VLAN access port in the enterprise campus.

Multiservice switches support a new parameter for IP telephony support that makes the access port a multi-VLAN access port. The new parameter is called an auxiliary VLAN. Every Ethernet 10/100/1000 port in the switch is associated with two VLANs:

■ A native VLAN for data service that is identified by the port VLAN ID (PVID)

■ An auxiliary VLAN for voice service that is identified by the voice VLAN ID (VVID)

During the initial CDP exchange with the access switch, the IP phone is configured with a VVID. The IP phone is also supplied with a QoS configuration using CDP. Voice traffic is separated from data and supports a different trust boundary.

Data packets between the multiservice access switch and the PC or workstation are on the native VLAN. All packets going out on the native VLAN of an IEEE 802.1Q port are sent untagged by the access switch. The PC or workstation connected to the IP phone usually sends untagged packets.

Voice packets are tagged by the IP phone based on the CDP information from the access switch.

The multi-VLAN access ports are not trunk ports, even though the hardware is set to the dot1q trunk. The hardware setting is used to carry more than one VLAN, but the port is still considered an access port that is able to carry one native VLAN and the auxiliary

VLAN. The **switchport host** command can be applied to a multi-VLAN access port on the access switch.

> **Note**   The switch downloads both the data (native) VLAN and the auxiliary (voice) VLAN to the phone. The IP phone marks any traffic on the voice VLAN by modifying the priority bits in the 802.1Q/p tag to CoS 5 (binary 111), which can later be easily mapped to a Layer 3 marking (for example, DSCP 46 or EF). The trust can also be extended to any CoS markings that may have been set by the attached PC (or can mark these values up or down as desired).

Soft Phones and Voice VLANs

When softphones are used instead of "hard" phones, this affects the implementation of QoS and security policies for the voice traffic. Because the softphone is simply an application running on a PC, the voice traffic is mixed with data traffic on the access VLAN that the PC is connected to. There is not 802.1Q tagging and 802.1P class of service (CoS) marking between the PC and the switch. This has some implications for the design and implementation of security and QoS policies for voice traffic.

There is not a VLAN separation between voice and data traffic, which means that all security policies that need to be applied to the voice and data traffic from PCs with softphones must be based on upper-layer characteristics of the traffic. VLAN or subnet cannot be used to classify traffic as voice or data traffic.

There is not a Layer 2 CoS marking in the frames, which means that implementation of a QoS policy for the voice traffic either depends on trusting DSCP markings set by the PC or on classification and marking of the traffic by the access switch.

QoS Considerations

Typical campus networks are built with oversubscription in mind. The network usually has multiple possible congestion points where important traffic may be dropped without QoS.

Most campus links are underutilized. Some studies have shown that 95 percent of campus access layer links are utilized at less than 5 percent of their capacity.

The rule-of-thumb recommendation for data oversubscription is 20:1 for access ports on the access-to-distribution uplink. The recommendation is 4:1 for the distribution-to-core links. When you use these oversubscription ratios, congestion may occur infrequently on the uplinks. QoS is needed for these occasions. If congestion is occurring often, the design does not have sufficient uplink bandwidth.

Recommended Practices for QoS

QoS helps manage oversubscription and speed-transitions in the design. The following are recommended best practices for QoS:

- Deployed end-to-end to be effective

- Ensures that mission-critical applications are not impacted by link or transmit queue congestion

- Enforces QoS policies at aggregation and rate transition points

- Uses multiple queues with configurable admission criteria, and scheduling effective QoS is deployed end-to-end with each layer supporting a role

Internet worms and denial-of-service (DoS) attacks can flood links even in a high-speed campus environment. QoS policies protect voice, video, and mission-critical data traffic while giving a lower class of service to suspect traffic.

Aggregation and rate transition points must enforce QoS policies to support preferred traffic and manage congestion. In campus networks, multiple queues with configurable admission criteria and scheduling are required on the LAN ports.

Transmit Queue Congestion

The type of congestion that is most common in a campus network is called transmit-queue (Tx-queue) starvation.

Both LANs and WANs are subject to Tx-queue congestion:

- During a transition from LAN to WAN, a router has to make the rate transition from 10/100 Ethernet to WAN speeds. When this happens, the router must queue the packets and apply QoS to ensure that important traffic is transmitted first. Tx-queue starvation occurs when incoming packets are received faster than outgoing packets are transmitted. Packets are queued as they wait to serialize out onto the slower link.

- In the campus, as the LAN infrastructure transitions from 10-Gbps or 1-Gbps uplinks in the distribution layer to 10/100/1000 Mbps to the desktop, packets must be queued as they wait to serialize out the 10-Mbps or 100-Mbps link.

The difference between a WAN router and a campus switch is the number of interfaces and the amount of memory associated with each. In the campus, the amount of Tx-queue space is much smaller than the amount of memory available in a WAN router. Because of the small amount of memory, the potential for dropped traffic because of Tx-queue starvation is relatively high.

QoS Role in the Campus

QoS features are used to prioritize traffic according to its relative importance and provide preferential treatment using congestion management techniques.

Using QoS in the campus network design ensures that important traffic such as voice and video is placed in a queue that is configured so that it optimizes memory usage.

However, the network should provide an adequate level of service for all network traffic, including lower-priority, best-effort traffic under normal circumstances. For best-effort traffic, there is an implied good-faith commitment that there are at least some network resources available.

QoS is also needed to identify and potentially punish out-of-profile traffic such as potential worms, distributed DoS (DDoS) attacks, and peer-to-peer media-sharing applications that may be placed in a scavenger class and marked with differentiated services code point (DSCP) class selector 1 (CS1). The scavenger class is intended to provide deferential services, or less-than best-effort services, to certain applications. During periods of congestion, scavenger-class traffic is the first to experience Tx-queue starvation and packet loss when the bandwidth is reserved for higher-priority traffic. As demand increases or capacity is reduced, best-effort traffic may also be affected. The minimum goal of high-availability network design is to ensure that high-priority voice, video, and mission-critical data applications are never affected by network congestion.

Campus QoS Design Considerations

Campus QoS design is primarily concerned with classification, marking, and policing, as illustrated in Figure 2-46.

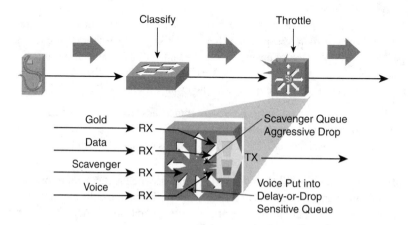

Figure 2-46   *Campus QoS Design Considerations*

Queuing is enabled at any node that has the potential for congestion. The edge traffic classification scheme is mapped to the upstream queue configuration. The applications are classified and marked as close to their sources as technically and administratively feasible. Traffic flows are policed as close to their sources as possible.

Multiple queues are the only way to guarantee voice quality, protect mission-critical data, and throttle abnormal sources:

■ Voice needs to be assigned to the hardware priority queue. VoIP deployments require provisioning-explicit priority servicing for VoIP traffic and a guaranteed bandwidth service for call-signaling traffic. Strict-priority queuing is limited to 33 percent of the capacity of the link.

■ At least 25 percent of the bandwidth of the link is reserved for the default best-effort class, which is the default class for data traffic. Under normal circumstances, the network should provide an adequate level of service for best-effort traffic.

■ Scavenger traffic needs to be assigned its own queue with a low threshold to trigger aggressive drops. Applications assigned to this class have little or no contribution to the organizational objectives of the enterprise. Assigning a minimal bandwidth queue to scavenger traffic forces it to be squelched to virtually nothing during periods of congestion, but allows it to be available if bandwidth is not being used for business purposes, which might occur during off-peak hours.

Cisco Catalyst Integrated Security Features

The Cisco Catalyst Integrated Security capabilities provide campus security on the Cisco Catalyst switches through the use of integrated tools:

■ Port security prevents MAC flooding attacks.

■ Dynamic Host Configuration Protocol (DHCP) snooping prevents client attacks on the DHCP server and switch.

■ Dynamic ARP inspection adds security to ARP using the DHCP snooping table to minimize the impact of ARP poisoning and spoofing attacks.

■ IP source guard prevents IP spoofing addresses using the DHCP snooping table.

Port Security Prevents MAC-Based Attacks

Port security can be used to prevent MAC-based attacks.

A MAC-based attack occurs when an attacker sends out floods of MAC addresses to a switch to overload the CAM table. When the CAM table limit is reached, the switch can no longer keep track of legitimate addresses and starts flooding all information to all ports.

Port security enables a network administrator to restrict the MAC addresses allowed or the maximum number of MAC addresses on a per-port basis. The allowed MAC addresses on a given port can be either statically configured by the administrator or dynamically learned by the switch. A security violation occurs when either the maximum number of MAC addresses on a given port is exceeded or a frame with an unsecure source MAC address is seen on that port. The port is then shut down, or alternatively, a Simple Network Management Protocol (SNMP) trap is generated. Aging with either inactivity or a predefined time interval can be configured with port security for the dynamic or static secure MAC addresses.

Note   When a port security violation occurs, the port takes one of three actions, depending on how the port is configured: The port will be shut down (Shutdown), frames will simply be ignored (Protect), or the frames will be ignored and the violation counter incremented (Restrict).

DHCP Snooping Protects Against Rogue and Malicious DHCP Servers

DHCP snooping can be used to protect against rogue and malicious DHCP servers.

In some cases, an intruder can attach a server to the network and have it assume the role of the DHCP server for that segment. This enables the intruder to give out false DHCP information for the default gateway and domain name servers, which points clients to the hacker's machine. This misdirection enables the hacker to become a "man in the middle" and gain access to confidential information, such as username and password pairs, while the end user is unaware of the attack. DHCP snooping can prevent this. DHCP snooping is a per-port security mechanism used to differentiate an untrusted switch port connected to an end user from a trusted switch port connected to a DHCP server or another switch. It can be enabled on a per-VLAN basis. DHCP snooping allows only authorized DHCP servers to respond to DHCP requests and to distribute network information to clients. It also provides the ability to rate-limit DHCP request on client ports, thereby mitigating the effect of DHCP DoS attacks from an individual client or access port.

Dynamic ARP Inspection Protects Against ARP Poisoning

Dynamic ARP inspection can provide protection against ARP poisoning.

ARP does not have any authentication. It is quite simple for a malicious user to spoof addresses by using tools such as ettercap, dsniff, and arpspoof to poison the ARP tables of other hosts on the same VLAN. In a typical attack, a malicious user can send unsolicited ARP replies (gratuitous ARP packets) to other hosts on the subnet with the attacker's MAC address and the default gateway's IP address. Frames intended for default gateways sent from hosts with poisoned ARP tables are sent to the hacker's machine (allowing the packets to be sniffed) or an unreachable host as a DoS attack. ARP poisoning leads to various man-in-the-middle attacks, posing a security threat in the network.

Dynamic ARP inspection helps prevent the man-in-the-middle attacks by not relaying invalid or gratuitous ARP replies out to other ports in the same VLAN. Dynamic ARP inspection intercepts all ARP requests and all replies on the untrusted ports. Each intercepted packet is verified for valid IP-to-MAC bindings, which are gathered via DHCP snooping. Denied ARP packets are either dropped or logged by the switch for auditing, so ARP poisoning attacks are stopped. Incoming ARP packets on the trusted ports are not inspected. Dynamic ARP inspection can also rate-limit ARP requests from client ports to minimize port-scanning mechanisms.

IP Source Guard Protects Against Spoofed IP Addresses

IP source guard is a unique Cisco IOS Software feature for Catalyst switches that helps mitigate IP spoofing.

IP source guard prevents a malicious host from attacking the network by hijacking its neighbor's IP address. IP source guard provides per-port IP traffic filtering of the assigned source IP addresses at wire speed. It dynamically maintains per-port VLAN ACLs based on IP-to-MAC-to-switch port bindings. The binding table is populated either by the DHCP snooping feature or through static configuration of entries. IP source guard is typically deployed for untrusted switch ports in the access layer.

Example Catalyst Integrated Security Feature Configuration

This configuration snippet shows the commands to enable the Catalyst Integrated Security features:

```
ip dhcp snooping
ip dhcp snooping vlan 2-10
ip arp inspection vlan 2-10
!c
interface fastethernet3/1
switchport port-security
switchport port-security max 3
switchport port-security violation restrict
switchport port-security aging time 2
switchport port-security aging type inactivity
ip arp inspection limit rate 100
ip dhcp snooping limit rate 100
ip verify source port-security
!
interface gigabit1/1
ip dhcp snooping trust
ip arp inspection trust
```

Summary

This chapter examined design models for high availability and fast convergence for the hierarchical layers of the Cisco enterprise campus architecture. High availability in the campus minimizes convergence time after link and node failures with appropriate redundancy.

For predictable fast convergence, VLANs should not span access switches in the campus. Layer 2 designs use RTSP when STP is required, define primary and secondary root switches, and use the Cisco STP Toolkit to harden Layer 2. Trunks and channels are tuned for predictable fast convergence. Aggressive mode UDLD is configured on all fiber links.

Oversubscription and bandwidth are managed to minimize complexity and provide deterministic behavior. Layer 3 designs should load balance traffic over redundant, equal-cost links built on triangles, not squares. Routing protocols should peer only on transit links and summarize at the distribution layer. HSRP and GLBP support fast convergence for end devices.

The Layer 2 to Layer 3 boundary is typically at the distribution layer, but it can be placed at the access layer. Campus network designs should avoid daisy chaining access layer switches, provide appropriate redundancy, and avoid asymmetric flooding.

Infrastructure service considerations such as IP telephony and QoS impact the end-to-end network. The access layer supports device attachment, inline power for devices, and multi-VLAN access ports. End-to-end QoS helps manage oversubscriptions and network speed transitions. Tx-queue starvation is the most common campus congestion issue. Cisco Catalyst Integrated Security features provide security at the network edge.

References

For additional information, refer to these resources:

Cisco Systems, Inc. *Designing a Campus Network for High Availability* at www.cisco.com/application/pdf/en/us/guest/netsol/ns432/c649/cdccont_0900aecd801 a8a2d.pdf

Cisco Systems, Inc. *High Availability Campus Network Design—Routed Access Layer using EIGRP or OSPF* at www.cisco.com/application/pdf/en/us/guest/netsol/ns432/c649/ccmigration_09186a0 0805fccbf.pdf

Cisco Systems, Inc. *Enterprise QoS Solution Reference Network Design Guide* at www.cisco.com/en/US/docs/solutions/Enterprise/WAN_and_MAN/QoS_SRND/ QoS-SRND-Book.html

Cisco Systems, Inc. *Cisco Nonstop Forwarding* at www.cisco.com/univercd/cc/td/doc/product/software/ios122s/122snwft/release/ 122s20/fsnsf20s.pdf

Cisco Systems, Inc. *Cisco IOS Software Modularity on the Cisco Catalyst 6500 Series Switch* at www.cisco.com/en/US/prod/collateral/switches/ps5718/ps708/prod_white_paper0900 aecd80313e09.html

Cisco Systems, Inc. *Cisco Catalyst Integrated Security-Enabling the Self-Defending Network* at www.cisco.com/en/US/prod/collateral/switches/ps5718/ps708/prod_ white_paper0900aecd8015f0ae.pdf

Review Questions

Answer the following questions, and then refer to Appendix A, "Answers to Review Questions," for the answers.

1. Which descriptions best define the core layer? (Choose two.)

    a. It aggregates end users and supports a feature-rich environment.

    b. It provides a high-speed, Layer 3 switching environment using hardware-accelerated services.

    c. It performs high-speed routing and packet manipulations.

    d. It provides scalability and fast policy-based connectivity.

    e. It provides the backbone for campus connectivity.

2. What hardware supports Cisco IOS Software Modularity? (Choose all that apply.)

    a. Cisco Catalyst 3750 series

    b. Cisco Catalyst 4500 series

    c. Cisco Catalyst 6500 series

    d. Cisco Catalyst XR series

    e. All Cisco Catalyst series switches

3. Which statements are correct descriptions of NSF? (Choose all that apply.)

    a. It allows the standby RP to take control of the device after a hardware or software fault on the active RP.

    b. It is a Layer 3 function that works with SSO to minimize the amount of time a network is unavailable to its users following a switchover.

    c. It is supported by the Cisco implementation of EIGRP, OSPF, RIP, and BGP protocols.

    d. It synchronizes startup configuration, startup variables, and running configuration.

    e. The main objective of NSF is to continue forwarding IP packets following an RP switchover.

4. If you need to implement STP, which version is recommended for the enterprise campus?

    a. CST

    b. HSRP

    c. MST

    d. PVST+

    e. RSTP

5. What is the enterprise recommendation regarding UDLD?

    a. Adjust the default hello timers to three seconds for Aggressive mode.

    b. Enable it to create channels containing up to eight parallel links between switches.

    c. Enable it in Global mode and on every interface you need to support.

    d. Enable it in Global mode to support every individual fiber-optic and Ethernet interface.

    e. Enable it in Global mode to support every individual fiber-optic interface.

6. Which statements are correct descriptions of EtherChannels? (Choose two.)

    a. EtherChannels can reduce the number of peers by creating a single logical interface.

    b. EtherChannels can increase the number of peers by creating multiple logical interfaces.

    c. OSPF running on a Cisco IOS Software-based switch will not notice a failed link in a bundle.

    d. EIGRP may not change the link cost if there is a failed link in a bundle.

    e. EtherChannel Min-Links feature is supported on PAgP EtherChannels.

7. Which statements are correct descriptions of EtherChannel load balancing? (Choose three.)

    a. Load balancing using an alternate input hash can be tuned with the **cef port-channel load-balance** command.

    b. Load balancing using an alternate input hash can be tuned with the **port-channel load-balance** command.

    c. The default input hash value of Layer 3 for the source and destination does not load balance across the links.

    d. The default input hash value of Layer 3 for source and destination and Layer 4 port does load balance across the links.

    e. To achieve the best load balancing, use alternating hashes in the core and distribution layer switches.

    f. To achieve the best load balancing, use two, four, or eight ports in the port channel.

8. What are the reasons that passive interfaces should be implemented at distribution layer ports facing the access layer? (Choose two.)

    a. To limit unnecessary peering across the access layer switches when the Layer 2 to Layer 3 boundary is in the distribution layer

    b. To limit unnecessary peering across the access layer switches when the Layer 2 to Layer 3 boundary is in the access layer

    c. To provide high availability in the event of a link or node failure

    d. To support transit traffic through the access layer in the event of a link or node failure

    e. To avoid transit traffic through the access layer in the event of a link or node failure

9. What are the advantages of GLBP in the distribution layer? (Choose two.)

    a. GLBP provides all the benefits of HSRP and includes load balancing when VLANs do not span the access switches.

    b. A convergence event on the uplink affects only half as many hosts as compared to HSRP when VLANs do not span the access switches.

    c. A convergence event on the uplink affects is processed in half the time as compared to HSRP when VLANs do not span the access switches.

    d. STP can block one of the access layer uplinks, and there is at most a two-hop Layer 2 path for upstream traffic when VLANs span access switches.

    e. STP can block one of the access layer uplinks, and there is at most a two-hop Layer 3 path for upstream traffic when VLANs span access switches.

10. What is a potential issue when daisy chaining access layer switches?

    a. It is not easy to determine where the root switch is located.

    b. It is very hard to determine how many ports will be in a blocking state.

    c. The design will black-hole traffic and be affected by multiple convergence events with a single network failure.

    d. There is a danger that black holes will occur in the event of a link or node failure when the distribution interconnection is Layer 2.

    e. There is a danger that black holes will occur in the event of a link or node failure when the distribution interconnection is Layer 3.

11. What is the best mechanism to prevent unicast flooding issues?

   a. Bias the routing metrics to remove equal-cost routes.

   b. Do not span VLANs across multiple access switches.

   c. Span VLANs across multiple access switches.

   d. Tune ARP timers so they exceed CAM timers.

   e. Tune CAM timers so they exceed ARP timers.

12. What hardware is supported by the Cisco Power Calculator? (Choose all that apply.)

   a. Cisco Catalyst 3750 series

   b. Cisco Catalyst 4500 series

   c. Cisco Catalyst 6500 series

   d. Cisco Catalyst XR series

   e. All Cisco Catalyst series switches

13. What features do Cisco Catalyst Integrated Security capabilities provide?
(Choose three.)

   a. DHCP snooping prevents rogue DHCP activities.

   b. Dynamic ARP inspection adds security to ARP to minimize the impact of ARP poisoning and spoofing attacks.

   c. DHCP snooping prevents client attacks on the DHCP server and switch using the dynamic ARP inspection table.

   d. IP source guard prevents IP spoofing using the DHCP snooping table.

   e. IP source guard prevents IP spoofing using the dynamic ARP inspection table

Chapter 3

Developing an Optimum Design for Layer 3

After completing this chapter, you will be able to

- Design IPv4 and IPv6 addressing solutions to support summarization

- Design IPv6 migration schemes

- Design routing solutions to support summarization, route filtering, and redistribution

- Design scalable EIGRP routing solutions for the enterprise

- Design scalable OSPF routing solutions for the enterprise

- Design scalable BGP routing solutions for the enterprise

This chapter examines a select number of topics on both advance IP addressing and design issues with Border Gateway Protocol (BGP), Enhanced Interior Gateway Routing Protocol (EIGRP), and Open Shortest Path First (OSPF). As one would expect, advanced IP addressing and routing protocol design encompasses a large amount of detail that has already filled a number of books on routing protocols and networking best practices.

Designing Advanced IP Addressing

Designing IP addressing at a professional level involves several advanced considerations. This section reviews the importance of IP address planning and selection and the importance of IP address summarization. It also discusses some applications of summary addressing.

Note In this chapter, IP (unless specified as IPv6) refers to IPv4.

IP Address Planning as a Foundation

Structured and modular cabling plant and network infrastructures are ideal for a good design with low maintenance and upgrade costs. In similar fashion, a well-planned IP addressing scheme is the foundation for greater efficiency in operating and maintaining a network. Without proper advanced planning, networks may not be able to benefit from route summarization features inherent to many routing protocols.

Route summarization is important in scaling any routing protocol. However, some existing IP addressing schemes may not support summarization. It takes time and effort to properly allocate IP subnets in blocks to facilitate summarization. The benefits of summarized addresses are reduced router workload and routing traffic and faster convergence. Although modern router CPUs can handle a vastly increased workload as compared to older routers, reducing load mitigates the impact of periods of intense network instability. In general, summary routes dampen out or reduce network route churn, making the network more stable. In addition, summary routes lead to faster network convergence. Summarized networks are simpler to troubleshoot because there are fewer routes in the routing table or in routing advertisements, compared to nonsummarized networks.

Just as using the right blocks of subnets enables use of more efficient routing, care with subnet assignments can also support role-based functions within the addressing scheme structure. This in turn enables efficient and easily managed access control lists (ACL) for quality of service (QoS) and security purposes.

In addition to allocating subnets in summarized blocks, it is advantageous to choose blocks of addresses within these subnets that can be easily summarized or described using wildcard masking in access control lists (ACL). With a well-chosen addressing scheme, ACLs can become much simpler to maintain in the enterprise.

Summary Address Blocks

Summary address blocks are the key to creating and using summary routes. How do you recognize a block of addresses that can be summarized? A block of IP addresses might be able to be summarized if it contains sequential numbers in one of the octets. The sequence of numbers must fit a pattern for the binary bit pattern to be appropriate for summarization. The pattern can be described without doing binary arithmetic.

For the sequential numbers to be summarized, the block must be x numbers in a row, where x is a power of 2. In addition, the first number in the sequence must be a multiple of x. The sequence will always end before the next multiple of x.

For example, any address block that matches the following can be summarized:

- 128 numbers in a row, starting with a multiple of 128 (0 or 128)

- 64 numbers in a row, starting with a multiple of 64 (0, 64, 128, or 192)

- 32 numbers in a row, starting with a multiple of 32

- 16 numbers in a row, starting with a multiple of 16

If you examine 172.19.160.0 through 172.19.191.0, there are 191 − 160 + 1 = 32 numbers in a row, in sequence in the third octet. Note that 32 is 2^5 power of 2. Note also that 160 is a multiple of 32 (5 * 32 = 160). Because the range meets the preceding conditions, the sequence 172.19.160.0 through 172.19.191.0 can be summarized.

Finding the correct octet for a subnet-style mask is fairly easy with summary address blocks. The formula is to subtract n from 256. For example, for 32 numbers in a row, the mask octet is 256 − 32 = 224. Because the numbers are in the third octet, you place the 224 in the third octet, to form the mask 255.255.224.0.

A summary route expressed as either 172.19.160.0, 255.255.224.0, or as 172.169.160/19 would then describe how to reach subnets starting with 172.19.160.0 through 172.19.191.0.

Summarization for IPv6

Although the address format of IPv6 is different from IPv4, the same principles apply. Blocks of subsequent IPv6 /64 subnets can be summarized into larger blocks for decreased routing table size and increased routing table stability. To an extent, routing summarization for IPv6 is simpler than for IPv4, because you do not have to consider variable-length subnet masking (VLSM). Most IPv6 subnets have a prefix length of 64 bits, so again, you are looking for contiguous blocks of /64 subnets. The number of subnets in this block should be a power of 2, and the starting number should be a multiple of that same power of 2 for the block to be summarizable.

For example, examine the block 2001:0DB8:0:A480::/64 to 2001:0DB8:0:A4BF::/64. A quick analysis of the address block shows that the relevant part is in the last two hexadecimal characters, which are 0x80 for the first subnet in the range and 0xBF for the last subnet in the range. Conversion of these numbers to decimal yields 0x80 = 128 and 0xBF = 191. This is a block of 191 − 128 + 1 = 64 subnets. After verifying that 128 is a multiple of 64, you can conclude that the block of subnets is can be summarized.

To calculate the prefix length, you need to find the number of bits represented by the block of 64 addresses. 64 = 2^6; therefore, 6 bits need to be subtracted from the original /64 prefix length to obtain the prefix length of the summary, which is /58 (64 − 6 = 58).

As a result, a summary route of 2001:0DB8:0:A480::/58 can be used to describe how to reach subnets 2001:0DB8:0:A480::/64 to 2001:0DB8:0:A4BF::/64.

Note   If you have a well-chosen IPv4 addressing scheme that summarizes properly, you might consider mapping those addresses to an IPv6 addressing scheme. For example, the issued /48 prefix, append the second and third octets from your network 10.x.y.0/24, voilà! Jeff Doyle and others advise that if you're tight on subnets, if your addressing doesn't summarize well, and for other such reasons, it is usually best to do IPv6 addressing from scratch, rather than tying it to a poorly conceived legacy IPv4 addressing scheme.

Changing IP Addressing Needs

IP address redesign is necessary to adapt to changes in how subnets are now being used. In some networks, IP subnets were initially assigned sequentially. Summary address blocks of subnets were then assigned to sites to enable route summarization.

However, newer specifications require additional subnets, as follows:

- **IP telephony:** Additional subnets or address ranges are needed to support voice services. In some cases, the number of subnets double when IP telephony is implemented in an organization.

- **Videoconferencing:** Immersive TelePresence applications are high bandwidth and sensitive to loss and latency. Generally, best practice is to segment these devices, creating the need for more subnets.

- **Layer 3 switching at the edge:** Deploying Layer 3 switching to the network edge is another trend driving the need for more subnets. Edge Layer 3 switching can create the demand for a rapid increase in the number of smaller subnets. In some cases, there can be insufficient address space, and readdressing is required.

- **Network Admission Control (NAC):** NAC is also being deployed in many organizations. Some Cisco 802.1X and NAC deployments are dynamically assigning VLANs based on user logins or user roles. In these environments, ACLs control connectivity to servers and network resources based on the source subnet, which is based on the user role.

- **Corporate requirements:** Corporate governance security initiatives are also isolating groups of servers by function, sometimes called segmentation. Describing "production" and "development" subnets in an ACL can be painful unless they have been chosen wisely. These new subnets can make managing the network more complex. Maintaining ad hoc subnets for voice security and other reasons can be time-consuming. When it is possible, describing the permitted traffic in a few ACL statements is a highly desirable. Therefore, ACL-friendly addressing which can be summarized helps network administrators to efficiently manage their networks.

Planning Addresses

The first step in implementing ACL-friendly addressing is to recognize the need. In an environment with IP phones and NAC implemented, you need to support IP phone subnets and NAC role subnets in ACLs. In the case of IP phones, ACLs will probably be used for both QoS and voice-security rules. For NAC role-based subnets, ACLs will most likely be used for security purposes.

Servers in medium-to-large server farms should at least be grouped so that servers with different functions or levels of criticality are in different subnets. That saves listing individual IP addresses in lengthy ACLs. If the servers are in subnets attached to different access switches, it can be useful to assign the subnets so that there is a pattern suitable for wildcarding in ACLs.

If the addressing scheme allows simple wildcard rules to be written, those simple ACL rules can be used everywhere. This avoids maintaining per-location ACLs that need to define source or destination addresses to local subnets. ACL-friendly addressing supports maintaining one or a few global ACLs, which are applied identically at various control points in the network. This would typically be accomplished with a tool such as Cisco Security Manager.

The conclusion is that it is advantageous to build a pattern into role-based addressing and other addressing schemes so that ACL wildcards can match the pattern. This in turn supports implementing simpler ACLs.

Note   For IPv6 access lists, the wildcard masks are not usually used. All source and destination addresses are notated in the form of prefixes. Therefore, it is important that subnets that are to be grouped in an access list falling within a summarized address range.

Applications of Summary Address Blocks

Summary address blocks can be used to support several network applications:

- Separate VLANs for voice and data, and even role-based addressing

- Bit splitting for route summarization

- Addressing for virtual private network (VPN) clients

- Network Address Translation (NAT)

These features are discussed in detail in the following sections.

Implementing Role-Based Addressing

The most obvious approach to implement role-based addressing is to use network 10. This has the virtue of simplicity. A simple scheme that can be used with Layer 3 closets is to use 10.number_for_closet.VLAN.x /24 and avoid binary arithmetic. This approach uses the second octet for closets or Layer 3 switches, the third octet for VLANs, and the fourth octet for hosts.

If you have more than 256 closets or Layer 3 switches to identify in the second octet, you might use some bits from the beginning of the third octet, because you probably do not have 256 VLANs per switch.

Another approach is to use some or all of the Class B private addressing blocks. This approach will typically involve binary arithmetic. The easiest method is to allocate bits using bit splitting. An example network is 172.0001 xxxx.xxxx xxxx.xxhh hhhh. In this case, you start out with 6 bits reserved for hosts in the fourth octet, or 62 hosts per subnet (VLAN). The x bits are to be split further.

This format initially uses decimal notation to the first octet and binary notation in the second, third, and fourth octets to minimize conversion back and forth.

If you do not need to use the bits in the second octet to identify additional closets, you end up with something like 172.16.cccc cccR.RRhh hhhh:

- The *c* characters indicate that 7 bits allow for 2^7 or 128 closet or Layer 3 switches.

- The *R* characters indicate 3 bits for a role-based subnet (relative to the closet block), or 8 NAC or other roles per switch.

- The *h* characters indicate 6 bits for the 62-host subnets specified.

This addressing plan is enough to cover a reasonably large enterprise network.

Another 4 bits are available to work with in the second octet if needed.

Using a role-aware or ACL-friendly addressing scheme, you can write a small number of global **permit** or **deny** statements for each role. This greatly simplifies edge ACL maintenance. It is easier to maintain one ACL for all edge VLANs or interfaces than different ACLs for every Layer 3 access or distribution switch.

Note   The role-based approach depends on the use of noncontiguous wildcard masks to match multiple subnets that fit a specific role. This dependency makes the method unsuitable for IPv6 and IPv4 (if devices in the path do not support discontiguous masks).

Bit Splitting for Route Summarization

The previous bit-splitting technique has been around for a while. It can also be useful in coming up with summary address block for routing protocols if you cannot use simple octet boundaries. The basic idea is to start with a network prefix, such as 10.0.0.0, or a prefix in the range 172.16.0.0 to 172.31.0.0, 192.168.n.0, or an assigned IP address. The remaining bits can then be thought of as available for use for the area, subnet, or host part of the address. It can be useful to write the available bits as *x*, then substitute *a*, *s*, or *h* as they are assigned. The *n* in an address indicates the network prefix portion of the address, which is not subject to change or assignment.

Generally, you know how large your average subnets need to be in buildings. (A subnet with 64 bits can be summarized and will cover most LAN switches.) That allows you to convert six *x* bits to *h* for host bits.

You can then determine the number of necessary WAN links and the amount you are comfortable putting into one area to decide the number of *a* bits you need to assign. The leftover bits are *s* bits. Generally, one does not need all the bits, and the remaining bits (the *a* versus *s* boundary) can be assigned to allow some room for growth.

For example, suppose 172.16.0.0 is being used, with subnets of 62 hosts each. That commits the final 6 bits to host address in the fourth octet. If you need 16 or fewer areas, you might allocate 4 *a* bits for area number, which leaves 6 *s* bits for subnet. That would be 2^6 or 64 subnets per area, which is many.

Example: Bit Splitting for Area 1

This example illustrates how the bit-splitting approach would support the addresses in OSPF area 1. Writing 1 as four binary bits substitutes 0001 for the *a* bits. The area 1 addresses would be those with the bit pattern 172.16.0001 ssss.sshh hhhh. This bit pattern in the third octet supports decimal numbers 16 to 31. Addresses in the range 172.16.16.0 to 172.16.31.255 would fall into area 1. If you repeat this logic, area 0 would have addresses 172.16.0.0 to 172.16.15.255, and area 2 would have addresses 172.16.32.0 to 172.16.47.255.

Subnets would consist of an appropriate third octet value for the area they are in, together with addresses in the range 0 to 63, 64 to 127, 128 to 191, or 192 to 255 in the last octet. Thus, 172.16.16.0/26, 172.16.16.64/26, 172.16.16.128/26, 172.16.16.192/26, and 172.16.17.0/26 would be the first five subnets in area 1.

One recommendation that preserves good summarization is to take the last subnet in each area and divide it up for use as /30 or /31 subnets for WAN link addressing.

Few people enjoy working in binary. Free or inexpensive subnet calculator tools can help. For those with skill writing Microsoft Excel spreadsheet formulas, you can install Excel Toolkit functions to help with decimal-to-binary or decimal-to-hexadecimal conversion. Then, build a spreadsheet that lists all area blocks, subnets, and address assignments.

IPv6 Address Planning

Because the IPv6 address space is much larger than the IPv4 address space, addressing plans for IPv6 are in many ways simpler to create. Subnetting an IPv4 address range is always a balancing act between getting the right number of subnets, the right number of hosts per subnet, and grouping subnets in such a way that they are easily summarizable, while also leaving room for future growth. With IPv6, creating an address plan is more straightforward.

It is strongly recommended that all IPv6 subnets use a /64 prefix. With 2^{64} hosts per subnet, a /64 prefix allows more hosts on each single subnet than a single broadcast domain could physically support. There is some concern that using /64 prefixes for every link, even point-to-point and loopback interfaces, unnecessarily wastes large chunks of IPv6 address space. For this reason, some organizations prefer to use /126 prefixes for point-to-point links and /128 prefixes for loopback interfaces.

Note   When using /126 prefixes, avoid overlap with router anycast and embedded RP addresses. Another consideration in the implementation of prefix lengths that are longer than /64 is that it could cause incompatibilities with future capabilities that assume a /64 prefix length for each subnet.

Using a /64 prefix for any subnet that contains end hosts removes any considerations about the number of hosts per subnet from the addressing plan. The second consideration in IPv4 addressing plans is to determine the right number of subnets for each site. For IPv6, this consideration is much less problematic. Local Internet Registries (LIR) commonly assign a /48 prefix from their assigned address blocks to each customer site. With 64 bits being used for the host part of the address, this leaves $128 - 64 - 48 = 16$ bits to number the subnets within the site. This translates to $2^{16} = 65,536$ possible subnets per site, which should be sufficient for all but the largest sites. If a single /48 prefix is insufficient, additional /48 prefixes can be obtained from the LIR.

Effectively, the 16 bits that are available for subnet allocation can be used freely to implement summarizable address plans or role-based addressing.

Note   For easy configuration and renumbering, the **ipv6 general-prefix** command can be used to define a base prefix in the configuration, such as the /48 prefix that is assigned by the LIR. You can then reference this prefix by name in the interface-level IPv6 address configuration commands.

Bit Splitting for IPv6

The 16 bits that are available for subnetting can be split in many different ways. Like IPv4, the IPv6 address plan is an integral part of the overall network design and should be synchronized with other design choices that are made. In an existing network, consider mapping the IPv6 address scheme to known numbers, such as VLANs or IPv4 addresses. This mapping eases network management and troubleshooting tasks, because network operators can relate the structure of the IPv6 addresses to existing address structures.

The following are examples of IPv6 addressing schemes that split the 16 subnet bits in different ways to support different design requirements:

- **Split by area:** If the site is split into areas, such as OSPF areas, the address structure should reflect this to support summarization between the areas. For example, the first 4 of the 16 bits could be used to represent the area, while the VLAN is coded into the last 12 bits. This scheme can support $2^4 = 16$ areas and $2^{12} = 4096$ subnets per area. A small range of VLAN numbers should be set aside to support point-to-point links and loopback interfaces within the area.

- **IPv4 mapping:** If the current IPv4 address structure is based on network 10.0.0.0/8 and all subnets are using /24 or shorter prefixes, the middle 16 bits in the IPv4 address can be mapped to the IPv6 address. For example, if a subnet has IPv4 prefix 10.123.10.0/24, the middle two octets 123.10 can be converted to hexadecimal: 123 = 0x7B and 10 = 0x0A. If the LIR-assigned prefix is 2001:0DB8:1234::/48, appending the 16 bits that are derived from the IPv4 address yields 2001:0DB8:1234:7B0A::/64 as the IPv6 prefix for the subnet. This method is convenient because it establishes a one-to-one mapping between the well known IPv4 addresses and the new IPv6 addresses. However, to use this method, the IPv4 address scheme needs to meet certain conditions, such as not using more than 16 bits for subnetting.

- **Role-based addressing:** For easier access list and firewall rule definition, it can be useful to code roles (for example, voice, office data, and guest users) into the address scheme. For example, the first 4 bits could be used to represent the role, the next 4 bits to represent the area, and the final 8 bits to represent the VLAN. This results in $2^4 = 16$ different roles that can be defined, $2^4 = 16$ areas within the site, and $2^8 = 256$ VLANs per area and per role. Using the first 4 bits for area makes it extremely easy to configure access lists or firewall rules, because all subnets for a specific role fall within a /52 address block. Summarization is slightly less efficient than in a scheme that is purely based on areas. Instead of one summarized address block per area, there is now a summarized block per role.

The methods that are shown here are just examples. When creating an address plan as part of a network design, carefully consider other address or network elements to define an address plan that matches and supports these elements.

Note   For further information about IPv6 address planning, see RFC 5375, *IPv6 Unicast Address Assignment Considerations.*

Addressing for VPN Clients

Focusing some attention on IP addressing for VPN clients can also provide benefits. As role-based security is deployed, there is a need for different groupings of VPN clients. These might correspond to administrators, employees, different groups of contractors or consultants, external support organizations, guests, and so on. You can use different VPN groups for different VPN client pools.

Role-based access can be controlled via the group password mechanism for the Cisco VPN client. Each group can be assigned VPN endpoint addresses from a different pool.

Traffic from the user PC has a VPN endpoint address as its source address.

The different subnets or blocks of VPN endpoint addresses can then be used in ACLs to control access across the network to resources, as discussed earlier for NAC roles. If the pools are subnets of a summary address block, routing traffic back to clients can be done in a simple way.

NAT in the Enterprise

NAT is a powerful tool for working with IP addresses. It has the potential for being very useful in the enterprise to allow private internal addressing to map to publicly assigned addresses at the Internet connection point. However, if it is overused, it can be harmful.

NAT and Port Address Translation (PAT) are common tools for firewalls. A common approach to supporting content load-balancing devices is to perform destination NAT. A recommended approach to supporting content load-balancing devices is to perform source NAT. As long as NAT is done in a controlled, disciplined fashion, it can be useful.

Avoid using internal NAT or PAT to map private-to-private addresses internally. Internal NAT can make network troubleshooting confusing and difficult. For example, it would be difficult to determine which network 10 in an organization a user is currently connected to.

Internal NAT or PAT is sometimes required for interconnection of networks after a corporate merger or acquisition. Many organizations are now using network 10.0.0.0 internally, resulting in a "two network 10.0.0.0" problem after a merger. This is a severely suboptimal situation and can make troubleshooting and documentation very difficult. Re-addressing should be planned as soon as possible. It is also a recommended practice to isolate any servers reached through content devices using source NAT or destination NAT. These servers are typically isolated because the packets with NAT addresses are not useful elsewhere in the network. NAT can also be utilized in the data center to support small out-of-band (OOB) management VLANs on devices that cannot route or define a default gateway for the management VLAN, thereby avoiding one management VLAN that spans the entire data center.

NAT with External Partners

NAT also proves useful when a company or organization has more than a couple of external business partners. Some companies exchange dynamic routing information with external business partners. Exchanges require trust. The drawback to this approach is that a static route from a partner to your network might somehow get advertised back to you. This advertisement, if accepted, can result in part of your network becoming unreachable. One way to control this situation is to implement two-way filtering of routes to partners: Advertise only subnets that the partner needs to reach, and only accept routes to subnets or prefixes that your staff or servers need to reach at the partner.

Some organizations prefer to use static routing to reach partners in a tightly controlled way. The next hop is sometimes a virtual Hot Standby Router Protocol (HSRP) or Gateway Load Balancing Protocol (GLBP) address on a pair of routers controlled by the partner.

When the partner is huge, such as a large bank, static routing is too labor intensive. Importing thousands of external routes into the internal routing protocol for each of several large partners causes the routing table to become bloated.

Another approach is to terminate all routing from a partner at an edge router, preferably receiving only summary routes from the partner. NAT can then be used to change all partner addresses on traffic into a range of locally assigned addresses. Different NAT blocks are used for different partners. This approach converts a wide range of partner addresses into a tightly controlled set of addresses and simplifies troubleshooting. It can also avoid potential issues when multiple organizations are using the 10.0.0.0/8 network.

If the NAT blocks are chosen out of a larger block that can be summarized, a redistributed static route for the larger block easily makes all partners reachable on the enterprise network. Internal routing then have one route that in effect says "this way to partner networks."

A partner block approach to NAT supports faster internal routing convergence by keeping partner subnets out of the enterprise routing table.

A disadvantage to this approach is that it is more difficult to trace the source of IP packets. However, if it is required, you can backtrack and get the source information through the NAT table.

Design Considerations for IPv6 in Campus Networks

This section discusses the three different IPv6 deployment models that can be used in the enterprise campus.

IPv6 Campus Design Considerations

As mentioned earlier, three major deployment models can be used to implement IPv6 support in the enterprise campus environment: the dual-stack model, the hybrid model, and the service block model. The choice of deployment model strongly depends on whether IPv6 switching in hardware is supported in the different areas of the network.

Dual stack is the preferred, most versatile, and highest-performance way to deploy IPv6 in existing IPv4 environments. IPv6 can be enabled wherever IPv4 is commissioned along with the associated features that are required to make IPv6 routable, highly available, and secure. In some cases, IPv6 may not be enabled on a specific interface or device because of the presence of legacy applications or hosts for which IPv6 is not supported. Inversely, IPv6 may be enabled on interfaces and devices for which IPv4 support is no longer necessary.

A key requirement for the deployment of the dual-stack model is that IPv6 switching must be performed in hardware on all switches in the campus. If some areas of the campus network do not support IPv6 switching in hardware, tunneling mechanisms are leveraged to integrate these areas into the IPv6 network. The hybrid model combines a dual-stack approach for IPv6-capable areas of the network with tunneling mechanisms such as Intra-Site Automatic Tunnel Addressing Protocol (ISATAP) and manual IPv6 tunnels where needed.

The hybrid model adapts as much as possible to the characteristics of the existing network infrastructure. Transition mechanisms are selected based on multiple criteria, such as IPv6 hardware capabilities of the network elements, number of hosts, types of applications, location of IPv6 services, and network infrastructure feature support for various transition mechanisms.

The service block model uses a different approach to IPv6 deployment. It centralizes IPv6 as a service, similar to how other services such as voice or guest access can be provided at a central location. The service block model is unique in that it can be deployed as an overlay network without any impact to the existing IPv4 network, and it is completely centralized. This overlay network can be implemented rapidly while allowing for high availability of IPv6 services, QoS capabilities, and restriction of access to IPv6 resources with little or no changes to the existing IPv4 network. As the existing campus network becomes IPv6-capable, the service block model can become decentralized. Connections into the service block are changed from tunnels (ISATAP or manually configured) to dual-stack connections. When all the campus layers are dual-stack capable, the service block can be dismantled and repurposed for other uses.

These three models are not exclusive. Elements from each of these models can be combined to support specific network requirements.

Ultimately, a dual-stack deployment is preferred. The hybrid and service block models are transitory solutions. The models can be leveraged to migrate to a dual stack design in a graceful manner, without a need for forced hardware upgrades throughout the entire campus. From an address-planning standpoint, this means that the IPv6 address plan should be designed to support a complete dual-stack design in the future.

Dual-Stack Model

The dual-stack model deploys IPv4 and IPv6 in parallel without any tunneling or translation between the two protocols. IPv6 is enabled in the access, distribution, and core layers of the campus network. This model makes IPv6 simple to deploy, and is very scalable. No dependencies exist between the IPv4 and IPv6 design, which results in easier implementation and troubleshooting.

Deploying IPv6 in the campus using the dual-stack model offers several advantages over the hybrid and service block models. The primary advantage of the dual-stack model is that it does not require tunneling within the campus network. The dual-stack model runs the two protocols as "ships in the night," meaning that IPv4 and IPv6 run alongside one another and have no dependency on each other to function except that they share network resources. Both IPv4 and IPv6 have independent routing, high availability, QoS, security, and multicast policies. The dual-stack model also offers processing performance advantages, because packets are natively forwarded without having to account for additional encapsulation and lookup overhead.

These advantages make the dual-stack model the preferred deployment model. The stack model requires all switches in the campus to support IPv6 forwarding.

Hybrid Model

The hybrid model strategy is to employ two or more independent transition mechanisms with the same deployment design goals. Flexibility is the key aspect of the hybrid approach. Any combination of transition mechanisms can be leveraged to best fit a given network environment. The hybrid model uses dual stack in all areas of the network where the equipment supports IPv6. Tunneling mechanisms are deployed for areas that do not currently support IPv6 in hardware. These areas can be transitioned to dual stack as hardware is upgraded later.

Various tunneling mechanisms and deployment scenarios can be part of a hybrid model deployment. This section highlights two common scenarios.

The first scenario that may require the use of a hybrid model is when the campus core is not enabled for IPv6. Common reasons why the core layer might not be enabled for IPv6 are either that the core layer does not have hardware-based IPv6 support at all, or has limited IPv6 support but with low performance.

In this scenario, manually configured tunnels are used exclusively from the distribution to aggregation layers. Two tunnels from each switch are used for redundancy and load balancing. From an IPv6 perspective, the tunnels can be viewed as virtual links between the distribution and aggregation layer switches. On the tunnels, routing and IPv6 multicast are configured in the same manner as with a dual-stack configuration.

The scalability of this model is limited, and a dual-stack model is preferred. However, this is a good model to use if the campus core is being upgraded or has plans to be upgraded, and access to IPv6 services is required before the completion of the core upgrade.

The second scenario focuses on the situation where hosts that are located in the campus access layer need to use IPv6 services, but the distribution layer is not IPv6 capable or enabled. The distribution layer switch is most commonly the first Layer 3 gateway for the access layer devices. If IPv6 capabilities are not present in the existing distribution layer switches, the hosts cannot gain access to IPv6 addressing router information (stateless autoconfiguration or Dynamic Host Configuration Protocol [DHCP] for IPv6), and then cannot access the rest of the IPv6-enabled network.

In this scenario, tunneling can be used on the IPv6-enabled hosts to provide access to IPv6 services that are located beyond the distribution layer. For example, the ISATAP tunneling mechanisms on the hosts in the access layer to provide IPv6 addressing and off-link routing. The Microsoft Windows XP and Vista hosts in the access layer must have IPv6 enabled and either a static ISATAP router definition or Domain Name System (DNS) A record entry that is configured for the ISATAP router address.

Using the ISATAP IPv4 address, the hosts establish tunnels to the IPv6-enabled core routers, obtain IPv6 addresses, and tunnel IPv6 traffic across the IPv4 distribution switches to the IPv6 enabled part of the network.

Terminating ISATAP tunnels in the core layer makes the layer appear as an access layer to the IPv6 traffic, which may be undesirable from a high-level design perspective. To avoid the blending of core and access layer functions, the ISATAP can be terminated on a different set of switches, such as the data center aggregation switches.

The main reason to choose the hybrid deployment model is to deploy IPv6 without having to go through an immediate hardware upgrade for parts of the network. It allows switches that have not reached the end of their normal life cycle to remain deployed and avoids the added cost that is associated with upgrading equipment before its time with the sole purpose of enabling IPv6.

Some drawbacks apply to the hybrid model. The use of ISATAP tunnels is not compatible with IPv6 multicast. Therefore, any access or distribution layer blocks that require the use of IPv6 multicast applications should be deployed using the dual-stack model. Manual tunnels support IPv6 multicast and can still be used to carry IPv6 across an IPv4 core. Another drawback of the hybrid model is the added complexity that is associated with tunneling. Considerations that must be accounted for include performance, management, security, scalability, and availability.

Service Block Model

The service block model has several similarities to the hybrid model. The underlying IPv4 network is used as the foundation for the overlay IPv6 network that is being deployed. ISATAP provides access to hosts in the access layer. Manually configured tunnels are utilized from the data center aggregation layer to provide IPv6 access to the applications and services that are located in the data center access layer. IPv4 routing is configured between the core layer and service block switches to allow visibility to the service block switches for terminating IPv6-in-IPv4 tunnels.

The biggest difference with the hybrid model is that the service block model centralizes IPv6 connectivity through a separate redundant pair of switches. The service block deployment model is based on a redundant pair of Cisco Catalyst 6500 series switches with a Cisco Supervisor Engine 32 or Supervisor Engine 720 card. The key to maintaining a highly scalable and redundant configuration in the service block is to ensure that a high-performance switch, supervisor, and modules are used to manage the load of the ISATAP, manually configured tunnels, and dual-stack connections for an entire campus network.

Note   As the number of tunnels and required throughput increases, it might be necessary to distribute the load across an additional pair of switches in the service block.

The biggest benefit of this model compared with the hybrid model is that the centralized approach enables you to pace the IPv6 deployment in a very controlled manner.

In essence, the service block model provides control over the pace of IPv6 service introduction by leveraging the following:

■   Per-user or per-VLAN tunnels, or both, can be configured via ISATAP to control the flow of connections and allow for the measurement of IPv6 traffic use.

■   Access on a per-server or per-application basis can be controlled via access lists and routing policies that are implemented on the service block switches. This level of control allows for access to one, a few, or even many IPv6-enabled services, while all other services remain on IPv4 until those services can be upgraded or replaced. This enables a "per-service" deployment of IPv6.

■   The use of separate dual redundant switches in the service block allows for high availability of ISATAP and manually configured tunnels as well as all dual-stack connections.

■   Flexible options allow hosts access to the IPv6-enabled ISP connections, either by allowing a segregated IPv6 connection that is used only for IPv6-based Internet traffic or by providing links to the existing Internet edge connections that have both IPv4 and IPv6 ISP connections.

■ Implementation of the service block model does not disrupt the existing network infrastructure and services. Because of its similarity to the hybrid model, the service block model suffers from the same drawbacks that are associated with the use of tunneling. In addition to those drawbacks, there is the cost that is associated with the service block switches.

Note For a detailed discussion of the three IPv6 deployment models, implementation guidelines, and examples, see the *Deploying IPv6 in Campus Networks* document at www.cisco.com/en/US/docs/solutions/Enterprise/Campus/CampIPv6.html.

Designing Advanced Routing

This section discusses elements of advanced routing solution design using route summarization and default routing. It also discusses utilizing route filtering and redistribution in advanced routing designs. The discussion in this section

■ Describes why route summarization and default routing should be used in a routing design

■ Describes why route filtering should be used in a routing design

■ Describes why redistribution should be used in a routing design

Route Summarization and Default Routing

Route summarization procedures condense routing information. Without summarization, each router in a network must retain a route to every subnet in the network. With summarization, routers can reduce some sets of routes to a single advertisement, reducing both the load on the router and the perceived complexity of the network. The importance of route summarization increases with network size, as shown in Figure 3-1.

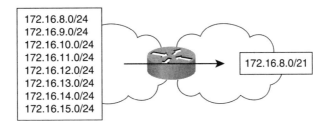

Figure 3-1 *Route Summarization*

Medium-to-large networks often require the use of more routing protocol features than a small network. The larger the network, the more important it is to have a careful design with attention to properly scaling the routing protocol. Stability, control, predictability, and security of routing are also important. Converged networks are increasingly used to support voice, IP telephony, storage, and other drop-sensitive traffic, and so networks must be designed for fast routing convergence.

Route summarization is one key network design element for supporting manageable and fast-converging routing. The Implementing Cisco IP Routing (ROUTE) course covers the configuration of route summarization and its benefits for routing and troubleshooting.

The design recommendations for summarizations are straightforward and include

■ Using route summarization to scale routing designs.

■ Designing addressing by using address blocks that can be summarized.

■ Using default routing whenever possible. Route summarization is the ultimate route summarization, where all other routes are summarized in the default.

Originating Default Routes

The concept of originating default routes is useful for summarization in routing. Most networks use some form of default routing. It is wise to have the default route (0.0.0.0 /0) advertised dynamically into the rest of the network by the router or routers that connect to Internet service providers (ISP). This route advertises the path to any route not found; more specifically in the routing table, as shown in Figure 3-2.

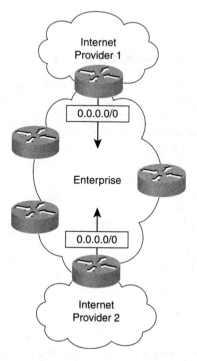

Figure 3-2   *Originating Default Routes*

It is generally a bad idea to configure a static default route on every router, even if recursive routing is used. In recursive routing, for any route in the routing table whose next-hop IP address is not a directly connected interface of the router, the routing algorithm looks recursively into the routing table until it finds a directly connected interface to which it can forward the packets. If you configure a static default route on every router to the ISP router, the next hop is the ISP-connected router rather than a directly connected peer router. This approach can lead to black holes in the network if there is not a path to the ISP-connected router. This approach also needs to be reconfigured on every router if the exit point changes or if a second ISP connection is added.

If manually configured next hops are used, more configuration commands are needed. This approach can also lead to routing loops and is hard to change. If there are alternative paths, this static approach might fail to take advantage of them.

The recommended alternative is to configure each ISP-connected router with a static default route and redistribute it into the dynamic routing protocol. Static default route configuration needs to be done only at the network edge devices. All other routers pick up the route dynamically, and traffic out of the enterprise uses the closest exit. If the ISP-connected router loses connectivity to the ISP or fails, the default route is no longer advertised in the organization.

You might need to use the **default-information originate** command, with options, to redistribute the default route into the dynamic routing protocol.

Note   The actual syntax of the command to inject a default route into an Interior Gateway Protocol (IGP) depends on the IGP being used. The command in the text works for RIP, OSPF, Intermediate System-to-Intermediate System (IS-IS), and BGP. For EIGRP, the **ip default-network** command is used. See the Cisco IP Command Reference for more in-depth study.

Stub Areas and Default Route

Explicit route summarization is not the only way to achieve the benefits of summarization. The various kinds of OSPF stub areas can be thought of as a simpler form of summarization. The point of using OSPF stub areas, totally stubby areas, and not-so-stubby areas (NSSA) is to reduce the amount of routing information advertised into an area. The information that is suppressed is replaced by the default route 0.0.0.0/0 (IPv4) or ::/0 (IPv6)

OSPF cannot filter prefixes within an area. It only filters routes as they are passed between areas at an Area Border Router (ABR).

OSPF stub areas do not work to IP Security (IPsec) virtual private network (VPN) sites such as with generic routing encapsulation (GRE) over IPsec tunnels. For IPsec VPN remote sites, the 0/0 route must point to the ISP, so stub areas cannot be used. An alternative to the default route is to advertise a summary route for the organization as a "corporate default" route and filter unnecessary prefixes at the ABR. Because OSPF cannot filter routes within an area, there still will be within-area flooding of link-state advertisements (LSA).

You can use this approach with the EIGRP, too. The **ip default-network** *network-number* command is used to configure the last-resort gateway or default route. A router configured with this command considers the network listed in the command as the candidate route for computing the gateway of last resort. This network must be in the routing table either as a static route or an IGP route before the router will announce the network as a candidate default route to other EIGRP routers. The network must be an EIGRP-derived network in the routing table or be generated by a static route that has been redistributed into EIGRP.

EIGRP networks typically configure the default route at ISP connection points. Filters can then be used so that only the default and any other critical prefixes are sent to remote sites. In many WAN designs with central Internet access, HQ just needs to advertise default to branch offices, in effect "this way to the rest of the network and to the Internet." If the offices have direct Internet access, a corporate summary can work similarly, "this way to the rest of the company."

In a site-to-site IPsec VPN network, it can be useful to also advertise a corporate summary route or corporate default route (which might be 10.0.0.0 /8) to remote sites. The advantage of doing so is that all other corporate prefixes need not be advertised to the IPsec VPN site. Even if the IPsec network uses two or three hub sites, dynamic failover occurs based on the corporate default. For the corporate default advertisement to work properly under failure conditions, all the site-specific prefixes need to be advertised between the hub sites.

Filtering the unnecessary routes out can save on the bandwidth and router CPU that is expended to provide routing information to remote sites. This increases the stability and efficiency of the network. Removing the clutter from routing tables also makes troubleshooting more effective and speeds convergence.

Route Filtering in the Network Design

This section discusses the appropriate use of route filtering in network design. Route filtering can be used to manage traffic flows in the network, avoid inappropriate transit traffic through remote nodes, and provide a defense against inaccurate or inappropriate routing updates. You can use different techniques to apply route filtering in various routing protocols.

Inappropriate Transit Traffic

Transit traffic is external traffic passing through a network or site, as shown in Figure 3-3.

With poorly configured topology, poorly configured filtering, or poorly configured summarization, a part of the network can be used suboptimally for transit traffic.

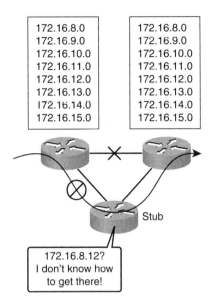

172.16.8.0	172.16.8.0
172.16.9.0	172.16.9.0
172.16.10.0	172.16.10.0
172.16.11.0	172.16.11.0
172.16.12.0	172.16.12.0
172.16.13.0	172.16.13.0
172.16.14.0	172.16.14.0
172.16.15.0	172.16.15.0

Stub

172.16.8.12?
I don't know how
to get there!

Figure 3-3 *Avoid Inappropriate Transit Traffic*

Remote sites generally are connected with lower bandwidth than is present in the network core. Remote sites are rarely desirable as transit networks to forward network from one place to another. Remote sites typically cannot handle the traffic volume needed to be a viable routing alternative to the core network. In general, when core connectivity fails, routing should not detour via a remote site.

In OSPF, there is little control over intra-area traffic. LSAs cannot be filtered within an area. OSPF does not allow traffic to arbitrarily route into and then out of an area. The exception is area 0, which can be used for transit when another area becomes discontiguous.

With EIGRP, it can be desirable to configure EIGRP stub networks. This informs central routers that they should not use a remote site as a transit network. In addition, the use of stub networks damps unnecessary EIGRP queries, speeding network convergence. Filtering can help manage which parts of the network are available for transit in an EIGRP network.

With BGP, the most common concern about transit traffic is when a site has two Internet connections. If there is no filtering, the connections advertise routes. This advertisement can put the site at risk of becoming a transit network. This should not be a problem with two connections to the same ISP, because the autonomous system number is present in the BGP autonomous system path. Based on the autonomous system path, the ISP router ignores any routes advertised from the ISP to the site and then back to the ISP.

When two ISPs are involved, the site might inadvertently become a transit site. The best approach is to filter routes advertised outbound to the ISPs and ensure that only the company or site prefixes are advertised outward. Tagging routes with a BGP community is an easy way to do this. All inbound routes received from the ISP should be filtered, too, so that you accept only the routes the ISP should be sending you.

Defensive Filtering

Route filtering can also be used defensively against inaccurate or inappropriate routing traffic. This is illustrated in Figure 3-4.

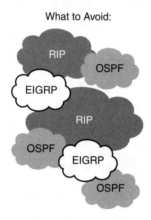

Figure 3-4   *Defensive Filtering*

One common problem some organizations experience is that they inherit inappropriate routes from another organization, such as a business partner. Your business partner should not be advertising your routing prefixes back to your network. Those destinations are not reached through the partner, unless you have a very odd network design. The default route should not be reached via the partner, unless the partner is providing your network with Internet connectivity.

Inappropriate partner advertisements can disrupt routing without filtering. For example, a partner may define a static route to your data center. If this route leaks into your routing process, a portion of your network might think that the data center has moved to a location behind the router of the partner.

Defensive filtering protects the network from disruptions due to incorrect advertisements of others. You configure which routing updates your routers should accept from the partner and which routing updates should be ignored. For example, you would not accept routing updates about how to get to your own prefixes or about default routing.

For security reasons, you should advertise to a partner only the prefixes that you want them to be able to reach. This provides the partner with minimum information about your network and is part of a layered security approach. It also ensures that if there is an accidental leak of another partner's routes or static routes into the dynamic routing process, the inappropriate information does not also leak to others.

The approach of blocking route advertisements is also called route hiding or route starvation. Traffic cannot get to the hidden subnets from the partner unless a summary route is also present. Packet-filtering ACLs should also be used to supplement security by route starvation.

Designing Redistribution

Redistribution is a powerful tool for manipulating and managing routing updates, particularly when two routing protocols are present in a network. This is shown in Figure 3-5.

What to Avoid:

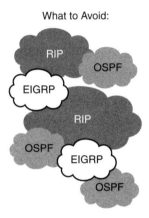

Figure 3-5   *Designing Redistribution*

In some situations, routing redistribution is useful and even necessary. These include migration between routing protocols, corporate mergers, reorganization, and support for devices that speak only RIP or OSPF.

However, redistribution should be used with planning and some degree of caution. It is easy to create routing loops with redistribution. This is particularly true when there are multiple redistribution points, sometimes coupled with static routes, inconsistent routing summaries, or route filters.

Experience teaches that it is much better to have distinct pockets of routing protocols and redistribute than to have a random mix of routers and routing protocols with ad hoc redistribution. Therefore, running corporate EIGRP with redistribution into RIP or OSPF for a region that has routers from other vendors is viable, with due care. On the other hand, freely intermixing OSPF-speaking routers with EIGRP routers in ad hoc fashion is just asking for major problems.

When more than one interconnection point exists between two regions using different routing protocols, bidirectional redistribution is commonly considered. When running OSPF and EIGRP in two regions, it is attractive to redistribute OSPF into EIGRP, and EIGRP into OSPF.

Filtered Redistribution

When you use bidirectional redistribution, you should prevent re-advertising information back into the routing protocol region or autonomous system that it originally came from. This is illustrated in Figure 3-6.

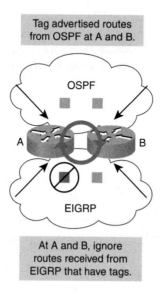

Figure 3-6   *Filtered Redistribution*

For example, filters should be used so that OSPF information that was redistributed into EIGRP does not get re-advertised into OSPF. You also need to prevent information that came from EIGRP into OSPF from being re-advertised back into the EIGRP part of the network. This is sometimes called a manual split horizon. Split horizon is a routing proto-col feature. The idea behind it is that it is counterproductive to advertise information back to the source of that information, because the information may be out of date or incorrect, and because the source of the information is presumed to be better informed.

If you do not do this filtering or use a manual split horizon, you will probably see strange convergence after an outage, you will probably see routing loops, and in general, you will experience routing problems and instability.

Both EIGRP and OSPF support the tagging of routes. A route map can be used to add the numeric tag to specific prefixes. The tag information is then passed along in routing updates. Another router may then filter out routes that match, or do not match, the tag. This is done using a route map in a distribution list.

One typical use of tags is with redistribution. In Figure 3-6, routers A and B can apply tags to routes from IGP X when they are advertised outbound into IGP Y. This in effect marks them as routes from IGP X. When routers A and B receive routes from Y, they would then filter out routes marked as from X when received from IGP Y, because both routers learn such routes directly from IGP X. The process of filtering also applies in the opposite direction.

The point is to get routes in the most direct way, not via an indirect information path that might be passing along old information.

Migrating Between Routing Protocols

This section discusses two common approaches for migrating between routing protocols. One approach for migrating between routing protocols is to use administrative distance (AD) to migrate the routing protocols. Another approach is to use redistribution and a moving boundary.

Migration by AD does not use redistribution. Instead, two routing protocols are run at the same time with the same routes. This assumes sufficient memory, CPU, and bandwidth are in place to support this on the routers running two routing protocols.

The first step in migration by AD is to turn on the new protocol, but make sure that it has a higher AD than the existing routing protocol so it is not preferred. This step enables the protocol and allows adjacencies or neighbors and routing databases to be checked but does not actually rely on the new routing protocol for routing decisions.

When the new protocol is fully deployed, various checks can be done with **show** commands to confirm proper deployment. Then, the cutover takes place. In cutover, the AD is shifted for one of the two protocols so that the new routing protocol will now have a lower AD.

Final steps in this process include the following:

■ Check for any prefixes learned only via the old protocol.

■ Check for any strange next hops (perhaps using some form of automated comparison).

With migration by redistribution, the migration is staged as a series of smaller steps. In each step, part of the network is converted from the old to the new routing protocol. In a big network, the AD approach might be used to support this conversion. In a smaller network, an overnight cutover or simpler approach might suffice.

To provide full connectivity during migration by redistribution, the boundary routers between the two parts of the network would have to bidirectionally redistribute between protocols. Filtering via tags would be one relatively simple way to manage this. The boundary routers move as more of the region is migrated.

Designing Scalable EIGRP Designs

This section focuses on designing advanced routing solutions using Enhanced Interior Gateway Routing Protocol (EIGRP). It describes how to scale EIGRP designs and how to use multiple EIGRP autonomous systems in a large network.

Scaling EIGRP Designs

EIGRP is tolerant of arbitrary topologies for small and medium networks. This is both a strength and a weakness. It is useful to be able to deploy EIGRP without restructuring the network. As the scale of the network increases, however, the risk of instability or long convergence times becomes greater. For example, if a network has reached the point where it includes 500 routers, EIGRP may stop working well without a structured hierarchy. As the size of the network increases, more stringent design is needed for EIGRP to work well.

Note   This mechanism contrasts with OSPF, where structured design is imposed at an early stage. The counterpart to using EIGRP with an arbitrary topology would be an OSPF design that puts everything into OSPF area 0. That also may work for small-to-medium networks, up to around 200 or 300 OSPF routers.

To scale EIGRP, it is a good idea to use a structured hierarchical topology with route summarization.

One of the biggest stability and convergence issues with EIGRP is the propagation of EIGRP queries. When EIGRP does not have a feasible successor, it sends queries to its neighbors. The query tells the neighbor, "I do not have a route to this destination any more; do not route through me. Let me know if you hear of a viable alternative route." The router has to wait for replies to all the queries it sends. Queries can flood through many routers in a portion of the network and increase convergence time. Summarization points and filtered routes limit EIGRP query propagation and minimize convergence time.

Feasible distance is the best metric along a path to a destination network, including the metric to the neighbor advertising that path. Reported distance is the total metric along a path to a destination network as advertised by an upstream neighbor. A feasible successor is a path whose reported distance is less than the feasible distance (current best path).

EIGRP Fast Convergence

Customers have been using EIGRP to achieve subsecond convergence for years. Lab testing by Cisco has shown that the key factor for EIGRP convergence is the presence or absence of a feasible successor. When there is no feasible successor, EIGRP uses queries to EIGRP peers and has to wait for responses. This slows convergence.

Proper network design is required for EIGRP to achieve fast convergence. Summarization helps limit the scope of EIGRP queries, indirectly speeding convergence. Summarization also shrinks the number of entries in the routing table, which speeds up various CPU operations. The effect of CPU operation on convergence is much less significant than the presence or absence of a feasible successor. A recommended way to ensure that a feasible successor is present is to use equal-cost routing.

EIGRP metrics can be tuned using the delay parameter. However, adjusting the delay on links consistently and tuning variance are next to impossible to do well at any scale.

In general, it is unwise to have a large number of EIGRP peers. Under worst-case conditions, router CPU or other limiting factors might delay routing protocol convergence. A somewhat conservative design is best to avoid nasty surprises.

EIGRP Fast-Convergence Metrics

This section discusses EIGRP fast-convergence metrics. Cisco tested convergence of various routing protocols in the lab, as shown in Figure 3-7.

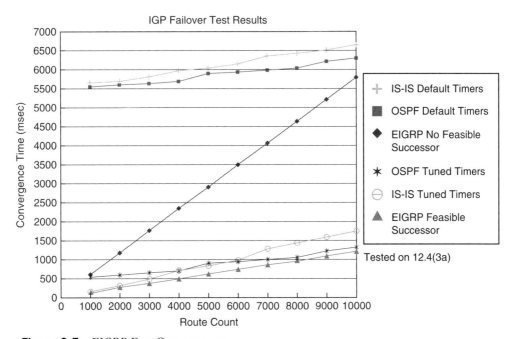

Figure 3-7   *EIGRP Fast Convergence*

EIGRP convergence time increases as more routes need to be processed. However, there is a much bigger impact for networks without EIGRP feasible successors than for networks with no feasible successors.

With a feasible successor present, EIGRP converges in times ranging from about 1/10 second for 1000 routes to about 1.2 seconds for 10,000 routes. Without the feasible successor, convergence times increased to 1/2 to 1 second for 1000 routes and to about 6 seconds for 10,000 routes.

Subsecond timers are not available for EIGRP. One reason is that the hello timer is not the most significant factor in EIGRP convergence time. Another is that experimentation suggests that setting the EIGRP timer below two seconds can lead to instability. The recommended EIGRP minimum timer settings are two seconds for hellos and six seconds for the dead timer. Subsecond settings are not an option.

Scaling EIGRP with Multiple Autonomous Systems

Implementing multiple EIGRP autonomous systems is sometimes used as a scaling technique. The usual rationale is to reduce the volume of EIGRP queries by limiting them to one EIGRP autonomous system. However, there can be issues with multiple EIGRP autonomous systems, as shown in Figure 3-8.

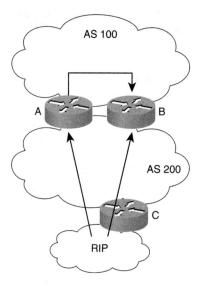

Figure 3-8 *Scaling EIGRP with Multiple Autonomous Systems*

One potential issue is with the external route redistribution. In Figure 3-8, a route is redistributed from RIP into autonomous system 200. Router A redistributes it into autonomous system 100. Router B hears about the route prefix in advertisements from both autonomous system 200 and autonomous system 100. The AD is the same because the route is external to both autonomous systems.

The route that is installed into the EIGRP topology database first gets placed into the routing table.

Example: External Route Redistribution Issue

If router B selects the route via autonomous system 100, it then routes to the RIP autonomous system indirectly, rather than directly via autonomous system 200, as illustrated in Figure 3-9.

Router B also advertises the route via autonomous system 100 back into autonomous system 200. Suppose B has a lower redistribution metric than router C does. If that is the case, A prefers the route learned from B over the route learned from C. In this case, A forwards traffic for this route to B in autonomous system 200, and B forwards traffic back to A in autonomous system 100. This is a routing loop!

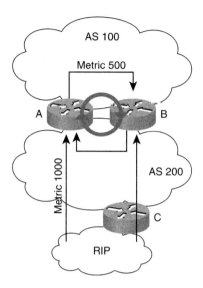

Figure 3-9   *Example: External Route Redistribution Issue*

If two EIGRP processes run and two equal paths are learned, one by each EIGRP process, both routes do not get installed. The router installs the route that was learned through the EIGRP process with the lower autonomous system number. In Cisco IOS Software Releases earlier than 12.2(7)T, the router installed the path with the latest time stamp received from either of the EIGRP processes. The change in behavior is tracked by Cisco bug ID CSCdm47037.

The same sort of behavior may be seen with redistribution between two routing protocols, especially for routes learned from the protocol with the lower AD.

Filtering EIGRP Redistribution with Route Tags

Outbound route tags can be used to filter redistribution and support EIGRP scaling with multiple EIGRP autonomous systems, as shown in Figure 3-10.

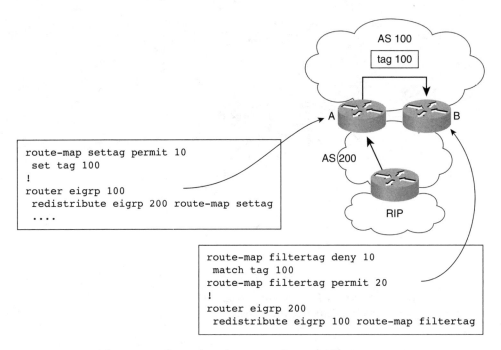

```
route-map settag permit 10
 set tag 100
!
router eigrp 100
 redistribute eigrp 200 route-map settag
 ....
```

```
route-map filtertag deny 10
 match tag 100
route-map filtertag permit 20
!
router eigrp 200
 redistribute eigrp 100 route-map filtertag
```

Figure 3-10 *Filtering EIGRP Redistribution with Route Tags*

External routes can be configured to carry administrative tags. When the external route is redistributed into autonomous system 100 at router A or B, it can be tagged. This tag can then be used to filter the redistribution of the route back into autonomous system 200. This filtering blocks the formation of the loop, because router A will no longer receive the redistributed routes from router B through autonomous system 200.

In the configuration snippets, when routers A and B redistribute autonomous system 200 routes into autonomous system 100, they tag the routes with tag 100. Any routes tagged with tag 100 can then be prevented from being redistributed back into autonomous system 200. This successfully prevents a routing loop from forming.

Filtering EIGRP Routing Updates with Inbound Route Tags

You can filter EIGRP routing updates with inbound route tags to support scaling with multiple EIGRP autonomous systems, as shown in Figure 3-11.

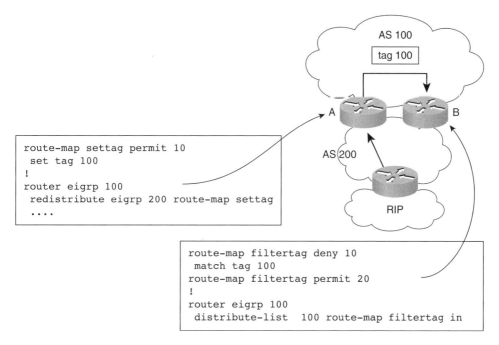

```
route-map settag permit 10
 set tag 100
!
router eigrp 100
 redistribute eigrp 200 route-map settag
 ....
```

```
route-map filtertag deny 10
 match tag 100
route-map filtertag permit 20
 !
router eigrp 100
 distribute-list  100 route-map filtertag in
```

Figure 3-11   *Filtering EIGRP Routing Updates with Inbound Route Tags*

Filtering outbound tags in the previous example does not prevent router B from learning the routes from autonomous system 100. Router B could still perform suboptimal routing by accepting the redistributed route learned from autonomous system 100.

The solution is to use inbound route tag filtering. This technique prevents routers from learning such routes, in which case they also will not be redistributed or advertised outbound. The Cisco bug fix CSCdt43016 provides support for incoming route filtering based on route maps. It allows for filtering routes based on any route map condition before acceptance into the local routing protocol database. This fix works for EIGRP and OSPF, starting with the Cisco IOS Software Releases 12.2T and 12.0S.

When routes are filtered to prevent router B from learning them, you prevent suboptimal routing by router B. The syntax shifts from using a route map with a **redistribute** command to using a route map with an inbound **distribute-list** command.

Note   This example shows how filtering and administrative tags can help prevent routing loops with redistribution and suboptimal routing.

Example: Queries with Multiple EIGRP Autonomous Systems

This example looks at the query behavior with multiple EIGRP autonomous systems. This is illustrated in Figure 3-12.

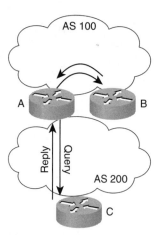

Figure 3-12   *Example: Queries with Multiple EIGRP Autonomous Systems*

If router C sends an EIGRP query to router A, router A needs to query its neighbors. Router A sends a reply to router C, because it has no other neighbors in autonomous system 200. However, router A must also query all of its autonomous system 100 neighbors for the missing route. These routers may have to query their neighbors.

In this example, the query from router C is answered promptly by router A, but router A still needs to wait for the response to its query. Having multiple autonomous systems does not stop queries; it just delays them on the way.

Note   The conclusion of this example is that using multiple EIGRP autonomous systems as an EIGRP query-limiting technique does not work.

What really stops a query is general scaling methods using summarization, distribution lists, and stubs.

Reasons for Multiple EIGRP Autonomous Systems

There are several valid reasons for having multiple EIGRP autonomous systems, including the following:

■   **Migration strategy after a merger or acquisition:** Although this is not a permanent solution, multiple autonomous systems are appropriate for merging two networks over time.

■   **Different groups administer the different EIGRP autonomous systems:** This scenario adds complexity to the network design, but might be used for different domains of trust or administrative control.

■   **Organizations with very large networks may use multiple EIGRP autonomous systems as a way to divide their networks:** Generally, this type of design approach uses summary routes at autonomous system boundaries to contain summary address blocks of prefixes in very large networks and to address the EIGRP query propagation issue.

These reasons for using multiple EIGRP autonomous systems can be appropriate, but pay careful attention to limiting queries.

Designing Scalable OSPF Design

The ability to scale an OSPF internetwork depends on the overall network structure and addressing scheme. As outlined in the preceding sections about network topology and route summarization, adopting a hierarchical addressing environment and a structured address assignment are the most important factors in determining the scalability of your internetwork. Network scalability is affected by operational and technical considerations.

This section discusses designing advanced routing solutions using OSPF. It describes how to obtain scale OSPF designs and what factors can influence convergence in OSPF on a large network. The concepts covered are

■   How to scale OSPF routing to a large network

■   How to obtain fast convergence for OSPF in a routing design

Factors Influencing OSPF Scalability

Scaling is determined by the utilization of three router resources: memory, CPU, and interface bandwidth. The workload that OSPF imposes on a router depends on these factors:

■   **Number of adjacent neighbors for any one router:** OSPF floods all link-state changes to all routers in an area. Routers with many neighbors have the most work to do when link-state changes occur. In general, any one router should have no more than 60 neighbors.

■   **Number of adjacent routers in an area:** OSPF uses a CPU-intensive algorithm. The number of calculations that must be performed given n link-state packets is proportional to $n \log n$. As a result, the larger and more unstable the area, the greater the likelihood for performance problems associated with routing protocol recalculation. Generally, an area should have no more than 50 routers. Areas that suffer with unstable links should be smaller.

■   **Number of areas supported by any one router:** A router must run the link-state algorithm for each link-state change that occurs for every area in which the router resides. Every ABR is in at least two areas (the backbone and one adjacent area). In general, to maximize stability, one router should not be in more than three areas.

■ **Designated router (DR) selection:** In general, the DR and backup designated router (BDR) on a multiaccess link (for example, Ethernet) have the most OSPF work to do. It is a good idea to select routers that are not already heavily loaded with CPU-intensive activities to be the DR and BDR. In addition, it is generally not a good idea to select the same router to be the DR on many multiaccess links simultaneously.

The first and most important decision when designing an OSPF network is to determine which routers and links are to be included in the backbone area and which are to be included in each adjacent area.

Number of Adjacent Neighbors and DRs

One contribution to the OSPF workload on a router is the number of OSPF adjacent routers that it needs to communicate with.

Each OSPF adjacency represents another router whose resources are expended to support these activities:

■ Exchanging hellos

■ Synchronizing link-state databases

■ Reliably flooding LSA changes

■ Advertising the router and network LSA

Some design choices can reduce the impact of the OSPF adjacencies. Here are some recommendations:

■ On LAN media, choose the most powerful routers or the router with the lightest load as the DR candidates. Set the priority of other routers to zero so they will not be DR candidates.

■ When there are many branch or remote routers, spread the workload over enough peers. Practical experience suggests that IPsec VPN peers, for example, running OSPF over GRE tunnels are less stable than non-VPN peers. Volatility or amount of change and other workload need to be considered when determining how many peers a central hub router can support.

Any lab testing needs to consider typical operating conditions. Simultaneous restarts on all peers or flapping connections to all peers are the worst-case situations for OSPF.

Routing Information in the Area and Domain

The workload also depends on the amount of routing information available within the area and the OSPF autonomous system. Routing information in OSPF depends on the number of routers and links to adjacent routers in an area.

There are techniques and tools to reduce this information. Stub and totally stubby areas import less information into an area about destinations outside the routing domain or the area then do normal areas. Therefore, using stub and totally stubby areas further reduces the workload on an OSPF router.

Interarea routes and costs are advertised into an area by each ABR. Totally stubby areas keep not only external routes but also this interarea information from having to be flooded into and within an area.

One way to think about Autonomous System Boundary Routers (ASBR) in OSPF is that each is in effect providing a distance vector-like list of destinations and costs. The more external prefixes and the more ASBRs there are, the more the workload for Type 5 or 7 LSAs. Stub areas keep all this information from having to be flooded within an area.

The conclusion is that area size and layout design, area types, route types, redistribution, and summarization all affect the size of the LSA database in an area.

Designing OSPF Areas

Area design can be used to reduce routing information in an area. Area design requires considering your network topology and addressing. Ideally, the network topology and addressing should be designed initially with division of areas in mind. Whereas EIGRP will tolerate more arbitrary network topologies, OSPF requires a cleaner hierarchy with a more clear backbone and area topology.

Geographic and functional boundaries should be considered in determining OSPF area placement.

As discussed previously, to improve performance minimize the routing information advertised into and out of areas. Bear in mind that anything in the LSA database must be propagated to all routers within the area. With OSPF, note that all changes to the LSA database need to be propagated; this in turn consumes bandwidth and CPU for links and routers within the area. Rapid changes or flapping only exacerbate this effect because the routers have to repeatedly propagate changes. Stub areas, totally stubby areas, and summary routes not only reduce the size of the LSA database, but they also insulate the area from external changes.

Experience shows that you should be conservative about adding routers to the backbone area 0. The first time people configure an OSPF design, they end up with almost everything in area 0. Some organizations find that over time, too many routers ended up in area 0. A recommended practice is to put only the essential backbone and ABRs into area 0.

Some general advice about OSPF design is this:

- Keep it simple.

- Make nonbackbone areas stub areas (or totally stubby areas).

- Have the address space compressible.

Area Size: How Many Routers in an Area?

Cisco experience suggests that the number of adjacent neighbors has more impact than the total number of routers in the area. In addition, the biggest consideration is the amount of information that has to be flooded within the area. Therefore, one network might have, for example, 200 WAN routers with one Fast Ethernet subnet in one area. Another might have fewer routers and more subnets.

It is a good idea to keep the OSPF router LSAs under the IP maximum transmission unit (MTU) size. When the MTU is exceeded, the result is IP fragmentation. IP fragmentation is, at best, a less-efficient way to transmit information and requires extra router processing. A large number of router LSAs also implies that there are many interfaces (and perhaps neighbors). This is an indirect indication that the area may have become too large. If the MTU size is exceeded, the command **ip ospf mtu ignore** must be used.

Stability and redundancy are the most important criteria for the backbone. Stability is increased by keeping the size of the backbone reasonable.

Note   As best practice each area, including the backbone, should contain no more than 50 routers.

If link quality is high and the number of routes is small, the number of routers can be increased. Redundancy is important in the backbone to prevent partition when a link fails. Good backbones are designed so that no that single link failure can cause a partition.

Current ISP experience and Cisco testing suggest that it is unwise to have more than about 300 routers in OSPF backbone area 0, depending on all the other complexity factors that have been discussed. As mentioned in the preceding note, 50 or fewer routers is the most optimal design.

Note   This number is intended as an appropriate indication that an OSPF design is unsatisfactory and should be reconsidered, focusing on a smaller area 0.

OSPF Hierarchy

OSPF requires two levels of hierarchy in your network, as shown in Figure 3-13.

Route summarization is extremely desirable for a reliable and scalable OSPF network. Summarization in OSPF naturally fits at area boundaries, when there is a backbone area 0 and areas off the backbone, with one or a few routers interconnecting the other areas to area 0. If you want three levels of hierarchy for a large network, BGP can be used to interconnect different OSPF routing domains. With advanced care, two OSPF processes can be used, although it is not recommended for most networks due to complexity and the chance of inadvertent adjacencies.

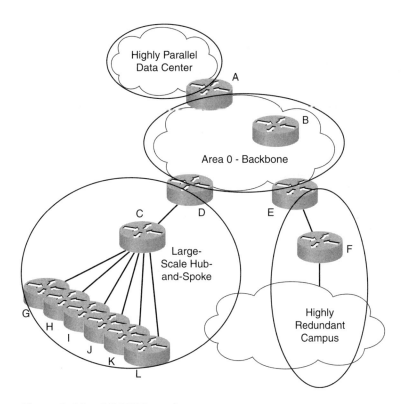

Figure 3-13   *OSPF Hierarchy*

One difficult question in OSPF design is whether distribution or core routers should be ABRs. General design advice is to separate complexity from complexity and put complex parts of the network into separate areas. A part of the network might be considered complex when it has a lot of routing information, such as a full-mesh, a large hub-and-spoke, or a highly redundant topology such as a redundant campus or data center.

ABRs provide opportunities to support route summarization or create stub or totally stubby areas. A structured IP addressing scheme needs to align with the areas for effective route summarization. One of the simplest ways to allocate addresses in OSPF is to assign a separate network number for each area.

Stub areas cannot distinguish among ABRs for destinations external to the OSPF domain (redistributed routes). Unless the ABRs are geographically far apart, this should not matter. Totally stubby areas cannot distinguish one ABR from another, in terms of the best route to destinations outside the area. Unless the ABRs are geographically far apart, this should not matter.

Area and Domain Summarization

There are many ways to summarize routes in OSPF. The effectiveness of route summarization mechanisms depends on the addressing scheme. Summarization should be supported into and out of areas at the ABR or ASBR. To minimize route information inserted into the area, consider the following guidelines when planning your OSPF internetwork:

■ Configure the network addressing scheme so that the range of subnets assigned within an area is contiguous.

■ Create an address space that will split areas easily as the network grows. If possible, assign subnets according to simple octet boundaries.

■ Plan ahead for the addition of new routers to the OSPF environment. Ensure that new routers are inserted appropriately as area, backbone, or border routers.

Figure 3-14 shows some of the ways to summarize routes and otherwise reduce LSA database size and flooding in OSPF.

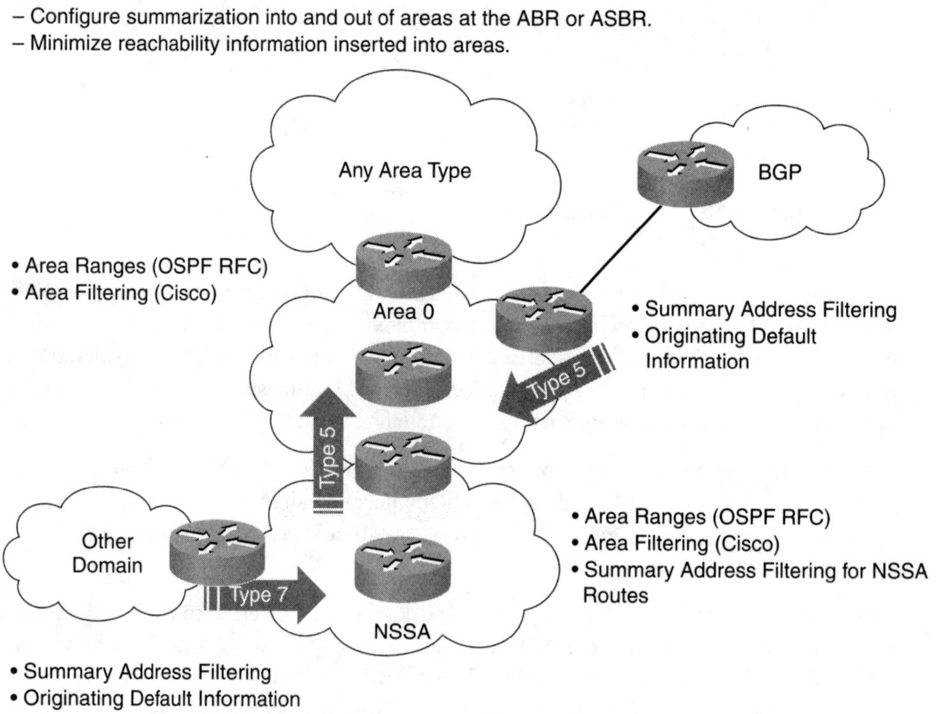

Figure 3-14   *Area and Domain Summarization*

■ **Area ranges per the OSPF RFCs:** The ability to inject only a subset of routing information back into area 0. This takes place only an ABR. It consolidates and summarizes routes at an area boundary.

- **Area filtering:** Filters prefixes advertised in type 3 LSAs between areas of an ABR.

- **Summary address filtering** Used on an ASBR to filtering on routes injected into OSPF by redistribution from other protocols.

- Originating default.

- Filtering for NSSA routes.

> **Note** OSPF Version 2 (OSPFv2) for IP Version 4 (IPv4) and OSPF Version 3 (OSPFv3) for IP Version 6 (IPv6) are implemented as two entirely independent protocols. This independence means that theoretically the area structure and ABRs could be entirely different for each of these protocols. However, from a design standpoint, it is often best to align the area structure and ABRs for both protocols to reduce operational complexity and ease troubleshooting. This approach implies that the IPv6 and IPv4 address blocks that are assigned to the areas should also be aligned to support summarization for both protocols.

OSPF Hub-and-Spoke Design

In an OSPF hub-and-spoke design, any change at one spoke site is passed up the link to the area hub and is then replicated to each of the other spoke sites. These actions can place a great burden on the hub router. Change flooding is the chief problem encountered in these designs.

Stub areas minimize the amount of information within the area. Totally stubby areas are better than stub areas in this regard. If a spoke site must redistribute routes into OSPF, make it a NSSA. Keep in mind that totally stubby NSSAs are also possible.

> **Note** A Cisco proprietary extension to stub areas is what is called totally stubby areas. Cisco indicates this by adding a **no-summary** keyword to the stub area configuration. A totally stubby area is one that blocks external routes and summary routes (inter-area routes) from going into the area. This way, intra-area routes and the default of 0.0.0.0 are the only routes injected into that area.

Limiting the number of spokes per area reduces the flooding at the hub. However, smaller areas allow for less summarization into the backbone. Each spoke requires either a separate interface or a subinterface on the hub router.

Number of Areas in an OSPF Hub-and-Spoke Design

For a hub-and-spoke topology, the number of areas and the number of sites per area need to be determined, as shown in Figure 3-15.

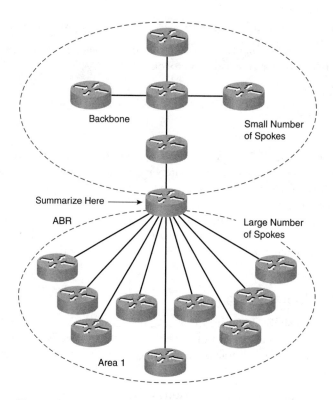

Figure 3-15   *Number of Areas in a Hub-and-Spoke Design*

As the number of remote sites goes up, you have to start breaking the network into multiple areas. As already noted, the number of routers per area depends on a couple of factors. If the number of remote sites is low, you can place the hub and its spokes within an area. If there are multiple remote sites, you can make the hub an ABR and split off the spokes in one or more areas.

In general, the hub should be an ABR, to allow each area to be summarized into the other areas.

The backbone area is extremely important in OSPF. The best approach is to design OSPF to have a small and highly stable area 0. For example, some large Frame Relay or ATM designs have had an area 0 consisting of just the ABRs, all within a couple of racks.

Issues with Hub-and-Spoke Design

Low-speed links and large numbers of spoke sites are the worst issues for hub-and-spoke design, as illustrated in Figure 3-16.

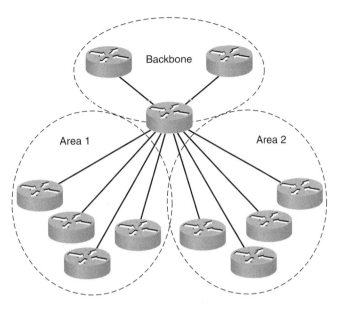

Figure 3-16 *Issues with Hub-and-Spoke Design*

Low-speed links and large numbers of spokes may require multiple flooding domains or areas, which you must effectively support. You should balance the number of flooding domains on the hub against the number of spokes in each flooding domain. The link speeds and the amount of information being passed through the network determine the right balance.

Design for these situations must balance

- The number of areas

- The router impact of maintaining an LSA database and doing Dijkstra calculations per area

- The number of remote routers in each area

In situations with low bandwidth, the lack of bandwidth to flood LSAs when changes are occurring or OSPF is initializing becomes a driving factor. The number of routers per area must be strictly limited so that the bandwidth is adequate for LSA flooding under stress conditions (for example, simultaneous router startup or linkup conditions).

The extreme case of low-bandwidth links might be 9600-bps links. Areas for a network would consist of, at most, a couple of sites. In this case, another approach to routing might be appropriate. For example, use static routes from the hub out to the spokes, with default routes back to the hub. Flooding reduction, as discussed in the "OSPF Flooding Reduction" section later in this chapter, might help but would not improve bandwidth usage in a worst-case situation. The recommendation for this type of setting is lab testing under worst-case conditions to define the bandwidth requirements.

OSPF Hub-and-Spoke Network Types

When using OSPF for hub-and-spoke networks, over nonbroadcast multiaccess access (that is, Frame Relay or ATM), you have several choices for the type of network you use. Figure 3-17 shows the details.

Network Type	Advantages	Disadvantages
Single Interface at the Hub Treated as an OSPF Broadcast or NBMA Network	• Single IP Subnet • Fewer Host Routes in Routing Table	• Manual Configuration of Each Spoke With the Correct OSPF Priority for DR/BDR • No Reachability Between Spokes or Labor-Intensive Layer 2 Configuration
Single Interface at the Hub Treated as an OSPF Point-to-Multipoint Network `ip ospf network-type point-to-multipoint`	• Single IP Subnet • No Configuration Per Spoke • Most Natural Solution	• Additional Host Routes Inserted in the Routing Table • Longer Hello and Dead Timer Intervals
Individual Point-to-Point Interface at the Hub for Each Spoke `ip ospf network-type point-to-point`	• Can Take Advantage of End-to-End Signaling for Down State • Shorter Hello and Dead Timer Intervals	• Lost IP Address Space • More Routes in the Routing Table • Overhead of Subinterfaces

Recommendation: Point-to-point or point-to-multipoint with hub-and-spoke.

Figure 3-17 *OSPF Hub-and-Spoke Network Types*

You must use the right combination of network types for OSPF hub and spoke to work well. Generally, it is wisest to use either the point-to-multipoint OSPF network type at the hub site or configure the hub site with point-to-point subinterfaces.

Configuring point-to-multipoint is simple. The disadvantage of a point-to-multipoint design is that additional host routes are added to the routing table, and the default OPSF hello and dead-timer interval is longer. However, point-to-multipoint implementations simplify configuration as compared to broadcast or nonbroadcast multiaccess (NBMA) implementations and conserve IP address space as compared to point-to-point implementations.

Configuring point-to-point subinterfaces initially takes more work, perhaps on the order of a few hours. Each subinterface adds a route to the routing table, making this option about equal to point-to-multipoint in terms of routing table impact. More address space gets used up, even with /30 or /31 subnetting for the point-to-point links. On the other hand, after configuration, point-to-point subinterfaces may provide the most stability, with everything including management working well in this environment.

The broadcast or NBMA network types are best avoided. Although they can be made to work with some configuration effort, they lead to less stable networks or networks where certain failure modes have odd consequences.

OSPF Area Border Connection Behavior

OSPF has strict rules for routing. They sometimes cause nonintuitive traffic patterns.

In Figure 3-18, dual-homed connections in hub-and-spoke networks illustrate a design challenge in OSPF, where connections are parallel to an area border. Traffic crossing the backbone must get into an area by the shortest path and then stay in that area.

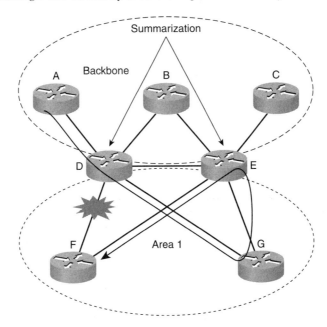

Figure 3-18 *OSPF Area Border Connection Behavior*

In this example, the link from D to E is in area 0. If the D-to-F link fails, traffic from D to F goes from D to G to E to F. Because D is an ABR for area 1, the traffic to F is all internal to area 1 and must remain in area 1. OSPF does not support traffic going from D to E and then to F because the D-to-E link is in area 0, not in area 1. A similar scenario applies for traffic from A to F: It must get into area 1 by the shortest path through D and then stay in area 1.

In OSPF, traffic from area 1 to area 1 must stay in area 1 unless area 1 is partitioned, in which case the backbone area 0 can be used. Traffic from area 1 to area 2 must go from area 1 to area 0, and then into area 2. It cannot go into and out of any of the areas in other sequences.

OSPF area border connections must be considered in a thorough OSPF design. One solution to the odd transit situation just discussed is to connect ABRs with physical or virtual links for each area that both ABRs belong to. You can connect the ABRs within each area by either of two means:

■   Adding a real link between the ABRs inside area 1

■   Adding a virtual link between the ABRs inside area 0

In general, the recommendation is to avoid virtual links when you have a good alternative. OSPF virtual links depend on area robustness and therefore are less reliable than a physical link. Virtual links add complexity and fragility; if an area has a problem, the virtual link through the area has a problem. Also, if you rely too much on virtual links, you can end up with a maze of virtual links and possibly miss some virtual connections.

If the ABRs are Layer 3 switches or have some form of Ethernet connections, VLANs can be used to provide connections within each area common to both ABRs. With multiple logical links, whether physical, subinterfaces, or VLANs between a pair of ABRs, the following options are recommended:

- Consider making sure that a link exists between the ABRs within each area on those ABRs.

- Implement one physical or logical link per area.

Fast Convergence in OSPF

Network convergence is the time that is needed for the network to respond to events. It is the time that it takes for traffic to be rerouted onto an alternative path when node or link fails or onto a more optimal path when a new link or node appears. Traffic is not rerouted until the data plane data structures such as the Forwarding Information Base (FIB) and adjacency tables of all devices have been adjusted to reflect the new state of the network. For that to occur, all network devices must go through the following procedure:

1. **Detect the event:** Loss or addition of a link or neighbor needs to be detected. This can be done through a combination of Layer 1, Layer 2, and Layer 3 detection mechanisms, such as carrier detection, routing protocol hello timers, and Bidirectional Forwarding Detection (BFD).

2. **Propagate the event:** Routing protocol update mechanisms are used to forward the information about the topology change from neighbor to neighbor.

3. **Process the event:** The information needs to be entered into the appropriate routing protocol data structures and the routing algorithm needs to be invoked to calculate updated best paths for the new topology.

4. **Update forwarding data structures:** The results of the routing algorithm calculations need to be entered into the data plane packet forwarding data structures.

At this point, the network has converged. The rest of this section focuses on the second and third steps in this procedure, because these are most specific to OSPF and tuning the associated parameters can greatly improve OSPF convergence times. The first step is dependent on the type of failure and the combination of Layer 1, Layer 2, and Layer 3 protocols that are deployed. The fourth step is not routing protocol specific, but depends on the hardware platform and the mechanisms involved in programming the data plane data structures.

Tuning OSPF Parameters

By default, OSPF LSA propagation is controlled by three parameters:

■ **OSPF_LSA_DELAY_INTERVAL:** Controls the length of time that the router should wait before generating a type 1 router LSA or type 2 network LSA. By default, this parameter is set at 500 ms.

■ **MinLSInterval:** Defines the minimum time between distinct originations of any particular LSA. The value of MinLSInterval is set to 5 seconds. This value is defined in appendix B of RFC 2328.

■ **MinLSArrival:** The minimum time that must elapse between reception of new LSA instances during flooding for any particular LSA. LSA instances received at higher frequencies are discarded. The value of MinLSArrival is set to 1 second. This value is defined in Appendix B of RFC 2328.

OSPF Exponential Backoff

The default OSPF LSA propagation timers are quite conservative. Lowering the values of the timers that control OSPF LSA generation can significantly improve OSPF convergence times. However, if the value for the timeout between the generation of successive iterations of an LSA is a fixed value, lowering the values could also lead to excessive LSA flooding.

This is why Cisco has implemented an exponential backoff algorithm for LSA generation. The initial backoff timers are low, but if successive events are generated for the same LSA, the backoff timers increase. Three configurable timers control the LSA pacing:

■ **LSA-Start:** The initial delay to generate an LSA. This timer can be set at a very low value, such as 1 ms or even 0 ms. Setting this timer to a low value helps improve convergence because initial LSAs for new events are sent as quickly as possible.

■ **LSA-Hold:** The minimum time to elapse before flooding an updated instance of an LSA. This value is used as an incremental value. Initially, the hold time between successive LSAs is set to be equal to this configured value. Each time a new version of an LSA is generated the hold time between LSAs is doubled, until the LSA-Max-Wait value is reached, at which point that value is used until the network stabilizes.

■ **LSA-Max-Wait:** The maximum time that can elapse before flooding an updated instance of an LSA. Once the exponential backoff algorithm reaches this value, it stops increasing the hold time and uses the LSA-Max-Wait timer as a fixed interval between newly generated LSAs.

What the optimal values for these values depends on the network. Tuning the timers too aggressively could result in excessive CPU load during network reconvergence, especially when the network is unstable for a period. Lower the values gradually from their defaults and observe router behavior to determine what the optimal values are for your network.

When you adjust the OSPF LSA throttling timers, it might be necessary to adjust the MinLSArrival timer. Any LSAs that are received at a higher frequency than the value of this timer are discarded. To prevent routers from dropping valid LSAs, make sure that the MinLSArrival is configured to be lower or equal to the LSA-Hold timer.

Note To reduce the impact of link flapping, IP event dampening can be implemented. For more information about this feature, see https://www.cisco.com/en/US/docs/ios/iproute_pi/configuration/guide/iri_ip_event_damp_ps10591_TSD_Products_Configuration_Guide_Chapter.html.

Figure 3-19 illustrates the OSPF exponential backoff algorithm. It is assumed that, every second, an event happens that causes a new version of an LSA to be generated. With the default timers, the initial LSA is generated after 500 ms. After that, a five-second wait occurs between successive LSAs.

Result of tuning OSPF LSA throttle timers:

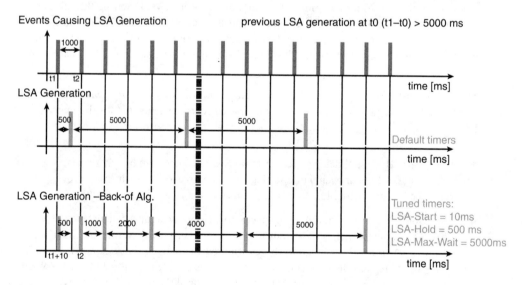

Figure 3-19 *Tuning OSPF LSA Throttle Timers*

With the OSPF LSA throttle timers set at 10 ms for LSA-Start, 500 ms for LSA-Hold, and 5000 ms for LSA-Max-Wait, the initial LSA is generated after 10 ms. The next LSA is generated after the LSA-Hold time of 500 ms. The next LSA is generated after 2 x 500 = 1000 ms. The next LSA is generated after 4 x 500 = 2000 ms. The next LSA is generated after 8 x 500 = 4000 ms. The next one would be generated after 16 x 500 = 8000 ms, but because the LSA-Max-Wait is set at 5000 ms, the LSA is generated after 5000 ms. From this point onward, a 5000 ms wait is applied to successive LSAs, until the network stabilizes and the timers are reset.

OSPF LSA Pacing

The LSA throttle timers control LSA generation by the originating routers. Another set of timers, the LSA pacing timers, controls the time it takes to propagate LSAs from router to router. By default, a router waits 33 ms between transmission of successive LSAs in the LSA flooding queue. There is a separate queue for LSA retransmissions, and LSAs in this queue are paced at 66 ms by default. If you adjust the LSA throttle timers to be low, you may also want to adjust these timers, because the total time for an LSA to propagate through the network is the initial LSA generation time plus the sum of the propagation delays between all routers in the path.

The intent of this timer is to ensure that you do not overwhelm neighboring routers with LSAs that cannot be processed quickly enough. However, with the increase of processing power on routers over the last decades this is not a major concern any more.

OSPF Event Processing

The LSA throttling and pacing timers control OSPF LSA propagation. The next element in OSPF convergence is event processing. The timing of successive OSPF SPF calculations is throttled in the same manner as LSA generation, using an exponential backoff algorithm.

The timers involved in OSPF SPF throttling are very similar to the LSA throttling timers. There are three tunable timers:

- **SPF-Start:** The initial delay to schedule an SFP calculation after a change.

- **SPF-Hold:** The minimum holdtime between two consecutive SPF calculations. Similar to the LSA-Hold timer, this timer is used as an incremental value in an exponential backoff algorithm.

- **SPF-Max-Wait:** The maximum wait time between two consecutive SPF calculations.

Considerations in adjusting these timers are similar to the LSA throttling timers. An additional factor to consider is the time it takes for an SPF calculation to complete on the router platform used. You cannot schedule a new SPF run before the previous calculation has completed. Therefore, ensure that the SPF-Hold timer is higher than the time it takes to run a complete SPF. When estimating SPF run times, you should account for future network growth.

Bidirectional Forwarding Detection

Bidirectional Forwarding Detection (BFD) is another feature that helps speed up routing convergence. One of the significant factors in routing convergence is the detection of link or node failure. In the case of link failures, there is usually an electrical signal or keepalive to detect the loss of the link. BFD is a technology that uses efficient fast Layer 2 link hellos to detect failed or one-way links, which is generally what fast routing hellos detect.

BFD requires routing-protocol support. BFD is available for OSPF, EIGRP, IS-IS, and BGP. BFD quickly notifies the routing protocol of link-down conditions. This can provide failure detection and response times down to around 50 ms, which is the typical SONET failure response time.

The CPU impact of BFD is less than that of fast hellos. This is because some of the processing is shifted to the data plane rather than the control plane. On nondistributed platforms, Cisco testing has shown a minor, 2 percent CPU increase above baseline when supporting 100 concurrent BFD sessions.

BFD provides a method for network administrators to configure subsecond Layer 2 failure detection between adjacent network nodes. Furthermore, administrators can configure their routing protocols to respond to BFD notifications and begin Layer 3 route convergence almost immediately.

Note BFD is currently supported only on Cisco 6500/7600 series routers, Cisco 12000 series routers, Cisco 10720 routers, Cisco Nexus 7000, and Cisco Carrier Routing System (CRS-1) routers.

Designing Scalable BGP Designs

Border Gateway Protocol (BGP) is commonly used in sites with multiple connections to the Internet. BGP is also frequently present in medium-to large networks to provide a controlled interconnection between multiple routing domains running OSPF or EIGRP. Large-scale internal BGP networks are also becoming more prevalent as large enterprises implement internal Multiprotocol Label Switching (MPLS) VPNs for security segmentation, business unit or brand isolation, and similar purposes.

This section discusses designing advanced routing solutions using BGP. It describes how to identify scaling issues in internal BGP designs and how to use techniques to alleviate these issues.

Scaling BGP Designs

This section discusses aspects of scaling in basic internal BGP (IBGP) design. This is illustrated in Figure 3-20.

BGP can provide a controlled interconnection between multiple routing domains running OSPF or EIGRP and support internal MPLS VPNs. IBGP requires a full mesh of BGP peers.

The full mesh of IBGP routers is needed because IBGP routers do not re-advertise routes learned via IBGP to other IBGP peers. This behavior is part of BGP protocol behavior that is used to prevent information from circulating between IBGP speaking routers in a routing information loop or cycle. External BGP (EBGP) relies on the autonomous system path to prevent loops. However, there is no way to tell whether a route advertised through several IBGP speakers is a loop. Because IBGP peers are in the same autonomous system, they do not add anything to the autonomous system path, and they do not re-advertise routes learned via IBGP.

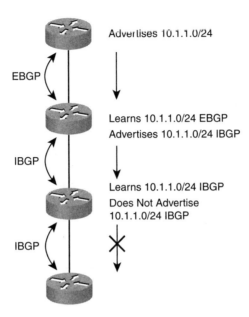

Figure 3-20   *IBGP Full-Mesh Requirement*

Note   BGP is commonly used in sites with multiple connections to the Internet. BGP is also common with MPLS VPNs and MPLS mixed with IP Security (IPsec) VPNs.

Full-Mesh IBGP Scalability

Because IBGP requires a full mesh of peers, scaling the full mesh is a concern. In general, for N peers in an IBGP full mesh, each would have $N - 1$ peers. There are $N(N - 1)/2$ peering relationships. This means that each peer would need the CPU, memory, and bandwidth to handle updates and peer status for all the other routers. This is not a hierarchical design, and it would not be cost-effective to scale for large networks.

There are two IBGP alternatives to scale IBGP:

■   Route reflectors

■   Confederations

The following sections explore the basic design and behavior of route reflectors and confederations and demonstrate how they can be used in a routing design.

Scaling IBGP with Route Reflectors

A BGP route reflector is an IBGP speaker that reflects or repeats routes learned from IBGP peers to some of its other IBGP peers. This is shown in Figure 3-21.

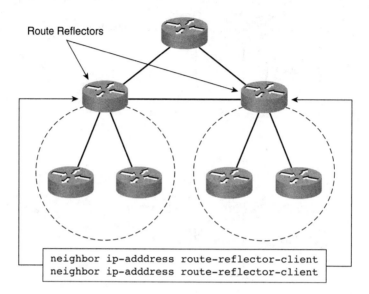

Route Reflectors

```
neighbor ip-adddress route-reflector-client
neighbor ip-adddress route-reflector-client
```

Figure 3-21 *BGP Route Reflectors*

To prevent loops, a route reflector adds an originator ID and a cluster list to routes that it reflects between IBGP speakers. These attributes act similarly to the autonomous system path attribute to prevent routing information loops.

All configuration of the route reflector is done on the route reflector itself. The configuration identifies which IBGP peers are route reflector clients.

Implementing route reflectors is fairly simple and can be done incrementally. Each client router needs to be configured as a client on the route reflector or on multiple route reflectors. Unnecessary peers can then be removed from the configuration on the client router. Often, route reflector clients peer only with the route reflectors. In a service provider network, route reflector clients might also be provider edge (PE) devices, which also peer with customers using EBGP.

To avoid a single point of failure, redundant route reflectors are typically used.

BGP Route Reflector Definitions

A route reflector client (shown in Figure 3-22) is an IBGP router that receives and sends routes to most other IBGP speakers via the route reflector. The route reflector client needs no special configuration, other than removing peering with some or all neighbors other than the route reflector.

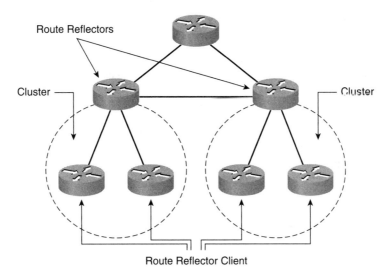

Figure 3-22 *BGP Route Reflector Definitions*

A cluster is a route reflector together with its clients. The route reflector relieves the route reflector client routers of needing to be interconnected via an IBGP full mesh.

Route reflector clusters may overlap.

A nonclient router (shown in Figure 3-23) is any route reflector IBGP peer that is not a route reflector client of that route reflector.

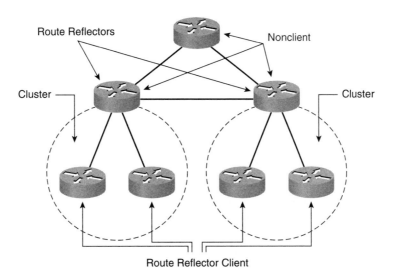

Figure 3-23 *Additional BGP Route Reflector Definitions*

Route reflectors are typically nonclients with regard to the other route reflectors in the network.

Route reflectors must still be fully IBGP meshed with nonclients. Therefore, route reflectors reduce meshing within clusters, but all mesh links outside the cluster must be maintained on the route reflector. The route reflector clients get information from IBGP speakers outside the cluster via the route reflector.

If a route reflector receives a route from a nonclient, it reflects it to route reflector clients but not to other nonclients. The route reflector receives the routes if it has a direct peering relationship to the original nonclient. The route reflector also sends the route to EBGP peers, which is standard behavior. IBGP routes get repeated to all EBGP peers.

Route Reflector Basics

This section briefly looks at how route advertisement works with route reflectors. This is illustrated in Figure 3-24.

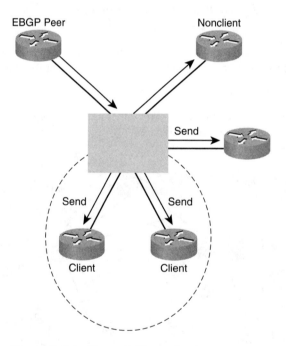

Figure 3-24 *Route Reflector Basics*

If a route reflector receives a route from an EBGP peer, it passes that route to all route reflector clients and nonclients, just as in normal IBGP peering behavior.

If the route reflector receives a route from a route reflector client, it reflects the route to the other clients within the cluster and nonclients. It also reflects the route to EBGP peers. Here's another way to think of this: The route reflector takes over the communication for the route reflector clients, passing along all the messages they would normally transmit directly via a peering session.

> **Note**   Route reflectors ignore the split-horizon design of IBGP and re-advertise routes they have received to any neighbor they have configured as a route reflector client.

Scaling IBGP with Confederations

BGP confederations are another way of scaling IBGP. Their behavior is defined in RFC 5065. Confederations insert information using the autonomous system path into BGP routes to prevent loops within an autonomous system. The basic idea with confederations is to divide a normal BGP autonomous system into multiple sub-autonomous systems. The outer or containing autonomous system is called the confederation autonomous system. This is all that is visible to the outside world.

Each of the inner autonomous systems is a smaller sub-autonomous system that uses a different autonomous system number, typically chosen from the private autonomous system number range of 64,512 through 65,534.

BGP Confederation Definitions

This section defines terms used with confederations (see Figure 3-25).

Peers within the same sub-autonomous system are confederation internal peers.

IBGP peers that are in a different sub-autonomous system are confederation external peers.

As IBGP information is passed around within a confederation autonomous system, the sub-autonomous system numbers are put into a confederation sequence, which works like an autonomous system path.

Confederation Basics

Route advertisement with confederations works similarly to that of route reflectors in the following ways:

- A route learned from an EBGP peer is advertised to all confederation external and internal peers.

- A route learned from a confederation internal peer is advertised to all confederation external peers, and to EBGP peers.

- A route learned from a confederation external peer is advertised to all confederation internal peers, and to EBGP peers.

Another way to understand this is that IBGP between sub-autonomous systems acts like EBGP. Private autonomous system numbers are used internally within the confederation autonomous system and removed from updates sent outside the confederation.

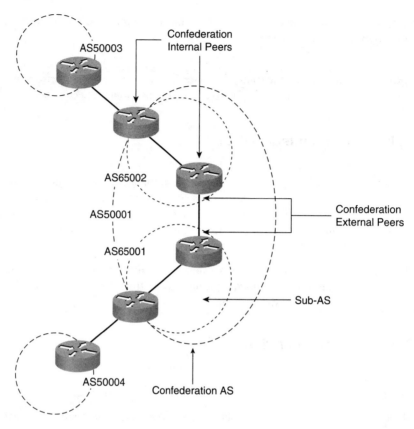

Figure 3-25   *Confederation Definitions*

> **Note**   Private autonomous system numbers are typically used within the confederation.

Confederations Reduce Meshing

Like route reflectors, confederations are used to reduce the amount of IBGP meshing needed. Without route reflectors or confederation, IBGP requires a full mesh of peering relationships, as illustrated in Figure 3-26.

> **Note**   The IBGP does not require peers to be directly connected.

However, confederations can reduce meshing requirements, as shown in Figure 3-27.

Routers in different sub-autonomous systems do not peer with each other, except at sub-autonomous system borders. It is generally recommended to use two or three links between sub-autonomous system borders. More links just consume CPU and memory in the border routers.

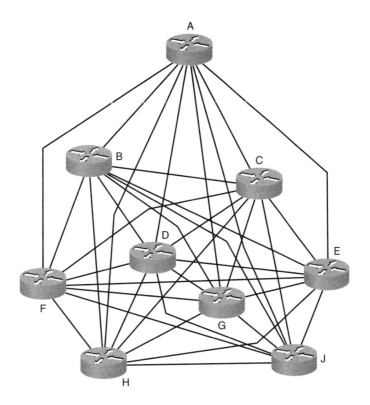

Figure 3-26   *IBGP Full-Mesh Peering*

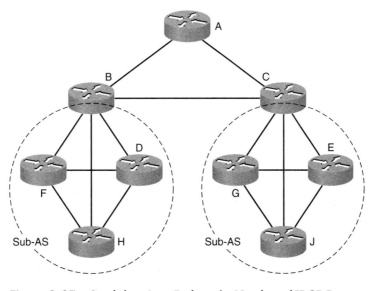

Figure 3-27   *Confederations Reduce the Number of IBGP Peers*

When you use sub-autonomous systems for confederations, the meshing is restricted to within the sub-autonomous systems, with some additional peering between sub-autonomous system border routers.

Route reflectors can be used within confederations to further reduce network complexity. Historically, service providers have not done this, but they are now starting to. Using route reflectors alleviates the need to fully mesh within a sub-autonomous system.

Deploying Confederations

In Figure 3-28, router B could be configured to set the BGP next hop to itself for advertisement to routers C and D. This is not normally done by IBGP routers. This would impose the constraint that routers C and D would need to have routes to the new next hop, router B.

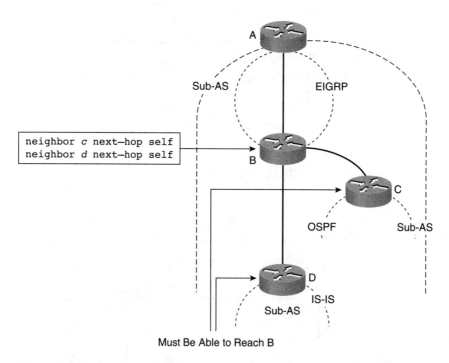

Figure 3-28 *Deploying Confederations*

Using this configuration breaks the confederation up from a next-hop perspective from both the IGP and BGP point of view. This scenario allows for more flexibility and scaling in very large networks. This deployment might make sense for large organizations that support separate entities such as government organizations that have distinct branches or divisions.

Using confederation sub-autonomous systems has other advantages. The IBGP policies can differ internally within and between the sub-autonomous systems. In particular, multi-exit discriminator (MED) acceptance or stripping, local preference settings, route dampening, and so on can vary between sub-autonomous systems. In addition, policy controls can be used on peerings between sub-autonomous systems.

This highlights some advantages of confederations. Confederations can ease the transition in an acquisition or merger. The new network can be treated as another sub-autonomous system and keep its IGP. It can also keep its EBGP policies with its customers.

A disadvantage of confederations is that there is no graceful way to migrate from full mesh to using confederations. The migration may well require downtime.

Table 3-1 compares how confederations and route reflectors provide various IBGP scaling features.

Table 3-1   *Comparing Confederations to Route Reflectors*

	Confederation	Route Reflector
Loop prevention	Autonomous system confederation set	Originator or set cluster ID
Break up a single autonomous system	Sub-autonomous systems	Clusters
Redundancy	Multiple connections between sub-autonomous systems	Client connects to several reflectors
External connections	Anywhere in the network	Anywhere in the network
Multilevel hierarchy	Reflectors within sub-autonomous systems	Hierarchical clusters
Policy control	Along outside borders and between sub-autonomous systems	Along outside borders
Scalability	Medium; still requires full IBGP within each sub-autonomous system	Very high
Migration	Very difficult (impossible in some situations)	Moderately easy (impossible in some situations)

In general, route reflectors are simpler to migrate to and relatively simple to use, whereas confederations are more flexible as to IGP and policy.

Summary

This chapter covered the elements of advanced routing design, and touched on the merits of a well-planned IP addressing scheme. The IP addressing scheme is the foundation for greater efficiency in operating and maintaining a network. Without proper planning in advance, networks might not be able to benefit from route summarization features inherent to many routing protocols.

Cisco favors a transition strategy from IPv4 to IPv6 that begins from the edges of the network and moves in toward the core. This strategy allows you to control the deployment cost and focus on the needs of the applications, rather than complete a full network upgrade to a native IPv6 network at this stage. Cisco IPv6 router products offer the features for a such an integration strategy. The various deployment strategies permit the first stages of the transition to IPv6 to happen now, whether as a trial of IPv6 capabilities or as the early controlled stages of major IPv6 network implementations.IPv6 can be deployed as dual stack, hybrid, and service block.

The general advanced routing design discussion can be encapsulated in the following key points:

- Route summarization and default routing are important in scaling routing designs.

- Route filtering can be used to manage traffic flows in the network, avoiding inappropriate transit traffic and as a defense against inappropriate routing updates.

- Redistribution can be useful for manipulating and managing routing updates but needs to be designed properly to prevent routing loops or other problems.

EIGRP converges quickly as long as it has a feasible successor. With no feasible successor, EIGRP sends queries out to its neighbors. To limit the scope of these queries, use route summarization and filtering. By limiting EIGRP query scope, you can speed up EIGRP convergence and increase stability. In addition, large numbers of neighbors should be avoided for any one router. Multiple autonomous systems may be used with EIGRP providing that you understand that they do not directly limit EIGRP query scope. You would use them to support migration strategies, different administrative groups, or very large network design.

OSPF scaling depends on summarization and controlling how much LSA flooding is needed. Simple, stub, summarized designs scale most effectively. Several techniques speed up convergence for OSPF, including fast hellos, and BFD.

Finally, IBGP requires a full mesh of all IBGP routers, but full-mesh peering does not scale gracefully. Route reflectors pass along routing information to and from their clients. The route reflector clients are relieved of the burden of most IBGP peering. Confederations allow an autonomous system to be divided into sub-autonomous systems, where the sub-autonomous system border routers peer with each other and then pass along routes on behalf of the other sub-autonomous system routers. Confederation sequences are used to prevent information loops. Sub-autonomous systems can have different BGP polices from each other.

The key points to remember include the following:

- IP address design allows for route summarization that supports network scaling, stability, and fast convergence.

- Route summarization, route filtering, and appropriate redistribution help minimize routing information in the network.

- EIGRP converges quickly as long as it has a feasible successor. Multiple autonomous systems with EIGRP may be used, with care, to support special situations, including migration strategies and very large network design.

- Simple, stub, summarized OSPF designs scale most effectively. Several techniques speed up convergence for OSPF, including fast hellos and BFD.

- IBGP designs can be scaled using route reflectors to pass routing information to and from their clients and confederations to allow an autonomous system to be divided into sub-autonomous systems.

References

Cisco Systems, Inc. *Deploying IPv6 in Campus Networks* at www.cisco.com/en/US/docs/solutions/Enterprise/Campus/CampIPv6.html

Shannon McFarland, Muninder Sambi, Nikhil Sharma, and Sanjay Hooda. *IPv6 for Enterprise Networks* (Cisco Press, 2011)

Cisco Systems, Inc. *Designing Large-Scale IP Internetworks* at www.cisco.com/en/US/docs/internetworking/design/guide/nd2003.html

Cisco IOS IP Routing: BGP Command Reference at www.cisco.com/en/US/docs/ios/iproute_bgp/command/reference/irg_book.html

Cisco IOS IP Routing: EIGRP Command Reference at www.cisco.com/en/US/docs/ios/iproute_eigrp/command/reference/ire_book.html

Cisco IOS IP Routing: ISIS Command Reference at www.cisco.com/en/US/docs/ios/iproute_isis/command/reference/irs_book.html

Cisco IOS IP Routing: ODR Command Reference at www.cisco.com/en/US/docs/ios/iproute_odr/command/reference/ird_book.html

Cisco IOS IP Routing: OSPF Command Reference at www.cisco.com/en/US/docs/ios/iproute_ospf/command/reference/iro_book.html

Cisco IOS IP Routing: Protocol-Independent Command Reference at www.cisco.com/en/US/docs/ios/iproute_pi/command/reference/iri_book.html

Cisco IOS IP Routing: RIP Command Reference at www.cisco.com/en/US/docs/ios/iproute_rip/command/reference/irr_book.html

The Internet Engineering Task Force. RFC 1793: *Extending OSPF to Support Demand Circuits* at www.ietf.org/rfc/rfc1793.txt

The Internet Engineering Task Force. RFC 2328: *OSPF Version 2* at www.ietf.org/rfc/rfc2328.txt

The Internet Engineering Task Force. RFC 4456: *BGP Route Reflection—An Alternative to Full Mesh IBGP* at www.ietf.org/rfc/rfc4456.txt

The Internet Engineering Task Force. RFC 5065: *Autonomous System Confederations for BGP* at www.ietf.org/rfc/rfc5065.txt

The Internet Engineering Task Force. RFC 4136: *OSPF Refresh and Flooding Reduction in Stable Topologies* at www.ietf.org/rfc/rfc4136.txt

Review Questions

Answer the following questions, and then refer to Appendix A, "Answers to Review Questions," for the answers.

1. Which three address blocks are summarizable?

   a. 172.16.20.0/24 to 172.16.27.0/24

   b. 172.16.20.0/24 to 172.16.23.0/24

   c. 10.16.0.0/16 to 10.31.0.0/16

   d. 10.16.0.0/16 to 10.47.0.0/16

   e. 2001:0DB8:C3B7:10A0::/64 to 2001:0DB8:C3B7:10DF::/64

   f. 2001:0DB8:1234:FB40::/64 to 2001:0DB8:1234:FB5F::/64

   g. 10.96.0.0/16 to 10.159.0.0/16

2. Which two can bit-splitting techniques be used for? (Choose two.)

   a. OSPF area design

   b. Summarizable address blocks with convenient role-based subnets

   c. Access list convergence

   d. Detecting summarizable address blocks

   e. Manual route summarization

3. Which is the recommended design approach for OSPF?

   a. Configure a static default route everywhere for predictability.

   b. Configure static default routes using recursive routing for consistency.

   c. Originate the default at the edge and redistribute it into dynamic routing.

   d. Make the OSPF backbone area 0 stubby.

   e. Do not use additional parameters with the originate default command.

4. Which two statements best describe redistribution?

    a. Redistribution works poorly with an arbitrary mix of routing protocols anywhere.

    b. Redistribution seldom requires route filters.

    c. Redistribution is not useful after a merger.

    d. Redistribution works well with a limited number of redistribution points.

    e. Redistribution prevents summarization.

5. Select the best statement concerning EIGRP and OSPF routing design.

    a. Routing design needs to be done most carefully for small networks.

    b. OSPF should not be used for small networks.

    c. Routing design needs to be done most carefully for large networks.

    d. Route summarization must be used in all network designs.

    e. OSPF works best with a full mesh.

6. Which three factors are the biggest influences on OSPF scalability?

    a. Flooding paths and redundancy

    b. Amount of routing information in the OSPF area or routing domain

    c. Number of routers capable of Cisco Express Forwarding

    d. Number of adjacent neighbors

    e. Other routing protocols in use

7. Which statement best describes basic IBGP?

    a. IBGP is a link-state protocol.

    b. IBGP requires a full mesh of peers because it has no other way to prevent looping of routing information.

    c. IBGP inherently handles all full-mesh scalability issues.

    d. IBGP uses split horizoning to prevent looping of routing information.

    e. IBGP uses the autonomous system path to prevent looping of routing information.

8. A route reflector reflects routes from a route reflector client to which three types of IBGP routers?

    a. Nonclient routers

    b. Sub-autonomous system members

    c. Other route reflector client routers

    d. EBGP peers

    e. IBGP peers configured for EIGRP or OSPF routing

Chapter 4

Advanced WAN Services Design Considerations

Upon completing this chapter, you will be able to

- Choose an appropriate advanced WAN technology based on customer requirements

- Describe the optical technologies used in support of advanced WAN technologies

- Describe Metro Ethernet, VPLS, and MPLS VPN technologies

- Discuss customer requirements and SLAs as part of a WAN design

This chapter reviews the key concepts associated with the design and selection of WAN services. The optical technologies Synchronous Optical Network (SONET), Synchronous Digital Hierarchy (SDH), coarse wavelength-division multiplexing (CWDM), dense wavelength-division multiplexing (DWDM), and Route Processor Redundancy (RPR) are considered along with their companion, Metro Ethernet services.

Advanced WAN Service Layers

Service providers are interested in providing advanced WAN services that can be supported with low impact on their existing fiber infrastructure. Managed services such as storage, content switching, web hosting, instant messaging, and security built on Ethernet allow the service provider to deliver advanced WAN functions to customers that are using Ethernet user-network interfaces (UNI). Figure 4-1 illustrates the relationship between the different WAN services layers and customer applications.

Customers have multiple reasons for requesting advanced WAN services based on Ethernet:

- Familiar equipment is used, and so customers can utilize their existing devices.

- A familiar protocol is implemented.

- Higher bandwidth is possible than with traditional WAN links.

■ Lower bits-per-second costs can be supported.

■ The underlying optical technologies allow the service provider to supply these advanced WAN services on their existing fiber infrastructure.

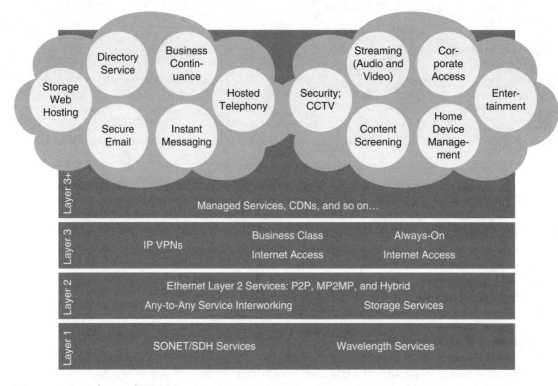

Figure 4-1 *Advanced WAN Services Layers*

Enterprise Optical Interconnections

Several common optical interconnection technologies are used to connect enterprise locations:

■ **SDH:** SONET is a North American high-speed baseband digital transport standard specifying incrementally increasing data stream rates for movement across digital optical links. SONET/SDH is the European standard for digital optical links.

■ **DWDM and CWDM:** DWDM and CWDM are technologies that increase the information-carrying capacity of existing fiber-optic infrastructure by transmitting and receiving data on different light wavelengths on a single strand of fiber.

■ **Dynamic Packet Transport (DPT) and Resilient Packet Ring (RPR):** DPT is an RPR technology designed for service providers to deliver scalable Internet service, reliable IP-aware optical transport, and simplified network operations, principally for metropolitan-area applications. DPT is based on Spatial Reuse Protocol (SRP), a Cisco-developed MAC layer protocol for ring-based packet internetworking.

These technologies can be used directly over leased dark fiber, or by a service provider as the transport mechanism underlying an Ethernet or other offering.

Overview of SONET and SDH

SONET is a time-division multiplexing (TDM) technique for framing voice and data onto a single wavelength on fiber. It typically utilizes fixed time division to allocate bandwidth between entry points on a ring. Many long-haul fiber connections are SONET, in part because SONET repeater technology is used in many service provider networks to boost signals that are carried across long distances. SONET was historically used to prevent dropped calls in a TDM environment. SONET can provide reliable transport with TDM bandwidth guarantees for TDM voice and public-safety voice and radio traffic.

The maximum distance for single-mode installations is determined by the amount of light loss in the fiber path. Good-quality single-mode fiber with very few splices can carry an OC-12c/STM-4 signal 50 miles (80 km) or more without a repeater. Good-quality multi-mode fiber can carry the signal up to 1640 feet (500 m).

SONET typically uses fiber rings. When the ring fails, traffic wraps the other way around the ring. One benefit of SONET is that some network equipment may not notice the 50-ms failure leading to a ring wrap, particularly if SONET access gear keeps Ethernet services on a link in an up state. One drawback to a SONET design is that it requires provisioning double the protected bandwidth. Bandwidth along SONET is committed as circuits between two points on the ring.

Not all SONET topologies are ring based. Sometimes, single or double pairs of fiber are run in linear fashion from a SONET network. Physical constraints such as river crossings can narrow the two sides of the ring into more of a figure 8, which is potentially a single point of failure. Although the high reliability of SONET is often mentioned in sales presentations, it is wise to verify that the entire SONET path being used is a true ring.

SONET can be used with SONET access equipment that may statistically multiplex Ethernet (10 Mbps, Fast Ethernet, or Gigabit Ethernet) onto a SONET circuit. This allows some degree of oversubscription of bandwidth. The actual oversubscription amount is typically not disclosed by the provider.

Optical Carrier (OC) rates are the digital hierarchies of the SONET and SDH standards. Table 4-1 illustrates the commonly deployed SONET and SDH rates.

Note   SONET is an ANSI specification. SDH is the SONET-equivalent specification proposed by the ITU. European carriers use SDH widely; Asian and Pacific Rim carriers use SONET more frequently. The primary differences between the SONET and SDH specifications are the basic transmission rate and some header information.

Table 4-1 *Common SONET and SDH Rates*

Hierarchy	OC-x	Speed	SONET	SDH
—	OC-1	51.85 Mbps	STS-1	STM-0
Level Zero	OC-3	155.52 Mbps	STS-3	STM-1
Level One	OC-12	622.08 Mbps	STS-12	STM-4
Level Two	OC-48	2.488 Gbps	STS-48	STM-16
Level Three	OC-192	9.953 Gbps	STS-192	STM-64
Level Four	OC-768	39.813 Gbps	STS-768	STM-256

In advanced WAN designs, the designer must balance the current and future uses of the transport and other network components, customer requirements, customer perceptions, and the costs of the various network components. Whether SONET (or SDH) is the best solution depends on the situation.

Enterprise View of SONET

From the enterprise customer perspective, SONET is the transport underlying some other form of connection. The connection might be TDM based, such as T1 or T3, or it may be one of the various types of Ethernet services offered by a service provider. SONET may be included as part of the Ethernet service because of its robustness, and the service-provider-installed base in SONET infrastructure. Traditional TDM circuits may also be aggregated and then transported over SONET.

You should ask several key questions of a service provider that offers SONET for your network transport:

- Is the service based on connecting across end-to-end SONET rings, or are there segments that are linear or otherwise not geographically diverse? You need to consider whether single points of failure exist in the transport.

- What path does your service follow? If you are buying services from two providers for redundancy, it might be useful to determine whether the provider's SONET follows different paths. Sometimes, different providers lease fiber from the same supplier or along the same rights of way, such as gas pipelines, train tracks, and high-voltage electrical wire paths.

- Is there oversubscription and sharing, or is bandwidth dedicated for your use? Although you might not get the oversubscription details, you should know what is being allocated for your use. If the service provider is managing the customer edge (CE) device, you should also be interested in the quality of service (QoS) procedures used to manage the rate transition from your site to the SONET network.

WDM Overview

A wavelength-division multiplexing (WDM) system uses a multiplexer (mux) at the transmitter to place multiple optical signals on a fiber and a demultiplexer (demux) at the receiver to split them off of the fiber. The signals use different wavelengths. Before being multiplexed, source signals might be converted from electrical to optical format, or from optical format to electrical format and back to optical format.

CWDM Technical Overview

CWDM is an optical technology for transmitting up to 16 channels, each in a separate wavelength or color, over the same fiber strand. The CWDM solutions help enable enterprises and service providers to increase the bandwidth of an existing Gigabit Ethernet optical infrastructure without adding new fiber strands.

Unlike DWDM, which can transmit up to 160 channels on the same fiber by tightly packing them, CWDM technology relies on wider spacing between channels. This design makes CWDM a relatively inexpensive technology for transmitting multiple gigabit-per-second signals on a single fiber strand as compared with DWDM because it can support less-sophisticated, and therefore cheaper, transceiver designs. In the point-to-point configuration shown in Figure 4-2, two endpoints are directly connected through a fiber link. The ITU has standardized a 20-nm channel-spacing grid for use with CWDM, using the wavelengths between 1310 nm and 1610 nm. Most CWDM systems support eight channels in the 1470- to 1610-nm range. The Cisco CWDM Gigabit Interface Converter (GBIC)/small form-factor pluggable (SFP) solution allows organizations to add or drop as many as eight channels (Gigabit Ethernet or Fibre Channel) into a pair of single-mode (SM) fiber strands. As a result, the need for additional fiber is minimized. You can create redundant point-to-point links by adding or dropping redundant channels into a second pair of SM fiber strands.

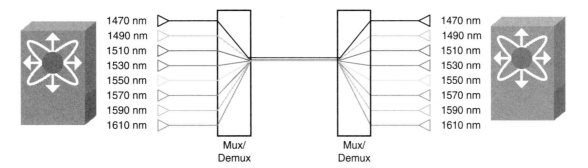

Figure 4-2 *CWDM Technical Overview*

CWDM multiplexing is achieved through special passive (nonpowered) glass devices known as filters. The filters act as prisms, directing lights from many incoming and outgoing fibers (client ports) to a common transmit and receive trunk port. Optical multiplexing in a ring with CWDM networks is supported with optical add/drop multiplexers (OADM). OADMs can drop off one or more CWDM wavelengths at a specific location and replace that signal with one or more different outbound signals.

The Cisco CWDM GBIC/SFP solution has two main components: a set of eight different pluggable transceivers (Cisco CWDM GBICs and Cisco CWDM SFPs), and a set of different Cisco CWDM passive multiplexers/demultiplexers or OADMs. Both the transceivers and the passive multiplexers are compliant with the CWDM grid defined in the ITU-T G.694.2 standards.

CWDM can be used by enterprises on leased dark fiber to increase capacity (for example, from 1 Gbps to 8 Gbps or 16 Gbps) over metro-area distances. One problem with CWDM is that the wavelengths are not compatible with erbium-doped fiber amplifier (EDFA) technology, which amplifies all light signals within their frequency range.

Note   EDFA technology is beginning to make repeaters obsolete. EDFA is a form of fiber-optical amplification that transmits a light signal through a section of erbium-doped fiber and amplifies the signal with a laser pump diode. EDFA is used in transmitter booster amplifiers, inline repeating amplifiers, and in receiver preamplifiers.

CWDM supports up to a 30-dB power budget on an SM fiber. This restricts the distances over which CWDM may be used. CWDM supports distances of approximately 60 miles (100 km) in a point-to-point topology and about 25 miles (40 km) in a ring topology.

In some areas, service providers use CWDM to provide lambda or wavelength services. A lambda service is where a provider manages equipment and multiplexes customer traffic onto one or more wavelengths for a high-speed connection, typically between two or more points.

DWDM Technical Overview

DWDM is a core technology in an optical transport network. The concepts of DWDM are similar to those for CWDM. However, DWDM spaces the wavelengths more tightly, yielding up to 160 channels.

The tighter channel spacing in DWDM requires more sophisticated, precise, and therefore more expensive transceiver designs. In a service provider's backbone network, the majority of embedded fiber is standard SM fiber (G.652) with high dispersion in the 1550-nm window. DWDM supports 32 or more channels in the narrow band around 1550 nm at 100-GHz spacing, or about 0.8 nm, as illustrated in Figure 4-3.

Note   Current Cisco DWDM cards can support 32 wavelengths.

Because of the EDFA compatibility of the wavelengths used, DWDM is also available over much longer distances than CDWM and supports metropolitan-area network (MAN) and WAN applications. In practice, signals can travel for up to 75 miles (120 km) between amplifiers if fiber with EDFA is used. At distances of 375 miles (600 km) to 600 miles (1000 km), the signal must be regenerated.

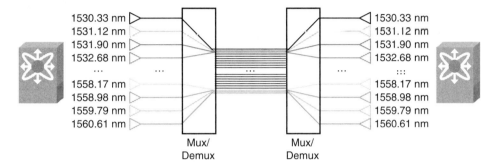

1530.33 nm				1530.33 nm
1531.12 nm				1531.12 nm
1531.90 nm				1531.90 nm
1532.68 nm				1532.68 nm
...	...	...	...	:::
1558.17 nm				1558.17 nm
1558.98 nm				1558.98 nm
1559.79 nm				1559.79 nm
1560.61 nm				1560.61 nm
	Mux/		Mux/	
	Demux		Demux	

Figure 4-3   *DWDM Technical Overview*

DWDM can be used as a high-speed enterprise WAN connectivity service. Typical DWDM uses include connectivity between sites and data centers for example 1-, 2-, or 4-Gbps Fibre Channel; IBM fiber connectivity (FICON) and Enterprise System Connection (ESCON); and Gigabit and 10 Gigabit Ethernet.

Protection options include client-side safeguards using rerouting, an optical splitter that allows the signal to go both ways around a ring or line-card-based protection that detects loss of signal and wraps.

DWDM Systems

DWDM typically uses a transponder, mux/demux, and an amplifier:

- **Transponder:** Receives the input optical signal (from a client-layer SONET/SDH or other signal), converts that signal into the electrical domain, and retransmits the signal using a 1550-nm band laser.

- **Multiplexer:** Takes the various 1550-nm band signals and places them onto an SM fiber. The terminal multiplexer may or may not also support a local EDFA. An OADM extracts a channel of signal and inserts (replaces it with) an outgoing signal from a site.

- **Amplifier:** Provides power amplification of the multiwavelength optical signal.

Figure 4-4 shows how DWDM can be used with the reconfigurable OADM (ROADM). A ROADM allows reconfiguration on-the-fly so that commands select the wavelengths to be dropped and added. Other forms of OADM are tied to specific wavelengths. Reconfiguration with older OADMs meant swapping cards to select different frequencies (wavelengths). This might require interrupting the entire set of channels.

The primary challenge with mux/demux is to minimize crosstalk and maximize channel separation so that the system can distinguish each wavelength.

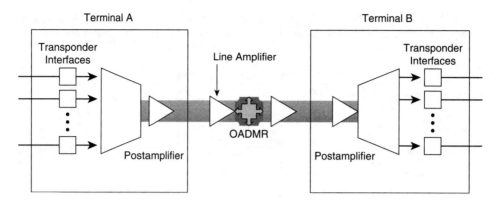

Figure 4-4 *DWDM Systems*

RPR Overview

RPR is a Layer 2 transport architecture providing packet-based transmission based on a dual counter-rotating ring topology. The June 2004 IEEE 802.17 standard defines RPR as a MAN technology supporting a ring structure using unidirectional, counter-rotating ringlets. Each ringlet is made up of links with data flow in the same direction. The use of dual fiber-optic rings provides a high level of packet survivability. If a station fails or fiber is cut, data is transmitted over the alternate ring.

RPR is similar to the older Cisco Spatial Reuse Protocol (SRP). SRP is implemented in the Cisco Dynamic Packet Transport (DPT) products. Newer Cisco DPT interfaces have been designed to include support for the 802.17 RPR protocol.

Whereas DPT and SRP use SONET/SDH as the physical medium, IEEE 802.17 RPR has been defined to use either SONET/SDH or the physical layer of Gigabit and 10 Gigabit Ethernet. DTP, SRP, and RPR can all support metro and long-distance use.

RPR in the Enterprise

Figure 4-5 illustrates how the customer views RPR—as a transport ring that supports connections between their locations. RPR overcomes some limitations of SONET/SDH. Because SONET/SDH is designed to support the characteristics of voice traffic, SONET and SDH are limited in their ability to efficiently carry bursty data traffic. Voice traffic typically has consistent, well-characterized usage patterns, but data traffic bursts as large files are transferred.

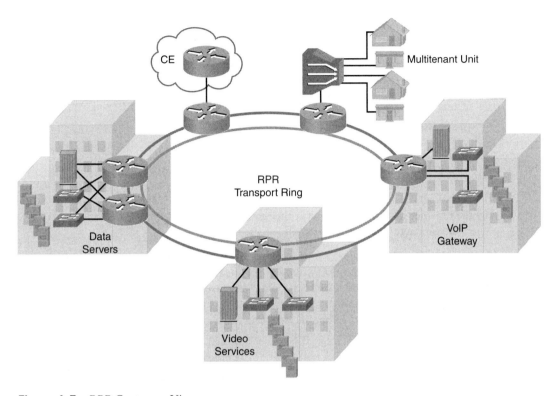

Figure 4-5 *RPR Customer View*

Unlike point-to-point voice traffic, data traffic is characterized by the predominance of point-to-multipoint and multipoint-to-multipoint transmission and bursty traffic. RPR efficiently supports data traffic on service provider networks because RPR can take advantage of the multiple QoS and class of service (CoS) features of data traffic. RPR can also offer network efficiency by sharing or oversubscribing core bandwidth.

From a customer's perspective, SONET typically provides TDM bandwidth guarantees, although they do not match up precisely with typical Ethernet speeds. The guarantee holds unless the provider performs edge oversubscription, with more access bandwidth than what is available across the SONET ring.

RPR is based on a statistical multiplexing approach that behaves more like Ethernet and does not provide TDM-style bandwidth guarantees. RPR can use QoS to protect and prioritize important traffic, but bandwidth guarantees are harder to provide. Service providers must be prepared to use a different approach with RPR to meet service-level agreements (SLA).

Metro Ethernet Overview

A Metro Ethernet is a flexible transport architecture that uses a combination of optical, Ethernet, and IP technologies in the metropolitan area. The mix of technologies depends on how the service provider has designed its infrastructure.

This section provides an overview of Metro Ethernet service models and architectures.

Metro Ethernet Service Model

Metro Ethernet leverages a service provider multiservice core.

The technology inside a Metro Ethernet network is not visible to customers; they see only the Ethernet services connection at their premises. The service provider is responsible for provisioning these functions across its core network.

Metro Ethernet is a large market for the service provider because there is an opportunity to provide services to customers with millions of existing Ethernet interfaces. Although the service provider might not want to disclose the backbone infrastructure, the more knowledge the customer has regarding the provider core, the more informed they can be about the quality of the services they will be receive and potential problems that might arise.

Note   Appropriate SLAs for the advanced WAN services are discussed in the "Implementing Advanced WAN Services" section of this chapter.

Metro Ethernet Architecture

The service provider administers Ethernet as a network infrastructure for metropolitan connectivity, possibly using various Layer 1 transport technologies. The Metro Ethernet architecture is illustrated in Figure 4-6.

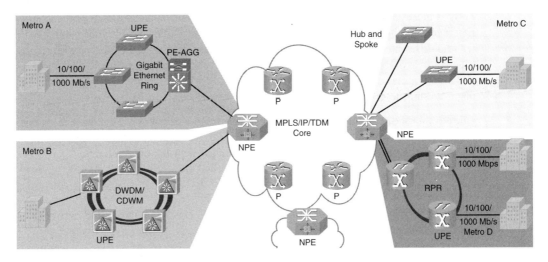

Figure 4-6   *Metro Ethernet Architecture*

The service provider may use SONET/SDH rings or point-to-point links, WDM, or RPR technology for its Metro Ethernet architecture. Edge aggregation devices or user provider edge (UPE) devices may multiplex multiple customers onto one optical circuit to the network provider edge (NPE) device. NPE devices connect to core provider (P) devices. The Ethernet service provided might include multiple services, such as LAN interconnection, IP telephony, and Internet access. It might also include varying levels of SLA and QoS for different customer needs. Edge aggregation allows the service provider to support oversubscription.

The actual implementation for the Metro Ethernet MAN service may be based on one or several of the following approaches:

- A pure Ethernet MAN uses only Layer 2 switches for all of its internal structure. The switches may be in a loop-free topology and may not be running Spanning Tree Protocol (STP).

- A SONET/SDH-based Ethernet MAN is usually utilized as an intermediate step in the transition from a traditional, time-division-based network, to a modern statistical network such as Ethernet. In this model, the existing SONET/SDH infrastructure is used to transport high-speed Ethernet connections.

- A Multiprotocol Label Switching (MPLS)-based Metro Ethernet network uses Layer 2 MPLS virtual private networks (VPN) in the provider network (P-network). The subscriber gets an Ethernet interface on copper or fiber, at 10-Mbps to 1-Gbps rates. The customer Ethernet packets are transported over MPLS, and the P-network may use Ethernet again as the underlying technology to transport MPLS.

Each of these approaches offers different oversubscription characteristics. Switched Ethernet and Ethernet over MPLS (EoMPLS) use statistical multiplexing (stat muxing), with no differentiation between customers or types of traffic unless QoS is provided. Ethernet over SONET implementations are not oversubscribed unless the SONET infrastructure does not go end to end in the P-network, in which case portions of the network might be subject to oversubscription.

One advantage of edge aggregation is that service providers can now customize the service to customers without changing the infrastructure. For instance, with oversubscription, a provider web page might allow customers to increase their bandwidth limits.

Metro Ethernet LAN Services

Cisco offers a scalable Metro Ethernet solution over an existing SONET/SDH network, switched Ethernet network, or IP MPLS network. This provides multiple classes of service and bandwidth profiles to support critical data, voice, video, and storage applications. The Cisco Optical Metro Ethernet solution supports several Metro Ethernet Forum (MEF) service types:

- **Ethernet Private Line (EPL) service:** A port-based point-to-point Ethernet-line (E-line) service that maps Layer 2 traffic directly onto a TDM circuit

- **Ethernet Relay Service (ERS):** A point-to-point VLAN-based E-line service that is used primarily for establishing a point-to-point connection between customer routers

- **Ethernet Wire Service (EWS):** A point-to-point port-based E-line service that is used primarily to connect geographically remote LANs over a P-network

- **Ethernet Multipoint Service (EMS):** A multipoint-to-multipoint port-based emulated LAN (ELAN) service that is used for transparent LAN applications

- **Ethernet Relay Multipoint Service (ERMS):** A multipoint-to-multipoint VLAN-based ELAN service that is used primarily for establishing a multipoint-to-multipoint connection between customer routers

Metro Ethernet services are characterized by the UNI and Ethernet virtual circuit (EVC) attributes. EVCs can be point-to-point or point-to-multipoint services. Some UNIs can support multiple EVCs. The EPL, ERS, and EWS service types map to the E-line services defined by the MEF. The EMS and ERMS service types map to the ELAN services defined by the MEF.

Cisco Ethernet services also include Layer 3 MPLS VPN services, which may be based on Ethernet or other underlying transport technologies. Figure 4-7 provides an illustrated overview of Cisco Ethernet-based services.

Ethernet services can be used in conjunction with Ethernet switches or routers. For organizations with the skills and interest for managing their own routing, Layer 2 Ethernet connectivity provides routing-neutral connectivity similar to that of leased lines, Frame Relay, and ATM circuits. One potential difference of service provider Ethernet services is that using multipoint Ethernet could vastly increase the number of routing peers in the organization.

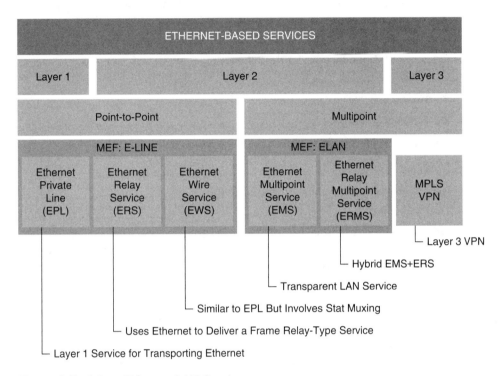

Figure 4-7 *Metro Ethernet LAN Services*

When implementing service provider Ethernet services, customers must decide whether they want to outsource routing to the service provider or perform their own routing. Outsourced routing, or routing in cooperation with the service provider, is typically done using Layer 3 MPLS VPNs.

Note   Metro Ethernet switching and large multipoint router-based architectures have design and scalability implications.

Ethernet Private Line Service

An EPL service is a dedicated point-to-point connection from one customer-specified location to another, with guaranteed bandwidth and payload transparency end to end.

EPL typically uses SONET/SDH transport. Because the bandwidth is dedicated with no oversubscription, a simple SLA concerning uptime may support all the customer requirements. SONET protection can provide high availability for EPL service.

The Cisco EPL service is ideal for transparent LAN interconnection and data center integration, for which wire-speed performance and VLAN transparency are important. Whereas TDM-based and OC-based facilities have been the traditional means of providing EPL service, the Cisco EPL service also supports DWDM/CWDM, Ethernet over SONET/SDH, and dedicated Ethernet platforms interconnected via fiber.

The EPL service is typically used for the following:

■   Mission-critical links

■   Mainframe-to-mainframe links

■   Data center or storage-area network (SAN) extension links

■   Business-continuity links

■   Network consolidation-joining sites in MANs

Note   Organizations need to be careful of provider-managed CE devices handling the speed transitions from the customer to the P-network, because the provider-managed CE devices may impede the organization from being able to easily implement their own QoS policies.

Ethernet Relay Service

Cisco ERS is a point-to-point VLAN-based E-line service that supports service multiplexing, where multiple instances of service or EVCs can be multiplexed onto a single customer UNI.

Service multiplexing means that many connections can be provided over one link. The multiplexed UNI supports point-to-point or point-to-multipoint connections between two or more customer-specified sites, similar to a Frame Relay service. Instead of the data-link connection identifier (DLCI), the connection identifier in ERS is a VLAN tag. Each customer VLAN tag is mapped to a specific Ethernet virtual connection.

Note   ERS uses the VLAN to indicate destination. Therefore, the Ethernet service is not transparent to Layer 2 Ethernet frames—the VLAN tag dictates destination. The ERS EVC does not act like a trunk where all VLANs go from one site to one or multiple sites.

ERS uses different point-to-point VLANs to connect one site to other remote sites.

Note   If multipoint connections are available, the service is referred to as an ERMS.

Service multiplexing provides scalability for large sites, minimizing the number of Ethernet connections to the MAN or WAN Ethernet service. A router is typically the customer premise device.

ERS also provides Ethernet access through service interworking to other Layer 2 services, such as Frame Relay and ATM, so that the customers can begin using Ethernet services without replacing their existing legacy systems. With service interworking, traffic on a DLCI or virtual path identifier/virtual channel identifier (VPI/VCI) at a remote site is converted to an Ethernet frame by the provider and arrives within a VLAN at headquarters.

The provider may offer tiers of service, based on bandwidth, CoS, and distance. A typical SLA might be based on committed information rate (CIR) or peak information rate (PIR), burst capacity, and packet-loss rate.

ERS is ideal for interconnecting routers in an enterprise network, and for connecting to Internet service providers (ISP) and other service providers for direct Internet access, VPN services, and other value-added services. Service providers can multiplex connections from many end customers onto a single Ethernet port at the service provider's point of presence (POP) for efficiency and ease of management.

Ethernet Wire Service

The Cisco EWS is a point-to-point connection between a pair of sites. Cisco EWS differs from Cisco EPLS in that it is usually provided over a shared, switched infrastructure within the service provider network that can be allocated among customers. Oversubscription of the service provider network is handled using stat muxing. The benefit of EWS to the customer is that it is typically offered with a wider choice of committed bandwidth levels up to wire speed. To help ensure privacy, the service provider segregates each subscriber's traffic by applying VLAN tags on each EVC, typically using queue-in-queue (QinQ) tunneling. Customer SLA capabilities are usually based on CoS.

EWS is considered a port-based service. With EWS, the carrier network is transparent to all customer Ethernet traffic. EWS provides all-to-one bundling, where all customer packets are transmitted to the destination port transparently and the VLAN tags from the customer are preserved through the P-network. The CE device might be a router or a switch.

EWS is commonly used for point-to-point LAN extension, access to storage resources, and data center connectivity.

Ethernet Multipoint Service

EMS is a multipoint-to-multipoint service that is typically provided over a shared, switched infrastructure within the P-network.

EMS is a multipoint version of EWS, and shares the same technical access requirements and characteristics.

In EMS, the P-network acts as a virtual switch for the customer. It provides the ability to connect multiple customer sites and allows for any-to-any communication. The enabling technology is Virtual Private Line Service (VPLS), implemented at the NPE. The service provider can use rate limiting to minimize the impact of a customer broadcast storm on other customers.

Oversubscription of the P-network is also handled with EMS using stat muxing. EMS is generally offered to the customer with a choice of committed bandwidth levels up to wire speed. To help ensure privacy, the service provider segregates each subscriber's traffic by applying VLAN tags on each EVC, typically using QinQ tunneling. Customer SLA capabilities are usually based on CoS.

EMS provides all-to-one bundling, where all customer packets are transmitted to the destination ports transparently. The VLAN tags from the customer are preserved through the P-network. The CE device might be a router or a switch.

For example, Verizon Transparent LAN Services (TLS) is a commercial EMS. It is based on a loop-free topology using Cisco 6500 switches and fiber-based Gigabit Ethernet links between them. TLS uses 802.1Q QinQ encapsulation to maintain customer traffic separation.

EMS is commonly used for multipoint LAN extension, LAN extension over the WAN, and disaster recovery.

Ethernet Relay Multipoint Service

ERMS is a hybrid of EMS and ERS.

ERMS offers the any-to-any connectivity characteristics of EMS and the service multiplexing of ERS. This combination enables a single UNI to support a customer's intranet connection and one or more additional EVCs for connection to outside networks, ISPs, or content providers. Some EVCs might be point to point, and others might be multipoint. The service provider can use rate limiting to minimize the impact of a customer broadcast storm on other customers.

ERMS can be used for many applications, including branch Layer 2 VPNs, Layer 3 VPNs for intranet and extranet access, Internet access through the ISP, and disaster recovery.

Any Transport over MPLS

MPLS technology is used in the core of many service provider networks. Originally, these MPLS networks were built to support IP-based services, such as Internet access and Layer 3 MPLS VPNs. Layer 2 services, such as Frame Relay, ATM, and Metro Ethernet, were traditionally built as separate Layer 2 networks on top of various Layer 1 transports, such as SONET, SDH, CWDM, and DWDM. Maintaining separate networks for Layer 3 and Layer 2 services comes at a cost. Efforts such as capacity planning, providing high availability, and managing infrastructure devices are replicated for each of the networks. This increases the overall cost of operations. Any Transport over MPLS (AToM) enables service providers to use an MPLS network as a transport network for Metro Ethernet services.

AToM provides a way for service providers to leverage their existing MPLS network to offer Layer 2 services in addition to Layer 3 services.

AToM provides a common framework to encapsulate and transparently convey different types of Layer 2 protocols over an MPLS network core. AToM currently supports transport of Ethernet, High-Level Data Link Control (HDLC), PPP, Frame Relay, and ATM. The AToM framework and transport options for the various Layer 2 protocols are defined in RFC 4447, RFC 4385, RFC 4448, RFC 4717, RFC 4618, and RFC 4619. In addition to these methods to transport Layer 2 protocols, RFC 4553 and RFC 4842 define methods to transport TDM-based services, such as T1/E1, T3/E3, and SONET/SDH, over a core MPLS network.

Using AToM, service providers can establish point-to-point Layer 2 pseudowires (PW) between two customer premises equipment (CPE) devices. The PW is presented to the CPE device as a standard Layer 2 circuit. Inside the cloud, the frame is encapsulated using AToM headers that are specific for the Layer 3 protocol. The encapsulated frames are then carried to the egress provider edge (PE) using a label-switched path (LSP) that is signaled between the ingress and egress PE during establishment of the PW.

AToM is most commonly used for like-to-like connections, such as EoMPLS, ATM over MPLS, or Frame Relay over MPLS (FRoMPLS). In addition, AToM supports interworking options that make it possible to establish circuits that use a different Layer 2 technology at each of the two ends of the circuit. For example, an Ethernet-based circuit could be used at the central site and Frame Relay at the branch sites. The interworking mechanisms enable gradual migration from legacy WAN connections to an Ethernet-based WAN. AToM can be leveraged to provide ERS and EMS type services. Because of the statistical multiplexing in the MPLS core network, QoS for AToM PWs is commonly implemented through a combination of MPLS traffic engineering (TE) and differentiated services (DiffServ) technologies.

Ethernet over MPLS

EoMPLS is one of the Layer 2 transport options that are defined in the AToM framework. Figure 4-8 shows a typical EoMPLS frame.

Figure 4-8 *EoMPLS Frame*

An EoMPLS virtual circuit (VC) is signaled and established through a targeted Label Distribution Protocol (LDP) session. During session establishment, essential parameters, such as the VC type, are exchanged, and an LSP is established between the ingress and egress PE routers. The EoMPLS VC is a point-to-point connection. Therefore, MAC address learning is unnecessary for the circuit. The EoMPLS circuit represents a virtual PW.

When Ethernet frames are received from the CE router or switch, the ingress PE strips the preamble and frame check sequence (FCS) and subsequently adds the following additional headers:

- **AToM control word:** The control word is optional for most Layer 2 protocols, except for Frame Relay and for ATM AAL5 (where it is required). The control word is 32-bit that is inserted between the VC label and the transported Layer 2 frame in case of AToM. The control word is used to carry extra information such as the protocol control information and the sequence number. This information is needed to correctly and efficiently carry the Layer 2 protocol across the network. This header is optional, and the use of the control word is negotiated when the VC is established.

- **Circuit label:** This is the inner MPLS label and represents the circuit. This label is not used in the MPLS core. It is exposed when the frame reaches the last hop and is used by the egress PE to determine the interface to forward the frame on. This label is exchanged through the targeted LDP session on circuit establishment.

- **Tunnel label:** This is the MPLS label that is used to switch the frame across the MPLS core to the egress PE. It identifies the egress PE and is obtained through the normal LDP that is used in the MPLS core between the PE and provider routers (P routers). If MPLS traffic engineering is used, this label could also be derived through Resource Reservation Protocol-Traffic Engineering (RSVP-TE). In certain scenarios, the tunnel label could actually consist of two separate labels: an LDP label and a TE label.

- **Core Layer 2 header:** With this header, the egress PE encapsulates the EoMPLS frame in the appropriate Layer 2 protocol and sends it to the next-hop router in the LSP.

EoMPLS can operate in two different modes: port and VLAN. The mode determines how IEEE 802.1Q VLAN tags are processed.

When the circuit operates in port mode (circuit type 5), it encapsulates and transmits the entire Layer 2 frame that it receives on the ingress interface, including the 802.1Q header if it is present. Port mode is entirely transparent and allows the customer to use the EoMPLS PW as a standard Ethernet link. 802.1Q trunking can be used to carry multiple VLANs across the PW. EoMPLS port mode implements an EWS.

When the circuit operates in VLAN mode (circuit type 4), the VLAN tag in the 802.1Q header of the incoming frame is examined to determine the circuit on which the frame needs to be transmitted. The incoming VLAN tag acts as a connection identifier, like the DLCI in Frame Relay or VPI/VCI in ATM. On egress, the 802.1Q header is rewritten to the VLAN that identifies the circuit at the other end; this may be a different VLAN. VLAN mode can be used to implement several VLAN-based VCs over a single physical Ethernet access link. This implementation is analogous to the implementation of VCs in a Frame Relay or ATM network. VLAN mode uses the VLAN tag to identify the circuit and is therefore not transparent. Customer-defined VLANs are not transparently carried across the circuit. Also, EoMPLS port mode requires an 802.1Q VLAN tag to be present in the received frame to select the outbound circuit. EoMPLS VLAN mode implements an ERS.

The AToM interworking feature allows EoMPLS VCs to be defined that use port mode on one end of the circuit and VLAN mode on the other side. This feature can be useful to implement a hub-and-spoke type of ERS. At the hub site, the circuit is operated in VLAN mode, and a different VLAN is used to identify each of the spokes. At the spoke sites, the circuit is operated in port mode, making it unnecessary for the spoke CE device to tag the frames. The link between the spoke CE and PE uses standard Ethernet frames, and the link between the hub CE and PE uses 802.1Q trunking to identify the traffic to and from the different spokes.

End-to-End QoS

Metro Ethernet offerings should provide end-to-end QoS across the network.

A service provider can use IEEE 802.1Q tunneling to support end-to-end QoS for its customers. In Figure 4-9, the CE device is connected to the service provider UPE device using 802.1Q. The CE device adds an 802.1Q tag to all frames and supports the CoS across the network. The UPE devices add a second 802.1Q frame to support QinQ encapsulation of the customer traffic. Depending on the agreement with the service provider, the type of QoS can be extended across the network. The two 802.1Q tags can be seen in the frame in the middle of the chart. The outer 802.1Q tag added by the UPE acts as a customer ID.

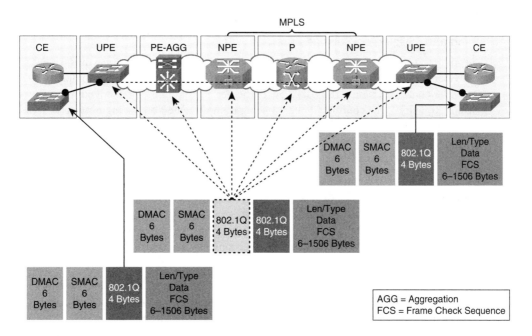

Figure 4-9 *End-to-End QoS*

Switches and other devices in the service provider backbone transport the encapsulated Ethernet frame based on the outer 802.1Q tag and ToS. The outer 802.1Q tag is stripped off when the frame reaches the destination or destinations indicated in the outer tag. At the remote UPE, the Ethernet frame is transparently forwarded based on the original CE 802.1Q tag with the original CoS.

The destination MAC is preserved end to end, so multicast traffic will be seen by the P-network as having a multicast destination MAC address. If the service is point to multi-point, one multicast frame sent into the P-network will be received at multiple customer sites, in accordance with multicast flooding within a VLAN.

Note   If any remote site receives a multicast stream, the stream floods to all sites in that VLAN.

Because the service providers do not need to coordinate the customer VLANs with QinQ encapsulation, the customer VLANs can be preserved across the network, and the network supports VLAN transparency. With the QinQ encapsulation, customer VLANs can overlap.

An example of the 802.1Q encapsulation technique is a large service provider using EoMPLS to break up VLAN domains with a routed domain in the middle.

Shaping and Policing on Subrate Ethernet WAN

In addition to the true Ethernet speeds of 10 Mbps, 100 Mbps, and 1000 Mbps, some providers offer subrate speeds on their Ethernet-based WAN services. For example, a provider could provision a 100-Mbps Fast Ethernet link but limit the bandwidth to 60 Mbps. To enforce the contracted rate, policing is implemented on the ingress interface of the provider router. The advantage of this approach is that it allows the bandwidth to be scaled up without changes to the underlying circuit. If the customer requires more band-width, the provider needs only to increase the configured traffic rate of the policer.

A common problem with this approach is that it can create a congestion point in the P-network. If in this example, the CPE router receives 100-Mbps worth of traffic, it trans-mits all the traffic on the Fast Ethernet interface connected to the provider router. The provider router subsequently drops 40 Mbps of the traffic. The customer does not have control over the type of packets that will be dropped by the provider, which makes it hard to apply any QoS policies on the WAN.

To implement QoS policies on this type of WAN, traffic shaping is usually deployed on the CPE router. If in this example, traffic shaping is implemented on the CPE to shape outbound traffic to 60 Mbps, traffic will not be dropped by the provider policing. Instead, the traffic accumulates in buffers on the CPE router, which eventually drops the packets that it cannot forward. However, this mechanism effectively moves the conges-tion point from the provider side of the link to the customer side of the link. This allows the customer to implement queuing policies for the traffic as it is being shaped and to distribute bandwidth or prioritize between classes of traffic. Instead of traffic being dropped randomly in the P-network, the customer now gets to choose which types of traffic will be dropped if congestion occurs, making it possible to implement QoS policies across the Ethernet-based WAN.

Choosing the Right Service

Figure 4-10 shows a decision tree that a customer can use to help choose the appropriate Layer 2 service. For example, customers that require only point-to-point service can use EPL, EWS, or ERS; whereas customers that require multipoint services should use EMS or ERMS.

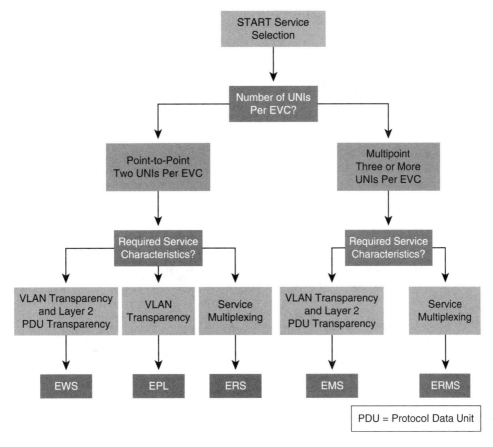

Figure 4-10 *Choosing the Right Service*

VPLS Overview

VPLS is a multipoint architecture that connects two or more customer devices using Ethernet bridging techniques over an MPLS network. In VPLS, the P-network emulates an IEEE 802.1D Ethernet bridge, with each EMS being analogous to a VLAN.

VPLS is an architecture that is still being defined. There are two RFCs that are distinct and incompatible with one another:

- **RFC 4761:** *Virtual Private LAN Service (VPLS). Using BGP for Auto-Discovery and Signaling is a standard proposed by Juniper*

- **RFC 4762:** *Virtual Private LAN Service (VPLS). Using Label Distribution Protocol (LDP) Signaling is a standard proposed by Cisco*

One of the major differences in the standard is in the VPLS PE discovery process, or how VPLS PE devices find each other, communicate capabilities, and perform tasks such as preprovisioning EVCs.

VPLS Architecture Model

In the VPLS architecture model, UPE devices act as IEEE 802.1D standard bridges or switches. They are interconnected in a full mesh of PWs. In Figure 4-11, the PWs cross a routed MPLS and IP provider backbone. From the point of view of the UPEs, these PWs are just Ethernet connections to another switch.

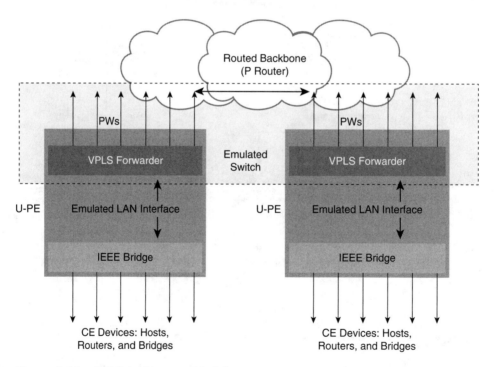

Figure 4-11   *VPLS Architecture Model*

VPLS will self-learn source MAC address to port associations, and frames are forwarded based on the destination MAC address. If the destination address is unknown, or is a broadcast or multicast address, the frame is flooded to all ports associated with the virtual bridge.

In the event of a provider outage, IP rerouting rapidly restores PW connectivity. In such a case, no MAC aging and relearning is needed.

To simplify processing, the VPLS core does not use STP. Instead, it uses split-horizon forwarding, so that Ethernet frames are not sent back out on the same PW on which they were received.

Broadcast and multicast traffic would always be flooded in VPLS.

VPLS in the Enterprise

VPLS is used as an enterprise WAN connectivity service.

VPLS looks like an Ethernet switch to the customer with the same inherent Layer 2 core issues:

- **Stability of the network as it grows:** Experience shows that purely STP-based VPLS does not scale gracefully. VPLS based on MPLS scales much better.

- **Impact of network outages:** A customer should ask what happens to their traffic in the event of an outage and receive enough details to justify the quoted speed of convergence.

- **Multicast and broadcast radiation between sites:** Because the VPLS network acts like a switch, customer multicasts and broadcasts sent into the VPLS cloud radiate to all sites of that customer. This can be somewhat controlled by using routers to connect to the VPLS network, but multicasts sent by the router flood to all the customer's sites.

- **Interior Gateway Protocol (IGP) peering scalability:** The VPLS network is one broadcast domain, so all attached routers are usually routing peers. As the number of routing peers increases, the full mesh of connections becomes a scaling issue. Designs using VPLS in a hierarchical fashion should be more scalable.

- **Impact of an STP loop of another customer:** Because VPLS uses stat muxing, all customers share bandwidth. It is reasonable to ask what the impact of a customer with a spanning-tree loop would be on other customers. If the customer is attached by a Layer 2 switch, all the packets from the loop are necessarily flooded within the links interconnecting their VPLS sites. If they connect at 1 Gbps and the provider trunks are 20 Gbps, this might not be so bad. If the provider links are 2 Gbps, the impact might be much greater, particularly if EtherChannel is in use. (Deterministic assignment of traffic to channels causes the traffic of other selected customers to share the problem customer's channels.)

A VPLS customer might also want to conduct due diligence to verify that the provider is aware of and has implemented adequate Layer 2 security measures.

Hierarchical VPLS Overview

Hierarchical VPLS (H-VPLS) provides scaling by only interconnecting the core MPLS NPE routers with a full mesh of PWs. The many UPE VPLS devices are then connected hierarchically by PWs to the NPE devices, not to each other. When there is redundancy, as shown in Figure 4-12, the software in the UPE blocks the PWs to all but the highest NPE IP address. H-VPLS partitions the network into several edge domains that are interconnected using an MPLS core.

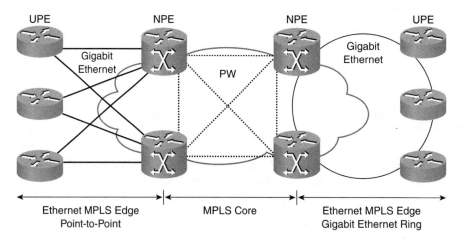

Figure 4-12 *Hierarchical VPLS Overview*

One advantage of the H-VPLS approach for the service provider is that the core of the network is an MPLS network, which may also be used for the transport of Layer 3 MPLS VPNs and other traffic. The MPLS core also serves to limit any edge spanning-tree domains, speeding up STP convergence and reducing any potential instability.

The physical topology of Ethernet edge H-VPLS (EE H-VPLS) can comprise point-to-point Ethernet connections, or Ethernet rings using an STP to provide redundancy and loop avoidance. Other edge architectures use an aggregation layer between the UPE and NPE, or use Ethernet over SONET/SDH (EoS), or RPR as a transport between the UPE and NPE.

H-VPLS provides an extremely flexible architectural model that also enables multipoint Ethernet services (VPLS) and Ethernet point-to-point Layer 2 VPN services and Ethernet access to Layer 3 VPN services.

Scaling VPLS

A service provider VPLS design must address three major scaling factors:

- **Scaling of the full mesh of PWs between PE devices:** As the number of PE devices scales, each edge device must form an adjacency with all other PE devices. This re-quires that the edge devices must have the IP address of all remote PEs in its routing table, and also requires the PE to exchange label information with all remote PE devices. That introduces an N − 1 control plane scaling issue.

H-VPLS helps address this issue by using UPE devices to spread the edge workload across multiple, less-costly devices. The lower number of PWs between the NPE devices helps scale the network by reducing the burden on the core for frame replication and forwarding.

- **Frame replication and forwarding:** VPLS forwards Ethernet frames using Layer 2 MAC addresses. The operation of VPLS is exactly the same as that found within IEEE 802.1 bridges in that the virtual switch self-learns the source MAC address-to-port associations and forwards frames based on the destination MAC address. If the destination address is unknown, or is a broadcast or multicast address, the frame is flooded to all ports associated with the virtual bridge. H-VPLS needs a lower number of PWs because only the NPE devices are connected in a full mesh. This helps reduce the burden on the core for frame replication and forwarding.

- **MAC address table size:** One of the biggest considerations in VPLS provider design is MAC address learning. PE devices need to be capable of handling MAC address tables for many customer devices and customers. That number is much greater than what a typical enterprise campus switch needs to handle today.

    H-VPLS allows MAC tables to be spread across multiple inexpensive devices to scale the edge. UPE devices need only learn of their local NPE devices and therefore do not need large routing table support. Core NPE devices still need to handle very large MAC address tables. Using MPLS in the core removes the MAC learning requirement from the P devices.

Note Interconnecting only customer routers and not switches by VPLS greatly simplifies scaling MAC learning, because then only the router MAC addresses need to be learned in VPLS devices. However, few providers are willing to limit their potential VPLS market by imposing such a requirement.

Some VPLS device vendors use proprietary MAC-in-MAC encapsulation schemes so that the NPE devices need learn only the MAC addresses of other UPE devices. This approach may also use supporting protocols, reminiscent of ATM LAN Emulation (LANE). At the time of this writing, Cisco devices do not implement these mechanisms.

How well the provider's design handles all these factors is of interest to the customer. Poor VPLS design can lead to scaling and stability problems as the provider's network grows. Although a customer should not have to be intimately familiar with VPLS designs to evaluate a provider's service, listening to a service provider's answers on these topics can provide insight into that provider's qualifications. At the customer level, VPLS can create excessive number of routing peers and thus cause scaling issues.

QoS Issues with EMS or VPLS

QoS is relatively easy to provide with point-to-point links. Oversubscription is managed by controlling what is allowed into the point-to-point link.

However, QoS for multipoint networks is harder because it requires coordination between multiple devices with unpredictable and rapidly changing traffic patterns. Careful consideration needs to be taken for interactive services such as video and IP telephony. The need for coordination implies that the service provider provide QoS, because it is not something the customer can layer on top of a connection, nor is it something the customer can just implement for their own use.

The technique of bandwidth slicing can be used by customers in an attempt to compensate for lack of provider QoS. In this approach, each CE device has a slice of the bandwidth to each remote location. Access lists then police traffic to each location, to try to ensure the remote link is not congested. The issue with this approach is that inside the VPLS cloud, Customer A traffic competes not only with Customer A traffic but also with the traffic from other customers. In addition, broadcast and multicast traffic fed into the VPLS cloud are received at every service provider edge site, consuming some of the bandwidth, too.

These issues illustrate that if the customer wants QoS, the service provider has to partner to provide it. Customers should expect that QoS is a premium service and determine bandwidth levels for each QoS class to help manage QoS.

EMS or VPLS and Routing Implications

One concern when using the Open Shortest Path First (OSPF) routing protocol is that the multiaccess network might not have consistent broadcast or multicast performance. If some sites experience greater packet loss levels, OSPF processing may consume more router CPU. In the extreme case, packet loss or delay might cause significant levels of OSPF instability. This is currently being seen in some large VPN networks that use generic routing encapsulation (GRE) over IP Security (IPsec) for OSPF routing.

Another concern is that retransmissions or flapping status with regard to one site might consume significant CPU resources on all its peer routers. As discussed in Chapter 3, "Developing an Optimum Design for Layer 3," it is advisable to manage the number of OSPF adjacencies in a full-mesh network and to use designs to limit the number of adjacencies.

Note A similar caution applies to Enhanced Interior Gateway Routing Protocol (EIGRP) routing over an EMS or VPLS service. You should avoid having high numbers of peers with EIGRP, too.

VPLS and IP Multicast

In a campus switched network, IP multicast in a VLAN floods to all ports in the VLAN, unless Internet Group Management Protocol (IGMP) snooping is in use. However, IGMP snooping is not an option with VPLS or EMS. A broadcast or multicast frame sent into the VPLS cloud ends up being sent out of the VPLS P-network to every CE device that has a port associated with the virtual switch.

Because the VPLS network has been designed for transparency by emulating a switch, the VPLS PE devices cannot provide any intelligence by delivering multicast only where it is needed. If the CE devices are routers, they discard undesired multicast packets they receive. IP multicast traffic in MPLS can result in wasted bandwidth and router CPU utilization spent discarding unnecessary traffic.

One conclusion is that VPLS designers with customer networks that have significant amounts of multicast need to use administrative scoping to limit the propagation of multicast packets, or else allow sufficient bandwidth for unnecessary multicast traffic at the edge links.

VPLS Availability

VPLS provides some advantages in the case of P-network outages.

An advantage to using VPLS is that PWs are the underlying technology for the data plane. In the case of a failure in the P-network, traffic is routed automatically along available backup paths in the P-network. Failover in this case is much faster than achievable with STP.

A cost applies to this fast failover. If redundant PWs are used from redundant PE devices, a failure might require aging of MAC addresses followed by unicast flooding. The resulting lost packets followed by a surge of traffic would have a negative impact on customer traffic.

PW rerouting around outages prevents this potential problem.

Note   Although this section has focused primarily on VPLS, many of the same considerations apply to any Ethernet service offering. Appropriate SLAs for the advanced WAN services are discussed in the "Implementing Advanced WAN Services" section in this chapter.

MPLS VPN Overview

As an alternative to Metro Ethernet services, some customers are implementing MPLS VPNs. MPLS VPN services are based on MPLS label paths that are automatically formed based on IP routing. MPLS VPNs experience the same level of stability as exhibited by Layer 3 networks in general. MPLS VPNs can support either Layer 2 transport (typically a long-haul or metro-area Ethernet point-to-point service) or a Layer 3 routed service. The characteristics of the MPLS VPNs vary depending on whether they are implemented at Layer 3 or Layer 2:

- **Layer 3 service:** Layer 3 MPLS VPNs forward only IP packets. The CE routers become peers of MPLS VPN provider routers. In this case, routing may well be a cooperative venture. Stability of the provider routing, their experience with routing, and speed of provider routing convergence are all valid customer considerations. Layer 3 VPNs can support any access or backbone technology. Service providers can use Layer 3 VPNs as a foundation to provide advanced WAN services.

- **Layer 2 service:** Layer 2 MPLS VPNs can forward any network protocol based on Layer 2 frames. There is no peering with the provider. Layer 2 service allows customer routers to peer directly with each other without a handoff to SP router. MPLS Layer 2 VPNs provide point-to-point service where the access technology is determined by the VPN type. MPLS Layer 2 VPNs may also be useful for service interworking, or converting Frame Relay or ATM into Ethernet for delivery on a high-bandwidth link at a central site or data center.

The choice of Layer 2 VPN over Layer 3 VPN depends on how much control the enterprise wants to retain. If an enterprise has a small staff or lacks routing skills, a managed router Layer 3 VPN service puts all CE routers in the hands of one or more providers and delegates all routing to the provider. Large organizations with considerable in-house routing skills may prefer Layer 2 VPNs because they can maintain control of their Layer 3 policies.

Customer Considerations with MPLS VPNs

When designing customer MPLS VPNs, consider the following:

- **Who does the routing?** A major decision when implementing MPLS VPN is who will do the routing. For a simple scenario, the customer may opt to use static routing, where there is no dynamic interaction with the service provider routing. Another option is for the customer to use External Border Gateway Protocol (EBGP), EIGRP, OSPF, or Intermediate System-to-Intermediate System (IS-IS) with the provider, depending on which PE-CE routing protocol the provider supports.

  If the customer redistributes routes learned via MPLS VPN routing into their IGP, these routes may become external routes. In the case of OSPF or EIGRP as the PE-CE routing protocol, the provider may be able to redistribute them as internal routes, which is generally preferable from the customer's perspective.

- **Who manages the CE devices?** Depending on the size and routing experience of the customer, they may choose to manage their own CE devices, or they might choose to buy managed services from the provider. The customer must also determine the level of redundancy needed, depending on whether one or two CE devices will be implemented.

- **Should one or two MPLS VPN providers be used?** Another key decision is whether to use one or two MPLS VPN providers. Having two providers provides better redundancy than dual-homing to one provider because two providers are less likely to experience a common failure event. However, two providers can add complexity to the design. If two MPLS VPN providers are used with two CE devices per location, the design needs to support using the appropriate default gateway with the appropriate first-hop redundancy protocol (FHRP) or other mechanism.

- **Is QoS needed?** If QoS is available from the service provider, the customer needs to decide whether to buy an MPLS service with QoS. Using Layer 3 VPNs allows the customer to implement QoS internally.

- **Is IP multicast supported?** With Layer 3 MPLS VPN, IP multicast may be supported. Doing IP multicast over a Layer 2 MPLS VPN requires service provider support and might cost extra. It may also require special configuration or working with the provider, particularly to support large IP multicast flows.

Routing Considerations: Backdoor Routes

Backdoor routes need to be considered when designing routing for a Layer 3 MPLS VPN WAN.

If there are internal backdoor routes (for example, a second path between locations through a GRE over IPsec tunnel or other WAN link), the internal route (even over slowed links) is preferred over the external route. This needs to be taken into account when designing the routing to properly use the Layer 3 MPLS VPN.

In general, sites with one WAN router do not have this problem. When the PE-CE routing protocol is BGP, EBGP has a better administrative distance (AD) than the IGP in use. The potential problem with backdoor routes arises when there are several Layer 3 devices at one site, especially if the WAN routing is split across them. If the provider follows the common practice of handing off routes through EBGP, the customer may end up running EBGP at every site. In addition, the customer may have EBGP with the route reflector over the IPsec VPN.

The service provider may be able to redistribute routes as internal routes for OSPF and EIGRP. Using a separate EIGRP autonomous system for the IPsec VPN is another approach to allow simple redistribution controls and metrics.

As a recommended practice, you should minimize the locations where you implement route redistribution. Route redistribution at many locations can adversely impact network stability.

Routing Considerations: Managed Router Combined with Internal Routing

If a managed router service is purchased, it can become awkward to do your own routing.

You might find with managed routers that you still want to control your own routing, perhaps when your company purchases managed router services from one MPLS provider, and then later purchases a similar service from another organization. If not otherwise specified, both providers may choose to use static routing.

In such a setting, the lack of dynamic routing makes it hard to automate dynamic failover in response to provider failure or problems. One approach is to add another layer of routers at each site and set up GRE tunnels between these routers, as shown in Figure 4-13. The GRE tunnels will allow an organization to control its own routing and run services such as IP multicast. The providers need to provide enough static routing to deliver packets between the added customer routers.

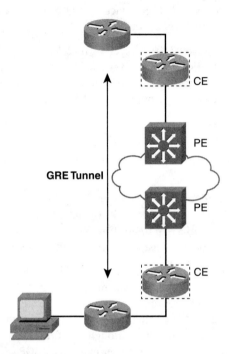

Figure 4-13 *Managed Router Combined with Internal Routing*

Several potential issues arise with this approach. The GRE tunnel adds to the cost and complexity of the network. You need another router at each site. It is more difficult to configure the network, and there are potential performance issues related to the impact of encapsulation and possibly maximum transmission unit (MTU) sizes leading to fragmentation.

Routing Considerations: Managed Router from Two Service Providers

In Figure 4-14, there is a managed CE router service from two different service providers; as a result, the issue of FHRP may arise.

With two service providers providing parallel paths between your locations, you need to consider what the primary path for specific traffic types is and how to support failover. Hot Standby Router Protocol (HSRP) or another FHRP can be used, but it can be challenging to get your two providers to cooperate with each other to provide the FHRP service.

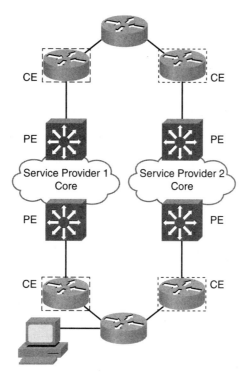

Figure 4-14   *Managed Router from Two Service Providers*

Note   If your site is large enough to use a router or Layer 3 switch in front of the service provider-managed routers, the FHRP is not an issue. However, if you are managing the Layer 3 device, you probably do not need managed router service.

You should negotiate this design with the service providers at contract time. Getting service providers to cooperate can be easier before signing agreements.

Implementing Advanced WAN Services

WAN service design involves a partnership between service providers and customers, where the service provider manages services for the customer on an ongoing basis. This section reviews issues that enterprise customers should consider when implementing advanced WAN services. Service providers should also understand these considerations to address customer concerns.

Advanced WAN Service Selection

It is important to know the actual characteristics of advanced WAN services. Sales presentations and marketing literature highlight the best features of a service but probably do not cover the weak or problem areas. It is up to the customer to ask good questions and do the research. If the service is something you are already using, measure its characteristics. This information can help you, your manager, and the business make an informed decision about supporting your business applications such as IP telephony over that service. When you are considering a new service, you cannot measure its ability to support your business application. You need to make decisions based on the underlying technology, the reputation of the vendor, customer references, trade literature, and other such factors.

One way to mitigate risk with WAN services is to use two providers. When you want to deploy a new technology such as an MPLS VPN, you can implement it on one provider, and continue to use the older service with your other provider in case there are problems. Using two providers also lets you experience their technical and customer service levels. If one is providing inadequate service and not meeting your requirements, it is easier to migrate to the other provider.

In general, an advanced WAN service is a partnership between the service provider and customer. An SLA provides contractual obligations for the service provider. A good WAN contract should have an escape clause that addresses what will occur if the WAN provider consistently fails to meet the SLA or provide reasonable levels of customer service. However, most problems are better solved by working the partner relationship. You should be able to explain issues to your service provider, ask what they will do to make things better, and observe the result. If nothing changes, you have the option of considering another provider.

Business Risk Assessment

Part of a good design is to assess the business risk and base design decisions on how critical the service will be.

Any technology has associated business risks. If a WAN service deployment fails, or if the underlying technology fails, it can have a severe business impact, costing lost business or productivity and amounting to a large cost per hour.

When selecting between providers of advanced WAN services, one factor to consider is risk and the likelihood of problems. It might not be worth saving 10 percent at the risk of repeated outages or a long outage. You need to consider the chance of such an outage happening. These are hard questions to answer, but a service provider can cite examples such as their experience, how long they have been in the business, and how long they have gone without a major outage on a particular service.

Another approach is due diligence questioning, where you conduct a survey, observe the network operations center (NOC), ask a lot of questions, and in general, try to assess the provider personnel's level of technical knowledge. There are several questions a customer can ask:

- Does the provider have several experts available for the specific technology?

- How skilled are the lower-level staff?

- How neat is the cabling?

- Are the devices and cables labeled?

- How old is the equipment?

- How big is the provider?

Note Service providers and/or vendors might be less likely to cooperate with smaller companies due to the size of potential revenue.

Obtaining more than a shallow level of information can be a challenge. Generally, providers do not like to provide these details. Patience and persistence can lead to eventually getting the information you desire.

In general, you should match risk to the purpose of the design. Noncritical internal Internet traffic might be serviced by a low-cost but riskier provider. More critical e-commerce traffic might instead be handled by a more established collocation or Internet provider.

Response to risk always involves trade-offs:

- The time and cost to get more information can be prohibitive.

- The cost of service may make due diligence questioning less practical.

- The value of the data compared to the cost of outage should be considered.

- The likelihood of an outage may not be easy to estimate.

Consultants and resellers can provide their views on risks of various technologies, but the decision of the correct risk versus cost trade-off is really up to the customer.

The scope of a possible outage is another consideration. If a network designer has seen a few STP loops, the designer might believe that a switch and STP-based P-network is risky, because a loop can bring down the entire STP domain. Because routing outages are usually much more localized, that line of reasoning could lead to preferring an MPLS VPN-based service.

WAN Features and Requirements

Customers need to understand what WAN features are available and what they need to support their organization.

Hasty WAN purchases can result in not getting adequate information. Although it might sound obvious, it can be useful to make sure all parties agree as to what the requirements are for the new WAN service being purchased. There are several important questions to ask:

- Will the routing work as it does currently, or will changes be required?

- Will existing VLANs be transparently supported across the service provider core?

- What QoS levels can be supported at what cost?

- Is IP multicast available? What is the cost for multicast?

- What level of security is provided to isolate customer traffic? Is there a cost for this service?

- What management services and tools are available at what cost?

Defining these requirements is important because advanced WAN services are not transparent transport connections the way that leased lines, Frame Relay, and ATM are. It is important to verify that traffic fed into the P-network will be transported appropriately across the service provider core.

It is important to define what WAN features are standard and what features are optional upgrades:

- In Layer 3 MPLS VPNs, the service provider's routing interacts with the customer routing in a secure way. IP multicast has to be handled differently by the provider than unicast routing, so it might not be available or might cost extra.

- With some Ethernet services, Cisco Discovery Protocol might not work or might be limited to a specific VLAN.

It is necessary to get the details of any managed service. To one service provider, network management may mean occasional ping tests and some console logging, and to another service provider it means in-depth Simple Network Management Protocol (SNMP) monitoring with access to the SNMP reports. Security services that merely inform you of a threat reported by an intrusion detection system (IDS) are not as useful as an indication of what triggered that alarm and other network activity going on at the time.

In general, buying WAN services requires asking questions to get details:

- What does "managed router" or "managed link" mean? What base services does the provider implement, such as ping testing, SNMP polling for CPU and link utilization, and other functions? What management services are optional upgrades?

- What is the process for changes? What are the costs for changes? How fast do requested configuration changes actually happen?

- Is the managed router cooperatively managed, or are all configuration decisions made by the provider based on some initial design?

- Can I review the configuration of the managed router? Can I poll it via SNMP? Can I receive syslog messages and SNMP traps from it?

- What does "QoS" mean? How many levels are supported, what sort of SLA or bandwidth guarantees are available, and how are the service levels protected and enforced?

SLA Overview

The SLA is a statement of intent from the provider.

The SLA should set customer expectations by specifying what service levels the service provider will deliver to the customer.

A good SLA covers common managed-service metrics, such as the following:

- **Mean time to repair (MTTR):** MTTR is a measure of how long it takes to repair failures.

- **Mean time between failures (MTBF):** MTBF is a measure of how often failures occur. MTBF can be used to project how often failures are expected

Outage severity and causes vary. For many customers, it is useful to keep a log that tracks major, intermediate, and minor outages; the date and time of the outage; the time the service was restored; and the root cause of the outage. By tracking outages and noting the clarity of communication and the causes of outages, customers have concrete information to discuss at contract renewal time.

A good SLA also includes technical metrics, such as the following:

- **Packet loss:** Packet loss occurs when one or more packets traveling across a network are lost and fail to reach their destination.

- **Latency:** Latency or delay is a measure of how much time it takes for a packet to get from one point in the network to another. Delay can be measured in either one-way or round-trip delay.

- **Jitter:** Jitter is the variable delay that can occur between successive packets. Based on network congestion, improper queuing, or configuration errors, the delay between each packet in a data stream can vary instead of remaining constant.

- **IP availability:** IP availability is a measure of the availability of IP services end to end across a network. TCP session breakage occurs after a component failure when the combination of convergence at Layer 2, Layer 3, and Layer 4 components causes a TCP session to fail.

Traffic throughput and general usefulness of a WAN link depend on very low packet loss rates (for example, 0.001 percent or lower), reasonably low latency, and low jitter. What these numbers should be depends on the type of traffic. VoIP requires good values for all. Best-effort Internet traffic is typically much more tolerant of latency and jitter. Layer 4 components such as Windows Server and Windows XP client stacks have about a 9-second tolerance for interruptions in IP availability.

Customers should avoid SLAs that average results across many devices or links. When averaging availability across enough routers, a device can be down for days and not violate some availability SLAs. Generally, customers want an SLA that covers the extreme behavior of any individual link or device.

SLA Monitoring

Customers should monitor the network status to track how well the service provider is doing at meeting the terms of the SLA.

Networks measurements let customers know what kind of service they are actually receiving. Measurements also provide a baseline for comparison when there are application issues. Measurements can help diagnose outages and performance problems, especially when it is unclear whether the problem is internal to the customer or with the service providers. Customers who receive and monitor alarms can help document the delay in notification or response from the provider after outages.

Some service providers allow their customers to view SLA performance data through a web portal. These measurements should be monitored as a way to track issues such as slow service due to congestion and to understand the health of the network. Even when service provider reports are accessible, many organizations also implement internal monitoring of key links. Internal monitoring can serve to activate an early response to a major outage, and can provide a cross-check that the service provider reports are not censoring the data shown.

Problems can arise if customers think they have been getting poor service because of violations of the SLA. Internal customer measurements can provide evidence of network issues to discuss with the service provider, especially if the service provider has not actively been measuring the service.

Note   SLAs can be monitored using the IP SLA feature embedded in the Cisco IOS Software that runs on routers and switches.

Application Performance Across the WAN

Application performance for critical business applications is a prime consideration in WAN service selection.

A WAN service has primary attributes that define the service, including the following:

■ Bandwidth

■ Bursting capacity

■ QoS classes and policies

■ Multicast support

An SLA defines expected service levels for secondary attributes:

■ MTTR

■ MTBF

■ Packet loss

■ Latency

■ Jitter

■ Availability

Application performance across a WAN is dependent on these attributes.

One of the main considerations in selecting a WAN service is how the business-critical applications will perform across the WAN. The WAN must accommodate the behavior and requirements of the applications that are running across it. Bandwidth requirements, the need for multicast support, QoS mechanisms, and maximum tolerances for latency, jitter, and packet loss are all determined by the demands of the business applications that use the WAN.

Therefore, knowing the requirements of the mix of business-critical applications that the WAN needs to support is vital in determining the required SLA and other attributes of the WAN, such as bandwidth, multicast support, and necessary QoS mechanisms.

If application performance is impaired because the characteristics of the WAN service do not support the requirements of the application, most of the business benefits that are associated with that application are lost.

The WAN is not the only factor that determines end-to-end application performance, although it is very important. A major challenge in ensuring skilled application perform-ance across a WAN is that many applications are designed, developed, and tested in a LAN environment. With abundant bandwidth, low latency and jitter, and relatively little contention for resources between applications, the LAN is an application-friendly environment. When that same application is run across a WAN, the user experience can suddenly be seriously degraded.

In the past, most of the applications were used across the LAN within the headquarters office, or within the branch office LANs between clients and application servers that all resided in the branch itself. This is rapidly changing. Users increasingly need the flexibility to work from anywhere on the network, while business applications are being consolidated in the data center. This changing environment brings the challenge of application performance across the WAN and the Internet to the forefront.

Theoretically, upgrading the WAN until it approaches LAN characteristics is a way to improve application performance. However, this approach is often practically cost-prohibitive or simply impossible.

WAN optimization technologies, such as Cisco Wide Area Application Services (WAAS), can help address this challenge. The Cisco WAAS solution provides application-specific acceleration that is validated by application vendors. Cisco WAAS transparently intercepts traffic and optimizes traffic flows at the transport and session layers. By altering the behavior of the traffic flows across the network, the application experience can approximate LAN-like application performance, while the underlying network still has WAN characteristics.

Cisco WAAS is just one of the solutions that can help improve application performance across the WAN. Other examples of technologies that can help optimize WAN application performance are video transcoding and translating for video applications, web caching for web-based applications, and QoS technologies to guarantee access to network resources for business-critical applications.

WAN CPE Selection Considerations

When selecting the CPE device to connect to a WAN service, consider the following:

■   Type of WAN service (Layer 2 or Layer 3)

■   Physical WAN interface

■   Performance limits

■   Support for additional services

There is a trade-off between cost, speed, and features. Remember RFC 1925, *The Twelve Networking Truths*:

■   "(7a) Good, Fast, Cheap: Pick any two (you can't have all three)."

■   "(9) For all resources, whatever it is, you need more."

Another major step in the process of designing a WAN solution is to select the appropriate CPE device to connect the branch and headquarters networks to the WAN service. Several factors need to be considered:

- **Type of WAN service:** If a Layer 3 service, such as a Layer 3 MPLS VPN has been selected, it is important that the CPE device supports the routing protocol that is used to interact with the provider routers (P routers). This could be as simple as static routing, but it is important that the enterprise routing policy matches the provider routing policy. If a Layer 2 service has been selected, the CPE should support the control protocols that are used between the central and branch sites.

- **Physical WAN interface:** Ethernet is becoming more common as a WAN interface, opening up the possibility to use a switch as the CPE device. If a different technology is used such as Frame Relay, xDSL, or ATM, it is important to select a CPE that supports the corresponding physical interface and speed. Feature set and scalability of the CPE must also be considered. Generally, a Layer 3 switch may not have the feature set or scalability of a router.

- **Performance limits:** WAN bandwidth has steadily increased over the years, and it is important that the CPE that you select can actually forward traffic at the rate that is used on the WAN interface. Routers often support higher-speed interfaces than what can actually be forwarded by the forwarding engine. A Gigabit Ethernet interface may be supplied on the chassis or a module to allow speeds of more than 100 Mbps, but this does not automatically mean that the router is capable of forwarding at 1 Gbps. Case in point is the Integrated Services Router (ISR) G1, ISR G2, Aggregation Services Router (ASR), and so on. Always verify published performance numbers that are based on tests to estimate whether the CPE that you select is capable of forwarding at the full speed of the selected WAN service. Switches are generally capable of forwarding at line rate for all their interfaces. Therefore, they might seem an attractive solution for high-speed Ethernet-based WAN services. However, switches tend to have limited feature support, which may make them unsuitable as a WAN CPE.

- **Support for additional services:** Many WAN and remote branch office connectivity designs require the deployment of various additional services, such as intrusion prevention, QoS, stateful firewalls, unified communications, and WAN acceleration. To support these services, separate appliances and devices can be deployed. Integrating these services into the WAN CPE device often leads to reduced operational complexity.

As with most design decisions, the choice of the appropriate CPE for a WAN service is a balancing act between performance, feature support, and cost. Also, always consider the projected future growth in traffic and feature support to ensure that the CPE device will not need to be prematurely decommissioned as the WAN evolves.

Cisco PfR Overview

Performance Routing (PfR), which was formerly known as Optimized Edge Routing (OER), is the general term used for features that take into account diverse WAN characteristics. It makes an informed-decision about the best path to reach a network or application, given multiple choices that may have varied performance characteristics. Unlike traditional routing protocols, PfR takes into account the network performance, delay, loss, and link loading. Traditional routing protocols typically rely on cost (total bandwidth) once reachability, in that a neighbor relationship exists between routers, exists across a WAN link

WAN access links are the largest end-to-end bottleneck in wide-area connectivity. Normally, the best outbound path is decided based on static routing or dynamic routing policies that evaluate a static set of criteria, such as bandwidth, delay, cost, or other static criteria. For example, Border Gateway Protocol (BGP) decides the outbound path that is based on the shortest autonomous system path, together with all the other BGP decision criteria.

Cisco PfR allows the path selection to be based on policies that can include measured reachability, delay, loss, jitter, synthetic mean opinion score (MOS) (for voice), load, throughput, and monetary cost.

Cisco PfR provides automatic outbound route optimization and load distribution for multiple connections by selecting the optimal exit point. Cisco PfR is an integrated Cisco IOS Software solution that allows users to monitor IP traffic flows and then define policies and rules that are based on prefix performance, link load distribution, link cost, and traffic type. Cisco PfR selects the best exit path. If BGP is used as the routing protocol, Cisco PfR can also monitor inbound traffic and influence routing or path selection for inbound traffic from outside the site by prepending BGP autonomous system numbers (ASN) to its outbound prefix advertisements.

To implement Cisco PfR, a site configures one or more border routers that communicate with a router that is chosen and configured as the master controller. The master controller makes decisions as to which outbound path to use, based on the configured policy. Because Cisco PfR influences the outbound routing decision, it can be used in any type of dual-homed site. This includes dual-homed branch sites that connect to the WAN and the Internet, data centers that have dual-homed connections to different ISPs, and remote users with dual Internet uplinks. When Cisco PfR is applied on both sides of a dual-homed WAN connection, it can be used to influence both outbound and inbound traffic between the sites. Figure 4-15 shows an example PfR deployment in the enterprise.

Cisco PfR Operations

Cisco PfR follows a cycle of learn, measure, apply policy, optimize, and verify.

Learn Phase

In the learn phase, the configuration identifies prefixes and traffic classes of interest.

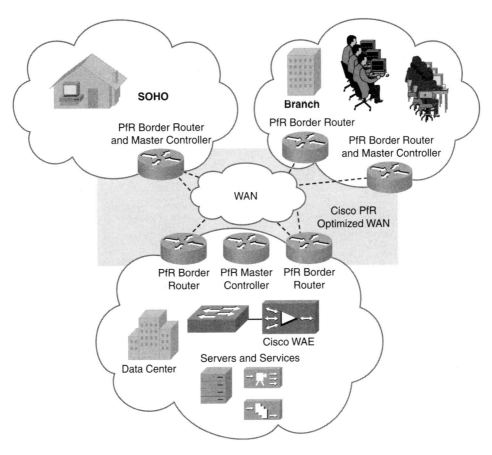

Figure 4-15 *Example of PfR in the Enterprise*

Measure Phase

In the measure phase, passive or active measurement provides calculations using each border router. Passive monitoring amounts to looking up NetFlow data in memory. The router observes what happens when packets are sent, and it records the results as internal NetFlow statistics. If no packets are being sent, there is no new data for the system. NetFlow data captures delay and throughput statistics. The delay measurements are based on TCP round-trip time (RTT) for the initial synchronization (SYN) to the following acknowledgment (ACK). Cisco PfR data also records packet loss (comparing highest TCP sequence number and received packets with lower sequence number) and unreachables (SYN with no received ACK) for passive measurements. Cisco PfR passive monitoring is based on TCP traffic flows for IP traffic. Passive monitoring of non-TCP sessions is not supported, because User Datagram Protocol (UDP) does not readily provide delay estimates, response counts, and other traffic data.

Active probing defaults to automatically configured IP SLA probes that are based on Internet Control Message Protocol (ICMP) echo and echo-reply.

Cisco PfR active probing can be configured to use additional IP SLA measurements other than the standard ICMP-based probes. This allows Cisco PfR to respond to delay, jitter, MOS, and packet loss in the network. Currently, Cisco PfR can use ICMP, TCP connections, or UDP echo for active probing. Note that the target for the last two must be capable of responding. If the target is a router, it must be configured with the **ip sla responder** command.

Cisco PfR can also use traceroute probes. These probes collect delay, loss, and reachability information for each hop from source address to probe target prefix. You can configure these probes to run in three ways: continuous, policy based (running only when the prefix is out of policy), or on demand.

Note   Repeated ping probing might trigger an intrusion detection system (IDS) or intrusion prevention system (IPS) intervention on the remote site.

Apply Policy Phase

In the apply policy phase, the master controller periodically gathers data from the border routers and applies the configured policy to determine the best route.

Optimize Phase

In the optimize phase, controls are applied either by adding a static or BGP route, or if traffic classes are to be controlled, through policy-based routing (PBR). Cisco PfR routing control is exerted by injecting routes into the border routers. The master controller is a pure control plane component. It does not need to be in the data path and does not need to participate in any routing protocol. The route injection is performed through Cisco PfR command messages from the master controller to the border routers, and not by inserting routes on the master controller. Currently, Cisco PfR can influence outbound routing in three ways:

■   Setting the BGP local preference for a specific prefix

■   Creating a temporary static route for a specific prefix

■   Creating a dynamic PBR policy

This routing change at the border routers influences the other routers in the internal network through one of the following methods:

■   Internal BGP peering

■   BGP or static route redistribution into the IGP

If the border routers are close to one another (namely, they have a high-speed LAN connection between them), you can use default routes to get packets to the border, and then have Cisco PfR shift some traffic for selected prefixes between the two exit routers. Cisco PfR is mainly concerned about preferring one border router to the other. The IGP routing comes into play only if you have to rely on your IGP to route traffic between the border routers or if you want optimal routing directly to the "correct" border router.

The injected BGP or static route is not advertised to external peers and has no routing impact outside the local site.

You can configure BGP routing to attempt to influence ingress routing. You do so by prepending additional autonomous system hops to the prefixes that are advertised to the upstream ISPs. Alternatively, a BGP community can be attached that signals a specific routing policy to the ISP. These methods may also cause an asynchronous traversal of traffic.

Verify Phase

In the verify phase, feedback from NetFlow confirms that traffic is using the selected exit path.

Cisco PfR Solution Topologies

Cisco PfR can prove useful in several design topologies.

The first example is a small office, home office (SOHO) or broadband site has two exit paths, such as a cable and a digital subscriber line (DSL) connection. The single edge router is configured to be both master controller and border router. The router selects between the two exit paths using Cisco PfR. This topology reflects a smaller site, which has redundant Internet access through two different ISPs, mainly for outbound traffic.

A second example is a remote office with two exit routers to two Internet or WAN service providers. This office uses Cisco PfR to select the best path to headquarters. One of the border routers is also the master controller. This topology might be a branch site that connects to the central site via an MPLS-based VPN but also has an IPsec-based VPN connection back to the central office across the Internet.

A third example is a larger office that has a master controller that is separate from the two border routers. Cisco PfR helps select the better outbound path through the two ISPs (ISP 1 or ISP 2). A typical scenario is an enterprise data center or headquarters site that hosts business-critical applications and uses two different ISPs for high availability.

Cisco PfR is generally used to influence outbound traffic path selection. In the third example, BGP autonomous system path prepending can attempt to influence inbound traffic.

Cisco PfR Design and Deployment Considerations

When integrating Cisco PfR in a WAN design, consider the following:

- Decide which routers will be border routers and master controllers. The routers at the egress point of each site should be configured as border routers. Each site needs its own master controller that controls the border routers for that site. The master controller is a control plane function and can be combined on a border router or run on a separate router. The main consideration is scale. On the branch site, the master controller function can easily be implemented on one of the border routers, because there will be only a few active prefixes to manage. On large sites, such as main WAN hubs or data center sites, it is better to implement a separate router as the master controller that can be scaled to support the projected number of prefixes.

■ Decide which traffic classes you want to apply your policies. By default, traffic is classified based on prefix. In addition, classes can be manually defined based on application.

■ Decide which performance metrics you want to measure. By default, delay, loss, and reachability are passively monitored for TCP traffic, and bandwidth is measured for all traffic through use of Cisco NetFlow technology. If additional measurements such as jitter, delay, or MOS scores are required for UDP, ICMP, and TCP traffic, you can enable active probing.

■ Decide which of the measurements are considered to be most important and what the critical thresholds are for each of these measurements.

■ Evaluate the routing protocols and policies that are used in the WAN, and decide how Cisco PfR will influence the routing decisions. Depending on the routing protocols that are used on the network, installation of static routes, manipulation of BGP attributes, or installation of PBR route maps can be used.

Note For specific deployment scenarios and configuration examples, see the Performance Routing Design Guide at *http://www.cisco.com/en/US/docs/solutions/ Enterprise/WAN_and_MAN/Transport_diversity/Transport_Diversity_PfR.html.*

Summary

WAN service design manages business risk and supports customer requirements. When designing a WAN, all the "trade-offs" need to be weighed to meet business requirements. Options such as WAAS, network security, and type of service should be carefully weighed.

SLAs define WAN service commitments by the service provider and should be monitored for compliance. *Doveryai, no proveryai.* (Russian: Trust, but verify.)

Application performance across the WAN is an important consideration in selecting a WAN service. Understanding the traffic patterns of an application and its service needs is paramount.

Cisco PfR can dynamically reroute traffic based on changing conditions on the WAN to optimize application performance.

References

For additional information, refer to these resources:

Cisco Systems, Inc. *Cisco CWDM Solution* at www.cisco.com/en/US/prod/collateral/modules/ps5455/ps6575/prod_brochure0900a ecd803a53ea.pdf

Cisco Systems, Inc. *Cisco CWDM GBIC and SFP Solution Data Sheet* at www.cisco.com/en/US/prod/collateral/modules/ps5455/ps6575/product_data_sheet0 9186a00801a557c_ps708_Products_Data_Sheet.html

Cisco Systems, Inc. *Cisco ONS 15454 DWDM Engineering and Planning Guide, Release 7.x*, Chapter 1, "DWDM Overview," at www.cisco.com/en/US/docs/optical/15000r7_0/dwdm/planning/guide/d7ovw.html

Cisco Systems, Inc. *Fundamentals of DWDM Technology* at www.cisco.com/univercd/cc/td/doc/product/mels/cm1500/dwdm/dwdm_ovr.htm

Cisco Systems, Inc. *MPLS Layer 2 VPNs—AToM* at www.cisco.com/en/US/docs/solutions/Enterprise/WAN_and_MAN/ngmaneover.html# wp1058927

Cisco Systems, Inc. *Virtual Private LAN Services (VPLS) Introduction* at www.cisco.com/en/US/products/ps6648/products_ios_protocol_option_home.html

Cisco Systems, Inc. *Ethernet Wide Area Networking, Routers or Switches and Making the Right Choice* at www.cisco.com/en/US/prod/collateral/routers/ps10538/white_paper_c11-564978_ps10537_Products_White_Paper.html

Miercom. *Lab Testing Summary Report Product Category: Integrated Services Router Generation 2* at www.miercom.com/cisco/isrg2/20091028.pdf

Cisco Systems, Inc. *Cisco Services Ready Engine Data Sheet* at www.cisco.com/en/US/prod/collateral/modules/ps10598/data_sheet_c78-553913.html

Cisco Systems, Inc. *Cisco Services Ready Engine Q&A* at www.cisco.com/en/US/prod/collateral/modules/ps10598/qa_c78_553916.html

Cisco Systems. Inc. *Enhancing the WAN Experience with PfR and WAAS* at www.cisco.com/en/US/prod/collateral/iosswrel/ps6537/ps6554/ps6599/ps8787/prod_ white_paper0900aecd806c5077.html

Cisco Systems, Inc. *Cisco Performance Routing* at www.cisco.com/en/US/prod/collateral/iosswrel/ps6537/ps6554/ps6599/ps8787/produ ct_data_sheet0900aecd806c4ee4.html

Cisco Systems, Inc. *Transport Diversity: Performance Routing (PfR)* at www.cisco.com/en/US/docs/solutions/Enterprise/WAN_and_MAN/Transport_diversit y/Transport_Diversity_PfR.html#wp44825

Cisco Systems, Inc. IP SLA at
www.cisco.com/en/US/tech/tk920/tsd_technology_support_sub-protocol_home.html

The Internet Engineering Task Force. RFC 4447: *Pseudowire Setup and Maintenance Using the Label Distribution Protocol (LDP)* at www.rfc-editor.org/rfc/rfc4447.txt

The Internet Engineering Task Force. RFC 4385: *Pseudowire Emulation Edge-to-Edge (PWE3) Control Word for Use over an MPLS PSN* at www.rfc-editor.org/rfc/rfc4385.txt

The Internet Engineering Task Force. RFC 4448: *Encapsulation Methods for Transport of Ethernet over MPLS Networks* at www.rfc-editor.org/rfc/rfc4448.txt

The Internet Engineering Task Force. RFC 4717: *Encapsulation Methods for Transport of Asynchronous Transfer Mode (ATM) over MPLS Networks* at www.rfc-editor.org/rfc/rfc4717.txt

The Internet Engineering Task Force. RFC 4618: *Encapsulation Methods for Transport of PPP/High-Level Data Link Control (HDLC) over MPLS Networks* at www.rfc-editor.org/rfc/rfc4618.txt

The Internet Engineering Task Force. RFC 4619: *Encapsulation Methods for Transport of Frame Relay over Multiprotocol Label Switching (MPLS) Networks* at www.rfc-editor.org/rfc/rfc4619.txt

IEEE 802 LAN/MAN Standards Committee. *IEEE 802.17 Resilient Packet Ring Working Group* at www.ieee802.org/17/

The Internet Engineering Task Force. RFC 4761: *Virtual Private LAN Service (VPLS) Using BGP for Auto-Discovery and Signaling* at www.ietf.org/rfc/rfc4761.txt

The Internet Engineering Task Force. RFC 4762: *Virtual Private LAN Service (VPLS) Using Label Distribution Protocol (LDP) Signaling* at www.ietf.org/rfc/rfc4762.txt

Review Questions

Answer the following questions, and then refer to Appendix A, "Answers to Review Questions," for the answers.

1. What technique does SONET use for framing voice and data onto a single wavelength on fiber?

    a. SHD

    b. SDH

    c. DPT

    d. TDM

    e. RPR

2. Which description best defines CWDM?

    a. A WDM system that is compatible with EDFA optical technology for transmitting up to 16 channels over multiple fiber strands

    b. A technology for transmitting multiple optical signals using less-sophisticated and less-costly transceiver designs than DWDM

    c. An optical technology for transmitting up to 32 channels over multiple fiber strands

    d. A technology for transmitting more closely packed optical signals using more sophisticated transceiver designs than DWDM

3. Which Ethernet-based services are point-to-point services? (Choose three.)

    a. EPL

    b. EPWS

    c. ERS

    d. EWS

    e. EMS

    f. ERMS

4. What definition best describes service multiplexing?

    a. Ability to multiplex services and UNIs on a single customer EVAC

    b. Ability to multiplex services and UNIs on a single customer EVC

    c. Ability to support multiple instances of services or EVACs on a single customer UNI

    d. Ability to support multiple instances of services or EVCs on a single customer UNI

    e. Ability to support multiple instances of services or UNIs on a single customer EVC

5. What are the characteristics of EMS? (Choose three.)

    a. Service multiplexing is supported.

    b. The P-network acts as a virtual switch for the customer.

    c. All customer packets are transmitted to the destination ports transparently.

    d. Oversubscription of the P-network is handled using stat muxing.

    e. Oversubscription of the P-network is handled using time-division multiplexing.

6. What is a PW in MPLS?

    a. A password used for MD5 authentication for the underlying IGP

    b. A physical wire between PE routers

    c. An Ethernet connection from the PE to the CE device

    d. Encapsulation of circuit data or PDUs at the ingress

    e. Carries encapsulated data across the tunnel and acts as a logical wire

7. What is a jitter?

    a. A measure of how much time it takes for a packet to get from one point in the network to another

    b. A measure of outage severity

    c. A measure of packets traveling across a network that fail to reach their destination

    d. A measure of the availability of IP services end-to-end across a network

    e. The variation in delay in the interval between successive packets

8. Why is a business risk assessment needed?

    a. Because the due diligence effort can be so time-consuming

    b. To define the value of the data

    c. As a basis for design decisions

    d. To support due diligence questioning

    e. To obtain more than a shallow level of service provider information

9. Which factors should you consider when selecting a CPE device for a WAN service? (Choose three.)

    a. Physical interface that is used by the WAN service

    b. Performance limits of the CPE device

    c. SLAs that are offered by the WAN provider

    d. Underlying optical technology that is used in the provider core

    e. Required additional services, such as VPN and QoS

    f. SLA reporting tools that are provided by the WAN service provider

10. Which of the following are the phases in Cisco PfR operations? (Choose three.)
(Source: *Advanced WAN Service Implementations*)

   a. Plan

   b. Optimize

   c. Measure

   d. Learn

   e. Prepare

   f. Implement

   g. Synchronize

Chapter 5

Enterprise Data Center Design

After completing this chapter, you will be able to

- Discuss design considerations for the core and aggregation layer infrastructures of the enterprise data center

- Discuss design considerations for the access layer of the enterprise data center

- Describe the access layer technologies and designs to support scaling the data center architecture

- Discuss network and server virtualization design

- Discuss designs and technologies to support scaling the data center and increasing availability

The data center is home to the computational power, storage, and applications necessary to support an enterprise business. The data center infrastructure is central to the IT architecture, from which all content is sourced or passes through. Proper planning of the data center infrastructure design is critical; and performance, resiliency, and scalability need to be carefully considered.

The data center network design is based on a proven layered approach, which has been tested and improved during the past several years in some of the largest data center implementations in the world. The layered approach is the basic foundation of the data center design that seeks to improve scalability, performance, flexibility, resiliency, and maintenance. Figure 5-1 shows the basic layered design.

Virtualization technologies are becoming pervasive. Virtualization allows optimization of the data center provides many services. It allows resources on demand, and optimization of computer and network resources. It also serves to enable the implementation of architectures such as cloud computing and borderless networks, Virtualization also lowers operating expenses (OPEX) by optimizing power; heating, ventilation, air conditioning (HVAC); and data center floor space.

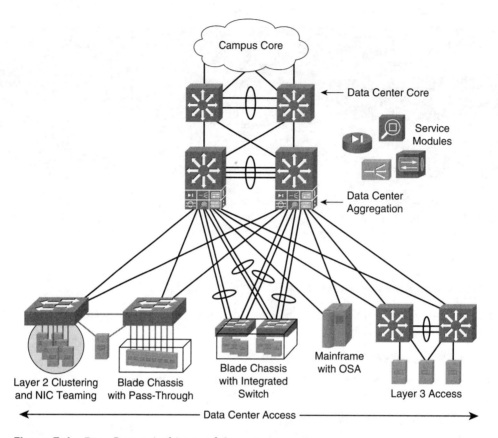

Figure 5-1   *Data Center Architectural Overview*

The chapter discusses the three layers of the data center architecture. It also covers considerations for using end-of-row (EOR) access compared to top-of-rack (TOR) access switch designs. Options for scaling the data center and for high availability are also reviewed.

Designing the Core and Aggregation Layers

This chapter covers the core and aggregation layer of data center architecture. Data center virtualization is also reviewed.

The data center architecture is based on a three-layer approach. The core layer provides a high-speed Layer 3 fabric for packet switching. The aggregation layer extends spanning-tree or Layer 3 routing protocols into the access layer, depending on which access layer model is used. The access later provides physical connectivity for the servers. This chapter examines the design considerations for the core and aggregation layers.

Data Center Architecture Overview

As mentioned in the introduction, the data center network design is based on a layered approach to improve scalability, performance, flexibility, resiliency, and maintenance. There are three layers of the data center design:

- **Core layer:** Provides the high-speed packet-switching backplane for all flows going in and out of the data center

- **Aggregation layer:** Provides service module integration, Layer 2 domain definitions, spanning-tree processing, default gateway redundancy, and other critical data center functions

- **Access layer:** Physically connects servers to the network

The multitier data center model is dominated by multitier HTTP-based applications that support web, application, and database tiers of servers. The access layer network infrastructure can support both Layer 2 and Layer 3 topologies and Layer 2 adjacency requirements that fulfill the various server broadcast domain or administrative requirements. The server components can consist of single and dual-attached one-rack unit (1RU) servers, blade servers with integral switches, blade servers with pass-through cabling, clustered servers, and mainframes with a mix of oversubscription requirements.

Multiple aggregation modules in the aggregation layer support scaling of connectivity from the access layer. The aggregation layer supports integrated service modules that provide services such as security, load balancing, content switching, firewall, Secure Sockets Layer (SSL) offload, intrusion detection, and network analysis.

Note An enterprise data center network in most instances has a three-tier design with an Ethernet access layer and an aggregation layer connected to the campus core layer. Small and medium data centers have a two-tier design, with the Layer 3 access layer connected to the backbone database core (collapsed core and aggregation layers). Three-tier designs allow for greater scalability in the number of access ports, but a two-tier design is ideal for small server farms.

Benefits of the Three-Layer Model

There are several benefits to the three-tier model for data center design. The separation of the data center architecture into access, aggregation, and core layers permits flexibility in the following areas:

- **Layer 2 domain sizing:** When a requirement exists to extend a VLAN from one switch to another, the domain size is determined at the aggregation layer. If the access layer is absent, the Layer 2 domain must be configured across the core for extension to occur. Extending Layer 2 through a core causes path blocking by the spanning tree, which might cause uncontrollable broadcast issues related to extending Layer 2 domains and should therefore be avoided.

- **Service module support:** A solution that uses the aggregation layer with the access layer and enables services to be shared across the entire access layer of switches. This lowers the total cost of ownership (TCO) and lowers complexity by reducing the number of components to configure and manage.

- **Support for a mix of access layer models:** The three-layer approach permits a mix of both Layer 2 and Layer 3 access models with 1RU and modular platforms, permitting a more flexible solution and allowing application environments to be optimally positioned.

- **Support for network interface card (NIC) teaming and high-availability clustering:** Supporting NIC teaming with switch fault tolerance and high-availability clustering requires Layer 2 adjacency between NICs, resulting in Layer 2 VLAN extension between switches. VLAN extension can also require extending the Layer 2 domain through the core, which is not recommended.

The three layers of hierarchy keep VLANs at or below the aggregation layer.

Note   The extension of VLANs across the data center core and other layers is not best practice. However, customer requirements such as clustering or virtual machine mobility across multiple data centers may require VLANs to be extended across the data center core. These cases significantly change the data center core design and introduce the risk of failures in one area of the network affecting the entire network. Therefore, network designers should investigate technologies such as Cisco Overlay Transport Virtualization (OTV) to overcome the drawbacks and mitigate the risks of stretching Layer 2 domains across a data center core.

The Services Layer

Network services such as load balancing and security services can be integrated in the aggregation layer of the data center or designed as a separate layer, as shown in Figure 5-2.

Load balancing, firewall services, and other network services are commonly integrated in the aggregation layer of the data center by using service modules that are inserted in the aggregation switches, as shown on the left in Figure 5-2.

An advantage of this approach is that it allows for a compact design, saving on power, rack space, and cabling. However, the service modules use slots in the aggregation layer switches that could otherwise be used to support additional access switches. When you run out of ports on the aggregation switches, you must add a new pair of aggregation switches, including additional service modules. Using this approach effectively links service scaling and aggregation layer scaling.

An alternative approach is to design a separate services layer that connects to the aggregation layer switches. By placing the service modules in separate Cisco Catalyst 6500 series service chassis, ports on the aggregation layer switches are freed up to connect additional access layer switches. If additional firewall, load balancing, or other service capacity is required, service modules can be added to existing or new service chassis. As a result, there is less dependency between aggregation layer scaling and scaling of network services.

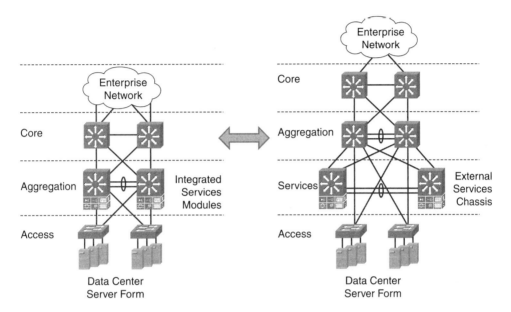

Figure 5-2   *Integrated Service Modules Versus Service Chassis*

Another design restriction that is removed when the services are moved to a separate layer is the use of Catalyst 6500 series switches for the aggregation layer. Currently, the Catalyst 6500 series switches are the only switches that support service modules. Therefore, if Nexus 7000 series switches are required in the aggregation layer to support a higher port density for 10 Gigabit Ethernet, at present, you cannot integrate the service modules in the aggregation layer switches. However, service modules may be introduced into the Nexus line in the future. At present, the services must be moved into separate Catalyst 6500 series chassis or implemented by using dedicated appliances for each of the services.

Using Dedicated Service Appliances

As mentioned, a services layer can be implemented by placing service modules in separate Catalyst 6500 series service chassis. Figure 5-3 displays service chassis implementation. Alternatively, network services can be implemented on external, standalone devices that are commonly referred to as appliances. Each of these methods has specific advantages and disadvantages.

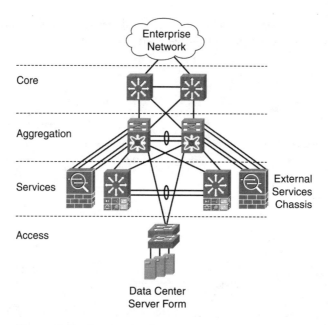

Figure 5-3   *Service Appliances*

When choosing between a design that is based on appliances or service chassis, you should consider the following design aspects:

■ **Power and rack space:** Combining several service modules in a single Catalyst 6500 series chassis may require less rack space and reduce the power requirements compared with using several external appliances.

■ **Performance and throughput:** The performance of some of the individual appliances, such as the Cisco ASA 5580 adaptive security appliance, can be higher than the corresponding service module, such as the Catalyst 6500 Series Firewall Services Module (FWSM).

■ **Fault tolerance:** In most designs, appliances are connected to only one of the aggregation layer switches. This configuration means that when that aggregation switch fails, any directly attached appliances are also lost. A service chassis can be dual-homed to two different aggregation switches. In this case, the loss of an aggregation layer switch does not cause the associated service chassis to be lost. However, when a service chassis fails, all the service modules that reside within that chassis are lost. The availability of the services depends on the exact combination of accessible features that are used in the different service modules, appliances, and switches.

■ **Required services:** Some services are supported on an appliance but not on the comparable service module. For example, a Cisco ASA can be used to serve as a firewall and terminate virtual private network (VPN) connections, and the Catalyst 6500 series FWSM provides firewall services but cannot be used to terminate VPN connections. However, there is now an ASA service module that no longer has this limitation.

The choice between using service chassis and appliances is not exclusive. It is possible to use appliances for some services while implementing a service chassis for others.

Data Center Core Layer Design

The data center core layer provides a fabric for high-speed packet switching between multiple aggregation modules. A data center core is not necessarily required but is recommended when multiple aggregation modules are used for scalability. Even when a small number of aggregation modules are used, it might be appropriate to use the campus core for connecting the data center fabric. Figure 5-4 illustrates how the data center interconnects with the campus core.

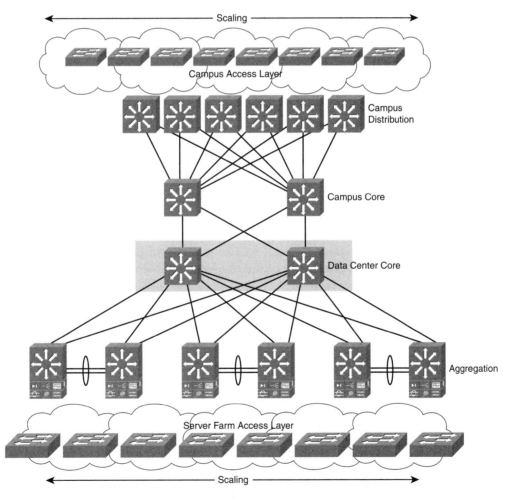

Figure 5-4   *Data Center Core Layer Overview*

When determining whether to implement a data center core, consider the following:

- **10 Gigabit Ethernet port density:** Depending on the switch type, a single pair of campus core switches might not support the number of 10 Gigabit Ethernet ports required to connect the campus distribution layer and the data center aggregation layer switches.

- **Administrative domains and policies:** Separate cores help isolate campus distribution layers and data center aggregation layers in terms of administration and policies, such as quality of service (QoS), access lists, troubleshooting, and maintenance.

- **Future growth:** The impact of implementing a separate data center core layer at a later date might make it worthwhile to implement it during the initial implementation stage.

The data center core layer is distinct from the campus core layer, with a different purpose and responsibilities. The data center core layer serves as the gateway to the campus core, where other campus modules connect, including the enterprise edge and WAN modules. Links connecting the data center core are terminated at Layer 3 and use a distributed, low-latency forwarding architecture and 10 Gigabit Ethernet interfaces for a high level of throughput and performance.

Layer 3 Characteristics for the Data Center Core

When designing the enterprise data center, consider where in the infrastructure to place the Layer 2 to Layer 3 boundary, as shown in Figure 5-5.

The recommended practice is for the core infrastructure to be implemented at Layer 3, and for the Layer 2 to Layer 3 boundary to be implemented either within or below the aggregation layer modules. Layer 3 links allow the core to achieve bandwidth scalability and quick convergence, and to avoid path blocking or the risk of uncontrollable broadcast issues related to extending Layer 2 domains. Layer 2 should be avoided in the core because a Spanning Tree Protocol (STP) loop could cause a full data center outage.

The traffic flow in the core consists primarily of sessions traveling between the campus core and the aggregation modules. The core aggregates the aggregation module traffic flows onto optimal paths to the campus core. Server-to-server traffic typically remains within an aggregation module, but backup and replication traffic can travel between aggregation modules by way of the core.

The core layer should run an interior routing protocol such as Open Shortest Path First (OSPF) or Enhanced Interior Gateway Routing Protocol (EIGRP), and load balance traffic between the campus core and core aggregation layers using Cisco Express Forwarding (CEF)-based hashing algorithms.

From a campus core perspective, at least two equal-cost routes to the server subnets permit the core to load balance flows to each aggregation switch in a particular module. By default, load balancing is performed using CEF-based load balancing on Layer 3 source and destination IP address hashing. An option is to use Layer 3 IP plus Layer 4 port-based CEF load-balance hashing algorithms. This usually improves load distribution because it presents more unique values to the hashing algorithm by leveraging the automatic source port randomization in the client TCP stack.

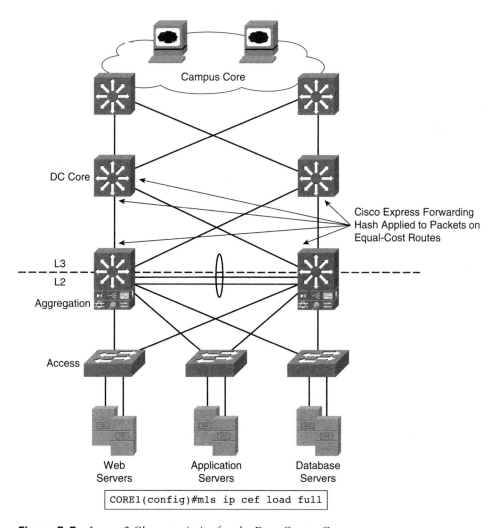

Figure 5-5 *Layer 3 Characteristics for the Data Center Core*

Note   To configure the CEF load balancing, use the **mls ip cef load-sharing** command in global configuration mode. To return to the default settings, use the **no** form of this command:

mls ip cef load-sharing [**full**] [*exclude-port* {*destination* | *source*}] [**simple**]

no mls ip cef load-sharing

OSPF Routing Protocol Design Recommendations

The OSPF routing protocol design should be tuned for the data center core layer, as shown in Figure 5-6.

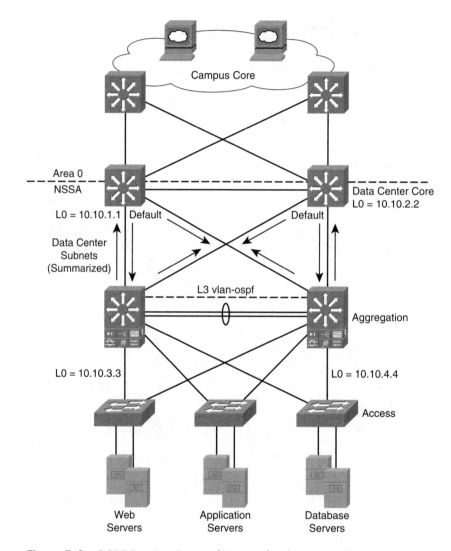

Figure 5-6   *OSPF Routing Protocol Design for the Data Center Core*

The OSPF routing protocol suggested configuration is as follows:

■   Use a not-so-stubby area (NSSA) from the core down. It limits link-state advertisement (LSA) propagation but permits route redistribution. You can advertise the default route into the aggregation layer and summarize the routes coming out of the NSSA.

- Use the **auto-cost reference-bandwidth 10000** command to set the bandwidth to a 10 Gigabit Ethernet value and allow OSPF to differentiate the cost on higher-speed links, such as 10 Gigabit Ethernet trunk links. This is needed because the OSPF default reference bandwidth is 100 Mbps.

The default reference bandwidth of 100 Mbps used in Cisco IOS is a legacy from prevalent network speeds at the time the OSFP Version 2 protocol was originally developed. This reference bandwidth results in 10-Gbps, 1-Gbps, and 100-Mbps interfaces to have the same cost. A common best practice in Cisco IOS configuration is to raise the reference bandwidth to a more reasonable number in the context of currently available link speeds. By raising the reference bandwidth to a larger number, such as 10,000 Mbps, it is the equivalent of 10 Gb. Therefore, a 10 Gigabit Ethernet interface has a cost of 1, and a 1-Gb interface has a cost of 10.

Cisco NX-OS automatically implements by default a more reasonable reference bandwidth of 40000 Mbps. This value provides greater flexibility with the development of 40-Gbps and 100-Gbps interfaces on the horizon in the Nexus 7000 platform. In a data center network with both NX-OS and IOS devices, the reference bandwidth setting should be adjusted so that all devices within an OSPF area use a consistent value. Configuration of reference bandwidth for OSPF in Cisco NX-OS is identical to Cisco IOS; it is done with the use of the **auto-cost reference-bandwidth** command.

EIGRP Routing Protocol Design Recommendations

The EIGRP routing protocol design should be tuned for the data center core layer, as shown in Figure 5-7.

Here are some recommendations on EIGRP design for the data center core layer:

- Advertise a default summary route into the data center access layer with the **ip summary-address eigrp** interface command on the aggregation layer.

- If other default routes exist in the network, such as from the Internet edge, you might need to filter them using distribute lists.

- Summarize the data center access layer subnets with the **ip summary-address eigrp** interface command from the aggregation layer.

- Use the **passive-interface default** command, and advertise only on the links that need to participate in the routing process using the **no passive-interface** *interface* command.

Aggregation Layer Design

The aggregation layer design is critical to the stability and scalability of the overall data center architecture. All traffic in and out of the data center not only passes through the aggregation layer but also relies on the services, path selection, and redundant architecture built in to the aggregation layer design.

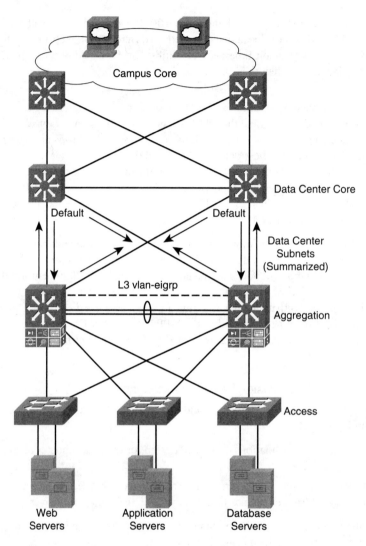

Figure 5-7 *EIGRP Routing Protocol Design for the Data Center Core*

The following aggregation layer design topics are discussed in this section:

■ Scaling the aggregation layer

■ STP design

■ Integrated services support

■ Service module placement considerations

■ STP, Hot Standby Router Protocol (HSRP), and service context alignment

- Active/standby service design
- Active/active service design
- Establishing path preference
- Using virtual routing and forwarding (VRF) instances in the data center

Scaling the Aggregation Layer

Multiple aggregation modules allow the data center architecture to scale as additional servers are added, as shown in Figure 5-8.

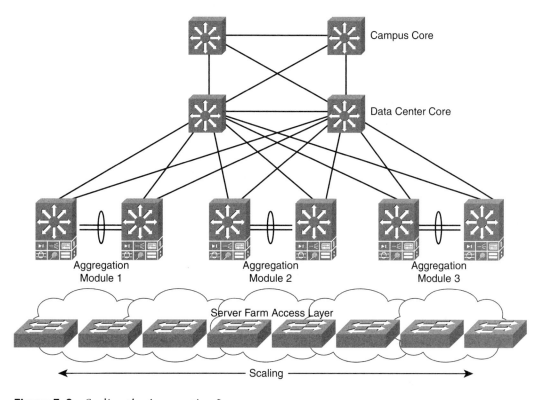

Figure 5-8 *Scaling the Aggregation Layer*

The aggregation layer in the enterprise data center model consists of pairs of interconnected aggregation switches referred to as modules. Multiple aggregation modules are used to scale the aggregation layer:

- **Spanning-tree scaling:** Layer 2 diameters are being pushed to scale further than ever before as Layer 2 domains continue to increase in size because of clustering, NIC teaming, and other application requirements. By using multiple aggregation modules, you can limit Layer 2 domain size and can limit failure exposure to a smaller domain.

- **Access layer density scaling:** As the access layer demands increase in terms of bandwidth and server interface requirements, the uplinks to the aggregation layer are migrating to 10 Gigabit Ethernet. This trend can create a density challenge in existing or new aggregation layer designs. Although the long-term answer might be higher-density 10 Gigabit Ethernet line cards and larger switch fabrics, a current proven solution is the use of multiple aggregation modules. Currently, the maximum number of 10 Gigabit Ethernet ports that can be placed in the aggregation layer switch is 64 when using the WS-X6708-10G-3C line card in the Cisco Catalyst 6509 switch. Using a data center core layer and implementing multiple aggregation modules provides a higher level of 10 Gigabit Ethernet density.

- **HSRP scaling:** The aggregation layer provides a primary and secondary router "default gateway" address for all servers on a Layer 2 access topology across the entire access layer. HSRP is the most widely used protocol for default gateway redundancy in the enterprise data center. Based on test results on the CPU processing requirements of HSRP, Cisco recommends the maximum number of HSRP instances in an aggregation module to be limited to approximately 500, with recommended timers of a 1-second hello and a 3-second hold time.

- **Application services scaling:** The aggregation layer supports applications on service modules across multiple access layer switches, scaling the ability of the network to provide application services. Some examples of supported applications are Server Load Balancing (SLB) and firewalls. The service modules can be deployed with virtual contexts, with each context behaving like an independent device with its own policies, interfaces, domains, and server.

STP Design

If you have Layer 2 in the aggregation layer, the STP design should be your first concern. The aggregation layer carries the largest burden with Layer 2 scaling because the aggregation layer establishes the Layer 2 domain size and manages it with a spanning tree protocol such as Rapid Per-VLAN Spanning Tree (RPVST+) or Multiple Spanning Tree (MST) This is illustrated in Figure 5-9.

Note   This book follows the Cisco documentation in referring to RPVST+ as RSTP because RPVST+ is the Cisco implementation of RSTP.

The aggregation modules permit the spanning-tree domain to be distributed. For the data center environment, RSTP is recommended over MST for these reasons:

- It has fast convergence characteristics. It already incorporates the Cisco proprietary enhancements of Per-VLAN Spanning Tree Plus (PVST+), including UplinkFast and BackboneFast. RSTP and MST are both valid design choices for the data center environment.

- MST and RSTP use the same underlying algorithms for convergence; therefore, they both have very fast convergence characteristics.

- Access layer uplink failures are detected quickly, typically within 300 ms to 2 seconds depending on the number of VLANs.

- RSTP and MST can be combined with root guard, BPDU guard (bridge protocol data unit), loop guard, bridge assurance and UniDirectional Link Detection (UDLD) to achieve a stable STP environment.

- MST requires careful and consistent configuration to avoid "regionalization" and reversion to a single global spanning tree. Most networks lose such consistency within one to two years.

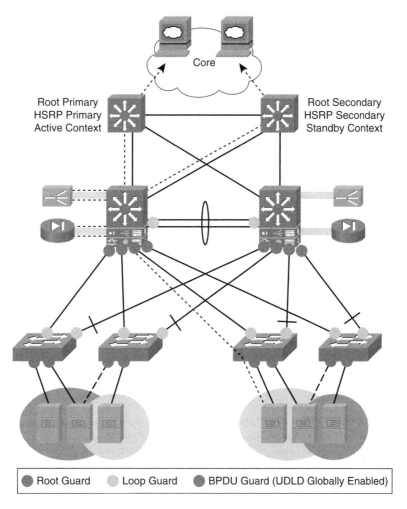

Figure 5-9   *STP Design*

Note   Bridge assurance is preferred over loop guard. If an access switch does not support bridge assurance, loop guard can be implemented between that access switch and the aggregation switch. Do not enable both bridge assurance and loop guard at the same time.

Understanding Bridge Assurance

Bridge assurance can be used as protection against certain problems that can cause bridging loops in the network. Specifically, bridge assurance is used to protect against a unidirectional link failure or other software failure and a device that continues to forward data traffic when it is no longer running the spanning-tree algorithm.

Bridge assurance is enabled by default and can only be disabled globally. It is enabled only on spanning-tree network ports that are point-to-point links. Finally, both ends of the link must have bridge assurance enabled. If the device on one side of the link has bridge assurance enabled and the device on the other side either does not support bridge assurance or does not have this feature enabled, the connecting port is blocked.

With bridge assurance enabled, BPDUs are sent out on all operational network ports, including alternate and backup ports, for each hello time period. If the port does not receive a BPDU for a specified period, the port moves into an inconsistent state (blocking) and is not used in the root port calculation. When that port receives a BPDU, it resumes the normal spanning-tree transitions.

Note   Bridge assurance is supported only by RPVST+ and MST and requires IOS 12.2(33)SXI and later releases. Bridge assurance is also available in NX-OS.

When UDLD is enabled globally, it is activated by default only on fiber ports. You must manually enable it on copper ports.

When choosing between RSTP and MST, consider the following design aspects:

- RSTP is easier to configure, deploy, and maintain.

- MST is an IEEE standard.

- MST is more resource efficient. In particular, the number of BPDUs that are transmitted by MST does not depend on the number of VLANs, as with RSTP.

- MST does not interact seamlessly with service appliances and service modules in transparent mode. Appliances or service modules that are running in Transparent mode bridge VLANs together. When using RSTP, the BPDUs can be bridged, and as a result the spanning trees for these two VLANs are merged. Bridging BPDUs through the appliance prevents bridging loops in case of an active/active misconfiguration on the appliances. MST does not allow BPDUs to be bridged through the appliance. Therefore, Cisco currently recommends the use of RSTP if appliances or services modules are deployed in Transparent mode.

Note   Do not mix MST and RSTP in the same Layer 2 domain. The interaction between MST and RSTP is suboptimal in terms of convergence time and resource utilization. Whether using MST or RSTP, it is recommended to use a consistent spanning-tree mode across the entire bridged domain.

Integrated Service Modules

Integrated service modules in the aggregation layer provide services such as content switching, firewall, SSL offload, intrusion detection, and network analysis. Layer 4 through Layer 7 services such as server load balancing, firewall, and SSL offload can be integrated in modules in the Cisco Catalyst 6500 series switches.

For redundancy, the integrated services may be deployed in one of two scenarios:

■ Active/standby pairs, where one appliance is active and the other appliance is in standby mode. This is the traditional deployment model for the Cisco Content Switching Module (CSM) and the older Cisco Catalyst 6500 series FWSM Version 2.x.

■ Active/active pairs, where both appliances are active and providing services. This newer deployment model can support the Cisco Application Control Engine (ACE) and Catalyst series FWSM Version 3.1.

Integrated service modules or blades can provide flexibility and economies of scale by optimizing rack space, cabling, and management. The integrated services supported influence many aspects of the overall design.

Service Module Placement Consideration

You might need to consider the underlying fabric when placing service modules in the Catalyst 6500 series switches. Figure 5-10 has details on service modules and placement configuration.

The Cisco Catalyst 6500 series Supervisor Engine 720 integrated switch fabric provides either one or two fabric channel connections per slot based on the switch chassis configuration. In the three-, four-, and nine-slot configurations, each slot has two fabric channel connections. Single-channel fabric-attached modules include the Secure Sockets Layer Module (SSSLM), the Network Analysis Module (NAM), and the Intrusion Detection System Module (IDSM). Dual-channel fabric-attached modules include the 6700 series line cards.

Although the Cisco Catalyst 6513 switch has a 13-slot configuration, 8 of the slots provide only a single fabric channel connection. Any module that requires two fabric channel connections, such as the Cisco 6748 line card, are not supported in the single fabric channel connection slots.

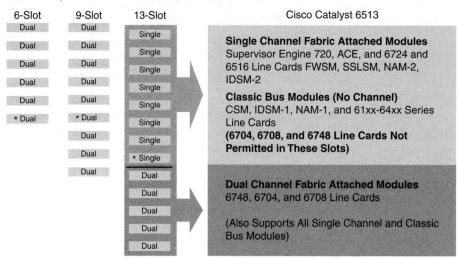

* Primary Catalyst 6500 Series Supervisor Engine 720 Placement

Figure 5-10   *Service Module Placement Consideration*

Note   The current integrated service modules require only a single fabric channel connection.

Based on the chassis, the Catalyst 6513 switch can support more single fabric channel integrated service modules, whereas the Catalyst 6509 switch can support more dual fabric channel Gigabit and 10 Gigabit Ethernet ports. Therefore, the 6509-E is the choice for higher speed and capacity.

Service Modules and the Services Layer

Data center services design consists of several major design choices around the physical and logical design. Each of these topics is explored.

There is no one single best design to implement network services in the data center. Many different choices can be made. Each choice affects the behavior of the total solution. The best choice for a particular data center deployment depends on the specific requirements of the applications in use. Aspects to consider when designing data center services include the following:

■   Determining the default gateway for the servers.

■   Service modules can be integrated in the aggregation layer switches or implemented as a separate services layer. This choice strongly depends on the other requirements of the aggregation layer switches. If the aggregation layer switches support service modules and have sufficient empty slots to insert the service modules in the aggregations switches, this is an efficient solution. If the aggregation switch platform does not support service modules or needs all slots to support access and core connection requirements, a separate services layer is more appropriate.

■   Service modules are efficient with regard to rack space, power, and cabling. However, in some cases, dedicated appliances may offer higher throughput or features that are unavailable on a service module.

These factors are most important in determining the physical design of the data center services module. After deciding on a physical design, there are still some choices to be made that affect the logical design:

■   High availability for service modules and appliances can be achieved by using an active/standby or an active/active design. In the active/standby design, all traffic flows through a single service chassis or chain of appliances. A second service chassis or appliance chain is provisioned and kept in a standby state, to take over only if components in the primary service chain fail. The active/active design leverages the fact that a physical service module or appliance can be divided into virtual contexts, such as firewall contexts on a Catalyst 6500 series FWSM or load-balancer contexts on the Cisco ACE Module.

Contexts are still provisioned as redundant pairs, where one of the two is active and the other is standby. However, by distributing the active contexts for each context pair over the physical pair of service modules or appliances, the hardware resources of both devices are actively used to forward data.

The active/standby model is simpler to deploy and more predictable in failure conditions, because the aggregate load can never exceed the capacity of a single service chain. The active/active model allows all available hardware resources to be used. However, the active/active model is more complex. Also, it is important to keep different active contexts that are combined into a service chain in the same physical service chassis or chain of appliances. If a single service chain consists of active contexts that are spread across multiple service chassis, it can result in unnecessary additional load on the link between the aggregation switches or the links between the aggregation and services layer.

■   Service modules, appliances, or device contexts can often be configured in two different modes: Routed mode and Transparent mode (sometimes also called Bridged mode). In Routed mode, the device or context acts as a router, and the different interfaces on the device or context belong to different VLANs. One of the advantages of routed mode is that it offers better separation between Layer 2 domains. However, routing protocols or static routing must be enabled to forward traffic through the device.

In Transparent mode, the device or context acts as a "bump in the wire." It passes traffic between VLANs transparently, and no control plane interaction occurs with other network components. It does not participate in STP or routing protocols. This lack of interaction makes Transparent mode easier to deploy and configure because it does not affect the logical topology that is implemented on the other devices. However, when using service modules, appliances, or device contexts in Transparent mode, take care to avoid potential bridging loops that might result if both devices or contexts in a failover pair become active at the same time because of misconfiguration.

■   Finally, it must be decided which redundant device pair will function as the default gateway for the servers on the access layer. If all service modules and appliances are deployed in Transparent mode, the default gateway for the servers is typically the aggregation switch, because that is the boundary between the Layer 2 and Layer 3 domains. If Routed mode is used on some of the devices or contexts, the default gateway is typically the first routed device or context in the service chain. This creates a dependency between the configuration of the servers and the configuration of the service module, appliance, or context. This dependency often makes it more complex to add or remove services in the service chain, because a change on the server side may be required.

To resolve this issue, VRFs or virtual device contexts (VDC) can be used to create an additional logical router hop between the servers and the service chain and aggregation switch. This shields the servers from changes in the service chain.

Each individual choice in this list affects the configuration and deployment of the services in different ways; understanding the impact of each individual choice can be daunting. To provide you with a number of proven tested designs, Cisco has created different validated designs that cover most common design requirements.

Active STP, HSRP, and Service Context Alignment

A recommended practice is to align the active STP, HSRP, and service context in the aggregation layer to provide a more deterministic environment.

Figure 5-11 shows alignment of the STP root, the primary HSRP instance, and the active service module. The active service module is known as the service context.

Note   The primary STP root can be established using the **spanning-tree vlan** *vlan_id* **root primary** command.
The primary HSRP instance can be configured using the **standby priority** command. The active service context can be aligned by connecting the service module on the aggregation switch supporting the primary STP root and primary HSRP instance.

Active component alignment prevents session flow from entering one aggregation switch and then hopping to a second aggregation switch to reach a service context. When the traffic enters the aggregation switch that is connected to the active service context, the traffic is forwarded to the service module directly and avoids the Inter-Switch Link (ISL). This recommended model provides a more deterministic environment and offers more efficient traffic flow and simplified troubleshooting.

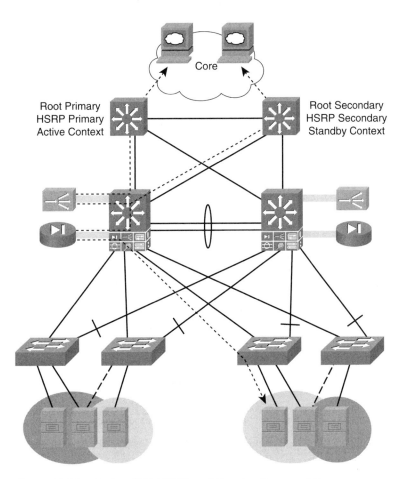

Figure 5-11 *Active STP, HSRP, and Service Content Alignment*

Active/Standby Service Module Design

The active/standby mode of operation is used by service modules that require Layer 2 adjacency with the servers.

The active/standby design typically supports the Cisco CSM, the Catalyst 6500 series FSWM 2.x, and the SSL integrated service modules.

Advantages to the active/standby design include the following:

■ It is a predictable deployment model.

■ This traditional model simplifies troubleshooting. It can be designed so that you know in the primary situation what service modules are active and where the data flows should occur.

Disadvantages to the active/standby design include the following:

■ It underutilizes the access layer uplinks because it may not use both uplinks.

■ It underutilizes service modules and switch fabrics because it does not use both modules.

This model uses the aligned spanning tree root, the primary HSRP, and the active service module.

Active/Active Service Module Design

The active/active mode of operation is used by service modules that support multiple contexts or multiple active/standby groups. This concept is illustrated in Figure 5-12.

Newer service modules can take advantage of active/active designs. The Cisco CSM supports active/standby per context, and the Catalyst 6500 series FSWM 3.1 can implement multiple active/standby groups. In both cases, each service module in the aggregation layer is active.

Advantages to the active/active design include the following:

■ It distributes the services and processing and increases the overall service performance.

■ It supports uplink load balancing by VLAN, so that the uplinks can be used more efficiently.

Note   This model aligns the spanning-tree root, the primary HSRP, and the service module per active context on each VLAN.

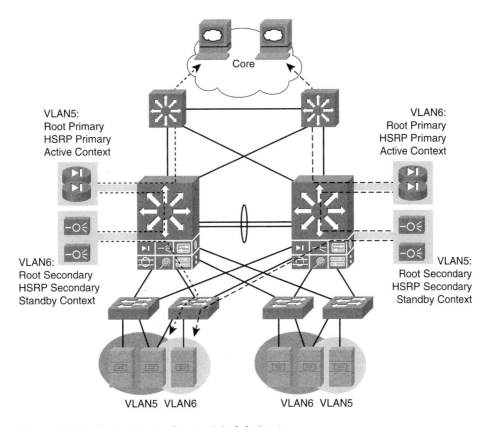

Figure 5-12 *Active/Active Service Module Design*

Establishing Inbound Path Preference

When active/standby service module pairs are used, it becomes important to align traffic flows so that the active primary service modules are the preferred path to a particular server application. This is illustrated in Figure 5-13.

Clients connect to the Cisco CSM by directing their requests to the virtual IP address of the virtual server. When a client initiates a connection to the virtual server, the Cisco CSM chooses a real physical server in the server farm for the connection based on configured load-balancing algorithms and policies such as access rules.

The Route Health Injection (RHI) feature allows a Cisco CSM or Cisco ACE in a Catalyst 6500 series switch to install a host route in the Multilayer Switch Feature Card (MSFC) if the virtual server is in the operational state. By using RHI with specific route map attributes to set the desired metric, a /32 route for the virtual IP address is injected into the routing table. This establishes a path preference with the enterprise core so that all sessions to a particular virtual IP address go to the aggregation layer switch where the primary service module is located. If context failover occurs, the RHI and path preference point to the new active server.

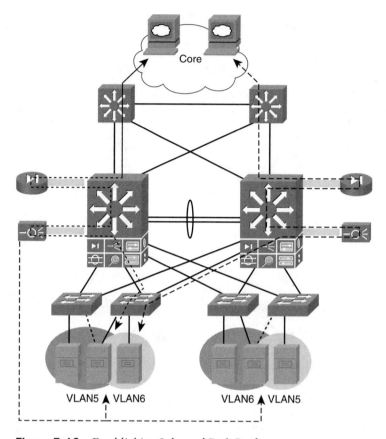

Figure 5-13   *Establishing Inbound Path Preference*

Note   Inbound path preference can be established using the **advertise active** SLB virtual server command and a **set metric route-map** command applied to the appropriate virtual IP address.

RHI can support the active context on Cisco ACE, Cisco CSM, Catalyst 6500 series FWSM, and SSL service modules. This design aligns the spanning-tree root and the active service module. RHI supports a deterministic inbound session flow to a specific aggregation switch, which avoids unnecessary use of the ISL and asymmetrical flows.

Using VRFs in the Data Center

Finally, separate VRFs can be used as a virtualization and management approach in data center designs, as shown in Figure 5-14.

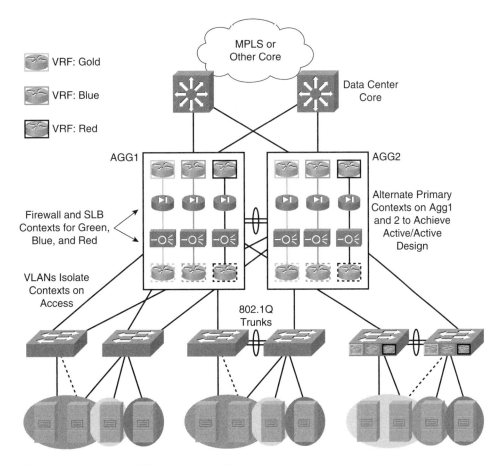

Figure 5-14 *Using VRFs in the Data Center*

Layer 3 routing virtualization can be supported using VRFs on the MSFC in the Cisco Catalyst 6500 series. VRFs enable the logical partitioning of network resources such as the MSFC, Cisco ACE, and Catalyst 6500 series FWSM.

VRFs support the provisioning of application services by context within multiple access topologies. VRFs can support path isolation from metropolitan-area network (MAN) and WAN designs, such as those that use Multiprotocol Label Switching (MPLS), down to the data center resources. VRFs could be used to map the virtualized data center to an MPLS MAN or WAN cloud. Security policy management and deployment can be implemented by user group or VRF.

Note   A Layer 3 access design that uses VRF can provide an aggregation layer service module solution, but this is beyond the scope of this book.

Using the Cisco Nexus 7000 Series in the Core and Aggregation Layer

This section covers the core and aggregation layer technologies that are supported by the Cisco Nexus 7000 series switches. Figure 5-15 displays the Nexus family positioning.

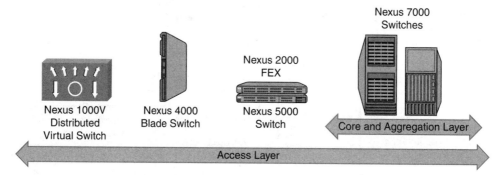

Figure 5-15   *Nexus Family of Switches*

The Cisco Nexus family of data center switches was specifically designed to meet the requirements of the data center. Features include the following:

■   **High availability:** All switches have redundant power supplies and hot-swappable fan trays. All Cisco Nexus switches use Cisco NX-OS Software, an operating system that is designed specifically for the data center and engineered for high availability, scala- bility, and flexibility. The Cisco NX-OS Software is modular in nature and has capa- bilities that improve the overall availability of the system. One of these capabilities is stateful process restart, which allows a network process to be restarted without hav- ing to relearn adjacencies, MAC addresses, or other state information.

■   **Cooling and power:** Most of the Cisco Nexus switches have front-to-back cooling to support hot-cold aisle designs.

■   **Cabling:** Access switches such as the Cisco Nexus 5000 series switches and Cisco Nexus 2000 series fabric extenders (FEX) have switch ports at the rear of the unit for close proximity to the servers that they support. The Cisco Nexus switches have all been designed to support a unified fabric, consolidating LANs and storage-area net- works (SAN) on a single network. This consolidation reduces the cabling by a factor two for servers that are both LAN and SAN attached.

■   **Virtualization:** The Cisco VN-Link technology provides virtual machine-aware net- work services. This technology is used in the Cisco Nexus 1000V Distributed

Virtual Switch, which integrates into the VMware vSphere virtualization platform. Other virtualization technologies that are supported in the Cisco Nexus family of switches are virtual port channels (vPC) and virtual device contexts (VDC).

- **High bandwidth:** The Cisco Nexus family of switches was designed for line rate 10 Gigabit Ethernet speeds at present and 40 and 100 Gigabit Ethernet speeds in the future to support the high-bandwidth requirements of the data center.

Although the Cisco Nexus 7000 switches can be deployed as high-density, highly available access switches in an EOR design, they have primarily been designed for the data center aggregation and core layers. The Cisco Nexus 7000 has been built for high-density 10 Gigabit Ethernet and is ready to support 40 and 100 Gigabit Ethernet in the future. The Cisco NX-OS Software that runs on the Cisco Nexus 7000 offers two major features that open up new design possibilities that previously did not exist. They are as follows:

- **VDCs:** Cisco Nexus 7000 switches that are running Cisco NX-OS Software have introduced the capability to divide a single physical switch into up to four virtual switches, referred to as virtual device contexts or VDCs. Each VDC operates like a standalone switch with a distinct configuration file, a complement of physical ports, and separate instances of necessary control plane protocols such as routing protocols and spanning tree. This feature provides the potential option to use a single physical switch pair to serve multiple roles within a data center topology. Different VDC design options can use this feature for service integration, enhanced security, administrative boundaries, or flexibility of hardware deployment during changing business needs. One common design replaces a core and an aggregation 6500 with a single Nexus 7010 using one VDC in each of the core and aggregation roles.

- **vPCs:** Two Cisco Nexus 7000 switches can be combined into a vPC domain, allowing multichassis Link Aggregation Control Protocol (LACP) port-channel connections across the pair. vPCs (also known as virtual channel ports) can be built between the vPC switch pair and other neighboring devices. Even though the vPCs are terminated on two different physical switches, the vPC switch pair represents itself as a single switch to neighboring devices that are connected on the vPCs. This allows the traditional triangles between the access and aggregation layers to be removed from the logical design. Physically, the access switches still connect to two different aggregation switches, but logically, the pair of Cisco Nexus 7000 switches acts as a single switch. The links between the access switch and aggregation switch pair are combined into a vPC, and STP treats the connection as a single link. As a result, STP does not block any of the links, and the complete bandwidth between the access and aggregation layers can be used. The concept of VPCs is similar to the Catalyst 6500 VSS (Virtual Switching System) technology. With vPCs, however, it is an "active/active" backplane model, whereas the Catalyst 6500 only has one supervisor active between VSS pair switches. This is discussed in more detail later. With VPC, the switches combine to provide FHRP services, and therefore both switches forward packets sent to a HSRP, VRRP, or GLBP virtual gateway MAC addresses, to avoid the routing polarization previously common to FHRPs.

VDCs

VDCs allow a single Cisco Nexus 7000 switch to be partitioned into a maximum of four logical switches: the default VDC and three additional VDCs. Initially, all hardware resources of the switch belong to the default VDC. When you first configure a Cisco Nexus 7000 switch, you are effectively configuring the default VDC: VDC 1. The default VDC has a special role. It controls all hardware resources and has access to all other VDCs. VDCs are always created from the default VDC. Hardware resources, such as interfaces and memory, are also allocated to the other VDCs from the default VDC. The default VDC can access and manage all other VDCs, and the additional VDCs have access to only the resources that are allocated to them They cannot access any other VDCs.

VDCs are truly separate virtual switches. They do not share any processes or data structures, and traffic can never be forwarded from one VDC to another VDC inside the chassis. Any traffic that needs to be passed between two VDCs in the same chassis must first leave the originating VDC through one of the ports that are allocated to it and then enter the destination VDC through one of the ports that are allocated to that VDC. VDCs are separated on the data plane, control plane, and management plane. The only exception to this is the default VDC, which can interact with the other VDCs on the management plane. Control and data plane functions of the default VDC are still separated from the other VDCs.

The default VDC has several other unique and critical roles in the function of the switch. They include the following:

- Systemwide parameters such as Control Plane Policing (CoPP), VDC resource allocation, and Network Time Protocol (NTP) may be configured from the default VDC.

- Licensing of the switch for software features is controlled from the default VDC.

- Software installation must be performed from the default VDC. All VDCs run the same version of software.

- Reloads of the entire switch may be issued only from the default VDC. Nondefault VDCs may be reloaded independently of other VDCs as of Cisco NX-OS Version 4.1(2). If it is anticipated that a switch may be used in a multi-VDC configuration, it is recommended to reserve the default VDC for administrative functions and configure production network connections in nondefault VDCs. This approach provides flexibility and higher security. Administrative access into the nondefault VDCs to perform configuration functions may easily be granted without exposing access to reload the entire switch or change software versions. No Layer 3 interfaces in the default VDC must be exposed to the production data network; only the management interface needs to be accessible through an out-of-band (OOB) management path. Unused interfaces may be retained in a shutdown state in the default VDC as a holding area until they are needed in the configuration of one of the nondefault VDCs. In this state, the default VDC may be maintained as an administrative context requiring console access or separate security credentials. Following this guideline effectively allows a single Cisco Nexus 7000 switch to perform the functional roles of up to three production switches.

Designs Enabled by VDCs

Because a VDC has the same functional characteristics as a physical switch, it can be used in many different places in the overall data center network design. A major advantage of using VDCs instead of separate physical switches is that physical ports can be easily reallocated to the various VDCs. This allows for easier changes and additions to the network design as the network evolves. Because a VDC has characteristics and capabilities that are similar to a separate physical switch, these are not VDC-specific topologies. They could also be built with separate dedicated switches in the roles that are occupied by VDCs. However, VDCs can provide additional design flexibility and efficiency in these scenarios.

The following are some examples of scenarios that could benefit from the use of VDCs:

- **Split-core topology:** VDCs can be used to build two separate redundant data center cores using only a single pair of Cisco Nexus 7000 switches. This technique can be useful to facilitate migration when the enterprise network must expand to support mergers and acquisitions. If sufficient ports are available on the existing data center core switches, two additional VDCs can be created for a separate data center core. This approach allows a second data center network to be built alongside the original one, without any impact on the existing network. Eventually, aggregation blocks could be migrated from one core to the other by reallocating interfaces from one VDC to the other.

- **Multiple aggregation blocks:** At the aggregation layer of the data center network, a single aggregation block consists of a pair of aggregation switches for redundancy and their associated access layer switches. If an enterprise has a business requirement to deploy separate aggregation blocks for different business units or functions, the use of VDCs may be considered to accomplish this logical segregation without the need to deploy separate physical switches. Administration and management can be delegated to different groups, and configuration changes in the VDC of one aggregation block cannot affect the VDCs for the other aggregation blocks. For example, a separate production and development aggregation block could be built using a single pair of aggregation switches.

- *"Services sandwich": In some data center designs, VRFs are used to create a Layer 3 hop that separates the servers in the access network from the services in the service chain and the aggregation layer. This approach creates a "sandwich" consisting of two VRFs with the services chain in between. Instead of VRFs, two VDCs could be used instead to create this services sandwich. In addition to control plane and data plane separation, a VDC provides management plane separation. The VDC services sandwich design increases security by logically separating the switches on the inside and the outside of the services chain.

In many cases, VDCs can be implemented where otherwise two separate physical switches would be required. However, some restrictions and design aspects should be taken into account. Consider the following aspects when using VDCs in your data center design:

- It is not recommended to use two VDCs from the same physical switch to construct any single layer of a hierarchical network design. For example, if you use two different VDCs inside the same physical switch as the two aggregation switches in an aggregation block, the whole aggregation block will fail when the physical switch fails. Distinct, physical box redundancy within a network layer is a key characteristic that contributes to the high availability of the hierarchical network design reference model.

- The control plane and management plane processes of different VDCs are separated and do not directly interact with each other. However, VDCs share the memory and CPU of the supervisor in the physical Cisco Nexus 7000 switch. This means that a VDC-based design can work well when neither of the two VDCs is pushing the limits of its capabilities in terms of scale factors such as routing table entries and STP virtual ports. Some resources are explicitly allocated to VDCs, while other resources are shared. For example, the minimum and maximum amounts of routing table memory that are allocated to each of the VDCs are configured when the VDCs are created (and can be changed later). Having several VDCs that each carry large routing tables could eventually exhaust routing table memory on the supervisor.

- Review the CoPP policy and rate limits of the switch to ensure that they are appropriate for the deployment environment. The system will apply CoPP collectively for all VDCs, because there is only one logical, in-band control plane interface. Ensure that the configured limits will satisfy the requirements of all necessary control plane traffic for all active VDCs.

- The ternary content-addressable memory (TCAM) on a line card is shared between all VDCs that have ports from that line card allocated to them. This means that allocating entire line cards to VDCs, instead of distributing ports on a line card over different VDCs results in more efficient TCAM usage. It is also wise to allocate ports to a VDC in port groups, even if it is not a card requirement. Features such as QoS and CoPP are performed on a port group basis to prevent configuration in one VDC from affecting behavior in another.

- Using VDCs instead of VRFs may require additional interfaces. While VRFs can share a physical link by using it as a trunk and then allocating the corresponding VLANs to each of the VRFs, VDCs do not allow a physical interface to be shared between VRFs.

- The 32-port 10 Gigabit Ethernet I/O module (N7K-M132XP-12) has specific constraints that are based on its architecture, where interfaces that are part of the same port group of four ports must be allocated to the same VDC. This means that it is not possible to allocate interfaces from the same port group to different VDCs.

vPCs

The vPC technology allows loop-free designs to be created in the access and aggregation layers, increasing the total forwarding capacity and simplifying the network topology. The vPC technology is a clustering technique that allows two Cisco Nexus 7000 switches to represent themselves as a single switch to other network devices. The vPC technology enables Layer 2 Multichassis EtherChannels (MEC) to be built between the other network device and the pair of Cisco Nexus switches.

Table 5-1 lists components used by vPC technology.

Table 5-1 *Critical Components Used by vPC Technology*

Component	Description
vPC domain	A vPC domain is group of two vPC peer switches using vPC. The vPC domain must have a unique identifier. A single vPC domain cannot consist of more than 2 switches. A single switch cannot be part of more than 1 vPC domain.
vPC peer switch	A vPC peer switch is a switch that forms a vPC domain with another vPC-enabled switch.
vPC	A vPC is an EtherChannel between the vPC peer switches and another network device that has links that are connected to the 2 different vPC peer switches.
vPC member port	A vPC member port is a physical port on a vPC peer switch that is associated to a vPC.
vPC peer link	This is the link between the vPC peer switches, used to exchange vPC control traffic. The peer link can also be used to forward vPC data if one of the links in a vPC fails. The availability of this link is vital to the operation of vPC, so it is recommended to configure it as a port channel with members spread across different line cards.
vPC peer keepalive link	When the vPC peer link is down, it is important to differentiate between the failure of the vPC peer link alone and the failure of the directly attached PC peer as a whole. The peer keepalive link allows the vPC peers to exchange heartbeat messages without using the vPC peer link. This mechanism is critical to prevent dual-active scenarios in case of vPC peer link failure. The vPC peer keepalive mechanism uses IP transport and can be routed across multiple hops if necessary.

Table 5-1   *Critical Components Used by vPC Technology*

Component	Description
Cisco Fabric Services protocol	The Cisco Fabric Services protocol is a reliable messaging protocol that is designed to support rapid stateful configuration message passing and synchronization. The vPC uses Cisco Fabric Services to transfer a copy of the system configuration for a comparison process and to synchronize protocol state information between the two vPC peer switches.
Orphan device	A device that is not connected to both switches in a vPC domain.
Orphan port	A port that connects an orphan device.

vPC Best Practices

The following are some best-practice recommendations to consider when deploying vPC:

- Connect the two Cisco Nexus 7000 switches through redundant 10 Gigabit Ethernet links (operated in Dedicated mode) from 10 Gigabit Ethernet line cards to form the peer link between vPC peers.

- Dual-attach all the access switches to the vPC peers (if possible). A switch or host that would only connect to one vPC peer would consume precious bandwidth on the peer link. In case of failure of the peer link or a vPC peer, it would also risk being entirely isolated from the network.

- If it is not possible to dual-attach a device, implement a separate trunk between the two vPC peer switches to carry the non-vPC VLANs.

- Carry only vPC VLANs on the vPC peer link (if possible). If vPC and non-vPC VLANs have to share the vPC peer link, consider using the **dual-active exclude interface-vlan** *non-vPC-vlan-list* command to decouple the switch virtual interface (SVI) status from the peer link failure.

- The vPC peer keepalive link should never be routed over the vPC peer link. The vPC peer link and peer keepalive link must be separate to ensure vPC system resiliency. A deadlock condition occurs when both the peer link and peer keepalive link are down. To form or recover a peer link, a working peer keepalive link must first exist, which is why they should be independent.

- Use a separate VRF and front-panel ports for the peer keepalive link. (Gigabit Ethernet is more than adequate.) Alternatively, use the supervisor OOB management interfaces for the vPC peer keepalive link. The peer keepalive link is a logical Layer 3 link. By default, it runs over the management network between the two vPC peers and consumes little bandwidth, allowing regular management traffic to leverage the same ports.

- When using redundant supervisors, only one management interface is active at a time on a given vPC peer. This means that the management interfaces cannot be connected back to back between vPC peers to create the peer keepalive link. An intermediate switch is required so that the peer keepalive heartbeats can be forwarded regardless of the active supervisor. Best practice is not to route over a vPC to L3 SVIs on the vPC peers. A better option is to use dedicated point-to-point links.

Designs Enabled by vPC

The biggest advantage of vPC is that it enables loop-free topologies where STP is no longer actively involved in maintaining the network topology and where no links between the access and aggregation layers are blocked. This increases the stability and efficiency of the aggregation blocks. Depending on the switch platform that is used in the access layer, you can use two common variations in the aggregation block design:

- **Single-sided vPC:** If the access switch platform does not support vPC, vPC is configured on the aggregation switches only, and standard EtherChannel configuration is used on the access switch. In a standard EtherChannel configuration, a maximum of eight links can be bundled in a single channel.

Figure 5-16 illustrates a single-sided vPC.

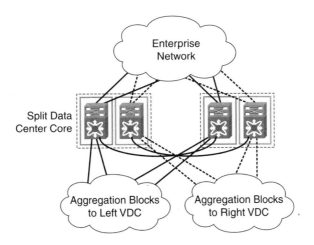

Figure 5-16   *Single-Sided VPC*

- **Double-sided vPC:** If the access switch platform also supports vPC, as does the Cisco Nexus 5000 series, vPC can be configured on both the aggregation and access layers. This configuration allows a maximum of 16 links to be bundled into a single vPC between the aggregation and access switches. In this type of design, vPC can also be used toward dual-homed servers on the access layer. Eventually, this results in having all links from the server all the way up to the aggregation layer actively forwarding traffic.

Layer 2 Multipathing

Layer 2 multipathing (L2MP), also known as Cisco FabricPath, allows the bandwidth between the access and aggregation layer to be scaled beyond what is possible with traditional spanning tree or vPC. At the same time, L2MP increases network stability by replacing the Spanning Tree Protocol with Layer 2 routing.

In modern data center environments, traditional oversubscription rules do not apply. In most campus environments, traffic tends to be "north-south" in nature. Traffic flows from the clients in the access layer to the campus core to access services in the data center or on the Internet. The data center environment is different; in addition to the "north-south" traffic, there is also a need to support high volumes of "east-west" traffic.

Servers do not only communicate with hosts outside the data center, but there is also a lot of traffic between servers inside the data center, such as database replication, vMotion traffic, and intercluster communication.

To accommodate these traffic patterns, a data center network design must be able to support high volumes of bandwidth in the access and distribution layers in the data center aggregation blocks. In traditional spanning-tree-based topologies, half of the links between the access and distribution layers are not used, because they are blocked by the spanning-tree loop-prevention mechanism. vPC solves this problem by allowing MECs between the access and distribution layer, which eliminate blocked ports. By definition, however, a vPC domain consists of a single pair of switches. It is not possible to expand a vPC domain to three or more switches to achieve better scalability and availability.

Another approach is to use Layer 3 routing between the access and distribution layer, because routing protocols can use full bandwidth between the layers through use of Equal Cost Multipath (ECMP). However, Layer 3 routing between the access and aggregation layer restricts the ability to span VLANs across multiple access switches. This is a desirable design trait in current data center networks because the ability to span VLANs across multiple access switches is a requirement for many server virtualization and clustering technologies. L2MP brings routing to the Layer 2 domain. It replaces the Spanning Tree Protocol with new control plane mechanisms based on the Intermediate System-to-Intermediate System (IS-IS) routing protocol. Similar to Layer 3 routing, L2MP leverages ECMP to provide traffic load balancing and allows a fully forwarding Layer 2 fabric to be built. Unlike vPC, L2MP is not limited to a single pair of switches in a domain and allows the data center access distribution blocks to scale beyond what is currently possible with vPC.

Note   For more information about L2MP and FabricPath, see the NX-OS configuration guide at www.cisco.com/en/US/docs/switches/datacenter/sw/5_x/nx-os/fabricpath/configuration/guide/fp_cliX.html.

Designing the Access Layer

The data center access layer provides the physical-level attachment to the server resources and operates in Layer 2 or Layer 3 modes. Either spanning-tree or Layer 3 routing protocols can be extended from the aggregation layer into the access layer, depending on which access layer model is used. This section covers data center access layer design considerations.

Overview of the Data Center Access Layer

The data center access layer is the first oversubscription point in the data center because it aggregates the server traffic onto Gigabit EtherChannel, 10 Gigabit Ethernet, or 10 Gigabit EtherChannel uplinks to the aggregation layer. The data center access layer provides the physical-level attachment to the server resources and can operate in Layer 2 or Layer 3 mode. The operational mode plays a critical role in meeting particular server requirements, such as NIC teaming, clustering, and broadcast containment. Spanning-tree or Layer 3 routing protocols are extended from the aggregation layer into the access layer, depending on which access layer model is used. The access layer is typically one of three models:

- **Layer 2 looped:** VLANs are extended into the aggregation layer. Layer 2 services such as NIC teaming, clustering, and stateful services from the aggregation layer such as a firewall, SLB, and SSL can be provided across Layer 2 models. Layer 3 routing is first performed in the aggregation layer.

- **Layer 2 loop free:** VLANs are not extended into the aggregation layer. Layer 2 services are supported. Layer 3 routing is first performed in the aggregation layer.

- **Layer 3:** Stateful services requiring Layer 2 connectivity cannot be provisioned from the aggregation layer. Layer 3 routing is first performed in the access layer.

The access layer has deterministic traffic flows to the active service modules by leveraging the aggregation layer alignment of the primary STP, primary HSRP, and active service module.

Note Cisco recommends that you implement access layer switches logically paired in groups to support either server redundant connections or diverse connections for production, backup, and management Ethernet interfaces.

Layer 2 Looped Designs

Access layer switches are primarily deployed in Layer 2 mode in the data center and are shown in Figure 5-17.

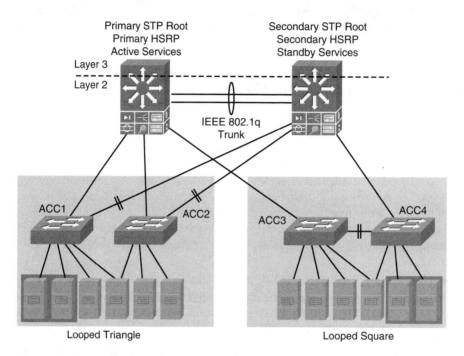

Figure 5-17 *Layer 2 Looped Design Benefits*

A looped Layer 2 access topology provides the following benefits:

- **VLAN extension:** The Layer 2 access topology provides the flexibility to extend VLANs between switches that are connected to a common aggregation module. The Layer 3 boundary in the aggregation layer is above the trunk link that connects the aggregation switches. This simplifies the provisioning of servers to a particular subnet or VLAN and removes issues about the physical placement of the server in a particular rack or row.

- **Layer 2 adjacency requirements:** NIC teaming, high-availability clusters, and database clusters are application examples that typically require NICs to be in the same broadcast domain or VLAN. The list of applications used in a clustered environment is growing, and Layer 2 adjacency is a common requirement.

- **Custom applications:** Because of either a lack of skills or available tools, many developers write custom applications without considering the Layer 3 network environment. These custom applications can create challenges in a Layer 3 IP access topology. Customer applications that depend on Layer 2 adjacency with other servers could require rewriting code when changing IP addresses.

- **Virtual machine mobility:** The use of virtualization in the data center often requires the same set of VLANs to be provisioned to all servers that run the virtualization hypervisor software. Virtual machines may be relocated between these hosts as required by resource or high-availability policies.

- **Service modules:** Layer 2 access permits services provided by service modules or appliances to be shared across the entire access layer. Examples of service modules include Cisco Catalyst 6500 series FWSM, Cisco CSM, and SSL Services Module (SSLSM). The active/standby modes of operation used by many service modules require Layer 2 adjacency with the servers that use them.

- **Redundancy:** Looped designs are inherently redundant. A redundant path exists through a second path that is blocking based on STP control. VLANs may be load balanced across access layer uplinks.

Layer 2 Looped Topologies

The two Layer 2 looped topologies are the looped triangle and the looped square.

The looped triangle topology, shown in the top of Figure 5-17, is currently the most widely implemented in the enterprise data center. This topology provides a deterministic design when the spanning-tree root, HSRP default gateway, and active service modules are aligned on the same aggregation switch. Network resiliency is achieved with dual-homing and Rapid Spanning Tree Protocol (RSTP). However, the uplink to the secondary switches is placed in blocking mode, thereby reducing the available bandwidth by 50 percent.

The looped square topology, shown in the lower part of Figure 5-17, has not been as common in the enterprise data center but is gaining more interest. This topology is similar to the triangle loop topology in terms of a deterministic design and network resilience, but differs in where the spanning-tree blocking occurs. The looped square topology uses a trunk between access switches, which increases the access layer switch density on the aggregation switches when compared to a triangle loop topology where 10 Gigabit Ethernet uplinks are used. The looped square topology optimizes the 10 Gigabit Ethernet port density on aggregation layer switches.

Figure 5-18 shows the spanning-tree blocking point on the link between the access switch pair. This topology aligns well to an active/active service module design deployed in the aggregation layer because it permits the uplinks to be load balanced without crossing the aggregation layer trunks. If active services are on only one access switch, it might be desirable to adjust the STP cost so that the uplink to the backup aggregation switch is blocking instead of the link between the access pair. This forces all traffic to the primary aggregation switch without having to traverse the aggregation layer ISL trunk. With this design, there is a larger failure domain. Access layer failures on one side of the network can impact the other areas of the access layer.

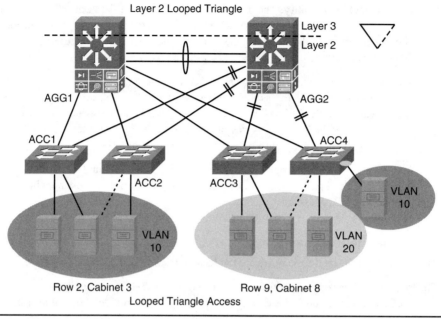

Looped Triangle Access

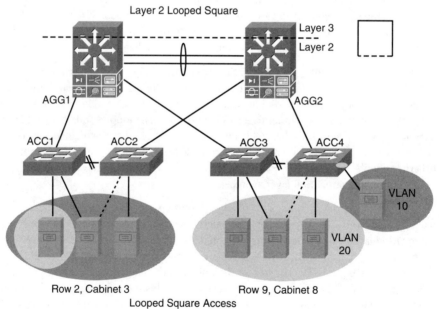

Looped Square Access

Figure 5-18   *Layer 2 Looped Topologies*

The Layer 2 looped triangle, shown in the upper part of Figure 5-18, has the following features:

■ Supports VLAN extension/Layer 2 adjacency across the access layer.

■ Resiliency is achieved with dual-homing and RSTP.

■ Quick convergence with RSTP.

■ Supports stateful services at the aggregation layer.

■ Proven and widely used.

The Layer 2 looped square, shown in the lower portion of Figure 5-17, has the following features:

■ Supports VLAN extension/Layer 2 adjacency across the access layer.

■ Resiliency is achieved with dual-homing and STP.

■ Quick convergence with 802.1w and 802.1s.

■ Supports stateful services at the aggregation layer.

■ Supports more access layer switches, optimizing 10 Gigabit Ethernet aggregation layer density.

■ Active/active uplinks align well to active/active service module designs.

The disadvantages of the square loop design relate to aggregation layer ISL use, because 50 percent of access layer traffic might cross the ISL to reach the default gateway's active service module. There can also be degradation in performance in the event of an uplink failure.

The disadvantage to the triangle loop is if the spanning tree root, HSRP default gateway, and active service modules are aligned on the same aggregation switch, in a failure sub-optimal and variable traffic flows can take place. This can make troubleshooting very difficult.

Layer 2 Looped Design Issues

The main drawback to looped Layer 2 design is that if a Layer 2 loop occurs, the fault has a severe impact across the entire Layer 2 domain, and the network may become unmanageable due to the infinite replication of frames.

Using RSTP with recommended STP practices improves stability and prevents loop conditions. However, conditions can occur that cause loops even when STP is being run. In addition to STP, the following loop-prevention mechanisms should be used:

■ **BPDU guard:** Used to protect the switched network from the problems that may be caused by the receipt of bridge protocol data unit (BPDU) on ports that should not be receiving them. The receipt of unexpected BPDUs may be accidental or may be part of an unauthorized attempt to add a switch to the network. BPDU guard disables the port upon BPDU reception if PortFast is enabled on the port.

- **Root guard:** Allows a device attached to the port configured with root guard to participate in STP so long as the device does not try to become the root. Root guard blocks the access from the device until the receipt of its superior BPDUs ceases.

- **UniDirectional Link Detection (UDLD):** Allows devices to monitor the physical configuration of the cables and detect when a unidirectional link exists. When a unidirectional link is detected, UDLD shuts down the affected port and alerts the user.

- **Bridge assurance:** When enabled, bridge assurance alters the spanning behavior to send BPDUs on all ports, as opposed to the normal behavior where BPDUs are only sent on designated ports. When a port that has been enabled for bridge assurance stops receiving BPDUs from its neighbor, it moves the port to BA Inconsistent state, preventing a potential bridging loop.

- **Loop guard:** Checks whether a root port or an alternate root port receives BPDUs. If the port is not receiving BPDUs, the loop guard feature puts the port into an inconsistent state until it starts receiving BPDUs again. Loop guard isolates the failure and lets the spanning tree converge to a stable topology without the failed link or bridge.

Layer 2 Loop-Free Designs

The loop-free Layer 2 model, illustrated in Figure 5-19, is an alternative design model used when looped topology characteristics are undesirable but Layer 2 support is required. Some reasons for using the loop-free Layer 2 include inexperience with Layer 2 STP, a need for all uplinks to be active, and previous bad experiences related to STP implementations.

Even with the loop-free design topology, it is still necessary to run STP as a loop-prevention tool. In the event that a cabling or configuration error creates a loop, STP prevents the loop from possibly bringing down the network.

A loop-free Layer 2 access topology has these attributes:

- **Active uplinks:** All uplinks are active, and none are blocking.

- **Layer 2 server adjacency:** Supported across a single pair of access switches with the loop-free U design, and across an aggregation switch pair with the loop-free inverted U design.

- **Stability:** Provides fewer chances for loop conditions due to misconfiguration than Layer 2 looped designs.

Note   Network virtualization technologies such as VSS and vPC enable additional loop-free designs that are based on MEC. The topologies described in this section assume that these technologies are not available on the platforms that are being used.

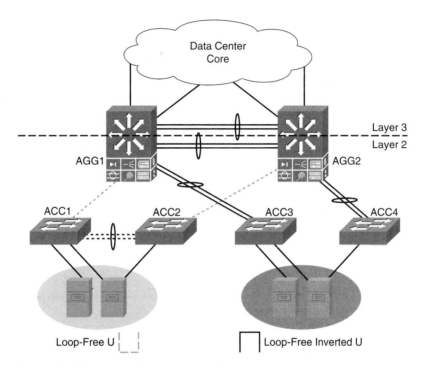

Figure 5-19 *Layer 2 Loop-Free Design*

Loop-Free Topologies

The two Layer 2 loop-free topologies are the loop-free U and the loop-free inverted U, as shown in Figure 5-20.

The following are characteristics of loop-free U access:

- VLANs are contained in switch pairs (no extension outside of switch pairs).

- No STP blocking; all uplinks are active.

- Layer 2 service modules black hole traffic on uplink failure.

The following are characteristics of loop-free inverted U access:

- Supports VLAN extension.

- No STP blocking; all uplinks are active.

- Access switch uplink failure black holes single attached servers.
- ISL scaling considerations.
- Supports all service module implementations.

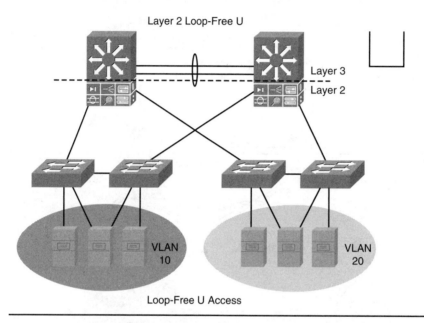

Loop-Free U Access

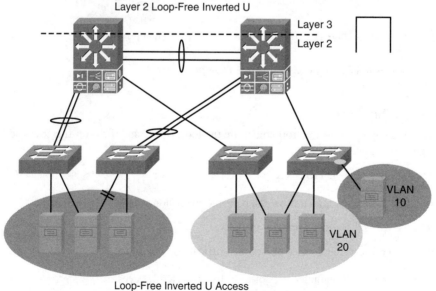

Loop-Free Inverted U Access

Figure 5-20 *Loop-Free Topologies*

For both topologies, all uplinks are active with no blocking. The Layer 2 to Layer 3 line of demarcation differs in each design. Both topologies provide a backup path in the event of an uplink failure and permit a higher density of access switches to be supported on the aggregation module than the looped designs.

In a loop-free U design, a VLAN is configured on each access switch, and on the trunk between access switches and its corresponding 802.1Q uplink. Redundancy is supported through the trunk between the access layer switches. VLANs are contained on an access switch pair. The trunk between aggregation switches is Layer 3. The main disadvantages to the loop-free U design are that VLANs cannot be extended between aggregation switches and that Layer 2 service modules will black hole traffic in the event of an uplink failure.

In a loop-free inverted U design, a VLAN is configured on each access switch and its corresponding 802.1Q uplink, and is extended between aggregation switches but is not extended between access switches. The trunk between aggregation switches is Layer 2. This permits active/standby hellos and session-state communications from service modules to take place to support redundancy. One issue with the loop-free inverted U design is that access switch uplink failures can black hole single attached servers. Redundancy can be improved using Gigabit EtherChannel or NIC teaming on servers. When an active/standby service module is being used, trunk scaling should be considered. The loop-free inverted U design model supports all service module implementations.

Example: Loop-Free U Design and Layer 2 Service Modules

The loop-free U design with Layer 2 service modules can experience black-holing of traffic in the event of an uplink failure.

For example, in Figure 5-21, if the uplink connecting the access switch and the primary aggregation switch goes down, the VLAN interface on the aggregation switch MSFC goes down, too, if the uplink is the only interface in that VLAN.

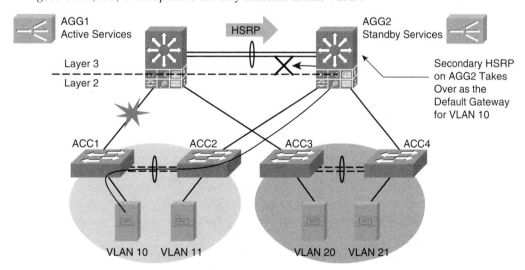

Figure 5-21 *Example: Loop-Free U Design and Layer 2 Service Modules*

In Figure 5-21, the SVI for VLAN 10 would go down if AGG1 loses connection to ACC1, which is supporting VLAN 10. The HSRP multicast hellos are no longer received by the AGG2 switch, which creates an active/active HSRP state for the VLAN 10 MSFC interfaces on both AGG1 and AGG2. However, the servers on ACC1 cannot reach the active service module context on AGG1 through AGG2 because there is no Layer 2 path between AGG1 and AGG2 for VLAN 10.

Note The active/standby modes of operation used by service modules require Layer 2 adjacency with the servers that use them.

Although the service module can be configured to switch over the active/standby roles by using the interface monitoring features, this requires the entire module to switch over (all contexts) on a single uplink failure. This is not a desirable condition and is further complicated if multiple uplink failures occur, or when maintenance requires taking down an access layer switch uplink.

Note Cisco does not recommend the use of the loop-free Layer 2 access design with active/standby Layer 2 service module implementations that do not support single-context failover.

Example: Loop-Free U Design and Cisco ACE Service Module

The loop-free U design is supported with newer service modules such as Cisco ACE, which supports per context failover with autostate, or with Catalyst 6500 series FWSM 3.1, which supports an active/active service module design.

In Figure 5-22, the Cisco ACE module supports autostate on the uplinks. If the uplink between AGG1 and ACC1 fails, the active Cisco ACE service module context can fail over to AGG2 in less than 1 second.

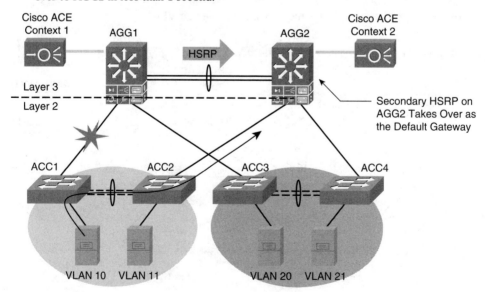

Figure 5-22 *Example: Loop-Free U Design and ACE Service Modules*

When Catalyst 6500 series FWSM 3.1 uses the active/active service module design, it supports the loop-free U topology, too. If the ACC1 uplinks fail for this design, the hosts uses the active Catalyst 6500 series FWSM 3.1 on AGG2.

Note Another option to overcome potential black-holing with service modules is to implement a "services sandwich" design, leveraging VRFs or VDCs. In such a design, HSRP is used on the subaggregation layer. If there is an uplink failure, the HSRP standby router in the subaggregation VRF or VDC takes over, and then forwards the traffic over the ISL to the active services chain in the other aggregation switch.

Layer 2 FlexLink Designs

FlexLink designs are a Layer 2 alternative to the looped access layer topology. In Figure 5-23, a pair of access switches is configured with FlexLinks.

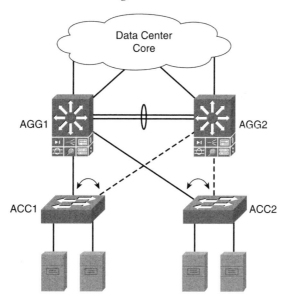

Figure 5-23 *Using FlexLinks in the Data Center*

FlexLinks provide an active/standby pair of uplinks defined on a common access layer switch. Here are some of the attributes of FlexLinks:

- FlexLinks are configured using the **switchport backup interface** *interface-id* command on the primary interface (the interface specified in the command is the port, which becomes the backup for the primary interface).

- An interface can belong to only one FlexLink.

- The pair can be of the same or different interface types (such as Gigabit Ethernet, 10 Gigabit Ethernet) or EtherChannel.

- FlexLinks automatically disable STP, so no BPDUs are propagated.

- Failover from active to standby is in the 1- to 2-second range, which is not as fast as with RST.

- FlexLinks operate using only a single pair of links.

- The aggregation layer switch is not aware of the FlexLink configuration. From the perspective of the aggregation switch, the links are up and STP logical and virtual ports are active and allocated.

Note   FlexLinks are currently supported on a variety of Cisco platforms as of IOS Release 12.2. See Cisco.com for specific information for the platform under consideration.

FlexLink Issues and Considerations

There are some potential issues and considerations with FlexLinks. Because STP is disabled on FlexLinks, a loop condition might exist in particular scenarios (for example, when a patch cable is mistakenly connected between access layer switches where at least one is configured for FlexLinks).

In Figure 5-24, a new link has been added between the ACC1 and ACC2 switches. If the access switch ports have BPDU guard enabled, BPDU guard sees the loop and disables the port.

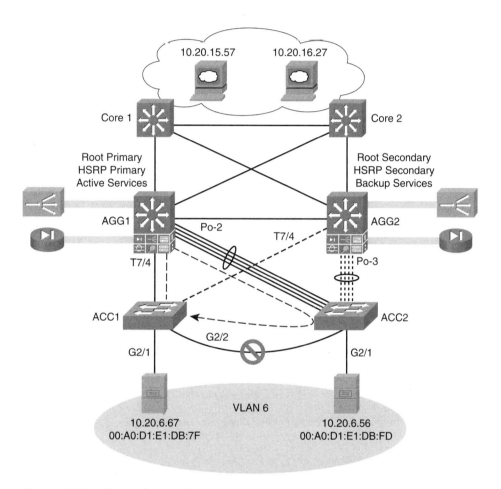

Figure 5-24   *FlexLink Considerations: Interaccess Switch Loop Issue*

There are some other considerations to take into account with FlexLink designs. You need to consider ISL bandwidth requirements under failover situations.

Another loop can occur if a second connection that is not part of the FlexLink channel group is made in parallel between the aggregation switch and an access switch.

In Figure 5-25, a new uplink has been added from the AGG1 to ACC1 G2/2. Because STP BPDUs are not passed along the FlexLink path, this parallel link creates a loop in the topology that cannot be detected by BPDU guard, and an endless replication of broadcast and multicast frames occurs, which negatively impacts the whole aggregation module.

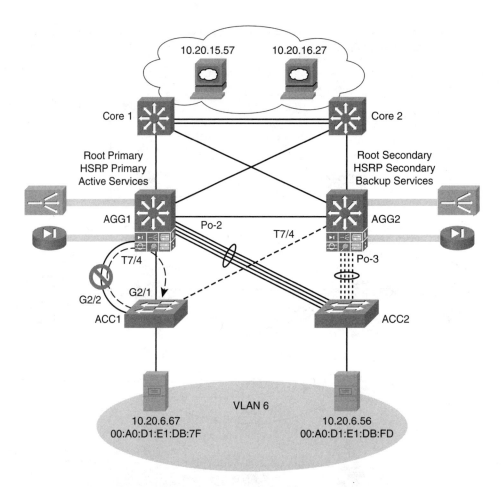

Figure 5-25   *Example: FlexLink with Parallel Link Loop Issue*

Note   Unless BPDU guard is enabled on access ports, the aggregation switch with a loop is subject to endless replication of broadcast or multicast frames and very high CPU usage, HSRP flapping, and other negative conditions.

Root guard on the aggregation switch is also ineffective in this scenario because AGG1 does not see a path to the root AGG2 through the access switch with FlexLinks enabled.

Note   FlexLink is recommended only in environments with high administrative control and limited changes.

Comparison of Layer 2 Access Designs

Table 5-2 compares the features of Layer 2 access designs.

Table 5-2   *Comparison of Layer 2 Access Designs*

	All Uplinks in Active State	VLAN Extension Supported	Service Module Black Holing[5] Issues	Single Attached Server Black Holing on Uplink Failure	Optimize Access Switch Density	Must Consider ISL Scaling
Looped triangle	No	Yes	No	No	No	No[3]
Looped square	Yes	Yes	No	No	Yes	Yes
Loop-free U	Yes	No	Yes[4]	No	Yes	No
Loop-free inverted U	Yes	Yes	No	Yes[1] Yes[2]	Yes[2]	Yes
FlexLinks	No	Yes	No	No	No	No
Star[6]	Yes	Yes	No	No	No	No

[1] Use of distributed EtherChannel greatly reduces chances of black-holing condition.

[2] NIC teaming can eliminate black-holing conditions.

[3] When service modules are used and active service modules are aligned to AGG1.

[4] Cisco ACE Module permits Layer 2 loop-free access with per context switchover on uplink failure.

[5] Applies when using Cisco ACE or Catalyst 6500 series FWSM in active/standby arrangement.

[6] Star designs are based on VSS, vPC, StackWise, or other technologies that use MEC.

The table column headings indicate whether the design provides these features:

■ **All uplinks in active state:** Some access layer designs can use both uplinks (active/active), whereas other designs have one link active and the other either blocked on a per-VLAN basis by spanning tree, or completely unused in a backup mode only.

■ **VLAN extension supported:** Some access design models permit a VLAN to be extended to all access switches that are connected to a common aggregation module.

■ **Service module black-holing issues:** Most access designs are susceptible to an uplink failure on the access layer switch breaking connectivity between the servers and the service modules.

- **Single attached server black holing on uplink failure:** If an access switch has a single uplink, it could be a large failure exposure point. Uplinks that use Distributed EtherChannel can reduce the chances of black holing. Another technique that can be used is server load balancing to a virtual IP address that includes servers physically connected across multiple access switches. NIC teaming can also be used.

- **Optimizes access switch density:** When 10 Gigabit Ethernet uplinks are used, port density at the aggregation layer can be a challenge. Some access layer designs permit a larger number of access layer switches per aggregation module than others.

- **Must consider trunk scaling:** Some access layer designs send all traffic toward the primary root aggregation switch, whereas other designs send traffic toward both aggregation switches. When sending to both aggregation switches, 50 percent of the traffic typically passes over the ISL to reach the active HSRP default gateway and active service module pair. The amount of bandwidth used for the trunks becomes important in these designs and can create scaling challenges.

Layer 3 Access Layer Designs

In a Layer 3 design, access switches connect to the aggregation switches using a Layer 3 uplink with a dedicated subnet. Layer 3 routing is first performed on the access switch. Layer 2 trunks between pairs of access switches support the Layer 2 adjacency requirements in the data center. This design limits Layer 2 adjacencies to access switch pairs, and VLAN extension across the data center is not possible as shown in Figure 5-26.

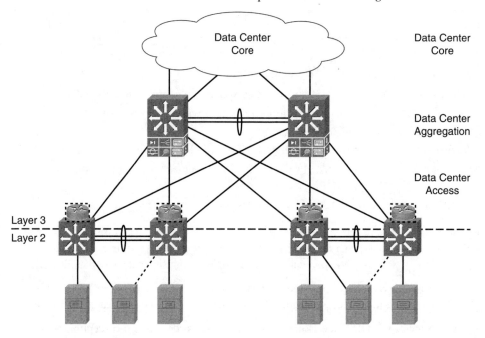

Figure 5-26 *Layer 3 Access Design Overview*

Note When you are using a Layer 3 access model, Cisco recommends running STP as a loop-prevention tool. STP would be active only on the interswitch trunk and server ports on the access layer switches.

The Layer 3 design is typically used to limit or contain broadcast domains to a particular size. Smaller broadcast domains reduce exposure to broadcast domain issues and can shelter particular servers that could be adversely affected by a particular broadcast level. Although Layer 3 access designs are stable, they are not as common as Layer 2 designs in the data center.

With a Layer 3 access design, all uplinks are active and use CEF load balancing up to the ECMP maximum. The current ECMP maximum is eight paths. Layer 3 designs can provide convergence times faster than STP, although RSTP is close.

Multicast Source Support

Historically, Layer 3 designs have been implemented to support many multicast sources. Multicast sources on Layer 2 access works well when Internet Group Management Protocol (IGMP) snooping is available. IGMP snooping at the access switch automatically limits multicast flow to interfaces with registered clients in the VLAN, as shown in Figure 5-27.

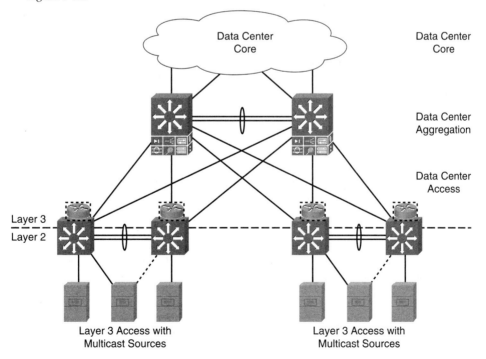

Figure 5-27 *Multicast Sources Support*

Drivers for Layer 3 designs include situations where IGMP snooping is not available at the access layer, or when particular Layer 3 administrative functions are required.

Benefits of Layer 3 Access

Here are some of the benefits of Layer 3 access designs:

■ Broadcast and failure domain sizes are minimized, which leads to a higher level of network stability.

■ Server stability requirements are supported, including isolation of particular applications from multicast traffic.

■ All uplinks are available paths and are active up to the ECMP maximum.

■ Fast uplink convergence is supported for failover and fallback. The aggregation switches do not need to rebuild Address Resolution Protocol (ARP) tables. Layer 3 designs can provide convergence times faster than STP, although RSTP is close.

Drawbacks of Layer 3 Access

IP address space management is more difficult with Layer 3 access than with Layer 2 access. Migrating to a Layer 3 design usually requires re-addressing the data center devices. When trying to migrate to Layer 3 access, it can be difficult to determine all the Layer 2 adjacencies in place and which custom applications use hard-coded addresses.

Layer 2 adjacency is limited to access pairs, which limits clustering and NIC teaming capabilities. It can also limit data center application deployments, such as with the VMware VMotion product that provides infrastructure services transferring virtual machines between servers. Service modules need to be deployed at each access layer pair to maintain Layer 2 adjacency with servers and provide stateful failover.

Blade Server Overview

Blade servers are a technology that is often implemented in the data center access layer. A blade server is a chassis that houses many servers on a blade or module. Typically, blade servers are used to replace older server farms where increased density is a requirement or where new applications that use clustering are being deployed. Blade servers allow the data center manager to reduce operational costs and save rack space. Blade servers are a growing portion of the server market today for many of the leading server vendors, including Cisco Systems, IBM, Hewlett-Packard, Sun Microsystems, and Dell.

Designs that use blade servers are becoming popular in the enterprise data center. Blade servers can support either integrated switches or pass-through modules for connecting servers to the network.

Blade servers present specific challenges related to designing and supporting the data center network that need to be considered:

■ **Administrative domains:** The design must define who is responsible for configuring and managing integral switches. Usually, the system administration team is responsible for the components inside of a server product, and the network team typically supports the configuration of the spanning tree and trunks. Change control and troubleshooting need to be supported, too.

■ **Interoperability:** Blade servers support many different vendor-specific switches, including Cisco, Nortel, and D-Link switches. Although many of the technologies in use are expected to meet interoperability standards such as spanning-tree IEEE 802.1W, they must be verified and tested to ensure proper operation in the data center network.

■ **Spanning-tree scaling:** The integrated switch on the blade server is logically similar to the external rack-based server switching design. The same challenges apply relative to the increase in spanning-tree logical and virtual ports, as shown in Figure 5-28.

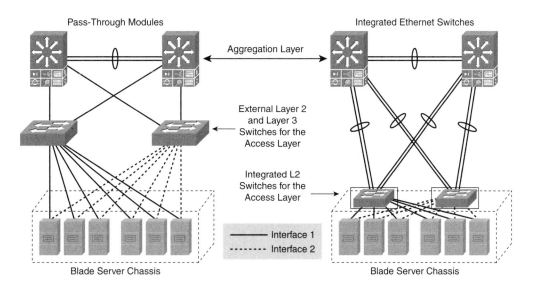

Figure 5-28 *Blade Server Overview*

■ **Pass-through cabling:** The pass-through module option on blade servers permits customers to use their existing external access switches for connecting the servers in the blade server chassis and to avoid the integrated switch option. Customers should examine the pass-through cabling system to make sure it can properly be supported in their physical cabinets.

■ **Switch trunk topologies:** Each vendor blade server implementation has unique internal and external switch trunk connectivity options. Make sure that the access layer topology chosen for your data center design meets requirements such as VLAN extension and NIC teaming while staying within the watermark values of the spanning tree.

> **Note** Watermark values are related to the maximum number of systemwide active logical instances and virtual port instances per line card that, if reached, can adversely affect convergence and system stability. These values are mostly influenced by the total number of access layer uplinks and the total number of VLANs. If a data center-wide VLAN approach is used (no manual pruning on links), the watermark maximum values can be reached fairly quickly.

- Environmental issues: The consolidation of many servers into one enclosure requires a greater amount of cooling. This could limit the number of blade servers in a particular area or rack, because too much warm air can circulate around the systems. Blade server enclosures in large data centers have been found to strain the weight limits of the data center's raised flooring and the available power.

Blade Server Connectivity Options

Blade servers connect servers to the network at the access layer. The access layer network infrastructure may need to support blade servers with integral switches or blade servers with pass-through cabling. Blade servers can support either Layer 2 or Layer 3 topologies, depending on the server broadcast domain or administrative requirements, as shown in Figure 5-29.

As previously discussed, a Layer 2 access design supports Layer 2 capabilities, including VLAN extension and NIC teaming. A Layer 3 access design can be used to provide Layer 3 capabilities, aggregate blade server uplinks, and optimize 10 Gigabit Ethernet densities in the aggregation layer.

Stacked or dual-tier Layer 2 access designs that use the blade server integrated switches with external Layer 2 switches should be avoided. Dual Layer 2 designs are susceptible to these factors:

- More complex STP design and blocking issues
- Oversubscription of uplinks and trunks
- Larger failure domain issues

The network designer may also consider implementing blade servers with integrated Cisco switches that support the trunk failover feature. Trunk failover allows rapid failover to the redundant switch in the blade enclosure if all uplinks from the primary switch fail. When the uplinks fail, the switch shuts down the ports connected to the blade servers and lets NIC teaming software direct traffic to the redundant switch.

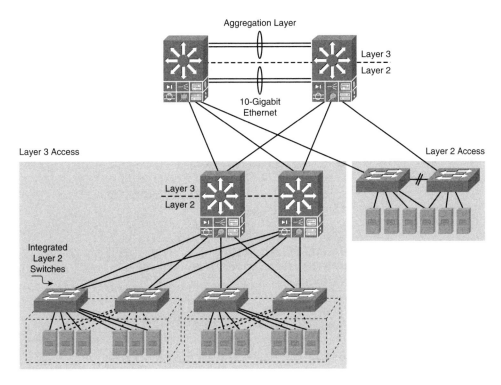

Figure 5-29   *Blade Server Connectivity Options*

Blade Server Trunk Failover Feature

Layer 2 trunk failover, which is also known as link-state tracking, is a feature of blade servers that provides Layer 2 redundancy in the network when used with server NIC adapter teaming. This is shown in Figure 5-30.

When you enable Layer 2 trunk failover on the integrated switch, the link state of the internal downstream ports is bound to the link state of one or more of the external upstream ports. An internal downstream port is an interface that is connected to the server. An external upstream port is an interface that is connected to the external network. When you associate a set of downstream ports to a set of upstream ports, if all the upstream ports become unavailable, trunk failover automatically puts all the associated downstream ports in an error-disabled state. This causes the server primary interface to failover to the secondary interface. This feature is dependent on the NIC feature set support for NIC teaming and failover.

When Layer 2 trunk failover is not enabled, if the upstream interfaces lose connectivity, the link states of the downstream interfaces remain unchanged. The server is not aware that external connectivity has been lost and does not failover to the secondary interface. Traffic is black holed.

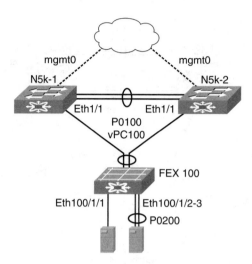

Figure 5-30   *Blade Server Trunk Failover Feature*

You can distribute trunk failover groups across accesses switches to achieve maximum bandwidth utilization from the blade server chassis. Although this is a loop-free topology that does not need STP blocking, STP should be enabled for loop protection.

Virtual Blade Switching

The Cisco Virtual Blade Switch (VBS) technology allows up to nine physical switches to be combined into a single logical switch. The VBS takes advantage of link virtualization to deliver improved levels of system and application availability through multiple layers of redundancy.

One of the traditional drawbacks of a blade switch solution is the increase in the total number of switches to manage. In a traditional TOR access switch deployment, there are typically two redundant TOR switches per rack, and servers are dual-homed to both switches. If, in that same rack, four blade chassis are deployed with two redundant blade switches per chassis, the total number of switches in the rack increases to eight. Also, if traditional triangular access designs are used, 16 uplinks to the aggregation layer are required rather than the 4 uplinks that are used in the traditional TOR deployment. The Cisco VBS technology that is used in the Cisco Catalyst 3100 series of blade switches overcomes these two issues. The Cisco VBS technology uses special high-speed intercon-nect cables to connect up to nine blade switches in a ring. The ring extends the backplane of the individual switches and combines them into a single logical switch.

This mechanism is similar to the Cisco StackWise technology that is embedded in the Cisco Catalyst 3750 series switches. A master switch is elected, which manages the entire Cisco VBS. Because the combined switches act as a single switch, EtherChannels can be created from member links that reside on different blade switches. This configuration simplifies the access layer topology and total number of required uplinks to the aggregation layer. Also, the number of managed devices is reduced from eight separate switches to a single switch.

Another advantage is that blade servers that are dual-homed to two physical blade switches are now logically connected to a single virtual switch. This enables the use of EtherChannel between the server and the Cisco VBS, improving load balancing and resiliency. The choice between a TOR and EOR design is a trade-off between the physical cabling requirements and the network requirements of the data center design.

Cisco Nexus Switch Family in the Access Layer

The Cisco Nexus family of switches was designed to support the requirements of the data center and several access layer technologies to enhance data center access layer designs.

TOR and EOR Designs

One of the major choices in the design of the access layer of the data center is whether to use a TOR or EOR design. This decision strongly depends on the cabling and other physical aspects of the data center design.

The Cisco Nexus 5000 can be combined with Cisco Nexus 2000 FEXs to create a design that combines the advantages of a TOR design with the advantages of an EOR design. Dual redundant Cisco Nexus 2000 FEXs are placed at the top of each rack. The uplink ports on the Cisco Nexus 2000 FEXs are connected to a Cisco Nexus 5000 switch that is installed in the EOR position. From a cabling standpoint, this design is a TOR design. The cabling between the servers and the Cisco Nexus 2000 FEX is contained within the rack. Only a limited number of cables need to be run between the racks to support the 10 Gigabit Ethernet connections between the Cisco Nexus 2000 FEXs and the Cisco Nexus 5000 switches in the EOR position. From a network design standpoint, however, this design is an EOR design. The FEXs act as remote line cards for the Cisco Nexus 5000 switches, which means that the ports on the Cisco Nexus 2000 act as ports on the associated Cisco Nexus 5000. In the logical network topology, the FEXs disappear from the picture, and all servers appear as directly connected to the Cisco Nexus 5000. From a network design perspective, this design has the simplicity that is normally associated with EOR designs.

Static and Dynamic Pinning

When deploying Cisco Nexus 2000 FEXs together with Cisco Nexus 5000 switches in a top-of rack design, you need to make a design choice whether to use the Cisco Nexus 2000 in Static Pinning of Dynamic Pinning mode.

In Static Pinning mode, the server ports on the Cisco Nexus 2000 FEX are statically pinned to one of the uplink ports. For example, when a Cisco Nexus 2000 FEX with 48 Gigabit Ethernet server ports is deployed in Static Pinning mode using four 10 Gigabit

Ethernet uplink ports to the Cisco Nexus 5000, 12 server ports are pinned to each uplink port. Ports 1 to 12 are pinned to the first uplink, ports 13 to 24 to the second uplink, ports 25 to 36 to the third uplink, and ports 37 to 48 to the fourth uplink. This results in an oversubscription ratio of 1.2 to 1, because a group of twelve 1-Gigabit Ethernet server ports shares the bandwidth of one 10 Gigabit Ethernet uplink. If one of the uplinks between the Cisco Nexus 2000 and the Cisco Nexus 5000 fails, the FEX disables the server ports that are pinned to that uplink port. For example, if the fourth uplink fails, server ports 37 to 48 are disabled, and the servers that are connected to these ports see the associated Ethernet link go down. If the servers are dual-homed and use some form of NIC redundancy, this mechanism is triggered, and the server fails over to the other NIC. A single-homed server simply loses connectivity if it is connected to one of the ports that are pinned to the failed uplink port. The oversubscription ratio on the other ports remains unchanged, because each of the other three groups of twelve 1-Gigabit Ethernet ports is still sharing the same 10 Gigabit Ethernet uplink port as before.

Cisco Nexus 2000 FEX Dynamic Pinning

In Dynamic Pinning mode, the server ports are not statically pinned to an uplink port, but all server ports share the combined bandwidth of the uplink ports. This is achieved by configuring an EtherChannel between the Cisco Nexus 2000 FEX and the Cisco Nexus 5000. Instead of statically assigning traffic from specific server ports to the uplink port that they are pinned to, traffic is now distributed over the uplinks based on the EtherChannel load-balancing hash algorithm.

Taking the same example as before, the oversubscription ratio is again 1.2 to 1, because the forty-eight 1-Gigabit Ethernet server ports now share the bandwidth of the four 10 Gigabit Ethernet uplink ports, resulting in a 48:40 = 1.2:1 oversubscription ratio. However, the behavior under failure conditions is different from the behavior when using Static Pinning mode. If one of the uplinks between the Cisco Nexus 2000 and the Cisco Nexus 5000 fails, the FEX does not disable any server ports, because there is no longer a direct relation between the uplink ports and the server ports. Instead, the traffic of the 48 server ports is now distributed over the remaining three 10 Gigabit Ethernet uplinks. The servers that are connected to the Cisco Nexus 2000 do not notice the failure and keep forwarding traffic on the NIC that is connected to the FEX. Single-homed servers do not lose connectivity when using dynamic pinning. Their traffic is simply redistributed over the remaining uplinks. Dual-homed servers do not fail over to the redundant NIC. However, this means that the oversubscription ratio for the remaining uplink ports changes. The oversubscription ratio for the remaining ports in the example is 48:30 = 1.6:1, which represents a 33 percent increase in traffic on each uplink port. If the uplinks are already running close to maximum utilization, it might cause traffic from all servers to be dropped, degrading performance for all servers.

As these examples show, the choice of pinning mode depends to a large extent on the way that servers are connected to the access switches. For dual-homed servers, static pinning results in more deterministic oversubscription ratios. However, for single-homed servers, dynamic pinning provides increased availability.

Virtual Port Channel in the Data Center Access Layer

The vPC feature can be used to build loop-free designs in the aggregation block. This feature does not require vPC to be enabled on the access layer switches. It is sufficient if the aggregation switches, such as the Cisco Nexus 7000 series, support the vPC feature. Standard EtherChannel technology can be used on the access switches. However, if the access switches, such as the Cisco Nexus 5000 switches, also support vPC, vPC can be used on both sides of the EtherChannel. This allows a unique 16-link EtherChannel to be built between the access and aggregation switches.

Another application of vPC on the Cisco Nexus 5000 is that it allows an EtherChannel to be built between a server and a redundant pair of Cisco Nexus 5000 switches. Normally, EtherChannels can be built only from a server that is dual-homed to a single switch. Using vPC allows the most efficient form of load balancing to be used on the server, while still maintaining the level of availability that is associated with dual-homing a server to two different access switches.

The third application of vPC on the Cisco Nexus 5000 is in the so-called active/active FEX configuration. The Cisco Nexus 5000 switch has a fixed single supervisor architecture and does not support redundant supervisors for increased availability. In a so-called straight-through FEX design, the Cisco Nexus 2000 FEXs are connected to a single Cisco Nexus 5000 switch, which controls the FEX. When the Cisco Nexus 5000 switch fails, servers that are single-attach connected to the Cisco Nexus 5000 lose their connection. Servers that are connected to the FEXs that are associated with the Cisco Nexus 5000 also lose their connection. A common way to increase the availability of the servers in this design is to dual-home the servers to two different FEXs, which are in turn associated with two different Cisco Nexus 5000 switches. The vPC can be used to build an EtherChannel between the server and the two Cisco Nexus 5000 switches, providing both high availability and load balancing. However, if single-homed servers are used in the straight-through FEX design, all these servers lose their connectivity if the Cisco Nexus 5000 switch that the FEXs are associated with fails.

To resolve this issue, the Cisco Nexus 2000 FEXs can be dual-homed to two different Cisco Nexus 5000 switches. In this scenario, a combination of dynamic pinning and vPC on the Cisco Nexus 5000 is used. The FEX is connected through an EtherChannel that is terminated on two different Cisco Nexus 5000 switches, which together form a vPC domain. Traffic from the server ports on the Cisco Nexus 2000 FEX is distributed across the uplinks to the two Cisco Nexus 5000 switches. If one of these switches fails, the traffic from the servers continues to be forwarded across the remaining links in the EtherChannel to the other Cisco Nexus 5000. The active/active FEX design effectively creates a single virtual switch from two Cisco Nexus 5000 switches and all their associated FEXs. However, unlike a chassis-based switch with dual supervisors, the control plane, and management plane on the dual Cisco Nexus 5000 switches are active simultaneously.

Straight-Through FEX Design

Cisco Nexus 2000 FEXs are connected to a single Cisco Nexus 5000 switch. Straight-through FEX design occurs when two Nexus 2000 FEXs are connected to a single Cisco 5000 switch. In summary,

- Static or dynamic pinning can be used between the Nexus 5000 and the FEXs.

- EtherChannels to dual-homed servers can be supported using vPC.

- Single-homed servers can lose connectivity when a Cisco Nexus 5000 fails. The straight-through design is the simplest to implement, as shown in Figure 5-30. It allows either static or dynamic pinning to be used between the Cisco Nexus 5000 switch and its associated Cisco Nexus 2000 FEXs. The vPC can be used to create EtherChannels between dual-homed servers and the redundant pair of Cisco Nexus 5000 switches, providing both high availability and load balancing. However, single-homed servers can lose connectivity if one of the Cisco Nexus 5000 switches fails. This design is the most appropriate for dual-homed servers. It allows all the different forms of NIC teaming on the server to be used and is simple and straightforward to implement.

Active/Active FEX Design

Active/active FEX design occurs when Nexus 2000 FEXs dual-homes to two Nexus 5000 switches. Figure 5-31 shows that each FEX is dual-homed with two Cisco Nexus 5000 series switches. The FEX-fabric interfaces for each FEX are configured as a vPC on both peer switches. The host interfaces on the FEX appear on both peer switches. If these host interfaces are bundled in a port channel, you must configure the port channel identically on both peer switches. Configuration synchronization helps keep the FEX configuration synchronized between the pair of vPC peer switches.

As shown in Figure 5-31, the active/active design is slightly more complex. The Cisco Nexus 2000 FEX can now be controlled and configured by two different Cisco Nexus 5000 switches. The FEX has to be configured on both Cisco Nexus 5000 switches in a consistent manner, and vPC has to be set up to combine the FEX uplinks into a single EtherChannel.

Note The two Cisco Nexus 5000 switches are configured independently. Therefore, configuration changes that are made to ports on a dual-homed Cisco Nexus 2000 FEX have to be manually synchronized between the two Cisco Nexus 5000 switches.

In Figure 5-31, the vPC is already operational. FEX 100 is dual-homed to both parent switches: N5k-1 and N5k-2 on FEX-fabric interfaces Ethernet 1/1. Because the FEX is pre-provisioned, there is no existing running configuration on Ethernet 1/1. FEX 100 is configured to have two types of host interfaces. One interface is Ethernet100/1/1, which is singly attached to a server (non-port-channel member), and the other interface is Ethernet 100/1/2-3, which is configured in a port channel to the server (port-channel member).

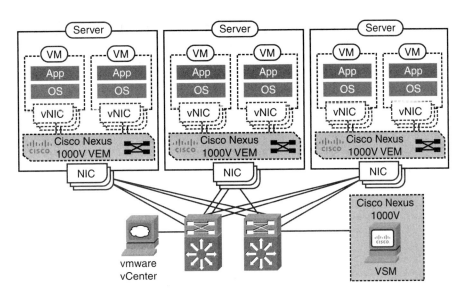

Figure 5-31 *Active/Active Topology*

A vPC-based EtherChannel is used between the FEXs and the switches, dynamic pinning is automatically used. Traffic is balanced across the FEX uplinks based on EtherChannel load balancing. When one of the FEX uplinks is lost, traffic is balanced across the remaining uplinks.

Because vPC is used between the FEXs and the switches, vPC cannot be used toward the servers. This means that EtherChannel cannot be configured between the server and the access switches. Active/standby and transmit load balancing can still be used as NIC teaming options to attain high availability and some extent of load balancing.

In this design, single-homed servers maintain connectivity if one of the Cisco Nexus 5000 switches fails. Therefore, this design increases the availability of single-homed servers to a level that is comparable to that of a single-homed server that is connected to a chassis-based switch with dual redundant supervisors.

The main advantage of the active/active design over the straight-through design is that it offers higher availability to single-homed servers. Therefore, it is most suitable to an environment in which most of the servers are single-homed.

The choice between straight-through or active/active is not exclusive. If the FEXs are deployed in a typical TOR design, it is possible to mix the two options. In racks that mainly contain dual-homed servers, the straight-through design could be used, and racks that contain mostly single-homed servers could be set up using the active/active design.

Cisco Nexus 1000V in the Data Center Access Layer

The Cisco Nexus 1000V, as shown in Figure 5-32, is a distributed virtual switch. It integrates in the VMware vSphere solution directly into the VMWare Kernel. The Cisco Nexus 1000V consists of Virtual Ethernet Modules (VEM) and one or two Virtual Supervisor Modules (VSM) to control and manage the VEMs. The Cisco Nexus 1000V VEMs integrate in the VMware ESX hypervisor software and connect the VMs to the network. The VMNICs in the ESX hosts serve as the uplinks to the physical access layer switches. This effectively creates an additional access layer in the virtualized data center network.

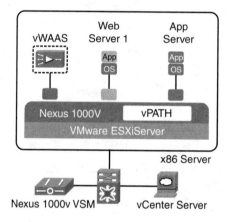

Figure 5-32 *Nexus 1000V Switching Architecture and vWAAS Architecture*

The Cisco Nexus 1000V switch can optimize the use of Layer 4 to Layer 7 services in a virtual machine environment through Cisco vPath architecture services. Cisco vPath technology is aware of all Layer 4 to Layer 7 policies associated with individual virtual machines. After the data packets of a specific virtual machine are identified and policies applied, the remaining data packets flow directly to the virtual machines.

Cisco Virtual Gateway (VSG) integrated with the Cisco Nexus 1000V switch provides trusted multitenant access with granular zone-based security policies for virtual machines. VSG delivers security policies across multiple servers, supporting virtual machine mobility across physical servers for workload balancing, availability, or scale for business growth in cloud computing.

Figure 5-32 displays the Cisco Virtual Wide Area Application Services (vWAAS). vWAAS is a WAN optimization solution (and the Nexus 1000V switching architecture, as mentioned earlier), and it is integrated with the Cisco Nexus 1000V switch to deliver assured application performance acceleration to IT users connected to enterprise data centers and enterprise.

The Cisco Nexus 1000V VEM is not a switch in the traditional sense. It does not participate in the STP and uses different frame forwarding rules than traditional Ethernet switches. It is better characterized as an Ethernet host virtualizer (EHV). It forwards traffic between the connected VMs and the physical access switches but will not allow transit traffic to be forwarded through the ESX host. The VEM never forwards traffic between VMNICs, but only between VMNICs and virtual network interface cards (vNIC), or between the vNICs within the ESX hosts.

Therefore, most of the considerations that are associated with the virtualized access layer design revolve around channeling and trunking to provide network connectivity for the VMs and the ESX host management and control. STP or other control plane protocols do not need to be considered.

Virtual Port Channel Host Mode

Virtual Port Channel Host Mode (vPC-HM), shown in Figure 5-33, allows a port channel from the Cisco Nexus 1000V to be terminated on two separate upstream switches, even if these switches do not support a clustering technology, such as vPC or VSS.

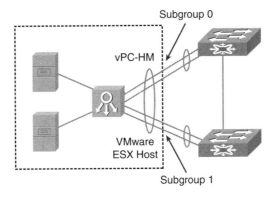

Figure 5-33 *vPC-HM*

For redundancy, ESX hosts are usually dual-homed to two different physical access switches to increase the availability of the host. Common scenarios use two, four, or six different physical NICs, called VMNICs, to connect the ESX host to two different access switches.

If the upstream access switches support some form of clustering technology, such as vPC or VSS, all interfaces can be grouped in a single EtherChannel, and traffic can be distributed using EtherChannel load-balancing hash algorithms. Alternatively, ports can be grouped by function, and separate EtherChannels can be created for each of the functions. For example, an ESX host with six VMNICs could be connected using two separate EtherChannels; one EtherChannel consisting of two links for management, control, storage, and VMotion traffic, and a second EtherChannel consisting of four links to carry the VM traffic.

If the upstream switches do not support vPC or VSS, it is important to ensure that traffic from a specific VM is always forwarded to the same upstream access switch. Distributing traffic across the two physical access switches would cause the MAC address table entry for that VM to be continually updated, resulting in unstable MAC address tables in the upstream switches.

To ensure that traffic is correctly distributed across upstream access switches, the Cisco Nexus 1000V supports vPC-HM. This allows a port channel to be created that contains links that are terminated on different physical access switches. The port channel is divided into two subgroups, one for each access switch. These subgroups can be automatically discovered through the Cisco Discovery Protocol or manually configured if the upstream switches do not support Cisco Discovery Protocol.

Traffic from individual virtual machine is assigned to a specific subgroup to ensure that the same upstream access switch is used for all traffic that is sourced by that virtual machine. If there are multiple links within a subgroup, traffic is load balanced using the regular EtherChannel load-balancing hash algorithms.

The vPC-HM does not require the upstream switches to support vPC. However, if a subgroup contains multiple links, a standard port channel should be configured on the physical access switch to bundle all the links in the subgroup into an EtherChannel.

Design Considerations for the Cisco Nexus 1000V

When designing a virtualized access layer with the Cisco Nexus 1000V, consider the following:

- It is recommended to separate management, control, VMotion, and storage traffic from the virtual machine production traffic. This requires two separate uplinks from each VEM (one that carries the management and control VLANs and one that carries the production VLANs). Because it is important that each of these two uplinks is redundant, each uplink should consist of an EtherChannel containing at least two physical links, which are connected to two different physical access switches. To meet this requirement, at least four VMNICs are required on the ESX host.

- The EtherChannels to the upstream switches can be configured as a standard EtherChannel if the upstream switches support vPC or VSS. If this is not the case, vPC-HM should be configured.

- If a group of ESX hosts supports VMotion, it is important that the virtual machine uplinks on the VEMs of these hosts are configured in a consistent manner. This requirement is most easily satisfied through configuration of uplink-port profiles.

- The Cisco Nexus 1000V VSM is a virtual machine that runs on one of the ESX hosts. There are two common ways to connect the VSM control, packet, and management VLANs to the network. The first method is to leave control, packet, and management interfaces on a standard VMware vSwitch, together with the VMware ESX service console and kernel interfaces. The VEM is then specifically used for VM production traffic. The second method is to move all these management interfaces to the VEM and connect the VEM to the management network in addition to the production network. The first method is safer because configuration errors on the VSM cannot cause the connections between the VSM, VEMs, service console, and vCenter to be disrupted. The second method provides additional control over the management traffic, because it allows the advanced features of the Cisco Nexus 1000V, such as NetFlow, Switched Port Analyzer (SPAN), and quality of service (QoS), to be applied to the management interfaces.

Cisco Nexus 1010

Cisco also has a hardware solution around Nexus 1000 technology. Cisco Nexus 1000V series switches, as shown in Figure 5-34, are intelligent virtual machine access switches that are designed for VMware vSphere environments running the Cisco NX-OS Software operating system. It operates inside the VMware ESX hypervisor.

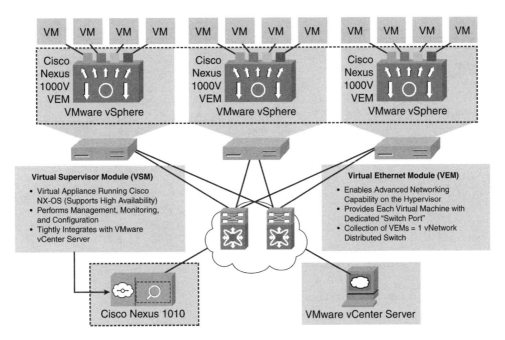

Figure 5-34 *Cisco Nexus 1010*

Benefits of such a platform include the following:

■ Placing management and control path elements, such as the Cisco Nexus 1000V Virtual Supervisor Module (VSM), on Cisco Nexus 1010 allows you to manage policies separate from VMware virtualization administrators. This makes it easier to attain compliance and audit requirements and reduces administrative errors.

■ Offloading VSM to a dedicated appliance delivers scalability and performance improvements to the virtualized data center infrastructure.

■ A virtual services platform close to, but not resident within, the virtualization infrastructure permits a virtual-machine-aware solution such as the Cisco Network

Analysis Module to gain accurate network statistics directly from data sources, including virtual ports.

■ Server virtualization decouples application development from physical server deployment.

Layer 2 or Layer 3 Access Design?

Is there a right way to design the access layer in the data center? Both approaches have merits, as summarized in Figure 5-35. There are many trade-offs to consider when choosing between Layer 2 or Layer 3 access designs.

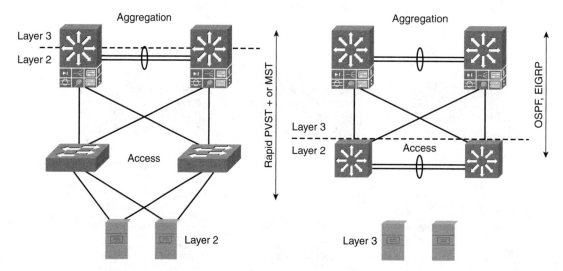

Figure 5-35 *Choosing Between Layer 2 and Layer 3 Access Designs*

A Layer 2 design has these advantages:

■ Provides NIC teaming and Layer 2 adjacency across a wider area

■ Supports high-availability clustering using Layer 2 adjacency

■ Extends VLANs to support server requirements

■ Supports custom application requirements

A Layer 3 design has these advantages:

■ Manages loops with less difficulty

■ Supports faster convergence of the network

■ Can minimize broadcast domain sizes, leading to better stability

■ Supports link utilization on all active uplinks

Depending on the organization and the network requirements, you also need to consider these factors:

- How skilled your staff is in Layer 2 or Layer 3 technology, which will impact the time to resolve issues.

- Oversubscription requirements for the aggregation layer switches, which impacts scaling capabilities.

- Service module support and placement, which impacts scaling and costs.

- The data center access layer provides physical attachment for servers using a Layer 2 or Layer 3 design.

- Layer 2 access designs can extend VLANs between aggregation switches and support more Layer 2 adjacency options.

- Looped designs provide a deterministic design that support network resiliency with dual-homing and RSTP.

- Loop-free designs provide most Layer 2 features without looped topologies.

- FlexLinks provide an active/standby pair of uplinks defined on a common access layer switch.

- Layer 3 access designs provide fast convergence and stability but support fewer adjacency options.

- Blade servers increase server density and support Layer 2 or Layer 3 access.

Scaling the Data Center Architecture

As data center applications grow, the need to scale the data center also grows. The choice of access layer switch design can affect how the data center can be scaled. EtherChannel technologies and service module designs also provide options for scaling the bandwidth and density of the data center aggregation layer.

TOR Versus EOR Designs

The access layer server components consist of 1RU servers, blade servers with integral switches, blade servers with pass-through cabling, clustered servers, and mainframes with Open Systems Adapters (OSA). The access layer network infrastructure consists of EOR switches, TOR configuration 1RU or two-rack unit (2RU) switches, and blade server switches.

There are trade-offs to consider when increasing the size of the data center with deployment. The most common considerations in choosing access layer platforms include the following:

■ **Cabling design:** Cable density in the server cabinet and under the floor can be difficult to manage and support. With a higher density of servers per rack, cable routing and management can become quite difficult to manage and maintain.

■ **Cooling requirements:** Cable bulk can create cooling challenges if air passages are blocked by the number of cables at the cabinet base entry. Servers in the rack may require more cooling volume because of their higher density. The use of TOR switches can improve the cabling design.

■ **Power requirements:** The increased density of components in the rack is driving a need for a larger power feed to the rack. Many data centers do not have the power capacity at the server rows to support this increase. Spreading out server racks in the data center can help resolve this issue.

■ **Density:** Considering the density of servers along with the maximum number of interfaces used per rack and per row can help determine whether an EOR or a TOR solution is a better fit. If multiple ports per rack are used, it might take many TOR switches in each rack to support them. EOR switches that are spaced out in the row might reduce the complexity in terms of the number of switches, and permit more flexibility in supporting varying numbers of server interfaces.

■ **10 Gigabit Ethernet and 10 Gigabit EtherChannel uplink support:** It is important to determine what the oversubscription ratio is per application. When this value is known, it can be used to determine the correct amount of uplink bandwidth that is required on the access layer switch. Choosing a switch that can support 10 Gigabit Ethernet and 10 Gigabit EtherChannel might be an important option when considering current or future oversubscription ratios. Another consideration in determining oversubscription ratios is the use of server virtualization. Server virtualization consolidates multiple logical servers inside a single physical server. This consolidation results in higher utilization of the server uplinks, meaning that the oversubscription ratio in the access layer should be lower than in a non-virtualized data center environment. Also, the effect of virtual machine mobility on the traffic patterns should be considered. Where in nonvirtualized environments, different types of applications and servers are deployed in fixed positions in the racks, virtual servers may be moved from host to host dynamically. This means that traffic patterns are less predictable, and the uplinks of all switches may have to be sized to support the bandwidth requirements of the most bandwidth-hungry applications.

■ **Resiliency features:** When servers are connected with a single NIC at the access layer, the access switch becomes a single point of failure. This makes features such as redundant power and redundant processors much more important in the access layer switch.

■ **Intended use:** A development network might not require the redundancy or the software-rich features that are required by the production environment.

The best solution is usually based on business requirements and can be a hybrid implementation.

Cabinet Design with TOR Switching

The advantage to the 1RU switching design is that it minimizes the number of cables needed from each cabinet, as shown in Figure 5-36.

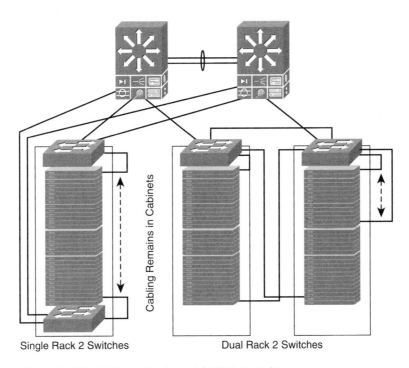

Single Rack 2 Switches   Dual Rack 2 Switches

Figure 5-36 *Cabinet Design with TOR Switching*

The access layer switch is located inside the cabinet with the servers, and the cabling from the servers to the access switch is contained in the cabinet. There are several considerations with TOR designs:

- **Cooling requirements:** Although it will be easier to provide cooling volumes with less cable bulk entering the cabinet, the cooling requirements of the servers typically do not permit a full rack of servers. You could expect to see 25 to 30 1RU servers in a rack.

- **Additional Gigabit EtherChannel (GEC) or 10 Gigabit Ethernet uplinks:** The increase in uplinks from the access layer switches requires higher GEC or 10 Gigabit Ethernet density at the aggregation layer or additional aggregation modules.

- **Higher STP processing:** For Layer 2 looped access layer topologies, the increase in uplinks increases the STP active logical ports and the virtual port per line card instances at the aggregation layer, creating more overhead and processing requirements.

- **More devices to manage:** The 1RU designs implement more network devices as compared to modular designs. The additional devices add to the management complexity.

- **Number of 1RU switches required:** The port density needs to support all the servers and all the features per server planned for the cabinet. There are typically three to four interfaces connected on a server for features such as NIC teaming and OOB management. Multiple 1RU switches might be needed, and they may require redundant power supplies. 1RU switches do not support redundant CPUs.

Example: Network Topology with TOR Switching Model

This example discusses the network topology needed to support 1000 servers using 1RU switching in the access layer. In Figure 5-37, 80 switches have been provisioned to support 1000 servers based on 25 servers per cabinet, 40 cabinets, and 2 1RU switches per cabinet. The 80 switches in the topology require 2 uplinks per switch or 160 uplinks to the aggregation layer.

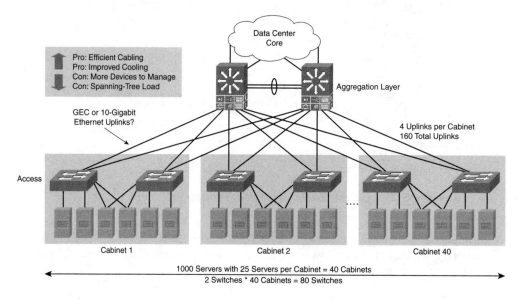

Figure 5-37   *Network Topology with TOR Switching Model*

> **Note**   Using a modular switch design with a Cisco Catalyst 6509 switch, the 1000 servers could be supported with about 8 access layer switches needing 16 uplinks to the aggregation layer.

The advantage to the 1RU switching model is efficient cabling, which supports improved cooling to the cabinet. The disadvantage of the 1RU switching model is the necessity to support an increased number of devices under network management and STP processing.

Cabinet Design with Modular Access Switches

The EOR design minimizes the number of switches needed to support the servers and the number of uplinks needed. The access layer switches are typically located outside of the server cabinet at the ends of the row or distributed within the row. Cabling from the servers to the access switch is routed under raised floors or in overhead trays.

There are several advantages with EOR designs:

- **Decreased management complexity:** There are fewer devices to manage, which makes this task less complex.

- **Decreased STP processing:** With fewer devices in the Layer 2 infrastructure and significantly fewer uplinks, there is less impact on STP processing.

- **Redundancy options:** Redundant switch power and CPUs can be supported on modular switches.

There are some disadvantages with EOR designs:

- **Cable bulk:** More cabling needs to be routed and managed.

- **Cooling constraints:** The cable bulk at the cabinet floor entry can be difficult to manage and can block cool airflow.

Example: Network Topology with Modular Access Switches

Figure 5-38 shows 8 Catalyst 6509 switches provisioned to support 1000 servers. The 8 switches in the topology require 2 uplinks per switch, or 16 uplinks to the aggregation layer.

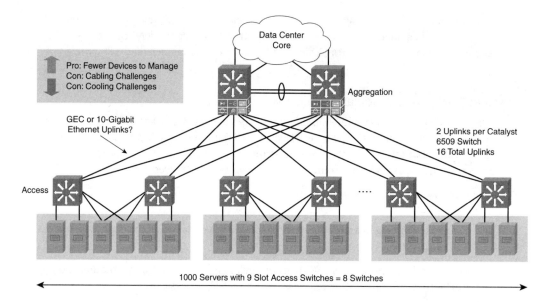

Figure 5-38 *Example: Network Topology with EOR*

> **Note** With the TOR switch design, the 1000 servers could be supported with about 80 access layer switches, requiring 160 uplinks to the aggregation layer.

The advantages to the EOR switching topology are fewer devices to manage and fewer uplinks to the aggregation layer. This lowers the STP processing requirements.

The disadvantage of the EOR switching model is that there are challenges inherent in implementing and managing the cabling from the servers to the access switches. The cable bulk at the cabinet entry location can significantly impede cooling. One technique to help manage the cabling is to install the copper cabling in trays above the equipment racks and install the fiber cabling below the floor.

Cabinet Design with Fabric Extenders

The Cisco Nexus 5000 switch can be combined with Cisco Nexus 2000 FEXs to create a unique solution that combines the best aspects of the TOR and EOR designs. The Cisco Nexus 2000 FEXs are 1RU devices that are placed in the same position as a traditional TOR switch inside the racks. The FEXs have 10 Gigabit Ethernet uplink ports that are cabled back to a pair of Cisco Nexus 5000 switches that are placed at the end or middle of a row of cabinets.

The cabling in this design is laid out in the same manner as the cabling in a traditional TOR design. The cables between the FEXs and the servers are connected inside the racks. Only a limited number of cables are run between the FEXs and the central Cisco Nexus 5000 switches.

However, the Cisco Nexus 2000 FEXs are not independent switches; they are configured and managed from the central Cisco Nexus 5000 switches. Thus, from a management standpoint, this design is like the EOR design. In fact, the Cisco Nexus 5000 switches can be compared to a modular switch, with Cisco Nexus 5000 taking the role of the supervisor and the FEXs taking the role of remote line cards. The remote line cards are placed in the top of each server cabinet, and the switch fabric of the Cisco Nexus 5000 is extended to the remote line cards through 10 Gigabit Ethernet links.

This design combines the two biggest advantages of the TOR and EOR designs—efficient cabling and a relatively small number of access switches—simplifying management and reducing the load on the aggregation switches.

Example: Network Topology with FEXs

This example discusses the network topology that is required to support 1000 servers using the Cisco Nexus 5000 switches and Cisco Nexus 2000 FEXs in the access layer, as shown in Figure 5-39, 80 FEXs have been provisioned to support 1000 servers based on 25 servers per cabinet, 40 cabinets, and 2 FEX switches per cabinet. A maximum of 12 FEXs per pair of Cisco Nexus 5000 switches can be supported in active/active mode.

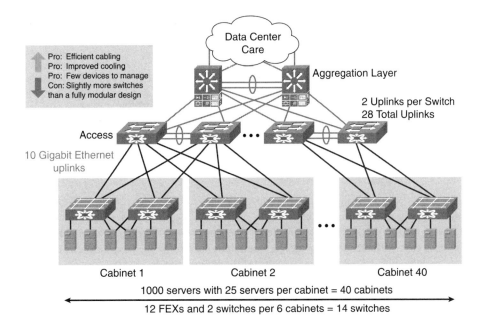

Figure 5-39 *Network Topology with FEXs*

Note In straight-through mode, 24 FEXs could be supported per pair of switches, but because that would reduce the availability of single-homed servers compared with the

> EOR design, the conservative number of 12 FEXs per pair of switches has been chosen for the calculations.

Twelve FEXs and two switches are necessary to support six racks. With a total of 40 racks, this means that 7 pairs of Cisco Nexus 5000 switches are needed, resulting in a total of 14 switches. With 2 uplinks per switch, 28 uplinks to the aggregation layer are required. (In reality, it is likely that more uplinks would be provisioned to support the aggregate bandwidth of the 1000 servers. Like the EOR design, only the minimum number of links that are required for a completely redundant design is calculated.)

This design requires a slightly higher number of switches than the EOR design, but far less than the TOR design based on 1RU switches. The intercabinet cabling requirements are drastically reduced compared with the EOR design.

Server NIC Density

The number of NICs required per server affects how many servers can be supported per switch. When planning for NIC support on switches, the data center designer should plan for at least three NICs per server:

- Front-end interface for public access.

- Storage interface on Gigabit Ethernet or Fibre Channel host bus adapter (HBA).

- Backup interface for server backup.

- Back-end interface for private access.

- OOB management interface. This is a low-bandwidth application, so it can be supported on low-end switches.

NIC port density has implications on network design. It may require more than two TOR switches per server cabinet. For example, if there are 30 servers in a rack, you could need 120 ports (30 * 4 ports = 120). This density requires three 48-port TOR switches per cabinet. As part of the data center design, you might need to implement hard limits on servers per rack to support the cabling capacity of the access switch.

Cross-cabinet cabling should be avoided because it is difficult to manage.

Hybrid Example with a Separate OOB Switch

Figure 5-40 shows a design that has both TOR and EOR switches in the design. Both TOR switches and EOR switches are implemented in cabinets at the end of the row of server switches.

The design provides a lot of flexibility if you have sufficient cabling infrastructure to support the server to access switch cabling. The hybrid design provides benefits of using both TOR switches and EOR switches. The TOR switches provide lower power consumption. The EOR switches provide options for redundant CPUs and power supplies for critical applications. The design can also support NIC teaming. Low-end 1RU switches can be implemented in server cabinets to provide OOB management support.

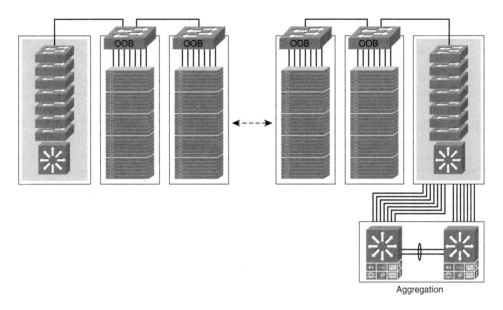

Figure 5-40 *Hybrid Example with Separate OOB Switches*

Oversubscription and Uplinks

To define the correct amount of uplink bandwidth that is required on the access layer switch, you need to determine what the oversubscription ratio is per uplink.

The oversubscription ratio per server value can be determined by dividing the total number of server Gigabit Ethernet connections by the total aggregated uplink bandwidth on the access layer switch. For example, the ratio for a Catalyst 6509 switch with four 10 Gigabit Ethernet ECMP uplinks that supports 336 server access ports can be calculated as follows:

> 336 Gigabit Ethernet connections with 40-Gb uplink bandwidth = 8.4:1 oversubscription ratio

The oversubscription ratio per server is important for several reasons:

- The ability to send a large file in a specific amount of time can be critical to cluster operation and performance.

- Future server platform upgrade cycles will increase levels of outbound traffic.

- The PCI-X or PCI-Express NICs provide a high-speed transfer bus speed and use large amounts of memory.

Choosing a switch that can support 10 Gigabit Ethernet and 10 Gigabit EtherChannel uplinks might be an important option when considering current or future oversubscription ratios. Depending on your future server requirements, you may want flexibility in adjusting the oversubscription ratio by upgrading to 10 Gigabit Ethernet or 10 Gigabit EtherChannel. This ability may be better supported in modular switches than in 1RU switches. Modular switches also support the ability to upgrade the CPU and switch fabric.

To support the increasing bandwidth requirements of servers, a data center access switch shouldsupport 10 Gigabit Ethernet uplinks, with the possibility to support 10 Gigabit EtherChannel to add bandwidth as needed. The Cisco Nexus 5000 switches offer up to twenty-six 10 Gigabit Ethernet ports in a 1RU switch. The Cisco Nexus 7000 series switch scales to very high densities of 1 Gigabit Ethernet ports. Modular switches, such as the Cisco Nexus 7000 or Cisco Catalyst 6500 series switches, also support the option to upgrade supervisor and switch fabric as more 10 Gigabit Ethernet ports are installed in the chassis.

Scaling Bandwidth and Uplink Density

This section covers scaling bandwidth and uplink density. The various technologies include the following:

- EtherChannel with load balancing

- EtherChannel with Min-Links

- Scaling with service layer switches

- Scaling service chains

Note   Transparent Interconnection of Lots of Links (TRILL) is beyond the current scope of this text and is not covered in this or the next section. TRILL replaces STP as a mechanism to find loop-free trees within Layer 2 broadcast domains to enable scaling.

Optimizing EtherChannel Utilization with Load Balancing

Test results show that EtherChannel ports configured with the default Layer 3 hash may not provide optimal utilization. Figure 5-41 shows Layer 3 versus Layer 4 load balancing with EtherChannel. The left side of Figure 5-41 shows the default Layer 3 hashing algorithm, and the right shows the Layer 4 hashing algorithm.

To enable the Layer 3 IP plus Layer 4 port-based CEF hashing algorithm for EtherChannel ports, use the **port-channel load-balance** command. This command can improve load distribution for EtherChannel ports because it presents more unique values to the hashing algorithm by leveraging the automatic source-port randomization in the client TCP stack.

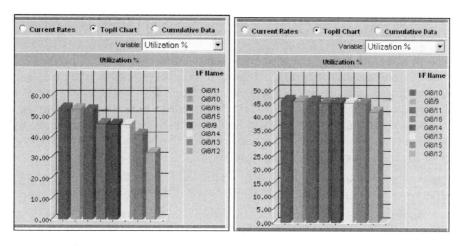

Figure 5-41   *Optimizing EtherChannel Utilization with Load Balancing*

Optimizing EtherChannel Utilization with Min-Links

The EtherChannel Min-Links feature allows a minimum number of available ports to be specified for a port channel to be considered a valid path, as shown in Figure 5-42.

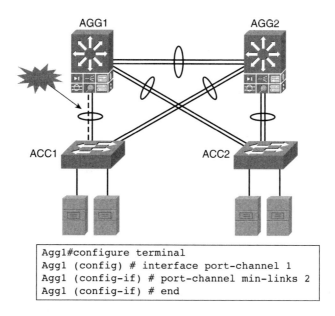

```
Agg1#configure terminal
Agg1 (config) # interface port-channel 1
Agg1 (config-if) # port-channel min-links 2
Agg1 (config-if) # end
```

Figure 5-42   *Optimizing EtherChannel Utilization with Min-Links*

This feature enables the user to set a minimum threshold for the number of links in an EtherChannel that must be in a link-up state, so that if fewer than the specified number of links are available, the port channel interface fails over to a standby EtherChannel. Min-Links are enabled with the **port-channel min-links** command.

The Min-Links feature is available as of Cisco IOS Software Release 12.2(18)SXF on LACP EtherChannels. The Min-Links feature works at the physical interface level and is independent of spanning-tree path selection. The access layer topology can consist of looped, loop-free, or FlexLink models. This feature can be useful in making sure that a higher-bandwidth uplink path is chosen as the active path in the data center access layer. It causes LACP EtherChannels to become inactive if they have too few active member ports to supply the required minimum bandwidth.

There are some implications to using Min-Links:

- **Active/standby service modules:** If active services are primarily on the Agg1 aggregation switch, a failure that forces Min-Links to use the path to the Agg2 aggregation switch will likely cause all traffic to also traverse the ISL between the aggregation switches.

- **Dual failures:** With Min-Links, it is possible to have a situation where both uplinks would be forced down if both EtherChannels do not have the minimum required port members, which would black hole all connected servers.

- **Looped topologies with the spanning tree:** If a looped access topology is used, it is possible to provide a similar capability by using the *spanning-tree pathcost method long* global option. This permits the spanning tree to use larger-cost values when comparing the cost of different paths to root, which in turn can differentiate the cost value of various paths when a port member fails.

Scaling with Service Layer Switches

As the access layer demands increase in terms of bandwidth and server interface requirements, the uplinks to the aggregation layer are migrating beyond Gigabit Ethernet or GEC speeds and moving to 10 Gigabit Ethernet to get the full bandwidth without the hash implications.

One mechanism for scaling 10 Gigabit Ethernet port density is to move services off of the aggregation layer switches onto service layer switches that are connected via EtherChannel or GEC. The service switch is connected to both aggregation switches with GEC or 10 Gigabit Ethernet links configured as IEEE 802.1Q trunks. This is illustrated in Figure 5-43.

Moving classic bus-based service modules out of the aggregation layer switch increases the number of available slots and improves aggregation layer performance. Service switches are useful when a farm of classic bus-based Cisco CSMs or SSL offload modules are required.

Note   When a single classic bus module exists in the aggregation switch, all line cards that are not distributed forwarding card (DFC) enabled must perform truncated header lookup. Performance in the aggregation layer is improved when the classic bus-based service modules are on service layer switches.

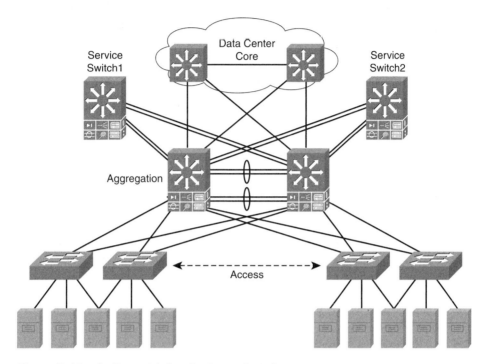

Figure 5-43 *Scaling with Service Layer Switches*

There are some implications to implementing service-level switches:

■ It might be necessary to implement QoS or separate links for fault-tolerant paths.

■ Only necessary Layer 2 VLANs should be extended to the service switches through 802.1Q trunks.

■ If a Cisco CSM in a service switch is configured for RHI, a Layer 3 link to the aggregation layer switch is necessary, because RHI knows how to insert a host route into only the routing table of the local MSFC. A Layer 3 link permits a routing protocol to redistribute the host route to the aggregation layer.

Scaling Service on Cisco ACE Modules

Another way to scale uplink port density and aggregation layer switch slots is to use Cisco ACE modules.

The Cisco ACE module can consolidate the functions of SLB, SSL acceleration, and firewall services such as protocol inspection and filtering into one service module. With the consolidation of functions, a TCP flow is terminated only once, at the Cisco ACE module, instead of at four or more places across the network. This saves time, processing power, and memory. The Cisco ACE module functions as a fabric-enabled line card and, depending on the license, can support 4-Gbps, 8-Gbps, or 16-Gbps throughput.

The Cisco ACE module can support active/active service module designs.

Scaling Spanning Tree and High Availability

As data centers grow, the ability to scale the STP design across the data center is often necessary to meet application requirements, such as Layer 2 adjacency, and to permit a high level of flexibility in administering the servers. As more resources are deployed in the data center, there is also an increased need for high-availability solutions.

Scalability

The ability to extend VLANs across the data center is not only necessary to meet application requirements such as Layer 2 adjacency, but to permit a high level of flexibility in administering the servers. STP designs should answer several scaling questions:

1. How many VLANs can be supported in a single aggregation module?

    Consolidating many data centers into a few is one of the drivers for larger Layer 2 domains.

2. Can a "VLAN anywhere" model be supported to avoid pruning?

    Customers want to meet server installation requirements without the need to place them in the same physical proximity, and want simplified management of additions, moves, and changes.

3. How many access switches can be supported in each aggregation module?

    Growth in data centers and 1RU access layer designs increase the number of access switches to be supported.

4. What are the maximum number of logical ports and virtual ports in STP?

    STP logical and hardware restrictions can impact the data center design.

Note   STP logical ports and virtual ports are discussed in this section.

STPs in the Data Center

The STPs recommended in data center design are IEEE 802.1W, which Cisco implements as an RSTP called Rapid Per-VLAN Spanning Tree Plus (RPVST+), and IEEE 802.1S or Multiple Spanning Tree (MST). Both RSTP and MST have quick convergence characteristics but differ in flexibility and operation.

RSTP is the most common STP used in the data center today, and is the implementation recommended by Cisco for the enterprise data center. RSTP has several desirable characteristics for the enterprise data center:

- It scales to a large size (about 10,000 logical ports).

- Coupled with UDLD, loop guard, root guard, and BPDU guard, it provides a strong and stable Layer 2 design solution.

- It is a proven solution that is easy to implement and scale.

MST is not as common in the enterprise data center because of its characteristics:

- It permits large-scale STP implementations (about 30,000 logical ports). This is typically more useful for service providers and application service providers.

- It is not as flexible as RSTP.

- It has service module implications for firewalls in Transparent mode.

- It is more commonly used with service providers and application service providers.

Note   This book focuses on the use of RSTP.

STP Scaling

Table 5-3 examines at the maximum scalability for STPs on aggregation switches in the data center.

Table 5-3   *Cisco STP Scaling Recommendations*

	Cisco Catalyst 6500 MST	Cisco Catalyst 6500 Rapid PVST+ (RSTP)	Cisco Nexus 7000 MST	Cisco Nexus 7000 Rapid PVST+ (RSTP)
Total active STP logical interfaces	50,000 total	10,000 total	75,000 total	16,000 total
Total virtual ports per line card	6000 per switching module[*]	1800 per switching module[*] (6700) 1200 for earlier modules	No per I/O module limit	No per I/O module limit

[*]10-, 10/100-, and 100-Mbps switching modules support a maximum of 1200 logical interfaces per module. See www.cisco.com/en/US/docs/solutions/Enterprise/Data_Center/ DC_Infra2_5/DCInfra_5.html.

In a Layer 2 looped topology design, spanning-tree processing instances are created on each interface for each active VLAN. These logical instances are used to process the spanning-tree-related packets for each VLAN. These instances are referred to as active logical ports and virtual ports.

Both active logical ports and virtual ports are important values to consider in spanning-tree designs, because they affect STP convergence time and stability. Table 5-3 shows the maximum number of logical interfaces and virtual ports that are supported on Cisco Catalyst 6500 series switches with a Catalyst 6500 series Supervisor Engine 720 using Cisco IOS Release 12.2SX, and the values for the Cisco Nexus 7000 series switches using Cisco NX-OS Software Release 4.2. These values are usually of concern only on the aggregation layer switches that have a larger number of trunks and VLANs configured than other layers in the data center topology.

When designing a large data center using extended Layer 2 VLAN topologies, it is necessary to calculate the spanning-tree logical and virtual ports to ensure that spanning tree operates with optimal convergence and stability characteristics.

STP Logical Interfaces

Active logical ports are a systemwide value that reflects the total number of spanning-tree processing instances used in the whole system.

Total active logical interfaces can be calculated by a formula:

Sum [(Each trunk on the switch) * (Active VLANs on each trunk)] + (Number of nontrunking interfaces on the switch)

In Figure 5-44, there are 10 VLANs on ACC1 and 20 VLANs on ACC2. There is an EtherChannel trunk between AGG1 and AGG2 on a pair of 10 Gigabit Ethernet links.

The total number of STP active logical interfaces on AGG1 in the figure is calculated like this:

[(10 on Te7/3) + (20 on Te7/4)] + (30 on EtherChannel Te7/1-2) = 60

> **Note** An STP instance for all 30 VLANs defined in the system configuration is present on each trunk unless manual VLAN pruning is performed. For example, on each trunk configuration, the **switchport trunk allowed vlan x, y** command must be performed to reduce the number of spanning-tree logical interfaces being used on that port. The automatic VLAN Trunking Protocol (VTP) pruning feature does not remove STP logical instances from the port.

You can also determine the active logical interfaces on a switch by using the **show spanning-tree summary total** command.

Virtual ports are STP instances allocated to each trunk port on a line card. Virtual ports are a per-line card value that reflects the total number of spanning-tree processing

instances used on a particular line card. The number of virtual ports per line card is calculated by another formula:

Sum (Each port used as a trunk or part of a port channel in a trunk) * (Active VLANs
on each trunk)

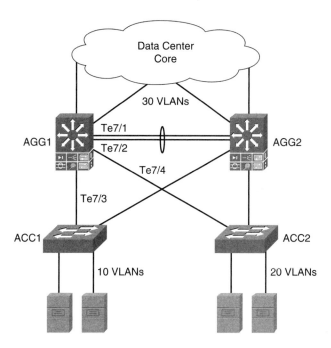

Figure 5-44   *STP Logical Interfaces*

Virtual ports are calculated per port in channel groups; so, for AGG1 in the figure, they
are calculated like this:

(30 on Te7/1) + (30 on Te7/2) + (10 on Te7/3) + (20 on Te7/4) = 90 virtual ports

You can also determine the virtual ports on a switch module by using the **show vlan
virtual-ports slot** command.

STP Scaling with 120 Systemwide VLANs

In Figure 5-45, the data center has a Layer 2 looped topology with 120 VLANs systemwide. No manual pruning is being performed on the trunks. This is a 1RU access switch
design, and 45 access switches are connected to each aggregation switch using 4 GECs.

The number of active logical interfaces is calculated like this:

(120 * 45 access links) + (120 instances on link to AGG2) = 5400 + 120 = 5520

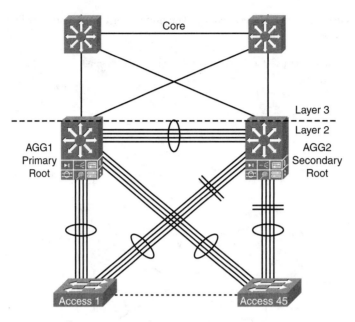

Figure 5-45   *Example: Active Logical Interfaces*

As you can see, 5520 is under the maximum recommendation of 10,000 active logical interfaces supported when using RSTP.

When you consider the virtual ports per line card, there are design issues with a port that uses 120 systemwide VLANs and 45 access links.

If a Cisco Catalyst 6748 Ethernet line card is used on AGG1 to terminate the access switches, it could connect 12 of the 45 access switches on 4 GECs.

The number of virtual ports is calculated like this:

(120 * 48 access links) = 5760

As you can see, 5750 is greater than 1800, which is the maximum number of recommended virtual ports per switching module when using RSTP.

The STP design recommendations are exceeded with 120 VLANs.

Note   The maximum number of VLANs that can be safely supported in this design is 37 (1800 divided by 48). In this case, MST should be used because it would be less than 6000, which is the maximum number of recommended virtual ports per switching module when using 802.1S/MST (*Cisco Data Center Infrastructure 2.5 Design Guide*, Chapter 5, 74–75).

This is not a supported design, and there will be problems when convergence situations arise. This example design will experience various issues such as long convergence times and possibly degraded system-level stability.

You can expect to see a larger network impact when interfaces change between the shutdown and no shutdown states because the large number of virtual interfaces will greatly slow STP convergence times. You will also get a large number of system messages.

STP in 1RU Designs

The use of 1RU access switch designs increases the chances of a larger spanning-tree diameter and the possibility of more STP issues.

The integral switch on the blade server is logically similar to the 1RU access switch design. The same challenges apply to 1RU and blade server designs relative to the increase in spanning-tree logical and virtual ports. There are a few STP issues to consider with these designs:

■ A higher number of access-link trunks increases STP logical port counts in the aggregation layer.

■ You should determine the spanning-tree logical ports, virtual interfaces in place, and STP domain limits before extending VLANs or adding trunks.

■ You can use multiple aggregation modules to scale STP and 10 Gigabit Ethernet density.

STP Scaling Design Guidelines

You have several options to choose from when scaling STP designs and reducing the total number of logical ports:

■ **Add aggregation modules:** Scale the design by dividing up the STP domain using multiple aggregation modules. When multiple aggregation modules are used, it permits the spanning-tree domain to be distributed. This reduces the total port count in any one domain, which would permit STP to function within the limits of the line card or switch.

■ **Limit HSRP instances:** The number of VLANs is typically tied to the number of HSRP instances. Cisco recommends a maximum of 500 HSRP instances on the Catalyst 6500 series Supervisor Engine 720 with default timers. This is somewhat dependent on other CPU-driven processes. The Cisco Nexus 7000 can support up to 2000 HSRP groups per system, with default timers.

■ **Perform manual pruning on trunks:** If the logical interfaces and virtual ports in a Layer 2 domain are near the upper limits, perform manual pruning on the trunks. Although this can be somewhat cumbersome, it dramatically reduces the total number of both active logical and virtual port instances used.

■ **Use MST if it meets the requirements:** If you cannot support the STP scaling issues with RSTP, you can consider implementing MST. MST supports a large number of logical port instances and is used in some of the largest data centers in the world. The drawbacks of using MST are that it does not have as much flexibility as other STPs, such as RSTP, and it might not be supported in certain service module configurations.

Scaling the Data Center Using Zones

A commonly used modular data center design approach is to build a group of similar server racks, access switches, and associated aggregation switches into a logical unit often referred to as a pod or a zone. The data center may then be scaled by replicating the model to encompass additional pods, or potentially different types of pods based on server functions or access switch cabling models.

Considerations such as the types of servers in use, server virtualization models, location of storage resources, power, and cooling must be assessed when developing a zone or pod model for a specific enterprise data center requirement. There are many variations to using the pod or zone concept to scale the data center topology.

A zone-based design approach has several benefits that help scaling data center designs. VLANs are not extended beyond the zone boundaries, which implies that virtual machine mobility and Layer 2 server clusters are also contained within a specific zone. This approach limits the size of failure domains and reduces potential spanning-tree scalability issues. The zone-based design approach also confines specific groups of servers and applications to a specific zone. This allows the design for a specific zone to be tuned for the requirements of the applications that inhabit that zone. A zone-based design approach may also help in complying with security policies and regulations in a virtualized data center environment, because applications and services are confined to specific zones of the data center.

High Availability in the Data Center

The common points of failure in the data center are on the path from the server to the aggregation switch. Single-attached servers connected to single-attached access switches are susceptible to failures in the server network adapter, the network media, and the access switch. This is illustrated in Figure 5-46.

These network failure issues can be addressed by deployment of dual-attached servers using network adapter teaming software connected to dual-attached access switches.

Common NIC teaming configurations are discussed in this section.

Common NIC Teaming Configurations

Servers with a single NIC can have many single points of failure. The NIC, the cable, and the switch to which it connects are all single points of failure. NIC teaming eliminates this single point of failure by providing special drivers that allow two NICs to be connected to two different access switches or different line cards on the same access switch. If one

NIC fails, the secondary NIC assumes the IP address of the server and takes over operation without disruption. The various types of NIC teaming solutions include active/stand-
by and active/active. All NIC teaming solutions require the NICs to have Layer 2 adjacency with each other. There are three common NIC teaming configurations, as shown in
Figure 5-47.

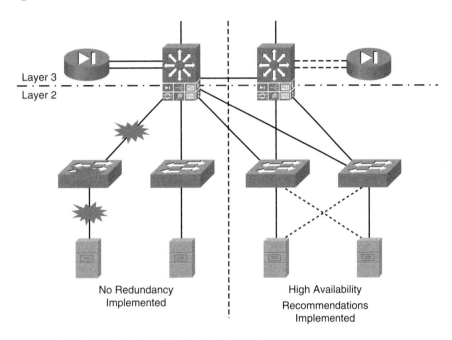

Figure 5-46   *High Availability in the Data Center*

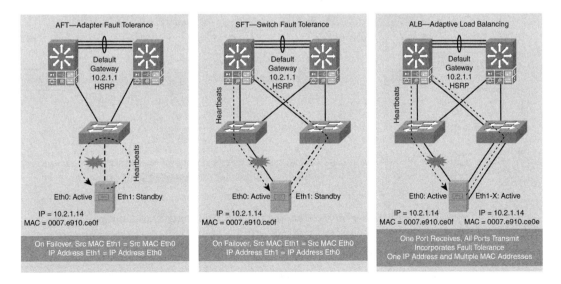

Figure 5-47   *Common NIC Teaming Configurations*

The three common NIC teaming configurations are as follows:

■ **Adapter fault tolerance (AFT):** With AFT designs, two NICs connect to the same switch. One adapter is active and the other standby, and they use one common IP address and MAC address.

■ **Switch fault tolerance (SFT):** With SFT designs, one port is active and the other standby, and they use one common IP address and MAC address.

■ **Adaptive load balancing (ALB):** With ALB designs, one port receives and all ports transmit using one IP address and multiple MAC addresses.

> **Note** NIC manufacturer drivers are changing and may operate differently. Also, some server operating systems have started integrating NIC teaming drivers.

Server Attachment Methods

EtherChannel is another means of providing scalable bandwidth for network servers such as large UNIX servers or PC-based web servers. Various attachments are illustrated in Figure 5-48.

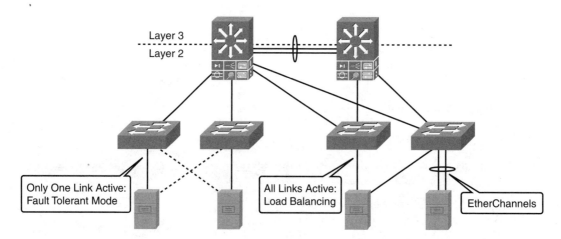

Figure 5-48 *Server Attachment Methods*

In addition to single- and dual-connected servers, EtherChannel allows servers to bundle multiple links to allow higher throughputs between servers and clients and to support redundancy.

Depending on the server, traffic from the server is distributed across the adapters in an EtherChannel based on a hash algorithm or in a round-robin fashion where packets are sent evenly across all adapters.

Incoming traffic to the server is also distributed across the adapters in the link. In addition, you can enable the Layer 3 IP plus Layer 4 port-based CEF hashing algorithm for

EtherChannel ports by using the **port-channel load-balance** command. This command can improve load distribution for EtherChannel ports because it presents more unique values to the hashing algorithm by leveraging the automatic source-port randomization in the client TCP stack.

Note   Because the traffic is distributed across the adapters, it will not permit full utilization of the EtherChannel bandwidth for applications such as backups.

High Availability and Failover Times

The main objective in building a highly available data center network design is to avoid TCP session breakage while providing convergence that is unnoticeable, or as fast as possible. Figure 5-49 summarizes and compares failover times for various technologies.

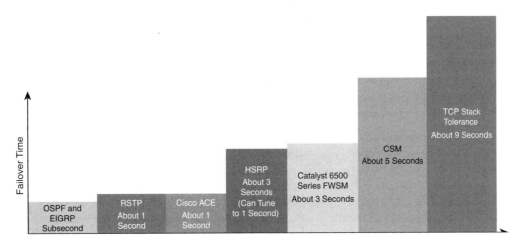

Figure 5-49   *High Availability and Failover Times*

The overall failover time in the data center is the combination of convergence at Layer 2, Layer 3, and Layer 4 components. The network components have different recovery times:

■   Tuned routing protocols can failover in less than 1 second. OSPF and EIGRP can both achieve subsecond convergence time with recommended timer configurations.

■   RSTP converges in about 1 second. RSTP permits subsecond convergence time for minor failures when logical ports are under watermarks, and can take 1 second to 2 seconds for major failure conditions.

■   EtherChannel can fail over in about 1 second. When a link fails, Cisco EtherChannel technology redirects traffic from the failed link to the remaining links in less than 1 second.

- Default HSRP timers are 3 seconds for the hello time and 10 seconds for the hold time. A recommended practice is to configure the timers with a hello time of 1 second and a hold time of 3 seconds so that convergence occurs in less than 3 seconds. Convergence can be adjusted down to subsecond values, but the CPU load must be considered.

- Stateful service modules typically fail over within three to 5 seconds. The convergence time for both the Cisco Catalyst 6500 series FWSM and the CSM is about 5 seconds with recommended timers. Cisco ACE can achieve failovers in about 1 second with its active/active configuration.

- The least tolerant TCP/IP stacks are the Windows Server and Windows XP client stacks, which have about a 9-second tolerance. Each of the TCP/IP stacks that are built in to the various operating systems has a different level of tolerance for determining when a TCP session will be dropped. Other TCP/IP stacks such as those found in Linux, HP, and IBM systems are more tolerant and have a longer window before tearing down a TCP session.

High Availability and Cisco NSF with SSO

The main objective in building a highly available data center network design is to avoid TCP session breakage while providing convergence that is unnoticeable, or as fast as possible. Cisco nonstop forwarding (NSF) with stateful switchover (SSO) are supervisor redundancy mechanisms that provide intrachassis SSO at Layers 2 to 4.

The worst-case convergence time is the event of a supervisor failure on AGG1 (illustrated in Figure 5-50), the primary aggregation switch, which results in all the components on the switch converging to the AGG2 aggregation switch. If the CSM is in use, this failover results in a minimum convergence time of about 5 seconds. This convergence time will most likely be more because tables such as the content-addressable memory (CAM) and ARP have to be rebuilt, so the maximum convergence time can approach the 9-second limit of the Windows TCP/IP stack.

This convergence time and possible lost sessions can be avoided by using dual Catalyst 6500 series Supervisor Engine 720 engines and Cisco NSF with SSO on the primary aggregation switch of the data center. SSO synchronizes the Layer 2 protocol state for trunks and ports; the Layer 2 and Layer 3 MAC, Forwarding Information Base (FIB), and adjacency hardware tables; and the access control list (ACL) and QoS tables. SSO is a prerequisite of Cisco NSF.

The main objective of Cisco NSF is to continue forwarding IP packets following a route processor switchover. Cisco NSF is supported by the EIGRP, OSPF, IS-IS, and Border Gateway Protocol (BGP). Routers running these protocols can detect a switchover and take the necessary actions to continue forwarding network traffic using CEF while recovering route information from the peer devices. With Cisco NSF, peer networking devices do not experience routing flaps.

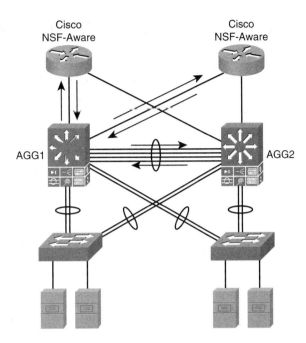

Figure 5-50 *High Availability and Failover Times*

The recommended data center design that uses service modules has a minimum convergence time of about 6 to 7 seconds, primarily because of service modules. If Cisco NSF with SSO is implemented, the service modules do not converge in the event of a supervisor failure. Implementing dual supervisors that use Cisco NSF with SSO can achieve increased high availability in the data center network.

With the current Cisco IOS Release 12.2(25), HSRP state is not maintained by Cisco NSF with SSO. During a switchover on AGG1 (the primary aggregation switch), the AGG2 (the backup aggregation switch) HSRP instances take over for SSO control plane recovery. Because the HSRP MAC address is statefully maintained on the Catalyst 6500 series Supervisor Engine 720 module primary switch standby, the sessions continue to flow through the primary switch, regardless of the active state that appears on the backup aggregation switch. After the control plane comes up on the primary aggregation switch, the HSRP hello messages begin to flow and preemptively move the active HSRP state back to the primary aggregation switch.

You should not set the Interior Gateway Protocol (IGP) timers so aggressively or tune them so low that Cisco NSF with SSO is defeated. The IGP process should not react to adjacent node failure before an SSO can be determined.

Describing Network Virtualization in More Detail

Definition of Virtualization

The term *virtualization* is used in many different technologies. What they have in common is that in all these technologies a pool of physical resources is used to create abstract logical entities, as shown in Figure 5-51.

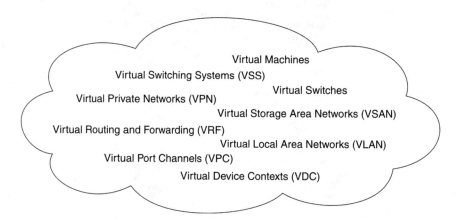

Figure 5-51   *Definition of Virtualization*

Virtualization is a term that is used in the field of IT for the concept of creating abstract entities from a pool of physical resources, while hiding these physical resources from the users or systems that interact with these abstract entities.

As such, virtualization covers many different technologies:

- **Virtual machine:** Virtual machines create multiple logical PCs or servers inside a single physical PC or server to allow sharing of hardware resources such as memory, CPU power, storage, and NICs.

- **VLAN:** VLANs create multiple, logically separated, switched networks on a shared, physical switched network.

- **Virtual SAN (VSAN):** VSANs create multiple, logically separated Fibre Channel fabrics on a shared, physical Fibre Channel fabric.

- **VPN:** VPNs create multiple, logically separated (private) networks on a shared physical network.

- **VDC:** VDCs create multiple logical devices, such as switches, firewalls, or load balancers, inside a single physical device.

- **VRF:** VRF creates multiple, logical Layer 3 routing and forwarding instances inside a single physical router. Each of these instances contains all the elements that are necessary to perform the Layer 3 routing and forwarding functions, such as a Routing

Information Base (RIB), FIB, and routing protocol instances. The various VRFs share the physical resources of the router, such as interfaces, memory, and CPU power.

- **VSS:** VSSs create a single logical switch by combining the physical resources of two separate Cisco Catalyst 6500 series switches.

- **vPC:** vPCs combine two Cisco Nexus 7000 series switches in such a way that they represent themselves as a single, logical switch to neighboring devices, in order to allow these neighboring devices to create an EtherChannel link to the virtual logical switch.

- **vSwitch:** vSwitches create a logical switch from software components that run inside servers.

Virtualization Categories

Although all virtualization technologies create logical entities from a pool of physical resources, the manner in which this action is accomplished may vary. There are several different categories of virtualization:

- **Network virtualization:** When business requirements demand that network traffic is separated on two different networks, the traditional solution is to build two separate physical networks. However, this solution often leads to suboptimal use of resources such as underutilized circuits and devices. Having separate physical networks can lead to rigid change procedures. Moving resources or users from one network to the other is by definition a physical change. Network virtualization technologies, such as VLANs, VSANs, and VPNs, allow you to combine the different networks onto a shared physical infrastructure while still keeping the logical separation to satisfy the original business requirements. This kind of technology allows for higher resource efficiency, while also reducing the time to perform network changes. Network virtualization typically consists of two components: separation of control and data plane functions for the virtual networks inside the network nodes (for example, VLANs inside a switch), and separation of traffic on the links between the nodes (for example, the use of IEEE 802.1Q tagging on a trunk between switches).

- **Device virtualization:** Device virtualization allows multiple logical devices of a certain type, which have different roles, to be run inside a single physical device, instead of using separate physical devices for each of these roles. For example, a solution such as VMware ESX, Microsoft Hyper-V, or Citrix XenServer allows you to run multiple virtual machines (servers or PCs) inside a single physical piece of server hardware. Other examples are the use of virtual device context in firewalls, load balancers, or switches. A major benefit of device virtualization is that several low-performance devices can be replaced by one high-performance device. This replacement typically yields a better price-to-performance ratio. Another benefit is the added flexibility that makes it easier to add, reassign, or repurpose resources in the system.

- **Device clustering:** Device clustering allows multiple physical devices to be combined into a larger logical device. The main benefit of clustering techniques is that they allow systems to scale beyond the size of a single system and attain a higher availability than what could be achieved by a single system. However, the number of logical devices, and hence the complexity of the overall system design, does not increase. The fact that the logical system actually consists of separate physical components is hidden from other devices in the system. An example of device clustering is a VSS, which combines two Catalyst 6500 series switches into a single logical switch. Other examples are combining multiple Catalyst 3750 or 3750E series switches into a stack using Cisco StackWise technology and using vPC on the Cisco Nexus family of switches.

These different virtualization technologies can also be combined into a single virtualization solution. For example, the Cisco Nexus 1000V distributed virtual switch combines device virtualization with device clustering: The Cisco Nexus 1000V series consists of a Virtual Supervisor Module (VSM) and Virtual Ethernet Modules (VEM). The VSM can be implemented as a virtual machine inside a VMware ESX server or as a physical appliance. The VEMs are software components that are embedded in the VMware ESX hypervisor.

Network Virtualization

Network virtualization and its incarnations such as VLANs, VPNs, and VSANs have been widely used in network infrastructures in past decades. The use of VLANs is so pervasive that you would not likely find an enterprise campus or data center environment that does not use VLANs in one form or another. In the WAN, service provider-based VPNs (such as Multiprotocol Label Switching [MPLS], Frame Relay, and IPsec VPNs) are commonly used to interconnect branch offices. The different types of network virtualization all aim to provide separated logical networks on a shared physical infrastructure. The degree of virtualization differs by technology. However, three major points independent of the technology used are the data, control, and management plane. Details of the planes are as follows:

■ **Data plane:** The objective of all network virtualization technologies is separation of the data plane, because this separation is typically mandated by the business needs. Data plane separation is maintained inside each network device by maintaining separate forwarding tables for each virtual network. Data plane traffic is also logically separated on the links between the devices, typically through some form of tagging, such as 802.1Q tagging for VLANs.

■ **Control plane:** The degree of separation on the control plane differs by technology and usually depends on the implementation of the vendor. On the edge of the virtualized domain, the control plane protocols should hide the use of virtualization by interacting with the edge devices in the exact same manner as on a physical network. Within the virtualized domain, the control plane for each virtual network can be entirely separate. For example, in a VSAN, a separate instance of the Fabric Shortest Path First (FSPF) protocol is used for each VSAN. Alternatively, the control plane for multiple virtual networks can be combined. For example, when using Multiple Spanning Tree (MST) in a switched environment, a single process maintains the network topology for all VLANs, and multiple VLANs are grouped by logical instance.

■ **Management plane:** In most forms of network virtualization, the management plane is not separated. Multiple virtual networks typically can be managed from a single device. New virtual networks can be created, and interfaces can be reassigned to different virtual networks as needed.

Virtual Routing and Forwarding

VLANs are virtual Layer 2 networks. Traffic is separated at Layer 2, and hosts in different VLANs cannot communicate at Layer 2. To communicate between VLANs, a router is needed and network policies and traffic control can be implemented on the router.

In most campus network designs, the routing function is implemented on the distribution layer, which is the Layer 2 to Layer 3 boundary. Therefore, VLAN separation alone does not automatically imply complete network separation. For example, voice and data traffic can be separated into two VLANs. However, this separation will not stop devices on the data VLAN from communicating with devices on the voice VLAN on Layer 3 via the distribution switches unless specific measures are taken to restrict the flow of traffic between the VLANs. To create multiple separated Layer 3 networks on a shared Layer 3 infrastructure, an additional layer of virtualization is necessary. To achieve the separation on Layer 3, the data plane and control plane functions of the router or Layer 3 switch need to be segmented into different Layer 3 VPNs, as shown in Figure 5-52. This process is similar to the way that a Layer 2 switch segments the Layer 2 control and data plane into different VLANs.

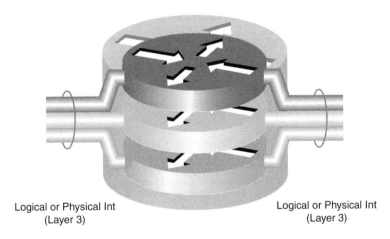

Logical or Physical Int
(Layer 3)

Logical or Physical Int
(Layer 3)

Figure 5-52   *Layer 3 VPN*

The core concept in Layer 3 VPNs is a virtual routing and forwarding (VRF) instance. This instance consists of all the data plane and control plane data structures and processes that together define the Layer 3 VPN. The virtualized network consists of Layer 2 VLANs and Layer 3 VRFs to provide logical, end-to-end isolation across the network. The number of VRFs and VLANs match the number separate paths needed and are mapped to each other.

A VRF includes the following components:

- **A subset of the router interfaces:** Similar to how Layer 2 ports are assigned to a particular VLAN on a Layer 2 switch, the Layer 3 interfaces of the router are assigned to a VRF. Because the elementary component is a Layer 3 interface, this component includes software interfaces, such as subinterfaces, tunnel interfaces, loopback interfaces, and SVIs. The VRF holds its own separate routing and forwarding tables. Interfaces are either associated with global routing or a particular VRF.

- **A routing table or RIB:** Because traffic between Layer 3 interfaces that are in different VRFs should remain separated, a separate routing table is necessary for each VRF. The separate routing table ensures that traffic from an interface in one VRF cannot be routed to an interface in a different VRF.

- **A FIB:** The routing table or RIB is a control plane data structure, and from it, an associated FIB is calculated, which is used in the actual packet forwarding. Clearly, this also needs to be separated by VRF.

- **Routing protocol instances:** To ensure control plane separation between the different Layer 3 VPNs, it is necessary to implement routing protocols on a per-VRF basis. To accomplish this task, you can run an entirely separate process for the routing protocol in the VRF. Or you can use a subprocess or routing protocol instance in a global process that is in charge of the routing information exchange for the VRF.

Layer 3 VPNs and Network Virtualization

With Layer 3 VPNs the routing and forwarding of traffic from the different VPNs must be separated inside the router or Layer 3 switch. You can accomplish this through the implementation of different VRFs for each VPN inside the router. It must be possible to identify the traffic that belongs to each VPN as it travels from router to router. The sending router should mark the traffic on egress in such a way that the receiving router can identify the originating VPN on ingress, as shown in Figure 5-53.

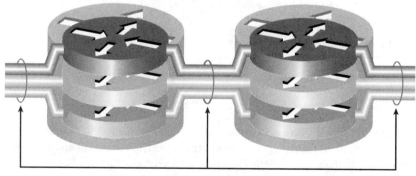

802.1q, GRE, MPLS, L2TPv3 Tags

Figure 5-53   *L2TPv3*

There are four major mechanisms that you can use to accomplish this action:

- **802.1Q VLAN tagging:** Multiple subinterfaces or SVIs are created for each physical link between two VPN-enabled routers. These subinterfaces or SVIs are then associated with the different VRFs. As a result, packets that are sent from a specific VRF are sent out a particular subinterface or SVI and use the associated VLAN tag for that subinterface or SVI. On ingress, a reverse process is applied. When the router receives the packet, the incoming subinterface or SVI is determined from the VLAN tag. The packet is then processed by the VRF that is associated with that subinterface or SVI. This method can be used only if there is a direct Ethernet connection between the two routers (or Layer 3 switches) that supports 802.1Q trunking.

- **GRE tunnels:** GRE tunnels are logical point-to-point links between two routers that encapsulate packets in a generic routing encapsulation (GRE) header. Multiple GRE tunnels are defined between the two VPN-enabled routers. The tunnel interfaces that correspond to these tunnels are then associated with the different VRFs. Packets that are sent from a specific VRF are sent out a particular tunnel interface and use the associated destination IP address for that tunnel. On ingress, the destination IP address is examined, and from this the associated incoming tunnel interface is determined. The packet is then processed by the VRF that is associated with that tunnel interface. The advantage of this method is that the GRE tunnel can span multiple routed hops. As a result, VPN enabled routers can be connected across a network that consists of routers that are not VPN enabled.

- **MPLS:** This method uses Multiprotocol Border Gateway Protocol (MP-BGP) to exchange MPLS labels for each of the different VPNs. When packets are sent by a specific VRF, two MPLS labels are applied: one label that identifies a label-switched path to the other router, and a second label that identifies the VPN. The first label is used to switch the packet across the MPLS cloud to the egress router. The egress router uses the second label to identify the correct VRF and destination subnet for the packet. This method is the most scalable method that you can use to build end-to-end Layer 3 VPNs. However, it is also the most complex method.

- **L2TPv3:** L2TPv3 (Layer 2 Tunneling Protocol Version 3) is a technology that allows Layer 2 frames, such as Ethernet, PPP, and Frame Relay to be transported across an IP network. L2TPv3 tunnels can be used to establish logical point-to-point links between two routers. Similar to the GRE method, multiple L2TPv3 tunnels can be used to separate the traffic of different VRFs and connect VPN-enabled routers across a network that consists of routers that are not VPN enabled.

Summary

This chapter reviewed design models, best practices, methodology, and virtualization for data centers in the Cisco enterprise architecture. The data center architecture is based on a three-layer approach consisting of the core, aggregation, and access layers. The core layer provides a high-speed Layer 3 fabric for packet switching. The aggregation layer extends spanning-tree or Layer 3 routing protocols into the access layer. The data center access layer provides the physical-level attachment to the server resources, and operates in Layer 2 or Layer 3 modes, often with either an EOR or TOR design. Care needs to be taken when scaling STP in the data center and managing the total number of logical interfaces and virtual ports in an STP domain. EtherChannel technologies and service module designs are options for scaling the bandwidth and density of the data center aggregation layer.

References

For additional information, refer to these resources:

Cisco Systems, Inc. *Enterprise Data Center Introduction* at www.cisco.com/web/partners/pr67/pr30/pr220/partners_strategic_solution_concept_home.html

Cisco Systems, Inc. *Cisco Application Control Engine (ACE) Module At-a-Glance*, at www.cisco.com/en/US/prod/collateral/modules/ps2706/ps6906/prod_brochure0900aecd804585e5.pdf

Cisco Systems, Inc. *Cisco Data Center Network Architecture and Solutions Overview* at www.cisco.com/en/US/solutions/collateral/ns340/ns517/ns224/ns377/net_brochure0900aecd802c9a4f.pdf

Cisco Systems, Inc. *Configuring EtherChannels and Layer 2 Trunk Failover and Link-State Tracking* at www.cisco.com/en/US/docs/switches/blades/3020/software/release/12.2_25_sef1/configuration/guide/swethchl.html

Cisco Systems, Inc. *Cisco Data Center Infrastructure 2.5 Design Guide* at www.cisco.com/univercd/cc/td/doc/product/lan/cat3750/12225see/scg/swethchl.pdf

Cisco Systems, Inc. *Nexus 1000v Release and General Information* at www.cisco.com/ en/US/products/ps9902/tsd_products_support_general_information.html

Cisco Systems, *Cisco Nexus 1010 Virtual Services Appliance* at www.cisco.com/en/US/products/ps10785/index.html

Cisco Systems, Inc. *Cisco Nexus 1000V Series Switches Deployment Guide Version 2* at www.cisco.com/en/US/prod/collateral/switches/ps9441/ps9902/guide_c07-

556626.html

Cisco Systems, Inc. *Data Center Design—IP Network Infrastructure* at
www.cisco.com/en/US/docs/solutions/Enterprise/Data_Center/DC_3_0/DC-
3_0_IPInfra.html

Cisco Systems, Inc. *Implementing Nexus 7000 in the Data Center Aggregation
Layer with Services* at
www.cisco.com/en/US/docs/solutions/Enterprise/Data_Center/ nx_7000_dc.html

Cisco Systems, Inc. *Data Center Service Integration: Service Chassis Design Guide*
at
www.cisco.com/en/US/docs/solutions/Enterprise/Data_Center/dc_servchas/servicecha
ssis_design.html

Cisco Systems, Inc. *Advanced Services' Building Cisco Enterprise Data Center
Architecture* at www.cisco.com/en/US/services/ps11/ps2696/ps2804/services_data_
sheet0900aecd80281d85.pdf

Review Questions

Answer the following questions, and then refer to Appendix A, "Answers to Review
Questions," for the answers.

1. What are the benefits of the three layer model for data center design? (Choose three.)

    a. Providing redundant Internet services

    b. Support for NIC teaming

    c. Support for Layer 2 domain sizing

    d. Support for one fixed access layer model

    e. Support for a mix of access layer models

2. What are the design recommendations for OSPF in the data center? (Choose three.)

    a. Use NSSA from the core layer down.

    b. Use NSSA from the aggregation layer down.

    c. Adjust the default bandwidth value with the **auto-cost reference-bandwidth**
        command.

    d. Adjust the default bandwidth value with the **auto-cost bandwidth** command.

    e. Tune the timers with the **timers throttle spf** command.

3. What are the characteristics of a Layer 2 looped design model? (Choose two.)

    a. VLANs do not extend to the aggregation layer.

    b. Layer 2 services from the aggregation layer such as NIC teaming are supported.

   c. Redundancy can be supported using a trunk between the access switches.

   d. VLANs are extended to the aggregation layer.

   e. STP is not needed for reliable operation.

   f. All uplinks are active, and none are blocking.

4. Which design is most susceptible to black holing of service module traffic in the event of an uplink failure?

   a. Layer 2 loop-free U

   b. Layer 2 looped square

   c. Layer 2 looped triangle

   d. Layer 2 loop-free inverted U

   e. Layer 2 looped inverted triangle

5. What are the characteristics of a Layer 3 access design model? (Choose three.)

   a. VLANs do not extend to the aggregation layer.

   b. VLANs are extended to the aggregation layer.

   c. All uplinks are active, and none are blocking.

   d. Layer 2 server adjacency is supported across a single pair of access switches.

   e. Layer 2 server adjacency is not supported across access switches.

6. What are the characteristics of top-of-rack access switch designs as compared to end-of-rack access switch designs? (Choose three.)

   a. VLANs do not extend to the aggregation layer.

   b. Cabling from the cabinet is minimized.

   c. Uplinks to the aggregation layer are minimized.

   d. Cooling requirements are eased.

   e. STP processing requirements are minimized.

   f. The number of devices to manage increases.

7. What command is used to enable an EtherChannel hash for Layer 3 IP plus Layer 4 port-based Cisco Express Forwarding?

   a. mpls ip cef

    b. port-channel ip cef

    c. mpls ip port-channel cef

    d. port-channel load-balance

    e. mpls ip load-balance

8. Where are service layer switches typically connected in the data center architecture?

    a. At the core layer in Layer 2 access layer designs

    b. At the service layer in Layer 3 access layer designs

    c. At the access layer in Layer 2 access layer designs

    d. At the access layer in Layer 3 access layer designs

    e. At the aggregation layer in Layer 2 access layer designs

    f. At the aggregation layer in Layer 3 access layer designs

9. What are STP virtual ports?

    a. A systemwide value that reflects the total uplinks that are not blocked

    b. The total number of trunking interfaces on a line card

    c. A systemwide value that reflects the total number of spanning-tree processing instances used

    d. A per-line card value that reflects the total number of spanning-tree processing instances used on a particular line card

    e. A per-line card value that is the sum of all ports used as trunks or part of a port channel in a trunk

10. The integral switch on a blade server is logically similar to what design?

    a. Layer 3 access design

    b. 1RU access switch design

    c. Enterprise-wide MST design

    d. Modular access switch design

    e. Multiple aggregation module design

11. Which component has the largest failover time?

    a. ACE Module

    b. FWSM

    c. Tuned EIGRP

    d. RSTP

    e. HSRP

12. Which three design options are enabled by the use of VDCs on the Cisco Nexus 7000 series switches?

    a. Balancing burger: using two VDCs on a Cisco Nexus 7000 switch to create a redundant pair of switches to dual-homed servers

    b. Split-core topology: building two separate data center cores using a single redundant pair of Cisco Nexus 7000 switches

    c. Services sandwich: using two VDCs on a Cisco Nexus 7000 switch to logically separate the switches below and above the services chain

    d. Consolidated aggregation: using two VDCs of a single Cisco Nexus 7000 switch as a redundant pair of aggregation switches in an aggregation block

    e. Multiple aggregation layers: using VDCs to create separate aggregation blocks by business unit or function from a single pair of Cisco Nexus 2000 FEXs

13. What are two characteristics of an access layer design based on Cisco Nexus 5000 series switches and Cisco Nexus 2000 fabric extenders?

    a. Cabling is similar to a top-of-rack design.

    b. Cabling is similar to an end-of-row design.

    c. Management and control characteristics are similar to a top-of-rack design.

    d. Management and control characteristics are similar to an end-of-row design.

Chapter 6

SAN Design Considerations

After completing this chapter, you will be able to

■ Describe SAN components and technologies

■ Discuss basic SAN design and SAN extension

■ Discuss SAN design using Cisco MDS 9000 series multilayer switches

■ Describe SAN extension considerations

■ Describe Unified Fabric Technology

■ Discuss integrated design considerations for supporting IP and SAN traffic on integrated fabric on the Cisco Nexus family of switches

The storage-area network (SAN) is a set of protocols and technologies that permit storage devices to have direct connections with servers over some distance. In addition, a SAN permits the storage devices to be shared among a number of servers based on select criteria. Finally, using VSAN technologies (virtual SAN), a group of discrete SANs can be connected together using a "virtual" SAN fabric.

This chapter introduces you to SAN design considerations. Beginning with the business drivers for storage-area networking, SAN components and technologies are explored. The protocols that govern SAN behavior are examined, along with references to Cisco MDS 9000 switches.

Traditional data centers often consist of multiple networks in order to meet the distinct requirements of LAN, SAN, and high-performance computing (HPC) traffic. Integrating these different types of traffic onto a single unified fabric result in a substantial reduction of access layer cabling, adapters, and switches. This is also a foundation for both "green" data centers and other important architectures to enable services such as cloud computing.

To enable a unified fabric, switched 10 Gigabit Ethernet can be used as the foundation. Fibre Channel SAN traffic can be transported across the Ethernet switched network using the Fibre Channel over Ethernet (FCoE) protocol. To interconnect the FCoE-connected servers to the Fibre Channel SAN, FCoE-enabled switches are necessary to support native Fibre Channel uplinks in addition to 10 Gigabit Ethernet FCoE interfaces. Fibre Channel traffic is extremely sensitive to packet loss; therefore, the FCoE standards prescribe that the underlying Ethernet network should be lossless.

The IEEE Data Center Bridging (DCB) Task Group has defined additional Ethernet standards that help achieve a lossless Ethernet network. The Cisco Nexus 5000 series switches and Cisco Nexus 2000 series fabric extenders (FEX) can be deployed to implement a unified fabric that consolidates LAN, SAN, and HPC traffic onto a single network. Integrating HPC traffic mainly requires inexpensive adapters with low latency (a common characteristic of 10-Gbps technology today).

Identifying SAN Components and Technologies

SAN technology is designed to remotely attach storage devices such as disk drives to host computers. SAN technology enables a high throughput and therefore high performance. For example, an advantage of a SAN is that data access is provided at a block level via the Small Computer Systems Interface (SCSI) protocol, as shown in Figure 6-1.

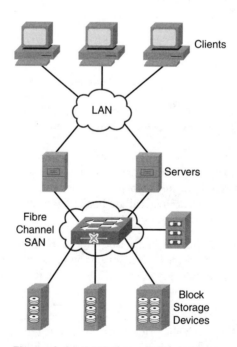

Figure 6-1 *SAN Overview*

In a SAN network, the clients request files from the servers, which have knowledge of the file system structure. The servers request specific blocks of data from a storage element in the back-end storage network.

SAN technology supports shared storage that is separate from the server or servers that use it. Storage resources are easily moved or allocated with no interruption of service on the servers. Managing a SAN tends to be more complex than direct-attached storage (DAS). However, SANs provide a lower total cost of ownership (TCO) because the storage is not captive to one server and so there is a more efficient utilization of storage resources. The consolidation of multiple lower-end storage systems into centralized, higher-end systems allows for reduced administrative overhead. Backup can be easier with SAN technology because it does not necessarily tie up host capacity, nor does it require a dedicated network or bandwidth on the main network. SAN technology also supports the fast implementation of high availability. SAN also allows the consolidation of storage. This not only optimizes backups, power, cooling, and space, it also decreases the administrative complexity of managing storage.

The hardware that connects servers to storage devices in a SAN is referred to as a fabric. Two separate fabrics are commonly used to provide high availability, which is necessary because failure recovery can drastically impact production servers.

The SAN fabric enables connectivity of any server to any storage device through the use of Fibre Channel switching technology. Fibre Channel switching technology is a standard from the T11 Technical Committee of the InterNational Committee for Information Technology Standards (INCITS), an American National Standards Institute (ANSI)-accredited standards committee. The SAN fabric provides a high-speed, full-duplex dedicated network, with high-availability features, high throughput, and very low latency. When storage resources are consolidated into the same fabric, organizations can more easily make use of many features, including data replication, data sharing, and centralized backups.

The following are some of the business drivers for SAN deployments:

- Escalating storage requirements

- Rising storage management costs

- Business continuity

- Requirement to share information

- Increasing levels of underutilized disk storage resources resulting in increased backup storage and backup handling costs

One disadvantage to SANs is that there is limited vendor interoperability.

SAN Components

There are three main components to a Fibre Channel SAN: host bus adapters (HBA), data storage devices, and storage subsystems.

An HBA is an I/O adapter that provides connectivity between a host server and a storage device. The HBA is used to connect a device to a SAN using a Fibre Channel interface. Intelligent HBAs perform many of the lower-level I/O functions to minimize the CPU impact on the host server. HBA connection methods can be either copper or fiber, similar to a typical LAN adapter.

The fundamental idea of SAN is to connect hosts to storage devices. Most data storage is done through the use of hard disk drives. Hard disk technology has been used in personal computers and servers for years. Hard disks use a number of different technologies. Interfaces on the hard disks can be one of the following:

■ SCSI

■ Fibre Channel

■ Advanced Technology Attachment (ATA)

■ Integrated Drive Electronics (IDE)

■ Serial ATA (SATA)

Disk drives themselves cannot sit directly on the network. The technologies listed represent the controller intelligence that enables the drives to be used. The means needed for physical connectivity may vary. There are several methods of connecting storage devices to their host CPUs:

■ **Parallel SCSI copper interconnects:** Provides historically based external server storage. Scalability tends to be a problem. Cable distances are limited.

■ **iSCSI:** iSCSI is an SCSI transport protocol for mapping of block-oriented storage data over TCP/IP networks. Conceptually, iSCSI+TCP+IP provide an equivalent of Layer 3/4 network transport, rather than alternatives of either parallel SCSI cable or Fibre Channel Protocol (FCP) (SCSI over Fibre Channel). The basic idea of iSCSI is to take advantage of the investment in existing IP networks to facilitate and extend SANs. This is accomplished by using the TCP/IP protocol to transport SCSI commands and data between host and SAN nodes.

■ **Optical direct connect:** Provides much longer distance capability than SCSI copper connections.

■ **Fibre Channel switch:** Provides the most scalability and complete feature set. The Fibre Channel switches are the basis for the Fibre Channel network.

■ **Host-based protocols:** Host-based protocols such as Network File System (NFS) and Server Message Block (SMB).

  ■ NFS was designed as a UNIX (now available in other OS such as Linux or Microsoft) protocol that runs over TCP (Version 3) or User Datagram Protocol (UDP) (Version 2). NFS was originally invented by Sun Microsystems and later submitted to the IETF as a standard in 1998. It allows a server to share its disks, independent of implementation (array or JBOD; SCSI, ATA, or FCP).

  ■ SMB is a protocol originally invented at IBM. It also allows the sharing of other peripherals such as printers. Its primary use is in Microsoft-based networks.

However, it can be used with other operating systems. Other storage devices include tape drives, flash drives, and read/write CD/DVD drives.

Storage systems connect storage devices to the network. Storage organization can be supported through various subsystems from simplistic to complex with large volumes of storage and many services available. Here are some examples of storage subsystems:

- **Just a bunch of disks (JBOD):** JBOD refers to a simple disk array. An example of a JBOD is a server with an external cable to a cabinet that has several pluggable hard disks in it. They share the cabinet and power. It may have a redundant array of independent/inexpensive disks (RAID) controller in it or it may not. The JBOD can be connected via SCSI technology. It can also use Fibre Channel technology. Fibre Channel-attached disks are connected to what is essentially a Fibre Channel hub.

- **Storage arrays:** Intelligent storage arrays are a group of devices that provide mass storage and other functions and services. Various internal architectures based on a bus architecture or a switched architecture are possible with storage arrays. To the SAN, the storage system internal architecture is not important. Storage arrays fundamentally include these components:

  - Connected devices (host connections) that can be supported through Fibre Channel or direct connections.

  - Disk drive technologies.

  - Cache that can support read-only and read-write access. Cache can be implemented with backup power sources to ensure data integrity.

- **RAID:** RAID is a technology in which disk drives are combined and configured to provide increased performance and fault tolerance.

RAID Overview

RAID is a method used to inexpensively put together a set of physical hard drives into a logical array of storage devices. RAID provides fault tolerance compared to standalone disk drives. RAID does this by mirroring data or implementing parity check operations. RAID can be performed using hardware or host-based software.

Several types of RAID can be used, including one or more of these:

- **RAID 0 (striping):** Two or more disk drives are concatenated together to form one large volume. Read and write operations can be done in parallel. RAID 0 is done for performance and increase capacity. It provides no redundancy.

- **RAID 1 (mirroring):** Data is duplicated on multiple disks. This can be done for increased reliability and availability. If Raid 1 is used on two drives, it provides twice the read transaction rate of single disks and the same write transaction rate as single disks. RAID 1 doubles the requirement for disk drives.

- **RAID 3 (error detection):** Data is striped across multiple disks, and a dedicated disk drive is used for maintaining error-correction information. This can be done for added reliability and availability. RAID 3 offers no protection for the parity disk, and therefore is rarely used.

■ **RAID 5 (error correction):** Data and parity information is striped across multiple disks. This is commonly done for added reliability and availability. The error-correction information is striped on all disks. This adds a level of protection to data and parity. Redundancy with RAID 5 is better than with RAID 3, because if one drive fails the array can still function, and when the drive is replaced the RAID controller dynamically rewrites the data on the new drive. RAID 5 is one of the most commonly used implementations of RAID.

■ **RAID 6 (error correction):** RAID 6 also stripes parity information across multiple disks like RAID 5. However, instead of storing one parity block, RAID 6 stores two parity blocks using different parity functions. Having an additional parity block protects RAID 6 against disk failure during a disk recovery operation. Effectively, RAID 6 increases reliability at the cost of storage efficiency.

Note Additional RAID levels exist but are not commonly used. RAID 2 is formally defined but is not in use, and RAID 4 has had little exposure. There are also proprietary forms of RAID, such as EMC's Parity RAID.

RAID technology can be used as a protection mechanism for SAN along with cache mirroring, data mirroring, and remote replication.

RAID levels can be combined. RAID 5 arrays can be "mirrored" with another RAID 5 array for an additional element of protection. This can make storage even more reliable.

Storage Topologies

Storage topologies come in one of two main types: direct-attached storage (DAS) and network-attached storage (NAS) topologies. DAS is a topology where the storage devices connect directly to the server. Storage devices that can be attached to the IP network are called NAS devices.

DAS

DAS is commonly described as captive storage. DAS is often implemented in a parallel SCSI implementation. Devices in a captive storage topology do not have direct access to the storage network and do not support efficient sharing of storage. For example, the only way to access the DAS devices in Figure 6-2 is by using the CPU of the host.

To access data on a DAS, a user must go through a front-end network. DAS devices provide little or no mobility to other servers and little scalability. DAS devices limit file sharing and can be complex to implement and manage.

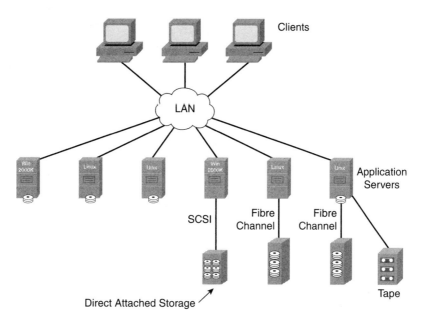

Figure 6-2 *Direct-Attached Storage*

For example, to support data backups, DAS devices require resources on the host and spare disk systems that cannot be used on other systems.

NAS

A NAS device is dedicated to file sharing. NAS devices have direct IP capabilities that allow access at a file level using a protocol such as Network File System (NFS) or Common Internet File System (CIFS) across an IP network. NAS devices provide data storage and access and the management of these functions. NAS devices support file-serving requests so that resources can be freed up on other servers. NAS servers commonly use SCSI and RAID technologies internally. A NAS device is directly connected to a front-end network. Storage devices can be shared between servers and between users as shown in Figure 6-3.

NAS devices respond to requests by providing portions of the file system. To retrieve a file, a NAS device has to open a directory, read it, locate the file, check permissions, and then transfer the file. If the file is several directories deep, the NAS device needs to perform repeated operations to retrieve one file. This process can require a lot of network traffic, although TCP can be tuned to help optimize the file transport.

Note   The block-level access operations on DAS devices are much faster than operations requiring a search of the file or directory system on a volume.

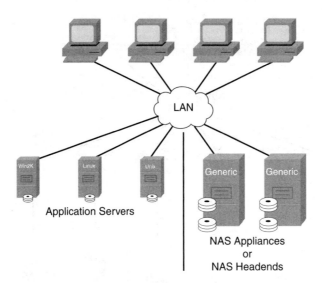

Figure 6-3   *Network-Attached Storage*

SAN Technologies

SAN devices communicate with each other using a variety of protocols. These protocols are introduced in the following sections. The Cisco MDS 9000 family of switches offers a number of enhancements for SCSI, and a brief overview of VSAN, IVR (inter-VSAN routing), and SANTap follows.

SCSI Overview

SCSI is a parallel interface technology used by hosts to attach peripheral devices, such as hard disks and tape drives.

SCSI technology supports writing blocks of one or more files or databases to an external disk in a SAN. The files are written using the host system attributes, including permissions, file size, and modification date. The SCSI channel used to transmit SCSI commands, data, and status is the foundation for all communications in a SAN based on SCSI devices. Connectivity between a SCSI host and a SCSI device can be supported on either an internal or external connection.

SCSI uses a bus technology that supports multiple devices attached to a controller and can support daisy chaining. Through the bus connection, a host can communicate with several SCSI devices using multiple half-duplex I/O channels. SCSI communication is commonly described as being between an initiator and a target. An initiator is typically the host computer. A target is typically the storage device.

The parallel SCSI specification contains these elements:

- Up to 75 foot (25 meter) bus length

- Shared channel bandwidth of up to 320 MBps

- Up to 16 devices per SCSI bus

- Half-duplex operation

Daisy chaining slightly increases SCSI scalability. Because daisy-chained storage devices are captive behind a server, this technology still has limitations from a networking perspective.

Note   The SCSI adapter can access seven other devices plus itself when the bus width is 8 bits. When the bus width is 16 bits, the adapter can access up to 15 other devices.

Fibre Channel Overview

Fibre Channel is a serial, data transfer architecture with a high level of scalability and a bandwidth that supports the extension of SCSI technologies.

The serial connectivity of Fibre Channel provides a mechanism for transporting SCSI information across high-speed networks. Fibre Channel provides high-speed transport for the SCSI payload but overcomes the distance and limitations that come with parallel SCSI technology.

Fibre Channel includes these features:

- Addressing for up to 16 million nodes

- Loop (shared) and fabric (switched) transport options

- Host speeds of 100 to 400 MBps, or an effective throughput of 1 to 4 Gbps on the fabric

- Segment distances of up to 6 miles (10 km)

- Support for multiple protocols

Fibre Channel is the integration of the best attributes of host channel and networking technologies. Fibre Channel implements attributes from channel technology in the mainframe environment, including reliability and scalability. Fibre Channel also implements attributes from networking, including connectionless services, high connectivity, and long distances.

Fibre Channel supports three topologies: point to point, arbitrated loop (similar to Token Ring), and switched fabric. Fibre Channel switching is point-to-point oriented. Both the initiator and storage target side are nodes in the storage network. Fibre Channel has become the dominant open systems protocol for connecting servers to storage.

Fibre Channel Communications Model

Fibre Channel communications is similar to TCP in the following aspects as summarized in Figure 6-4.

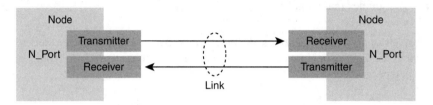

Figure 6-4   *Similarities Between Fibre Channel and TCP*

■ Fibre Channel communications are point-to-point oriented. A session is established between the two points through the device login. This session establishment is similar to TCP session establishment.

■ Fibre Channel supports a logical node connection point between node ports (N_ports). This is similar to TCP and UDP sockets.

■ Fibre Channel Protocol (FCP) supports flow control on a hop by hop basis using a buffer-to-buffer credit (BB_Credit) method. In BB_Credit flow control, the source and destination set the number of buffer credits allowed to accumulate before the source stops sending data. Each frame sent from the source must be acknowledged by the destination, and a buffer credit supports an unacknowledged frame. If an initiator wants to talk to a target, it first negotiates with the target for the number of BB_Credits allowed. During transmission, the source keeps a running count of buffer credits. If the number of credits reaches the maximum buffer credit, the source stops sending until it receives an acknowledgment from the destination. Flow control with Fibre Channel is similar to TCP flow control except that the Fibre Channel mechanism has no drops.

■ Fibre Channel supports acknowledgments for certain classes of traffic. For example, the Cisco MDS 9000 FCIP TCP stack is optimized for transporting storage traffic. It uses packet shaping to minimize the possibility of dropped packets and uses selective acknowledgment (SACK) and fast retransmit to recover quickly from congestion conditions. The classes are labeled 1, 2, 3, and F. For example, class 2 uses acknowledgments for guaranteed delivery. The Fibre Channel support for acknowledgments for certain classes of traffic is similar to the TCP and UDP acknowledgment models.

■ Fibre Channel enables multiple sessions to be maintained per device. This mechanism is similar to multiple TCP and UDP sockets.

VSAN

A virtual SAN (VSAN), shown in Figure 6-5, is a logical SAN that provides isolation among devices that are physically connected to the same fabric.

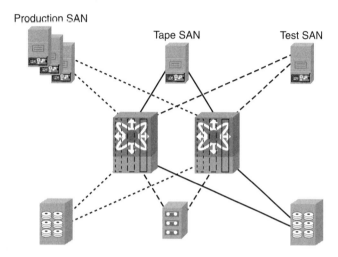

Figure 6-5 *Virtual SANs*

A SAN island is a physically isolated switch or group of switches used to connect hosts to storage devices. The initial SAN deployments were more typically islands consisting of two to four switches.

The Cisco MDS 9000 SAN fabric family supports VSAN technology. VSANs provide the capability to overlay multiple virtual fabric environments within a single fabric infrastructure. This VSAN capability is sometimes called fabric virtualization. VSANs are a way to support independent virtual fabrics on a single switch. VSANs improve consolidation and simplify management by allowing for more efficient SAN utilization. Inter-VSAN routing (IVR) allows a resource on any individual VSAN to be shared by users of a different VSAN without merging the fabrics. Each VSAN divides the fabric into smaller failure domains, creating greater resilience.

An expansion port (E_Port) is an interface that functions as a fabric expansion port by connecting to another E_Port on another switch. E_Ports carry frames between switches for configuration and fabric management. The Cisco MDS 9000 series uses the Enhanced Inter-Switch Link (EISL) frame format to support virtual fabric trunking across trunking E_Ports (TE_Ports). Trunking enables interconnected ports to transmit and receive frames in more than one VSAN over the same physical link.

A good SAN design is required to build a large SAN and ultimately use a high number of ports. In Figure 6-5, there are several SAN islands. Instead of using different switches at each island, you can use VSANs. You can consolidate the islands into a single physical fabric but maintain logical separation. This cuts down on the physical connections needed to the various targets shared by different islands.

IVR

IVR is also known as fabric routing. IVR provides connectivity between fabrics without merging them. The connectivity is supported at Layer 3. By routing between VSANs, devices can maintain a level of separation in terms of fabric services and fabricwide events required for the highest level of availability and take advantage of data sharing across thousands of devices. This is illustrated in Figure 6-6.

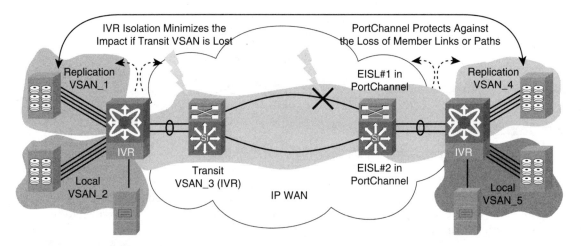

Figure 6-6   *Inter-VSAN Routing*

IVR includes these features:

- Sharing of centralized storage services, such as tape libraries and disks across VSANs. Without IVR, you would be forced to merge the separate fabrics to share information between VSANs.

- Enabling devices in different VSANs to communicate.

- Enabling selective features between VSANs. One example is to enable replication across VSANs while preventing local devices from traversing the WAN.

IVR is not limited to VSANs present on a common switch. Routes that traverse one or more VSANs across multiple switches can be established, if necessary, to create proper interconnections. IVR used in conjunction with Fibre Channel over IP (FCIP) can provide efficient business continuity or disaster recovery solutions.

FSPF

Fabric Shortest Path First (FSPF) is the standard path-selection protocol used by Fibre Channel fabrics. IVR uses FSPF to calculate the best path to a remote fabric.

FSPF supports multiple paths and automatically computes an alternative path around a failed link. It provides a preferred route when two equal paths are available.

The FSPF routing protocol has these characteristics and features:

- Supports multipath routing.

- Bases path status on a link state routing protocol.

- Routes hop by hop, based on only the domain ID.

- Runs on only E_Ports or TE_Ports and provides a loop-free topology.

- Runs on a per-VSAN basis. Connectivity in a given VSAN in a fabric is guaranteed only for the switches configured in that VSAN.

- Uses a topology database to keep track of the state of the links on all switches in the fabric and associates a cost with each link.

- Guarantees a fast reconvergence time in case of a topology change. FSPF uses the standard Dijkstra algorithm (OSPF uses this algorithm, as well), but there is a static dynamic option for a more robust, efficient, and incremental Dijkstra algorithm. The reconvergence time is fast and efficient because the route computation is done on a per-VSAN basis.

Zoning

Zoning is a way to enable access between an initiator and a storage target. Zoning is a logical grouping of fabric-connected devices within a SAN or VSAN. Zoning can be used to establish access control. Devices within a zone can access each other, as shown in Figure 6-7.

Zoning provides a means of restricting visibility and connectivity between devices connected to a common Fibre Channel SAN or VSAN. Zoning increases security, because limiting access prevents unauthorized access. Zoning allows the SAN administrator to overlay a security map dictating which host devices can see which targets, thereby reducing the risk of data loss. Because hosts are notified when targets connect or disconnect, zoning can also limit visibility of and notification concerning storage changes to the hosts that might actually connect to that storage. Zoning is often done per initiator, because specifying what each host can connect ends up being much simpler to maintain than a mix of hosts and targets that grows randomly over time.

There are two zoning types: software based and hardware based. Software-based zoning makes use of Domain Name System (DNS) queries. Hardware-based zoning is more common and more secure. Zoning is effective at managing connectivity between end devices within a storage network. However, zoning does not offer any capability to control the path selection and flow through a storage network between zoned devices.

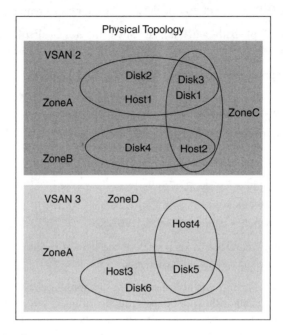

Figure 6-7 *Zoning*

VSANs and zoning are two powerful tools to aid the SAN designer in building robust, secure, and manageable networking environments while optimizing the use and cost of switching hardware. VSANs are first created as isolated logical fabrics within a common physical topology; then, individual unique zone sets can be applied as necessary within each VSAN.

FICON

Fiber Connectivity (FICON) is an upper-layer protocol developed by IBM that uses the lower layers of Fibre Channel transport for connecting IBM mainframes with control units.

FICON is the next-generation replacement for the older Enterprise System Connection (ESCON) protocol, which was a 200-Mbps unidirectional serial bit transmission protocol from IBM. This is illustrated in Figure 6-8. FICON is bidirectional, and runs over Fibre Channel at gigabit-per-second rates. One of the main advantages of FICON is the lack of the performance degradation over distance that is seen with ESCON. FICON can reach a distance of 60 miles (100 km) before experiencing any significant drop in data throughput.

The MDS 9000 series supports both FCP and FICON capabilities using VSAN technology for hardware-enforced, isolated environments within a single physical fabric. This provides both secure sharing of physical infrastructure and enhanced FICON mixed support.

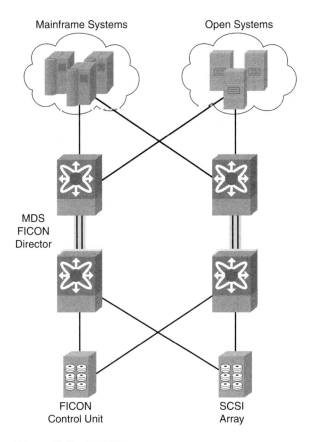

Figure 6-8 *FICON*

The FICON support that the MDS 9000 series provides includes traffic and management isolation, advanced distance extension, quality of service (QoS), and scaling. Because both FICON and Fibre Channel with FCP use Fibre Channel transports, these systems can share a common network and I/O infrastructure, commonly known as an intermix.

SANTap

SANTap is one of the Intelligent Storage Services features supported on the Storage Services Module (SSM) in the Cisco MDS 9500 series multilayer fabric directors and Cisco MDS 9200 multilayer fabric switches (see Figure 6-9).

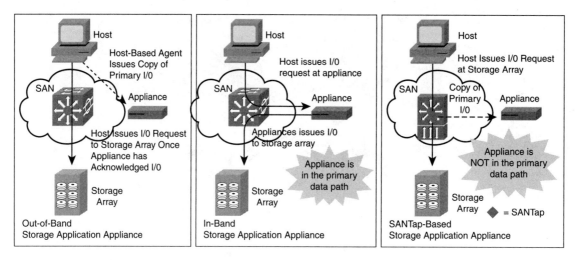

Figure 6-9   *SANTap*

The SANTap feature allows third-party data storage applications, such as long-distance replication and continuous backup, to be integrated into the SAN. SANTap enables data being written to a storage device to be duplicated at another appliance within the fabric. The appliance need not be in the primary data path. By duplicating write data to a storage target, third-party storage appliances can create either backups or replicas of primary data.

The SANTap protocol enables transparent insertion of appliance-based storage applications. End users can take advantage of a wide range of SANTap solutions from several third-party appliance and application vendors to perform heterogeneous data migration, remote replication, snapshots, continuous data protection, and information lifecycle management through intelligent tiered storage. Cisco SANTap provides a high-performance, reliable, heterogeneous platform that integrates easily into existing environments.

A SANTap solution provides these benefits:

■   Transparent insertion and provisioning of appliance-based storage applications

■   No disruption of the primary I/O from the server to the storage array

■   On-demand storage services

■   Scalable commodity appliance-based storage applications

Designing SAN and SAN Extension

Basic SAN design using the Cisco MDS 9000 series multilayer switches is based on port counts and performance. The underlying principles of SAN design are relatively straightforward, as shown in Figure 6-10 (which shows two fabrics that are not in the same failure domain).

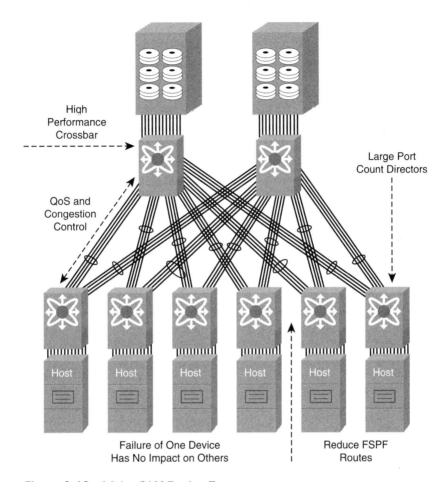

High
Performance
Crossbar

Large Port
Count Directors

QoS and
Congestion
Control

Host   Host   Host   Host   Host   Host

Failure of One Device
Has No Impact on Others

Reduce FSPF
Routes

Figure 6-10 *Major SAN Design Factors*

When designing a SAN, important concepts to plan for include the following:

■   Plan a network topology that can handle the number of ports for both present and
     future needs.

■   Design a network topology with a given end-to-end performance and throughput
     level in mind, taking into account any physical requirements of a design.

■   Provide the necessary connectivity with remote data centers to handle the business
     requirements of continuity and disaster recovery.

Port Density and Topology Requirements

The single most important factor in determining the most suitable SAN design is determining the number of end ports required both now and over the anticipated lifespan of
the design. For example, the design for a SAN that must handle a network with 100 end

ports differs significantly from the design for a SAN that has to handle a network with 1500 end ports. You can determine the number of ports required by answering these questions:

- How many ports are needed now?

- How many ports will be needed in the future?

- What is the expected life of the SAN?

A recommended practice is to design the SAN switches with the capacity to support future requirements. This does not mean that you need to install all the ports now, but you should plan for future requirements to avoid costly retrofits.

The SAN design should also consider topology and physical space requirements. Some questions to consider are these:

- Is the data center located on one floor?

- Is the data center located in one building?

- Do you want to use an IP SAN extension for disaster recovery connectivity?

Any design should also consider an increase in future port speeds, protocols, and densities that could be supported by unused module slots in switches. Under building the SAN switch infrastructure could result in the need for a "forklift upgrade" if more capacity is needed, while overbuilding could result in unused capacity. The choice is a business decision based on the forecasting of capacity versus the initial capital expenditure (CAPEX).

Device Oversubscription

All SAN designs should have some degree of oversubscription or fan-out from storage devices to hosts. It is a common practice for storage subsystem vendors to share one port on the storage subsystem among multiple host bus adapters (HBA) on multiple servers. Most major disk subsystem vendors provide guidelines as to the recommended fan-out ratio of subsystem client-side ports to server connections in the range of 7:1 to 15:1. This ratio balances different server platforms and applications across these subsystem ports to fully utilize available bandwidth. The ratio assumes that the storage subsystem ports have access to full line-rate performance and that the Fibre Channel switching fabric is nonblocking.

Note Some Fibre Channel switch line cards are designed to work in an oversubscribed mode. For example, on the Cisco MDS 9000 32-port Fibre Channel line card, the forwarding rate is 2.5 Gbps, for a 3.2:1 oversubscription ratio at Fibre Channel interface speeds of 2 Gbps or a 1.6:1 ratio at 1-Gbps speeds.

The fan-out ratio also implies that the Fibre Channel switch ports that the server HBAs are connected to are being underused most of the time. A general principle in optimizing design fan-out is to group applications or servers that burst high I/O rates at different time slots within the daily production cycle.

Traffic Management

For some SAN designs, it makes sense to implement traffic management policies that influence traffic flow and relative traffic priorities. You should consider the answers to the following questions:

■ Do different application servers have different performance requirements?

■ Should bandwidth be reserved for specific applications?

■ Is preferential treatment and QoS necessary for some traffic?

■ Given two alternate paths for traffic between data centers, should traffic use one path in preference to the other?

Fault Isolation

Consolidation of storage into a single fabric means increased storage utilization and reduced administration overhead. The major drawback is that faults are no longer isolated. Another consideration is that SANs are more complex than simple storage, so a higher skill level is needed to manage the SAN. Technologies such as VSANs enable consolidation of storage while increasing security and stability by logically isolating devices that are physically connected to the same set of switches. Faults or mistakes in one VSAN fabric are contained and do not impact other VSAN fabrics.

Convergence and Stability

Fast convergence and stability are the primary reasons storage vendors set limits on the number of switches and devices they have certified and qualified for operation in a single fabric.

Recommended practices for supporting fast convergence and SAN stability include the following:

■ Minimize the processing required with a given SAN topology by minimizing the number of switches in a SAN and the number of parallel links in a SAN.

■ Implement appropriate levels of redundancy in the network layers and redundant hardware components within the fabric.

SAN Designs with the Cisco MDS 9000 Family

The MDS 9000 series consists of Cisco MDS 9500 series multilayer directors, Cisco MDS 9100 series and Cisco MDS 9200 series multilayer fabric switches, and the Cisco MDS 9020 series fabric switch. The product line is designed to meet requirements for storage networks of all sizes and architectures. The MDS 9000 series delivers intelligent network services, such as VSANs, comprehensive security, advanced traffic management, sophisticated diagnostics, and unified SAN management. In addition, the Cisco MDS 9500 series multilayer directors and MDS 9200 series multilayer fabric switches provide multiprotocol and multitransport integration and an open platform for embedding intelligent storage services such as network-based volume management.

SAN Consolidation with VSANs

SAN consolidation refers to increasing the number of devices such as servers, storage arrays, and tape drives that have access to a SAN infrastructure while simplifying existing SAN topology layouts. If the number of devices connected to a SAN is increased, the cost and provisioning of storage resources becomes more flexible. The flexibility leads to cost reduction based on an increase in storage usage and increased management efficiencies.

Interconnecting smaller SAN islands to form larger connected fabrics or using VSANs simplifies SAN topology layouts and can lower costs by reducing physical SAN build-outs.

Comprehensive SAN Security

SAN security refers to processes and solution features that protect the integrity and availability of data stored on storage networks. There are four aspects to a comprehensive SAN security solution:

- Secure roles-based management with centralized authentication, authorization, and logging of all changes

- Centralized authentication of devices connected to the network to ensure that only authorized devices can be connected to the network

- Traffic isolation and access controls to ensure that a device connected to the network can securely send and receive data and is protected from activities of other devices in the network

- Encryption of all data leaving the storage network for business continuance, remote vaulting, and backup

Simplified SAN Management

SAN management refers to provisioning and operating a storage infrastructure while also ensuring availability, reliability, recoverability, and optimal performance.

For companies requiring large SANs, the need to simplify the management of networks has become critical. Managing multiple SAN islands with many points of management can become extremely complex. In addition, as enterprise SANs grow, end users are increasingly cautious about the lack of effective troubleshooting tools for storage networks. Many users have not had the confidence to build large SANs, in part because of the lack of troubleshooting tools and the complexity caused by the need to manage many Inter-Switch Links (ISL) across multiple SAN islands.

Note   The SAN ISL protocol should not be confused with the legacy LAN switching protocol of the same name.

Large enterprise end users require management tools that are centralized, easy to use, provide significant troubleshooting capabilities to help to resolve potential problems quickly, and are standards based in an effort to integrate seamlessly with other management tools.

Storage networking solutions that incorporate Cisco Fabric Manager deliver a centralized, secure point of management with industry-leading troubleshooting and monitoring tools that help large enterprise users scale their networks. Along with the intelligent networking features built in to the MDS 9000 series, end users can easily consolidate multiple SAN islands, build SAN extension solutions for business continuance, and lower costs by moving intelligent fabric applications into the network for efficient resource provisioning and utilization.

Single-Switch Collapsed-Core Design

The collapsed-core single-switch design takes a traditional core-edge topology and collapses it into a single chassis. Instead of using many small switches to provide sufficient port density, a single chassis with a high port count replaces the smaller switches. This design reduces the number of ISLs required in the network so that all available ports can be deployed for host or storage connections, leading to 100 percent port design efficiency.

In Figure 6-11, the backplane of the MDS in the collapsed-core design replaces all the ISL links. This design can also provide a lower fan-out ratio than the multiple small switches because the availability of more advanced blades for the MDS. Empty slots on the MDS can support future growth on new line cards.

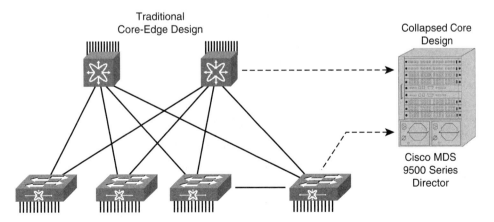

Figure 6-11   *Single-Switch Collapsed-Core Design*

The collapsed-core design on a first-generation switch has limited capabilities with regard to high availability. With later-generation Cisco MDS series switches, dual redundant crossbar switch fabrics are used on all director switches to provide low-latency, high-throughput, nonblocking, and non-oversubscribed switching capacity between line card modules. In addition, the port bandwidth reservation feature guarantees dedicated performance for those devices that require it.

Note   Second-generation MDS 9500 series director switches are fully redundant with no single point of failure with dual supervisors, crossbar switch fabrics, clock modules, or power supplies. Nonetheless, note that this design still has a single point of failure with the one chassis.

Small-Scale, Dual-Fabric Collapsed-Core Design

Figure 6-12 shows a small-scale design that makes use of two Cisco MDS 9216 multilayer fabric switches. Each fabric is a storage switch and its connections. A dual fabric provides a connection from each host or storage device to each SAN fabric.

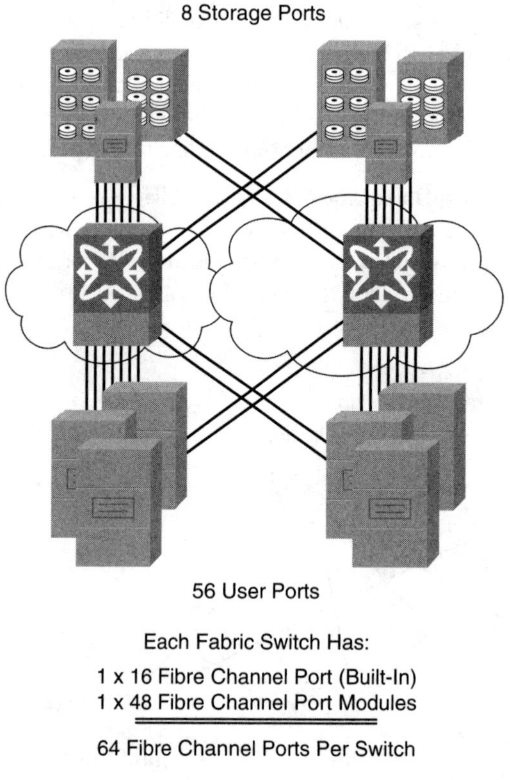

8 Storage Ports

56 User Ports

Each Fabric Switch Has:

1 x 16 Fibre Channel Port (Built-In)
1 x 48 Fibre Channel Port Modules

64 Fibre Channel Ports Per Switch

Figure 6-12   *Small Scale Dual Fabric: Collapsed Core Design*

A total of 64 ports per switch are supported when the 48-port Fibre Channel blade is added to the MDS 9216 switches with 16 built-in ports. This small-scale design can support a departmental SAN.

Note   The dual physical fabric is recommended for highly redundant SAN design systems. The dual-fabric design removes the single point of failure that comes with the single-switch design.

Figure 6-12 shows a small-scale design that uses a 7:1 fan-out ratio between host devices and storage ports. Each switch has a total of 64 ports. Fifty-six ports are used for host devices, and eight ports are used for storage per switch. The fan-out ratio is then calculated at 56:8, or simply 7:1. All available ports are deployed for host or storage connections.

MDS 9216 switches can provide VSAN support and port channels to other switches to scale the design in the future.

Medium-Scale, Dual-Fabric Collapsed-Core Design

Figure 6-13 illustrates a medium-scale collapsed-core design with dual fabric that can support up to 528 ports per switch. This solution might be useful for a medium-size enterprise. The solution makes use of a dual-fabric design so that each host and each storage port has connections to two fabric switches. No ISLs are needed for this design to interconnect core and edge switches, so all the port density is used to connect hosts and storage devices. The only links needed are to the hosts and storage devices. Port bandwidth reservations can be used to guarantee performance for those devices that require it. The design can also provide VSAN support and port channels to other switches to scale the design in the future.

Note   A dual physical fabric is recommended for highly redundant SAN design systems. Using a dual-fabric design removes the single point of failure that comes with the single-switch design.

This design uses a 10:1 fan-out ratio between host ports and storage ports. This means that 480 hosts will have access to 48 storage device ports.

Note   The collapsed-core SAN design can use a large SAN device for efficiency. When the SAN port requirements outgrow the largest SAN device, the core-edge approach is needed to support the SAN.

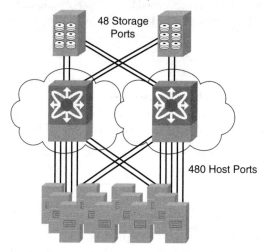

Per Director:
11 x 48-Port Modules
528 Ports Total
48 Ports for Storage
480 Ports for Hosts
10:1 Oversubscription

48 Storage Ports

480 Host Ports

Figure 6-13   *Medium-Scale, Dual-Fabric Collapsed-Core Design*

Large-Scale, Dual-Fabric Core-Edge Design

A large-scale SAN solution requires a core-edge design to provide sufficient host and storage port density. Figure 6-14 shows a design capable of more than 2000 host and storage ports.

The design makes use of both a core layer and an edge layer set of switches. Two core switches provide non-oversubscribed interconnectivity on the ISLs to the four edge layer switches. There are 128 storage ports per core switch, which are connected on 2-Gbps connections. The edge switches are connected to each core switch with a 16-port port channel running at 4 Gbps per port to provide 64 Gbps to each core switch. Each core supports 4 * 64 Gbps = 256 Gbps from the edge switches and 2 * 128 Gbps = 256 Gbps to the directly connected storage devices with no oversubscription.

In this design, the port bandwidth reservation feature is used to dedicate forwarding resources on edge switches for ISL connectivity from the edge to the core. The edge switches provide port density for 1984 host ports, with each edge switch supporting 496 host ports at 2 Gbps. The fan-out between host ports to storage ports across the edge and core switches is calculated like this:

1984 * 2 Gbps : 256 Gbps * 2 = 7.75:1

Each Core Switch:
- 128 Storage Ports at 2 G
- 64 ISL Ports to Edge at 4 G
- 1:1 Ratio of ISLs to Storage

Each Edge Switch:
- 496 Host Ports at 2 G
- 32 ISL Ports to Core at 4 G
- 7.75:1 Ratio of Hosts to Storage

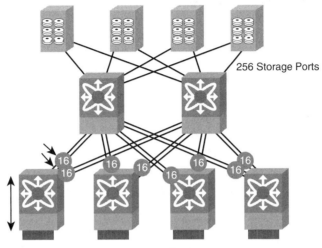

256 Storage Ports

1984 Host Ports

SAN System:
- 1984 Host Ports at 2 G
- 256 Storage Ports at 2 G
- 7.75:1 Ratio of Hosts to Storage

Figure 6-14 *Large-Scale, Dual-Fabric Core-Edge Design*

Note ISLs are needed between the switches. The edge-core design will scale to support much larger port densities than the collapsed-core design. A SAN of more than 2000 ports can be considered a large SAN, although SANs of more than 4000 ports can be found today.

Another measure of SAN size is the number of switches.

SAN Extension

SAN extension refers to transporting storage traffic over distances such as metropolitan-area networks (MAN) and WANs. Over short distances, such as within a data center, SANs are typically extended over optical links with multimode optical fiber. As the distance increases, such as within a large data center or campus, single-mode fiber or single-mode fiber with coarse wavelength-division multiplexing (CWDM) is typical. Over metropolitan distances, dense wavelength-division multiplexing (DWDM) is preferable. DWDM is also used where higher consolidation density or aggregation of FICON, ESCON, and 10 Gigabit Ethernet data center links are required. SAN extension across a MAN or WAN allows the enterprise to support applications such as distributed replication, backup, and remote storage (see Figure 6-15).

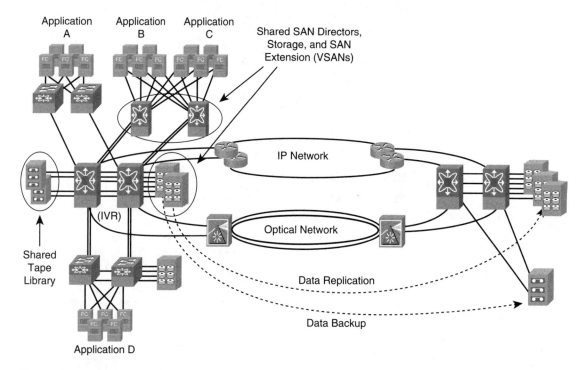

Figure 6-15 *SAN Extension*

In contrast, FCIP can be used to extend a Fibre Channel SAN across any distance. FCIP can be used over metro and campus distances or over intercontinental distances where IP might be the only transport available. With a single instance of synchronous disk replication, typically 15 MBps to 20 MBps of network bandwidth is required. To support this bandwidth, Optical Carrier 3 (OC-3) circuits at 155-Mbps rates are almost a minimum requirement. However, few SAN disaster recovery designs actually require synchronous replication over the FCIP, so bandwidth at or below OC-3 rates should initially be adequate for the typical SAN extension design. QoS is highly recommended to ensure the priority of the FCIP traffic and to ensure any performance degradation resulting from network delays and congestion is kept to an absolute minimum.

The Internet Small Computer Systems Interface (iSCSI) is another protocol that can support SAN extension. iSCSI is a protocol that carries SCSI commands, responses, and data over an IP network. With iSCSI, transport is supported over a TCP/IP network and not over a Fibre Channel network.

The primary use for iSCSI (which is also known as Internet SCSI) is for host-to-storage connectivity through an IP LAN. SCSI commands and data are encapsulated into iSCSI, adding a special header. The iSCSI data is then encapsulated directly into a TCP packet. No Fibre Channel is used at all, so this is an alternative to SAN fabric.

SAN Extension Protocols

SANs can use different protocol and transport stacks to transfer SCSI commands and data. The FCIP and iSCSI stacks support block-level storage for remote devices. Both FCIP and iSCSI are used to carry SCSI commands and status. Each uses the TCP/IP protocol suite as a transport mechanism. As a result, they support leveraging the existing network infrastructure to connect storage devices.

Fibre Channel over IP

Although they have similarities, these protocols also differ. FCIP is Fibre Channel encapsulated in IP. Its purpose is to provide connectivity between two separate SANs over a WAN, as shown in Figure 6-16. FCIP is a tunneling protocol. It encapsulates Fibre Channel packets and carries them within a TCP socket. The SCSI commands are encapsulated into a Fibre Channel frame. The Fibre Channel packet is encapsulated into FCIP. The FCIP protocol data unit (PDU) is then carried over TCP/IP. The result has the same effect as trunking Fibre Channel between switch fabrics over the WAN.

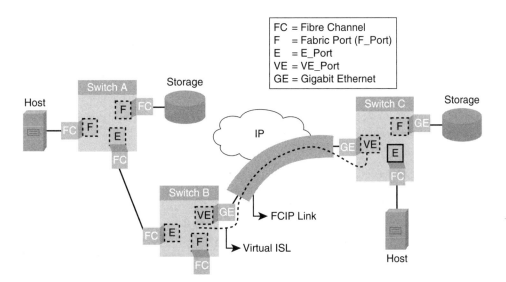

Figure 6-16   *FCIP*

Both FCIP and iSCSI have demanding QoS requirements. They both need high throughput with no to very few drops, low latency, and low jitter. Mixing FCIP and iSCSI traffic with other enterprise traffic can be a worst-case scenario for QoS. Often, dedicated IP connections are used to support FCIP and iSCSI.

FCIP is a standards-based protocol, outlined in RFC 3821. Before FCIP, to extend the SAN between networks you needed to extend the Fibre Channel connections from one network to another. Separate dedicated connections had to be purchased and maintained for the Fibre Channel connections. With the proper QoS mechanisms, FCIP uses the existing IP infrastructure to connect SANs.

Note Although it is typically used for SAN extension, FCIP can also be used for host attachment.

FCIP is a means of providing a SAN extension over an IP infrastructure, enabling storage applications such as asynchronous data replication, disaster recovery, remote tape vaulting, and host initiator to remote pooled storage to be deployed, which have low sensitivity to latency and distance. FCIP tunnels Fibre Channel frames over an IP link, using TCP to provide a reliable transport stream with a guarantee of in-order delivery.

SAN extension using FCIP typically has many cost benefits over other SAN extension technologies. It is relatively common to have existing IP infrastructure between data centers that can be leveraged at no incremental cost. In addition, IP connectivity is typically available at a better price point for long-distance links compared to pricing for optical Fibre Channel transport services.

iSCSI

iSCSI is a protocol used to carry SCSI commands, responses, and data over an IP network. With iSCSI, transport is supported over a TCP/IP network and not over a Fibre Channel network. File access is at the block level.

Figure 6-17 shows a connection that uses iSCSI between the iSCSI host and Switch B. Physical connectivity is achieved using a Gigabit Ethernet port on the switch.

Note The iSCSI Server Load Balancing (iSLB) feature in Cisco MDS 9000 SAN-OS Software Release 3.0 and later provides consolidation of Gigabit Ethernet ports and further simplifies configuration. iSLB enables multiple Gigabit Ethernet interfaces, spanning across different line cards or different Cisco MDS 9000 series switches within the same physical fabric, to act as a single iSCSI target portal. Hundreds or thousands of servers can be configured with just one target portal IP address for iSCSI storage access. The iSLB feature in the MDS 9000 series automatically assigns each server to a specific Gigabit Ethernet port. iSLB provides load balancing of iSCSI hosts within a physical fabric and a redundancy capability using Virtual Router Redundancy Protocol (VRRP).

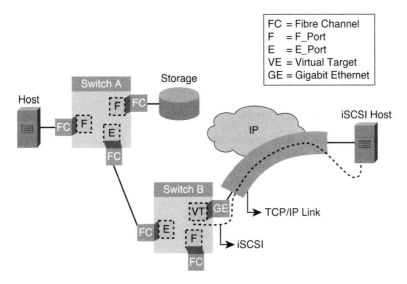

Figure 6-17   *iSCSI*

It is recommended practice that the LAN segment used for iSCSI is its own VLAN. Diffie-Hellman Challenge Handshake Authentication Protocol (DH-CHAP) authentication should also be used to enhance security on the LAN. DH-CHAP is an authentication protocol that authenticates the devices connecting to a switch. Fibre Channel authentication allows only trusted devices to be added to a fabric, thus preventing unauthorized devices from accessing the switch. IP Security (IPsec) can also be run between the switch and host to further enhance security if desired.

Note   Encrypting gigabytes of data can get very costly.

Although it can be complex to manage, iSCSI comes with significant advantages compared to FCIP, including the following:

■   Standard networking equipment can be used in the iSCSI network.

■   iSCSI provides a lower overall cost of ownership when compared to building a Fibre Channel fabric.

■   Like FCIP, iSCSI is a standards-based protocol, outlined in RFC 3720.

Scaling iSCSI can be done via a TCP/IP offload engine (TOE). TOE is a special network interface card (NIC) in the host computer that has some additional capabilities. The TCP/IP stack runs on the NIC instead of consuming CPU on the server for TCP/IP processing. The TOE also allows for the iSCSI device to do a network boot.

The host initiator port is an NIC. iSCSI makes the NIC look like a SCSI adapter to your host. Network portals exist on both the initiator and target. The network portal on the initiator is the IP address that the host will attach to. Hosts can have multiple portals for functions such as primary and backup use. The network portal on the target device might be a port on the IP services blade on the SAN switch. IP is stripped off at the iSCSI target and SCSI is presented to the logical units.

SAN Extension Developments

The SAN extension is becoming faster and more practical because of the technologies shown in Figure 6-18.

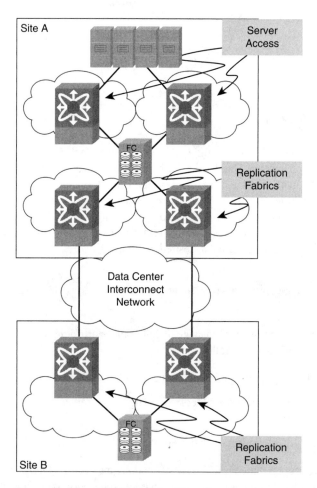

Figure 6-18 *SAN Extension Developments*

Benefits of a SAN solution include the following:

■ **Tape acceleration:** Speeds up the I/O transactions that occur during remote backups. This reduces the latency commonly associated with backup over a WAN and considerably reduces the time required for long-distance backups.

■ **FCIP write acceleration:** Speeds up I/O transactions between servers and disk-based storage devices such as a disk array.

■ **Hardware-assisted data compression over FCIP:** Achieves high data compression rates over WAN links. Through data compression, storage administrators can efficiently use the available bandwidth and send more storage traffic between data centers.

■ **Hardware-based IPsec encryption:** Ensures secure SAN extension transactions, an important consideration when transporting storage traffic outside the confines of data centers.

High-Availability SAN Extension

The conventional approach for a high-availability SAN extension design is achieved with dual fabrics such as a yellow VSAN and a blue VSAN in Figure 6-19. This design provides protection against failures in either fabric. It is common to augment the design with additional network protection via port channels and optical protection schemes.

In Figure 6-19, servers are connected to storage arrays over a long distance with two replication fabrics for high availability. The use of multipath software is required by the host to utilize the dual paths.

Integrated Fabric Designs Using Cisco Nexus Technology Overview

This section discusses the benefits and enabling technologies of a unified fabric.

Most traditional data centers consist of multiple networks. Each server is connected to the data center Ethernet-based LAN network, and many servers also have connections to a Fibre Channel-based SAN. In addition, a traditional network may deploy an InfiniBand network to satisfy the low-latency requirements of HPC clusters. InfiniBand is a switching technology that provides infrastructure that interconnects discreet server resources using a 20-Gbps, low-latency fabric.

Note   Cisco has since declared end of life for all InfiniBand switches.

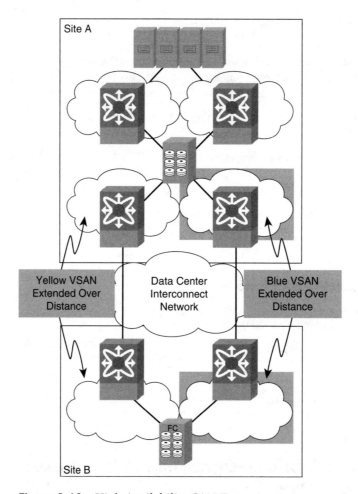

Figure 6-19   *High-Availability SAN Extension*

Unified Fabric Technologies

Unified fabric provides simplicity and economy of scale to the data center design.

Cabling and interface types are often different for each of the networks. Cables must be routed to different access switches based on the type of connection. Servers commonly have to support multiple types of adapters to connect to each of the different networks. Each of the different networks is managed separately and often under the administration of different groups in the data center support organization. The use of multiple networks with their own individual network adapters and access switches also leads to increased demand for power and cooling. At the same time, the amount of cabling that is required to support the different networks could impede airflow within the racks and underneath the floors.

I/O Consideration in the Data Center

Consolidation of these different networks onto a single data center network infrastructure brings substantial benefits, as shown in Figure 6-20.

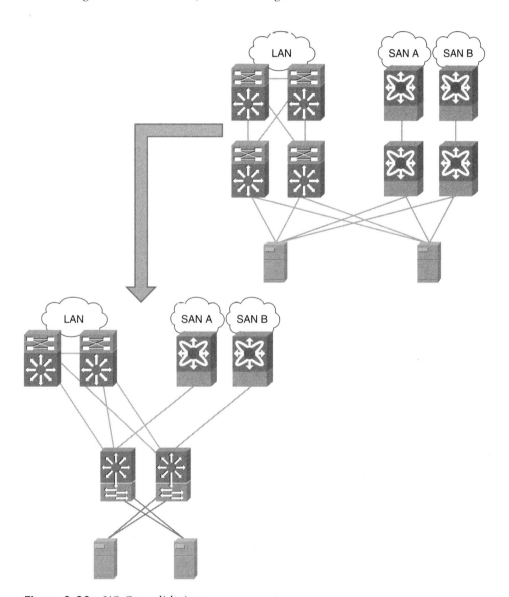

Figure 6-20   *I/O Consolidation*

Benefits of a unified fabric include the following:

- **Reduced cabling:** Multiple Fibre Channel and Ethernet connections can be replaced with a single 10 Gigabit Ethernet connection or a dual 10 Gigabit Ethernet connection for redundancy. In many cases, access layer cabling can be reduced by 50 per-, cent, or even more if the server uses multiple 1 Gigabit Ethernet connections.

- **Fewer access layer switches:** In a typical top-of-rack (TOR) design, shown at the top of Figure 6-20, each rack contains at least four separate switches: two Ethernet switches to support redundant LAN connections and two Fibre Channel switches to support redundant SAN connections. By consolidating LAN and SAN connectivity on a single network, as shown in the lower part of Figure 6-20, each rack needs just two access switches that can provide both redundant LAN and SAN connectivity.

- **Fewer network adapters per server:** By combining LAN and SAN connectivity on a single 10 Gigabit Ethernet adapter, the number of network adapters that need to be installed in each server is heavily reduced. A single converged network adapter (CNA) can replace the combination of a Fibre Channel HBA and one or more Gigabit Ethernet adapters.

- **Power and cooling savings:** Reducing the number of access switches per rack and the number of network adapters per server leads to a reduced demand for power. The less power that is used, the less heat that is generated. This also leads to a reduction in cooling requirements. The lower number of access layer cables can also improve airflow in the data center, which can lead to more efficient use of the available cooling.

- **Management integration:** Combining LAN, SAN, and interprocess communication (IPC) networks on a single network infrastructure not only reduces the number of managed devices but also the overall management complexity.

- **Wire once:** Using a single type of connection, such as 10 Gigabit Ethernet, for LAN, SAN, and IPC eliminates the need to recable racks to provision storage or network connectivity to a server.

Challenges When Building a Unified Fabric Based on 10 Gigabit Ethernet

A number of challenges arise when building a unified fabric implementation that is based on 10 Gigabit Ethernet, including the following:

- Traditional Ethernet switching technology must be enhanced to create highly available and lossless fabric to meet the demands of storage traffic.

- The unified fabric must integrate easily into existing Fibre Channel-based SANs.

- The architecture of the Ethernet switches must provide low port-to-port latencies to support IPC traffic.

- High availability and a lossless network are required to carry storage traffic.

- Integration issues with existing storage networks.

To consolidate LAN, SAN, and IPC traffic on a single network infrastructure, a medium has to be selected to support the requirements of all three traffic types and make financial sense in the existing data center environment.

To support LAN traffic, Ethernet is the most obvious choice. It is the dominant technology in IP networks. Moving away from Ethernet for IP connectivity is nearly impossible. Many applications assume Ethernet as the underlying technology, and the existing investment in Ethernet technology is too large to replace it with something entirely different. Another reason to use Ethernet (more specifically, 10 Gigabit Ethernet) is that it provides sufficient bandwidth for the increased demand for I/O in the data center. Currently, 10 Gbps is enough bandwidth to satisfy the combined requirements for storage, network, and IPC traffic at the same time. With 40 Gigabit Ethernet and 100 Gigabit Ethernet in the future, there is also a clear path for future growth as the demand for I/O bandwidth increases.

The primary requirements for IPC traffic are low latency, high bandwidth, and the support of zero-copy mechanisms in the adapter to allow the CPU to fully utilize the available I/O bandwidth.

The most important requirement for SAN traffic is that the network have close to zero packet loss. Because the Fiber Channel is extremely sensitive to packet drops, losing frames is not an option. Another important requirement is easy integration into an existing Fibre Channel SAN and compatibility with Fibre Channel management and provisioning mechanisms. Most enterprises have huge existing investments in Fibre Channel technology. Storage provisioning is based on Fibre Channel concepts, such as naming and zoning. To enable gradual migration to a completely unified fabric, it is important that the technology of choice can be easily integrated into existing Fibre Channel SANs.

These combined requirements make 10 Gigabit Ethernet a logical choice as the foundation for a unified fabric. It is readily available, relatively inexpensive, and it provides sufficient bandwidth for the combined requirements of LAN, SAN, and HPC traffic.

To meet the demands of IP-based LAN traffic and HPC traffic, it is sufficient to provide a low-delay, high-bandwidth Ethernet infrastructure. However, to meet the requirements of storage traffic, additional technologies are required. Cisco has chosen to build its unified fabric technology on FCoE. FCoE was standardized by the Technical Committee T11 of the International Committee for Information Technology Standards (INCITS), which oversees the development of Fibre Channel standards.

The FCoE technology uses 10 Gigabit Ethernet as the underlying physical and data link layer transport. As shown in Figure 6-21, a host using FCoE encapsulates Fibre Channel frames inside regular Ethernet frames. A special EtherType is used to signify that the frame contains FCoE, and an additional FCoE header following the Ethernet header contains some additional control information.

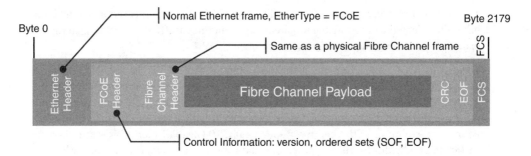

Figure 6-21   *FCoE Frame*

The maximum payload size of a Fibre Channel frame is 2112 bytes. Adding the 24-byte Fibre Channel frame header and 4-byte cyclic redundancy check (CRC) results in 2140 bytes. The 28-byte FCoE header, 4-byte start of frame (SOF), and 4-byte end of frame (EOF) add another 36 bytes for a total of 2176 bytes. Finally, FCoE is commonly encapsulated using an IEEE 802.1Q header to tag it with a VLAN and class of service (CoS) value. This adds another 4 bytes, for a total of 2180 bytes of data that are to be included in the Ethernet frame. This means that to support forwarding of FCoE frames, the Ethernet network should support so-called "baby giant" frames with a maximum transmission unit (MTU) of 2180 bytes.

Another requirement that is imposed by the T11 Fibre Channel Backbone 5 (FC-BB-5) standard is that the underlying Ethernet network should be full duplex and lossless. The standard does not specifically prescribe how this lossless behavior should be achieved, as long as it provides behavior that is like the one that is provided by the native Fibre Channel buffer-to-buffer mechanism.

To satisfy the demands of FCoE traffic, the IEEE DCB Task Group has defined a set of additional mechanisms that enhance traditional Ethernet to provide lossless behavior. One of these mechanisms is described in the 802.1Qbb priority-based flow control (PFC) standard. The mechanism is specifically mentioned in the T11 FC-BB-5 standard as a way to achieve lossless behavior on a full-duplex Ethernet network.

Because FCoE simply encapsulates Fibre Channel frames, it provides easy integration with existing Fibre Channel networks. Existing Fibre Channel mechanisms and concepts such as zoning and naming can be used to manage and provision storage on an FCoE network.

SAN Protocol Stack Extensions

Figure 6-22 compares FCoE with other SCSI-based SAN technologies, such as iSCSI and FCIP. The first thing that stands out is that FCoE, FCIP, and Fibre Channel all use the Fibre Channel Protocol (FCP) and Fibre Channel framing. This means that both FCoE and FCIP can easily be integrated into existing Fibre Channel SANs.

FCIP is primarily used as a switch-to-switch protocol and is utilized as a SAN extension technology to allow a SAN to be extended to a remote data center across an IP-based core network. FCoE was initially developed to be employed as an access layer protocol to connect hosts and storage to a Fibre Channel SAN. However, as the use of a unified fabric becomes more common, FCoE can also be leveraged as a switch-to-switch extension protocol.

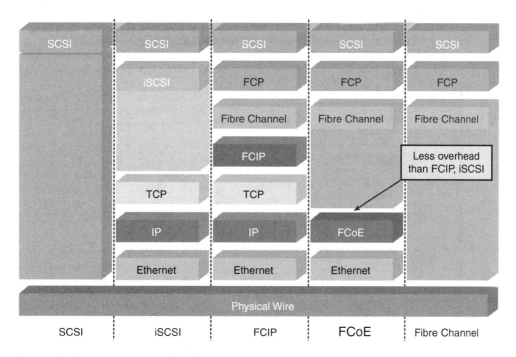

Figure 6-22 *SAN Protocol Stack*

Because FCIP uses TCP and IP on the network and transport layer, it has higher overhead than FCoE.

The iSCSI protocol is even more different. It does not use FCP but encapsulates SCSI directly into TCP/IP. As a result, iSCSI always requires gateway functionality to integrate it into an existing Fibre Channel network. Like FCIP, the overhead of iSCSI is higher than FCoE.

Note that the difference in encapsulation overhead is not the determining factor in protocol performance. Other factors, such as protocol offload in the network adapter and the use of jumbo frames, also have major influence on storage performance. The main differentiator between FCoE and iSCSI is the easy integration of FCoE in Fibre Channel SANs.

FCoE Components: Converged Network Adapter

FCoE in the access layer requires CNAs on the servers and Ethernet switches that can act as Fibre Channel forwarders (FCF). To create a lossless Ethernet fabric, both components need to support the IEEE DCB Ethernet extensions.

A converged network adapter (CNA), as shown in Figure 6-23, is a specialized 10 Gigabit Ethernet adapter that combines the functions of a standard Ethernet adapter and a Fibre Channel HBA. It allows a server to support Ethernet-based LAN traffic and FCoE-based SAN traffic on a single connection. FCoE frames and regular Ethernet frames are multiplexed onto a single wire. Contention between the different types of traffic is managed through the 802.1Qaz enhanced transmission selection and 802.1Qbb priority flow control mechanisms that are defined in the IEEE DCB standards.

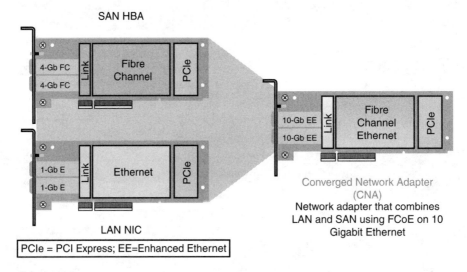

Figure 6-23   *CNA*

Although the CNA is a single physical adapter, it presents itself to the operating system as two separate devices: a Fibre Channel HBA and a 10 Gigabit Ethernet adapter. From a server management perspective, the server is configured the same as if a separate physical HBA and Ethernet NIC were present in the system.

The CNA implements the FCoE node (ENode) functions that are outlined in the FC-BB-5 standard. It implements the FCoE Initialization Protocol (FIP) and the DCB extensions that are necessary to support FCoE.

FCoE Components: Fibre Channel Forwarder

An FCF, or Fibre Channel forwarder, is a device used in FCoE that combines the functions of an Ethernet and Fibre Channel switch. Figure 6-24 displays the logical implementation of an FCF. The FCM, or Fibre Channel mapper, provides the encapsulation and encapsulation of frames. It can be used to connect Fibre Channel SANs, FCoE hosts, and FCoE servers.

To connect servers that are using CNAs to support FCoE, a special type of Ethernet switch is required. The switch should not only implement standard Ethernet bridging functions; it should also be capable of switching Fibre Channel frames and implement all the control and management plane functions that are required of a Fibre Channel switch. In terms of the FC-BB-5 standard, such a switch is also called an FCF.

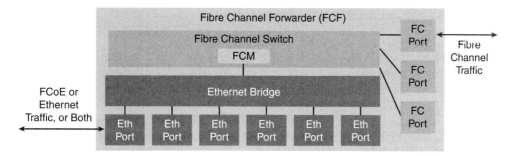

Figure 6-24 *Fibre Channel Forwarder*

An FCF consists of an Ethernet bridge, which connects to the Ethernet ports, and a Fibre Channel switch, which connects to the Fibre Channel ports that connect Fibre Channel switches or nodes. The Ethernet bridge and Fibre Channel switch are connected through an FCoE mapper (FCM). This is the component that de-encapsulates and encapsulates the Fibre Channel frames as they are passed from the Ethernet bridge to the Fibre Channel switch.

Data Center Bridging Standards

IEEE 802.1 Data Center Bridging (DCB) is a collection of standards-based extensions to classical Ethernet. It provides a lossless data center transport layer that helps enable the convergence of LANs and SANs onto a single unified fabric.

In addition to supporting FCoE, DCB can enhance the operation of iSCSI, NAS, and other business-critical storage traffic

The IEEE is in charge of creating LAN standards, including the Ethernet standards. Within the IEEE, the DCB Task Group aims to provide enhancements to existing 802.1 bridge specifications to satisfy the requirements of protocols and applications in the data center. The DCB Task Group recognizes that existing high-performance data centers typically comprise multiple application-specific networks that run on different data link layer technologies (for example, Fibre Channel for storage, InfiniBand for HPC, and Ethernet for network management and LAN connectivity). The specifications from the DCB Task Group enable 802.1 bridges to be used for the deployment of a converged network where all applications can be run over a single physical infrastructure.

As part of this effort, the DCB Task Group has adopted the following draft standards:

- **802.1Qbb PFC:** This standard specifies protocols, procedures, and managed objects that enable flow control per traffic class on IEEE 802 full-duplex links. DCB networks (bridges and end nodes) are characterized by limited bandwidth-delay product and limited hop count. Traffic class is identified by the VLAN tag priority values. PFC is intended to eliminate frame loss due to congestion. This is achieved by a mechanism that is similar to the IEEE 802.3x PAUSE but operates on individual priorities. This mechanism, with other DCB technologies, enables support for higher-layer protocols that are highly loss sensitive without affecting the operation of traditional LAN protocols utilizing other priorities.

Note The bandwidth delay product (BDP) is a formula that determines the amount of data that can be in transit in the network. It is calculated by as the product of bandwidth and latency.

- **802.1Qaz Enhanced Transmission Selection (ETS):** This standard specifies enhancement of transmission selection to support allocation of bandwidth among traffic classes. When the offered load in a traffic class does not use its allocated bandwidth, ETS allows other traffic classes to use the available bandwidth. The bandwidth-allocation priorities coexist with strict priorities. It includes managed objects to support bandwidth allocation.

- **802.1Qau Congestion Notification:** This standard specifies protocols, procedures, and managed objects that support congestion management of long-lived data flows within network domains of limited bandwidth delay product. This is achieved by enabling bridges to signal congestion information to end stations capable of transmission rate limiting to avoid frame loss. This mechanism enables support for higher-layer protocols that are highly loss or latency sensitive. VLAN tag-encoded priority values are allocated to segregate frames that are subject to congestion control, allowing simultaneous support of both congestion control and other higher-layer protocols.

- **Data Center Bridging Capability Exchange (DCBX) Protocol:** This protocol uses IEEE 802.1ab (Link Layer Discovery Protocol, or LLDP) extensions to discover DCB-capable devices and exchange configuration information, such as the per-class bandwidths that are used by ETS and the VLAN and CoS values that are used for the various traffic classes on the link.

- **FC-BB-5:** The FC-BB-5 standard prescribes that FCoE should be implemented on top of a lossless Ethernet fabric. The standard, however, does not specifically prescribe how this lossless behavior should be achieved. The exact implementation details are left up to the Ethernet vendors and standardization bodies.

Through implementation of these standards, specifically PFC and ETS, a lossless Ethernet fabric can be provided in support of FCoE traffic.

Unified Fabric Design Considerations

This section discusses the design aspects that need to be considered when designing a unified fabric using the Cisco Nexus family of switches The Cisco Nexus 5000 series switch can be deployed as an FCF to create a unified fabric.

The Cisco Nexus 5000 series of switches was specifically designed to support a unified fabric that is based on FCoE. The Cisco Nexus 5010 switch supports twenty 10 Gigabit Ethernet ports in a one-rack unit (1RU) chassis. The Cisco Nexus 5020 Switch supports forty 10 Gigabit Ethernet ports in a two-rack unit (2RU) chassis. All 10 Gigabit Ethernet ports support FCoE and can be used to connect to server CNAs using copper Twinax cables. In addition to the 10 Gigabit Ethernet ports, the Cisco Nexus 5000 series switches have expansion slots that can be used to install Fibre Channel interfaces. These interfaces can be used as uplinks to connect to the core Fibre Channel SAN switches.

The Cisco Nexus Operating System (NX-OS) Software that runs on the Cisco Nexus 5000 switches allows the switches to act as FCF. Cisco Nexus 5000 switches can operate in two different modes: Switch mode and N_Port Virtualization (NPV) mode. In Switch mode, the Cisco Nexus 5000 switch operates as a fully functional Fibre Channel switch, and the complete set of SAN switching features that are embedded in the Cisco NX-OS Software can be used to control and manage the FCoE-based SAN and the interconnections to the Fibre Channel SAN switches. In NPV mode, the Cisco Nexus 5000 switch does not implement complete Fibre Channel switching functions but acts as a forwarder and proxy between the attached FCoE interfaces and the Fibre Channel uplinks.

Note   A switch in NPV mode is not a fabric member and does not require a domain ID or other associated configuration.

The Cisco Nexus 5000 switch can be deployed as a TOR switch to attach directly to FCoE-enabled servers in the racks. Alternatively, it can be deployed together with the Cisco Nexus 2232 FEX in a fabric extension design.

Deploying Nexus in the Access Layer

In the initial phase of unified fabric deployment, depicted on the left side in Figure 6-25, FCoE (that is, single-hop FCoE) is used only in the access layer between the servers and the access layer switches. This layer is where the benefits of FCoE are the most obvious. The highest density of dedicated Fibre Channel cabling and hardware resides at this layer. Consolidating the access layer Fibre Channel adapters, cables, and switches can deliver a substantial reduction in equipment, cabling, energy use, and cooling. This leads to the reduction of operating expenses (OPEX).

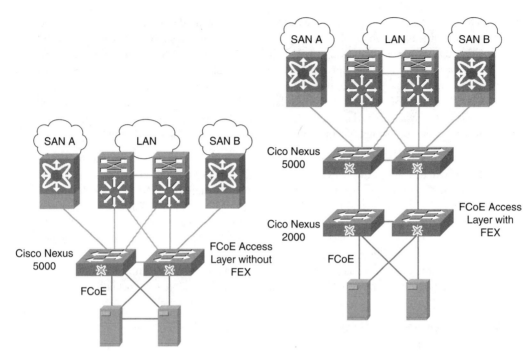

Figure 6-25 *Nexus in the Access Layer*

In a typical access layer unified fabric design, FCoE is used between the servers and the access layer switches, such as the Cisco Nexus 5000 switches. The access switch de-encapsulates the FCoE traffic and forwards the Fibre Channel frames to the connected aggregation or core layer SAN switch. Regular Ethernet traffic is forwarded normally to the aggregation layer LAN switches.

Note that in most SAN designs, redundancy and high availability is achieved in a different manner than in LAN designs. Instead of building a single fabric with redundant uplinks and switches, it is common to build two physically separate SAN fabrics. Servers and storage arrays are dual-homed to both fabrics, and fault detection and failover functions are implemented in dual-pathing software on the servers. If a server loses connectivity to its storage across the primary fabric, it reconnects to the storage across the alternate fabric. In unified fabric designs, this principle is maintained. The servers are dual-homed to two Cisco Nexus 5000 switches. One of these switches is connected to the SAN A fabric, while the other switch is connected to the SAN B fabric.

> **Note** It is important that separation between the two SAN fabrics be maintained. If it is not, the fabrics merge. During the merge process, both fabrics are down, so applications have no SAN connectivity for seconds if not tens of seconds. Proper care should be taken so that FCoE VLANs are not carried across the trunks between the Cisco Nexus 5000 switches.

On the LAN side of the unified fabric design, the Cisco Nexus 5000 switches in the access layer typically have redundant uplinks to the aggregation layer switches. A virtual port channel (vPC) can be leveraged to avoid blocking links between the access layer and aggregation layer. If the CNA supports EtherChannel based on the Link Aggregation Control Protocol (LACP). Because the traffic is Ethernet, a vPC can be used to load balance the traffic between the server and the access switches.

Note   Multiple CAN ports cannot be in a port channel to the same Nexus 5000.

Note   The Ethernet driver of the CNA manages the EtherChannel functionality. FCoE traffic is not affected by it. The storage driver and SAN multipathing software determine the forwarding path for the SAN traffic.

Nexus 5000/2000 Deployment Options in the Data Center

The Cisco Nexus 5000 switches can be deployed as TOR switches, connecting directly to the servers within the rack. Alternatively, as depicted on the right side of Figure 6-25, the FCoE-capable Cisco Nexus 2232PP FEX can be deployed in the TOR position, and up to eight 10-Gigabit Ethernet uplinks can be used to connect the FEX to a Cisco Nexus 5000 switch in the end-of-row (EOR) or middle-of-row (MOR) position. The FEX functions as a remote line card of the Cisco Nexus 5000 switch; it is not an active switching component. All FCoE frames are forwarded across the FEX uplinks to the Cisco Nexus 5000 switch, which will perform the Ethernet and Fibre Channel switching functions.

You can also extend the Cisco Nexus switch architecture by connecting up to 32 Cisco Nexus 2248 FEXs as remote I/O modules to a Nexus 7000. Each FEX provides TOR connectivity for up to 48 hosts. Each FEX becomes an extension of the parent Cisco Nexus 7000 series switch fabric, with the FEX and the switch becoming a virtual modular system. The FEX forwards all 1 Gigabit Ethernet traffic from the hosts to the switch over 10-Gbps uplinks. Traffic flows from the switch to the FEX over the 10-Gbps uplinks and to the individual hosts over 100/1000-Mbps Ethernet downlinks. You connect a FEX to the Cisco Nexus 7000 series switch through the 32-port M1 series Ethernet I/O modules installed in the switch. You can connect each FEX to one port in a set of four shared ports to get the fully dedicated 10-Gbps bandwidth.

FCoE VLAN to VSAN Mapping, VLAN Trunking, and the CNA

In Figure 6-26, there are two FCoE concepts. First is of VLAN to VSAN mapping. A unique, dedicated VLAN must be configured at every converged access switch to carry traffic for each virtual fabric (VSAN) in the SAN (for example, VLAN 100 for VSAN 100, VLAN 200 for VSAN 200, and so on). The second is VLAN trunking when using FCoE.

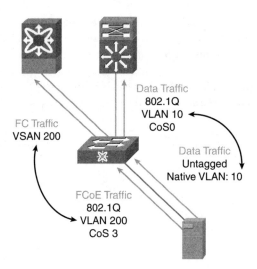

Figure 6-26 *FCoE VLAN to VSAN Mapping and VLAN Trunking*

Note   If Multiple Spanning Tree (MST) is enabled, a separate MST instance must be used for FCoE VLANs.

In Figure 6-26, the link between the server CNA and the access switch uses 802.1Q tagging to separate the FCoE storage traffic and the application traffic. FCoE traffic and data traffic are classified into two separate VLANs.

FCoE traffic is sent as 802.1Q-tagged Ethernet frames, marked with an explicitly configured FCoE VLAN and CoS value. CoS value 3 has been designated to be used for FCoE traffic. When the FCoE traffic is de-encapsulated and sent to the upstream Fibre Channel switch, the FCoE VLAN is mapped to a Fibre Channel VSAN. It is common practice to use the same values for the VLAN and VSAN numbers, but this is not required. It is possible to map a VSAN to a VLAN with a different number should the VLAN or VSAN number that matches already happen to be in use.

The regular Ethernet data traffic can use the native VLAN of the 802.1Q trunk between the server and the access switch, meaning that it is sent untagged. Effectively, this indicates that the VLAN that would normally be configured as the access VLAN of the port connecting to the server has to be configured as the trunk native VLAN on that same port in this type of configuration. The trunks toward the aggregation switches typically use a different VLAN as the native VLAN. Therefore, the traffic is tagged as it is sent to the aggregation layer. Because the data traffic is sent as untagged frames between the server and the access switch, the default CoS value of 0 is applied when the traffic is sent on the trunks toward the aggregation layer.

The FCoE VLAN is configured on the access switch, and its value is negotiated between the switch and the CNA that is using the FIP. FIP is used for a CNA to determine which

VLANs a FCF can be found on and to negotiate what MAC address to use after selecting one such FCF for each FCoE port. FIP allows a more complex topology, rather than simple point-to-point topology. The CoS value is negotiated using the DCBX protocol together with other DCB capabilities, such as the PFC and ETS parameters.

Switch Mode Versus NPV Mode

Cisco Nexus 5000 switches can be operated in two different modes: Switch mode and NPV Mode.

In switch mode, the Cisco Nexus 5000 switch acts as a Fibre Channel switch. It participates in all Cisco fabric services and executes all protocols that are commonly implemented on Fibre Channel switches, such as the Fabric Shortest Path First (FSPF) protocol and principal switch election. The link between the Cisco Nexus 5000 switch and the upstream SAN switch is treated as an ISL and can be used as a trunk to carry multiple VSANs. In Switch mode, all the advanced Fibre Channel features such as zoning and VSANs are available.

When Cisco Nexus 5000 switches are deployed in Switch mode, they fully participate in Cisco fabric services and routing functions. In large deployments, this can result in many switches in the SAN fabric. Although the Fibre Channel address structure theoretically allows for 239 different switches in a single fabric, practical limitations often reduce that number to 30 to 50 switches per fabric. Another challenge is that the Cisco Nexus 5000 switches are effectively acting as a SAN switch, and the management of these switches must be integrated in the SAN management systems and tools.

To address some of the challenges that are inherent in the use of Switch mode, NPV mode can be used instead. In NPV mode, the Cisco Nexus 5000 switch does not function as a Fibre Channel switch but simply forwards Fibre Channel traffic that is received on its FCoE server interfaces to an upstream Fibre Channel switch. The link between the Cisco Nexus 5000 switch and the Fibre Channel switch is not considered to be an ISL. Instead, the Cisco Nexus 5000 switch presents itself as an end host to the upstream switch. In NPV mode, the Cisco Nexus 5000 logs in to the fabric using a fabric login (FLOGI) on the port that connects to the upstream Fibre Channel switch. When the Cisco Nexus 5000 receives a FLOGI request from a server on one of its FCoE interfaces, it converts the FLOGI request to a fabric discovery (FDISC) request to allow the host to log in to the upstream Fibre Channel switch. This mechanism is part of the N_Port ID Virtualization (NPIV) feature, which needs to be supported by the upstream switch in order to be able to use the Cisco Nexus 5000 switch in NPV mode. Originally, NPIV was developed to allow multiple virtual machines running inside a physical VMware to share a single HBA and allow multiple FLOGIs on a single physical Fibre Channel link, in effect distinguishing between the virtual machines from the SAN perspective. In NPV mode, the Cisco Nexus 5000 switch presents itself as a host to the upstream Fibre Channel switch and proxies the login requests from its server ports to the uplink ports.

NPV mode has several advantages. Because the Cisco Nexus 5000 does not perform Fibre Channel switching functions in NPV mode, the total number of Fibre Channel switches in the fabric is much lower compared with Switch mode. Another advantage is that NPIV is a standard Fibre Channel feature, and there are no compatibility issues when connecting a Cisco Nexus 5000 switch to a third-party Fibre Channel switch fabric, as long as the upstream switch supports NPIV. When connecting a Cisco Nexus 5000 switch in Switch mode to a third-party fabric, possible compatibility issues must be considered.

A disadvantage of NPV mode is that it does not allow VSAN trunking between the Cisco Nexus 5000 switch and the upstream switch. Each uplink port can be member of only a single VSAN. If working with a single Cisco Nexus 5000 access switch, it might be necessary to use Switch mode. However, as mentioned earlier, a switch in NPV mode is not a fabric member.

In NPV mode, a separate physical link is required for each VSAN that needs to be extended. Also, in NPV mode, there is no local switching between the FCoE ports. All Fibre Channel traffic is switched on the upstream Fibre Channel switch. In most designs, this is hardly a limitation, because the FCoE ports are used to connect SCSI initiators, while the SCSI targets reside in the Fibre Channel SAN. However, if native FCoE storage devices are attached to the Cisco Nexus 5000 switch, traffic between the FCoE-attached hosts and FCoE-attached storage is switched through the upstream SAN switch instead of being locally switched on the Cisco Nexus 5000 switch.

Unified Fabric Best Practices

In this section, unified fabric best practices are discussed. Careful planning is important to create a successful operating architecture, and so best-practice guidelines should be considered when deploying a unified fabric. It is recommended to configure dedicated VLANs for each VSAN on the converged access switches:

- Configure a unique dedicated VLAN at every converged access switch to carry traffic for each virtual fabric (VSAN) in the SAN (for example, VLAN 2001 for VSAN 1, VLAN 2002 for VSAN 2). Do not map VSANs to VLANs that are used for regular Ethernet traffic.

- If enabling MST, you use a separate MST instance for FCoE VLANs.

- Do not configure the FCoE VLANs as members of Ethernet links that are not designated to carry FCoE traffic. It is recommended to limit the scope of the Spanning Tree Protocol (STP) for the FCoE VLAN unified fabric links only. If the converged access switches need to be connected to each other on an Ethernet link to provide a LAN alternate path, such links must explicitly be configured to exclude all FCoE VLANs from membership. Excluding these VLANs ensures that the scope of the STP for the FCoE VLANs is limited to unified fabric links only.

- Use separate FCoE VLANs for SAN A and SAN B in dual-fabric SAN designs to ensure SAN fabric separation.

- Configure the unified fabric links as trunk ports. It is recommended to configure all FCoE VLANs as members of the unified fabric links. Do not configure the FCoE VLAN as a native VLAN. The native VLAN is used to carry application data.

- Configure the unified fabric links as spanning-tree edge ports.

- When using FCoE on the Cisco Nexus 2000 FEXs, these FEXs should be connected straight through. Active/active FEX configuration is not supported for FCoE.

Summary

This chapter introduced the concept of SANs and unified fabric.

SAN technology supports shared storage that is separate from the servers that use it. Storage resources are easily moved or allocated with no interruption of service on the servers. The consolidation of multiple lower-end storage systems into centralized, higher-end systems allows for reduced administrative overhead. Backup is easier with SAN technology because it does not tie up host capacity, nor does it require a dedicated network or bandwidth on the main network. SAN technology also supports the rapid implementation of high availability.

SAN design involves determining port counts, appropriate oversubscription ratios, and convergence and stability characteristics. Commonly used designs are the dual-fabric collapsed-core and core-edge designs. SAN extensions are commonly used to extend SANs across multiple data centers for disaster recovery. Technologies such as FCIP and iSCSI can be used as the foundation of a SAN extension design

Traditional data centers often consist of multiple networks to meet the distinct requirements of LAN, SAN, and HPC traffic. Integrating the different types of traffic onto a single unified fabric results in a substantial reduction of access layer cabling, adapters, and switches. The Cisco Nexus 5000 series switches and Cisco Nexus 2000 series FEXs can be deployed to implement a unified fabric that consolidates LAN, SAN, and HPC traffic onto a single network.

References

For additional information, refer to these resources:

Cisco Systems, Inc. *Unified Fabric* at www.cisco.com/en/US/netsol/ns945/index.html

Cisco Systems, Inc. *Advanced SAN Design Using Cisco MDS 9500 Series Multilayer Directors* at www.cisco.com/en/US/partner/products/ps5990/ products_white_ paper0900aecd8044c807.shtml

Cisco Systems, Inc. *Unified Fabric White Paper—Fibre Channel over Ethernet (FCoE)* at www.cisco.com/en/US/docs/solutions/Enterprise/Data_Center/UF_FCoE_ final.html

Cisco Systems, Inc. *Configuring FCoE* at www.cisco.com/en/US/docs/switches/ datacenter/nexus5000/sw/fcoe/421_n1_1/Cisco_n5k_fcoeconfig_gd_re_421_n1_1_ chapter3.html

Cisco Systems, Inc. *Cisco MDS 9000 Statement of Direction* at www.cisco.com/en/US/solutions/collateral/ns340/ns394/ns259/at_a_glance_c45-465839.pdf

Cisco Systems, Inc. *Design Zone for Data Centers* www.cisco.com/en/US/netsol/ns743/networking_solutions_program_home.html

Review Questions

Answer the following questions, and then refer to Appendix A, "Answers to Review Questions," for the answers.

1. What are characteristics of Fibre Channel? (Choose three.)

   a. Parallel standard

   b. Full duplex

   c. Half duplex

   d. Addresses more than 16 million nodes

   e. Segment lengths of up to 6 miles (10 km)

   f. Bus lengths of up to 75 feet (25 meters)

2. What technology allows multiple logical SANs to exist in the same physical fabric?

   a. FICON

   b. IVR

   c. Zoning

   d. VSAN

   e. SANTap

3. What is a means of restricting visibility and connectivity between devices connected to a common Fibre Channel SAN or VSAN?

   a. IVR

   b. FICON

   c. Zoning

   d. SANTap

   e. VSAN

4. What are the characteristics of a large-scale SAN design? (Choose two.)

    a. Uses a collapsed core to support much larger port densities than the core-edge design FICON

    b. Uses a core-edge design to support much larger port densities than the collapsed-core design

    c. Has a lower port-density efficiency as compared to small- or medium-scale designs

    d. Has the highest port-density efficiency as compared to small- or medium-scale designs

    e. Uses oversubscribed interconnectivity on the ISLs

    f. Does not use ISLs

5. What can be a factor in SAN design? (Choose three.)

    a. Port density and topology

    b. Fast convergence and stability

    c. Fast routing protocol reservations

    d. Fault isolation using VSAN

    e. Simplified SAN management through storage captivity

    f. Network-attached file service

6. Which three are benefits of a unified fabric?

    a. Reduced cabling

    b. Improved network performance

    c. Reduced bandwidth requirements

    d. Fewer network adapters per server

    e. Power and cooling savings

    f. IP-enabled storage

7. Which of these types of adapters is used by a server when deploying FCoE? (Choose two.)

    a. HBA

    b. Ethernet NIC

    c. CNA

    d. HBA and Ethernet NIC

    e. HBA and CNA

    f. CNA and Ethernet NIC

8. Which three are best-practice guidelines for unified fabric design?

   a. If you enable MST, you should ensure that the MST instance for the FCoE VLANs is the same as the instance for the data VLANs.

   b. If you enable MST, you should use a separate MST instance for FCoE VLANs.

   c. Use separate FCoE VLANs for SAN A and SAN B in dual-fabric SAN designs.

   d. Use identical FCoE VLANs for SAN A and SAN B in dual-fabric SAN designs.

   e. When using FCoE on the Cisco Nexus 2000 FEXs, these FEXs should be connected straight through.

   f. When using FCoE on the Cisco Nexus 2000 FEXs, these FEXs should be connected as active/active extenders.

9. Which are DCB standards? (Choose three.)

   a. 802.1Qbb PFC

   b. 802.1w STP

   c. 802,1Qau Congestion Notification

   d. 802.1Qaz ETS

   e. 802.1F SAN over MAN

Chapter 7

E-Commerce Module Design

Upon completing this chapter, you will be able to

■ Discuss the importance of high availability for e-commerce designs

■ Discuss how firewalls, server load balancers, and multiple ISP connections are used in e-commerce designs

■ Discuss how to integrate firewalls and server load balancers into functioning e-commerce designs

■ Describe tuning techniques for improving the performance and availability of an e-commerce module design

■ Discuss design approaches for the e-commerce network module using common components and technologies

■ Compare and contrast several common design options that can provide an integrated ecommerce topology

The e-commerce module enables organizations to support e-commerce applications through the Internet. The module uses multiple component design techniques that have been discussed in this book. The first section examines common uses of firewalls, server load balancers, and connections to multiple Internet service providers (ISP) in e-commerce designs. The second section discusses the integration process of network components into e-commerce designs that provide varying levels of security. The final section examines tools and techniques for tuning e-commerce designs.

Designing High Availability for E-Commerce

This section discusses the importance of high availability for the e-commerce module. It also describes the significance of technical and nontechnical components that must be integrated into an e-commerce design.

E-Commerce High-Availability Requirements

E-commerce applications represent the public face of an organization. Therefore, the e-commerce module has strict design requirements so that web and application responses to users are fast and downtime is minimized. E-commerce downtime is particularly harmful because it reflects negatively on an organization and lost business can cost millions of dollars per hour.

Components of High Availability

High availability aims to prevent outages, or at least to minimize downtime. Achieving high availability takes ongoing effort and usually requires iterative improvements.

High availability requires integrating the following five components:

- Redundancy
- Technology (including hardware and software features)
- People
- Processes
- Tools

The redundancy and technology components are relatively straightforward to implement because they can be purchased and deployed. A network designer expects to be involved with these two aspects of high availability.

However, no matter how much and how well redundancy and technology have been designed and deployed, high availability will not be achieved unless the people component (for example, having sufficient staff with the right skills, training, and mindset), the processes component (including managing organizational expectations, change control processes, and so on), and the tools component (including network management, good documentation, and so forth) are present. If any one of these last three high-availability components is missing, incidents will likely happen and outages will probably occur and take longer to resolve. Unfortunately, network designers might not be able to influence these areas of an organization. All too often, a consultant doing a post-outage review is the person who first discusses these components and suggests changes.

These five components are detailed in the following sections.

Redundancy

Redundancy means using additional equipment or network links to reduce or eliminate the effects of a failure.

Redundancy in designs attempts to eliminate single points of failure, where one failed device or design element causes a service to go down. The following are examples of redundancy mechanisms that may be used:

- Geographic and path diversity

- Dual devices and links

- Dual WAN providers

- Dual data centers, especially for large organizations with large e-commerce sites

- Dual facilities, dual telephone central office facilities, and dual power substations

Redundant designs must trade off costs versus benefits. For example, it takes time to plan redundancy and verify the geographic diversity of service providers, and additional links and equipment cost money to purchase and maintain. These items need to be balanced against the risk and costs of downtime and so forth. The time and money invested in redundancy design should be spent where they will have the most impact. Consequently, redundancy is most frequently found in network, data center, or e-commerce module cores, and in critical WAN links or ISP connections. Within e-commerce module designs, duplicate elements may be specified in the path between users and applications, and in the applications and back-end databases and mainframes.

Technology

The use of appropriate technologies, including Cisco technologies, can improve high availability. For example, several Cisco routing continuity capabilities, such as Cisco non-stop forwarding (NSF), stateful switchover (SSO), and graceful restart, can improve availability. These technologies allow processor failover without causing links to flap (bounce or continuously go down and up), continued forwarding of packets, and maintenance of Border Gateway Protocol (BGP) adjacencies.

Techniques for detecting failure and triggering failover to a redundant device include service monitoring on server load balancers (SLB), Enhanced Object Tracking (EOT) for Cisco IOS IP service-level agreements (SLA), and Cisco Optimized Edge Router (OER).

Note   SLBs, EOT, IP SLAs, and OER are described later in this chapter.

Other technologies that contribute to high availability include fast routing convergence and firewall stateful failover (to allow user or application sessions to be maintained across a firewall device failover).

> **Note**   Firewall stateful failover is discussed in more detail in Chapter 8, "Security Services Design."

People

Using redundant equipment and links and advanced technologies is just the beginning of high availability. People are one of the most critical components of high availability. For example, staff work habits can impact high availability, planning and attention to detail enhances high availability, and carelessness hurts availability.

The level of staff skills and technical training is also important. For example, staff with the proper skills can configure devices correctly and conduct appropriate testing to understand the circumstances under which failover will activate and what failover will and will not accomplish. Thorough testing often translates into less downtime. For example, nonstateful firewall failover may adequately pass traffic. However, understanding how a particular application behaves may result in doing other tests that show that with non-stateful failover the application sessions lock up for an extended period of time until the application timeout causes the sessions to be reestablished. Designs that include failover must be tested to see how the entire system operates under failure conditions, not just how individual components fail over.

Good communication and documentation are also important. For example, network administrators need to be able to communicate with other network, security, application, and server teams. Network documentation should indicate why things are designed the way they are, how the network is supposed to work, and expected failover behavior.

Often, if people are not given the time to do a job right, they have to cut corners; testing and documentation are typically the first items they eliminate. A lack of thorough testing and documentation can have long-term consequences on the ability to maintain, opti-mize, and troubleshoot a network.

If possible, staff teams should be aligned with services. For example, if the corporate web page and e-commerce site depends on staff who report to the Engineering or Operations department managers, the manager of the e-commerce site may be competing for staff time with these other managers. This organizational structure may cause priority con-flicts and make it difficult to have routine testing or maintenance done for the e-com-merce site. The owner of, or expert on, key service applications and other e-commerce components should also be identified and included in design (and redesign) efforts.

Processes

Implementing sound, repeatable processes is important to achieving high availability; continual process improvement is part of the Cisco prepare, plan, design, implement, operate, and optimize (PPDIOO) methodology. Tasks that are implemented as though they are one-time occurrences and not repeatable processes are lost opportunities for learning.

The following are some ways that organizations can build repeatable processes:

■   By documenting change procedures for common changes (for example, Cisco IOS Software upgrades)

■   By documenting failover planning and lab testing procedures

■   By documenting a network implementation procedure and revising and improving it each time components are deployed

Some processes are specifically related to lab testing. Labs should be used appropriately, such as in the following ways:

■   Ensuring that lab equipment accurately reflects the production network

■   Ensuring that failover mechanisms are tested and understood

■   Ensuring that new code is systematically validated before deployment

Change control processes should be meaningful and not waste time. Examples of good change control processes include the following:

■   Specifying that all changes must be tested before deployment

■   Ensuring that planning includes rollback details

■   Ensuring that all departments within the organization have been made aware of the proposed change (so that all repercussions of the change can be considered)

Management of operational changes is also important and includes the following:

■   Ensuring that regular capacity management audits are performed

■   Ensuring that Cisco IOS versions are tracked and managed

■   Ensuring that design compliance is tracked, including when recommended practices change

■   Ensuring that plans for disaster recovery and continuity of operations are developed

■   Conducting a realistic and thorough risk analysis

Tools

Organizations should monitor service and component availability. With proper failover, services should continue operating when single components fail. Without component monitoring, if a failed redundant component is not detected and replaced, an outage may occur if the second component subsequently fails.

Performance thresholds and reporting the top N devices with specific characteristics (top N reporting) are useful, both for noticing when capacity is depleting, and for correlating slow services with stressed network or server resources. Monitoring packet loss, latency, jitter, and drops on (at least) WAN links or ISP connections is also important. These metrics might be the first indication of an outage or of a potential SLA deterioration that could affect the delivery of services.

Good documentation is a valuable tool and includes the following:

- Network diagrams help in planning and in fixing outages more quickly. Out-of-date documentation can lead to design errors, lack of redundancy, and other undesirable consequences.

- Documentation of how and why the network is designed the way it is helps capture knowledge that can be critical when a different person needs to change the design, reexamine how failover works, or make other changes.

- Addresses, VLAN numbers, and servers should be accurately documented to aid in troubleshooting, network redesign, and so forth.

- Accurate documentation that indicates how services map to applications, how applications map to virtual servers, and how virtual servers map to physical servers can be incredibly useful when troubleshooting.

Common E-Commerce Module Designs

The e-commerce module includes routing, switching, firewall, and server content load-balancing components.

This section reviews common e-commerce designs using firewalls and SLBs and common approaches for connecting to multiple ISPs. These elements may be integrated into the more complex e-commerce module designs shown in the "Integrated E-Commerce Designs" section, later in this chapter.

Common E-Commerce Firewall Designs

This section reviews common firewall designs for the e-commerce module, starting with a typical e-commerce module topology. Designs that use a server as an application gateway are described, followed by a discussion of virtualization using firewall contexts. Designs using virtual firewall layers are examined, and firewall modes are described.

Typical E-Commerce Module Topology

The e-commerce module is typically implemented in a data center facility and is connected to the Internet via one or multiple ISPs. Because there are multiple firewall layers inside the e-commerce module, this design is sometimes referred to as a firewall sandwich. The design is illustrated in Figure 7-1. The firewall connections in the figure are either in an active or standby state. A large site might use three layers of firewalls, whereas smaller sites might use only two layers of firewalls. The firewalls may consist of physical or virtual devices depending on the configuration and traffic needs.

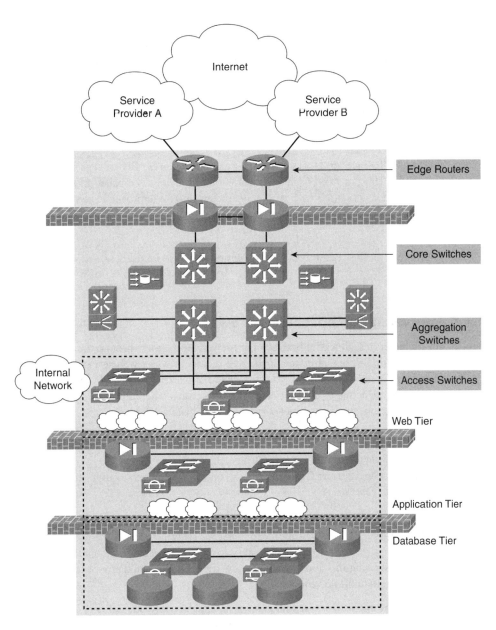

Figure 7-1   *Typical E-Commerce Module Topology*

As shown in Figure 7-1, a web tier (the outer demilitarized zone [DMZ] that supports the web servers) is typically protected from the Internet by a pair of firewalls. The web servers communicate with the application tier (application or middleware servers in the data center) through a second pair of firewalls. The application tier communicates with the database tie (the mainframes or databases) through the third pair of firewalls.

Although the specific connection is not shown in Figure 7-1, the e-commerce servers connect through the firewalls back to the internal network. This connectivity permits staff to update the applications and servers and do other maintenance and monitoring. When the e-commerce module is collocated with the corporate network, the edge routers may also provide the connection back to the corporate internal network. If the e-commerce module resides within a data center, the innermost firewalls may provide the connection back to the internal network.

Note   Sites requiring high levels of security sometimes implement firewalls using different operating systems. This practice ensures that if the outer firewall is breached, the same compromise does not permit a breach of the inner firewall. This approach is more difficult to manage and support, however.

Some variations on this "firewall sandwich" design may also be used, as shown in the following sections.

Using a Server as an Application Gateway

In some architectures, all traffic between the firewall layers goes through the servers. For example, in Figure 7-2, one interface of the web servers provides web services, and a separate interface connects through another firewall to application servers. In this design, the web tier servers are acting as application-specific gateways. The outer and inner sets of interface connections on the web tier servers are on separate VLANs.

Note   Figure 7-2 shows a logical representation of the application-specific gateway design. Usually, the two web tier server interfaces connect to a switch (or four interfaces connect to two switches).

This application-specific gateway approach increases security because a hacker would have to penetrate the firewall and the web server operating system to attack the middle layer of firewalls. Using this approach may allow the network administrator to avoid operating firewalls from multiple vendors.

A variation of the application-specific gateway design has only one connection from each server to each switch, but uses a port-specific access control list (ACL) on the firewalls. The ACL on the Internet edge firewall pair allows only web and related traffic to go to the web servers. Similarly, the middle firewall allows only application traffic, from the web servers, to the application servers.

If some traffic must go between firewalls, a single VLAN can connect to both firewall layers. For example, this might be needed if an application tier server needs to communicate directly with some devices on the Internet or with some devices in the internal corporate network (if the internal network is accessed via the Internet edge firewalls).

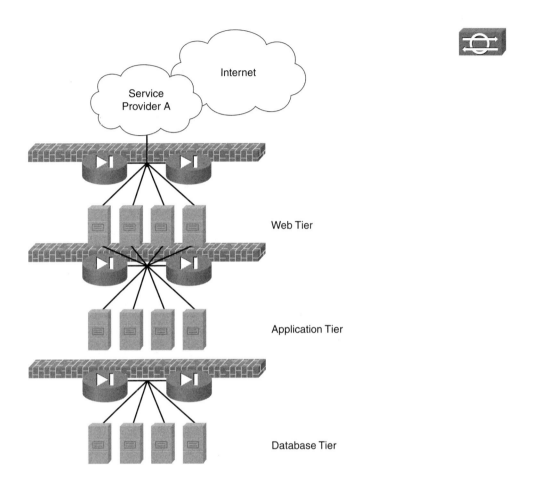

Figure 7-2 *Logical Representation of Using a Server as an Application Gateway*

Virtualization with Firewall Contexts

A physical Cisco firewall or Cisco Application Control Engine (ACE) module can be virtualized or divided into separate *firewall contexts*. These virtual firewall contexts operate similarly to separate physical firewall devices. The physical firewall resources that each firewall context is allocated can be controlled, for example, to prevent a problem in one firewall context from affecting another.

Figure 7-3 shows a server farm connected to a firewall in which firewall contexts are used to provide virtual firewalls to different servers. The firewall contexts retain the secure separation of rules and other customer features, such as Network Address Translation (NAT), ACLs, protocols, and so forth. For example, in enterprise networks, firewall contexts can be used to separate different Internet-facing e-commerce blocks and different layers of a firewall sandwich. Firewall contexts can also be used in Cisco Catalyst 6500 series Firewall Services Modules (FWSM).

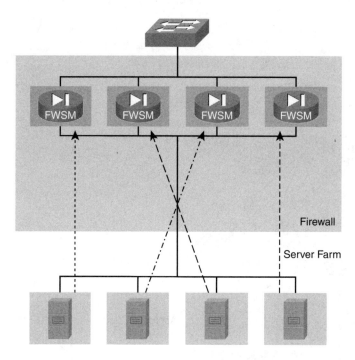

Figure 7-3   *Implementing Virtualization with Firewall Contexts*

Note   Virtual firewalls are discussed in Chapter 8.

Virtual Firewall Layers

A multitiered e-commerce module may use a single pair of firewall devices using virtual firewall layers. For example, a pair of Catalyst 6500 series FWSMs might be used rather than individual firewalls, as illustrated in the example in Figure 7-4.

The different types of lines on the left side of Figure 7-4 correspond to different layers in the logical traffic-flow diagram shown in the right side of the figure. Traffic from the Internet passes through the firewall to the web tier, passes through the firewall again to get from the web tier to the application tier, and passes once more through the firewall to get to the databases, mainframe, or internal network.

If a virtual firewall design is used, it is a good idea to provide a logical diagram showing the VLANs internal to the switch, similar to the right side of Figure 7-4. Routing and default gateway logic can also be superimposed on this diagram to indicate how packets flow, why traffic can or cannot flow from a tier directly to or from the Internet, how failover works, and so on. This design can also be documented using a firewall sandwich diagram, with notes indicating that the different firewall layers in the diagram are implemented in the same physical device.

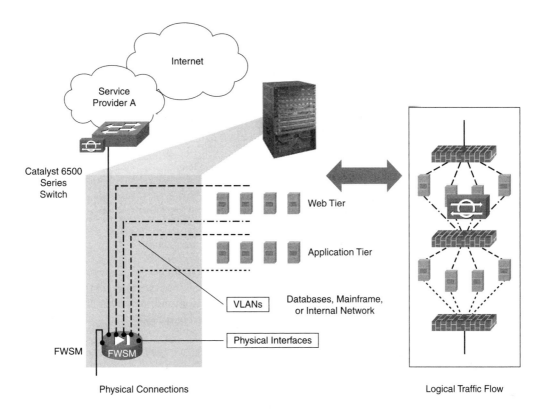

Figure 7-4 *Virtual Firewall Layers Represent Logical Traffic Flows*

Note   If such a design is used, it is a good idea to provide a logical switch diagram showing the VLANs that are internal to the switch. Routing or default gateway can be superimposed to document how packets flow, reachability, how failover works, and so on.

Firewall Modes

Cisco firewall technology allows firewall designs in which the firewall operates in either Transparent (Bridged) mode, or in traditional Routed mode, as illustrated in Figure 7-5. The mode can be established on a per-context basis, depending on licensing.

One VLAN usually corresponds to one subnet. However, in Transparent mode, the firewall bridges two VLANs together, switching traffic at Layer 2 between the two VLANs, which together constitute one IP subnet. As shown on the left side of Figure 7-5, any traffic that goes through the firewall is subject to stateful IP address-based ACLs and other firewall features. This Transparent mode is sometimes described as a bump-in-the-wire mode.

A firewall in Transparent mode can isolate less-secure servers from more-secure servers within the same VLAN and subnet. This would allow deployment without changing IP subnets or re-addressing the servers. Object-oriented ACLs can be used to support the process of securing the servers of different security levels.

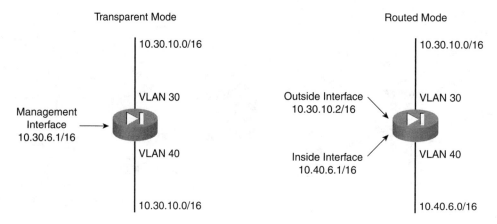

Figure 7-5   *A Firewall Runs in Either Transparent or Routed Mode*

In the traditional Routed mode, shown on the right side of Figure 7-5, the firewall routes traffic between VLANs (or interfaces). As traffic is routed, it passes through the firewall and is subject to stateful IP address-based ACLs, inspection, and other firewall configuration options. Most current designs use firewalls in routed mode.

Note   Firewall modes are discussed further in Chapter 8.

An example of using a firewall in Transparent mode is when there is a need to isolate a set of servers from other servers on the same VLAN. One solution to this requirement is shown in Figure 7-6. In this example, the "more secure" server ports are placed on VLAN 11. The Catalyst 6500 series FWSM is configured in transparent mode to bridge VLANs 10 and 11 together. The Multilayer Switch Feature Card (MSFC) in the Catalyst 6500 series switch routes traffic for the subnet onto the combined VLANs 10 and 11. The FWSM uses an IP ACL to control which traffic passes from VLAN 10 into VLAN 11. Recabling and re-addressing are not needed to support this implementation.

An alternative solution to this requirement is to use switch VLAN ACLs (VACL) to control traffic within a VLAN at the IP address level. Using private VLANs (PVLAN) is another way to secure the server ports.

Note   PVLANs are discussed further in Chapter 8.

Using router ACLs in the switch would require server re-addressing to move some of the servers onto a different VLAN and subnet. This is difficult to do quickly and might require a lot of work from server and application staff.

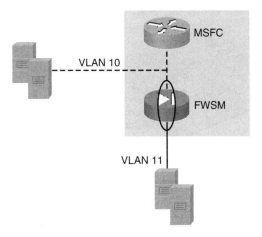

Figure 7-6   *Example Use of a Firewall in Transparent Mode*

> **Note**   Maintaining VACLs can be difficult. Many organizations prefer to use Catalyst 6500 series FWSM devices for their object-oriented configuration because the FWSM devices allow for logical grouping of IP addresses and ports, making for simpler rules.

Common E-Commerce Server Load Balancer Designs

This section introduces common e-commerce module design approaches using SLBs.

Functions of a Server Load Balancer

A Server Load Balancer (SLB), also called a content load balancer, supports both scaling and high availability by distributing client requests for service across active servers, as shown in Figure 7-7. The SLB provides a public IP address, also called a virtual IP (VIP) address, for *each service*. Clients resolve this address through Domain Name System (DNS) requests. The SLB intelligently passes traffic to a pool of physical servers, based on the load and on configured rules. The SLB rewrites the source and destination IP or MAC addresses, depending on the mode in which it operates.

The SLB monitors the health and performance of the servers. For example, when a server needs to be taken down for maintenance, it is removed from the server pool, and the SLB continues providing the services using the remaining servers. Similarly, additional server capacity can be added to the pool if needed. These features contribute to enhanced availability for e-commerce modules.

Pairs of SLB devices can function in various failover configurations. Sophisticated service monitoring can be used to ensure that services fail over to the redundant device if the primary SLB device loses connectivity.

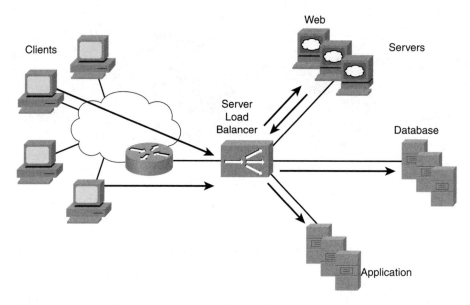

Figure 7-7   *A Server Load Balancer Represents Multiple Servers*

SLB Design Models

The following are three basic design approaches used with SLB devices:

- **Router mode:** The SLB device routes between outside and inside subnets.
- **Bridge mode (inline):** The SLB device operates in Transparent Bridging mode.
- **One-armed or two-armed mode:** The one-armed or two-armed mode can be implemented in several ways such that replies from servers pass back through the SLB on their way to the end user. The server default gateway can be set to the SLB device, policy-based routing (PBR) can be used, or client NAT can be used.

The following redundancy options can also be included with any of the three basic design approaches:

- With active/passive redundancy, one active SLB device is backed up by the other passive SLB device.
- With active/active redundancy, one SLB device is active for some VIP addresses (representing some services), and another SLB device is active for other VIP addresses (services). The SLB devices back each other up.

There are also various configuration options for how failover is triggered.

These design approaches are detailed in the following sections.

Note   A discussion of failover triggers is beyond the scope of this book.

SLB Router Mode

Using the SLB Router mode is a popular SLB design approach and is illustrated in Figure 7-8.

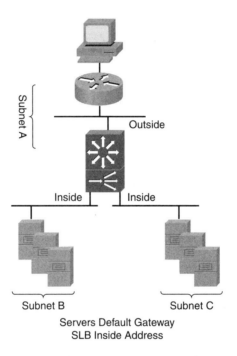

Figure 7-8   *A SLB in Router Mode Routes Between Outside and Inside Subnets*

In this approach, the SLB device routes between outside and inside subnets. The services' VIP addresses are usually in a globally routable public IP subnet. In Figure 7-8, the public network is subnet A. The physical servers are typically in a private IP subnet. The private subnets are subnets B and C in Figure 7-8. The SLB routes packets between the public and the private subnets.

The servers typically use the SLB inside address as their default gateway. As reply traffic from the server to the end user passes through the SLB, the SLB changes the server's IP address to the appropriate VIP address. Therefore, the end user has no way of telling that there is a SLB device in the path, nor does the end user see the IP address of the real server. Therefore, using private IP addresses for the real servers protects them from direct attacks across the Internet; would-be hackers cannot route traffic directly to the real servers.

Application Control Engine

Application Control Engine (ACE) is a design that is easy to deploy and works well with many server IP subnets. It is the recommended approach for appliance-based content load balancers. The real servers typically use the SLB inside address as their default gateway. As the return reply traffic passes through the SLB device, the source real IP is changed to the VIP address. Therefore, the end user has no direct way of telling that there is a SLB device in the path. The end user does not see the IP address of the physical server.

Note   You may need to re-address some network devices to support SLB deployments.

SLB Inline Bridge Mode

The SLB device may also be used in an Inline Bridge mode, as illustrated in Figure 7-9.

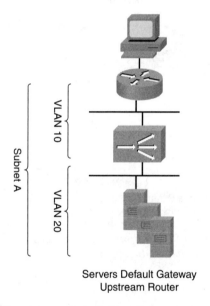

Servers Default Gateway
Upstream Router

Figure 7-9   *A SLB in Inline Bridge Mode Bridges Between VLANs in a Single Subnet*

This mode operates much like the firewall Transparent Bridging mode discussed earlier. The content load balancer or SLB device acts as a "bump in the wire" or transparent bridge between the servers and the upstream firewall or Layer 3 device (a router in Figure 7-9). The servers use the IP address of the firewall or Layer 3 device as their default gateway.

In this design, the physical servers are in a globally routable IP subnet, subnet A in Figure 7-9. The VIP addresses of services can be in the same or a different IP subnet. However, each server farm must be in one IP subnet because the SLB changes the MAC address associated with the VIP to the specific MAC address of a physical server to direct traffic to the appropriate physical server.

This design is one suggested configuration for integrated load balancers. However, if SLB devices are deployed in a redundant configuration, spanning-tree implications must be considered in the design. Configuring and designing with SLB devices that use Routed mode is typically simpler than with devices using bridged mode because troubleshooting SLB spanning-tree issues can be complicated.

SLB One-Armed Mode

The one-armed (or two-armed) mode is another popular approach for deploying SLB devices, as illustrated in Figure 7-10.

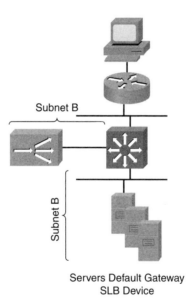

Figure 7-10 *A SLB in One-Armed Mode Is Not Inline with the Traffic*

In this out-of-band approach, the SLB device is connected to a switch, typically with one or two connections. It is not directly inline with the traffic path as it is in the previous designs discussed. In the one-armed approach, the SLB VIP and the physical servers are in the same VLAN or subnet. In the two-armed approach, the SLB device routes traffic to the physical server subnet, which can be a private subnet.

Inbound end-user traffic is routed to the VIP on the SLB device. The SLB device then translates the IP destination address to a physical server IP address and forwards the traffic to the physical server, the same as it does in Routed mode. The main difference is that return traffic must be forced to go to the SLB device so that the source IP address of traffic from the physical server can be translated back to the VIP that the end user device thinks it is communicating with.

The simplest way to cause return traffic to go through the SLB device is to set the server default gateway to the SLB device, rather than the router.

Another approach is to use PBR to "push" or "deflect" the appropriate outbound server traffic to the SLB device as next hop.

A third approach is to use client NAT, in which the client source address is replaced with the SLB address. The server then sends its reply back to the SLB device. The SLB changes the destination address back to the real end-user address and forwards the packet, based on a connection table in the SLB. This approach is not as popular because many organizations want to know the original end-user IP address, for logging and marketing purposes or for security audit trail purposes.

Note   Client NAT is also called source NAT.

One advantage of the one-armed or two-armed approach is that not all inbound and outbound traffic has to go through the SLB device. For example, PBR can allow the real server to do a file transfer or backup directly, without having to burden the SLB device with processing those packets. This might be helpful in scaling the e-commerce module to support greater traffic volumes.

Another advantage is that scaling by adding SLB devices is simple. Different VIPs can be used to send traffic to different SLB devices, and PBR or client NAT can steer replies back through the correct SLB device. Server default gateways can be used to provide services using different server pools.

Misconfigured SLB One-Armed Mode Flows

Figure 7-11 shows how traffic would flow in a misconfigured network with a one-armed SLB.

The steps shown in Figure 7-11 are as follows:

1. The client sends traffic to the VIP. The traffic is routed by the edge router, which uses its MAC address as the source MAC address. The router looks up the VIP in its routing table and uses the SLB MAC address as the destination MAC address.

2. The SLB device forwards the traffic, using its MAC address as the source MAC address and the selected server MAC and IP addresses as destination addresses.

3. If the server default gateway, PBR, or client NAT is not configured or is not configured correctly, the physical server reply goes directly to the client, causing a problem because the client receives traffic from a different IP address than the VIP to which its connection was established. In Figure 7-11, this problem is shown as a Reset. The problem results from no mechanism forcing replies back through the SLB device.

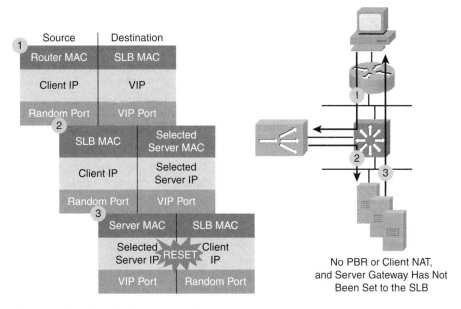

Figure 7-11   *Traffic Flow with Misconfiguration*

Properly Configured SLB One-Armed Mode Using Client NAT

Figure 7-12 shows the same network as in Figure 7-11, but with the SLB device doing client NAT.

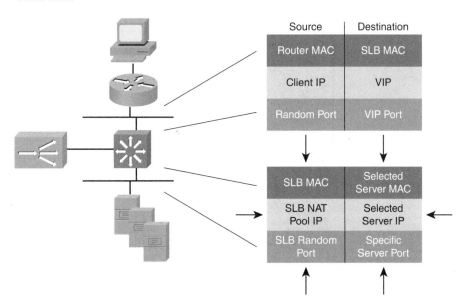

Figure 7-12   *Traffic Flows Correctly When the One-Armed SLB Is Configured with Client NAT*

With client NAT, the client information is rewritten before the packet goes to the server. Note that everything about the source (MAC address, IP address, and port) is rewritten by client NAT. Therefore, when the server replies, it replies to the SLB device.

As discussed, one potential issue with client NAT is accountability; the server traffic logs show only the IP address of the SLB, not the client's real IP address.

Common E-Commerce Design Topologies for Connecting to Multiple ISPs

One of the key components for e-commerce is ISP connectivity. This section discusses common topology designs for e-commerce modules connected to multiple ISPs.

One Firewall per ISP

Figure 7-13 shows a common approach to dual-homing (connecting a site to two ISPs using a router, a firewall, or both to connect to each ISP). This approach is commonly used in small sites because it is relatively easy to set up and administer.

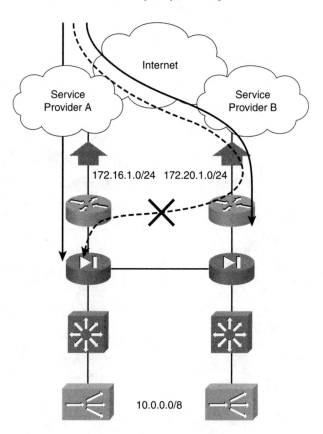

Figure 7-13   *Using One Firewall per ISP*

Note In Figure 7-13 and subsequent figures in this chapter, all addresses shown are private addresses. In reality, public addresses would probably be used on the ISP connections.

Note With the Cisco IOS firewall features, one device might be used for both routing and firewall functions. Another variation of this design uses one router to support both ISP connections.

External DNS resolves the organization's site name to an address from either ISP's external address block (172.16.1.0/24 or 172.20.1.0/24 in Figure 7-14). If DNS resolves using a round-robin approach, external users are approximately load balanced across the two paths to the organization's web server. The traffic is routed to the outside of the relevant NAT device or firewall.

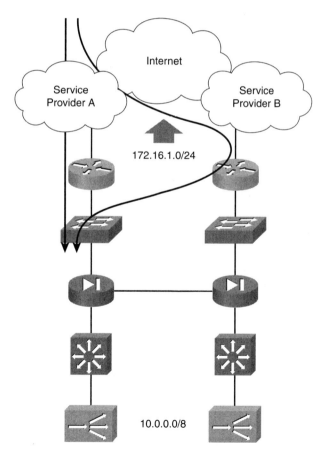

Figure 7-14 *Using Stateful Failover with a Common External Prefix*

On each edge router, NAT translates the address block provided by the ISP to the inside address of the e-commerce servers.

An issue with this design is that any failure on an edge router results in a loss of session because the failover between edge routers is not performing stateful NAT. Dual routers and dual connections per ISP can be used for more robust connectivity to each ISP, but the nonstateful failover still occurs if connectivity through one ISP is lost. Also, the external DNS must be aware if a site loses connectivity through one ISP so that it can stop resolving to addresses that are down.

Stateful Failover with Common External Prefix

A more sophisticated way to dual-home an e-commerce site to two ISPs uses stateful failover with a common external prefix, as illustrated in Figure 7-14.

In this case, the firewall pair and the NAT devices support some form of stateful failover. The NAT devices translate addresses to a block that both ISPs are willing to advertise for the site (172.16.1.0 /24 in the figure). This might be an address block obtained from one of the providers, or it could be a large organization's address block.

The edge routers advertise this block via BGP to both ISPs, which advertise it to their peers.

Note   BGP configuration requires special care and should use an assigned autonomous system number (ASN) to prevent the site from becoming a transit link between the ISPs and to prevent routing loops.

Note   Configuring basic BGP is covered in the *Implementing Cisco IP Routing (ROUTE) Foundation Learning Guide: Foundation learning for the ROUTE 642-902 Exam* by Diane Teare (Cisco Press, 2010).

If one provider loses routing or connectivity, BGP automatically fails over to the other path to the site. The firewalls support stateful failover with an active/active design to handle a failure internal to the site's switches or links. First-hop redundancy protocols (FHRP), such as Hot Standby Router Protocol (HSRP), are used for failover in case a switch-to-router link fails.

Distributed Data Centers

Very large e-commerce sites with critical services (such as banks) may use distributed data centers, as illustrated in Figure 7-15.

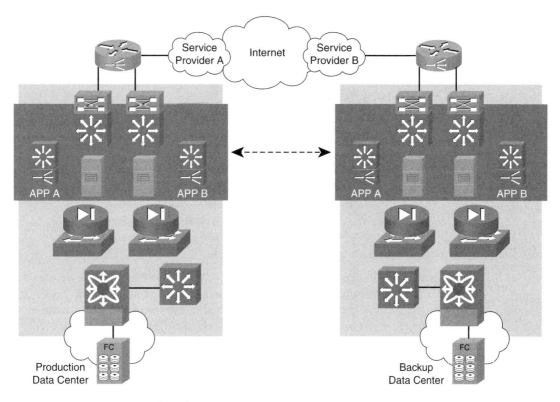

Figure 7-15   *Using Distributed Data Centers*

Just as deploying two chassis provides greater failover flexibility than deploying one chassis with dual components (such as power and supervisor modules), using two sites increases overall high availability while lessening the uptime requirements for each individual site. When e-commerce modules are implemented in well-designed distributed data centers, one site can occasionally be taken offline for maintenance without disrupting customer service. Using two e-commerce sites also protects against regional problems.

Note   GLSB and GSS are discussed in the next section.

Design Option: Distributed Data Centers

Very large e-commerce sites often use distributed data centers.

A two-chassis deployment can provide more failover flexibility than having one chassis with dual components such as power and supervisor modules. Similarly, having two sites increases overall high availability while lessening the uptime requirements for each individual site.

When the e-commerce modules are implemented in well-designed distributed data centers, this approach also means that one site can occasionally be taken offline for maintenance without disrupting customer service. Using two e-commerce sites also protects against regional problems. This feature is becoming a requirement for banks and other critical services.

To support the distributed data center design, applications need to be migrated to technology allowing active-active hot databases as opposed to active database and mirrored hot spare database. Another key element when using distributed sites is technology to detect when a site is "off the air" and should be failed over. The devices that detect the need for failover and respond are often external to the two sites. This technology can be an external service or can be provided by equipment at one or more service provider collocation facilities. The off-the-air detection might be provided by an external service, such Akamai or UltraDNS. It might also be provided using the Cisco GSS technology, typically within a provider collocation facility. The function that is provided is called global server load balancing (GSLB).

Some organizations dislike any DNS-based failover techniques because DNS or browser caches retain old DNS values for quite some time, and many implementations do not exhibit proper behavior regarding DNS TTL values. Also, implementations could incorrectly use source IP to guess user location, or do reordering when a DNS server or GSS provides an ordered list of addresses. Nonetheless, various large sites do use GSLB and believe strongly that it improves their service offering.

Another consideration at some sites is diversity of DNS, which affects the degree of protection against DDoS on DNS servers. Large external DNS services using anycast IP are one way to protect DNS from attacks. Other approaches that you might consider are site-controlled external DNS servers or GSS devices in collocation facilities.

One design approach for distributed e-commerce modules is to tie together the redundant sites via an internal WAN link to avoid the need for an external failover response. With this approach, DNS provides the addresses of servers at either site, addressed from a block of addresses that are advertised through the ISPs of both sites. If the connectivity from one site to the Internet fails, both Internet and internal routing redirect traffic to go through the other connection. Delay in failover and the impact of any routing instability are potential drawbacks to this approach. Conversely, failover at the Internet level cannot be too rapid; if it is, instability results.

Additional Data Center Services

Firewall protection and load balancing are common services in the e-commerce module. In addition, Secure Sockets Layer (SSL) offload and intrusion prevention systems (IPS) can be added to the data center service chains. Figure 7-16 shows this type of a configuration.

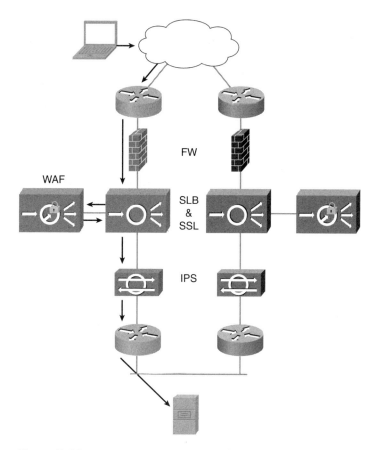

Figure 7-16 *Data Center Services Include Stateful Firewall, SSL Offload, SLB, WAFs, IPS*

As mentioned, firewall protection and load balancing are two utilities that are commonly implemented in the e-commerce module to provide a secure, resilient, and scalable infrastructure. Other services that can be provided to enhance server security and performance in the e-commerce module include the following:

- **SSL offload:** SSL is commonly used to encrypt sensitive web application traffic. Servers use locally installed certificates to authenticate and encrypt web connections from clients. SSL encryption and decryption is a CPU-intensive task that may affect the performance of the servers. The Cisco ACE can offload this task from the servers to improve server efficiency. The Cisco ACE stores server certificates locally, allowing it to proxy SSL connections for client requests and forward the client request in clear text to the server. This mechanism is also useful to ensure that a web application firewall (WAF) or IPS can inspect the payload of the SSL session for malicious content.

- **Cisco ACE WAF:** Many common attacks that target the e-commerce module attempt to exploit vulnerabilities on the application layer. These attacks may include cross-site scripting (XSS) attacks, Structured Query Language (SQL) and command injection, privilege escalation, cross-site request forgeries (CSRF), buffer overflows, cookie tampering, and denial-of-service (DoS) attacks. The Cisco ACE WAF provides a full-proxy firewall solution for both HTML- and XML-based web applications.

- **IPS:** An IPS provides deep packet and anomaly inspection to protect against both common and complex embedded attacks.

WAFs and IPSs complement each other in detecting and preventing attacks targeting the e-commerce servers. The WAF specifically focuses on attacks that are targeted at HTML- and XML-based web applications, inspecting the application layer conversation between client and server. The IPS detects and mitigates a broad range of network attacks by inspecting packets for suspicious patterns at the lower layers of the Open Systems Interconnection (OSI) model.

The SSL offload capability of the Cisco ACE enables the use of WAF and IPS systems for SSL-based applications. It decrypts the traffic before sending it in clear text to the WAF and IPS for further inspection.

Integrated E-Commerce Designs

This section illustrates more complex e-commerce module designs that incorporate elements from the earlier section, "Common E-Commerce Module Designs"

Base E-Commerce Module Design

This section describes a base e-commerce module design, an example of which is illustrated in Figure 7-17.

In the base design, the core layer supports the first stage of firewalls. In Figure 7-17, the core layer uses Cisco Catalyst 6509 switches with integrated FWSMs. In Layer 3 Routed mode, aggregation and access layers are considered trusted zones; therefore, there is no security between the web, application, and database tiers in this base design. If one of the servers is compromised, the attacker may have full access to the other servers and to the internal network.

The aggregation layer supports connectivity to the SLB devices or firewalls, in Routed mode. The default gateway for the e-commerce servers is the VIP address on these SLB devices or firewalls. In Figure 7-17, Cisco Catalyst 6513 switches with Cisco ACEs. ACEs are used as SLB devices; other SLB devices such as the Cisco ACEs could be used instead. The default gateway for the Cisco ACE is an HSRP address on the MSFC on the same Catalyst 6513 switch. Because the MSFC is directly connected to the SLB device, it is possible to support host routes with route health injection (RHI).

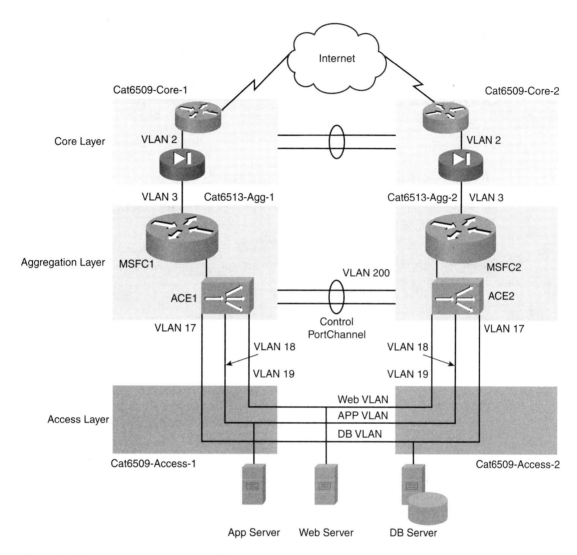

Figure 7-17 *Base E-Commerce Module Design*

Note   The RHI feature allows the SLB device to inject or remove host routes for its virtual servers, based on the health of the servers and applications. These routes to the virtual servers can then be propagated to the rest of the network. The RHI feature can be used to load balance a virtual server across multiple SLB devices. It can also be used as a disaster recovery mechanism; in this case, the route to a specific virtual server is propagated with a different metric for different SLB devices, either within the same data center or across data centers.

The access layer includes switches (not shown in Figure 7-17) to connect the web servers, application servers, and database servers. In more complex designs, the database servers or mainframes may be inside the main data center, isolated by firewalls from the e-commerce module.

In this design, all e-commerce traffic travels via the Cisco ACE. Additional Cisco ACE configuration is needed if direct access to the servers is required and for non-load-balanced sessions initiated by the servers.

Base Design Routing Logic

Routing in this e-commerce module design is mostly static, using VIP addresses to support failover. Figure 7-18 clarifies how the routing is intended to work.

The left side of Figure 7-18 shows how traffic is routed by using static routes to next-hop addresses to the VIP of a service on the Cisco ACE and then to a server IP address. The right side of the figure shows how traffic is routed from servers by using default routes to next-hop addresses to the Internet.

Inbound, the ISP uses a static or BGP route to direct traffic to the e-commerce network. The e-commerce module border router typically uses a static route with the next-hop address set to the outside IP address of the firewall. (Alternatively, Open Shortest Path First [OSPF] routing might be used.)

The firewall uses a static route with the next-hop address set to the HSRP address of the MSFC in the switch. The MSFC uses a connected route to reach the Cisco ACE, and static routes to reach the server's actual IP addresses. If RHI is used, it provides the necessary routes to the VIPs. The server's subnets are directly connected to the Cisco ACE.

Outbound, servers use the Cisco ACE as their default gateway. From there, a default route causes traffic to go to the HSRP address on the MSFCs, and then to the firewall's inside IP address, and then to the HSRP address of the border router pair, and finally to the connected interface of the ISP router.

The VLAN connections between the aggregation layer switches are used for FHRPs and failover heartbeat detection.

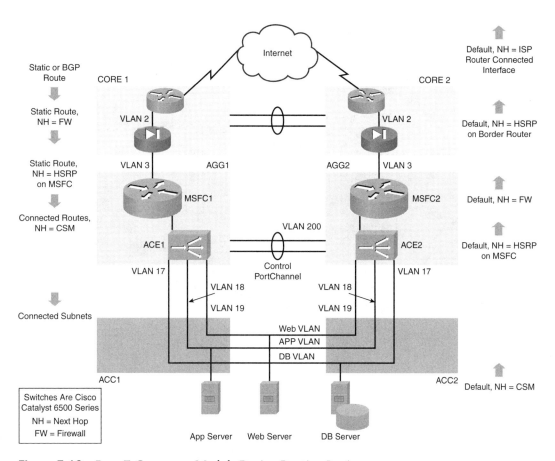

Figure 7-18 *Base E-Commerce Module Design Routing Logic*

Base Design Server Traffic Flows

Figure 7-19 shows representative flows going to and from a web server in this design. The left side of the figure shows a load-balanced session flow. The right side of the figure shows a server management session flow (for example, a Secure Shell [SSH] connection to a server).

In both of these flows, the firewall handles security logic, and the Cisco ACE handles the SLB decision or passes management traffic directly to a specific server.

> **Note**   Sometimes, special server management addresses are used to make it easier to con-figure the Cisco ACE to pass management traffic directly to the server. In other cases, the actual server address is used, rather than the VIP of the service, to indicate management traffic to the SLB module.

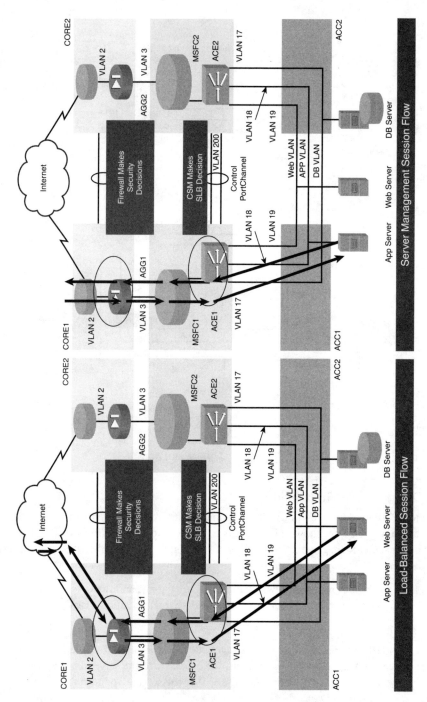

Figure 7-19   *Base E-Commerce Module Design Server Traffic Flows*

Two Firewall Layers in the E-Commerce Module Design

For more protection than in the base design, a firewall can be inserted into the aggregation layer. In the design in Figure 7-20, FWSM modules have been added to the aggregation switches. The additional FWSM is a Layer 3 firewall with a single context. It provides security between the web, application, and database tiers. Even if the exterior-facing web servers are compromised, a high degree of protection exists for the application and database servers and any connections to the rest of the internal data center network or mainframe.

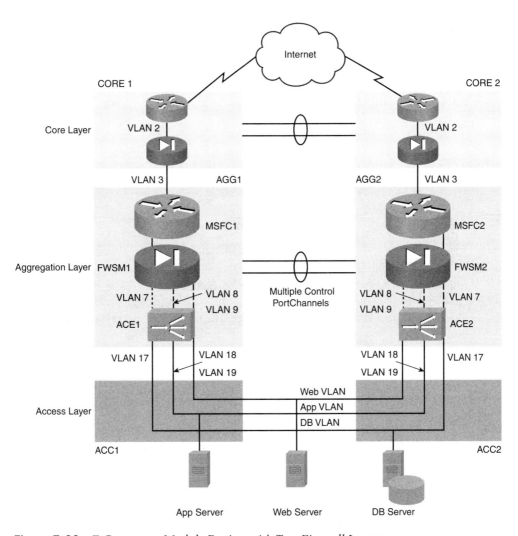

Figure 7-20 *E-Commerce Module Design with Two Firewall Layers*

With this design, the Cisco ACE can be used in Routed mode, as was done in the base design, or it can be used in Bridged mode to bridge between multiple VLAN pairs.

Figure 7-20 illustrates a bridged approach where the default gateway for the servers is the primary FWSM interface in the aggregation switch, rather than an address on the Cisco ACE.

The aggregation switch FWSM routes traffic directly to the server subnets. This traffic is bridged through the Cisco ACE, so the traffic burden on the Cisco ACE is not reduced. However, no extra configuration is needed for direct access to the servers (for example, for deterministic testing from outside) or for non-load-balanced sessions initiated by the servers (for example, FTP downloads).

Note   The ACE default gateway is also the FWSM's primary IP address. In this scenario, because the MSFC is not directly connected to the ACE or on the same subnet as the Cisco ACE, RHI is not possible.

The VLANs between the aggregation layer switches are used for FHRP or failover heart-beat detection.

Note   Cisco ACE modules could be used in place of the aggregation layer FWSMs, although ACEs are not full firewalls.

Traffic Flows in a Two-Firewall Layer Design

Figure 7-21 shows representative flows going to and from a web server in a design with two firewall layers.

Load-balanced user web traffic is shown in the left half of Figure 7-21. In this design, the perimeter firewall at the core still makes security decisions. The aggregation layer firewall provides an internal DMZ protecting the servers. The Cisco ACE makes the SLB decisions, as it does in the base design.

The right half of Figure 7-21 shows the traffic flow from the web server to the application server. The traffic from the web server is bridged through the Cisco ACE, to the default gateway for that subnet on the aggregation switch FWSM. The FWSM then routes the traffic to the application server subnet. The traffic from the FWSM is bridged through the Cisco ACE to the application server.

Return traffic from the application server to the web server is handled similarly. The application server subnet default gateway directs traffic to the FWSM, which routes it back onto the web server subnet.

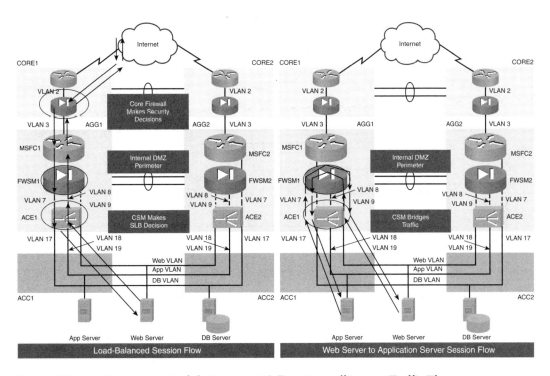

Figure 7-21   *E-Commerce Module Design with Two Firewall Layers Traffic Flows*

One-Armed SLB Two-Firewall E-Commerce Module Design

Figure 7-22 illustrates an e-commerce module design using a one-armed SLB device with two firewall layers.

In a one-armed design with two firewall layers, the Cisco ACE is moved such that selected traffic to and from the servers does not go through it. The design can be scaled by adding additional Cisco FWSMs and ACE modules to the switch chassis as needed.

The FWSM at the aggregation layer again provides security between the web, application, and database tiers.

In this design, the default gateway of the servers is still the appropriate primary IP address on the FWSM in the aggregation switch. The default gateway of the Cisco ACE, however, is the HSRP address on the MSFCs.

Inbound traffic is routed to the Cisco ACE as a connected route to the VIP of the service on the ACE. The Cisco ACE then statically routes inbound traffic to the aggregation switch FWSM, which routes it to the connected server subnet. Traffic bound directly for a real server IP address bypasses the Cisco ACE.

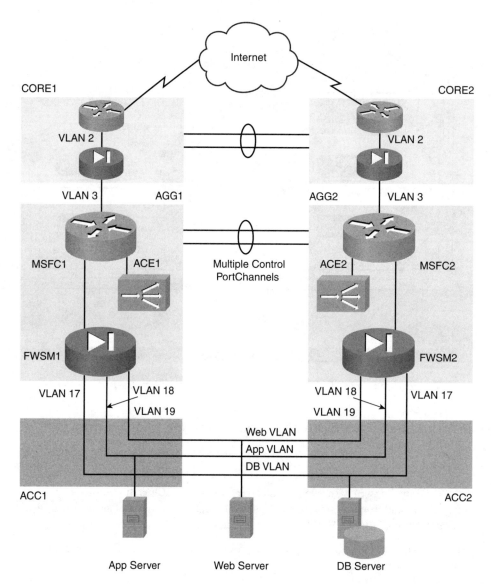

Figure 7-22 *E-Commerce Module One-Armed SLB Design with Two Firewall Layers*

The appropriate outbound traffic from the servers is directed by PBR or client NAT to the Cisco ACE. The MSFC is directly connected to the Cisco ACE, and so RHI is possible. No extra configuration is needed for direct traffic to and from the servers. All non-load-balanced traffic to and from the servers bypasses the Cisco ACE.

Traffic Flows in a One-Armed SLB Two-Firewall Layer Design

Figure 7-23 shows representative flows going to and from a web server in the one-armed SLB design with two firewall layers.

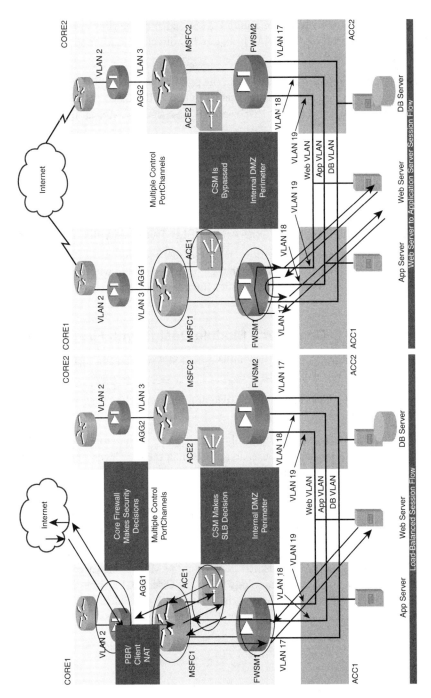

Figure 7-23 *E-Commerce Module One-Armed SLB Design with Two Firewall Layers Traffic Flows*

The traffic flow in the left half of Figure 7-23 is similar to the flow in Figure 7-21. The difference is that PBR or client NAT is required to direct the outbound server traffic from the MSFC to the SLB.

The right half of Figure 7-23 differs from the previous design in Figure 7-21. The traffic from the web server to the application server bypasses the Cisco ACE in this design. The FWSM routes traffic between the web server VLAN and the application server VLAN.

If server load balancing is desired for traffic from the web server to the application server, a more complex approach is required. For example, a VIP address in another subnet would allow routing of traffic from the web server to a virtual application server address, via the Cisco ACE.

Direct Server Traffic Flows in a One-Armed SLB Two-Firewall Layer Design

Figure 7-24 shows representative flows for server management traffic and direct Internet traffic going to and from a web server in the one-armed design with two firewall layers. The Cisco ACE is not in the traffic path for this type of traffic to and from the servers.

One-Armed SLB E-Commerce Module Design with Firewall Contexts

Figure 7-25 illustrates a design using a one-armed SLB with an aggregation firewall supporting multiple firewall contexts.

The aggregation FWSM is used in Transparent mode, with the MSFC routing between the server VLANs.

A firewall context is also placed logically in the Layer 2 path before traffic reaches the MSFC, eliminating the need for a separate firewall in the core layer. There is firewall protection from the outside, internally, and for each DMZ. The MSFC is on a secure internal segment with protection from each connected network.

The default gateway of the servers is the HSRP primary IP address on the MSFC. No extra configuration is needed for direct access to the servers or for non-load-balanced server-initiated sessions.

The ACE default gateway is the HSRP address on the MSFC. The Cisco ACE is deployed in routed mode in a one-armed topology. With the Cisco ACE in one-armed mode, non-load-balanced traffic can easily bypass the ACE. RHI is possible in this design because the MSFC is directly connected to the ACE.

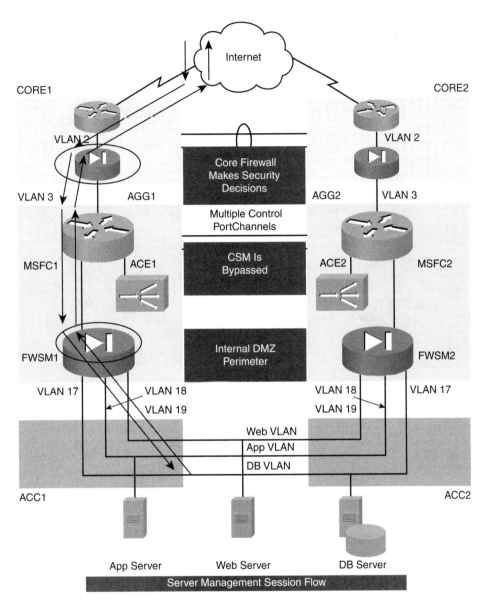

Figure 7-24 *Direct Server Traffic Flows in an E-Commerce Module One-Armed SLB Design with Two Firewall Layers*

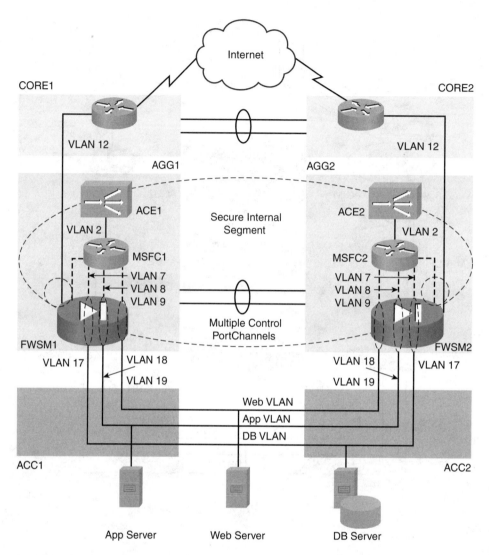

Figure 7-25   *E-Commerce Module One-Armed SLB Design with Firewall Contexts*

Traffic Flows in a One-Armed SLB Design with Firewall Contexts

Figure 7-26 shows representative flows going to and from a web server in the one-armed SLB design with multiple firewall contexts.

On the left side of Figure 7-26, inbound traffic reaches the core router and is routed to the MSFC in the aggregation layer switch. To reach the MSFC, it passes through a FWSM firewall context in Transparent mode for security checks and ACL filtering. The MSFC then routes inbound packets to the VIP on the Cisco ACE, which performs destination NAT processing on the packets. The Cisco ACE then routes the packets to the web server subnet. The FSWM applies ACLs and security enforcement because it is logically between the MSFC and the web server VLAN.

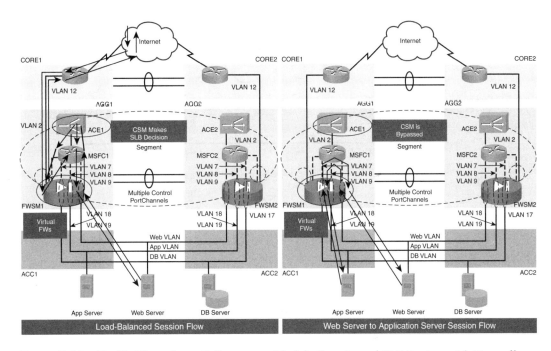

Figure 7-26 *Traffic Flows in an E-Commerce Module One-Armed SLB Design with Firewall Contexts*

Note Each subnet (web, application, and database) encompasses two VLANs that are bridged by the FWSM.

Outbound traffic from the web server goes through the FWSM to the MSFC, is routed to the Cisco ACE via PBR, and then is routed to the core router.

The right side of Figure 7-26 shows traffic being routed by the MSFC between the web server subnet and the application server subnet. This traffic passes through the FWSM twice; the FWSM enforces ACLs and security policies both times. Return traffic also passes through the FWSM twice. All routing next-hop addresses use HSRP virtual addresses, either on the MSFCs or on the core routers.

With minimal configuration effort, traffic from the web servers to the application servers can be sent through the Cisco ACE.

Note The trunk between the switches is necessary to support failover.

One-Armed SLB E-Commerce Module Design with ACE

Figure 7-27 illustrates a one-armed SLB design with ACE load-balancing appliance switches.

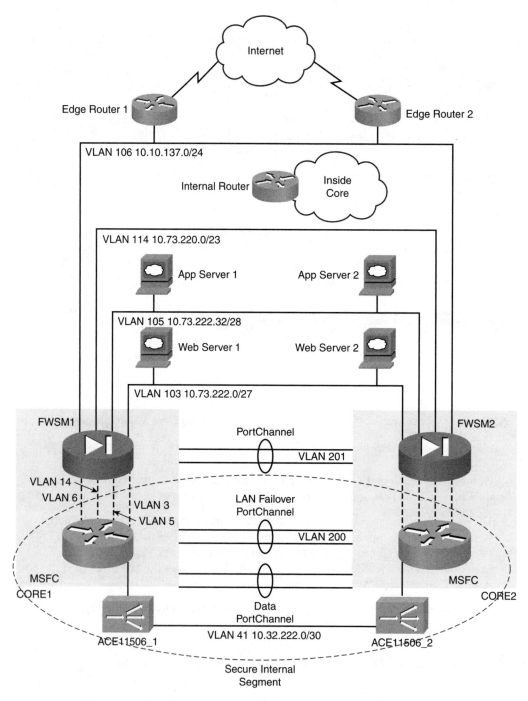

Figure 7-27   *E-Commerce Module One-Armed Design with ACE*

In Figure 7-27, the FWSMs are Layer 2 firewalls with multiple security contexts. There are several DMZs, with firewall perimeters outside, inside, and at each DMZ. The aggregation layer MSFC is on a secure internal segment with protection from each connected network, including from any malicious activity on data center networks.

The external ACE appliance is used in one-armed fashion; the dual ACE devices are connected with ports in the same VLANs.

NAT is implemented on the MSFC (because the transparent firewall does not support this function). Alternatively, an additional routed context on the FWSM could support NAT.

The ACE default gateway is the HSRP address on the MSFC. The dual ACE devices are directly connected at Layer 2 to the MSFCs, so RHI is possible.

The servers' default gateway is the HSRP primary IP address on the MSFC. Non-load-balanced traffic to and from the servers bypasses the ACE devices because the ACEs are in one-armed mode.

Testing E-Commerce Module Designs

As discussed, it is important to test failover conditions within e-commerce designs as thoroughly as possible to improve high availability. This testing first requires designers to do a preliminary analysis to understand how network devices detect different types of failures and how they will fail over. Testing not only confirms correct device configuration but can also help identify modes where failover does not occur. For example, applications may operate differently when packets are silently dropped (for example, because of the loss of NAT information or stateful firewall state) than when a TCP reset or Internet Control Message Protocol (ICMP) unreachable message is received.

Failover testing includes simulating failures as close to the real failure conditions as possible. For example, simulating a link failure by unplugging an Ethernet connection causes the switch or other device to detect the loss of the Ethernet, but this creates a relatively static condition. Silent packet drops can also be simulated.

One way that silent packet drops can be simulated is by sending traffic in a VLAN on a trunk and disallowing the VLAN at the other end of the trunk. Alternatively, some network prefixes can be routed to the NULL0 interface, causing packets to those destination prefixes to be discarded. On the other hand, implementing passive interfaces or otherwise altering routing to delete the route to a destination will not simulate a silent discard because the router normally sends "Destination network unreachable" packets back to the sender when packets are received for a prefix that is not in the routing table.

Layer 3 switches might experience a system failure (simulated by turning the power off) or a partial failure (simulated by removing one module). In the case of a partial failure, Layer 3 operations might stop functioning, but Layer 2 operations may continue. Neighboring devices would then experience loss of traffic and connectivity but not loss of Ethernet link status. This could be simulated by configuring the **no ip routing** command on the MSFC or route processor on a Layer 3 switch.

Creating testing procedure documentation aids in future troubleshooting. When an incident occurs in the production network, the test procedure documentation should be updated, reflecting lessons learned and possibly presenting alternatives to simulate the observed failure mode. Testing and the associated documentation can also be used to validate new software releases and configuration changes. For example, regression testing ensures that new software or configuration enhancements have not unnecessarily changed failover behavior.

Summary

In this chapter, you learned about e-commerce module design.

High availability is important to the e-commerce module and includes the following five components:

- Redundancy, including duplicate equipment and network links to reduce the effects of a single point of failure

- Technology, including hardware and software features

- People, including staff skills and training

- Processes, including change processes and failover testing

- Tools, including proper documentation

Common e-commerce module firewall designs include the following:

- The "firewall sandwich" design that separates the web tier, the application tier, and the database tier with redundant firewall layers.

- Using servers, such as web servers, as application gateways to increase security.

- Virtualizing a physical firewall, such as an FWSM, to create firewall contexts.

- Using virtual firewall layers within physical firewalls.

- Using firewalls in Routing or Transparent (Bridging) modes. Transparent firewalls bridge two VLANs together, switching traffic at Layer 2 between the two VLANs, which together constitute one IP subnet.

SLB devices map a VIP address for each service to a pool of real physical servers. SLB devices include the ACE appliance and module and are used in Router, Bridge (Inline), or one-armed (out-of-band) mode.

Common topologies for connecting to multiple ISPs include using one firewall per ISP with separate NAT pools, using a common external prefix advertised through BGP with a single NAT pool, and using distributed data centers with different ISPs.

The base e-commerce design includes firewalls only in the core layer. The aggregation and access layers are considered trusted zones; therefore, there is no security between the web, application, and database tiers in the base design.

A design with firewall services in the core and aggregation layers provides additional security between the web, application, and database tiers.

A SLB in one-armed mode can be used with two firewall layers to provide security. The SLB is deployed off to the side so that selected traffic to and from the servers does not go through it.

A one-armed SLB design with multiple firewall contexts can be used to provide firewall perimeters outside, inside, and at each DMZ. This design also eliminates the need for a separate firewall in the core layer. This one-armed SLB design can be further enhanced with ACE appliance or module.

References

For additional information, refer to the following:

Cisco Systems, Inc. *Service Module Design with ACE and FWSM* at www.cisco.com/en/US/partner/docs/solutions/Enterprise/Data_Center/ACE_FWSM.html

Cisco Systems, Inc. *Security and Virtualization in the Data Center* at www.cisco.com/en/US/docs/solutions/Enterprise/Data_Center/DC_3_0/dc_sec_design.html

Cisco Systems, Inc. *Application Control Engine Module Routing and Bridging Configuration Guide* at www.cisco.com/en/US/docs/interfaces_modules/services_modules/ace/vA4_1_0/configuration/rtg_brdg/guide/AceRteGd.pdf

Cisco Systems, Inc. *Configuring Enhanced Object Tracking* at www.cisco.com/univercd/cc/td/doc/product/software/ios124/124cg/hiap_c/haipbtrk.pdf

Cisco Systems, Inc. *Cisco GSS CLI-Based Global Server Load-Balancing Configuration Guide* at www.cisco.com/en/US/partner/docs/app_ntwk_services/data_center_app_services/gss4400series/v3.0/configuration/cli/gslb/guide/cli_gslb.html

Review Questions

Answer the following questions, and then refer to Appendix A, "Answers to Review Questions," for the answers.

1. Where is an e-commerce design typically implemented?

    a. In the aggregation layer

    b. In the application tier

    c. In the core layer

    d. In the data center

    e. In the web tier

2. What are three functions of SLB?

  a. Providing a private IP address or virtual IP address for each service

  b. Providing a public IP address or virtual IP address for each service

  c. Resolving DNS requests for destination IP addresses for each service

  d. Rewriting source and destination IP or MAC addresses, depending on SLB mode

  e. Supporting scaling and high availability by distributing client requests for service across active servers

3. What are three characteristics of SLB one-armed mode?

  a. Return traffic does not require special handling.

  b. The SLB is directly in line with the default traffic path.

  c. The SLB is not directly in line with the default traffic path.

  d. The SLB VIP and the real servers are in the same VLAN or subnet.

  e. Return traffic can use PBR to deflect appropriate outbound server traffic over to the SLB as next hop.

  f. The SLB routes traffic to the real server subnet if the real servers are not in the same VLAN or subnet as the SLB VIPs.

4. Where is the firewall perimeter in a basic e-commerce design?

  a. At the Internet

  b. At the core layer

  c. At the core and aggregation layers

  d. At the aggregation and access layers

  e. Between the aggregation layer router and the e-commerce servers

5. Which two choices describe the e-commerce design with two firewall layers when the Cisco ACE is not in Routed mode?

  a. Outbound traffic from servers may need to be directed by PBR or client NAT to the Cisco ACE.

  b. The aggregation switch Cisco FWSM routes traffic to the server subnets.

  c. The MSFC is directly connected to the Cisco ACE.

  d. The MSFC is not directly connected to the Cisco ACE.

  e. The SLB is moved to a position where selected traffic to and from the servers does not go through the SLB.

Security Services Design

Upon completing this chapter, you will be able to

- Design security-intelligent network services for performance, scalability, and availability to specified enterprise network needs

- Discuss design considerations for firewall services in the enterprise

- Describe design considerations for using network admission control services in the enterprise

- Discuss design considerations for intrusion-detection and -prevention services in the enterprise

As enterprises continually expand their mission-critical networks with new intranet, extranet, and e-commerce applications, network security is increasingly vital to prevent corruption and intrusion and to eliminate network security vulnerabilities. Without precautions, enterprises could experience major security breaches that could result in serious damages or loss.

This chapter examines security design in the enterprise. It looks at design considerations for firewall services, network admission control, and intrusion-detection and -prevention services. Readers should already know how to implement firewalls and security features such as access control lists (ACL), IP Security (IPsec) connections, Network Address Translation (NAT), and Port Address Translation (PAT).

Designing Firewalls

Firewalls have long provided the first line of defense in network security infrastructures. This is accomplished by comparing corporate policies on network access rights for users to the connection information surrounding each access attempt. User policies and connection information must match. Otherwise, the firewall does not grant access to network resources.

This section examines firewall design considerations. It discusses options for firewall deployment and topologies, including firewall modes, virtual firewalls, asymmetric routing using active/active topologies, scaling firewall performance, private VLANs (PVLAN), and zone-based firewalls.

Firewall Modes

Firewalls are commonly deployed in different areas of the network. They control access to network resources and apply deep packet inspection to network traffic, mitigating denial-of-service (DoS) attacks and enforcing protocol compliance. Firewalls are an indispensable tool in the company security policies enforcement. They are a key component of the Cisco's secure blueprint for enterprise networks (SAFE).

The principle goal of SAFE is to provide best practice information to interested parties on designing and implementing secure networks. SAFE serves as a guide to network designers considering the security requirements of their network. It takes a defense-in-depth approach to network security design. This type of design focuses on the expected threats and their methods of mitigation rather than on "Put the firewall here, put the intrusion-detection system there." This strategy results in a layered approach to security where the failure of one security system is not likely to lead to the compromise of network resources. SAFE is based on Cisco products and those of its partners.

The Cisco SAFE architecture divides the network into modules and defines detailed design and implementation guidelines for each of these modules. Current Cisco SAFE modules include data center, campus, WAN edge, extranet, Internet edge, e-commerce, branch, partner, and teleworker. In each of these modules, firewalls can be used to implement aspects of the overall integrated security solution.

The Cisco SAFE architecture is a key component of the Cisco Borderless Networks reference architecture.

A firewall can run in either routed or transparent mode, as shown in Figure 8-1.

In the traditional routed mode, the firewall is considered to be a Layer 3 device in the network. It can perform NAT between connected networks. Routed mode supports many interfaces. Each interface is on a different subnet and requires an IP address on that subnet.

Transparent mode is a newer mode available as of Firewall Service Module (FWSM) Release 2.2 and Cisco ASA and PIX Firewall Software Version 7.0.

In transparent mode, the firewall is a Layer 2 device, not a router hop. Transparent mode basically connects two VLANs at Layer 2 and utilizes security policy without creating separate Layer 3 subnets.

Firewalls can support multiple pairs of inside and outside interfaces as a bridge group. Each bridge group connects to a different network. A transparent firewall has one IP address assigned to the entire bridge group and uses this management address as the source address for management packets originating on the firewall.

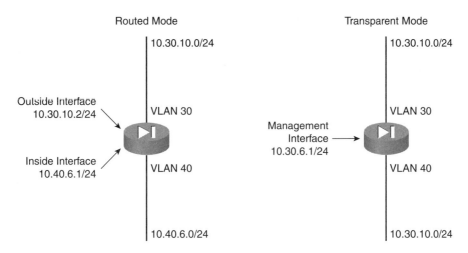

Figure 8-1   *Firewall Mode: Routed or Transparent*

Transparent mode can allow certain types of traffic in an access list that is blocked by routed mode, including unsupported protocols. Routing protocol adjacencies are supported through a transparent firewall. Open Shortest Path First (OSPF), Routing Information Protocol (RIP), Enhanced Interior Gateway Routing Protocol (EIGRP), and Border Gateway Protocol (BGP) traffic is allowed based on an extended access list. Protocols such as Hot Standby Router Protocol (HSRP), Virtual Router Redundancy Protocol (VRRP), and IP multicast can be supported through a transparent firewall. Transparent mode can also optionally use Ethertype access lists to allow non-IP traffic.

Transparent mode is also useful if it is required for the firewall to pass or filter IP multicast traffic.

Note   The Adaptive Security Appliance (ASA) performs stub multicast routing and protocol independent multicast (PIM) routing. However, you cannot configure both concurrently on a single security appliance.

The ASA and FWSM have different ACL mechanisms for controlling traffic:

■   The PIX firewall, by default, allows traffic to flow freely from an inside network (higher security level) to an outside network (lower security level).

■   The ASA allows IPv4 traffic through the routed or transparent firewall mode automatically from a higher security interface to a lower security interface without an access list. Address Resolution Protocol (ARP) packets are allowed through the transparent firewall in both directions without an access list. For Layer 3 traffic traveling from a lower security level interface to a high security level interface, an extended access list is required.

- The FWSM does not allow traffic to pass between interfaces unless it is explicitly permitted with an ACL. The only traffic allowed through the transparent firewall without an ACL is ARP traffic. Layer 3 traffic, such as IP traffic, cannot pass through the FWSM (even though the transparent mode acts as a bridge) unless the traffic is explicitly permitted with an extended ACL.

Note Cisco's initial firewall was called the PIX (Private Internet Exchange) and has been replaced by the ASA.

Zone-Based Policy Firewall

The zone-based policy firewall configuration model is a new design that is supported by the Cisco IOS Firewall Feature Set that can be run on integrated service routers (ISR) and asymmetric routers (ASR).

The zone-based policy firewall changes the design model from the older interface-based model to a zone-based configuration model. The zone-based policy firewall configuration model assigns interfaces to zones, and applies an inspection policy to traffic that is moving between the zones. Zones establish the security borders of the network. A zone defines a boundary where traffic is subjected to policy restrictions as it crosses to another region of the network.

A security zone is configured for each region of relative security within the network so that all interfaces that are assigned to the same zone are protected with a similar level of security. For example, Figure 8-2 shows an access router with three interfaces, each assigned to its own zone.

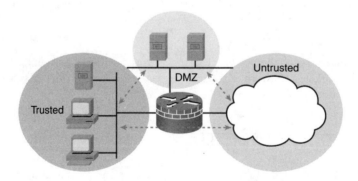

Figure 8-2 *Simple Zone-Based Firewall with Three Zones*

Characteristics of a zone-based firewall include the following:

- One interface is connected to the public Internet or another untrusted zone, such as an extranet or guest network.

- One interface is connected to a private trusted LAN that must not be accessible from the public untrusted Internet.

- One interface is connected to an Internet service DMZ, where a web server, Domain Name System (DNS) server, and email server must be accessible to the public Internet.

In Figure 8-2, each zone holds only one interface. If an additional interface is added to the private zone, the hosts that are connected to the new interface in that zone would be able to pass traffic to all hosts on the existing interface in the same zone. Traffic to hosts in other zones would be similarly affected by existing policies.

Suppose, for example, this scenario wanted to add a fourth network, a private wireless LAN or LAN from another building (in the private zone, as mentioned earlier). The LAN would need full connectivity to the other LAN and would have the same security policy. Therefore, it would be placed in the same zone.

Zone-based policy firewalls allow a more flexible, easily configured model. Firewall policy troubleshooting is based on the explicit policy on interzone traffic. The zone-based policy firewall default policy between zones is to deny all. If a policy is not explicitly configured, all traffic moving between zones is blocked. This is a significant departure from the stateful inspection model, in which traffic was implicitly allowed unless it was explicitly blocked with an ACL. By default, traffic is implicitly allowed to flow among interfaces that are members of the same zone.

Interzone policies offer considerable flexibility and granularity, so different inspection policies can be applied to multiple host groups that are connected to the same router interface. Multiple traffic classes and actions can be applied per zone pair. Zone-based policy firewalls can tie to Cisco Security Manager (CSM) mechanisms for ACL deployment and management.

Note   Recent IPsec virtual private network (VPN) enhancements simplify firewall policy configuration for VPN connectivity. IPsec virtual tunnel interface (VTI) and generic routing encapsulation (GRE) with IPsec allow the confinement of VPN site-to-site and client connections to a specific security zone, by placing the tunnel interfaces in a specified security zone. Connections can be isolated in a VPN DMZ if connectivity must be limited by a specific policy. If VPN connectivity is implicitly trusted, VPN connectivity can instead be placed in the same security zone as the trusted inside network.

Virtual Firewall Overview

A virtual firewall separates multiple firewall security contexts on a single firewall. The virtual firewall methodology enables a physical firewall to be partitioned into multiple standalone firewalls. Each standalone firewall acts and behaves as an independent entity with its own configuration, interfaces, security policies, routing table, and administrators. In Cisco ASA, these virtual firewalls are known as security contexts.

Specific VLANs are tied to a specific security context, as shown in Figure 8-3. In routed mode, up to 256 VLANs can be assigned to a context. The FWSM has an overall limit of 1000 VLAN interfaces divided among all contexts. Up to 250 contexts are supported on an FWSM depending on the software license. Each context has its own policies, such as NAT, access lists, and protocol fixups.

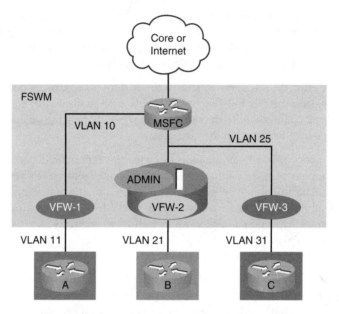

Figure 8-3   *Virtual Firewall Overview*

Note   At this time, licensing for contexts is available in 50, 100, or 250 contexts per firewall.

The FSWM uses the administrative context for network management connectivity. Each context may also be managed individually as if they were distinct and separate firewalls. This granularity allows different groups to administer their own firewall. The system context is used to add VLANS, create contexts, and assign VLANs to contexts. With the default FWSM software, up to two security contexts (the administrative and system context) are provided.

Note   The FWSM does not include any external physical interfaces. VLAN interfaces are assigned to the FWSM in a way that is similar to how a switched virtual interface (SVI) is assigned to the Multilayer Switch Feature Card (MSFC). The FWSM includes an internal interface to the Switch Fabric Module (SFM) (if present) or to the shared bus.

Firewall Context Design Considerations

Resource classes are important to firewall operations because multiple contexts can use a resource class. By default, all security contexts on a multiple-context FWSM have unlimited access to the resources of the FWSM, except where maximum limits per context are enforced. However, if you find that one or more contexts use too many resources, and they cause other contexts to be denied connections, you can configure resource management to limit the use of resources per context.

An attack or anomaly on one context can impact another context. All contexts belong to the default class if they are not assigned to another class, as illustrated in Figure 8-4. If a context belongs to a class other than the default class, those class settings always override the default class settings. However, if a class has any settings that are not defined, the member context uses the default class for those limits. By default, all security contexts have unlimited access to the resources of the FWSM or security appliance, except where maximum limits per context are enforced. If one or more contexts use too many resources, they cause other contexts to be denied connections.

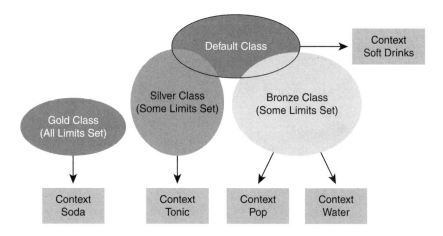

Figure 8-4   *Firewall Context Design Considerations*

Note   The FWSM does not limit the bandwidth per context. However, the switch containing the FWSM can limit the bandwidth per VLAN.

The FWSM and security appliances are subject to oversubscription if more than 100 percent of the resources are assigned across all contexts. For example, if the Bronze class is set to limit connections to 20 percent per context, and 10 contexts are assigned to the class, a total of 200 percent is allocated. If contexts concurrently use more than the system limit, each context gets less than the 20 percent you intended, and some connections will be denied because the system limit is reached.

MSFC Placement

The MSFC can be placed on the inside or the outside of the firewall depending on the VLANs assigned to the FWSM.

On the right side of Figure 8-5, the MSFC is outside of the firewall when VLAN 200 is assigned to the outside interface of the FWSM. The FWSM processes and protects all traffic to the inside VLANs 2, 4, and 6. The MSFC routes between the Internet and the switched networks. Placing the MSFC outside the FWSM makes design and management easier.

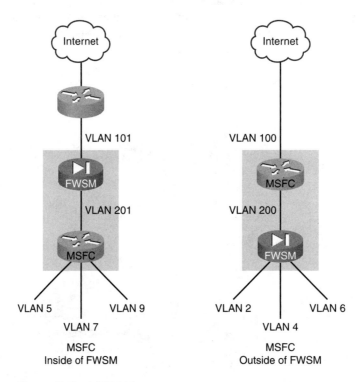

Figure 8-5 *MSFC Placement*

The MSFC is inside of the firewall on the left side of Figure 8-5 when VLAN 101 is assigned to the outside interface of the FWSM. The MSFC routes between VLANs 201, 5, 7, and 9. No inside traffic goes through the FWSM unless it is destined for the Internet. The FWSM secures the MSFC.

For multiple-context mode, if the MSFC is placed inside the FWSM, it should connect to only a single context. If the MSFC connects to multiple firewall contexts, the MSFC routes between the contexts, which might not be your intention.

Active/Active Firewall Topology

The active/active firewall topology uses two firewalls that are both actively providing firewall services.

When an FWSM is running in virtual firewall mode, it is possible to use active/active redundancy. In the active/active topology, the security contexts on the FWSM are divided into failover groups. A failover group is a logical group of one or more security contexts. The FWSM supports a maximum of two failover groups. The administrative context is always a member of failover group 1, and any unassigned security contexts are, by default, also members of failover group 1.

In Figure 8-6, FWSM 1 and FWSM 2 are each configured with two failover groups. FSWM 1 is active for group 1 and standby for group 2. FSWM 2 is active for group 2 and standby for group 1. The first virtual firewall is mapped to group 1, and the second virtual firewall is mapped to group 2.

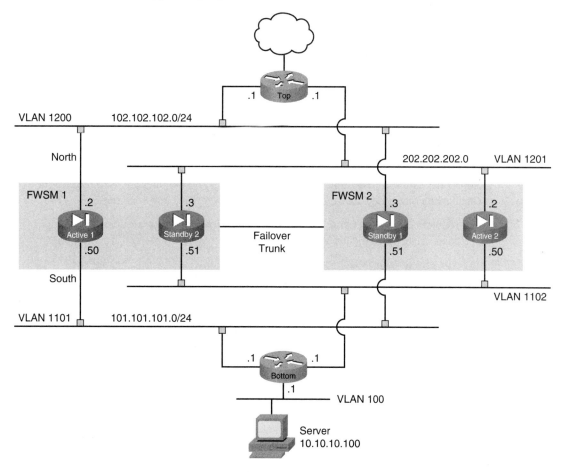

Figure 8-6   *Active/Active Firewall Topology*

Active/Active Topology Features

The active/active failover configuration requires two identical FWSMs connected to each other through a failover link associated with a dedicated VLAN and optionally a state-link VLAN using an interchassis design.

Note The active/active failover configuration can also be supported with redundant FWSM in a single chassis. The failover link is a VLAN.

Note All information sent over the failover and stateful failover links is sent in clear text. If FWSM is used to terminate VPN tunnels, this information includes any usernames, passwords, and preshared keys used for establishing the tunnels. Cisco recommends securing the failover communication with a failover key.

The health of the active interfaces and units is monitored to determine whether specific failover conditions are met. If those conditions are met, failover occurs. The MAC address of the primary unit is used by all interfaces in the active contexts. When an active failover group fails, it changes to the standby state and the associated standby failover group becomes active. The interfaces in the failover group that becomes active assume the MAC address and IP addresses of the interfaces in the failover group that failed.

This design supports preemption so that the FWSM with a higher priority will resume an active role after recovering from a failure condition.

Additional redundancy is supported if links from separate modules are used to form the Gigabit Ethernet EtherChannels supporting the failover trunk and state traffic VLANs.

Both devices can pass network traffic in an active/active topology; this design can support load balancing in the network.

Asymmetric Routing with Firewalls

The FWSMs support asymmetric routing where return traffic for a session is received through a different interface than the interface from which the traffic originated.

Asymmetric routing most commonly occurs when two interfaces on a single FWSM, or two FWSMs in a failover pair, are connected to different service providers and the outbound connection does not use a NAT address. By default, the FWSM drops the return traffic because there is no connection information for the traffic received through a different interface than the interface where the traffic originated.

Asymmetric routing of the return traffic is supported by using the **asr-group** interface command. The FSWM supports up to 32 ASR groups. Each ASR group supports a maximum of eight interfaces. Asymmetric routing is supported in the active/active failover redundancy mode, and in designs without failover redundancy in either single mode or within a virtual firewall by using ASR groups. Asymmetric routing is supported in both the routed and transparent modes of firewall operation.

Asymmetric Routing with ASR Group on a Single FWSM

Interfaces inside a common ASR group allow packets belonging to a given session to enter and leave from any interface within the ASR group, as shown in Figure 8-7.

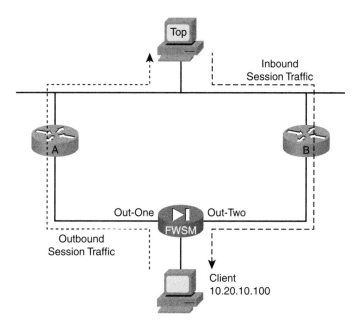

Figure 8-7   *Asymmetric Routing with ASR Groups on a Single FWSM*

When an interface configured with the **asr-group** command receives a packet for which it has no session information, it checks the session information for the other interfaces that are in the same group. If it does not find a match, the packet is dropped. If it finds a match and the incoming traffic originated on a different interface on the same unit, some or the entire Layer 2 header is rewritten and the packet is re-injected into the stream and forwarded to the intended host.

After valid synchronization (SYN) is sent out an ASR group interface, the FWSM accepts a returning synchronization-acknowledgment (SYN ACK) on another interface in the ASR group.

Asymmetric Routing with Active/Active Topology

Interfaces inside a common ASR group in an active/active topology also support asymmetric routing.

In the active/active topology, when an interface configured with the **asr-group** command receives a packet for which it has no session information, it checks the session information for the other interfaces that are in the same group. If it does not find a match, the packet is dropped. If it finds a match and the incoming traffic originated on a peer unit that was active for the context, some or all of the entire Layer 2 header is rewritten and the packet is redirected to the active peer.

Figure 8-8 shows that the traffic is forwarded through the outside interface of context A on the unit, where context A is in the standby state and returns through the outside interface of context A on the unit where context A is in the active state. This redirection continues as long as the session is active.

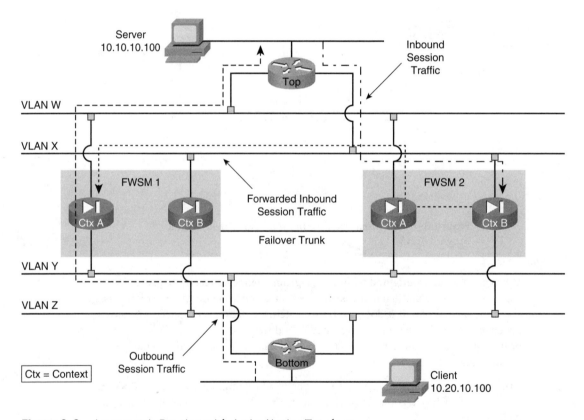

Figure 8-8   *Asymmetric Routing with Active/Active Topology*

Performance Scaling with Multiple FWSMs

For high throughput, up to four FWSMs can be installed in a single chassis using an active/active design. This section discusses two methods to load balance multiple FWSMs:

- Traffic engineering (TE) mechanisms, such as policy-based routing (PBR), to selectively steer traffic through multiple FWSMs

- Routing, such as static or Equal Cost Multipath (ECMP) routing, to direct flows per FWSM

Example: Load Balancing FWSMs Using PBR

PBR is a mechanism for implementing packet forwarding and routing according to policies defined by the network administrator rather than paths selected by traditional routing methods. Instead of routing by the destination address as determined by a routing protocol, PBR uses more-flexible methods such as source IP addresses or application types to match on the identity of the user and then selects the forwarding path. A redundant path could be configured in the event of a link failure or the device going down.

Figure 8-9 shows multiple FWSMs load balanced in an active/active design using PBR supported by the gateway router. A source-based selection method is used to determine the destination firewall path. This is a static load-sharing method based on class maps and route maps to divide traffic among multiple FWSMs. The route maps are configured in such a way that if the first FWSM goes down a backup FWSM is used.

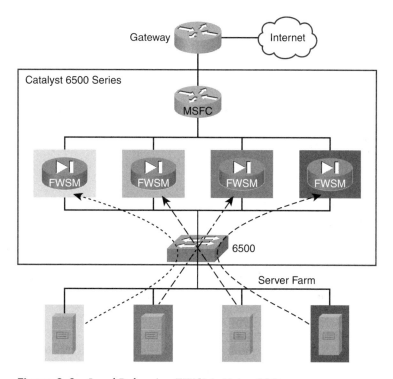

Figure 8-9   *Load Balancing FWSMs Using PBR*

Load Balancing FWSMs Using ECMP Routing

Static routing or ECMP routing can also be used to selectively route traffic through each of the FWSMs. Take care to ensure that the return path goes through the same firewall or that the FWSM supports asymmetric routing in an active/active design.

Figure 8-10 illustrates multiple FWSMs load balanced in an active/active design using ECMP routing. The standard destination-based selection method is used by the routing protocol to determine which FWSM to use. If an FWSM goes down, the routing protocol automatically load balances the traffic across the remaining FWSMs.

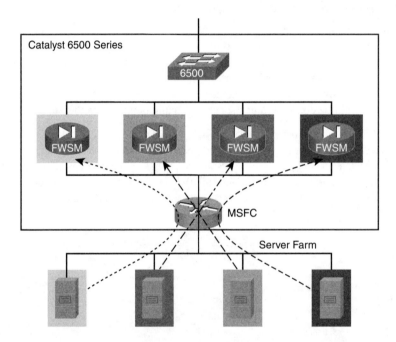

Figure 8-10   *Load Balancing FWSMs Using ECMP Routing*

PVLAN Security

PVLANs allow Layer 2 isolation between ports within a VLAN. Figure 8-11 illustrates the PVLAN architecture, which is explained in more detail in this section.

In a regular VLAN, all ports can communicate. PVLANs provide Layer 2 isolation between the ports within the same PVLAN without assigning ports to separate VLANs or assigning individual hosts to different Layer 3 IP networks. PVLANs provide a logical separation of the network that keeps traffic isolated.

The ports that belong to a PVLAN are associated with a primary VLAN. In addition, within the primary VLAN, ports are associated with either an isolated VLAN or a community VLAN. A PVLAN domain has one primary VLAN. Every port in a PVLAN domain is a member of the primary VLAN. Secondary VLANs provide Layer 2 isolation between ports within the same PVLAN domain. There are two types of secondary VLANs:

■ **Isolated VLANs:** Ports within an isolated VLAN cannot communicate with any other port on the switch other than the promiscuous port.

■ **Community VLANs:** Ports within a community VLAN can communicate with each other but cannot communicate with ports in other communities or other isolated ports.

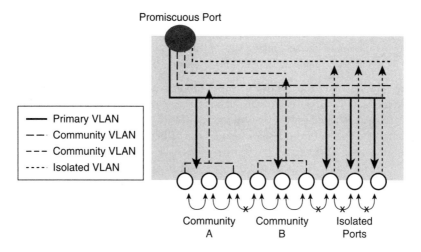

Figure 8-11   *PVLAN Review*

There are three types of PVLAN ports:

■ **Promiscuous:** This port communicates with all other PVLAN ports and is the port used to communicate with network devices, including routers, backup servers, and administrative workstations. This port listens to the secondary VLANs and sends traffic using the primary VLAN.

■ **Isolated:** This port has complete Layer 2 separation from the other ports within the same PVLAN with the exception of the promiscuous port. Even with static ARP entries, private ports cannot communicate with each other. Isolated ports use a secondary VLAN to send traffic out and block any traffic coming from the secondary VLAN. All the isolated ports in the system can share the same secondary VLAN.

■ **Community:** These ports communicate among themselves and with their promiscuous ports. These ports are isolated at Layer 2 from all other ports in other communities and from isolated ports. A separate secondary VLAN is allocated for each community.

Note   If a broadcast or multicast packet comes from the promiscuous port, it is sent to all the ports in the PVLAN domain, including all community and isolated ports.

FWSM in a PVLAN Environment: Isolated Ports

FWSM 3.1 supports PVLANs with Cisco IOS Release 12.2(18)SXF and later.

PVLANs provide an easy way to implement Layer 2 traffic segregation within a VLAN. This feature is popular in DMZ and server farm designs.

On a Cisco Catalyst 6500 series switch, the primary and secondary VLANs are configured on the Supervisor Engine. From the perspective of the routing function integrated in the switch, the FWSM is sitting on a promiscuous port and sees all traffic to and from the PVLAN. Only the primary VLAN is assigned to the FWSM, but it is made aware of the primary and secondary VLAN mappings through the MSFC. The FWSM automatically supports isolation of the secondary VLAN traffic to the community and isolated VLANs. The FWSM acts as a gateway between hosts on the PVLANs and the outside world.

Figure 8-12 illustrates the use of PVLANs supporting isolated ports with the FWSM in routed mode. Isolated ports are separated at Layer 2 by the switch processor. Outbound traffic from an isolated port is sent by the FSWM to the MSFC, which routes the traffic appropriately. The FWSM does not forward traffic between isolated ports, because for a single subnet the FWSM does not route packets back out the interface they came in from. Inbound traffic for the isolated port is sent by the MSFC to the FWSM, which sends it to the switch processor. The switch processor forwards the packets to the isolated port based on the MAC address.

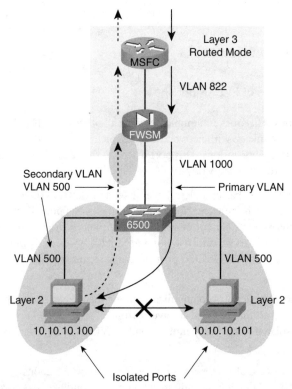

Figure 8-12 *Isolated Ports on FWSM in Routed Mode*

FWSM in a PVLAN Environment: Community VLANs

Community VLANs are supported by Layer 2 functions in the switch processor.

Figure 8-13 illustrates the use of community VLANs with the FWSM in routed mode. Community ports are interconnected at Layer 2 by the switch processor. Outbound traffic from a community port is seen by all devices on the community VLAN, including the FWSM. The FSWM forwards outbound traffic to the MSFC, which routes the traffic appropriately. Inbound traffic for the community port is sent by the MSFC to the FWSM, which sends it to the community VLAN. The Layer 2 switch processor forwards it to the appropriate community port or ports based on the MAC address.

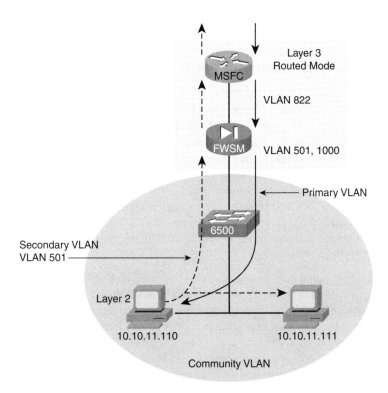

Figure 8-13 *Community Ports on FWSM in Routed Mode*

Designing NAC Services

Network Admission Control (NAC) is a set of technologies and solutions built on an industry initiative led by Cisco. NAC uses the network infrastructure to enforce security policy compliance on all devices seeking to access network computing resources, thereby limiting damage from emerging security threats such as viruses, worms, and spyware. Customers using NAC can allow network access to only compliant and trusted endpoint devices (PCs, servers, and personal digital assistants [PDA], for example) and can restrict the access of noncompliant devices.

Network Security with Access Control

An essential part of securing the network is controlling access to network resources. Access control is one of the functions that are part of the Cisco SAFE architecture framework. Access control or admission control consists of several elements that are key functions of the Cisco SAFE architecture, including the following:

■ **Identify:** As part of access control procedures, the identity of the user must be established and the network access rights of the user must be verified.

■ **Enforce:** Security policies often mandate the use of security-related software, such as virus scanners and firewall software. Part of an access control strategy is to enforce the use of security software before allowing network access.

■ **Isolate:** Endpoints that do not meet the requirements of the company security policy can be isolated and forced to remediate to the situation before being allowed onto the network.

Cisco Identity Based Networking Services (IBNS) is an integrated solution combining several Cisco products that offer authentication, access control, and user policies to secure network connectivity and resources. The Cisco IBNS solution enables greater security while simultaneously offering cost-effective management of changes throughout the organization. The Cisco IBNS framework allows enterprises to manage user mobility and reduce the overhead costs associated with granting and managing access to network resources. IEEE 802.1X authenticates clients requesting Layer 2 (data link layer) access to the network. However, with Cisco extensions to 802.1X, users and devices are authenticated and allowed admission to the network based on who or what they are, but not their condition.

NAC helps ensure that only trustworthy client devices, such as workstations and end-user PCs, are granted full network access. The Cisco NAC Appliance Agent (NAA) loaded on the client device queries antivirus, patch management, and personal firewall client software to assess the condition or posture of a client device before allowing that device to access the network. NAC can help ensure that a network client has an up-to-date virus signature set, the most current operating system patches, and is not infected. If the client requires an antivirus signature update or an operating system update, NAC directs the client to complete the necessary updates before allowing access to the protected network resources. If the client has been compromised or if a virus outbreak is occurring on the network, NAC places the client into a quarantined network segment. After the client has completed its update process or disinfection, the client is checked again. Clients with a healthy status are permitted normal network access.

Cisco 802.1X/IBNS and NAC provide complementary functions: user authentication and posture validation. Both can provide per-user group VLAN assignment and access control.

NAC Comparison

Cisco supports two types of NAC, as shown in Figure 8-14.

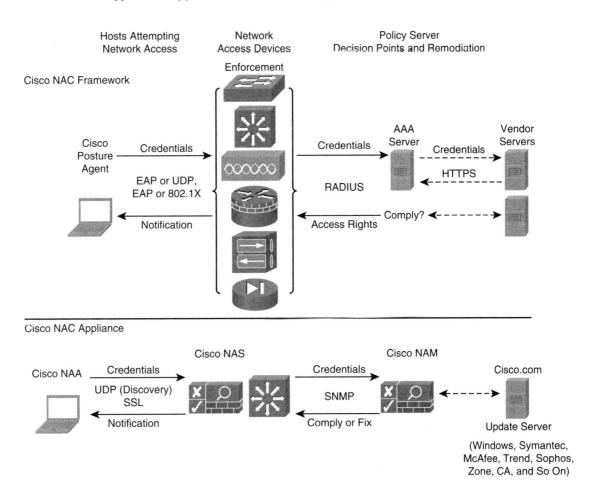

Figure 8-14 *NAC Comparison*

This list includes the following:

■   **Cisco NAC Framework** is a technology standard that integrates an intelligent network infrastructure with solutions from more than 60 manufacturers of leading antivirus and other security and management software solutions to enforce security policy compliance on all devices seeking to access network computing resources. NAC

Framework is embedded software within NAC-enabled products that provides ubiquitous control across all network access methods. Posture information can be gathered and access policy enforced for hosts attempting network access through routers, switches, wireless access points, and VPN concentrators. NAC Framework leverages multiple Cisco products and vendor products that support NAC.

■   Cisco NAC Appliance (formerly called Cisco Clean Access) is a turnkey solution for controlling and securing networks. Cisco NAC Appliance condenses NAC capabilities into an appliance. Cisco NAC Appliance client, server, and manager products enable network administrators to authenticate, authorize, evaluate, and remediate wired, wireless, and remote users and their machines before allowing users onto the network. Cisco NAC Appliance identifies whether networked devices such as laptops, IP phones, PDAs, and printers comply with the security policies of an organization and repairs any vulnerabilities before permitting access to the network.

Cisco NAC Appliance Fundamentals

This section discusses fundamentals of the Cisco NAC Appliance, including components and terminology.

Cisco NAC Appliance Components

Cisco NAC Appliance provides admission control and enforces compliance. Cisco NAC Appliance contains the following components:

■   **Cisco NAC Appliance Manager (Cisco NAM):** The administration server for Cisco NAC Appliance deployment where the policies are defined. The secure web console of the Cisco NAM is the single point of management for up to 20 Cisco NAC Appliance Server (NAS) devices in a deployment (or 40 Cisco NAS devices in a super-NAM installation). Cisco NAM acts as the authentication proxy to the authentication servers that reside on the back end. For out-of-band (OOB) deployment, the Cisco NAM console allows control of switches and VLAN assignment of user ports through the use of SNMP.

■   **Cisco NAC Appliance Server (Cisco NAS):** The enforcement server between the untrusted (managed) network and the trusted network. Cisco NAS enforces the policies defined in the Cisco NAM web console, including network access privileges, authentication requirements, bandwidth restrictions, and Cisco NAC Appliance system requirements. It can be deployed in-band (inline with user traffic) or OOB (inline with user traffic only during authentication and posture assessment). It can also be deployed in Layer 2 mode (users are adjacent to Cisco NAS) or Layer 3 mode (users are multiple hops away from the Cisco NAS).

- **Cisco NAC Appliance Agent (Cisco NAA):** An optional read-only agent that resides on Microsoft Windows clients. Cisco NAA checks applications, files, services, or Registry keys to ensure that clients meet specified network and software requirements before gaining access to the network.

- **Cisco NAC Profiler:** Enables network administrators to keep a real-time, contextual inventory of all devices in a network. It greatly facilitates the deployment and management of Cisco Network Admission Control (NAC) systems by discovering and tracking the location and type of all LAN-attached endpoints, including those that are not capable of authenticating. It also uses the information about the device to determine the correct policies for NAC to apply.

- **Cisco NAC Appliance policy updates:** Regular updates of prepackaged policies and rules that can be used to check the up-to-date status of operating systems and antivirus, antispyware, and other client software. The Cisco NAC Appliance policy updates currently provide built-in support for 24 antivirus vendors and 17 antispyware vendors.

- **Cisco NAC Guest Server:** Cisco NAC Guest Server is a core component of the Cisco TrustSec solution that can be added to Cisco NAC wired or wireless deployments to integrate secure guest access. Cisco NAC Guest Server facilitates the creation of guest accounts for temporary network access by permitting any internal user to sponsor a guest and create the guest account in a simple and secure manner. In addition, the entire process is recorded in a single place and stored for later reporting, including details of the network access activity.

Cisco NAC Appliance Policy Updates

Cisco provides automatic security policy updates as part of the standard software maintenance package. These updates deliver predefined policies for the most common network access criteria, including policies that check for critical operating system updates, common antivirus software virus definition updates, and common antispyware definition updates.

The Cisco NAC Appliance is preconfigured to offer policy checks for more than 200 applications from 50 vendors.

Note   For the latest supported applications, review the *Cisco NAC Appliance (Clean Access)* release notes at http://www.cisco.com/en/US/products/ps6128/prod_release_notes_list.html.

In addition to the preconfigured checks, the customer has full access to the Cisco NAC Appliance rules engine and can create any custom check or rule for any other third-party application.

Process Flow with the Cisco NAC Appliance

Figure 8-15 illustrates the process flow with the Cisco NAC Appliance.

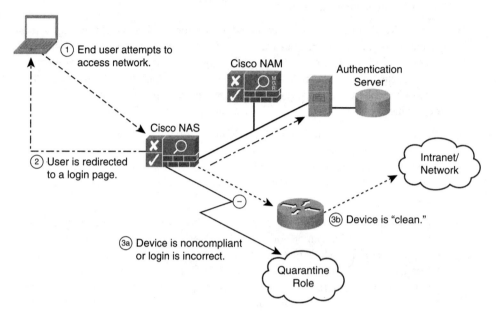

Figure 8-15   *Process Flow with the NAC Appliance*

The process is as follows:

1. The end user attempts to access a web page or use the intranet.

2. The user is redirected to a login page. Cisco NAC Appliance validates the username and password and performs device and network scans to assess vulnerabilities on the device.

3. If the device is noncompliant with corporate policies or the login is incorrect, the user is denied access to the network and assigned to a quarantine role with access only to online remediation resources.

Note   After remediation, the user returns to Step 2 for validation and scanning.

4. If the login is correct and the device complies with the policies, the device is placed on the certified devices list and is granted access to network.

Cisco NAS Scaling

There are three levels of Cisco NAM for supporting Cisco NAC Appliance solutions:

■ Cisco NAC Appliance Lite Manager manages up to 3 Cisco NAS devices, supporting 100, 250, or 500 users per server.

■ Cisco NAC Appliance Standard Manager manages up to 20 Cisco NAS devices, supporting from 1500 to 5000 users per (NAS) depending on which model is deployed.

■ Cisco NAC Appliance Super Manager manages up to 40 Cisco NAS devices, supporting from 1500 to 5000 users per (NAS) depending on which model is deployed.

The number of users supported on a server is a measure of concurrent users that have been scanned for posture compliance, not network devices such as printers or IP phones.

The number of users supported per server is influenced by many factors that consume CPU and server resources, such as the following:

■ The number of new user authentications per second

■ The number of posture assessments per second

■ How many checks are in each posture assessment

■ The number of agentless network scans per second

■ The number of plug-ins per scan

■ Rescan timer intervals

■ Per-role and total online timer intervals

■ Bandwidth controls

■ Filters and access controls

Note   Interface bandwidth is the least important calculation for determining how many users a Cisco NAS can support.

Cisco NAS Deployment Options

This section describes the deployment options for Cisco NAS.

There are four deployment variables with Cisco NAS deployments:

■ **Virtual or real gateway mode:** Determines whether the Cisco NAS acts as a Layer 2 or Layer 3 device in the network

■ **In-band or out-of-band operating mode:** Defines when traffic flows through the Cisco NAS

■ **Layer 2 or Layer 3 client access mode:** Defines whether user devices are Layer 2 or Layer 3 adjacent to the Cisco NAS

■ **Central or edge physical deployment:** Determines whether the Cisco NAS device is physically inline with the traffic path

Cisco NAS Gateway Modes

There are three Cisco NAS gateway modes, as shown in Figure 8-16.

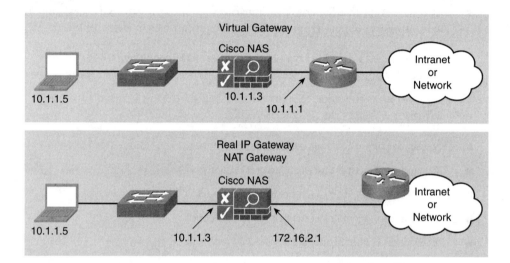

Figure 8-16 *Cisco NAS Gateway Modes*

The Cisco NAS can operate as a logical Layer 2 or Layer 3 network device depending on the gateway mode configured:

■ **Virtual gateway mode:** Cisco NAS operates as a standard Layer 2 Ethernet bridge but with added functionality provided by the IP filter and IPsec module. This configuration is typically used when the untrusted network already has a Layer 3 gateway. It is the most common deployment option. This option is the easiest to deploy. However, it may require additional equipment (Layer 3 gateway) and hinder throughput.

■ **Real IP gateway mode:** Cisco NAS operates as the Layer 3 default gateway for untrusted network (managed) clients. All traffic between the untrusted and trusted network passes through Cisco NAS, which applies the IP filtering rules, access policies, and any other traffic-handling mechanisms that are configured. Cisco NAS is designated as a default gateway for the managed subnet and can perform Dynamic Host Configuration Protocol (DHCP) services or act as a DHCP relay.

■ **NAT gateway mode:** Cisco NAS functions similarly to the way it does in the real IP gateway configuration, as a Layer 3 gateway, but with added NAT services. With NAT, clients are assigned IP addresses dynamically from a private address pool. The

Cisco NAS performs the translation between the private and public addresses as traffic is routed between the untrusted (managed) and external network. Cisco NAS supports standard, dynamic, and one-to-one NAT. In one-to-one NAT, a one-to-one correlation exists between public and private addresses and port numbers, and IP addresses can be mapped for translation.

Note The NAT gateway mode is primarily intended to facilitate testing because it requires the least amount of network configuration and is easy to initially set up. However, because it is limited in the number of connections it can handle, NAT gateway mode (in-band or out-of-band) is not supported for production deployment.

The installation type and operating mode determines the services Cisco NAS will provide. For example, Cisco NAS can operate as a bridge between the untrusted and trusted network, or it can operate as a gateway for the untrusted network.

Cisco NAS Operating Modes

Cisco NAS has two traffic flow deployment models: in-band or out-of-band.

Any Cisco NAS can be configured for either method, but only one Cisco NAS method can be deployed at a time. Selection of mode is based on whether the customer wants to remove the Cisco NAS from the data path after posture assessment.

In-band traffic flow is the easiest deployment option. The Cisco NAS remains in the traffic path before and after posture assessment. In-band operation provides ongoing ACL filtering and bandwidth throttling, and role-based access control.

In out-of-band traffic flow, the Cisco NAS is in the traffic path only during the posture assessment. Out-of-band mode provides VLAN port-based and role-based access control. ACL filtering and bandwidth throttling are provided only during posture assessment.

Note In-band traffic flow is supported with the Cisco NAS connected to any switch, hub, or access point. Out-of-band traffic flow is supported with the Cisco NAS connected to most common Cisco switches with recent software releases.

Cisco NAS Client Access Modes

The client access deployment mode selection is based on whether the client is Layer 2 adjacent to the Cisco NAS:

- **Layer 2 mode:** The MAC address of the client device is used to uniquely identify the device. This mode supports both virtual and real IP gateway operations in both in-band and out-of-band deployments. This is the most common deployment model for LANs.

- **Layer 3 mode:** The client device is not Layer 2 adjacent to the Cisco NAS. The IP address (and MAC address, starting with Cisco NAA Version 4.0 in Layer 3 OOB applications) of the client is used to identify the device. This mode supports both virtual and real IP gateway operations with in-band and out-of-band deployments.

Any Cisco NAS can be configured for either client access method, but only one Cisco NAS method can be configured at a time. Client access mode is configured independently from Cisco NAS operating mode.

Physical Deployment Models

The edge deployment model is the easiest physical deployment option to understand. The Cisco NAS is physically and logically inline to the traffic path. VLAN IDs are passed straight through the device when in virtual gateway mode. This deployment option can become complex when there are multiple access closets.

The central deployment model is the most common option and the easiest deployment option. In this option, the Cisco NAS is logically inline but not physically inline.

When the NAC appliance is configured as a virtual gateway, it acts as a bridge between the end users and default gateway (router) for the client subnet that is managed. For a given client VLAN, the NAC appliance bridges traffic from its untrusted interface to its trusted interface. When it acts as a bridge from the untrusted side to the trusted side of the appliance, two VLANs are used. For example, Client VLAN 110 is defined between the wireless LAN controller (WLC) and the untrusted interface of the NAC appliance. There is no routed interface or switched virtual interface (SVI) associated with VLAN 110 on the distribution switch. VLAN 10 is configured between the trusted interface of the NAC appliance and the next-hop router interface/SVI for the client subnet. A mapping rule is made in the NAC appliance that forwards packets that arrive on VLAN 110 out VLAN 10 when it swaps VLAN tag. The process is reversed for packets that return to the client. Note that, in this mode, bridge protocol data units (BPDU) are not passed from the untrusted-side VLANs to their trusted-side counterparts. The VLAN mapping option is usually chosen when the NAC appliance is positioned logically inline between clients and the networks that are protected. This bridging option must be used if the NAC appliance is to be deployed in the virtual gateway mode with a Unified Wireless deployment. Because the NAC server is aware of upper-layer protocols, by default it explicitly allows protocols that require it to connect to the network in Authenticated Role (for example, DNS and DHCP).

Cisco NAC Appliance Designs

This section reviews some common Cisco NAC Appliance designs.

As a recommended practice, the Cisco NAC Appliance solutions are implemented with full redundancy. A failover bundle is either a pair of Cisco NAM devices or NAS devices. The Cisco NAM failover bundle provides management redundancy. The Cisco NAS failover bundle provides redundant Cisco NAS operations for the protected devices.

In the Figure 8-17, the network has two sets of Cisco NAS failover bundles. One Cisco NAS failover bundle supports devices on VLANs 110, 120, and 130. The other Cisco NAS failover bundle supports devices on VLANs 140, 150, and 160. All components in the design are in an active/standby state. Each failover bundle shares a virtual MAC and virtual IP address. Because of the shared MAC address, Layer 2 connectivity is required between components. The redundant distribution switches are interconnected with a Layer 2 trunk.

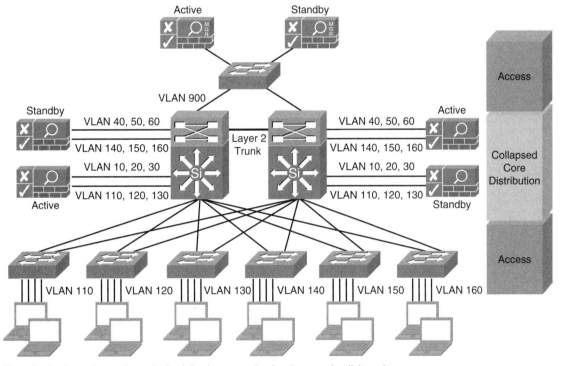

Note: Redundancy is not shown in the following examples for diagram simplicity only.

Figure 8-17 *Cisco NAC Appliance Redundancy Design*

Note   The VLANs do not span the access layer switches in this design. The Layer 2 trunk between the distribution switches is needed only to provide Layer 2 connectivity between the Cisco NAS failover bundles.

Cisco NAM devices connect to the redundant distribution switches and support all the Cisco NAS devices in the network.

Note   Redundancy is not shown in the rest of the figures in this section for simplicity only. Every design that follows can, should, and would have redundancy.

Layer 2 In-Band Designs

The Layer 2 in-band topology is the most common deployment option. The Cisco NAS is logically inline with the client traffic, but is not physically inline. When the virtual gateway mode is implemented, the VLAN IDs are mapped by the Cisco NAS.

In Figure 8-18, VLAN 110 is mapped to VLAN 10 by the Cisco NAS. All client traffic passes through the Cisco NAS. The Cisco NAS securely manages all traffic after posture assessment. The MAC address of the client is used to identify the device. VLAN 90 and VLAN 91 are the management VLANs for the Cisco NAS and the NAM.

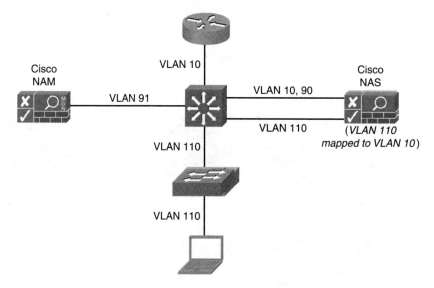

Figure 8-18 *Layer 2 In-Band Designs*

This is the most scalable design in large L2-to-distribution environments, because this design can be transparently implemented in the existing network supporting multiple access layer switches. It supports all network infrastructure equipment. The Cisco NAS supports per-user ACLs.

Note   This NAC design approach is not useful in L3-to-the-closet designs.

Example: Layer 2 In-Band Virtual Gateway

Figure 8-19 illustrates a Layer 2 in-band virtual gateway design. The Cisco NAS maps traffic from VLAN 110 to VLAN 10. VLAN 90 and VLAN 91 are the management VLANs for the Cisco NAS and NAM. The Layer 3 distribution switch has SVIs for the VLANs connecting to the Cisco NAM, NAS, and access switches. The distribution switch is the DHCP server and the default gateway for the access layer devices. The existing IP addressing in the network is not changed when the virtual gateway is implemented.

Chapter 8: Security Services Design   435

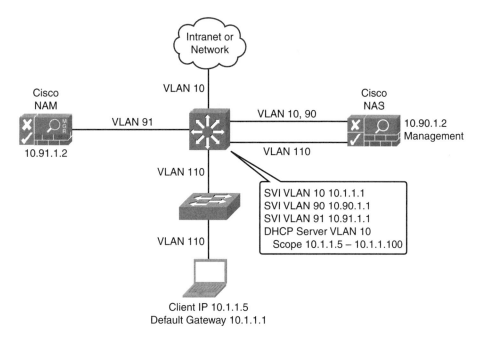

Figure 8-19   *Layer 2 In-Band Virtual Gateway*

Example: Layer 2 In-Band Real IP Gateway

Figure 8-20 illustrates a Layer 2 in-band real IP gateway design. The Cisco NAS is now the DHCP server and the default gateway for the access layer devices. The Cisco NAS has static routes to the other subnets in the organization. The Layer 3 distribution switch has SVIs for the VLANs connecting to the Cisco NAM, NAS, and access switches. The existing IP addressing in the network changes when the real IP gateway is implemented. VLAN 90 and VLAN 91 are the management VLANs for the Cisco NAS and NAM.

One drawback of this design is that it requires static routes at the access switches of the organization.

Layer 2 Out-of-Band Designs

The connections of the Layer 2 out-of-band design are similar to the Layer 2 in-band design, except that the link from the access switch to the distribution switch is now a trunk supporting both the posture assessment VLAN and the network access VLAN.

The client is inline with the Cisco NAS before and during posture assessment. The user VLAN is changed and Cisco NAS is bypassed only after a successful login and assessment. The Cisco NAS securely manages traffic only during assessment. ACLs to manage users need to be applied to the user-assigned VLAN, not the Cisco NAS, because after posture assessment user traffic does not pass through the Cisco NAS.

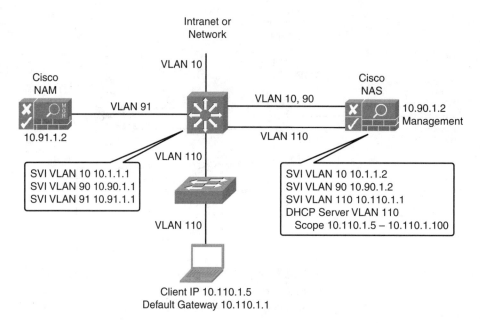

Figure 8-20   *Layer 2 In-Band Real IP Gateway*

Note   Cisco NAM can support either dynamic VLAN assignment based on roles or geographic VLAN assignment based on the VLANs on the switch. Only one MAC address is supported per switch port except for IP telephony devices.

This design requires use of supported out-of-band switches.

Note   For a list of switches and versions that Cisco NAC Appliance supports, see http://www.cisco.com/en/US/docs/security/nac/appliance/support_guide/switch_spt.html.

Cisco NAM uses SNMP for traps to detect user access (PC link-state up condition) and perform switch configuration.

Example: Layer 2 Out-of-Band Virtual Gateway

Figure 8-21 shows addressing with a Layer 3 out-of-band virtual gateway design. Cisco NAS maps traffic from VLAN 110 to VLAN 10 during the posture assessment. The Layer 3 distribution switch has SVIs for the VLANs connecting to the Cisco NAM, NAS, and access switches. The distribution switch is the DHCP server, and the default gateway for the access layer devices. The existing IP addressing in the network is not changed when the virtual gateway is implemented.

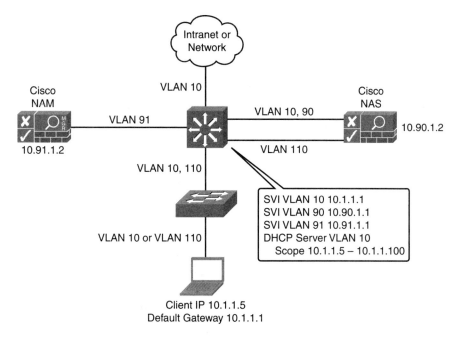

Figure 8-21   *Example: Layer 2 Out-of-Band Virtual Gateway*

Layer 3 In-Band Designs

In the Layer 3 in-band topology, the client device is not adjacent to the Cisco NAS. The IP address of the client is used to identify the device because the MAC address provided to the Cisco NAS is not from the client. This design is used to securely manage traffic from remote sites or for VPN concentrators.

Example: Layer 3 In-Band Virtual Gateway

Figure 8-22 illustrates a Layer 3 in-band virtual gateway design. The Cisco NAS maps traffic from VLAN 110 to VLAN 10. The Layer 3 distribution switch has SVIs for the VLANs connecting to the Cisco NAM, NAS, and access switches. The distribution switch is the default gateway for the access layer devices. The DHCP server is typically a remote router.

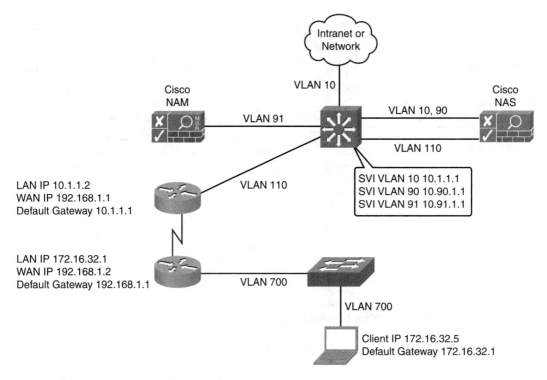

Figure 8-22   *Layer 3 In-Band Virtual Gateway*

All traffic from the remote site goes through Cisco NAS.

This design also supports VPN concentrators. Instead of the remote router pair, the VPN concentrator connects to the distribution switch. Traffic from the VPN concentrator is forwarded through the Cisco NAS for posture assessment and management.

Example: Layer 3 In-Band with Multiple Remotes

Figure 8-23 illustrates a Layer 3 in-band virtual gateway design with multiple remote sites. The Cisco NAS maps traffic from VLAN 110 to VLAN 10. Traffic to centralized hosts and Internet goes through Cisco NAS.

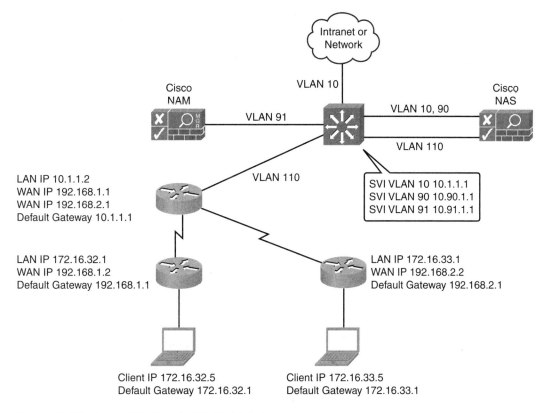

Figure 8-23 *Layer 3 In-Band with Multiple Remotes*

Note   Unless additional configuration steps are taken, traffic between clients at remote sites does not go through Cisco NAS, because the campus router allows routing between the edge routers. To securely manage traffic between the remote sites, you can implement networking technologies such as policy-based routing (PBR) or virtual routing and for-warding instances to isolate the remote sites. Implementing Cisco NAS at the remote sites will also secure the traffic.

Layer 3 Out-of-Band Designs

Layer 3 support for out-of-band deployments enables administrators to deploy Cisco NAS out-of-band centrally in the core or distribution layer to support users behind Layer 3 access switches and remote users behind WAN routers in some instances. With Layer 3 out-of-band, users who are multiple Layer 3 hops away from Cisco NAS can be support-ed for authentication and posture assessment. After authentication and posture assess-ment, the client traffic no longer passes through the Cisco NAS.

With the Layer 3 out-of-band topology, the IP address (and MAC address, starting with Cisco NAA Version 4 Layer 3 out-of-band applications) of the client is used to identify the device, because the MAC address (before the Cisco NAA Version 4 client) provided to the Cisco NAS is from the last-hop router. This design requires use of supported out-of-band switches with the appropriate software image and configuration. The NAM uses SNMP for traps and switch configuration. PBR is needed to direct the user traffic appropriately.

> **Note**   For a list of switches and versions that Cisco NAC Appliance supports, see http://www.cisco.com/en/US/docs/security/nac/appliance/support_guide/switch_spt.html.

Example: Layer 3 OOB with Addressing

Figure 8-24 shows an example of addressing with a Layer 3 out-of-band virtual gateway design supporting remote users. Cisco NAS maps traffic from VLAN 110 to VLAN 10 during the posture assessment. The Layer 3 distribution switch has SVIs for the VLANs connecting to Cisco NAM, NAS, and access switches. The remote-site edge router is the DHCP server and the default gateway for the client devices. The remote-site edge router uses a trunk to the remote-access switch to support either the production VLAN or the posture assessment VLAN. PBR is used to direct the user traffic appropriately.

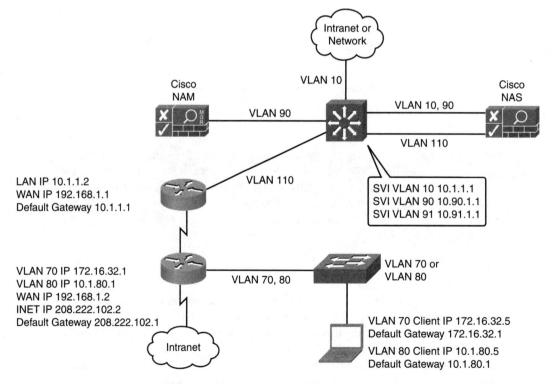

Figure 8-24   *Layer 3 OOB with Addressing*

NAC Framework Overview

NAC Framework is as an architecture-based framework solution designed to take advantage of an existing base of both Cisco network technologies and existing deployments of security and management solutions from other manufacturers. Figure 8-25 illustrates the key components of the NAC Framework architecture covered in this section.

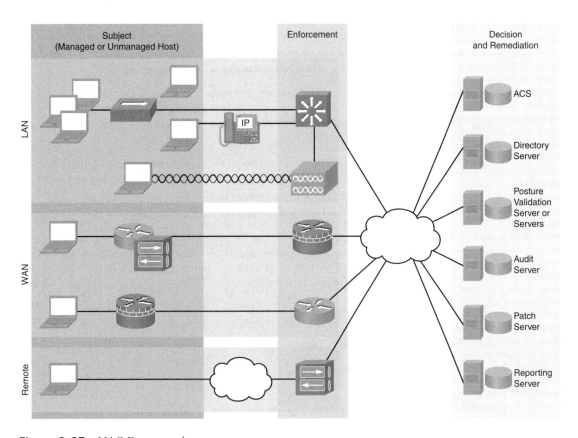

Figure 8-25 *NAC Framework*

The NAC Framework assesses the state, or posture, of a host to prevent unauthorized or vulnerable endpoints from accessing the network. The Cisco NAC posture validation process has three major architectural components:

■ **Subjects:** Managed or unmanaged hosts that are accessing the network on which NAC is enforced. Typical hosts are desktop computers, laptops, and servers, but may also include IP phones, network printers, and other network-attached devices. The subjects use posture agent software to communicate with NAC devices. The Cisco Trust Agent is the Cisco implementation of the posture agent.

■ **Enforcement devices:** Network devices that are acting as a NAC enforcement point. These may include Cisco access routers, VPN gateways, Cisco Catalyst Layer 2 and Layer 3 switches, and wireless access points.

■ **Decision and remediation devices:** Many network devices support the NAC Framework architecture:

   ■ **Authentication, authorization, and accounting (AAA) server:** The central policy server that aggregates one or more authentications or authorizations into a single system authorization decision and maps this decision to a network access profile for enforcement by the network access device (NAD). Cisco Secure Access Control Server (ACS) is the Cisco AAA server product that supports NAC.

   ■ **Directory server:** A centralized directory server for performing user or machine authentication. Possible directory services include Lightweight Directory Access Protocol (LDAP), Microsoft Active Directory, Novell Directory Services (NDS), and one-time password (OTP) servers.

   ■ **Posture validation server (PVS):** A PVS from one or more third parties acts as an application-specific policy decision point in NAC for authorizing a set of posture credentials from one or more posture plug-in against a set of policy rules. Examples include antivirus servers and security application servers.

   ■ **Remediation server:** A management solution used to bring noncompliant hosts into compliance. This could be a specialized patch management application or as simple as a website for distributing software. The better and more efficient your host patching and remediation is, the less risk.

   ■ **Audit server:** A server or software that performs vulnerability assessment (VA) against a host to determine the level of compliance or risk of the host before network admission.

Router Platform Support for the NAC Framework

The NAC Layer 3 IP method uses Extensible Authentication Protocol over User Data Protocol (EAPoUDP). Routers that support the NAC Layer 3 IP method are considered NAC Release 1.0 devices. They can act as a network intrusion-prevention system (NIPS) device. NAC Layer 3 IP was first introduced as part of the initial release of NAC in mid-2004. NAC Layer 3 IP shipped in June 2004 in Cisco IOS Software Release 12.3(8)T. It is included in Cisco IOS Software T-train images with security; the same image which includes firewall, NIPS, and cryptographic support. NAC Layer 3 IP is a posture-only credential check that supports authorization capabilities, URL redirect, and download-able ACLs. NAC Layer 3 IP is triggered by a Layer 3 packet entering a router interface with an IP admission ACL configured. NAC Layer 3 IP is mainly positioned for aggregation deployments (WAN, VPN, WLAN, and so on). The current deployment options preclude the use of NAC Layer 3 IP in the distribution layer of a campus infrastructure because the Catalyst Layer 3 switches do not currently support NAC Layer 3 IP.

NAC agentless host (NAH) is a mechanism in NAC that allows network access to hosts that do not or cannot perform NAC or other compliance authorizations. NADs that fall into this category often include printers, scanners, photocopiers, cameras, sensors, badge readers, and specialized equipment. NAH devices may also include computers with unsupported operating systems, hardened operating systems, embedded operating systems, and personal firewalls. Static exceptions can be configured to allow hosts to bypass the posture validation process based on specified MAC or IP address. Static exceptions can be configured in ACS to allow any specified hosts to bypass the posture validation process based on MAC address. Both individual and wildcard addresses can be specified.

Devices that support either the NAC Layer 2 IP method that uses EAPoUDP or the NAC Layer 2 802.1X (EAP over 802.1X) method, are NAC Release 2.0 devices. NAC Layer 2 IP is triggered by ARP or optionally DHCP traffic on a switch interface. NAC Layer 2 IP is also a posture-only credential check that supports authorization capabilities, URL redirect, and downloadable ACLs. NAC Layer 2 IP sessions are active for as long as the host responds to periodic status query messages implemented using ARP probes or until they are terminated. The ACLs that set the default policy for the switch port on the NAC Layer 2 IP switches are implemented in hardware. One of the main benefits of NAC Layer 2 IP is that it was designed to support multiple hosts per port. The network administrator needs to be aware that unlike NAC Layer 3 IP, only a limited number of hosts per port can be supported in NAC Layer 2 IP. Some network module switches for the Cisco ISR platforms support NAC Layer 2 IP or the NAC Layer 2 802.1X.

Note For NAC Framework router platform support, see http://www.cisco.com/en/US/ solutions/ns340/ns394/ns171/ns466/ns617/net_design_guidance0900aecd8040bc84.pdf.

Switch Platform Support for the NAC Framework

NAC performs posture validation at the Layer 2 network edge for hosts with or without 802.1X enabled. Vulnerable and noncompliant hosts can be isolated, given reduced network access, or directed to remediation servers based on organizational policy. By ensuring that every host complies with security policy, organizations can significantly reduce the damage caused by infected hosts.

Specific switching platforms are supported for this deployment.

Note For a list of supported switches, see http://www.cisco.com/en/US/docs/security/ nac/appliance/support_guide/switch_spt.html.

IPS and IDS Overview

Cisco intrusion-detection and intrusion-prevention solutions are part of the Cisco SAFE architecture. Designed to identify and stop worms, network viruses, and other malicious traffic, these solutions can help protect networks. Cisco provides a broad array of solutions for intrusion detection and prevention at both the network and at the endpoint.

This section gives an overview of intrusion-detection systems (IDS) and intrusion-prevention systems (IPS) that are used in enterprise networks.

Threat Detection and Mitigation

Detecting and mitigating threats and attacks is an important part of a network security strategy.

Because of increasingly sophisticated attacks, point security solutions are no longer effective. The present environment requires higher degrees of visibility that are only attainable with infrastructure-wide security intelligence and collaboration. Cisco SAFE uses various forms of network telemetry that are present on networking equipment, security appliances, and endpoints to achieve consistent and accurate visibility into network activity. Logging and event information that is generated by routers, switches, firewalls, IPSs, and endpoint protection software is collected, trended, and correlated. The architecture also utilizes the collaborative capabilities of security platforms such as IPSs, firewalls, and endpoint protection software.

Cisco SAFE implements the infrastructure-wide intelligence and collaboration capabilities that are provided by Cisco products to control and mitigate well-known and zero-day attacks. IPSs, firewalls, NAC, endpoint protection software, and monitoring and analysis systems work together to identify and dynamically respond to attacks. The architecture has the ability to identify the source of the threat, visualize the attack path, and to suggest (and even dynamically enforce) response actions. Possible response actions include isolation of compromised systems, rate limiting, connection resets, packet filtering, and source filtering.

IDS and IPS are vital components of network wide threat mitigation and response systems. IPS and IDS can be hardware appliances or part of the Cisco IOS firewall software (hardware acceleration/offloading is also an option). IPS is usually capable of both inline (IPS feature) and promiscuous (IDS feature) monitoring, but IDS is capable of promiscuous monitoring only.

IDSs

IDSs passively listen to network traffic, as shown in Figure 8-26. The IDS is not in the traffic path, but listens promiscuously to copies of all traffic on the network. Typically, only one promiscuous interface is required for network monitoring on an IDS. Further promiscuous interfaces could be used to monitor multiple networks. When IDS detects malicious traffic, it sends an alert to the management station. An IDS may can also send a TCP reset to the end host to terminate any malicious TCP connections.

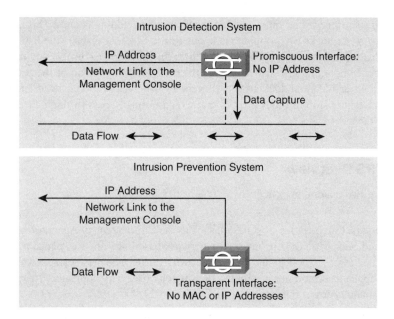

Figure 8-26 *IDS and IPS Overview*

In promiscuous mode, packets do not flow through the sensor. The sensor analyzes a copy of the monitored traffic rather than the actual forwarded packet. The advantage of operating in promiscuous mode is that the sensor does not affect the packet flow with the forwarded traffic. The disadvantage of operating in promiscuous mode, however, is that the sensor cannot stop malicious traffic from reaching its intended target for certain types of attacks, such as atomic attacks (single-packet attacks). The response actions implemented by promiscuous sensor devices are post-event responses and often require assistance from other networking devices (for example, routers and firewalls) to respond to an attack.

Intrusion-Prevention Systems

IPSs are active devices in the traffic path, as shown in Figure 8-26. An IPS listens to inline network traffic and permits or denies flows and packets into the network. The inline interfaces have no MAC or IP address and cannot be detected directly. All traffic passes through the IPS for inspection. Traffic arrives on one IPS interface and exits on another. When an IPS detects malicious traffic, it sends an alert to the management station and can block the malicious traffic immediately. The original and subsequent malicious traffic is blocked as the IPS proactively prevents attacks protecting against network viruses, worms, malicious applications, and vulnerability exploits. An IPS resembles a

Layer 2 bridge or repeater. By default, an IPS passes all packets unless specifically denied by a policy.

Operating in inline interface pair mode puts the IPS directly into the traffic flow and affects packet-forwarding rates, making them slower by adding latency. This allows the sensor to stop attacks by dropping malicious traffic before it reaches the intended target, thus providing a protective service. Not only is the inline device processing information on Layers 3 and 4, but it is also analyzing the contents and payload of the packets for more sophisticated embedded attacks (Layers 3 to 7). This deeper analysis lets the system identify and stop or block attacks that would normally pass through a traditional firewall device.

IDS and IPS Overview

There are two major components in an IDS or IPS solution:

- **Sensors:** Can be either host based, such as the Cisco Security Agent, or network based, such as an IPS appliance. The network-based sensors use specialized software and hardware to collect and analyze network traffic. The network-based sensors can be appliances, modules in a router, or a switch or security appliance. There are three common types of IDS/ or IPS technologies:

    - A signature-based IDS or IPS looks for specific predefined patterns or signatures in network traffic. Traffic patterns are compared to a database of known attacks and trigger an alarm or drop traffic if a match is found.

    - An anomaly-based IDS or IPS checks for defects or anomalies in packets or packet sequences and verifies whether there is any anomaly traffic behavior.

    - A policy-based IDS or IPS is configured based on the network security policy and detects traffic that does not match the policy.

- **Security management and monitoring infrastructure:** Configures the sensors and serves as the collection point for alarms for security management and monitoring. The management and monitoring applications performs alert collection, aggregation, and correlation. CSM is used to centrally provision device configurations and security policies for Cisco firewalls, VPNs, and IPSs and provides some light monitoring functions. Cisco Security Monitoring, Analysis, and Response System (MARS) provides security monitoring for network security devices and host applications. Cisco IPS Device Manager (IDM) is a web-based Java application that allows configuration and management of IPS sensors. IDS Event Viewer is a Java-based application that enables network managers to view and manage alarms for up to five sensors.

Note The Cisco IPS Device Manager has been replaced with the Cisco IPS Manager Express. The IPS Manager Express (IME) combines the IDM with the IDS Event Viewer, while adding enhanced health monitoring and the ability to manage up to five sensors. IME requires 6.1 sensor software release to provide the advanced dashboard and health monitoring features. IME is not designed to work with Cisco IOS Software sensor implementations. For more information, see http://www.cisco.com/en/US/products/ps9610/index.html.

Host Intrusion-Prevention Systems

Host intrusion-prevention system (HIPS) deployments include two components:

- **Endpoint agents:** Enforces the security policy received from the management server. Endpoint agents send event information to the management server, and interact with the user if necessary. The goal of an endpoint agent is to provide threat protection for the end system. Cisco Security Agent is the Cisco endpoint agent that provides threat protection for server and desktop computing systems. Cisco Security Agent consists of host-based agents that report to the Cisco Management Center for Cisco Security Agents. The Cisco Security Agent software resides between the applications and the kernel on a PC, enabling maximum application visibility with minimal impact to the stability and performance of the underlying operating system.

- **Management server:** Deploys security policies to endpoints. The management server is responsible for configuring and maintaining the environment. The server receives and stores events information and sends alerts to administrators. The management server may deploy software such as endpoint agent software updates. The interface to a HIPS management server is typically a GUI console that allows policy configuration and event viewing. For highly scalable environments, it is possible to have a dedicated database running where the configuration and event information is stored. The management center for Cisco Security Agents provides all management functions for Cisco Security Agent deployments.

IDS and IPS Design Considerations

The underlying security policy should be the same for an IDS or an IPS deployment. To deny traffic, an IPS solution must be deployed inline with the network, whereas an IDS sensor is connected in promiscuous mode, where packets do not flow through the sensor. The IDS sensor analyzes a copy of the monitored traffic rather than the actual forwarded packet. If your security policy does not support denying traffic, use an IDS deployment.

Note   It is common practice to deploy a sensor initially in IDS mode while baselining the network.

IDS or IPS sensors are placed in the network where they can effectively support the underlying security policy. Deployment decisions are often based on where you need to detect or stop an intrusion as soon as possible. Typical scenarios include placing the sensors at the perimeter of the network outside a firewall where the network is most exposed, internal to the network inside the firewall between boundaries between zones of trust, and at critical servers where an incident would be most costly. For example, placement outside the firewall generates many warnings that have relatively low value because no action is likely to be taken on this information.

> **Note**   Some environments deploy an IDS outside the firewall to assist in event correlation and to determine the effectiveness of the firewall. Sensor placement depends on an organization's security policy, which is a reflection of that organization's security needs.

Traffic impact considerations are increased with inline IPS sensors over IDS deployments. A failure of the IDS means traffic monitoring has stopped. A failure of the IPS can disrupt network traffic flow unless bypass methods are implemented. An IPS deployment also impacts inline traffic. The latency through the IPS sensor should generally be under a millisecond and as low as possible. The IPS sensors have bandwidth limitations on the amount of traffic that can be supported through the device. Exceeding the performance of a sensor results in dropped packets and a general degradation of network performance.

IDS or IPS Deployment Considerations

IDS or IPS sensors can be deployed based on the priority of targets. Internet and extranet connections are typically secured first because of their exposure. An IDS outside the firewall can detect all attacks and will generate a lot of alarms but is useful for analyzing what kind of traffic is reaching the organization and how an attack is executed. An IDS inside the firewall can detect firewall misconfigurations by showing what kind of traffic passes through the firewall. An IPS can provide more focused application protection and firewall augmentation for extranet and DMZ resources.

Management networks and data centers are often next in priority. A layered approach for maximum protection is appropriate for the high-security areas. There might be one system installed after the firewall and a second system at the entry point to the high-security area, such as the data center. Host-specific IDS can detect attacks against a specific server. An IPS can be used to block application-specific traffic which should not reach the server.

IPS deployments at remote and branch offices can both protect the branch from corporate incidents and protect the corporate resources from security incidents arising from branch practices. Remote-access systems need protection, too.

IPS Appliance Deployment Options

When you are placing an IPS sensor in an enterprise network, you have multiple options available depending on the infrastructure and the desired results. Figure 8-27 illustrates each of the following options.

- Two Layer 2 Devices (No Trunk)

- Two Layer 3 Devices

- Two VLANs On the Same Switch

- Two Layer 2 Devices (Trunked)

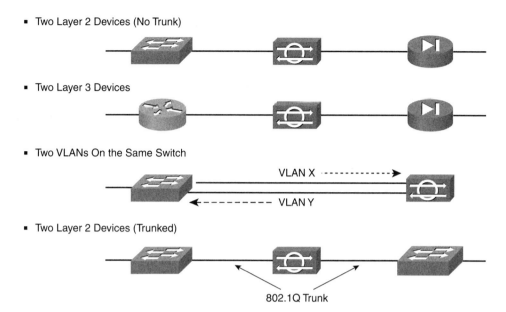

Figure 8-27 *IPS Appliance Deployment Options*

- **Two Layer 2 devices (no trunk):** Sensor placement between two Layer 2 devices without trunking is a typical campus design. In this deployment, the IPS appliance is placed between two switches. The IPS can be between the same VLAN on two different switches or between different VLANs with the same subnet on two different switches. Scenarios include placement between different security zones in a campus environment or between critical devices in a data center.

- **Two Layer 3 devices:** Sensor placement between Layer 3 devices is common in Internet, campus, and server farm designs. The two Layer 3 devices are in the same subnet. One advantage in these scenarios is the ease of configuration because the integration can take place without touching any other device.

- **Two VLANs on the same switch:** This design allows a sensor to bridge VLANs together on the same switch. The sensor brings packets in on one VLAN and out a different VLAN for traffic in the same subnet.

- **Two Layer 2 devices (trunked):** Sensor placement on a trunk port between switches is a common scenario providing protection of several VLANs from a single location.

Note   Deployments using IPS modules follow the same general guidelines as deployments for IPS appliances.

Feature: Inline VLAN Pairing

The IPS can associate VLANs in pairs on a physical interface. Packets received on one of the paired VLANs are analyzed and then forwarded to the other VLAN in the pair. The sensor brings packets in on one VLAN and out a different VLAN on the same trunk link for traffic in the same subnet. The sensor replaces the VLAN ID field in the IEEE 802.1Q header of each received packet with the ID of the egress VLAN on which the sensor forwards the packet. This design supports multiple VLAN pairs per physical interface and reduces the need to have many physical interfaces per chassis.

IPS Deployment Challenges

Asymmetric traffic patterns and high availability are challenges for IPS deployments.

Traditional packet flows in a network are symmetrical and consist of connections that take the same path through the network in both directions. Many newer network designs do not guarantee symmetrical flows and engineer the network to take advantage of all available links. This greatly increases the chance that traffic may use multiple paths to and from its destination.

This asymmetric traffic flow can cause problems with inline IPS devices. Because an IPS sensor inspects traffic statefully and needs to see both sides of the connection to function properly, asymmetric traffic flows may cause valid traffic to be dropped.

High availability is another deployment challenge. A failure of any redundant component in the network should not cause an interruption in network availability. This implies that existing sessions should continue to flow normally and not be dropped.

The current Cisco IPS 6.0 solutions do not support asymmetric flows or high availability natively in the product. A design workaround uses the network to mirror all traffic between two sensors in a "failover" pair. The IPS sensors in the pair see all packets traversing a point in the network. If one sensor fails for any reason, the network reroutes all traffic through the other sensor because it is the only available path. The secondary sensor has already seen all the packets and has built a complete state table for the flows, so traffic is not interrupted. Asymmetric traffic is also supported by this mirroring technique.

IDS or IPS Management Interface Deployment Options

Monitoring an IDS or IPS solution is one of the crucial elements to provide fast detection of any suspicious activity and an indication of prevented attacks. IDS or IPS management consolidates and centralizes alarms from multiple sources to provide the required view of the network.

Buying an IDS or IPS without proper staffing and tools greatly reduces the value. The key difference is that IDS without eyeballs does nothing to block malicious traffic. IDP without eyeballs (that is, security operations center) support results in cutting off a user. If the user is cut off by a false positive, that user is likely to be quite irate. Compensating for lack of staff (IDS solution) with an IPS is not usually conducive to good user relations.

On the network boundary, the sensors are usually installed adjacent to a firewall. The monitoring and management interfaces of an IPS sensor can therefore be connected to two different networks. This is especially critical when the outside sensor needs to communicate with the inside network.

One option is to connect the monitoring interface to the outside network and the management interface directly to the inside network. All management is done in-band over the internal network. This type of setup is simple, but provides a path around the firewall if the sensor is compromised. This design is not recommended.

A preferred design places the monitoring interface on the outside network, and the management interface on a separate inside VLAN. With this setup, the management interface is isolated by an IPS management VLAN from the rest of the inside network. If the VLAN is sufficiently trusted, this design provides good separation of the IDS or IPS sensor. A recommended practice is to use Secure Shell (SSH) or Secure Sockets Layer (SSL) protocol for management access to the IDS or IPS sensors.

Note   Using PVLANs to put all sensors on isolated ports is recommended because the sensors do not need to talk to each other except when distributed blocking is used. This prevents the compromise of a single sensor, which helps to prevent other sensors from being compromised.

In-Band Management Through Tunnels

Another option for deploying IDS or IPS uses a combination of management through an OOB network and management through secure tunnels depending on the location of the sensors.

For devices outside the perimeter firewall, the monitoring interface remains on the outside network, but the management interface is terminated on a separate DMZ. Management is supported in-band across an encrypted tunnel. The firewall protects the outside sensor from the inside devices and provides better separation compared to the previous solution. For internal devices in more secure areas, management is provided through a separate management VLAN.

IDS and IPS Monitoring and Management

Cisco Security MARS and CSM are part of the Cisco Security Management Suite, which delivers policy administration and enforcement for the Cisco Self-Defending Network. Both tools should be implemented in the management VLAN in a protected place such as the server farm or data center.

Cisco Security MARS provides multivendor event correlation and proactive response, distributing IPS signatures to mitigate active threats. Cisco Security MARS proactively identifies active network threats and distributes IPS signatures to mitigate them:

■   Cisco Security MARS ships with a set of predefined and easy-to-customize compliance reports.

■   Cisco Security MARS stores event information from every type of device. This information can be grouped in one single report.

For a small-size to medium-size organization, a centralized Cisco Security MARS implemented as a local controller is a typical deployment.

Note In Cisco Security MARS, a *local controller* is the name given to the hardware appliance that supports the features discussed in this section for monitoring, analysis, and response. The global controller is an appliance used to support the centralized operation and management of multiple local controllers in distributed deployments.

CSM enables organizations to manage security policies on Cisco security devices. CSM supports integrated provisioning of VPN and firewall services across Cisco IOS routers, Cisco PIX and ASA security appliances, and Cisco Catalyst 6500/Cisco 7600 service modules. It also supports IPS technologies on routers, service modules, and IPS devices. CSM supports provisioning of many platform-specific settings (for example, interfaces, routing, identity, QoS, and logging).

CSM, through its Cisco IPS Manager component, supports the management and configuration of Cisco IPS sensors (appliances, switch modules, network modules, and Security Service Modules [SSM]) and Cisco IOS IPS devices (Cisco IOS routers with IPS-enabled images and Cisco ISRs). Users configure IPS sensors and Cisco IOS IPS devices through the use of policies, each of which defines a different part of the configuration of the sensor. Whereas CSM 3.0 allowed the user to cross-launch the CiscoWorks IPS Management Center to access IPS functionality, Cisco Security Manager 3.1 provides fully integrated IPS features.

CSM enables organizations to manage security policies on Cisco security devices. CSM supports integrated provisioning of firewall, IPS, and VPN (site to site, remote access, and SSL). It provides integrated IPS provisioning services. Starting in Version 3.1, CSM provisions many platform-specific settings. Some examples include interfaces, routing, identity, QoS, and logging. It provides support for the following features on IPS devices:

- Virtual sensors

- Anomaly detection

- Passive operating system fingerprinting

- Simplified custom signature creation

- Signature Update Wizard and preview and tuning of new signatures

- IPS signature update license management

- External product interface (linkage of IPS sensor with Management Center for Cisco Security Agent)

Scaling Cisco Security MARS with Global Controller Deployment

The Cisco Security MARS global controller enables network monitoring scaling, as shown in Figure 8-28.

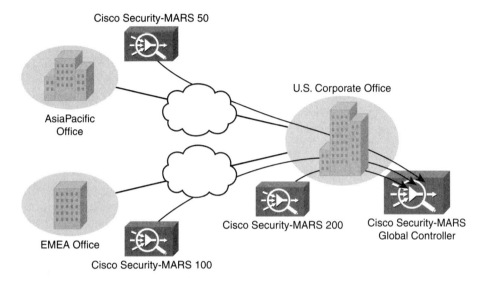

Figure 8-28   *Scaling Cisco Security MARS with Global Controller Deployment*

If an organization is supporting multiple Cisco Security MARS local controllers, they can deploy a distributed solution using a global controller to summarize the findings of two or more local controllers and manage the local controllers.

The global controller communicates over Hypertext Transfer Protocol Secure (HTTPS) using certificates. Only incidents from global rules are rolled up into the global controller. The global controller can distribute updates, rules, report templates, access rules, and queries across the local controller.

Summary

In this chapter, you learned about firewalls, NAC, and IPSs, and IDSs.

Firewalls have long provided the first line of defense in network security infrastructures. They accomplish this by comparing corporate policies on network access rights for users to the connection information surrounding each access attempt. User policies and connection information must match; otherwise, the firewall does not grant access to network resources.

NAC is a set of technologies and solutions that is built on an industry initiative led by Cisco. The NAC Framework uses the network infrastructure to enforce security policy compliance on all devices seeking to access network computing resources, thereby limit-

454 Designing Cisco Network Service Architectures (ARCH) Foundation Learning Guide

ing damage from emerging security threats such as viruses, worms, and spyware by using embedded software modules within NAC-enabled products. Customers using NAC can allow network access only to compliant and trusted endpoint devices (PCs, servers, and PDAs, for example) and can restrict the access of noncompliant devices. Cisco NAC Appliance condenses NAC capabilities into an appliance form where client, server, and manager products enable network administrators to authenticate, authorize, evaluate, and remediate wired, wireless, and remote users and their machines before allowing users onto the network.

Cisco intrusion-detection and -prevention solutions are part of the Cisco Self-Defending Network. Designed to identify and stop worms, network viruses, and other malicious traffic, these solutions can help protect networks. Cisco provides a broad array of solutions for intrusion detection and prevention at both the network and at the endpoint.

References

For additional information, refer to these resources:

Cisco Systems, Inc. *Cisco SAFE Solution Overview* at http://www.cisco.com/en/US/docs/solutions/Enterprise/Security/SAFESolOver.html

Cisco Systems, Inc. *Cisco SAFE Reference Guide* at http://www.cisco.com/en/US/docs/solutions/Enterprise/Security/SAFE_RG/SAFE_rg.html

Cisco Systems, Inc. *Catalyst 6500 Series Switch and Cisco 7600 Series Router Firewall Services Module Configuration Guide 4.0* at http://www.cisco.com/en/US/partner/docs/security/fwsm/fwsm40/configuration/guide/fwsm_cfg.html

Cisco Systems, Inc. *Network Admission Control Framework Deployment* Guide at http://www.cisco.com/en/US/solutions/ns340/ns394/ns171/ns466/ns617/net_design_guidance0900aecd80417226.pdf

Cisco Systems, Inc. *Release Notes for Network Admission Control, Release 2.1* at http://www.cisco.com/en/US/partner/docs/security/nac/2.1/release_notes/NAC21RN.html

Cisco Systems, Inc. *Cisco NAC Appliance (Clean Access) Release Notes* at http://www.cisco.com/en/US/products/ps6128/prod_release_notes_list.html

Cisco Systems, Inc. *Cisco NAC Appliance Switch and Wireless LAN Controller Support* at http://www.cisco.com/en/US/partner/docs/security/nac/appliance/support_guide/switch_spt.html

Cisco Systems, Inc. *Cisco NAC Appliance Data Sheet* at http://www.cisco.com/en/US/partner/prod/collateral/vpndevc/ps5707/ps8418/ps6128/product_data_sheet0900aecd802da1b5.html

Cisco Systems, Inc. *Cisco NAC Appliance—Clean Access Server Configuration Guide* at http://www.cisco.com/en/US/partner/docs/security/nac/appliance/configuration_guide/47/cas/47cas-book.html

Cisco Systems, Inc. *Cisco NAC Appliance—Clean Access Manager Configuration Guide* at http://www.cisco.com/en/US/partner/docs/security/nac/appliance/configuration_guide/47/cam/47cam-book.html

Cisco Systems, Inc. *Configuring the Cisco Intrusion Prevention System Sensor Using the Command Line Interface 7.0* at http://www.cisco.com/en/US/partner/docs/security/ips/7.0/configuration/guide/cli/cliguide7.html

Cisco Systems, Inc. *Cisco Secure Services Client Introduction* at http://www.cisco.com/ en/US/products/ps7034/index.html

Cisco Systems, Inc. *Installing and Using Cisco Intrusion Prevention System Device Manager 7.0* at http://www.cisco.com/en/US/partner/docs/security/ips/7.0/configuration/guide/idm/idmguide7.html

Cisco Systems, Inc. *Cisco Security Agent Version 6.0.2 Data Sheet* at http://www.cisco.com/en/US/partner/prod/collateral/vpndevc/ps5707/ps5057/data_sheet_c78_601195.html

Cisco Systems, Inc. *Cisco Trust Agent 2.0 Data Sheet* at http://www.cisco.com/en/US/partner/prod/collateral/vpndevc/ps5707/ps5923/product_data_sheet0900aecd80119868.html

Cisco Systems, Inc. *Zone-Based Policy Firewall Design and Application Guide* at http://www.cisco.com/en/US/products/sw/secursw/ps1018/products_tech_note09186a00808bc994.shtml

Review Questions

Answer the following questions, and then refer to Appendix A, "Answers to Review Questions," for the answers.

1. What is a virtual firewall?

    a. A logical separation of multiple firewall security contexts on a single firewall

    b. A physical separation of multiple firewall security contexts in a single chassis

    c. A routed firewall mode

    d. A transparent firewall mode

    e. An administrative context for network connectivity

2. Which command provides support for asymmetric routing?

    a. **asr-active** interface command on FWSM 2.1

    b. **asr-active** interface command on FWSM 3.0

    c. **asr-group** interface command on FWSM 2.1

    d. **asr-group** interface command on FWSM 3.0

      e. **asr-redundancy** interface command on FWSM 2.1

      f. **asr-redundancy** interface command on FWSM 3.0

3. What are three components of a PVLAN?

      a. Communications VLAN

      b. Community VLAN

      c. Isolated VLAN

      d. Isolation VLAN

      e. Primary VLAN

      f. Promiscuous VLAN

4. What are two methods to provide network security with access control?

      a. 802.1X posture alignment

      b. 802.1X posture assessment

      c. IBNS authentication

      d. INBS authentication

      e. NAC posture alignment

      f. NAC posture assessment

5. How many NAC Appliance Servers can Cisco NAC Appliance Super Manager manage?

      a. 3

      b. 5

      c. 20

      d. 40

      e. 50

6. What are two characteristics of real IP gateway mode?

      a. The Cisco NAM has an IP address for every managed VLAN.

      b. The Cisco NAM operates as a standard Ethernet bridge, but with added functionality.

      c. The Cisco NAS does not operate as the default gateway for untrusted network clients.

      d. The Cisco NAS has an IP address for every managed VLAN.

      e. The Cisco NAS operates as a standard Ethernet bridge, but with added functionality.

      f. The Cisco NAS operates as the default gateway for untrusted network clients.

7. What are two typical NAC agentless hosts?

   a. Cisco Secure Services clients

   b. Enforcement devices

   c. Printers

   d. Scanners

   e. Windows 2000 devices

   f. Windows XP devices

8. Which two of the following are characteristics of an IPS sensor?

   a. It is an active device in the traffic path.

   b. It passively listens to network traffic.

   c. A permissive interface is used to monitor networks.

   d. A promiscuous interface is used to monitor the network.

   e. Traffic arrives on one IPS interface and exits on another.

9. What are two challenges for IPS deployments?

   a. Supporting inline VLAN pairing

   b. Supporting asymmetric traffic flows

   c. Natively supporting symmetric traffic flows

   d. Natively bridging VLANs on two switches

   e. Supporting failover without dropping valid traffic

10. Which mechanism can be used to scale Cisco Security MARS deployments?

   a. Inline VLAN pairing for local controllers

   b. Symmetric traffic flows to a central controller

   c. A global controller to summarize multiple local controllers

   d. A central controller to summarize multiple local and global controllers

   e. HTTPS certificates for each global controller

11. Access control or admission control consists of which three elements?

   a. Identify

   b. Shun

   c. Enforce

   d. Isolate

   e. Interrupt

   f. Log and alert

Chapter 9

IPsec and SSL VPN Design

Upon completing this chapter, you will be able to

- Discuss design considerations for remote-access VPNs

- Discuss design considerations for site-to-site VPNs

- Discuss technologies for implementing VPNs

- Discuss managing and scaling VPNs

This chapter reviews virtual private network (VPN) design in the enterprise. VPNs are networks deployed on a public or private network infrastructure. VPNs are useful for telecommuters, mobile users, and remote offices. Customers, suppliers, and partners also find them useful.

For enterprises, VPNs are an alternative WAN infrastructure, replacing or augmenting existing private networks that use dedicated WANs based on leased-line, Frame Relay, ATM, or other technologies. Increasingly, enterprises are turning to their service providers for VPNs and other complete service solutions tailored to their particular business.

Designing Remote-Access VPNs

Remote-access VPNs permit secure, encrypted connections between mobile or remote users and their corporate networks through a third-party network, such as a service provider. Deploying a remote-access VPN enables enterprises to reduce communications expenses by leveraging the local packet-switching infrastructures of Internet service providers (ISP). Cisco remote-access VPN solutions deliver both IP Security (IPsec) and Secure Sockets Layer (SSL) technologies on a single platform with unified management.

Remote-Access VPN Overview

Remote-access VPNs using IPsec or SSL technologies, as shown in Figure 9-1, permit secure, encrypted connections between mobile or remote users and their corporate network across public networks.

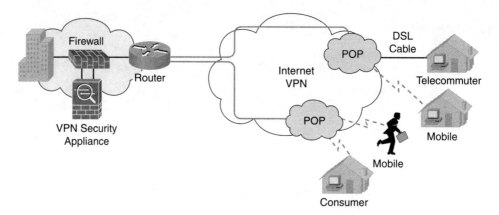

Figure 9-1   *Remote-Access VPNs*

Note   In SSL VPN, the delivery mechanism is Secure HTTP (HTTPS).

VPN technology is essential in securing connectivity across public or semipublic networks. Several components of the Cisco SAFE architecture leverage VPN technologies to provide authenticated connections and data confidentiality and integrity.

Site-to-site IPsec VPN technology is used in the WAN to secure the connections between the main enterprise sites and remote branch offices. Site-to-site VPN connections can also be used to build a secure extranet between an organization and its partners.

Remote-access IPsec and SSL VPNs are used to securely connect teleworkers or other remote mobile users to the corporate network. Separate access policies can be established for different groups of users, such as employees and partners.

There are three remote-access VPN components:

■   VPN termination device or headend supporting a high number of endpoints.

■   End clients (mobile or fixed). The remote-access client can be built inside of an operating system or application or can be installed as a Layer 3 software client (for example, the Cisco VPN Client).

■   Technology that connects the VPN headend and the end clients. The two main protocols supporting remote-access VPNs are IPsec and SSL, as follows:

   ■   IPsec is used primarily for data confidentiality and device authentication, but extensions to the standard allow for user authentication and authorization to occur as part of the IPsec process.

■ The main role of SSL is to provide security for web traffic. With SSL, the browser client supports the VPN connection to a host. SSL is a default capability in leading browsers.

Both IPsec and SSL remote-access VPNs are mechanisms to provide secure communication:

■ Authenticity identifies the trusted party by asking for username and password or a credential.

■ Integrity checking verifies that packets were not altered or tampered with as they traveled across the network.

■ Confidentiality is supported using encryption to ensure communications were not read by others.

Example: Cisco Easy VPN Client IPsec Implementation

Cisco Easy VPN provides simple IPsec VPN deployments for remote offices and teleworkers.

The Cisco Easy VPN Server allows Cisco routers and security appliances to act as IPsec VPN headend devices in remote-access and site-to-site VPNs.

For remote-access VPNs, the Cisco Easy VPN Server terminates VPN tunnels initiated by remote workers running the Cisco VPN Client software on PCs. This capability allows mobile and remote workers to access critical data and applications on their corporate intranet. The Cisco Easy VPN Server pushes configurations and security policies defined at the central site to the remote client device, helping to ensure that those connections have appropriate information and current policies in place before the connection is established. Cisco Easy VPN Server can pass a variety of information to the client, including IP address and mask, information about the internal Domain Name System (DNS) and Windows Internet Naming Service (WINS) server, and organization policies.

Note   Cisco Easy VPN Server is discussed in more detail in the section, "Using IPsec VPN Technologies."

SSL VPN Overview

SSL is a protocol designed to enable secure communications on an unsecure network such as the Internet.

SSL is a technology developed by Netscape to provide encryption between a web browser and a web server. SSL supports integrity of communications along with strong authentication using digital certificates:

■ Web server certificates authenticate the identity of a website to visiting browsers. When a user wants to send confidential information to a web server, the browser accesses the digital certificate of the server. The certificate, which contains the public key of the web server, is used by the browser to authenticate the identity of the web server and to encrypt information for the server using SSL technology. Because the web server is the only entity with access to its private key, only the server can decrypt the information.

■   Root certificates are self-signed digital certificates that are generated during the creation of a certificate authority (CA). "Trusted" root certificates refer to CA certificates that are stored in the trust lists that are natively embedded in the leading web browsers. There are a limited number of CA certificates, which come embedded in the web browsers from Microsoft and Netscape.

SSL for VPNs can be more than a basic web page supporting secure access to the applications available as static web pages on HTTP servers:

■   SSL VPNs can fit into existing networks and application environments and provide support for complex applications such as corporate directory and calendar systems, e-commerce applications, file sharing, and remote system management.

■   SSL VPNs can support the same authentication mechanisms and often-extensive application lists as those available for IPsec.

SSL VPNs have multiple access mechanisms:

■   Content rewriting and application translation using embedded clientless access and Layer 7 features. Clientless access is where a user can connect with little requirements beyond a basic web browser.

■   Port forwarding, which is known as a thin client. With a thin client, a small applet or application, generally less than 100 KB in size, provides access to a subset of resources.

■   Dynamic VPN client with full network access, which is known as a thick client. With a thick client, a larger client, generally around 500 KB, is delivered to the end user. The applications that can be reached through the thick client are similar to those available via IPsec VPNs. This client is delivered via a web page and never needs to be manually distributed or installed.

Clientless Access

The SSL VPN system supports clientless access by proxying web pages. The system connects to a web server, downloads and translates a web page, and then transfers it over an SSL connection to the browser of the end user. The SSL VPN system rewrites or translates content so that the internal addresses and names on a web page are accessible to the end users.

Only web-enabled and some client/server applications (such as intranets, applications with web interfaces, email, calendaring, and file servers) can be accessed using a clientless connection. This limited access is suitable for partners or contractors that need access to a limited set of resources on the network.

Several content-rewriting functions are involved in proxying the remote applications:

■ Translating the protocol in use by the application to HTTP

■ Delivering an HTML user interface

■ Supporting file sharing

Clientless access for SSL VPNs does not require specialized VPN software on the user desktop (because all VPN traffic is transmitted and delivered through a standard web browser), and so provisioning and support concerns are minimized.

Thin Client

Organizations that have not implemented web-based applications can often rely on the thin clients that support port forwarding, as shown in Figure 9-2. Port forwarding requires a small application (often in the form of Java or Microsoft ActiveX) that runs on the end-user system. The port forwarder acts as a local proxy server. The client application listens for connections on a port defined for an application on a local host address. It tunnels packets that arrive on this port inside of an SSL connection to the SSL VPN device, which unpacks them and forwards them to the real application server. Port forwarding maintains the native application look and feel for the end user.

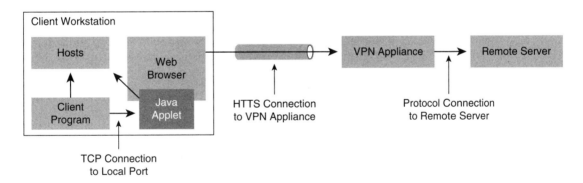

Figure 9-2 *Thin Client Functionality*

Port forwarding is an effective technique, but it also has some limitations. For port forwarding to work, the applications need to be well behaved and predictable in their network connectivity ports, patterns, and needs. Examples of applications that are not web enabled but can be addressed with port forwarding are common mail protocols, including Simple Mail Transfer Protocol (SMTP), Post Office Protocol Version 3 (POP3), Messaging Application Programming Interface (MAPI), and remote shell programs, such as Telnet. ActiveX or Java applet support may also be required on the client machine, along with the permissions in the browser to run them.

Thick Client

SSL VPN network extension connects the end-user system to the corporate network with access controls based only on network layer information, such as destination IP address and port number. Network extension uses a thick client that provides authorized users with secure access to the entire corporate LAN.

The thick client, shown here in Figure 9-3, is automatically delivered through the web page and does not need to be manually distributed or installed. The thick client requires administrative access to the local system for installation. The Layer 3 thick client provides a virtual adapter for the end user, typically using ActiveX and Java. The applications that can be accessed with the thick client are similar to those available through an IPsec VPN. Cisco AnyConnect is a Cisco implementation of the thick client.

Figure 9-3 *Thick Client (Port Forwarding)*

Because the SSL VPN network extension runs on top of the SSL protocol, it is simpler to manage and has greater robustness with different network topologies such as firewalls and Network Address Translation (NAT) than the higher security of IPsec. The thick client is typically a smaller installation than the IPsec client.

Thick mode should be used when users need full application access and IT wants tighter integration with the operating system for additional security and ease of use.

Remote-Access VPN Design Considerations

When deploying remote-access VPNs, it is important to determine where to terminate the service. The decision is impacted by the organization's firewall architecture, routing and addressing schema, and authentication policy. The following subsections examine these elements and their impact on remote-access VPN design.

VPN Termination Device and Firewall Placement

The VPN termination device can be deployed in parallel with a firewall, inline with a firewall, or in a demilitarized zone (DMZ). For best security, a recommended practice is to place the public side of the VPN termination device in a DMZ behind a firewall.

Note   The firewall could be the VPN termination device.

The firewall policies should limit traffic coming in to the VPN termination device to IPsec and SSL. Any IPsec tunnels should terminate on the VPN appliance. For extra security, send traffic through another firewall for additional inspection after it passes through the VPN appliance.

You should also enforce endpoint security compliance on the remote system.

Routing Design Considerations

Routing design considerations are mainly a VPN headend consideration for remote-access VPNs.

For nonlocal subnet IP addresses, the most common configuration is that the internal routers use static routes for the address blocks for remote devices pointing to the private interfaces of the headend device.

If a large number of networks exist behind each headend device, the configuration of static routes becomes difficult to maintain. Instead, it is recommended that you use Reverse Route Injection (RRI). RRI automatically inserts static routes into the routing table of the gateway router for those networks and hosts protected by a remote tunnel endpoint. These static routes can then be redistributed to the other routers in the network.

Note   Smaller organizations typically configure a few static routes to point to the VPN device and do not need RRI. The RRI function is usually of more benefit to larger organizations that have more complex requirements (for example, organizations that do not have a dedicated scope of Dynamic Host Configuration Protocol [DHCP] addresses that are associated to a specific VPN headend).

Address Assignment Considerations

For IPsec, thin, and thick clients, there are three common addressing techniques:

- The simplest and most common address assignment design is to use internal address pools per VPN headend and to implement a static route for this subnet to the VPN headend. With this approach, access control lists (ACL) on an internal firewall can support group-based address pools for incoming user policies.

- Another popular choice is to use DHCP to assign addresses. A recommended practice is to associate a dedicated scope of DHCP addresses to a specific VPN headend.

■ For situations where the remote user needs a static IP address assignment to support a specific application, organizations must deploy RADIUS or Lightweight Directory Access Protocol (LDAP) with an attribute to assign the user the same IP. In this case, RRI may be needed.

An IP address is not assigned for clientless end-user devices:

■ The headend device will proxy Address Resolution Protocol (ARP) on behalf of all local subnet IP addresses.

■ Because the clientless users do not receive a unique IP address on the corporate network, their traffic looks like it originates from the headend interface IP. This is good for scalability but is harder to monitor.

Other Design Considerations

Two other design considerations are authentication and access control.

Authentication

SSL can use other methods of authentication instead of a digital certificate. The simplest approach is to use a username and password, but security-conscious organizations use stronger authentication methods, such as security tokens and one-time password (OTP).

Customers who are focused on convenience sometimes authenticate to an internal LDAP (such as Microsoft Active Directory) or other authentication, authorization, and accounting (AAA) password database. Any type of static password configuration leaves the organization vulnerable to brute-force password attacks.

Access Control

Access control rules allow organizations to restrict network access. Some companies choose to maintain all access rules on an internal firewall based on the source IP of the client. This scenario supports addresses that are assigned to a specific pool based on group assignment. That is, user authentication determines group, group determines IP pool, and IP pool then allows enforcement of different security policies for different groups of users.

Access control rules can be defined at a per-group basis on the VPN headend device. This approach is easy to deploy but can be more difficult to maintain with large numbers of policies or across multiple devices. Access control rules can also be defined on the headend RADIUS server, although generic RADIUS has a 4-KB packet size limit. The Cisco Secure Access Control Server (ACS) offers a downloadable ACL feature that can be used with Cisco headend devices to support large policies.

Tunnel-based VPNs (IPsec and SSL VPN clients) provide Layer 3 control at the protocol, port, and destination IP level. Clientless SSL VPNs can provide more granular Layer 7 access control, including URL-based access or file server directory-level access control.

Example: VPN Architecture

Figure 9-4 shows an example of a VPN design architecture that supports employees and partners. The employees connect across the Internet using an IPsec VPN client. The noncorporate users connect using SSL. The IPsec or SSL clients are authenticated using the AAA server. Both IPsec and SSL VPNs come in on the public interface of the VPN cluster and are terminated. Load balancing is used for resiliency, stateless failover, and capacity growth on the VPN cluster. The private interface of the VPN headend connects through routers to the internal corporate network. Inbound ACLs on the internal edge routers provide access control rules to permit traffic to specific internal resources.

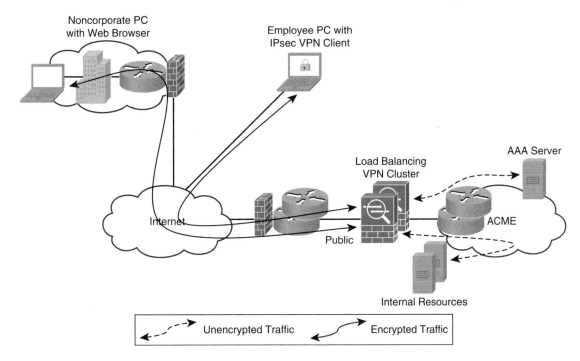

Figure 9-4   *VPN Architecture*

Users and partners are organized into various groups with appropriate security policy profiles and user authentication and authorization information. Both Cisco IPsec VPN and SSL VPN clients are supported, as is clientless SSL VPN with an optional port-forwarding feature.

Designing Site-to-Site VPNs

Site-to-site VPNs are an alternative WAN infrastructure used to connect branch offices, home offices, or business partners to all or portions of an enterprise network. VPNs do not inherently change private WAN requirements, such as support for multiple protocols, high reliability, and extensive scalability, but instead meet these requirements more cost-effectively and with greater flexibility but possibly lower performance or service-level agreements (SLA). Site-to-site VPNs use the most pervasive transport technologies available today, such as the public Internet or service provider IP networks, by using tunneling and encryption for data privacy and quality of service (QoS) for transport reliability.

Site-to-Site VPN Applications

Site-to-site VPNs can be used to replace costly WAN services or serve as a backup for disaster recovery purposes. Site-to-site VPNs can also help organizations meet regulatory requirements by providing encryption for sensitive data. This section examines these common uses for site-to-site IPsec VPNs.

WAN Replacement Using Site-to-Site IPsec VPNs

WAN replacement, as shown in Figure 9-5, is one of the main reasons organizations implement IPsec VPNs.

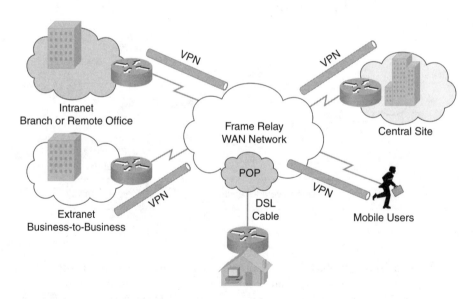

Figure 9-5   *WAN Replacement with VPN*

Up to 40 percent of typical enterprise employees work in branch offices, away from the central sites that provide mission-critical applications and services required for business operations. As these services are extended to branch office employees, requirements increase for bandwidth, security, and high availability.

IPsec VPNs can provide a cost-effective replacement for a private WAN infrastructure. Often, the cost of a relatively high-bandwidth IP connection, such as an ISP connection,

IP VPN service provider connection, or broadband digital subscriber line (DSL) or cable access, is lower than existing or upgraded WAN circuits.

Organizations can use IPsec VPNs to connect remote branches or offices, teleworkers, and mobile users to the corporate resources as the central site. Organizations also use IPsec VPNs to provide extranet connectivity for business-to-business applications.

There are four key components of site-to-site VPN:

- **Headend VPN devices:** Serve as VPN headend termination devices at a central campus
- **VPN access devices:** Serve as VPN branch-end termination devices at branch office locations
- **IPsec and generic routing encapsulation (GRE) tunnels:** Interconnect the headend and branch-end devices in the VPN
- **Internet services from ISPs:** Serve as the WAN interconnection medium

WAN Backup Using Site-to-Site IPsec VPNs

As shown in Figure 9-6, another common business application use for IPsec VPNs is backing up an existing WAN.

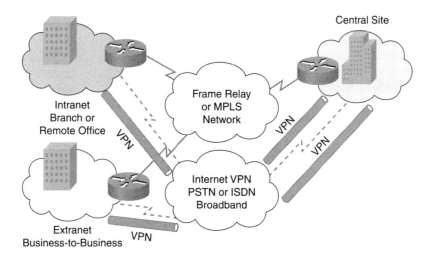

Figure 9-6   *WAN Backup via VPN*

When a primary network connection malfunctions, the remote branch office can rely on Internet VPN connectivity while waiting for the primary connection to be restored.

IPsec VPNs over a high-speed ISP connection or broadband cable or DSL access can provide a cost-effective secondary WAN connection for branch offices. Many customers continue to route their most critical traffic across their private WAN circuits and route higher-bandwidth, less-critical traffic across IPsec VPNs as a secondary connection path.

If a failure occurs on their primary WAN circuit, the IPsec VPN can also function as an established backup path.

Note   The Internet VPN option does not offer QoS and SLAs, which might be necessary for applications such as IP telephony.

Regulatory Encryption Using Site-to-Site IPsec VPNs

Another common business application use for IPsec VPNs is for mandatory or regulatory encryption.

Regulations such as the Health Insurance Portability and Accountability Act (HIPAA), the Sarbanes-Oxley Act (SOX), Payment Card Industry Data Security Standard (PCI DSS), and the Basel II agreement recommend or mandate the need for companies to implement all reasonable safeguards to protect personal, customer, and corporate information. IPsec VPNs inherently provide a high degree of data privacy through establishment of trust points between communicating devices, and data encryption with the Triple Data Encryption Standard (3DES) or Advanced Encryption Standard (AES).

Site-to-site VPNs support regulatory constraints and business policies. As network security risks increase and regulatory compliance becomes essential, organizations are using IPsec VPNs to encrypt and protect data such as medical records, corporate or personal financial data, and sensitive information such as legal, police, and academic records, whether a private WAN, IP VPN, or the Internet is used for connectivity.

Site-to-Site VPN Design Considerations

The design of site-to-site VPNS is impacted by the organization's routing and addressing schema. Other important design considerations are the size, scale, and performance expectations for the site-to-site VPN. These requirements drive the selection of and appropriate platform to provision the service. The following subsections examine these elements and their impact on site-to-site VPN design.

IP Addressing and Routing

An IPsec VPN is an overlay on an existing IP network.

The VPN termination devices need routable IP addresses for the outside Internet connection. Private IP addresses can be used on the inside of the VPN. Just as good IP network design supports summarization, the VPN address space needs to be designed to allow for network summarization. NAT may be needed to support overlapping address space between sites in an organization.

Most IPsec VPNs forward data across the network using IPsec tunnel mode, which encapsulates and protects an entire IP packet. Because tunnel mode encapsulates or hides the IP header of the pre-encrypted packet, a new IP header is added so that the packet can be successfully forwarded.

Many larger enterprise WANs need dynamic routing protocols such as Enhanced Interior Gateway Routing Protocol (EIGRP) and Open Shortest Path First (OSPF) to provide routing and maintain link state and path resiliency. All Interior Gateway Protocol (IGP) routing protocols use either broadcast or IP multicast as a method of transmitting routing table information. However, basic IPsec designs cannot transport IGP dynamic routing protocols or IP multicast traffic. When support for one or more of these features are required, IPsec should be used in conjunction with other technologies such as GRE.

Scaling, Sizing, and Performance

The task of scaling large IPsec VPNs while maintaining performance and high availability is challenging and requires careful planning and design. Many factors affect scalability of an IPsec VPN design, including the number of route sites, access connection speeds, routing peer limits, IPsec encryption engine throughput, features to be supported, and applications that will be transported over the IPsec VPN.

The number of remote sites is a primary factor in determining scalability of a design and affects the routing plan, high-availability design, and ultimately the overall throughput that must be aggregated by the VPN headend routers. Different routers can support different numbers of tunnels.

IPsec VPN throughput depends on several factors, including connection speeds, capacity of the crypto engine, and CPU limits of the router. An IPsec crypto engine in a Cisco IOS router is a unidirectional device that must process bidirectional packets. Outbound packets must be encrypted by the IPsec crypto engine, and inbound packets must be decrypted by the same device. For each interface having packets encrypted, it is necessary to consider the bidirectional speed of the interface. For example, a T1 connection speed is 1.544 Mbps, but the IPsec throughput required is 3.088 Mbps.

Cisco recommends the following practices for VPN device performance limits:

- The redundant headend device should be deployed in a configuration that results in CPU utilization less than 50 percent. The 50 percent target includes all overhead incurred by IPsec and any other enabled features, such as firewall, routing, intrusion-detection system (IDS), and logging. This performance limit allows the headend device to handle failover of the other headend device. As with any WAN implementation, a best practice is to test the termination devices throughput and application performance using the type of traffic used in the production network.

- Because branch devices need to support fewer additional tunnels in a failover event, branch devices can be deployed in a configuration with less than 65 percent CPU utilization.

Cisco Router Performance with IPsec VPNs

Because IPsec VPN connections do not normally have a bandwidth associated with them, the overall physical interface connection speeds of both the headend and branch routers largely determine the maximum speeds at which the IPsec VPN must operate.

Table 9-1 *Cisco Router Performance with IPsec VPNs*

Cisco VPN Security Router	Maximum Number of Tunnels	3 DES Throughput	AES Throughput
Cisco 850 series	5	8 Mbps	8 Mbps
Cisco 870 series	10	30 Mbps	30 Mbps
Cisco 1841 Integrated Services router with AIM-VPN/BPII	800	95 Mbps	95 Mbps
Cisco 2801 Integrated Services with AIM-VPN/BPII	1500	100 Mbps	100 Mbps
Cisco 2811 Integrated Services with AIM-VPN/EPII	1500	130 Mbps	130 Mbps
Cisco 2821 Integrated Services with AIM-VPN/EPII	1500	140 Mbps	140 Mbps
Cisco 2851 Integrated Services with AIM-VPN/EPII	1500	145 Mbps	145 Mbps
Cisco 3825 Integrated Services with AIM-VPN/EPII	2000	175 Mbps	175 Mbps
Cisco 3845 Integrated Services with AIM-VPN/EPII	2500	185 Mbps	185 Mbps
Cisco 7200VXR series with a Single Cisco SA-VAM2+	5000	260 Mbps	260 Mbps
Cisco 7301 router with Cisco SA-VAM2+	5000	370 Mbps	370 Mbps
Cisco Catalyst 6500/7600 router with 1 IPsec VPN SPA	8000	2.5 Gbps	2.5 Gbps

Table 9-1 shows best-case scenarios with minimal features running IPsec VPNs in a lab with 1400-byte packets.

Note Additional information, including the ISR G2 numbers, can be found at http://www.cisco.com/en/US/partner/prod/collateral/routers/ps10536/white_paper_c11_595485.pdf (Cisco.com login needed).

However, the packets-per-second (PPS) rate matters more than throughput bandwidth (in bits per second) for the connection speeds being terminated or aggregated. In general, routers and crypto engines have upper boundaries for processing a given number of PPS. The size of packets used for testing and throughput evaluations can understate or overstate true performance. For example, if a device can support 20 Kbps, 100-byte packets lead to 16 Mbps throughput, and 1400-byte packets at the same packet rate lead to 224 Mbps throughput. Because of such a wide variance in throughput, it is generally better to use PPS for scalability than bits per second.

Each time a crypto engine encrypts or decrypts a packet, it performs mathematical computations on the IP packet payload using the unique crypto key for the trust point, agreed upon by the sender and receiver. If more than one IPsec tunnel is terminated on a router, the router has multiple trust points and therefore multiple crypto keys. When packets are to be sent to or received from a different tunnel from the last packet sent or received, the crypto engine must swap keys to use the right key matched with the trust point. This key swapping can degrade the performance of a crypto engine, depending on its architecture, and increase the router CPU utilization. For some Cisco platforms, such as Cisco 7200VXR series routers with Cisco Service Adapter VPN Acceleration Module 2+ (SA-VAM2+), as the number of tunnels increases, throughput of the IPsec crypto engine decreases. For other Cisco platforms, such as Cisco 7600 series routers with VPN Shared Port Adapter (SPA), performance is relatively linear, with the same throughput for a single tunnel as for 1000 or even 5000 tunnels.

The Cisco Integrated Services Routers Generation 2 (ISR G2) provides a robust platform for delivering WAN services, unified communications, security, and application services to branch offices. These platforms are designed to support existing WAN access circuits and offer the performance that is needed for the transition to Ethernet-based access services. Table 9-2 shows comparable models from Generation 1 (G1) to Generation 2 (G2).

Cisco ISR G2 routers support faster interface and application module form factors, including a service module, an enhanced high-speed WAN interface card (EHWIC), and an internal services module. The new Cisco 1941W Integrated Services Router offers an IEEE 802.11N wireless option. Also included are system innovations such as the multigigabit fabric (MGF) for module-to-module communication, dual Compact Flash memory slots, and a Universal Serial Bus (USB) console interface.

Table 9-2   *Comparison of ISR G1 and G2*

Cisco ISR G1 Models	Comparable Cisco ISR G2 Models
1841	1941 and 1941W
2801	2901
2811	2911
2821	2921
2851	2951
3825	3925 and 3925E
3845	3945 and 3945E

All Cisco ISR G2 routers have an embedded encryption processor. The processor provides hardware-based acceleration for IPsec and SSL VPNs. For IPsec encryption, the acceleration chip performs the actual mathematical encryption, while relying on the router CPU to identify traffic for encryption, negotiate the security associations, and forward packets. This way, the encryption chip offloads the mathematically intensive part of the overall process, but the CPU is still involved in the overall processing and forwarding of the encrypted traffic.

Cisco ISR G2 routers have a higher-performing, onboard encryption accelerator than the original Cisco ISRs. The new encryption accelerator increases the VPN performance to two to three times that of the first generation of Cisco ISRs.

Note   The performance numbers in a production environment may differ.

Cisco ASA 5500 Series Performance

ASA 5500 series all-in-one Adaptive Security Appliances (ASA) deliver enterprise-class security and VPN services to small- and medium-size businesses and large enterprise networks in a modular, purpose-built appliance. The ASA 5500 series incorporates a wide range of integrated security services, including firewall, intrusion-prevention system (IPS), and anti-X services with SSL and IPsec VPN services in an easy-to-deploy, high-performance solution. The ASA 5500 series is the most feature-rich solution for SSL- and IPsec-based remote access that Cisco offers, and it supports robust site-to-site connectivity. The series provides higher scalability and greater throughput capabilities than the end-of-life Cisco VPN 3000 series concentrators.

Table 9-3 shows some best-case performance measures for the ASA 5500 series.

Table 9-3   *Cisco ASA 5500 Series Performance*

Model	SSL/IPsec Scalability	Maximum VPN Throughput
Cisco ASA 5505	25 simultaneous SSL sessions 25 simultaneous VPN sessions	100 Mbps
Cisco ASA 5510	250 simultaneous SSL sessions 250 simultaneous VPN sessions	170 Mbps
Cisco ASA 5520	750 simultaneous SSL sessions 750 simultaneous VPN sessions	225 Mbps
Cisco ASA 5540	2500 simultaneous SSL VPN sessions 5000 simultaneous VPN sessions	325 Mbps
Cisco ASA 5550	5000 simultaneous SSL sessions 5000 simultaneous VPN sessions	425 Mbps
Cisco ASA 5580	10,000 simultaneous SSL sessions 10,000 simultaneous VPN sessions	1 Gbps

Note   The performance numbers in a production environment may differ.

Typical VPN Device Deployments

Table 9-4 shows where Cisco VPN devices are typically deployed.

Table 9-4   *Typical VPN Device Deployment*

Location	Models
Teleworkers	Cisco 860, 880, and 890
Small office/home office (SOHO) Small business	Cisco 860, 880, and 890Cisco ASA 5505
Small branch	Cisco 1900 Cisco ASA 5510
Medium branch	Cisco 2900 Cisco ASA 5520
Enterprise branch	Cisco 3900 Cisco ASA 5540 and 5550
Enterprise edge	Cisco ASR 1000
Enterprise headquarters Data center	Catalyst 6500 Cisco ASR 1000 ASA 5580

The ASA 5500 series supports both IPsec VPNs and SSL-based remote-access VPN services deployments on a single integrated platform. Cisco ISRs and Cisco Catalyst switches support site-to-site IPsec VPNs of any topology, from hub and spoke to the more complex fully meshed VPNs on networks of all sizes, integrating security services with extensive Cisco IOS Software capabilities that include QoS, multiprotocol, multicast, and advanced routing support.

Design Topologies

A peer-to-peer IPsec VPN provides connectivity between two sites through a tunnel that secures traffic.

Typically, remote peers are connected to the central site over a shared infrastructure in a hub-and-spoke topology with tunnels from the multiple spokes to the headend hub. The hub-and-spoke topology scales well. However, a performance penalty applies for traffic between spoke sites because of the two encryption/decryption cycles such traffic requires. A meshed topology may be the appropriate design to use when there are multiple locations with a large amount of traffic flowing between them. To eliminate the performance penalty due to two encryption/decryption cycles for spoke-to-spoke traffic, a partial-mesh topology can be used. The partial-mesh topology is similar to a hub-and-spoke topology, but it supports some direct spoke-to-spoke connectivity.

The full-mesh topology provides direct connectivity between all locations. There are scaling issues as the number of IPsec tunnels needed grows exponentially as number of sites increases. This topology is also more difficult to provision.

> **Note**   Design topologies are discussed in more detail in the section, "Using IPsec VPN Technologies."

VPN Device Placement Designs

The following subsections provide an overview of various design options for placement of VPN devices in the network.

VPN Device Parallel to Firewall

The VPN device can be placed parallel to a firewall in the network, as shown in Figure 9-7.

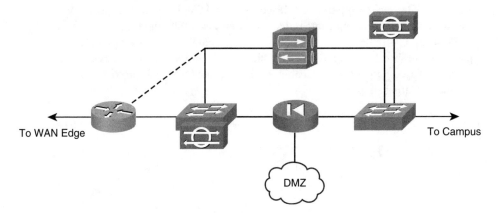

To WAN Edge   To Campus

DMZ

Figure 9-7   *VPN Device Placement: Parallel to Firewall*

There are advantages in placing the VPN device parallel to the firewall:

■ Simplified deployment because firewall addressing does not need to change

■ High scalability because multiple VPN devices can be deployed in parallel with the firewall

There are some disadvantages to placing the VPN device parallel to the firewall:

■ IPsec decrypted traffic is not firewall inspected. This issue is a major concern if the traffic is not subject to a stateful inspection.

■ No centralized point of logging or content inspection is implemented.

VPN Device on a Firewall DMZ

The VPN device can be placed in the demilitarized zone (DMZ) on the firewall in the network, as shown in Figure 9-8.

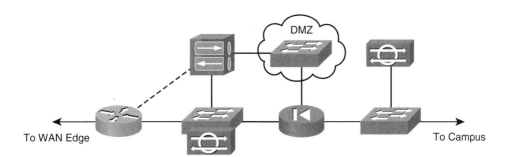

Figure 9-8 *VPN Device on a Firewall DMZ*

There are advantages to placing the VPN device in the DMZ of a firewall:

■ The firewall can statefully inspect the decrypted VPN traffic. The design supports the layered security model and enforces firewall security policies.

■ The design supports moderate-to-high scalability by adding additional VPN devices. Migration to this design is relatively straightforward with the addition of a LAN interface to firewall.

There are disadvantages to placing the VPN device in the DMZ of a firewall:

■ The configuration complexity increases because additional configuration on the firewall is required to support the additional interfaces. The firewall must support policy routing to differentiate VPN versus non-VPN traffic.

■ The firewall may impose bandwidth restrictions on stacks of VPN devices.

Integrated VPN and Firewall

Another option is an integrated VPN and firewall device in the network, as shown in Figure 9-9.

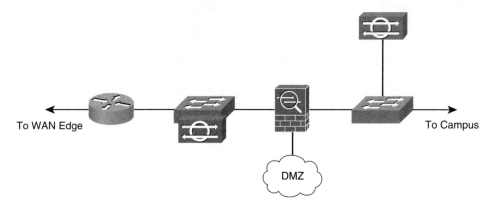

Figure 9-9   *Integrated VPN and Firewall*

There are advantages to integrating the VPN device and the firewall:

■   The firewall can statefully inspect the decrypted VPN traffic. The design supports the layered security model and enforces firewall security policies.

■   The design may be easier to manage with the same or fewer devices to support.

There are disadvantages to placing the VPN device in the DMZ of a firewall:

■   Scalability can be an issue because a single device must scale to meet the performance requirements of multiple features.

■   The configuration complexity increases because all the configurations are applied to one device.

Using IPsec VPN Technologies

Several types of IPsec VPNs are used to permit secure, encrypted communication between network devices.

IPsec VPN Overview

IPsec functionality provides data encryption at the IP packet level, offering a robust, standards-based security solution. Figure 9-10 shows the versatility of an IPsec VPN that allows significant client mobility.

Basic IPsec provides secure point-to-point tunnels between two peers, such as two routers. These tunnels are actually sets of security associations (SA) that are established between two IPsec peers. The SAs define which protocols and algorithms should be applied to sensitive packets and specify the keying material to be used by the two peers. SAs are unidirectional and are established per security protocol, either Authentication Header (AH) or Encapsulating Security Payload (ESP).

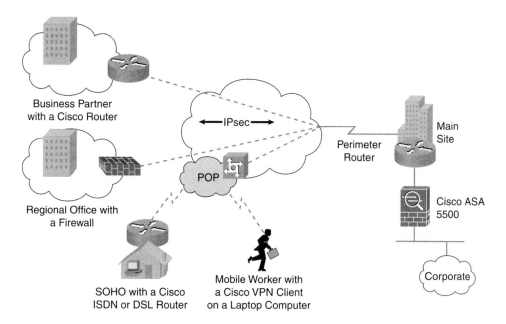

Figure 9-10 *IPsec VPN*

With IPsec, the network manager can define which traffic should be protected between two IPsec peers by configuring ACLs and applying these ACLs to interfaces by way of crypto maps. The ACLs used for IPsec are used only to determine which traffic should be protected by IPsec, not which traffic should be blocked or permitted through the interface. Separate ACLs define blocking and permitting at the interface.

IPsec can support certain traffic that is receiving one combination of IPsec protection (for example, authentication only) and other traffic that is receiving a different combination of IPsec protection (for example, both authentication and encryption) by using two different crypto ACLs to define the two different types of traffic. These different ACLs are then used in different crypto map entries, which specify different IPsec policies.

Standard IPsec VPNs support only unicast traffic, which is an issue for deploying them within an enterprise.

Extensions to Basic IPsec VPNs

Several site-to-site VPN solutions extend the capabilities of basic IPsec VPNs.

Cisco provides several site-to-site VPN solutions that support routing to deliver reliable transport for complex mission-critical traffic, such as voice and client/server applications. These solutions are built on five underlying VPN technologies:

- Cisco Easy VPN

- GRE tunneling

- Dynamic Multipoint VPN (DMVPN)

- Virtual tunnel interfaces (VTI)

- Group Encrypted Transport VPN (GET VPN)

Each technology is customized to meet specific deployment requirements.

Cisco Easy VPN

The Cisco Easy VPN solution provides simple VPN deployments for remote offices and teleworkers.

Ease of deployment is critical when technical resources are not available for VPN configuration at remote offices and for teleworkers. The Cisco Easy VPN solution centralizes VPN management across all Cisco VPN devices and reduces the management complexity of VPN deployments. The Cisco Easy VPN Remote feature and the Cisco Easy VPN Server feature offer flexibility, scalability, and ease of use for site-to-site and remote-access VPNs.

The Cisco Easy VPN Remote feature allows Cisco routers running Cisco IOS Software Release 12.2(4)YA (or later releases), Cisco ASA firewalls, and Cisco hardware clients to act as remote VPN clients. These devices can receive predefined security policies and configuration parameters from the VPN headend at the central site, which minimizes the VPN configuration required at the remote location. Parameters such as internal IP addresses, internal subnet masks, DHCP server addresses, Microsoft WINS server addresses, and split-tunneling flags are all pushed to the remote device.

The Cisco Easy VPN Server feature, available in Cisco IOS Software Release 12.2(8)T or later releases, increases compatibility of Cisco VPN products, and allows Cisco VPN concentrators, Cisco ASA firewalls, and Cisco routers to act as VPN headend devices in site-to-site or remote-access VPNs. With this feature, security policies defined at the headend can be pushed to the remote-office devices running the Cisco Easy VPN Remote feature.

Overview of Cisco Easy VPN Server Wizard on Cisco SDM

The Cisco Router and Security Device Manager (SDM) Easy VPN Server Wizard can configure the Cisco Easy VPN Server on Cisco routers.

Note SDM is end of life, but is included here because it is within the domain of the exam. For more information, as well as its replacement with Cisco Configuration Professional, see http://www.cisco.com/en/US/prod/collateral/routers/ps5318/eol_c51-620445.html.

The Cisco Easy VPN solution is ideal for remote offices with little IT support or for large customer deployments where it is impractical to individually configure multiple remote devices. This feature makes VPN configuration as easy as entering a password, which minimizes local IT support, increases productivity, and lowers costs. Figure 9-11 shows the starting Cisco SDM screen for the Easy VPN Server Wizard.

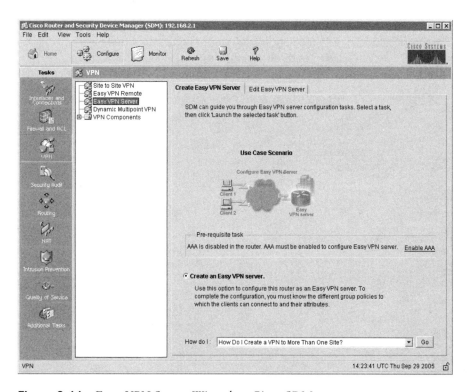

Figure 9-11 *Easy VPN Server Wizard on Cisco SDM*

The Easy VPN Server Wizard guides network administrators in performing the following tasks to successfully configure a Cisco Easy VPN Server on a router:

■ Selecting the interface on which the client connections will terminate

■ Configuring Internet Key Exchange (IKE) policies

■ Configuring the Group Policy lookup method

■ Configuring user authentication

- Configuring group policies on local database, if needed

- Configuring an IPsec transform set

Note   Cisco SDM supports VPNs with basic IPsec tunnels, GRE over IPsec tunnels, and DMVPN.

Note   The replacement for Cisco SDM is Cisco Configuration Professional (CCP). For more information about this product, see http://www.cisco.com/go/ciscocp.

Overview of Easy VPN Remote Wizard on Cisco SDM

The Cisco SDM Easy VPN Remote Wizard can configure the Cisco Easy VPN Remote devices. Figure 9-12 illustrates the SDM graphical configuration interface.

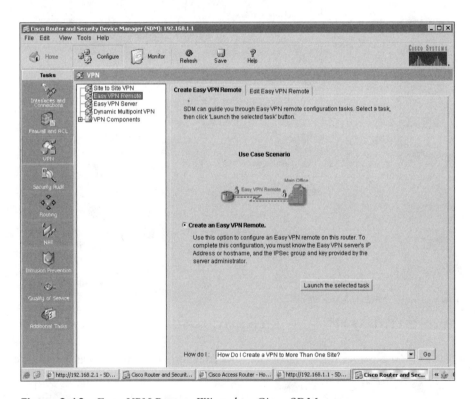

Figure 9-12   *Easy VPN Remote Wizard on Cisco SDM*

The Cisco SDM Easy VPN Remote Wizard can configure a remote router that will be connecting to the Cisco Easy VPN Server router. To launch the wizard in Cisco SDM, on the Tasks list on the left, click **VPN**. Select **Easy VPN Remote** in the tree hierarchy on the left. With the Create an Easy VPN Remote option selected, click the **Launch the Selected Task** button.

> **Note**   The Cisco Adaptive Security Device Manager (ASDM) can be used to configure Cisco Easy VPN Server or Remote operation on the Cisco ASA 5500 series appliances, Cisco PIX 500 series security appliances (running Cisco PIX Security Appliance Software Version 7.0 or later), and the Cisco Catalyst 6500 series Firewall Services Module (FWSM) Version 3.1 or later.

GRE over IPsec Design Recommendations

Basic IPsec designs cannot transport IGP dynamic routing protocols or IP multicast traffic because the IPsec ESP only tunnels unicast IP traffic. To support the routing or IP multicast requirements of most enterprises, IPsec should be used in conjunction with other technologies, such as GRE.

GRE tunneling, as shown in Figure 9-13, encapsulates non-IP and IP multicast or broadcast packets into IP unicast packets. These GRE packets can be encrypted by the IPsec tunnel. At the remote end of the IPsec tunnel, both the IPsec encapsulation and the GRE encapsulation are removed to recover the original packet. With GRE over IPsec designs, the hub router uses a single GRE interface for each spoke.

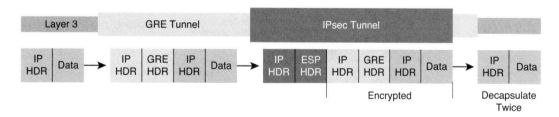

Figure 9-13   *Tunnels and IPsec*

GRE over IPsec Design Recommendations

A routing protocol can dynamically rebalance traffic across redundant headend routers on failover recovery. Although IPsec can typically scale to thousands of tunnels on some platforms, a routed point-to-point GRE over IPsec design is generally limited by the routing protocol being used and the number of routing peers exchanging routing information. In an aggressive design, the headend routing protocol can scale up to 500 peers:

■   Up to 500 peers for the Cisco 7200VXR series routers with Network Processing Engine-G1 (NPE-G1)

■   Up to 600 peers for the Cisco 7200VXR series with NPE-G2

■   Up to 1000 peers for the Cisco 7600 series router (or Cisco Catalyst 6500 series switches) with Supervisor Engine 720

EIGRP is recommended as the routing protocol because of its conservative use of router CPU and network bandwidth and its quick convergence times. EIGRP also provides a range of options for address summarization and default route propagation. It also permits much tighter control of routes advertised by allowing filtering at any point in the design, unlike OSPF. This can be a major scaling benefit for IPsec designs with many peers.

GRE keepalives can be used for failure detection in case of static routing on point-to-point tunnels. Beginning in Cisco IOS Software Release 12.2(8)T, the GRE keepalive feature is available for use on tunnel interfaces. This functionality allows the line protocol of the tunnel interface to track the reachability between the two tunnel endpoints. If GRE keepalives are sent and acknowledged by the remote router, the line protocol is "up." If successive GRE keepalives are not acknowledged, based on the configured interval and number of retries, the tunnel line protocol is marked "down."

Figure 9-14 shows a simple hub-and-spoke network with multiple headend devices for redundancy. Point-to-point GRE and crypto tunnels functionally coexist on the same router CPU on the headend devices. The headend supports multiple point-to-point GRE over IPsec tunnels for a prescribed number of branch-office locations. In addition to terminating the VPN tunnels at the central site, the headend can advertise branch routes using IP routing protocols such as EIGRP and OSPF.

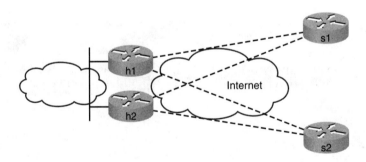

Figure 9-14   *GRE over IPsec*

To avoid asymmetric routing when routing is running over the tunnels, one of the GRE tunnels between the headend routers and each remote site must be favored. The routing metric should be consistent both upstream and downstream to prevent asymmetric routing. Preventing asymmetric routing allows more deterministic behavior of the traffic patterns.

There are options for configuring different paths in this design with slightly different metrics to provide preference between the tunnels:

■ Use the **delay** command under the GRE tunnel interface.

■ Set the bandwidth value for the GRE interface on both ends to match the speed of the actual link. This practice avoids unrealistic bandwidth settings that might affect the flow control of EIGRP.

Hub-and-spoke topologies are the most common topologies in a point-to-point GRE over IPsec design:

■ Although partial-mesh topologies are available, they are limited by both the routing protocol and the availability of static public IP addresses for the spokes.

■ Full-mesh topologies in a point-to-point GRE over IPsec design are also available and have the same limitations as partial-mesh topologies. With the administrative overhead involved, a full-mesh topology is not recommended in a point-to-point GRE over IPsec design.

DMVPN

Hub-and-spoke designs do not scale well for more than ten sites. With a traditional hub-and-spoke topology, all spoke-to-spoke traffic is through the hub. As more nodes are added to the topology, the configuration task becomes more complex because a separate GRE interface is needed on the hub for every spoke and all tunnels need to be predefined. In addition, the number of IPsec SAs grows as the number of spokes increases.

In these cases, dynamic peer discovery and on-demand tunnel creation mechanisms are required. When there is more than 20 percent spoke-to-spoke traffic or a full-mesh VPN topology is required, a DMVPN solution should be considered.

DMVPN Overview

DMVPN is a technology that supports IPsec VPNs with simplified configuration through crypto profiles and dynamic discovery of tunnel endpoints.

DMVPN enables dynamic configuration and reduces the maintenance and configuration on the hubs. DMVPN has a backbone hub-and-spoke topology, but allows direct spoke-to-spoke functionality using tunneling to enable the secure exchange of data between two branch offices without traversing the head office. DMVPN is a combination of IPsec, GRE, and Next Hop Resolution Protocol (NHRP).

DMVPN has several advantages:

■ With a dynamic mesh, the number of active tunnels is much lower on each spoke than with a full-mesh design. Smaller routers can be used at the spokes.

■ The configuration scales better because there is no need for static definitions for each spoke in the hub.

■ It is easier to add a node to the topology because there is no need to configure the new spoke on all the other nodes.

■ The spokes can have dynamic address or be behind NAT.

Note   You can use Cisco SDM to configure a router as a DMVPN hub or as a spoke router in a DMVPN network.

Example: DMVPN Topology

Figure 9-15 shows an example of a DMVPN topology. DMVPN does not alter the standards-based IPsec VPN tunnels, but it changes their configuration.

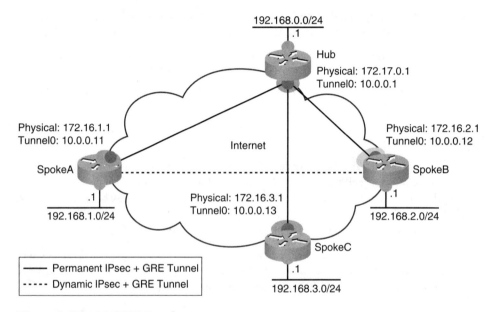

Figure 9-15   *DMVPN Topology*

The hub router maintains an NHRP database of public interface addresses for each spoke. The hub uses a single multipoint GRE (mGRE) tunnel interface to support multiple IPsec tunnels.

The spokes have a permanent IPsec tunnel to the hub but not to the other spokes. The spokes register as clients of the NHRP server. The spoke learns of all private networks on the other spokes and the hub through routing updates sent by the hub. A spoke queries the NHRP database for the real address of a destination spoke when it needs to communicate to another destination. The spoke uses the real destination address to build a dynamic IPsec tunnel to the target spoke. The spoke-to-spoke tunnel is also built over an mGRE interface. After the spoke-to-spoke tunnel is built, the IP next hop for the remote spoke network is the spoke-to-spoke tunnel interface. After a programmable timeout period, the NHRP entries age out, triggering IPsec to break down the dynamic spoke-to-spoke tunnel.

In Figure 9-15, spoke A uses the real IP address of 172.16.2.1 to bring up a tunnel to spoke B.

DMVPN Design Recommendations

Cisco recommends several practices for DMVPN with the hub-and-spoke topology:

- Use tunnel protection mode to associate a GRE tunnel with the IPsec profile on the same router. Tunnel protection mode specifies that IPsec encryption is performed after the GRE headers are added to the tunnel packet. Both ends of the tunnel need to be protected.

- Use IPsec in tunnel mode.

- Configure 3DES or AES for encryption of transported data.

- Use digital certificates or public key infrastructure (PKI) for scalable tunnel authentication. Typically, the CA is located on the private subnet of the hub.

- Configure EIGRP with route summarization for dynamic routing.

- Deploy hardware acceleration of IPsec to minimize router CPU overhead to support traffic with low-latency and -jitter requirements and for the highest performance for cost.

- Use an NHRP network ID and password key to prevent unauthorized nodes from joining the VPN. Provide each mGRE tunnel interface with a unique tunnel key, NHRP network ID, and IP subnet address. The mGRE tunnel key configured on the spokes must match the hub, and it is a recommended practice that the network ID matches on both sides of the tunnel.

- Use multiple NHRP servers on multiple hubs for backup and redundancy.

Note   For additional design and deployment recommendations for DMVPN, see the *DMVPN Design Guide* at http://www.cisco.com/en/US/partner/docs/solutions/ Enterprise/WAN_and_MAN/DMVPDG.html (Cisco.com login required).

Virtual Tunnel Interfaces Overview

Another mechanism for supporting VPNs is with IPsec virtual tunnel interfaces (VTI). IPsec VTIs provide a routable interface type for terminating IPsec tunnels and an easy way to define protection between sites to form an overlay network. A VTI supports native IPsec tunneling, and allows interface commands to be applied directly to the IPsec tunnels. The IPsec tunnel endpoint is associated with a virtual interface. Because there is a routable interface at the tunnel endpoint, many common interface capabilities can be applied to the IPsec tunnel.

The IPsec VTI supports QoS, multicast, and other routing functions that previously required GRE. VTIs allow for the flexibility of sending and receiving both IP unicast and multicast encrypted traffic on any physical interface, such as in the case of multiple paths. Traffic is encrypted or decrypted when it is forwarded from or to the tunnel interface and is managed by the IP routing table. Dynamic or static IP routing can be used to route the traffic to the virtual interface.

VTI simplifies VPN configuration and design. Customers can use the Cisco IOS virtual template to clone new virtual access interfaces for IPsec on demand. Using IP routing to forward the traffic to the tunnel interface simplifies the IPsec VPN configuration compared to the more complex process of using ACLs with the crypto map in native IPsec configurations. GRE or Layer 2 Tunneling Protocol (L2TP) tunnels are not needed for encapsulation. Dynamic VTIs (DVTI) function like any other real interface, so QoS, firewall, and other security services can be applied as soon as the tunnel is active. In addition, existing management applications now can monitor separate interfaces for different sites.

The use of VTIs improves network scaling. IPsec VTIs use single SAs per site, which cover different types of traffic and enable improved scaling as compared to GRE. A major benefit associated with IPsec VTIs is that the configuration does not require a static mapping of IPsec sessions to a physical interface. This also allows an ACL to be applied, unlike a standalone crypto map.

Both static VTIs (SVTI) and DVTIs are available. SVTI configurations can be used for site-to-site connectivity in which a tunnel provides always-on access between two sites. The advantage of using SVTIs as opposed to crypto map configurations is that users can enable dynamic routing protocols on the tunnel interface without the extra 4 bytes that are required for GRE headers, thus reducing the bandwidth for sending encrypted data. DVTIs can provide highly secure and scalable connectivity for remote-access VPNs. The DVTI technology replaces dynamic crypto maps and the dynamic hub-and-spoke method for establishing tunnels. DVTIs can be used for both the server and remote configuration.

Note   You can use Cisco SDM to configure Cisco Easy VPN Server and Cisco Easy VPN Remote with IPsec DVTIs.

VTIs support interoperability with standards-based IPsec installations of other vendors.

Both Cisco Easy VPN Server and Remote support DVTIs. The tunnels provide an on-demand separate virtual access interface for each Cisco Easy VPN connection. The Cisco Easy VPN with DVTI configuration provides a routable interface to selectively send traffic to different destinations, such as a Cisco Easy VPN concentrator, a different site-to-site peer, or the Internet. The IPsec DVTI configuration does not require a static mapping of IPsec sessions to a physical interface. This allows for the flexibility of sending and receiving encrypted traffic on any physical interface, such as in the case of multiple paths. Traffic is encrypted when it is forwarded from or to the tunnel interface.

Group Encrypted Transport VPN

The Cisco Group Encrypted Transport VPN (GET VPN) feature is a Cisco IOS Software solution that provides a tunnel-less technology to provide end-to-end security for voice, video, and data in a native mode for a fully meshed network. GET VPN can secure IP multicast group traffic or unicast traffic over a private WAN. It uses the ability of the core network to route and replicate the packets between various sites within the enterprise. GET VPN preserves the original source and destination addresses in the encryption header for optimal routing; hence, it is largely suited for an enterprise running a Multiprotocol Label Switching (MPLS) or IP VPN networks, where the enterprise private addresses are capable of being routed by the medium transporting the GET VPN traffic.

GET VPN is enabled in customer-edge routers without using tunnels. GET VPN uses Group Domain of Interpretation (GDOI) as the keying protocol with IPsec for efficiently encrypting and decrypting the data packets.

GET VPN enables the router to apply encryption to nontunneled (that is, "native") IP multicast and unicast packets and eliminates the requirement to configure tunnels to protect multicast and unicast traffic.

GET VPN is supported on Cisco IOS Software Release 12.4(11)T and on Cisco VPN acceleration modules:

- Cisco AIM-VPN/SSL module for Cisco ISRs

- Cisco VPN Acceleration Module 2+ (VAM2+) for Cisco 7200 series routers and Cisco 7301 routers

GET VPN Topology

GET VPN uses a group management model in which the GDOI protocol operates between a group member and a group controller or key server. The GET VPN architectural components are illustrated in Figure 9-16.

The key server, shown in Figure 9-16, establishes SAs among authorized group members. GDOI is protected by a Phase 1 Internet Security Association and Key Management Protocol (ISAKMP) SA.

Three traffic flows are necessary for group members to participate in a group:

- The group member registers with the key server to get the IPsec SA or SAs that are necessary to communicate with the group. The group member provides the group ID to the key server to get the respective policy and keys for this group. The key server authenticates and authorizes the group members and downloads the IPsec policy and keys that are necessary for them to encrypt and decrypt IP multicast packets. The key server is responsible for maintaining the policy and creating and maintaining the keys for the group.

- Group members exchange IP multicast packets that are encrypted using IPsec.

■ Because the key server is also responsible for rekeying the group before existing keys expire, the key server pushes a rekey message to the group members. The rekey message contains new IPsec policy and keys to use when old IPsec SAs expire. Rekey messages are sent in advance of the SA expiration time to ensure that valid group keys are always available.

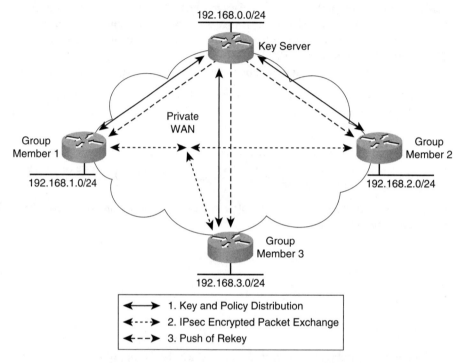

Figure 9-16 *GET VPN Topology*

Table 9-5 summarizes the differences in the different IPsec VPN types.

Table 9-5 *Comparison of IPsec VPN Types*

	Dynamic Routing	IP Multicast	Tunnels Traffic	Dynamic Meshing
IPsec direct encapsulation	No	No	Yes	No
Point-to-point GRE over IPsec	Yes	Yes	Yes	No
DMVPM	Yes	Yes	Yes	Yes
VTI	Yes	Yes	Yes	
GET VPN	Yes	Yes	No	Yes

Managing and Scaling VPNs

The Cisco security management products and internal processes can be used for scalable VPN administration and enforcement. Scaling VPNs involves several considerations, including crypto engine performance for real-time traffic and routing characteristics and metrics.

Recommendations for Managing VPNs

There are several recommended practices for managing VPNs:

- Use dedicated management interfaces if possible for out-of-band (OOB) management. If this is not possible, use a VPN for secure management and restrict access over the tunnel to management protocols only.

- Take precautions when managing a VPN device across the Internet. You should use strong authentication, integrity, and encryption practices. You should use a different username for configuration management and for troubleshooting. If you cannot use IPsec to connect to remote devices, use Secure Shell (SSH) or SSL for access.

- Use static public IP addresses at remote sites and static crypto maps at the headend to manage remote devices through a VPN tunnel. Be aware that some services such as TFTP do not always use the public IP address as the source address.

- Use the available IPsec information. IPsec information can be accessed minimally through syslog information or with the IPsec Message Information Base (MIB) via Simple Network Management Protocol (SNMP).

Considerations for Scaling VPNs

Scaling VPNs depends on many factors, but the primary issue is the offered load, in number of PPS, from the branch routers. The rate in PPS matters more than throughput bandwidth for the connection speeds being terminated or aggregated. In general, routers and crypto engines have upper boundaries for processing a given number of packets per second. Each time a crypto engine encrypts or decrypts a packet, it performs mathematical computations on the IP packet payload using the crypto key for the tunnel. The crypto engine performance measured in PPS is the key for sizing the headend.

The scalability of a VPN design depends on a number of elements, as listed here. Carefully consider these when selecting the technologies and platforms that are most appropriate for a given VPN design:

- **Number of branch offices:** The number of branch offices that will be aggregated over the IPsec VPN is a primary factor in determining scalability of a design. In addition to being a primary factor of the design, the number of branch offices affects the routing plan, the high-availability design, and ultimately, the overall throughput that must be aggregated by the VPN headend router or routers.

- **Connection speeds and packets per second:** Because individual IPsec VPN connections do not have a bandwidth associated with them, the overall physical interface connection speeds of both the headend and branch routers largely determine the maximum speeds at which the IPsec VPN must operate. When selecting a platform for the headend and branch routers, the VPN throughput in PPS and the physical interface speed should be considered.

- **IGP routing peers:** For routed IPsec VPN designs, the number of IGP routing peers that must be maintained by the headend aggregation routers is a primary determining factor in the scalability of the design. Specific performance depends on the aggregation router platform and its CPU capacity, which IPsec design is implemented, the number of peer branch routers exchanging routing, and whether there are secondary and backup IPsec tunnels to alternate headends for high availability.

- **High availability:** The nature of the high-availability design requirements affects the scalability of the deployment. If multiple headends are deployed at a single or different geographic sites, with each branch router having an IPsec tunnel to primary or secondary and possibly backup headends, the number of total IPsec tunnels that needs to be aggregated is doubled, tripled, or even quadrupled.

- **Supported applications:** The expected traffic mix on the VPN network is a major factor in estimating the required packets-per-second rates, and the traffic mix is determined by the applications that will be transported over the VPN. Another major design factor is whether the design needs to support multicast, which is also determined by the applications to be used across the VPN.

The marketing numbers for crypto performance rate performance in megabits per second, with 100 percent CPU usage, and using even maximum transmission unit (MTU)-size (approximately 1400-byte) packets to achieve the best results. This is an unrealistic traffic pattern. Internet mix (IMIX) traffic contains a mixture of frame sizes in a ratio to each other that approximates the overall makeup of frame sizes observed in real Internet traffic. Using IMIX traffic provides a better simulation of real network traffic. Converged traffic with a mix of 30 percent voice traffic at a maximum of 80 percent CPU utilization is the most realistic simulation of real network traffic for enterprise networks. Figure 9-17 compares the relative performance of three types of traffic on a router.

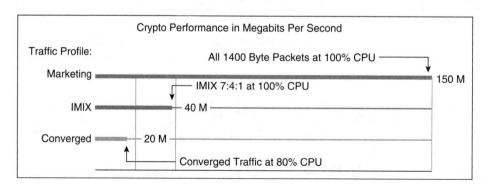

Figure 9-17 *Packets per Second Versus Megabits per Second*

PPS is a more critical metric than the number of tunnels, although the number of tunnels impacts the routing processes on the CPU. The number of tunnels also impacts crypto processing; if more than one IPsec tunnel is terminated on a router, the router has multiple crypto keys. When packets are to be sent or received to a different tunnel than the last packet sent or received, the crypto engine must swap keys. This key swapping can degrade the performance of a crypto engine, depending on its architecture, and increase the router CPU utilization.

Determining PPS

The number of packets per second per connection is determined by user applications on the network. High megabit-per-second throughput in the network typically corresponds to a large byte size per packet. The presence of VoIP in network decreases the average packet size and increases the number of packets per second.

To correctly simulate network behavior, test tools must emulate real application behavior. Using packet-blasting tools for testing is a poor indicator of real-world performance.

Enterprise WAN Categories

By categorizing enterprise WANs as shown in Table 9-6, it's possible to estimate the type of traffic to expect from the remote branches when scaling the VPN.

Table 9-6   *Enterprise WAN Categories*

	Point of Sale	Teleworker or Tele-Agent	Integrated Services Branch
Number of branches	Extra large: 1000–10,000	Large: 1000–3000	Medium: 500–1000
VoIP support	No	Yes, usually 1 call	Yes, 33% bandwidth
IP multicast	Generally not	Nice to have	Yes
Availability	Required (asynchronous dial backup)	Too costly (dial bandwidth insufficient for VoIP)	Multiple WAN links
Physical interface	Broadband or POTS	Broadband	Leased line

Table 9-6 illustrates how enterprise WANs can be categorized into three groups:

- **Point-of-sale WANs:** These WANs typically support a high number of retail branches for credit card and point-of-sale applications. The number of branches here may be 2000 or more. They have low data volume and do not support VoIP or IP multicast. The WANs need availability that the routing protocol provides. The physical interface for the remote sites is typically broadband or dialup plain old telephony service (POTS).

- **Teleworker or tele-agent WANs:** These WANs typically support a single user with an IP phone at the remote end. In the Cisco enterprise architecture, this is the "branch of one" or "teleworker" design. There can be large numbers of remote sites to support. Support for IP multicast is nice to have but might not be present. Backup availability is typically not provided because dial backup bandwidth is insufficient for the VoIP application. The remote sites typically connect using broadband.

- **Integrated services branch WAN:** These WANs typically connect remote enterprise branches to the central site. They also have high or bursty data volume and a relatively high number of branches, from 500 to 1000. They are likely to support converged applications, including voice, video, and IP multicast. VoIP traffic is typically 30 percent of the bandwidth. Backup availability is provided with multiple WAN links. The physical interface is typically a leased line or high-speed DSL.

Traffic Profiles per Branch Router

The major factor in headend VPN scaling is the PPS load of the hub for switching packets. Packet switching is impacted by the size of the packets. Based on field testing, the Cisco Enterprise Systems Engineering group has developed the following traffic profiles for representing real enterprise branch routers in the lab. Table 9-7 shows how the average packet size is influenced by the applications in use in the traffic profile.

Table 9-7   *Traffic Profiles per Branch Router*

Point of Sale	Teleworker or Tele-Agent	Integrated Services Branch Enterprise Mixed Voice and Video-Enabled VPN
TCP, 18 HTTP get, 300 bytes up, 1000 bytes down 2 FTP (1 up, 1 down, and 120K file size)	UDP, 1 G.729 voice call (100 PPS), 1 DNS, 1 POP3, 1 call setup (CS3), 1 TN3270 (best effort), 1 TN3270 (AF21), 1 HTTP (best effort), 1 HTTP (AF21), 1 FTP (1 up 240,000 file)	UDP, 33% bandwidth for G.729 VoIP (100 PPS per call), 9 calls per T1, 9 DNS, 4 POP3, 6 TN3270 (best effort), 6 TN3270 (AF21), 3 HTTP (best effort), 3 HTTP (AF21), 4 FTP (2 up, 2 down, 768,000 file)

Traffic pattern profiling considerations include the following:

- Does traffic mix include VoIP, video, or IP multicast? What VoIP codec is in use (G.711 at 4 Kbps versus G.729 at 8 Kbps)?

- Do the devices support changing interface MTU? Do devices use path MTU discovery? Is the router configured to adjust TCP maximum segment size (MSS)?

- What applications are in use? Is application optimization, such as HTTP pipelining, in place?

- Scaling considerations at the headend are also impacted by the number of neighbors per hub, which impacts path selection overhead.

Example: Enterprise Mix Packet Size

Figure 9-18 shows the average packet sizes for representative downstream and upstream traffic captured with NetFlow. The key point to notice is that the average packet size with VoIP traffic in the mix is significantly smaller than the 1400-byte packets used to describe marketing performance.

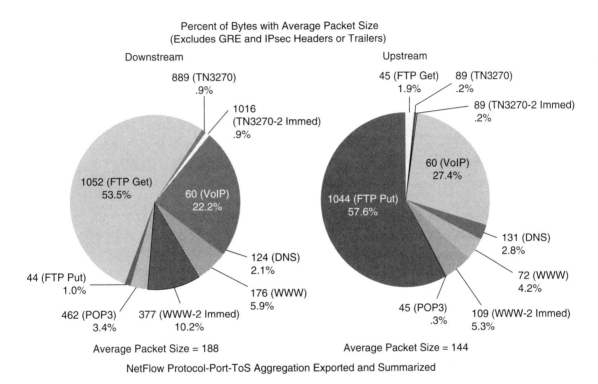

Figure 9-18 *Enterprise Mix Packet Size*

Note Because average packet size varies depending on the applications used, you should measure average packet size in your own environment.

Estimated PPS Based on Branch Profile

To accurately size the headend device, you need to measure the average and busy hour PPS rate of the branch routers. Figure 9-19 illustrates rough PPS estimates.

The Enterprise Systems Engineering group has the following rough PPS estimates that can be a starting point for VPN scaling:

■ A point-of-sale branch on a low speed link that supports only data may have only an average of 50 PPS of traffic.

- A teleworker on a higher-speed link has higher traffic requirements. The teleworker may generate 125 to 800 PPS depending on the link speed and network configuration.

- The integrated services branch may need to support multiple voice calls. If we use the general principle that 30 percent of the bandwidth is used for voice, a T1 line could support 9 voice calls of 100 or 50 PPS in both directions. The headend would need to support 900 PPS for VoIP traffic plus the data requirements of the remote site.

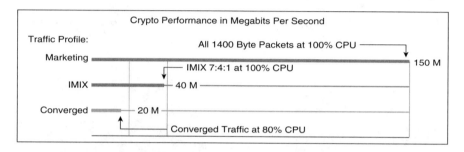

Figure 9-19   *Estimated PPS Based on Branch Profile*

Determining the PPS Rate

If you are migrating an existing network, you can measure the average and busy hour PPS rate of the existing branch routers.

Measuring traffic rates at the remote branches at the busy hour will provide useful data because most network managers do not know the details of bandwidth use. Many network managers, when asked, do not have any details and may reply, "I have 500 branches and a 45-Mbps link at the headend." Network designers need to know details of bandwidth use, not just how the network is implemented.

The measurement can be as simple as using the **show interfaces fastethernet** *number* | **include rate** command. You can also use network management tools to query SNMP or NetFlow data.

Example: Packet and Application View from NetFlow Analyzer 5

Figure 9-20 illustrates a view from the AdventNet ManageEngine NetFlow Analyzer 5 of the packets per hour and types of packets for a teleworker that supported a conference call, web-based data backup, and some web surfing during the day.

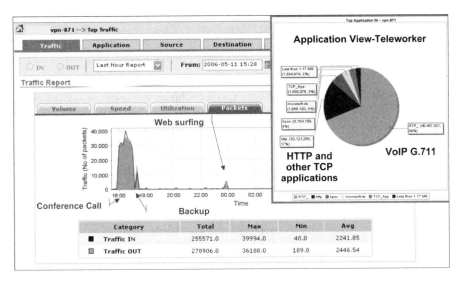

Figure 9-20 *Packet and Application View from NetFlow Analyzer 5*

Routing Protocol Considerations for IPsec VPNs

Both EIGRP and OSPF are appropriate enterprise routing protocols that can be supported on IPsec with GRE tunnels, DMVPNs, VTIs, and GET VPNs.

The distance vector characteristics of EIGRP are typically better for the hub-and-spoke
VPN topology:

- EIGRP can summarize per interface. By summarizing to the core and to the spoke, the
  branch routers will have fewer routes in the routing table.

- EIGRP is a "quiet" protocol when it is configured with stubs. There is no need to
  flood the topology database with EIGRP.

- EIGRP stub eliminates queries to spokes. As a recommended practice, configure the
  branch routers as stubs. The stub routers receive the default route from the headend
  router and advertise back up the branch subnets.

There are some disadvantages to the link-state characteristics of OSPF for hub-and-spoke
IPsec VPNs:

- OSPF needs to synchronize router databases periodically.

- OSPF brings hierarchy decisions into the hub-and-spoke topology. The number of
  routers per area needs to be allocated. A recommended practice is to use a power of
  two subnets for best summarization.

- OSPF stubs require the use of default routes. However, the default route in OSPF typically points to the Internet, not a tunnel.

- OSPF does not permit filtering of routes per se. Totally stubby areas are about the only way to really limit the information propagated by OSPF across multiple WAN (IPsec) sites.

With either protocol, increasing the number of neighbors increases the amount of process switching the hub routers need to support. Buffer tuning can help maintain network stability by minimizing the number of buffer misses and failures that may equate to losing or dropping neighbors.

EIGRP Metric Component Consideration

The EIGRP metric components can impact IPsec VPNs.

EIGRP calculates delay as the cumulative network delay. It adds the delay from all the hops to the source network. EIGRP delay is based on the input interface value of the receiving router.

EIGRP uses the minimum bandwidth for all the links to a network. The default bandwidth value for a tunnel is 9000 bps. EIGRP updates are throttled to 50 percent of bandwidth of the interface. You should consider matching tunnel bandwidth to physical link value if you send more than the default route and a summary route across a link because the EIGRP process can be throttled by the 9000 default bandwidth value of the tunnel.

Summary

VPNs allow organizations to securely connect remote offices and remote users using cost-effective, third-party Internet access rather than expensive dedicated WAN links. By deploying VPNs over high-bandwidth transport such as DSL, Ethernet, and cable, organizations can easily reduce their connectivity costs while simultaneously increasing remote connection bandwidth. VPNs are an alternative to Frame Relay and leased-line WAN infrastructures used to provide network connectivity for branch offices, home office intranets, and business partner extranets. Encrypted VPNs also provide the highest possible level of security through advanced encryption and authentication protocols to protect data from unauthorized access. With encrypted VPNs, corporations are able to increase the capacity of data, users, and connections, without significantly adding to an existing infrastructure. Encrypted VPNs provide more flexibility and scalability than Frame Relay and leased-line connections by enabling corporations to take advantage of the easy to provision Internet infrastructure within ISPs and easily add new users. As a result, corporations are able to dramatically increase capacity without the need to significantly expand infrastructure.

The two types of encrypted VPNs are site-to-site VPNs and remote-access VPNs:

- Site-to-site encrypted VPNs provide the same benefits as a private WAN, ensuring private communications from one trusted site to another, providing multiprotocol support, high reliability, and extensive scalability. In addition, site-to-site encrypted VPNs are cost-effective, secure, and allow for greater administrative flexibility than legacy private WANs.

- Remote-access VPNs are also a flexible and cost-effective alternative to private dialup solutions, and, in fact, VPNs have become the logical solution for remote access connectivity. Deploying a remote-access VPN helps reduce organizations' communications expenses by using the local dialup infrastructures of ISPs. Similarly, remote-access VPNs allow mobile workers, telecommuters, partners, and day extenders to take advantage of broadband connectivity.

This chapter covered the following VPN topics:

- Remote-access VPNs permit secure, encrypted connections between mobile or remote users and their corporate networks using IPsec and SSL technologies.

- Site-to-site VPNs are an alternative WAN infrastructure used to connect branch offices, home offices, and business partners to all or portions of an enterprise network using service provider networks.

- Several types of technologies can support IPsec VPNs, including Cisco Easy VPN, GRE over IPsec, DMVPN, VTI, and GET VPN.

- Both products and internal processes are needed for managing VPNs. Scaling VPNs involves several considerations, including crypto engine performance for real traffic and routing characteristics.

References

For additional information, refer to these resources:

Cisco Systems, Inc. *Cisco Virtual Office Whitepapers* at http://www.cisco.com/en/US/netsol/ns855/networking_solutions_white_papers_list.html

Cisco Systems, Inc. *IPsec VPN WAN Design Overview* at http://www.cisco.com/application/pdf/en/us/guest/netsol/ns171/c649/ccmigration_09186a008074f22f.pdf

Cisco Systems, Inc. *Point-to-Point GRE over IPsec Design Guide* at http://www.cisco.com/application/pdf/en/us/guest/netsol/ns171/c649/ccmigration_09186a008073a0c5.pdf

Cisco Systems, Inc. *Dynamic Multipoint VPN (DMVPN) Introduction* at http://www.cisco.com/en/US/partner/products/ps6658/index.html

Cisco Systems, Inc. *Dynamic Multipoint VPN (DMVPN) Design Guide* at
http://www.cisco.com/en/US/partner/docs/solutions/Enterprise/WAN_and_MAN/
DMVPDG.html

Cisco Systems, Inc. *IPsec Virtual Tunnel Interface* at http://www.cisco.com/univercd/
cc/td/doc/product/software/ios124/124cg/hsec_c/part17/ch10/hipsctm.pdf

Cisco Systems, Inc. *Cisco Group Encrypted Transport VPN* at http://www.cisco.com/
univercd/cc/td/doc/product/software/ios124/124newft/124t/124t11/htgetvpn.pdf

Cisco Systems, Inc. *Cisco IPsec and SSL VPN Solutions Portfolio* at
http://www.cisco.com/warp/public/cc/so/neso/axso/rmax/ipss_ds.pdf

AdventNet, Inc. *AdventNet ManageEngine NetFlow Analyzer User Guide* at
http://manageengine.adventnet.com/products/netflow/NetFlowAnalyzer_UserGuide.pdf

Cisco Systems, Inc. *Cisco AnyConnect VPN Client Administrator Guide, Release
2.4* at http://www.cisco.com/en/US/docs/security/vpn_client/anyconnect/anyconnect24/
administration/guide/anyconnectadmin24.html

Cisco Systems, Inc. *Cisco Configuration Professional Introduction* at
http://www.cisco.com/en/US/products/ps9422/index.html

Cisco Systems, Inc. *Enterprise Branch Security Design Guide* at
http://www.cisco.com/en/US/docs/solutions/Enterprise/Branch/E_B_SDC1.html

Cisco Systems, Inc. *Cisco Easy VPN* at
http://www.cisco.com/en/US/products/sw/secursw/ps5299/index.html

Cisco Systems, Inc. *ISR G2 'at a glance'* at
http://www.cisco.com/en/US/prod/collateral/routers/ps10538/aag_c45_556315.pdf

Cisco Systems, Inc. *ASR 10000 'at a glance'* at
http://www.cisco.com/en/US/solutions/collateral/ns341/ns524/ns562/ns592/at_a_
glance_c45-451487.pdf

Review Questions

Answer the following questions, and then refer to Appendix A, "Answers to Review
Questions," for the answers.

1. What is the recommended practice for deploying the VPN termination device for
    best security?

    a. To terminate any IPsec tunnels on an inline firewall

    b. To place the VPN termination device in line with a firewall

    c. To place the VPN termination device parallel to a firewall

    d. To place the private side of the VPN termination device in a DMZ behind a firewall

    e. To place the public side of the VPN termination device in a DMZ behind a firewall

2. What is the most common address assignment design for remote-access VPNs?

   a. Using a dedicated scope of DHCP addresses associated with a specific VPN headend

   b. Using internal address pools per VPN headend and implementing a static route for these subnets to the VPN headend

   c. Using RRI when IPsec tunnels are terminated on an inline firewall

   d. Using static IP address assignment for end users with LDAP and RRI

   e. Using static IP address assignment for end users with RADIUS and RRI

3. Of the following, which are site-to-site VPN applications? (Choose two.)

   a. WAN replacement

   b. Content rewriting

   c. Port forwarding

   d. Data privacy through 3DES or AES

   e. Mandated or regulatory encryption

4. What is the typical IPsec deployment design?

   a. Basic IPsec tunnels transporting IP unicast and multicast traffic

   b. Full-mesh topology with direct connectivity between all locations

   c. Partial-mesh topology with direct connectivity between many locations

   d. Remote peers connected over a shared infrastructure in a spoke to-spoke topology

   e. Remote peers connected to the central site over a shared infrastructure in a hub-and-spoke topology

5. What are two characteristics of the Cisco Easy VPN solution?

   a. Use of the GDOI protocol

   b. Mesh design scalability for greater than ten sites

   c. Reduced management complexity for VPN deployments

   d. Use of Cisco Easy VPN Remote and Easy VPN services features

   e. Centralized VPN management across all Cisco VPN devices

6. Of the following, which are advantages of implementing DMVPN tunnels? (Choose two.)

 a. IP broadcast and multicast traffic support

 b. Deterministic mesh availability with fewer active tunnels on each spoke

 c. Dynamic mesh availability with fewer active tunnels on each spoke

 d. Hub-and-spoke tunnel creation dynamically based on traffic requirements

 e. Spoke-to-spoke tunnel creation dynamically based on traffic requirements

7. Of the following, which are characteristics of GET VPN? (Choose two.)

 a. It is a set of software features that provides a tunnel-less technology for end-to-end security.

 b. It provides a routable interface type for terminating IPsec tunnels.

 c. It secures IP multicast group traffic or unicast traffic over a private WAN.

 d. It supports interoperability with standards-based IPsec installations of other vendors.

 e. It uses a NHRP network ID and password key to prevent unauthorized nodes from joining the VPN.

8. What are three recommendations for managing VPNs?

 a. Use in-band management if possible.

 b. Use dedicated management interfaces if possible.

 c. Use the same username for configuration management and for troubleshooting.

 d. Use a different username for configuration management and for troubleshooting.

 e. Use IPsec rather than SSH or SSL for access to VPN devices across the Internet.

 f. Use SSH or SSL rather than IPsec for access to VPN devices across the Internet.

9. What is the primary issue in scaling VPNs?

 a. Crypto engine performance for large packets

 b. Megabits-per-second capacity of a headend router

 c. Number of routes in network

 d. Number of tunnels terminated at a headend router

 e. Packets-per-second capacity from remote routers

10. Which routing protocol is recommended for large-scale enterprise IPsec VPNs?

    a. BGP

    b. EIGRP

    c. OSPF

    d. RIPv2

    e. Static routing

11. Which VPN type does not tunnel traffic?

    a. IPsec direct encapsulation

    b. Point-to-point GRE over IPsec

    c. DMVPN

    d. VTI

    e. GET VPN

    f. All of the above

Chapter 10

IP Multicast Design

Upon completing this chapter, you will be able to

■ Provide an overview of IP multicast

■ Describe IP multicast design recommendations

■ Discuss security IP multicast considerations

Note Some of the information in this introduction and the first main section of this chapter is derived from the *Authorized Self-Study Guide: Building Scalable Cisco Internetworks (BSCI), Third Edition*, by Diane Teare and Catherine Paquet, Cisco Press, 2006 (ISBN 1-58705-223-7), which provides a detailed introduction to IP multicast and its associated protocols. Some questions related to this material in the "Review Questions" section at the end of this chapter also derive from those in this BSCI book.

Many types of data can be transferred between devices over an IP network, including document files, voice, and video. However, a traditional IP network is not efficient when sending the same data to many locations; the data is sent in unicast packets and is therefore replicated on the network for each destination. For example, if a CEO's annual video address is sent out on a company's network for all employees to watch, the same data stream must be replicated for each employee. Obviously, this consumes many resources, including precious WAN bandwidth.

Note In this chapter, the term *IP* refers to IP Version 4 (IPv4).

IP multicast technology enables data to be sent over networks to a group of destinations in the most efficient way. The data is sent from the *source* as one stream; this single data stream travels as far as it can in the network. Devices replicate the data only if they need to send it out on multiple interfaces to reach all members of the destination group, called the *receivers*.

Multicast groups are identified by Class D IP addresses, which are in the range from 224.0.0.0 to 239.255.255.255. IP multicast involves some new protocols for network devices, including two for informing network devices which hosts require which multicast data stream (Internet Group Management Protocol [IGMP] and Cisco Group Management Protocol [CGMP]) and one for determining the best way to route multicast traffic (Protocol Independent Multicast [PIM]).

This chapter first introduces IP multicast technologies and then explores IP multicast design recommendations. The chapter concludes with a discussion of security considerations for networks with IP multicast traffic.

IP Multicast Technologies

This section introduces IP multicast and the Internet Group Management Protocol (IGMP), Cisco Group Management Protocol (CGMP), and Protocol Independent Multicast (PIM) protocols.

Introduction to Multicast

This section compares multicast with unicast and introduces the concept of a multicast group. The types of applications that benefit from the use of multicasting are discussed, multicast adoption trends are reviewed, and how an application or user learns about available multicast sessions is described. The advantages and disadvantages of multicast are described, and the basics of IP and Layer 2 multicast addresses and multicast address assignment are introduced. The section concludes with an introduction to the Cisco multicast architecture.

Multicast Versus Unicast

When IP multicast is used to send data packets to multiple receivers, the packets are not duplicated for every receiver, but instead are sent in a single stream. Downstream routers replicate the packets only on links where receiving hosts exist. The sender, or source, of multicast traffic does not have to know the unicast addresses of the receivers.

In contrast, unicast transmission sends multiple copies of data packets, one copy for each receiver, addressed to the receiver's unicast address.

The unicast example at the top of Figure 10-1 shows a host transmitting three copies of a data packet and a network forwarding each packet to three separate receivers. The host sends to only one receiver at a time; it has to create a packet with a different destination address for each receiver.

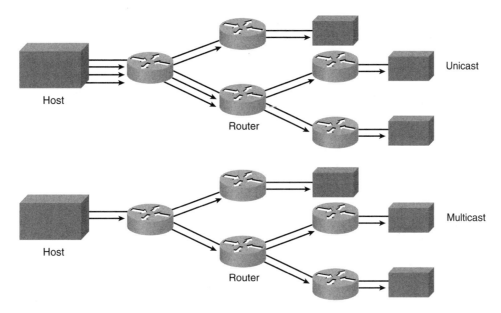

Figure 10-1 *Unicast Versus Multicast*

Unicast transmission requires a large amount of bandwidth. With unicast, the same information has to be sent multiple times, even on shared links. A large number of clients can impact the scalability of the network. If unicast is used as the means for transmitting the same data to multiple recipients, network managers must take the number of user connections and the number of replicated unicast transmissions into consideration. If the number of user connections or the amount of data to be sent becomes large, the network, or at least parts of it, might get overloaded.

The multicast example in the lower part of Figure 10-1 shows a host transmitting one copy of a data packet and a network replicating the packet at the last possible router for each receiver.

Note that there is only a single copy of each multicast packet on any given network segment. A host sends to multiple receivers simultaneously by sending only one packet, with one multicast destination address (the multicast group address). Downstream multicast routers replicate and forward the data packet to segments where there may be receivers.

IP Multicast Group Membership

With unicast IP addresses, a packet is routed from a source address to a destination address, traversing the IP network on a hop-by-hop basis.

IP multicast relies on the concept of a group address. In IP multicast, the destination address of a packet does not represent to a single destination, but instead represents a group of devices. When a receiver joins a multicast group, packets addressed to the group address flow to that receiver. All members of the group receive the packet.

The source address for multicast packets is always a unicast source address; multicast addresses are not used as source addresses.

A device must be a member of a group to receive the group's traffic. However, any multicast source device can transmit at any time to any group without joining that group. When a device sends multicast data to the group, all members of the group receive the data.

Figure 10-2 illustrates that packets that are sent to group addresses go to all group members but are not delivered to nongroup members. As shown in the figure, however, nongroup members can send packets to a group.

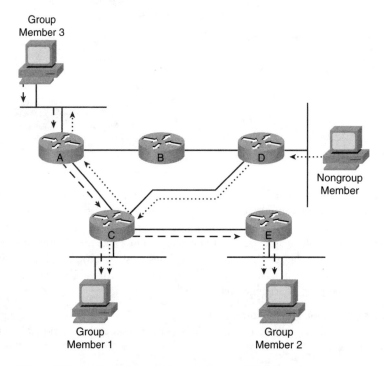

Figure 10-2 *IP Multicast Groups Define Who Receives Multicast Data*

Multicast Applications and Multicast Adoption Trends

IP multicast is used when simultaneous delivery for a group of receivers is required; hence, it is also called a *simulcast*.

There are various types of multicast applications. Two of the most common models are one to many and many to many.

In one-to-many applications, one sender sends data to many (two or more) receivers. This type of application may be used for audio or video distribution, push-media, announcements, monitoring, and so on. If a one-to-many application needs feedback from receivers, it may become a many-to-many application.

In many-to-many applications, any number of hosts send to the same multicast group. Two or more receivers also act as senders and a host can be a sender and a receiver simultaneously. Receiving data from several sources increases the complexity of applications and creates different management challenges. Using a many-to-many multicast concept as a foundation, a whole new range of applications may be built (for example, collaboration, concurrent processing, and distributed interactive simulations).

Other models (for example, many to one or few to many) are also used, especially in financial applications. The many-to-one multicast model is when many receivers are sending data back to one sender (via unicast or multicast) and may be used for resource-discovery, data-collection, auctions, polling, and similar applications.

Many new multicast applications are emerging as demand for them grows. Real-time applications include live TV, radio, and corporate broadcasts; financial data delivery; whiteboard collaboration; e-learning; and videoconferencing.

Non-real-time applications include file transfer, data and file replication, and video on demand (VoD). Ghosting multiple PC images simultaneously is a common file transfer application. Some forms of e-learning are also non-real-time applications.

Initially, multicast was adopted primarily by the research community. The first major enterprise deployments were in the financial services communities. E-learning (also called distance learning) and corporate communications were in the next wave of multicast applications. Content provisioning, multicast virtual private networks (VPN), IP Version 6 (IPv6) multicasting, and security surveillance are some of the more recent multicast applications.

Learning About Multicast Sessions

Whenever a multicast application is started on a receiver, the application has to learn about the available sessions or streams, which typically map to one or more IP multicast groups. The application may then request to join the appropriate multicast groups.

There are several possibilities for applications to learn about the sessions, including the following:

- The application may join a well-known, predefined group to which another multicast application sends announcements about available sessions.

- Some type of directory services may be available, and the application may contact the appropriate directory server.

- The application may be launched from a web page on which the sessions are listed as URLs.

- An email may be sent announcing the session; the user clicks the link in the email to join the session.

Another option is the use of the application called Session Directory (sd), which acts like a TV guide for displaying multicast content. A client application runs on a user's PC and lets the user know what content is available. With this application, the multicast group range of 224.2.0.0 through 224.2.255.255 (224.2/16) is the SDP/SAP Multicast Block, which is reserved for applications that send and receive multimedia session announcements using the SAP described in RFC 2974. An example of an application that uses SAP is the Session Directory tool (SDR), which transmits global scope SAP announcements on groups 224.2.127.254 and 224.2.127.255.

Advantages of Multicast

Multicast transmission provides many advantages over unicast transmission in a one-to-many or many-to-many environment, including the following:

- **Enhanced efficiency:** Available network bandwidth is used more efficiently because multiple streams of data are replaced with a single transmission. Server and CPU loads are also reduced. Multicast packets do not impose as high a rate of bandwidth utilization as unicast packets, so there is a greater possibility that they will arrive almost simultaneously at the receivers.

- **Optimized performance:** Multicast eliminates traffic redundancy because fewer copies of the data require forwarding and processing. The sender also needs much less processing power and bandwidth for the equivalent amount of multicast traffic.

- **Support for distributed applications:** As demand and usage grows, distributed multipoint applications will not be possible with unicast transmission, because it does not scale well (traffic levels and the number of clients increase at a 1:1 rate with unicast transmission). Multicast enables a whole range of new applications that were not possible with unicast, including for example, VoD.

Disadvantages of Multicast

Most multicast applications are User Datagram Protocol (UDP) based. This foundation results in some undesirable consequences when compared to similar unicast, TCP-based applications.

TCP supports only unicast transmissions. TCP is a connection-oriented protocol that requires a three-way handshake to establish communications. TCP enforces end-to-end reliability of packet delivery with sequence numbers and acknowledgments. TCP also supports flow control.

In contrast, UDP can support both unicast and multicast transmissions. UDP is a connectionless protocol that does not use a handshake to establish communication. UDP has no reliability mechanisms, so reliability issues have to be addressed in multicast applications if reliable data transfer is necessary.

Some of the disadvantages of multicast that need to be considered include the following:

- UDP's best-effort delivery results in occasional packet drops. Therefore, multicast applications must not expect reliable delivery of data and should be designed accordingly; in other words, the multicast application itself must be reliable (at the application layer).

■ Many multicast applications that operate in real time (for example, video and audio) may be affected by these losses; requesting retransmission of the lost data at the application layer in these real-time applications is not feasible. For example, high packet-drop rates in voice applications may result in jerky, missed speech patterns that can make the content unintelligible. Moderate to heavy drops in video are sometimes tolerated by the human eye and appear as unusual "artifacts" in the picture. However, some compression algorithms may be severely affected by even low drop rates, which might cause the picture to become jerky or to freeze for several seconds while the decompression algorithm recovers.

■ UDP's lack of congestion control (due to not having a windowing or slow-start mechanism like TCP has) may result in network congestion and overall network degradation as the popularity of UDP-based multicast applications grow. If possible, multicast applications should attempt to detect and avoid congestion conditions.

■ Duplicate packets may occasionally be generated when multicast network topologies change. Multicast applications should be designed to expect occasional duplicate packets to arrive and must handle them accordingly.

■ Out-of-sequence delivery of packets to the application may also result during network topology changes or other network events that affect the flow of multicast traffic. Multicast applications must be designed to handle these packets appropriately.

■ Multicast security is still evolving. For example, the issue of how to restrict multicast traffic to only a selected group of receivers to avoid eavesdropping has not yet been sufficiently resolved.

Some commercial applications (for example, financial data delivery) will become possible only when these reliability and security issues are fully resolved.

Multicast IP Addresses

Multicast IP addresses use the Class D address space, which is indicated by the high-order 4 bits set to binary 1110. Therefore, the Class D multicast address range is 224.0.0.0 through 239.255.255.255.

The Internet Assigned Numbers Authority (IANA) assigns ranges and specific multicast addresses. You can find a current list of assignments at http://www.iana.org/assignments/multicast-addresses.

Local scope addresses are addresses in the range 224.0.0.0 through 224.0.0.255 and are reserved by the IANA for network protocol use. This range of addresses is also known as the *local network control block*. Packets with multicast addresses in this range are never forwarded off the local network regardless of the Time to Live (TTL) field in the IP packet header; the TTL is usually set to 1. Examples of local scope IP multicast addresses include the following:

- **224.0.0.1**: All hosts

- **224.0.0.2**: All multicast routers

- **224.0.0.4**: All Distance Vector Multicast Routing Protocol (DVMRP) routers

- **224.0.0.5**: All Open Shortest Path First (OSPF) routers

- **224.0.0.6**: All OSPF designated routers (DR)

- **224.0.0.9**: All Routing Information Protocol Version 2 (RIPv2) routers

- **224.0.0.10**: All Enhanced Interior Gateway Protocol (EIGRP) routers

Globally scoped addresses are in the range 224.0.1.0 through 238.255.255.255. Some of these addresses have been reserved through the IANA for use by multicast applications, including the range 224.0.1.0 to 224.0.1.255, and 232.0.0.0/8 and 233.0.0.0/8. The rest of the addresses in this range are transient addresses that are dynamically assigned and then returned for others to use when they are no longer needed.

Limited, or administratively, scoped addresses are in the range 239.0.0.0 through 239.255.255.255. As defined by RFC 2365, *Administratively Scoped IP Multicast*, these addresses are reserved for use inside private domains. Enterprises usually define multicast boundaries at the borders of their network so that traffic in the administratively scoped range can neither enter nor leave the enterprise network. The administratively scoped multicast address space includes the following scopes, per the IANA:

- Site-local scope (239.255.0.0/16; 239.252.0.0/16, 239.253.0.0/16, and 239.254.0.0/16 are also reserved for this purpose)

- Organization-local scope (239.192.0.0 to 239.251.255.255)

The IANA has further refined these ranges, as detailed in the IANA multicast address assignment list referenced earlier.

> **Note** *The Guidelines for Enterprise IP Multicast Address Allocation* white paper, at http://www.cisco.com/en/US/prod/collateral/iosswrel/ps6537/ps6552/ps6592/prod_white _paper0900aecd80310d68.pdf, provides more details.

Layer 2 Multicast Addresses

Normally, devices on a LAN segment receive only frames destined for their own MAC address or the broadcast MAC address. For multicast to work, some means had to be devised so that multiple hosts could receive the same frame and still be capable of differentiating among multicast groups. The IEEE LAN specifications have provisions for the transmission of broadcast and multicast frames. In the IEEE 802.3 standard, bit 0 of the first octet is used to indicate a broadcast/multicast frame, as illustrated in Figure 10-3.

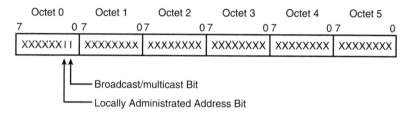

Figure 10-3   *IEEE 802.3 MAC Address Format*

This bit indicates that the frame is destined for an arbitrary group of hosts (multicast) or all hosts on the network (broadcast); in the case of broadcast, the broadcast address is 0xFFFF.FFFF.FFFF. IP multicast makes use of this bit to transmit IP packets to a group of hosts on a LAN segment.

The IANA owns a block of Ethernet MAC addresses that start with hexadecimal 01:00:5E. The lower half of this block is allocated for multicast addresses, resulting in the range of available MAC addresses of 0100.5E00.0000 through 0100.5E7F.FFFF.

The translation between IP multicast and Layer 2 multicast MAC addresses is achieved by the mapping of the low-order 23 bits of the IP (Layer 3) multicast address into the low-order 23 bits of the MAC (Layer 2) address, as shown in Figure 10-4.

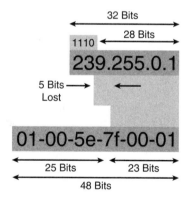

Figure 10-4   *IP Multicast to Ethernet MAC Address Mapping*

Because there are 28 bits of unique address space for an IP multicast addresses (32 minus the first 4 bits containing the 1110 Class D prefix) and there are only 23 bits mapped into the IEEE MAC address, there are five (28 – 23 = 5) bits of overlap. These 5 bits represent $2^5 = 32$ addresses. Therefore, there is a 32:1 overlap of IP addresses to MAC addresses, so 32 IP multicast addresses map to the same MAC multicast address.

Table 10-1 *Many IP Multicast Addresses Match One MAC Address*

224.10.0.1	225.10.0.1	226.10.0.1	227.10.0.1	228.10.0.1
229.10.0.1	230.10.0.1	231.10.0.1	232.10.0.1	233.10.0.1
234.10.0.1	235.10.0.1	236.10.0.1	237.10.0.1	238.10.0.1
239.10.0.1	224.138.0.1	225.138.0.1	226.138.0.1	227.138.0.1
228.138.0.1	229.138.0.1	230.138.0.1	231.138.0.1	232.138.0.1
233.138.0.1	234.138.0.1	235.138.0.1	236.138.0.1	237.138.0.1
238.138.0.1	239.138.0.1			

For example, all the IP multicast addresses in Table 10-1 map to the same Layer 2 multicast MAC address 01-00-5E-0A-00-01.

Note Organizations should avoid using IP multicast addresses that map to the 224.0.0.x or 224.0.1.x MAC addresses of 0x0100.5E00.00.xx or 0x0100.5E00.01.xx because these addresses will be flooded by the switch hardware.

Multicast Address Assignment

Layer 3 IP multicast addresses are typically assigned statically.

Aggregation and summarization of multicast group addresses are meaningless because any multicast source can send to any group address and any multicast client can receive data for any group without regard to geography. Administratively scoped, or private, address space can and should be used within the enterprise unless multicast traffic will be sourced to the Internet, requiring a unique group address. Multicast addresses can be allocated globally or locally, as follows:

■ **Enterprise internal group address assignment:** Static address allocation methods are typically used by enterprise network administrators to allocate specific addresses or address ranges from the administratively scoped address range, 239.0.0.0/8. The Multicast Address Dynamic Client Allocation Protocol (MADCAP) allows a client workstation to "lease" a multicast address from a MADCAP server in a manner similar to how a workstation can "lease" an IP address from a Dynamic Host Configuration Protocol (DHCP) server.

■ **Global group address assignment:** Static multicast addresses can be assigned by the IANA on a permanent basis so that they are valid everywhere and in all networks. This technique permits applications and hardware devices to have these addresses hard-coded into their software or microcode. In the late 1990s, when native multicast was beginning to be deployed on the Internet, several content providers planned to begin multicasting some of their audio and video content. An experimental form of static address allocation was proposed by the Internet Engineering Task Force (IETF). This allocation methodology, called GLOP addressing, which is defined in RFC 3180, *GLOP Addressing in 233/8*, uses the multicast group range of 233.0.0.0/8.

This block was assigned by the IANA and is an experimental, statically assigned range of multicast addresses intended for use by content providers, Internet service providers (ISP), or anyone wanting to source content into the global Internet. GLOP addresses have the high-order octet set to 233 (decimal). The next two octets contain the 16-bit Abstract Syntax Notation (ASN) of the content provider or ISP that is sourcing the multicast traffic. The remaining octet is used for group assignment.

Note   GLOP is not an acronym and does not stand for anything.

Cisco Multicast Architecture

Figure 10-5 illustrates the Cisco multicast architecture and the protocols used to support multicast in the enterprise, in both campus multicast solutions and interdomain multicast solutions.

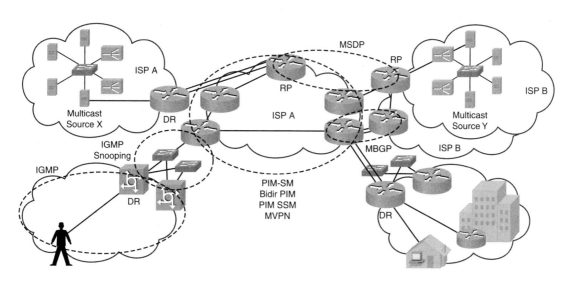

Figure 10-5   *Cisco Multicast Architecture*

For the campus, these protocols include the following:

■   IGMP for host-to-router communication

■   IGMP snooping on switches (or CGMP between Cisco routers and switches) for Layer 2 optimization

■   PIM sparse mode (SM) (PIM-SM) or bidirectional PIM (bidir-PIM) for routers

For interdomain multicast, these protocols include the following:

- Multiprotocol Border Gateway Protocol (MBGP) for multicast routing across domains

- Multicast Source Discovery Protocol (MSDP) with PIM-SM for multicast source discovery

- PIM source-specific multicast (SSM) for multicast from specific sources

- Multicast virtual private network (MVPN) for secure connectivity

Note MBGP, MPVN, and MDSP are not discussed further in this book. The other protocols are discussed in the remainder of this chapter.

Note The DR notation in Figure 10-5 indicates designated routers, which are elected by the PIM routers and are used to avoid duplicating multicast traffic for connected hosts. The PIM router with the highest IP address on a LAN becomes the DR for that LAN.

IGMP and CGMP

This section first introduces Internet Group Management Protocol (IGMP), which has evolved through three versions (1, 2, and 3). Multicasting in Layer 2 switches is also discussed in this section. Without control, Ethernet switches flood multicast packets in the same way that unknown unicast frames are flooded. IGMP snooping and Cisco Group Management Protocol (CGMP) are used to solve this problem and are also described in this section.

IGMP is used between hosts and their local router. Hosts use IGMP to register with the router to join (and leave) specific multicast groups; the router is then aware that it needs to forward the data stream destined to a specific multicast group to the registered hosts.

IGMP Version 1

With IGMPv1, specified in RFC 1112, *Host Extensions for IP Multicasting*, multicast routers periodically send membership *queries* (usually every 60 to 120 seconds) to the all-hosts multicast address 224.0.0.1.

Hosts wanting to receive specific multicast group traffic send membership *reports* to the multicast address of the group they want to join. Hosts either send reports when they want to first join a group or in response to membership queries. On each subnet, only one member per group responds to a query, to save bandwidth on the subnet and minimize processing by hosts. This process is called *report suppression*.

There must be at least one active member of a multicast group on a local segment if multicast traffic is to be forwarded to that segment.

IGMPv1 does not have a mechanism defined for hosts to leave a multicast group. IGMPv1 hosts therefore leave a group silently, at any time, without any notification to the router. This is not a problem if there are multiple members on a segment, because the multicast traffic must still be delivered to the segment. However, when the last member on a segment leaves the multicast group, there will be a period when the router continues to forward the multicast traffic onto the segment needlessly. The IGMPv1 router times out the group after several query intervals without a response. This process is inefficient, especially if there are many groups or there is a lot of traffic in the groups.

IGMP Version 2

Because of some of the limitations discovered in IGMPv1, work was begun on IGMPv2 in an attempt to remove these restrictions. IGMPv2 is specified in RFC 2236, *Internet Group Management Protocol, Version 2*. Most of the changes between IGMPv1 and IGMPv2 deal with the issues of leave and join latencies and ambiguities in the original protocol specification. IGMPv2 is backward compatible with IGMPv1.

The following are some important changes in IGMPv2:

- Group-specific queries

- Leave Group message

- Querier election mechanism

- Query-interval response time

A group-specific query enables a router to query membership in a single group instead of in all groups, providing an optimized way to quickly find out whether any members are left in a group without asking all groups for a report. The difference between the group-specific query and the membership query is that a membership query is multicast to the all-hosts (224.0.0.1) address, whereas a group-specific query for group G is multicast to the group G multicast address.

A Leave Group message enables hosts to tell the router that they are leaving the group. This information reduces the leave latency for the group on the segment when the member who is leaving is the last member of the group. The specification includes the timing of when Leave Group messages must be sent. After receiving a Leave Group message, the router sends a group-specific query to see whether any other group members are present.

When there are two IGMP routers on the same segment (the same broadcast domain), the router with the lowest IP address is the designated querier.

The query-interval response time is used to control the "burstiness" of reports and is specified in a query. It indicates to the members how much time they have to respond to a query by issuing a report.

IGMP Version 3

IGMPv3 is a proposed standard, documented in RFC 3376, *Internet Group Management Protocol, Version 3*, that adds the ability to filter multicasts based on the multicast source so that hosts can indicate that they want to receive traffic only from particular sources within a multicast group. This enhancement makes the utilization of routing resources more efficient; routers need only forward traffic from specific sources from which receivers have requested traffic.

For example, as illustrated in Figure 10-6, a joining member sends an IGMPv3 report to 224.0.0.22 immediately upon joining. This report might specify a source list, which is used for source filtering. A source list is a list of multicast sources that the host will accept packets from or a list of multicast sources that the host will not accept packets from. Using a source list, a multicast router can, for example, avoid delivering multicast packets from specific sources to networks where there are no interested receivers.

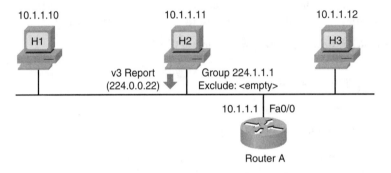

Figure 10-6   *IGMPv3: Joining a Group*

> **Note**   In IGMPv3, reports are sent to 224.0.0.22; the corresponding address used in earlier IGMP versions is 224.0.0.2. Note that in the IANA multicast addresses document referenced earlier, 224.0.0.22 is called the IGMP address.

Multicast with Layer 2 Switches

In a typical network, hosts are not directly connected to routers but are connected to a Layer 2 switch, which is in turn connected to a router.

IGMP is a network layer (Layer 3) protocol. Therefore, Layer 2 switches do not participate in IGMP and are not aware of which hosts attached to them might be part of a particular multicast group. By default, Layer 2 switches flood multicast frames to all ports within a VLAN (except the port from which the frame originated), which means that all multicast traffic received by a switch would be sent out on all ports within a VLAN, even if only one device on one port required the data stream.

One method Cisco Catalyst switches use to circumvent this is by allowing the administrator to configure the switch to manually associate a multicast MAC address with various ports. For example, the administrator may configure ports 5, 6, and 7 so that only those ports receive the multicast traffic destined for a specific multicast group. This method works but is not scalable because IP multicast hosts dynamically join and leave groups using IGMP to signal to the multicast router.

To improve the behavior of the switches when they receive multicast frames, many multicast switching solutions have been developed, including IGMP snooping and CGMP.

Note   The *Multicast Catalyst Switches Support Matrix* document, available at http://www.cisco.com/en/US/tech/tk828/technologies_tech_note09186a0080122a70.shtml, includes a list of which switches support CGMP and which switches support IGMP snooping.

IGMP Snooping

With IGMP snooping, the switch eavesdrops on the IGMP messages sent between routers and hosts, and updates its MAC address table accordingly.

IGMP snooping constrains IP multicast traffic at Layer 2 by configuring the Layer 2 LAN ports dynamically to forward IP multicast traffic only to those ports that want to receive it.

As its name implies, a switch must be IGMP aware to listen in on the IGMP conversations between hosts and routers. The switch's processor must examine, or "snoop," network layer information to identify and intercept all IGMP packets flowing between routers and hosts and vice versa, including IGMP membership reports and IGMP Leave Group messages.

When the switch sees an IGMP report from a host for a particular multicast group, the switch adds the port number on which the host is attached to the associated multicast table entry. After this port association is made, any multicast traffic received by the switch destined for the particular multicast group is forwarded *only* to the ports associated with that group in the multicast table. Similarly, when the switch sees an IGMP leave group message from a host, the switch removes the associated multicast table entry. IGMP snooping is used on subnets that include end users (receiver clients) and allows a Layer 2 switch to more efficiently handle IP multicast.

A switch may have to intercept all Layer 2 multicast packets to identify IGMP packets. This processing can have a significant impact on switch performance. Therefore, switches must effectively become Layer 3 aware to maintain forwarding throughput when performing IGMP snooping. Current Cisco switches support IP multicast data packet forwarding using special hardware (Layer 3 application specific integrated circuits [ASIC]) that can distinguish IGMP information packets from other multicast packets. In addition, the Cisco Catalyst and Nexus switches support multicast packet replication in hardware, which more efficiently copies multicast packets to the network interfaces where the multicast path flows diverge.

CGMP

CGMP is a Cisco Systems proprietary protocol that runs between a multicast router and a switch. The routers inform each of their directly connected switches of IGMP registrations that were received from hosts through the switch (in other words, from hosts accessible through the switch). The switch then forwards the multicast traffic only to ports that those requesting hosts are on rather than flooding the data to all ports.

CGMP is based on a client/server model, where the router may be considered a CGMP server, and the switch a CGMP client.

When the router sees an IGMP control message, it creates a CGMP packet that contains the request type (join or leave), the Layer 2 multicast MAC address, and the actual MAC address of the client.

This packet is sent to the well-known CGMP multicast MAC address 0x0100.0cdd.dddd to which all CGMP switches listen. The switch interprets the CGMP control message and creates the proper entries in its MAC address table (also called its forwarding table or (content-addressable memory [CAM] table) to constrain the forwarding of multicast traffic for this group to only the appropriate ports.

Figure 10-7 illustrates the interaction of the IGMP and CGMP protocols. Hosts A and D register, using IGMP to the router, to join the multicast group to receive data from the server. The router informs both switches of these registrations, using CGMP. When the router forwards the multicast data to the hosts via the switches, the switches ensure that the data only goes out of the ports on which hosts A and D are connected. The ports on which hosts B and C are connected do not receive the multicast data.

PIM Routing Protocol

PIM is used by routers that are forwarding multicast packets. The "protocol-independent" part of the name indicates that PIM is independent of the unicast routing protocol (for example, EIGRP or OSPF) running in the network.

PIM uses the normal routing table, populated by the unicast routing protocol, in its multicast routing calculations. Unlike other routing protocols, no routing updates are sent between PIM routers.

EIGRP, OSPF, and so forth are called *unicast routing protocols* because they are used for creating and maintaining unicast routing information in the routing table. Recall, however, that unicast routing protocols use multicast packets (or broadcast packets in some protocols) to send their routing update traffic.

Note   A variant of OSPF, called multicast OSPF, supports multicast routing. Cisco routers do not support multicast OSPF.

This section explores the operation of PIM.

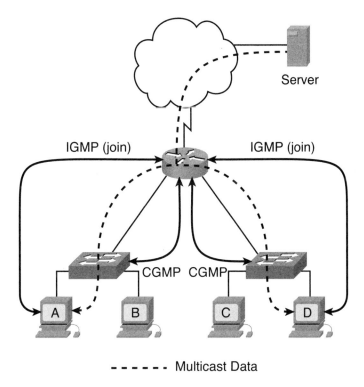

Figure 10-7 *IGMP and CGMP Inform Network Devices About Which Hosts Want Which Multicast Data*

PIM Terminology

When a router is forwarding a unicast packet, it looks up the destination address in its routing table and forwards the packet out of the appropriate interface. However, when forwarding a multicast packet, the router might have to forward the packet out of multiple interfaces, toward all the receiving hosts.

Multicast routing is connection oriented: Multicast traffic does not flow to the destinations until connection messages are sent toward the source to set up the flow paths for the traffic.

Multicast-enabled routers use PIM to dynamically create *distribution trees* that control the path that IP multicast traffic takes through the network to deliver traffic to all receivers. Building multicast distribution trees via connection messages is a dynamic process; when network topology changes occur, the distribution trees are rebuilt around failed links.

Distribution Trees

There are two types of distribution trees: source trees and shared trees.

A *source tree* is created for each source sending to each multicast group. The source tree has its root at the source and has branches through the network to the receivers. Source trees are also called source-routed or shortest path trees (SPT) because the tree takes a direct path (the shortest path) from source to its receivers.

A *shared tree* is a single tree that is shared between *all* sources for each multicast group. The shared tree has a single common root, called a rendezvous point (RP). Sources initially send their multicast packets to the RP, which in turn forwards data through a shared tree to the members of the group.

Multicast Distribution Tree Creation

Multicast-capable routers create distribution trees that control the path that IP multicast traffic takes through the network to deliver traffic to all receivers.

Figure 10-8 illustrates an example of the creation of a multicast distribution tree, based on the source address. A host sends a request to join the multicast group 224.1.1.1 and to get the multicast data from the source 10.1.1.1. Router E selects interface E0 as the best path to the source, using its unicast routing table. Interface E0 is added to the multicast routing entry for group 224.1.1.1. The join request is forwarded to Router B. Router B selects the best path to the source, using its unicast routing table. Router B adds the interface on which it received the join request as the outgoing interface in its multicast routing table and the interface it selected as the best path to the source as the incoming interface in its multicast routing table. Router B forwards the join request to Router A. The join request is forwarded to the source and the multicast tree is built, with a forwarding state from the source to the receiver. Multicast data flows from the source down the multicast distribution tree to the receiver.

Reverse Path Forwarding

Multicast routers consider the source address and the destination address of the multicast packet, and use the distribution tree to forward the packet away from the source toward the destination.

Forwarding multicast traffic away from the source, rather than to the receiver, is called *reverse path forwarding* (RPF); this is just the opposite of unicast routing. For multicast, the source IP address denotes the known source, and the destination IP address denotes a group of unknown receivers.

To avoid routing loops, RPF uses the unicast routing table to determine the upstream (toward the source) and downstream (away from the source) neighbors and ensures that only one interface on the router, to the upstream neighbor, is considered to be an incoming interface for data from a specific source. For example, data received on one router interface and forwarded out another interface might loop around the network and come back into the same router on a different interface; RPF ensures that this data is not forwarded again.

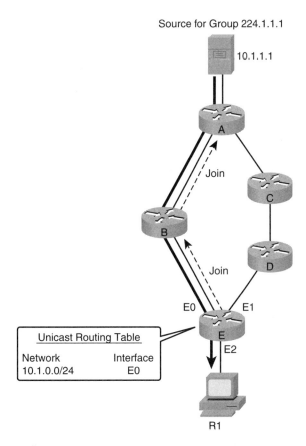

Figure 10-8 *Multicast Distribution Trees Are Created by Routers*

A router will forward a multicast packet only if it is received on the upstream interface; this interface is also called the *RPF interface.*

When a multicast packet arrives at a router, the router performs the following RPF check on the packet:

- The router looks up the source address in the unicast routing table to determine whether the packet has arrived on the interface that is on the reverse path back to the source.

- If the packet has arrived on the interface leading back to the source, the RPF check succeeds and the packet is forwarded.

- If the RPF check fails, the packet is dropped.

Source Distribution Trees

Figure 10-9 illustrates a source tree between Source 1, 192.168.1.1, and Receiver 1 and Receiver 2, in group 224.1.1.1. The path between the source and receivers over Routers A, C, and E is the path with the lowest cost. In this figure Source 1, 192.168.1.1, is forwarding to the receivers.

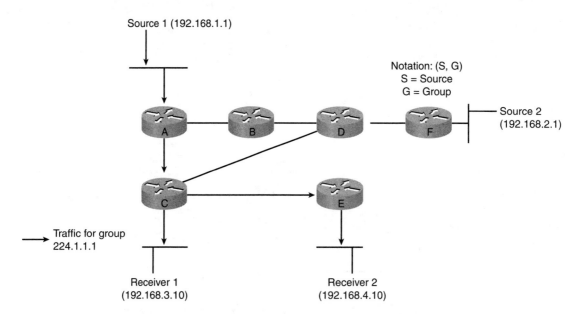

Figure 10-9   *Source Distribution Tree for Source 1*

Packets are forwarded according to the source and group address pair along the tree. For this reason, the forwarding state associated with the source tree is referred to by the notation (S,G) (pronounced "S comma G"), where S is the IP address of the source, and G is the multicast group address. The state for the source tree in Figure 10-9 is (192.168.1.1,224.1.1.1).

Figure 10-10 shows the same network as in Figure 10-9, but with Source 2, 192.168.2.1, active and sending multicast packets to Receiver 1 and Receiver 2. A separate source tree is built for this purpose, this time with Source 2 at the root of the tree. The state for this source tree is (192.168.2.1,224.1.1.1).

Therefore, with source trees, a separate tree is built for every source S sending to group G.

Source trees have the advantage of creating the optimal path between the source and the receivers. This advantage guarantees the minimum amount of network latency for forwarding multicast traffic. However, this optimization comes at a cost: The routers must maintain path information for each source. In a network that has thousands of sources and thousands of groups, this overhead can quickly become a resource issue on the routers. Memory consumption due to the size of the multicast routing table is a factor that network designers must consider. The multicast routing table is required to maintain current values, called state, that determine multicast routing behavior.

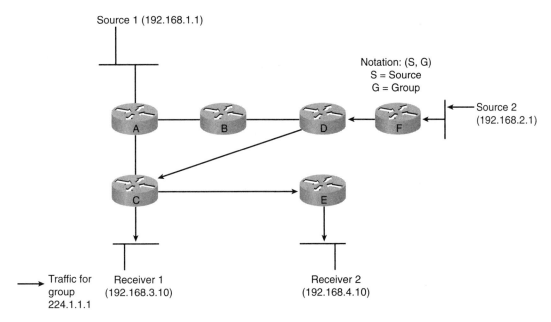

Figure 10-10 *A Separate Source Tree Is Built for Source 2 Sending to the Group*

Shared Distribution Trees

Figure 10-11 shows a shared distribution tree for group 224.2.2.2. Router D is the root of this shared tree, the RP. The tree is built from Router D to Routers C and E toward Receiver 1 and Receiver 2.

Packets are forwarded down the shared distribution tree to the receivers. The default forwarding state for the shared tree is identified by the notation (*,G) (pronounced "star comma G"), where * is a wildcard entry, meaning any source, and G is the multicast group address. The state for the shared tree in Figure 10-11 is (*,224.2.2.2).

Figure 10-12 illustrates the operation of the network in Figure 10-11. Source 1 and Source 2 are sending multicast packets toward the RP via source trees; from the RP, the multicast packets are flowing via a shared distribution tree toward Receiver 1 and Receiver 2. The shared tree is unidirectional. If a receiver is located between the source and the RP, that receiver will be serviced directly.

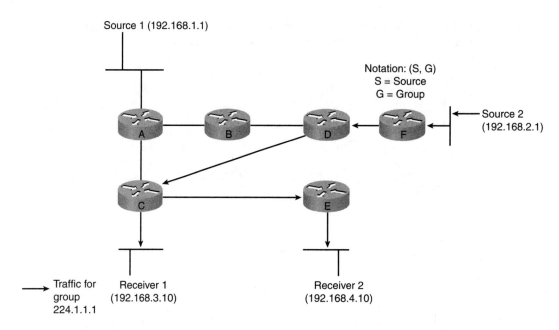

Figure 10-11   *The RP Is the Root of the Shared Distribution Tree*

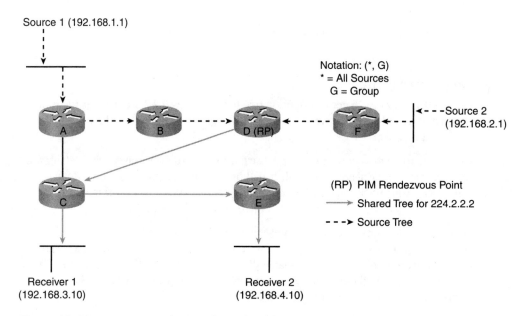

Figure 10-12   *Sources Send Toward the RP and the RP Sends to the Receivers*

Shared trees have the advantage of requiring the minimum amount of state in each router. The disadvantage of shared trees is that under certain circumstances the paths between the source and receivers might not be the optimal paths, which might introduce some latency in packet delivery. For example, in Figure 10-12, the shortest path between Source 1 and Receiver 1 would be through Router A and Router C. Because Router D is being used as the root for the shared tree, the traffic must traverse Routers A, B, D, and then C.

Multicast Distribution Tree Notation

To summarize, the multicast forwarding entries that appear in multicast forwarding tables are read in the following way:

- (S,G): For the source S sending to the group G; traffic is forwarded via the shortest path from the source. These entries typically reflect a source tree, but may also appear on a shared tree.

- (*,G): For any source (*) sending to the group G; traffic is forwarded via an RP for this group. These entries reflect a shared tree, but are also created in Cisco routers for any existing (S,G) entry.

(S,G) source tree state entries use more router memory because there is an entry for each source and group pair. The traffic is sent over the optimal path to each receiver, therefore minimizing the delay in packet delivery.

Shared distribution tree state entries (*,G) consume less router CPU and memory but may result in suboptimal paths from a source to receivers, thus introducing extra delay in packet delivery.

Deploying PIM and RPs

Multicast deployments require three elements: the application, the network infrastructure, and client devices. This section discusses how PIM is used in the network infrastructure and considerations for deploying RPs in multicast networks using shared trees.

PIM Deployment Models

The three main PIM deployment models used to support multicast services and applications are as follows:

- **Any Source Multicast (ASM):** ASM uses a combination of the shared and source trees and RPs. ASM is also known as PIM-SM and is described in RFC 4601, *Protocol Independent Multicast - Sparse Mode (PIM-SM): Protocol Specification (Revised)*. The majority of deployed multicast networks use this model.

- **Bidir-PIM:** Bidir-PIM exclusively uses shared trees and is recommended to support many-to-many host applications. Bidir-PIM drastically reduces the total (S,G) state information that is needed in the network.

- **SSM:** SSM exclusively uses source trees and is recommended to support one-to-many applications. SSM greatly simplifies the network and eliminates the need for RP engineering.

- **PIM Dense:** Flood and prune (obsolete).

These deployment models are described further in the following sections.

ASM or PIM-SM

ASM, or PIM-SM, uses a "pull" model to send multicast traffic. PIM-SM forwards multicast traffic only to network segments with active receivers that have explicitly requested the data. PIM-SM distributes information about active sources by forwarding data packets on shared trees. Because PIM-SM uses shared trees at least initially, it requires the use of an RP. The RP must be administratively configured in the network.

PIM-SM Shared Tree Join

In PIM-SM, sources register with the RP. Routers along the path from active receivers that have explicitly requested to join a specific multicast group register to join that group. These routers calculate, using the unicast routing table, whether they have a better metric to the RP or to the source itself. They forward the join message to the device with which they have the better metric. Data is forwarded down the shared tree to the receivers that have joined the group. The edge routers learn about a particular source when they receive data packets on the shared tree from that source through the RP. When a receiver requests to join a group, the edge router sends PIM (S,G) join messages toward that source.

Figure 10-13 illustrates an example. In this network, an active receiver (attached to the leaf Router E at the bottom of the figure) wants to join multicast group G.

The last-hop router (Router E in this figure) knows the IP address of the RP router for group G, and it sends a (*,G) join for this group toward the RP. This (*,G) join travels hop by hop toward the RP, building a branch of the shared tree that extends from the RP to the last-hop router (Router E) directly connected to the receiver. At this point, group G traffic can flow down the shared tree to the receiver.

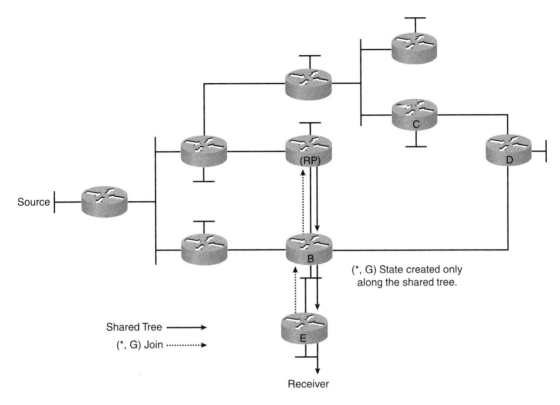

Figure 10-13 *PIM-SM Shared Tree Join*

PIM-SM Sender Registration

In PIM-SM, multicast sources register with the predefined RP using a sender registration.

The steps in the PM-SM sender registration process include the following, as illustrated in Figure 10-14:

1. An active source for group G sends a packet to its first-hop router, Router B.

2. The first-hop router, Router B, is responsible for registering the source with the RP (Router A) and requesting the RP to build a tree back to that router. During the sender registration process, the source router encapsulates the multicast data from the source in a special PIM-SM message called the Register message and unicasts that data to the RP.

3. When the RP receives the Register message, it de-encapsulates the multicast data packet inside of the Register message and forwards it down the shared tree to receivers in group G.

4. The RP also sends an (S,G) join message back toward the source S to create a branch of an (S,G) source tree. This results in an (S,G) state being created in all the routers along the source tree, including in the RP (Router A) and the router connected to the source (Router B).

5. The source tree is built from the source router (Router B) to the RP (Router A).

6. Multicast traffic then begins to flow from source S to the RP.

7. When the RP begins receiving multicast data on the source tree from source S, the RP sends a Register-Stop message to the source's first-hop router (Router B) to inform it that it can stop sending the unicast Register messages.

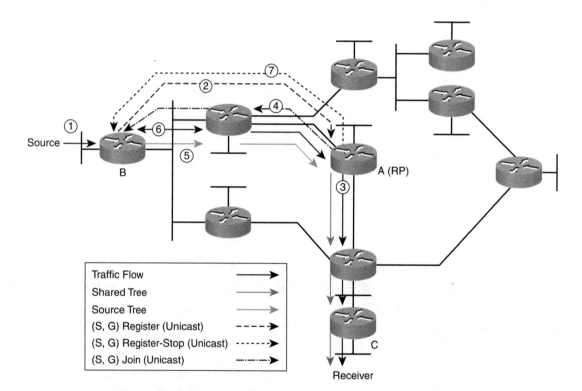

Figure 10-14 *PIM-SM Sender Registration Process*

PIM-SM SPT Switchover

PIM-SM includes the capability, known as SPT switchover, for last-hop routers (that is, routers with directly connected active receiver group members) to switch to an SPT (a source tree) and bypass the RP if the traffic rate is above a set threshold, called the SPT threshold. SPT switchover allows PIM-SM to more efficiently support multicast traffic.

The SPT threshold can be configured on Cisco routers using the **ip pim spt-threshold** {*kbps* | **infinity**} [**group-list** *access-list*] global configuration command; the default value of the SPT threshold is 0 Kbps. With this default setting, the switch from shared to source tree happens upon the arrival of the first data packet at the last-hop router. This means that the default behavior for PIM-SM last-hop, or leaf, routers attached to active receivers is to immediately join the source tree to the source when the first packet arrives via the (*,G) shared tree.

If the **infinity** keyword is used in the command, all sources for the specified group use the shared tree, never switching to the source tree.

Figure 10-15 provides an example. The last-hop router sends an (S,G) join message toward the source to join the SPT, therefore bypassing the RP. The (S,G) join message travels hop by hop to the first-hop router (the router connected directly to the source), thereby creating another branch of the SPT. This also creates an (S,G) state in all the routers along this branch of the SPT.

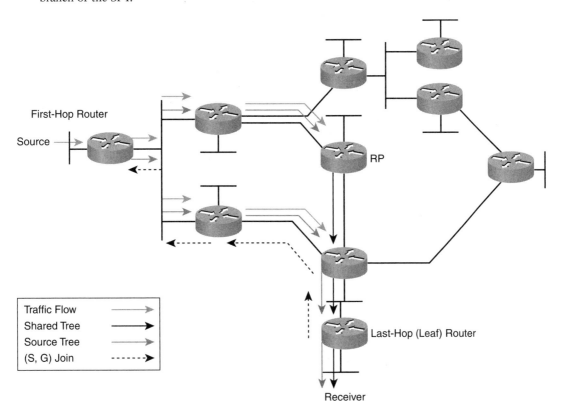

Figure 10-15 *PIM-SM Source Tree Switchover*

Bidirectional PIM

Bidir-PIM is an enhancement of the PIM protocol that was designed for efficient many-to-many communications within an individual PIM domain. Bidir-PIM is defined in RFC 5015, *Bidirectional Protocol Independent Multicast (BIDIR-PIM)*.

The shared trees created by PIM-SM are unidirectional. Source data cannot flow *up* the shared tree to the RP. Instead, a source tree must be created to bring the data stream to the RP (the root of the shared tree) so that the data can be forwarded *down* the branches of the shared tree to the receivers.

Several multicast applications use a many-to-many model where each host is both a receiver and a sender. In a PIM-SM deployment, routers that support such hosts would need to have a source tree *to* the RP for each host, and a common shared tree *from* the RP for each group. In a PIM-SM domain supporting a large number of many-to-many hosts, (*,G) and (S,G) entries appear everywhere along the path between the hosts and the associated RP, resulting in increased memory and protocol overhead. This large number of sources can create a huge (S,G) state problem.

Bidir-PIM allows packets to be forwarded from a source to the RP using only the shared tree state. In bidirectional mode, traffic is routed through a bidirectional shared tree that is rooted at the RP for the group. Therefore, only (*,G) entries appear in multicast forwarding tables; there are no (S,G) entries and no source trees. With bidir-PIM, the path taken by packets flowing from a host (whether it is a source or receiver) to the RP and back from the RP to the host is the same.

In bidirectional mode, multicast groups can scale to include an arbitrarily large number of sources, with only a minimal amount of additional overhead.

Figure 10-16 shows a bidirectional shared tree. Data from the source flows up the shared tree (*,G) toward the RP and then down the shared tree to the receivers. There is no registration process, and no source tree (S,G) is created.

Bidir-PIM uses a designated forwarder (DF) on each link. The DF ensures that bidirectional sources can reach the RP and decides which packets need to be forwarded upstream toward the RP. Figure 10-16 shows an example where the source, Host A, is also a receiver. Traffic originating from Host A travels against the usual direction of the shared tree, breaking the rule that shared trees only accept traffic on their RPF interface. In bidir-PIM the same shared tree is used to distribute traffic both from the RP to the receivers and from the sources to the RP.

The algorithm to elect the DF is straightforward. All the PIM neighbors in a subnet advertise their unicast route to the RP, and the router with the best route is elected as the DF. This process selects the shortest path between every subnet and the RP without creating any (S,G) entries.

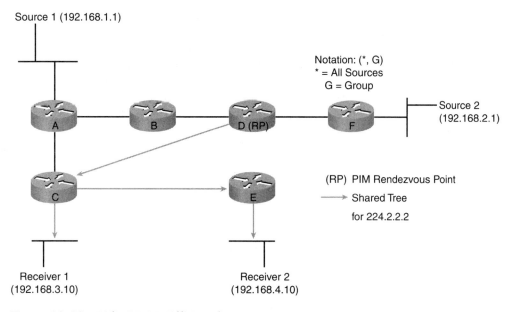

Figure 10-16 *Bidir-PIM Is Efficient for Many-to-Many Communication*

The RP in bidir-PIM only serves the function of getting sources and receivers to learn about each other. All routers establish a loop-free spanning-tree topology rooted in the IP address of the RP. This IP address need not be a router address but can be any unassigned IP address on a network that is reachable throughout the PIM domain. Traffic from the source is forwarded hop by hop toward the RP by the DF mechanism, and join messages from the receivers are sent to the RP.

Source-Specific Multicast

SSM is an extension of the PIM protocol that allows for an efficient data delivery mechanism in one-to-many communications.

In traditional multicast implementations, source devices running multicast applications join an IP multicast group, and traffic is distributed to the entire IP multicast group. If two applications with different sources and receivers use the same IP multicast group address, receivers of both applications receive traffic from both sources, which can include unwanted network traffic.

SSM enables a receiver, after it has learned about a specific multicast source through a directory service, to receive content directly from that specific source, instead of receiving it using a shared RP. Receivers are responsible for source and group discovery and receivers select which traffic they want from a group.

SSM only uses source trees; there are no shared trees and therefore an RP is not required.

The prerequisite for SSM deployment is a mechanism that allows hosts not only to report the group they want to join but also the specific source in the group. As discussed earlier, in the "IGMP Version 3" section, this mechanism is built in to the emerging IGMPv3 standard. In an SSM-enhanced multicast network, a receiver sends a request to join a specific multicast source in a multicast group to its last-hop router (the router closest to the receiver). The receiver identifies the specific source in the group by using the IGMPv3 include mode. The last-hop router sends the request directly to the specific source rather than to a common RP, as is done in PIM-SM. The first-hop router (the router closest to the source) starts forwarding the multicast traffic down the source tree to the receiver as soon as the source tree is built. This happens when the first (S,G) join request is received.

The IANA has reserved the global address range 232.0.0.0/8 for SSM applications and protocols. This assigned address range simplifies the address allocation for content and service providers. These providers can use the same group address range to deliver differing content from each source. Each (S,G) flow is unique. Routers running in SSM mode route data streams based on the full (S,G) address. Assuming that a source has a unique IP address on the Internet, any (S,G) from this source also would be unique.

The ability for SSM to explicitly include and exclude particular sources also provides limited security. Traffic from a source to a group that is not explicitly listed on the include list will not be forwarded to uninterested receivers. Only explicitly requested flows are forwarded to receivers.

Note   RFC 3569, *An Overview of Source-Specific Multicast (SSM)*, provides an outline of SSM.

SSM Join Process

Figure 10-17 illustrates an example of the SSM join process.

The process is follows:

1. A receiver determines the source address and group address for multicast data it wants to receive, such as from a web server.

2. The receiver sends a source-specific IGMPv3 join request to its closest router, the last-hop router (Router E in this example).

3. The last-hop router sends a PIM (S,G) join request to the first-hop router, the router closest to the source (Router A in this example).

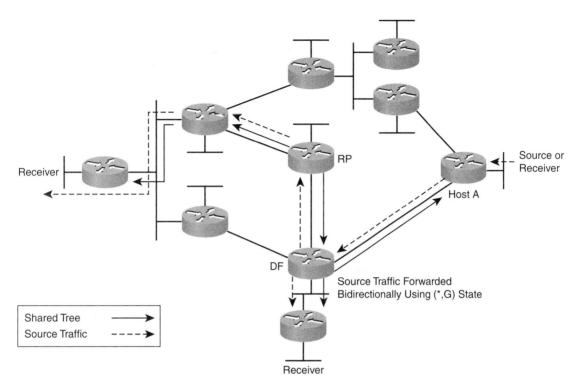

Figure 10-17 *SSM Join Process*

SSM Source Tree Creation

Figure 10-18 continues this example with the first-hop router, Router A, building the source tree to the last-hop router, Router E. The first-hop router starts forwarding the multicast traffic down the source tree to the receiver.

SSM is easy to install and provision in a network because it does not require the network to maintain which active sources are sending to which multicast groups. SSM is a recommended practice for Internet broadcast-style (one-to-many) applications.

PIM Dense Mode

PIM can operate in two operational modes: dense mode or sparse mode. Almost all current multicast deployments are based on sparse mode operation. PIM dense mode is considered to be obsolete. However, for historical reasons PIM may be deployed using a hybrid mode called PIM sparse-dense mode. In this mode, there is a risk of falling back to dense mode behavior in the absence of an RP. Therefore, it is beneficial to have an understanding of PIM dense mode.

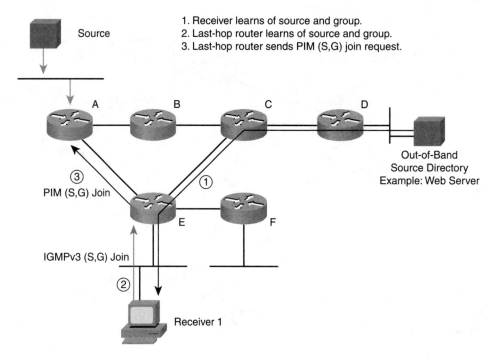

Figure 10-18   *SSM Source Path Tree Creation*

PIM dense mode builds source-based multicast distribution trees that operate on a flood-and-prune principle. Multicast packets from a source are flooded to all areas of a PIM dense mode network. PIM routers that receive multicast packets and do not have directly connected multicast group members or PIM neighbors send a prune message back up the source-based distribution tree toward the source of the packets. As a result, subsequent multicast packets are not flooded to pruned branches of the distribution tree. However, the pruned state in PIM dense mode times out approximately every three minutes, and the entire PIM dense mode network is reflooded with multicast packets and prune messages. This reflooding of unwanted traffic throughout the PIM dense mode network consumes network bandwidth.

RP Considerations

An RP is required only in networks with a shared tree. Therefore, an RP is required in networks running PIM-SM and bidir-PIM, not in networks running SSM.

This section discusses considerations for deploying RPs, including the following:

- Static RP addressing

- Anycast RP

- Auto-RP

- Bootstrap router (BSR)

Static RP Addressing

With static RP, every router in the network is manually configured with the IP address of a single RP. However, if this RP fails, the routers cannot fail over to a standby RP.

The only case in which a static RP can fail over is if anycast RPs are used and MSDP is running between each RP in the network, as described in the next section.

Anycast RP

Anycast is an IPv6 term that refers to an address that is shared by devices performing the same function. In IPv6, a packet addressed to an anycast address is sent to the *closest* device with that anycast address, as determined by the routing table; therefore, anycast provides load-sharing capabilities.

Anycast RP is a technique for configuring a PIM-SM network to provide fault tolerance and load sharing within a single multicast domain.

IPv4 has no defined anycast addresses. However, anycast RP allows two or more RPs to share the load for source registration and to act as a hot backup for each other. To perform the anycast RP function within IPv4, a unicast host address (with a /32 mask) is assigned as an anycast address, as illustrated in the example in Figure 10-19. This address is configured on a loopback interface on *all* the RPs, and is therefore added to the unicast routing table on the RPs. Notice in Figure 10-19 that the address 10.1.1.1/32 is assigned to *both* routers A and B.

All the downstream routers are configured to use this anycast address as the IP address of their local RP. IP routing automatically selects the topologically closest physical RP for each source and receiver to use. Because some sources and receivers might end up using different RPs, there needs to be some way for the RPs to exchange information about active sources. This is done with MDSP. MSDP announces the source addresses of the sources sending to a group. All RPs are configured to be MSDP peers of each other so that each RP knows about the active sources in the other RPs. If any of the RPs fail, IP routing converges, and one of the remaining RPs becomes the active RP in the area of the failed RP.

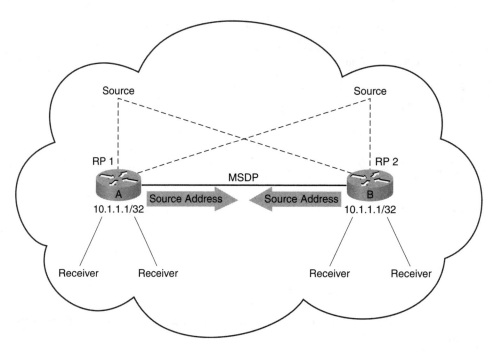

Figure 10-19   *With Anycast RP the RPs Load Share and Act as a Hot Backup for Each Other*

Note   The RPs are used only to set up the initial connection between sources and receivers in PIM SM. After the last-hop routers join the source tree (assuming PIM-SM SPT switchover is enabled), the RP is no longer necessary.

Auto-RP

The Auto-RP protocol is a dynamic way for every router in the network to learn the RP information.

The IANA has assigned two group addresses, 224.0.1.39 and 224.0.1.40, for Auto-RP. With Auto-RP, one or more routers are designated as RP mapping agents, which receive the RP announcement messages from candidate RPs (C-RPs) and arbitrate conflicts. The network administrator configures one or more routers in the network to be the C-RPs. The C-RPs announce their willingness to serve as an RP for a particular group range by periodically multicasting Auto-RP Announce messages to the Cisco announce multicast group, 224.0.1.39, as illustrated in Figure 10-20.

A *mapping agent* is a router that joins the Cisco RP announce group, 224.0.1.39. A mapping agent listens to all RP candidate announcements and builds a table with the information it learns. If several routers announce themselves as C-RPs for a multicast group range, the mapping agent chooses the C-RP with the highest IP address to be the RP.

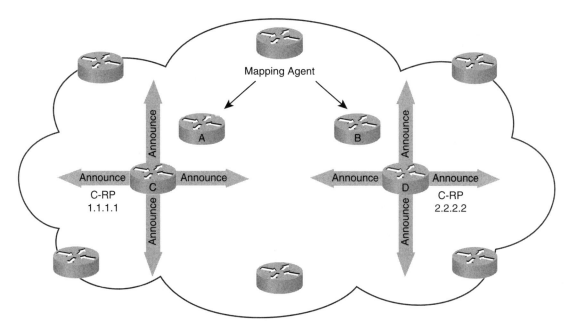

Figure 10-20   *Auto-RP Announcements Go to 224.0.1.39*

The RP mapping agent sends the consistent multicast group-to-RP mappings to all other routers in an RP discovery message addressed to 224.0.1.40, in dense mode. Mapping agents send this information, as illustrated in Figure 10-21, by default every 60 seconds.

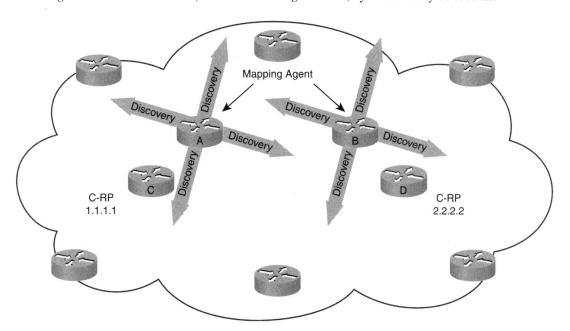

Figure 10-21   *Auto-RP Discovery Messages Go to 224.0.1.40*

Note   PIM dense mode (PIM-DM) uses a "push" model that floods multicast traffic to the entire network. Dense mode uses source trees. In PIM-DM, routers that have no need for the data (because they are not connected to receivers that want the data or to other routers that want it) request that the tree be pruned so that they no longer receive the data.

All PIM-enabled routers automatically join the Cisco RP discovery group, 224.0.1.40, allowing them to receive all group-to-RP mapping information. When the network routers receive an RP discovery message, they store the information about the elected RP in their group-to-RP mapping cache so that they know which RP to use for each group range.

Note   A C-RP and a mapping agent can be on the same router.

DM Fallback and DM Flooding

DM fallback is a condition in which the PIM mode goes from sparse mode (which requires an RP) to dense mode (which uses source trees and therefore does not use an RP). PIM-DM starts by flooding the multicast traffic, and then stops flooding on each link where it receives a Prune message. In earlier Cisco IOS Software releases, PIM-DM reflooded all the multicast traffic every three minutes. DM fallback occurs when RP information is lost. By default, PIM-DM fallback is enabled on Cisco routers, and a multicast group that loses its RP information falls back to dense mode, regardless of the interface configuration.

Using earlier Cisco IOS Software versions with Auto-RP requires that all interfaces be configured in sparse-dense mode using the **ip pim sparse-dense-mode** interface configuration command. An interface configured in sparse-dense mode works in either sparse mode or dense mode of operation, depending on the mode in which the multicast group operates. If a multicast group has a known RP, the interface works in sparse mode. If a multicast group has no known RP, the interface works in dense mode and data is flooded over the interface.

Note   To configure the address of a PIM RP, use the **ip pim rp-address** [**vrf** *vrf-name*] **rp-address** *rp-address* [*access-list*] [**override**] [**bidir**] global configuration command. The **override** keyword permits the statically defined RP address to take precedence over Auto-RP learned group-to-RP mapping information.

Two new Cisco IOS Software configuration commands are available to prevent DM flooding and DM fallback: the **ip pim autorp listener** command and the **no ip pim dm-fallback** command.

The **ip pim autorp listener** global configuration command causes IP multicast traffic for the two Auto-RP groups, 224.0.1.39 and 224.0.1.40, to be flooded, using PIM-DM, across interfaces operating in PIM-SM. This command allows Auto-RP to operate in PIM-DM, and multicast traffic to operate in PIM-SM, bidir-PIM, or SSM mode. This command is available starting with Cisco IOS Software Releases 12.3(4)T, 12.2(28)S, and 12.2(33)SRA.

If the **ip pim autorp listener** command is not supported on the devices in your network, Cisco recommends configuring a *sink RP* for all possible multicast groups in the network, because it is possible for an unknown or unexpected source to become active. A sink RP is also known as an *RP of last* resort and is a statically configured RP that may or may not actually exist in the network, so that there is always an RP defined. If no RP is configured to limit source registration, the group reverts to dense mode operation and is flooded with data.

Configuring a sink RP does not interfere with Auto-RP operation because by default Auto-RP messages supersede static RP configurations.

The **no ip pim dm-fallback** global configuration command disables DM fallback and blocks all multicast traffic for groups not specifically configured. This command is available starting with Cisco IOS Software Releases 12.3(4)T, 12.2(28)S, and 12.2(33)SRA. When IP multicast is used in mission-critical networks, PIM-DM should be avoided. If Auto-RP is configured or a BSR (described in the next section) is used to distribute RP information, a risk exists that RP information may be lost if all RPs, Auto-RP, or the BSR for a group fails because of network congestion. This failure can lead to the network either partially or fully falling back into PIM-DM. If a network falls back into PIM-DM, DM flooding occurs. Routers that lose RP information switch all existing states into DM, and any new states that must be created for the failed group are created in DM.

Boot Strap Router

BSR is another dynamic RP selection protocol that also supports interoperability between vendors.

BSR performs similarly to Auto-RP in that it uses candidate routers for the RP function and for relaying the RP information for a group. The network administrator configures one or more routers in the network to serve as candidate BSRs (C-BSRs).

At network startup, all C-BSRs participate in the BSR election process by sending a PIM BSR message, containing its BSR priority, out all interfaces, as illustrated in Figure 10-22. This information is distributed through link-local multicast messages that travel from PIM router to PIM router. These BSR messages are flooded hop by hop throughout the entire network. At the end of the BSR election interval, the BSR with the highest BSR priority is elected as the active BSR.

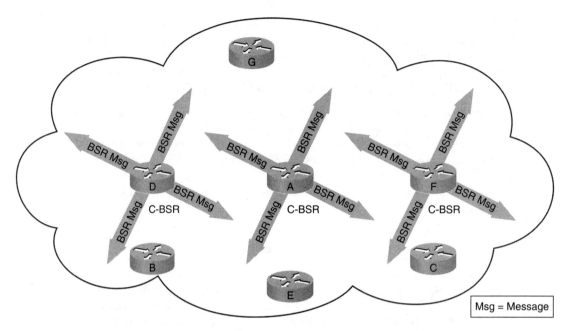

Figure 10-22 *To Elect an Active BSR, C-BSRs Send BSR Messages on All Interfaces*

Note   The BSR election process is similar in nature to the root-bridge election mechanism in the Spanning Tree Protocol (STP).

All routers in the network, including C-RPs, know which C-BSR has been elected as the currently active BSR. The C-RPs unicast their C-RP Announcement messages directly to the active BSR, as illustrated in Figure 10-23. The active BSR stores all incoming C-RP announcements in its group-to-RP mapping cache. The active BSR sends the entire list of C-RPs from its mapping cache in periodic BSR messages that are flooded hop by hop throughout the entire network, as also shown in Figure 10-23. As each router receives a copy of these BSR messages, it updates the information in its local group-to-RP mapping cache so that it knows the IP address of all C-RPs in the network.

Unlike Auto-RP where the mapping agent elects the active RP for a group range and announces the election results to the network, the BSR does not elect the active RP for a group. This task is left to each individual router in the network. Each router in the network elects the currently active RP for a particular group range using a well-known hashing algorithm. Because each router is running the same algorithm against the same list of C-RPs, they all elect the same RP for a particular group range.

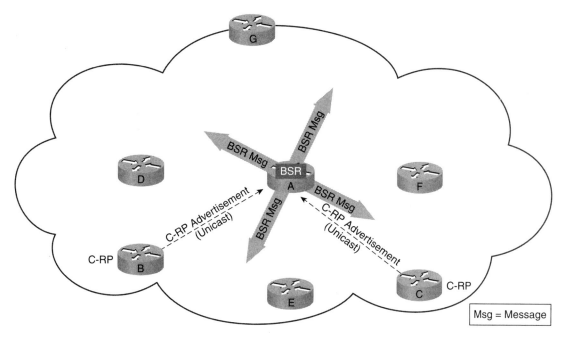

Figure 10-23 *The Active BSR Sends the Entire List of C-RPs in Periodic BSR Messages*

Securing IP Multicast

Multicast deployments have added security considerations compared to unicast routing environments. Some of the factors that distinguish multicast routing are the state information, replication process, join process, and unidirectional flows. Both multicast security considerations, access control mechanisms, and support for IP multicast over IPsec.

Security Considerations for IP Multicast

This section introduces security considerations for IP multicast environments.

Security Goals for Multicast Environments

The main goal for security of multicast networks is to keep the network running even if there are configuration errors, malfunctions, or network attacks (such as a denial-of-service [DoS] attack from an unknown server). Multicast security involves managing network resources and access control for multiple senders (sources) and receivers by defining what multicast traffic should be allowed in the network. Multicast security must also protect against rogue servers or RPs that should not be in the network. Network resource utilization must be managed; this includes managing multicast state information in the network and services participating in multicast activity.

You can use a wide range of tools and technologies t to manage multicast security. Control and enforcement of multicast networks includes answering the following four questions:

- **Why?** Network administrators want to control which users and servers have access to network resources, to support an organization's policies or protect access to resources and resource availability with permissions and controls.

- **How?** Control in multicast environments can include managing state creation and providing packet-level control by policing, filtering, and encryption techniques.

- **What?** Network administrators want to protect the content of the multicast service, protect the control plane of the network devices from being overloaded, and protect the data plane of the network from overloading the links between the devices.

- **Where?** Controls can be enforced in multiple locations, but most are configured locally on a router or switch. These controls may implicitly protect the service across the network. There are also protocols that can be coordinated to provide protection on a hop-by-hop basis and mechanisms that rely on policy servers to provide authentication, authorization, and accounting (AAA).

The following sections examine unicast and multicast state and replication requirements, attack traffic in unicast and multicast networks, and the use of scoped addresses.

Unicast and Multicast State Requirements

Unicast and multicast routing have different state requirements. For unicast routing, the state of the network resides in the unicast routing table. The state is relatively stable, only changing when the network topology changes. The router CPU is active after network topology changes, but end-user activity does not impact the state or the activity on the router other than the traffic through the links. The main network design constraint is the link bandwidth requirements.

For multicast routing, the state includes the unicast routing state plus the multicast state. The multicast state information increases when sources and receivers participate in multicast applications. The router CPU is active when application state changes occur and when network topology changes occur. PIM and IGMP create more periodic CPU activity than unicast protocols create. A multicast network design must take into consideration the number of multicast applications and sources to provide a robust network.

Throughput concerns are also different in unicast and multicast routing. Unicast routing is concerned with the amount of traffic received, called the *ingress* packet rate.

Multicast routing is also concerned with the amount of traffic sent, called the *egress* packet rate, and the ability to replicate outgoing packets.

Even low-input packet rates can potentially overload the capacity of the router to support the egress load because of the requirements for packet replication. Egress throughput impacts both routers and Layer 3 switches supporting IGMP snooping.

As shown in Figure 10-24, with IP multicast there is state information associated with ingress lookups per application or source. The memory requirements of the ingress state information increases with the number of applications or sources. As shown in Figure 10-24, the egress state information is concerned with the replication of packets to multiple interfaces for supporting receiver branches in the distribution tree. The egress state information increases with the number of applications across the number of receiver branches on outgoing interfaces.

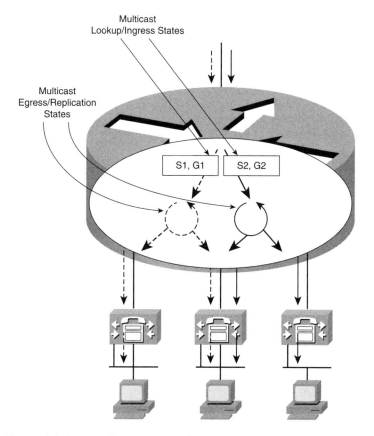

Figure 10-24 *Multicast State Information Increases with the Number of Sources and Receivers*

Hardware acceleration provides the optimal multicast performance, but limits apply to the amount of hardware state information permitted, based on the available chipsets on specific platforms. However, there are also limits in memory on software platforms, restricting the amount of state information permitted. These software limits are higher than the hardware limits.

Unicast and Multicast Replication Requirements

Multicast replication impacts where access control should be applied, as illustrated in the example in Figure 10-25.

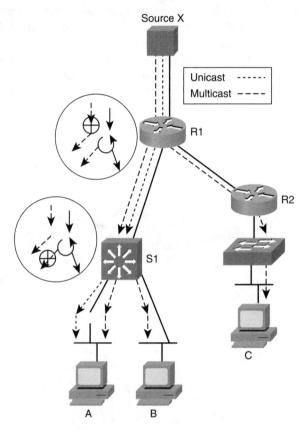

Figure 10-25 *Multicast Replication Impacts Where Access Control Should Be Applied*

In this example, the network engineer wants to ensure that Receiver A does not receive traffic from Source X. For unicast traffic, a filter can be put anywhere along the path, based on the source and receiver addresses. However, this model does not work for multicast because the receiver address is a group address.

For multicast traffic, filtering for receivers must always be placed after the last replication point to other potential receivers. In Figure 10-25, the filtering must occur on switch S1 egress, to avoid impacting Receiver B. Similarly, filtering sources must happen before the first potential replication point so that source information is blocked throughout the network.

Attack Traffic from Rogue Sources to Receivers

First, consider attack traffic from rogue sources to hosts (receivers). In unicast routing, any device can send a packet to another device. There is no implicit protection of receivers from sources. Firewalls and access control lists (ACL) can be used to protect against unwanted traffic.

In multicast routing, source devices do not send traffic to specific devices but to a multicast group. A receiver in a branch of the network needs to explicitly join a multicast group before traffic is forwarded to that branch. Therefore, multicast implicitly protects receivers against packets from unknown sources or potential attackers.

With SSM, unknown source attacks are not possible because receivers must join a specific source host in a specific multicast group. Traffic from unknown sources will only reach the first-hop router (the router closest to the source) and then be discarded; this traffic does not even create state information in the first-hop router.

With ASM (PIM-SM) and bidir-PIM, an end device receives traffic only when it joins a group. Therefore, an attacker cannot attack a specific receiver host but can only attack against a multicast group or the entire network.

Attack Traffic from Sources to Networks Without Receivers

Another type of network attacks targets network devices, using attack traffic from rogue sources to networks without receivers.

Multicast DoS attacks are often referred to as control plane attacks or state attacks. The aim of the attacker is usually to increase the multicast state information in routers above a manageable level so that the device experiences extremely slow convergence or it crashes. Multicast DoS can also be the result of misbehaving applications.

SSM networks drop traffic from unknown sources at the first-hop router closest to the source, and so are not affected by these types of attacks. However, multicast DoS attacks can impact ASM and bidir-PIM multicast implementations.

For ASM (PIM-SM) networks, attacks from rogue sources increase the number of (S,G) states and the (*,G) states created on the first-hop router and on the RP. The first-hop router sends unicast Register messages to the RP with a (*,G) join request. The RP joins to the first-hop router with an (S,G) join if it has active receivers downstream. This state information remains for 260 seconds by default. However, for example, if an attacker is able to generate 100 IGMPv3 (S,G) joins a second for each of 10 sources, after 260 seconds there would be 260,000 state entries. One way to limit this type of attack is to limit the rate of Register messages to the RP.

If the RP does not have active receivers downstream, it sends a Register-Stop message to the first-hop router. When the first-hop router receives the Register-Stop message, it stops sending Register messages to the RP, putting the source on hold.

For bidir-PIM networks, all receiverless traffic is carried across a single route to the RP in a (*,G) route. An attack using this type of traffic is similar to a unicast traffic attack to the

RP. In new Cisco IOS implementations, this does not create new (*,G) states. However, in earlier implementations, the receiverless traffic creates new (*,G) state information, except on the Cisco Catalyst 6500 series switches and the Cisco 7600 series routers.

Attack Traffic from Rogue Receivers

Receivers might also attack the network. Multicast receivers can create state attacks; there is no equivalent action in unicast networks. The following are three types of receiver attacks:

■ **Attack against content:** The rogue receiver attempts to gain access to content that the receiver is not unauthorized to access.

■ **Attack against bandwidth:** The receiver attempts to overload network bandwidth. This attack is typically against shared network bandwidth and is therefore actually an attack against other receivers.

■ **Attack against routers and switches:** The receiver tries to create more state information than the router or switch can handle by sending multiple join requests. Processing these multiple join requests from the receiver can increase the convergence time of other states or cause the network device to reboot.

An example of a receiver attack is a user requesting many Internet TV broadcasts from the available channels.

Scoped Addresses

Scoping addresses can provide some architectural security.

Unicast addresses have two scopes: public and private. RFC 1918, *Address Allocation for Private Internets*, defines the private address ranges for IPv4.

As discussed in the "Multicast IP Addresses" section, earlier in this chapter, multicast addresses have various scopes, including those defined by the IANA and as deployed within an organization. Recall that administratively, or limited, scoped addresses are in the 239.0.0.0/8 range. Although organizations can use the site-local addresses and organization-local addresses (within the administratively scoped address range) as a geographic form of access control for applications with these local addresses, there is no automatic enforcement of scopes. Figure 10-26 shows an example of a multicast address range allocation.

Routers configured with ACLs can prevent multicast traffic in an address range from flowing outside an autonomous system or any user-defined domain. Within an autonomous system or domain, the administratively scoped address range can be further subdivided so that local multicast boundaries can be defined. This address subdivision is called *address scoping* and allows for address reuse between these smaller domains.

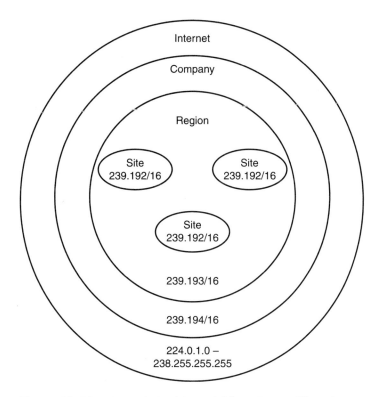

Figure 10-26   *Example Multicast Address Range Allocation*

Routers can also be configured to change the TTL threshold of multicast packets being forwarded out of an interface, using the **ip multicast ttl-threshold** *ttl* interface configuration command. This command allows only packets with a TTL value greater than the threshold specified to be forwarded out of the interface. For example, the TTL threshold on a border router interface could be set to 200, a very high value. Most multicast applications typically set the TTL value to well below 200, so no packets with a TTL lower than 200 would be forwarded out of the interface on this border router.

Multicast Access Control

This section describes access controls that can be used to secure IP multicast networks.

Packet Filter-Based Access Control

Cisco IOS Software supports packet filter-based ACLs that can help control traffic in a multicast network. These ACLs are typically implemented in hardware on most router platforms. If the packet-based ACL that filters traffic is deployed at the network ingress interface on the data plane before multicast processing, no state is created for the dropped traffic.

Figure 10-27 illustrates an example network. Example 10-1 provides the ACL configuration on the router in this network. A named ACL called check-source is created. This ACL permits any IP traffic from source address 10.0.0.0/8 to destination address 239.0.0.0/9 (239.0.0.0 to 239.127.255.255). Traffic to 224.0.0.0/4 is permitted and logged. All other traffic is denied and logged. This ACL is applied inbound on the router's E0 interface. As a result, the packet from the PC (10.0.0.1) to 239.10.244.1 is permitted, but the packet from the hacker (10.0.1.1) to 239.244.244.1 is denied.

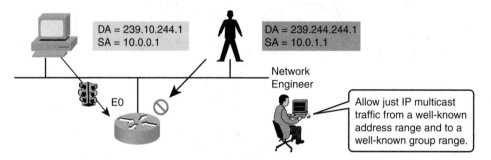

Figure 10-27   *Network for Packet Filter-Based Access Control Shown in Example 10-1*

Example 10-1   *Packet Filter-Based Access Control Configuration for Router in Figure 10-27*

```
ip access-list extended check-source
  permit ip host 10.0.0.0 0.255.255.255 239.0.0.0 0.127.255.255
  permit ip any 224.0.0.0 15.255.255.255 log
  deny ip any any log
interface ethernet0
  ip address 10.1.1.1 255.255.255.0
  ip access-group check-source in
```

The main advantage of this approach is simplicity and clarity. The disadvantages include the effort required to apply an ACL to any inbound interface on which a multicast source might be, including all subnets on which users or servers reside.

Note   When using ACLs, be sure to allow appropriate unicast traffic and routing protocol multicast traffic.

Although packet filters can also be used to filter outbound traffic, *protocol* filtering is typically preferred for outbound (egress) traffic.

Host Receiver-Side Access Control

IGMP access groups can be used to provide host receiver-side access control.

The **ip igmp access-group** interface configuration command is used to filter groups in IGMP reports by using a standard access list, or to filter sources and groups in IGMPv3 reports by using an extended access list. The latter use of this command restricts receivers to join only the specific (S,G) channels permitted by the extended ACL.

When an IGMP extended access list is referenced in the **ip igmp access-group** command on an interface, the (S,G) pairs in the permit and deny statements of the extended access list are matched against the (S,G) pair of the IGMP reports received on the interface. The first part of the extended access list clause (the *source address* part) filters the source (the multicast sender); the second part of the extended access list clause (the *destination address* part) filters the multicast group.

For example, if an IGMP report with (S1,S2,...Sn,G) is received, the router first checks the group (*,G) against the access list statements. If the *group* is denied, the entire IGMP report is denied. If the group is permitted, each individual (S,G) pair is checked against the access list. Denied *sources* are taken out of the IGMP report, thereby denying any sources that match the access list from sending to the group.

Figure 10-28 illustrates an example network with two hosts. Example 10-2 provides the ACL configuration on the router. The ACL controls IGMP entries into the router. Any host is permitted to join group 225.2.2.2, and any host in network 10.0.0.0/8 is permitted to join groups in the 232.0.0.0/8 range. All other traffic is denied. The ACL is applied to the router's E0 interface. As a result, the join to group 225.2.2.2 is permitted, whereas the join to group 224.1.1.1 is denied.

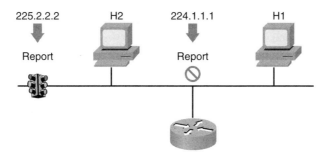

Figure 10-28   *Network for Host Receiver-Based Access Control Configuration Shown in Example 10-2*

Example 10-2   *Host Receiver-Based Access Control Configuration for Router in Figure 10-28*

```
ip access-list extended allowed-multicast-igmp
  permit ip any host 225.2.2.2
  permit ip 10.0.0.0 0.255.255.255 232.0.0.0 0.255.255.255
  deny ip any any
```

```
interface ethernet 0
 ip igmp access-group allowed-multicast-igmp
```

PIM-SM Source Control

PIM-SM register messages can be filtered on a candidate RP router using the **ip pim accept-register** global configuration command.

This command prevents unauthorized sources from registering with the RP. If an unauthorized source sends a register message to the RP, the RP immediately sends back a Register-Stop message. The filter can be based on the source address using a standard ACL or based on the (S,G) pair using an extended ACL.

Figure 10-29 illustrates an example network. Example 10-3 provides the ACL configuration on the RP router. Only a source with address 192.168.1.1 is permitted to register with the RP; therefore when the source 192.168.2.2 sends a register message, the RP returns a Register-Stop message.

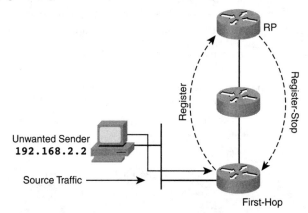

Figure 10-29 *Network for PIM-SM Source Control Configuration Shown in Example 10-3*

Example 10-3 *PIM-SM Source Control Configuration on the RP in Figure 10-29*

```
ip pim accept-register list 10

access-list 10 permit 192.168.1.1
```

This command allows for a limited form of centralized source control with PIM-SM. However, it does not inhibit (S,G) state creation on the first-hop router. Receivers that are on same first-hop router will still receive traffic from invalid sources.

An advantage of this approach is that it is configured only on the RPs, not on all the edge LAN interfaces.

Disabling Multicast Groups for IPv6

Cisco IOS Software supports disabling multicast groups by range for IPv6. The **ipv6 multicast group-range** *access-list-name* global configuration command enables a network administrator to specify an authorized IPv6 group range. If the group is denied by the referenced ACL, multicast protocol actions and traffic forwarding for unauthorized groups or channels are disabled for all interfaces. All control packets for the group are dropped, no state information is created for the group, and all data packets are dropped on hardware discarding platforms.

> **Note**   The **ipv6 multicast group-range** command is supported in Cisco IOS Software Release 12.4(4)T for IPv6. and IPv4.

Multicast over IPsec VPNs

Multicast is becoming more common as a transport for business-critical applications. With the growing adoption of multicast, protecting the content that is embedded in the multicast streams also becomes more critical. IPsec is commonly used to provide data authentication, data integrity, and data confidentiality for unicast traffic. As multicast becomes more common in enterprise networks, there is also an increased demand to protect multicast data using IPsec.

Numerous scenarios require multicast over IPsec to be considered in enterprise network designs.

An organization may already be deploying multicast in parts of their network and might need to extend multicast to their existing IPsec-based VPN. This requires a close examination of the existing IPsec deployment, to determine whether it can support multicast and which restrictions apply. Another scenario may be an organization that currently has a multicast-enabled WAN and is looking to replace or extend this multicast-enabled WAN with an IPsec-based VPN solution. A third scenario may be an organization that needs to add data security to an existing multicast-enabled network. For example, a company may be using a multicast-enabled Multiprotocol Label Switching virtual private network (MPLS VPN), and new regulations require that all traffic across the VPN is protected through IPsec.

Unfortunately, multicast support is not automatic for most types of IPsec VPNs. Even if multicast is supported for the specific type of IPsec VPN, there may be restrictions or performance issues to consider.

Two major challenges for IPsec VPNs to support multicast are as follows:

■   Multicast requires packets to be replicated to deliver a traffic stream to multiple destinations. Normally, this replication can happen on any router in the multicast-enabled network. In most types of IPsec VPNs, this is not a viable approach because the key that was used to encrypt the packet is not recognized by all the receiving routers. It is valid only for a specific IPsec peer. As a result, in most types of IPsec VPNs, the data needs to be replicated before it is encrypted. However, this can have a significant impact on the encrypting router, because a single multicast stream may need to be encrypted many times.

■ Another design consideration in certain types of IPsec VPNs is the reverse path forwarding (RPF) mechanism that is used by multicast. When multicast packets are received on an interface, a router verifies whether they are received on the interface that points back to the source according to the uncast routing table. Also, packets are never forwarded back to the RPF interface. This principle can cause challenges in multipoint IPsec VPNs, such as Dynamic Multipoint VPN (DMVPN).

Traditional Direct Encapsulation IPsec VPNs

Traditional direct encapsulation IPsec VPNs do not support multicast even if the underlying network supports multicast; multicast replication cannot be performed in the underlying network. Security associations (SA) are established between pairs of routers, and a common key is used to encrypt and decrypt packets. This key is unique to the pair of routers and is not known on any other router. This point-to-point relation between routers requires that the destination of the packet be known before it is encrypted. Routers in the transit path between the two IPsec pairs cannot replicate the packet and forward it to other routers in the IPsec VPN because they do not have the proper key to decrypt the packet.

To overcome this restriction, an overlay of point-to-point IPsec tunnels can be used. Packets should be replicated before encryption takes place. When a multicast packet arrives at the IPsec router, it should first determine which of its IPsec peers need to receive the packet and then create a copy for each of the peers. Subsequently, the replicated packets should be encrypted with the appropriate key for the corresponding peer and encapsulated in a unicast packet that is destined for that peer.

For this model to work, it is necessary that the router recognizes which of its peers are interested in the multicast stream. PIM is commonly used. However, although a point-to-point IPsec SA is established between the two peers, no corresponding point-to-point interface can be used to establish a PIM adjacency. The only interface that is used in traditional IPsec deployments is the physical WAN interface. Effectively, the IPsec VPN acts as a nonbroadcast multiaccess (NBMA) network, which prohibits the use of PIM and unicast routing protocols across the VPN.

A second potential issue is that on a nonbroadcast network, multicast packets can never be replicated to the interface on which they were received because of the RPF check. This means that a full mesh of IPsec peerings would be necessary to allow proper replication from any site to any site.

The IPsec virtual tunnel interface (VTI) feature removes this limitation. It associates a point-to-point tunnel interface with each of the IPsec peers. This association allows routing protocol adjacencies and PIM adjacencies to be established across the logical point-to-point link between the peers. It also eliminates the RPF issues, because traffic that is received on a particular VTI can be replicated to other VTIs

VTI is a relatively new feature and may not be supported in all Cisco IOS Software versions. A second and more widely available option is to use generic routing encapsulation (GRE) together with IPsec to create logical point-to-point links between IPsec VPN peers.

Multicast over IPsec GRE

GRE and IPsec can be used to create an overlay VPN that supports IP multicast.

GRE is a tunneling mechanism that can be used to establish a logical point-to-point link between two routers. If GRE tunneling is combined with IPsec, a secure tunnel is created to support unicast, broadcast, and multicast traffic between the two peers.

Routing protocols, such as Open Shortest Path First (OSPF) and Enhanced Interior Gateway Routing Protocol (EIGRP), can establish routing adjacencies across a GRE tunnel. Alternatively, static routes can be pointed to the corresponding tunnel interface. PIM can also establish adjacencies across a GRE tunnel, allowing multicast routing between the peers. Because unicast routes between the peers point to the tunnel interface, the multicast RPF check passes for multicast packets that are sourced from the peer site. Each GRE tunnel between two peers is a separate logical point-to-point link, so packets can be replicated and forwarded between tunnels. Therefore, multicast is supported between any two sites as long as they have IP connectivity.

When designing a GRE IPsec VPN to support multicast, consider the following:

- In this type of deployment, multicast replication takes place before encryption. In a typical hub-and-spoke design, a stream from the hub site to many spokes generates a burst of packets that all need to be encrypted at the same time. The overhead associated with replicating and then encrypting the multicast packets can add up quickly if a stream needs to be replicated to many different sites.

- The topology of the overlay VPN determines the unicast traffic paths and multicast distribution trees. This may result in suboptimal routing. For example, in a hub-and-spoke design, all multicast traffic between spokes flows through the hub. To optimize the traffic flow, it might be necessary to build additional tunnels to connect the spokes directly.

Multicast over DMVPN

DMVPN can be used to create a scalable multipoint IPsec VPN that supports limited IP multicast.

Traditional hub-and-spoke GRE designs do not scale well. With a traditional hub-and-spoke topology, all spoke-to-spoke traffic transits through the hub. As more nodes are added to the topology, the configuration task becomes more complex because a separate GRE interface is needed on the hub for every spoke and all tunnels need to be predefined. DMVPN enables dynamic configuration and reduces the maintenance and configuration on the hubs. DMVPN has a backbone hub-and-spoke topology, but it allows direct spoke-to-spoke functionality using tunneling to enable the secure exchange of data between two branch offices without traversing the head office. DMVPN is a combination of IPsec, GRE, and Next Hop Resolution Protocol (NHRP).

Instead of using point-to-point GRE tunnels, a multipoint GRE (mGRE) tunnel is created. Dynamic routing is used only between the hub and the spokes. When spokes need to communicate with each other directly, NHRP is used to determine the external IP address from the spoke router for a particular route, and a spoke-to-spoke IPsec tunnel is established on demand. To support IP multicast routing, PIM adjacencies are established between the hub and the spokes. No multicast adjacencies exist between the spoke sites. Unlike unicast traffic, multicast traffic does not trigger the establishment of spoke-to-spoke tunnels and cannot be sent directly from spoke to spoke.

Because of these limitations, multicast is only partially supported on DMVPN. Hub-to-spoke multicast flows are supported. Spoke-to-spoke multicast is not supported because a stream that is received from one of the spokes can never be forwarded back out the RPF interface to the other spokes.

Consider the following when designing a DMVPN to support multicast:

- Spoke-to-spoke multicast is not supported, which limits the types of multicast applications that can be used across the DMVPN. For example, distributing market data from the hub site to spoke sites would work well. However, a many-to-many application, such as multimedia conferencing, will not work in this type of environment.

- The NBMA nature of the DMVPN network also prevents multicast from operating correctly if the RP for a multicast is located at a spoke. Therefore, RPs should be located at the hub sites in a multicast DMVPN design.

- In DMVPN, multicast replication is performed at the hub site before encryption takes place, similar to hub-and-spoke GRE IPsec deployments. Therefore, DMVPN suffers from the same potential performance issues when a multicast stream is replicated to many different spokes.

- To alleviate the impact of multicast replication on DMVPN headend performance, the mGRE and encryption functions can be separated. The multicast replication, routing, and tunnel termination functions are performed by the mGRE headend; then, the encryption function is performed by a separate IPsec encryption headend. The separation of these functions allows for increased scalability.

Note For additional details regarding scaling multicast over IPsec VPN, refer to the Multicast over IPsec VPN Design Guide at http://www.cisco.com/en/US/docs/solutions/Enterprise/WAN_and_MAN/V3PNIPmc.html.

Multicast Using GET VPN

Group Encrypted Transport VPN (GET VPN) provides secure transport for unicast and multicast traffic on an existing private network.

Tunnel-based IPsec VPN solutions, such as IPsec direct encapsulation, IPsec GRE, and DMVPN, create overlay VPNs on top of an existing IP network. Traditional IPsec tunneling solutions suffer from multicast replication issues, because multicast replication must be performed before tunnel encapsulation and encryption at the IPsec router that is closest to the multicast source. Multicast replication cannot be performed in the underlying network, because encapsulated multicasts appear to the core network as unicast data.

Cisco GET VPN introduces the concept of a trusted group to eliminate point-to-point tunnels and their associated overlay routing. All group members share a common SA, also known as a group SA. This enables group members to decrypt traffic that was encrypted by any other group member. The group SA is negotiated with a central key server, using the Group Domain of Interpretation (GDOI) group key management protocol that is defined in RFC 3547.

In traditional IPsec, tunnel endpoint addresses are used as the new packet source and destination. The packet is then routed over the IP infrastructure, using the encrypting gateway source IP address and the decrypting gateway destination IP address. With GET VPN, IPsec-protected data packets encapsulate the original source and destination packet addresses of the host in the outer IP header to preserve the IP address.

Because tunnel header preservation is combined with group SAs, multicast replication can be offloaded to the provider network. Every group member shares the same SA, so the IPsec router that is closest to the multicast source does not need to replicate packets to all its peers and is no longer subject to the multicast replication issues that are seen in traditional IPsec solutions.

GET VPN only provides data security; it relies on the underlying network for routing. Therefore, you can use multicast to send the GET VPN packets to multiple destinations, which makes GET VPN very scalable.

Unlike IPsec direct encapsulation, VTI, IPsec GRE, and DMVPN, GET VPN does not create an overlay VPN. GET VPN can be used to secure data transport on an existing private core network or VPN, but it does not create the core network. Scalability and convergence characteristics of the GET VPN solution are dependent on the underlying network.

Because multicast replication is performed in the core, GET VPN does not suffer from scalability issues that are caused by multicast replication on hub sites.

GET VPN leverages the routing, forwarding, and replication functions of the core network, which means that the core network needs to support multicast in order for the DMVPN solution to support multicast. For correct end-to-end unicast and multicast routing, control plane interaction must occur between the core network and the edge networks.

GET VPN can be used across an existing semiprivate network, such as an MPLS VPN. GET VPN is less suited to be used to transport multicast across public networks, such as the Internet.

Summary

In this chapter, you learned the basics of IP multicast and the design and security recommendations for IP multicast networks including VPN technology.

With unicast transmission, multiple packets must be sent from a source to reach multiple receivers. In contrast, an IP multicast source sends a single packet; downstream routers replicate the packets only on links where receiving hosts exist.

An IP multicast group address is the destination address to which packets for the group are sent. A device must be a member of a group to receive the group's traffic.

Multicast applications can use a variety of models, including one to many or many to many. Using multicast provides advantages including enhanced efficiency and performance and support for distributed applications. However, because multicast applications are UDP based, reliability, congestion control, duplicate packets, out-of-sequence packets, and security may become issues.

Multicast addresses are in the range 224.0.0.0 through 239.255.255.255. Within this range, the multicast address scopes are shown in Table 10-2.

Table 10-2   *Multicast Address Scopes*

Range of Addresses	Description
224.0.0.0 through 224.0.0.255	Local scope addresses
224.0.1.0 through 238.255.255.255	Globally scoped addresses
239.0.0.0 through 239.255.255.255	Limited, or administratively, scoped addresses
239.255.0.0/16, 239.252.0.0/16, 239.253.0.0/16, and 239.254.0.0/16	Site-local scope addresses
239.192.0.0 to 239.251.255.255	Organization-local scope addresses

IP multicast addresses are mapped to Layer 2 multicast addresses by mapping the low-order 23 bits of the IP multicast address into the low-order 23 bits of the MAC (Layer 2) address, resulting in a 32:1 overlap of IP addresses to MAC addresses.

Multicast addresses are typically statically assigned. Alternatively, MADCAP allows a client workstation to "lease" a multicast address from a MADCAP server.

IGMP is used between hosts and their local router. There are three versions of IGMP. IGMPv2 additions to IGMPv1 include Leave Group messages. IGMPv3 adds the ability to filter multicasts based on the multicast source so that hosts can indicate that they want to receive traffic only from particular sources within a multicast group.

With IGMP snooping, the switch eavesdrops on the IGMP messages sent between routers and hosts and updates its MAC address table accordingly.

CGMP is a Cisco Systems proprietary protocol that runs between a multicast router and a switch; the routers inform each of their directly connected switches of IGMP registrations that were received from hosts accessible through the switch.

The PIM routing protocol is used by routers to forward multicast traffic. PIM uses the normal routing table, populated by the unicast routing protocol, in its multicast routing calculations. PIM terminology includes the following:

- **Source tree:** A distribution tree created for each source sending to each multicast group. (S,G) multicast forwarding entries represent source S sending to the group G.

- **Shared tree:** A single distribution tree that is shared between *all* sources for each multicast group. (*,G) multicast forwarding entries represent any source sending to the group G. Traffic is forwarded via an RP for the group.

- **RP:** The common root of a shared tree.

- **RPF:** Forwarding multicast traffic away from the source, rather than to the receiver.

The three main PIM deployment models are as follows:

- ASM (PIM-SM), using a combination of shared and source trees, for general-purpose applications

- Bidir-PIM, using only shared trees, for many-to-many applications

- SSM, using only source trees, for one-to-many applications

Considerations for deploying an RP include the following:

- Static RP addressing, when the RP address is manually configured. If the RP fails, routers cannot fail over to a standby RP.

- Anycast RP to provide RP load-sharing and hot-backup capabilities.

- Auto-RP, a dynamic way for routers to learn the RP information.

- BSR, another RP dynamic selection protocol that also supports interoperability between vendors.

Multicast security considerations include unicast and multicast state and replication requirements, various types of attack traffic, and scoped addresses.

Multicast access control mechanisms include packet filter-based ACLs, IGMP access groups, and PIM-SM Register message filtering. Multicast group ranges can be disabled for IPv6 multicast.

Multicast is not natively supported on most IPsec VPNs, and IPsec VPNs should be carefully designed to support IP multicast traffic. GET VPN leverages the routing, forwarding, and replication functions of the core network, which means that the core network needs to support multicast for the DMVPN solution to support multicast. For correct end-to-end unicast and multicast routing, control plane interaction must occur between the core network and the edge networks.

References

For additional information, refer to the following:

The IANA's IP multicast addressing assignments reference at http://www.iana.org/assignments/multicast-addresses

"The Internet Protocol Multicast" chapter of the *Internetworking Technology Handbook* at http://www.cisco.com/en/US/docs/internetworking/technology/handbook/IP-Multi.html

Cisco Systems, Inc. *Multicast in a Campus Network: CGMP and IGMP Snooping* at http://www.cisco.com/en/US/products/hw/switches/ps708/products_tech_note09186 a00800b0871.shtml

Cisco Systems, Inc. *IP Multicast Technology Overview* at http://www.cisco.com/univercd/cc/td/doc/cisintwk/intsolns/mcst_sol/mcst_ovr.pdf

Cisco Systems, Inc. *Bidirectional PIM Deployment Guide* at http://www.cisco.com/en/US/prod/collateral/iosswrel/ps6537/ps6552/ps6592/prod_white_paper0900aecd80310db2.pdf

Cisco Systems, Inc. *Guidelines for Enterprise IP Multicast Address Allocation* at http://www.cisco.com/en/US/tech/tk828/technologies_white_paper09186a00802d4 643.shtml

Cisco Systems, Inc. *Cisco IOS IP Multicast Configuration Guide, Release 12.4* at http://www.cisco.com/en/US/docs/ios/ipmulti/configuration/guide/12_4/imc_12_4_book.html

Cisco Systems, Inc. *Configuring a Virtual Tunnel interface with IP Security* at http://www.cisco.com/en/US/technologies/tk583/tk372/technologies_white_paper09 00aecd8029d629_ps6635_Products_White_Paper.html

Williamson, Beau. *Developing IP Multicast Networks, Volume I*, Indianapolis, IN: Cisco Press; October, 1999

Cisco Systems, Inc. *The Multicast Security Toolkit* at http://www.cisco.com/web/about/security/intelligence/multicast_toolkit.html

Cisco Systems, Inc. *Multicast over IPsec VPN Design Guide* at http://www.cisco.com/application/pdf/en/us/guest/netsol/ns171/c649/ccmigration_09186a008074f26a.pdf

The Internet Engineering Task Force. RFC 1112, *Host Extensions for IP Multicasting* at http://www.ietf.org/rfc/rfc1112.txt

The Internet Engineering Task Force. RFC 2974 *Session Announcement Protocol* at http://www.ietf.org/rfc/rfc2974.txt

The Internet Engineering Task Force. RFC 3376, *Internet Group Management Protocol, Version 3* at http://www.ietf.org/rfc/rfc3376.txt

The Internet Engineering Task Force. RFC 4601, *Protocol Independent Multicast - Sparse Mode (PIM-SM)* at http://www.ietf.org/rfc/rfc4601.txt

The Internet Engineering Task Force. RFC 3569, *An Overview of Source-Specific Multicast (SSM)* at http://www.ietf.org/rfc/rfc3569.txt

Cisco Systems, Inc. *Multicast VPN* at http://www.cisco.com/en/US/products/ ps6651/products_ios_protocol_option_home.html

Review Questions

Answer the following questions, and then refer to Appendix A, "Answers to Review Questions," for the answers.

1. What is a benefit of using IP multicast to deliver source traffic to multiple receivers?

   a. It guarantees packet delivery.

   b. It reduces network bandwidth consumption.

   c. It is highly efficient for sending single-stream application traffic.

   d. It replicates packets at all network devices to enable multiple client requests.

2. For a broadcast to flood packets out all interfaces, except those incoming from the source, multicast routing uses what?

   a. Unicasts

   b. Multicast routers

   c. RPF

   d. OSPF

   e. SPT

3. Which purpose is served by IGMP in IP multicast?

   a. To perform the RPF check

   b. To join hosts in a multicast group

   c. To provide reliable multicast transport

   d. To perform the multicast forwarding function

4. In which type of environments would PIM-SSM be efficiently used?

    a. Deployments that use shared distribution trees

    b. Deployments in which switches are used pervasively

    c. Deployments in which only a few receivers need IP multicast content

    d. One-to-many applications

    e. Many-to-many applications

5. Which three statements about ASM are correct?

    a. RPs are not needed.

    b. It is also known as PIM-SSM.

    c. Deployments use shared distribution trees.

    d. Deployments use source distribution trees.

    e. It is the traditional form for PIM deployments.

6. Which deployment model does not track (S,G) state?

    a. Anycast RP

    b. ASM

    c. Bidir-PIM

    d. PIM-SM

    e. SSM

7. Which two protocols use candidate RPs?

    a. Anycast RP

    b. Auto-RP

    c. BSR

    d. C-BSR

    e. Dense mode fallback

    f. MSDP

8. What are three characteristics of multicast state information?

    a. It does not include the unicast routing state information.

    b. It grows when sources and receivers run multicast applications.

    c. It includes the unicast routing state information.

    d. It changes only when the network topology changes.

    e. State changes do not affect CPU utilization.

    f. State changes affect CPU utilization.

9. How is packet filter-based access control typically deployed?

    a. At the network egress interface on the control plane after multicast processing

    b. At the network egress interface on the data plane after multicast processing

    c. At the network ingress interface on the control plane before multicast processing

    d. At the network ingress interface on the data plane before multicast processing

10. In which two types of environments would PIM-SSM be efficiently used?

    a. Deployments that use shared distribution trees

    b. Deployments in which switches are used pervasively

    c. Deployments in which only a few receivers need IP multicast content

    d. One-to-many applications

    e. Many-to-many applications

11. Which three statements about ASM are correct?

    a. RPs are not needed.

    b. It is also known as PIM-SSM.

    c. Deployments use shared distribution trees.

    d. Deployments use source distribution trees.

    e. It is the traditional form for PIM deployments.

12. What are three of the benefits of GET VPN?

    a. It can take advantage of quick branch-to-branch connectivity while improving core meshing capability

    b. It is an excellent solution for VPNs over the public Internet.

    c. It decreases processing power required for encryption by offloading encryption to intermediary Layer 2 switches that support CGMP.

    d. Encryption is supported for native multicast and unicast traffic with Group Encrypted Transport's GDOI protocol.

    e. It uses multicast to send the GET VPN packets to multiple destinations, which makes GET VPN very scalable.

Chapter 11

Network Management Capabilities Within Cisco IOS Software

Upon completing this chapter, you will be able to

- Identify the rationale for using embedded management functionality in network infrastructure devices

- Discuss design considerations for NetFlow

- Discuss design considerations for NBAR

- Discuss design considerations for IP SLAs

The Cisco IOS Software includes embedded management functionality that enables network engineers to achieve efficient network performance, scalability, and availability. These management tools provide critical data for establishing baselines, capacity planning, and determining network bottlenecks. This chapter discusses the importance, requirements, and considerations for implementing the embedded Cisco IOS Software management tools in an enterprise design.

Cisco IOS Embedded Management Tools

Network management includes a broad range of policies, procedures, and purpose-built hardware and software that are used to manage computer networks. Network management affects the performance, reliability, and security of the entire network. Embedded management describes software subsystems within Cisco IOS Software that help manage, monitor, and automate actions within a router or switch that is running Cisco IOS Software. Embedded management capabilities add a dimension to the management infrastructure by enabling devices to automatically collect data and take action, helping the network manager to better manage devices and the network.

Embedded Management Rationale

Network management is a set of tools and processes to help manage the network. Network administrators administer it so that they can be confident in the network's performance for the following reasons:

- To verify that the network is working well and behaving in the planned manner

- To characterize the performance of the network

- To understand the amount and location of traffic in the network

- To provide tools and information in order to troubleshoot the network

Network Management Functional Areas

To provide a clear focus and strategy for running a network safely and efficiently, the International Organization for Standardization (ISO) developed a network management model known as the FCAPS (Fault, Configuration, Accounting, Performance, Security) model. This model identifies five key areas of network management, as follows:

- **Fault management:** Fault management is concerned with detecting, diagnosing, and correcting network and system faults. Fault management products typically provide for alert handling and event management functions and can include the diagnostic tools necessary to isolate faults and facilitate corrective or alternative actions.

- **Configuration management:** Configuration management is concerned with the installation, identification, inventory removal, and configuration of hardware (including components such a cards, modules, memory, and software), software, firmware, and services. It also provides for monitoring and managing the deployment status of a device. The configuration management functional area includes software management, change control, and inventory management.

- **Accounting management:** Accounting management is concerned with tracking the use of resources in a network. An example is the allocation of billing costs for both time and services rendered by a service provider. It also addresses billing for utilization of communications and computing facilities and billing for tracking user access to networks and the resources accessed by those users. Accounting management systems typically include knowledge of tariff structures.

- **Performance management:** Performance management is concerned with the measurement and analysis of both short-term and long-term network and system statistics related to utilization, response time, availability, and error rates. It is also used to monitor any outages on a network. Ideally, this data can be used to prevent future failures by helping network planners identify trends that suggest capacity utilization or other issues before such problems affect users or services. Performance management tools are also used to assist in planning, design, and performance tuning for improved network and systems efficiency.

- **Security management:** Security management is concerned with controlling access to network resources and preventing unauthorized use or tampering with the network. Among other things, security management tasks address user access rights, data privacy, alarms, and audit trails of security attacks/breaches, the management of security mechanisms, and password distribution.

When designing a network management solution, consider each of these functional areas for its importance to the network and business it supports.

Designing Network Management Solutions

The requirements that a network management solution design is based on includes several different sources. Some requirements may be driven by business needs, whereas others may be driven by operational procedures. The network architecture and the devices that are deployed on the network may impose restrictions on the choice of network management technologies and influence how network management solutions are deployed. Examples of requirements include the following:

- **Business goals:** A service provider may need a network accounting solution in order to bill customers for network usage.

- **Network operations:** Change management procedures in a large enterprise may require that any configuration change made to a network device be logged.

- **Network architecture:** Measuring network traffic for baselining purposes may be relatively easy on a hub-and-spoke network because all traffic passes through the hub. A partially or fully meshed network may require a distributed network management solution to collect all the necessary traffic statistics.

- **Device technology:** Designing a solution to monitor service-level agreements (SLA) for the WAN is much simpler when all routers support the IP SLA feature. In this case, the existing infrastructure can be leveraged, whereas without IP SLA support on the routers, separate devices may need to be deployed to perform the SLA measurements.

Note   Cisco IOS IP SLAs allow the measurement of the performance of mission-critical data, voice, video, and other applications.

Cisco IOS Software Support of Network Management

Nonmanaged equipment is difficult to support. When something goes wrong, it can be extremely difficult to figure out the problem and cause if the device does not provides any information or just Remote Monitoring (RMON) data. This is a total cost of ownership (TCO) issue.

Managed equipment can provide various information, such as the equipment deployed, how it is connected, and version of software that it is running. Cisco IOS Software provides extensive management capabilities, such as the following:

■ A broad range of show commands that provide network information available for both in-band and out-of-band (OOB) management.

■ Cisco devices support many Simple Network Management Protocol (SNMP) Management Information Bases (MIB). Through these MIBS, you have SNMP access to vast amounts of information.

■ Network Configuration Protocol (NETCONF) is a new network management protocol. It defines a simple mechanism through which a network device can be managed or configuration data information can be retrieved. New configuration data can be uploaded and manipulated. NETCONF uses Extensible Markup Language (XML)-based data encoding for the configuration data and protocol messages. NETCONF relies on the Secure Shell (SSH) protocol as a secure transport for the protocol messages.

■ Device management applications such as the Cisco Router and Security Device Manager (SDM) and the Cisco Adaptive Security Device Manager (ASDM) provide web-based tools for managing single devices.

Embedded management software subsystems within Cisco IOS Software that help manage, monitor, and automate network management include the following:

■ Cisco IOS syslog

■ NetFlow

■ Network-Based Application Recognition (NBAR)

■ Cisco IOS SLAs

Note SDM is an end-of-life product, but it is included here because it is within the domain of the ARCH course and exam.

Note The embedded management software subsystems are the focus of this section.

Application Optimization and Cisco IOS Technologies

Traditional network management processes focus on managing WAN links because of their scarce bandwidth and susceptibility to issues, including the following:

■ The expense of WAN connections, sometimes resulting in organizations implementing lower-speed, lower-cost links.

- Speed mismatches between LAN and WAN links, leading to congestion, packet loss, and degraded application performance.

- Different types of application traffic with different delivery requirements using the same WAN links. Real-time applications such as voice and video are especially sensitive to congestion and suffer from degraded performance due to delay, jitter, and packet loss. (Jitter is the variance of delay.)

However, there is increasing interest in extending network management to support application optimization at the data center and throughout the enterprise. The embedded Cisco IOS technologies provide network management support for application optimization in the network, as illustrated in Figure 11-1.

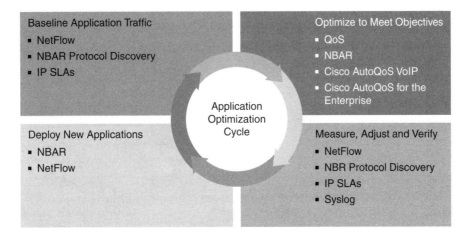

Figure 11-1 *Cisco IOS Technologies Support Application Optimization*

The phases in the application optimization cycle shown in Figure 11-1 are as follows:

- **Baseline application traffic:** In the first phase, a baseline is developed that measures network data so that the network manager can understand the basic traffic and application flows and the default network performance. Cisco IOS Software technologies that support this phase include NetFlow, NBAR Protocol Discovery, and IP SLAs.

- **Optimize to meet objectives:** After establishing the baseline, the network manager can apply policies and prioritize traffic so that each application has an optimal portion of network resources. Resources are allocated based on their value to the organization. Quality of service (QoS) is used to reduce congestion, prioritize specific traffic, and optimize end-to-end performance of critical applications. Cisco IOS Software technologies that support this phase include QoS, NBAR, Cisco AutoQoS VoIP, and Cisco AutoQoS for the Enterprise.

- **Measure, adjust, and verify:** In the third phase of the application optimization cycle, the network manager uses ongoing measurements and proactive adjustments to verify that the optimization techniques and QoS provide the network resources needed to meet the service objectives of the applications. This information is also used to resolve network issues that may occur. Several Cisco IOS Software features help measure network performance, including NetFlow, NBAR Protocol Discovery, IP SLAs, and syslog.

■ **Deploy new applications:** In this phase, network engineers determine the service objectives for new applications, estimate the network resources that will be needed to support these objectives, and allocate resources for new applications. Network management tools and processes enable the network manager to have the confidence to deploy new applications based on an understanding of the existing applications. NBAR and NetFlow are common Cisco IOS technologies used to support this phase.

As shown in Figure 11-2, Cisco IOS technology can be used to measure and monitor application performance, facilitating application optimization.

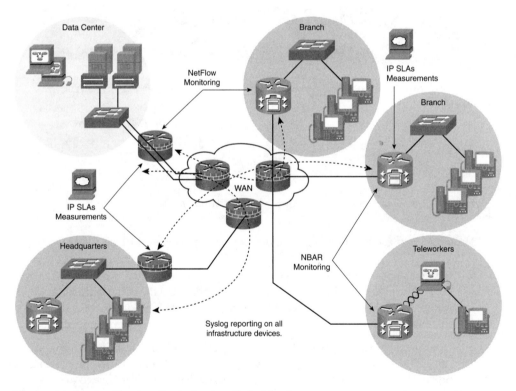

Figure 11-2 *Application Optimization Technologies*

Figure 11-2 highlights the location that Cisco IOS technologies are commonly deployed in the enterprise environment. Syslog should be positioned on every device. NetFlow, NBAR, and IP SLA monitoring are deployed on selected locations in the network.

Networks should be configured for manageability and security. Using a predefined template to structure network management configuration and reporting information is a recommended practice.

Syslog Considerations

The Cisco IOS system message logging (syslog) process enables a device to report and save important error and notification messages; the messages can be saved either locally or to a remote logging server. Syslog messages can be sent to local console connections, terminal monitor connections (vty and tty), the system buffer, or to remote syslog servers. Syslog sends text messages to a syslog server using UDP port 514.

Syslog provides a very comprehensive reporting mechanism that logs system messages in plain English text. The syslog messages include both messages in a standardized format (called system logging messages, system error messages, or simply system messages) and output from **debug** commands. These messages are generated during network operation to assist in identifying the type and severity of a problem or to aid users in monitoring router activity such as configuration changes.

The Embedded Syslog Manager (ESM) feature provides a programmable framework that allows a network manager to filter, escalate, correlate, route, and customize system logging messages before delivery by the Cisco IOS system message logger. ESM also allows system messages to be logged independently as standard messages, XML-formatted messages, or ESM-filtered messages. These outputs can be sent to any of the traditional syslog targets. A network manager, for example, could enable standard logging to the console connection, XML-formatted message logging to the buffer, and ESM-filtered message logging to the monitor. Similarly, each type of output could be sent to different remote hosts. A benefit of separate logging processes is that if there is some problem with the ESM filter modules, standard logging will not be affected.

ESM should not be confused with IOS Embedded Event Manager (EEM). EEM supports more than 20 event detectors that are highly integrated with different Cisco IOS Software components to trigger actions in response to network events. Your business logic can be injected into network operations using IOS EEM policies. These policies are programmed using either simple command-line interface (CLI) or using a scripting language called Tool Command Language (TCL).

Cisco IOS Syslog Message Standard

Figure 11-3 shows the standard output for a syslog message. The protocol was invented in the 1980s as the logging subsystem for the UNIX operating system. It is still used by UNIX, Linux, and other operating systems (such as Cisco IOS).

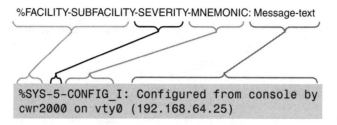

Figure 11-3 *Syslog Message Standard*

Figure 11-3 breaks down the syslog message into the following fields (which are part of the messages):

- **Facility:** A code consisting of two or more uppercase letters that indicate the hardware device, protocol, or a module of the system software.

- **Severity:** A single-digit code from 0 to 7 that reflects the severity of the condition. The lower the number, the more serious the situation.

- **Mnemonic:** A code that uniquely identifies the error message.

- **Message-text:** A text string describing the condition. This portion of the message sometimes contains detailed information about the event, including terminal port numbers, network addresses, or addresses that correspond to locations in the system memory address space.

Again, as Figure 11-3 shows, a typical message indicates that the operating system (FACILITY = SYS) is providing a notification (SEVERITY = 5) that it has been configured (MNEMONIC = CONFIG). The message text indicates that a user on vty0 from IP address 192.168.64.25 made this change.

Note   Not shown in Figure 11-3 is the optional time stamp that can be added to the syslog message by using the IOS command **logging timestamp**. Adding a time stamp is a best practice for monitoring purposes.

Note   For more information about syslog formats, see Appendix B of the *CiscoWorks Resource Manager Essentials (RME) User Guide*.

Issues with Syslog

This section describes some of the issues with syslog.

The severity of messages is not used consistently across the different Cisco platforms, so documentation for each Cisco IOS Software release is necessary to explain the meaning of these messages. This can cause confusion if network managers manually filter to extract information at certain levels of severity if devices inside the same network are running different software releases.

Syslog is verbose and can provide too many informational messages (along with the useful ones) for a specific problem or condition. Network managers can use filters or scripts to pull out important messages.

Note   CiscoWorks RME contains a syslog analyzer that can be referenced in Chapter 15 of the *RME User Guide*. In addition, some third-party products process syslog messages.

The syslog delivery communication mechanism is based on User Datagram Protocol (UDP); this is usually not a problem for a monitoring and alerting tool. However, RFC 3195 provides a specification for a reliable delivery mechanism for syslog. Cisco IOS Software provides support for the reliable delivery for syslog over Blocks Extensible Exchange Protocol (BEEP) feature that allows a device to be customized for receipt of syslog messages. This feature provides reliable and secure delivery for syslog messages using BEEP. In addition, it allows multiple sessions to a single logging host, independent of the underlying transport method, and provides a filtering mechanism that is called a message discriminator.

Note   Syslog is not a secure mechanism. However, this should not preclude the network manager from using syslog. Secure practices include establishing access control lists (ACL) to allow receipt of syslog packets only from internal resources.

NetFlow

NetFlow is an important embedded Cisco IOS Software technology that provides visibility into network behavior and how network assets are being used. This section describes how both traditional and Flexible NetFlow can help the network manager understand the behavior of traffic in the network.

NetFlow Overview

Cisco IOS NetFlow efficiently provides a key set of services for IP applications, including network traffic accounting, usage-based network billing, network planning, security, denial-of-service (DoS) monitoring capabilities, and network monitoring. NetFlow provides valuable information about network users and applications, peak usage times, and traffic routing. Cisco invented NetFlow in 1996, and is the leader in IP traffic-flow technology.

NetFlow answers the questions of what, when, where, and how traffic is flowing in the network. NetFlow data can be exported to network management applications that further process the information, resulting in display tables and graphs for accounting and billing or as an aid for network planning.

The Cisco IOS NetFlow Version 9 was used as the foundation for the Internet Engineering Task Force (IETF) IP Flow Information Export (IPFIX) standard that is defined in RFCs 5101, 5102, and 5103. The new generic data-transport capability within Cisco routers, IPFIX can be used to transport any performance information from a router or switch. New information—including Layer 2 information, new security detection and identification information, IP Version 6 (IPv6), multicast, Multiprotocol Label Switching (MPLS), Border Gateway Protocol (BGP) information, and more—is being exported using the NetFlow Version 9 export format.

Principal NetFlow Uses

Organizations use NetFlow in different ways, depending on the focus of the organization. Both service providers and enterprises use NetFlow to analyze new applications and their impact on the network. Understanding who is using the network and the endpoints of traffic flows is important for service providers for network planning and traffic engineering, and it is important to enterprises for monitoring network resources, users, and applications. For example, NetFlow data can be used to determine application ports for ACLs.

While a service provider is concerned about customer accounting and billing, enterprises may be concerned about chargeback billing for their departments. In addition, NetFlow can help organizations avoid costly bandwidth upgrades by identifying the applications causing congestion and thus help reduce peak WAN traffic.

Both types of organizations use NetFlow for security monitoring and troubleshooting the network. NetFlow can help in diagnosing slow network performance, determining bandwidth hogs and providing bandwidth utilization in real time, and can be used to confirm that appropriate bandwidth has been allocated to each class of service (CoS). NetFlow can help detect unauthorized WAN traffic and support anomaly detection and worm diagnosis.

Definition of a Flow

A flow is a unidirectional stream of packets between a given source and destination (both defined by a network layer IP address and source and destination port numbers). Traditionally, a flow in NetFlow is identified as the combination of the following seven key fields:

- **IP source address:** Defines who is originating the traffic

- **IP destination address:** Defines who is receiving the traffic

- **Source port:** Characterizes the source application that is utilizing the traffic up to Layer 4

- **Destination port:** Characterizes the destination application that is utilizing the traffic up to Layer 4

- **Layer 3 protocol field:** Characterizes the application that is utilizing the traffic

- **Type of service (ToS) byte:** Identifies the CoS or priority of the traffic

- **Input interface (ifIndex):** Defines interface that the info came in on

All packets with the same source and destination IP address, source and destination ports, protocol, input interface, and ToS are grouped into a flow with traditional NetFlow. For each flow, NetFlow tallies the packets and bytes.

Traditional IP Flows

As shown in Figure 11-4, in the traditional NetFlow implementation, seven key attributes are used to determine whether a packet is unique or similar to other packets. The key attributes methodology of determining a flow is quite scalable because a large amount of network information is condensed into a database of NetFlow information (called the NetFlow cache).

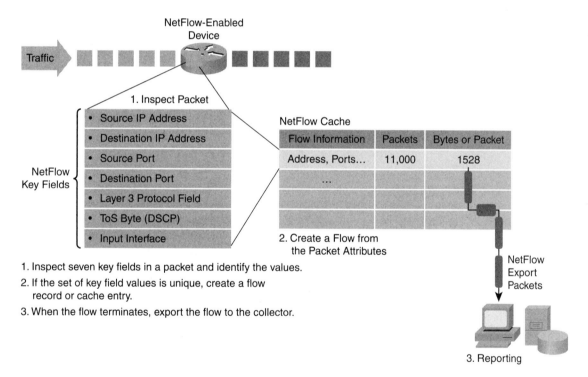

Figure 11-4   *Traditional IP Flows*

NetFlow operates by creating a NetFlow cache that contains the data for all active flows. A flow record is maintained within the NetFlow cache for all active flows. Each flow record in the NetFlow cache contains key fields that can be later used for exporting data to a collection device. NetFlow export, unlike Simple Network Management Protocol (SNMP) polling, pushes information periodically to the NetFlow reporting collector. In general, the NetFlow cache is constantly filling with flows. Software in the router or switch is searching the cache for flows that have terminated or expired. These flow records are exported to the NetFlow collector server.

Each flow record is created by identifying packets with similar characteristics and counting or tracking the packets and bytes per flow. The details or cache information is exported to the NetFlow collector server periodically, based on flow timers. The NetFlow collector (also called Flow Collector) contains a history of flow information that was switched within the Cisco device. NetFlow is efficient, with the amount of export data being about 1.5 percent of the switched traffic in the router. NetFlow accounts for every packet in nonsampled mode and provides a highly condensed and detailed view of all network traffic that entered the router or switch.

Network managers review NetFlow information by using either Cisco IOS Software **show** commands or by exporting NetFlow to the Flow Collector server.

Flow Record Creation

As shown in Figure 11-5, NetFlow inspects packets for key field values. These values are compared with existing flows in the cache. If the set of values is unique, NetFlow creates a new flow record in the cache. Additional information is included to the flow record in nonkey fields in both forms of NetFlow. Nonkey fields are added to the flow entry in the NetFlow cache and exported. The nonkey fields are not used to create or characterize the flows but are exported and just added to the flow in traditional NetFlow. If a field is nonkey, such as the outbound interface, normally only the first packet of the flow is used for the value in this field.

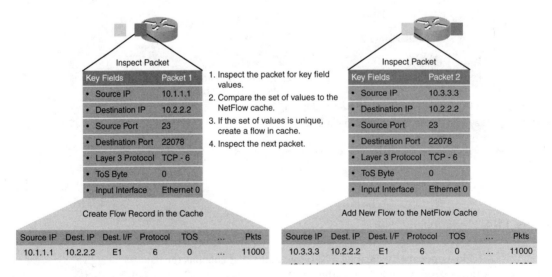

Figure 11-5 *Flow Record Creation*

In Figure 11-6, two unique flows are created in the cache because there are different values in the source IP address key fields in the figure.

Srclf	SrcIPadd	Dstlf	DstIPadd	ToS	Pkts	Src Port	Dst Port	NextHop	Bytes/ Pkt	Start Time	End Time
Fa1/0	172.16.21.2	Fa0/0	10.0.227.12	0	11,000	00A2	00A2	10.0.23.2	1,528	..	..
Fa1/0	172.16.3.2	Fa0/0	10.0.227.12	0	2,491	0015	0015	10.0.23.2	740	..	..
Fa1/0	172.16.20.2	Fa0/0	10.0.227.12	0	10,000	00A1	00A1	10.0.23.2	1,428	..	..
Fa1/0	172.16.6.2	Fa0/0	10.0.227.12	0	2,210	0019	0019	10.0.23.2	1,040	..	..

Figure 11-6 *NetFlow Data Before QoS Deployment*

NetFlow records contain the ToS field in the IP header and application ports, traffic volumes, and time stamps. This information allows the network manager to understand traffic profiles per CoS for traffic including data, voice, and video. The user of NetFlow can verify the QoS levels that are achieved and optimize bandwidth for specific classes of service.

Figure 11-6 and Figure 11-7 illustrate how the ToS key field distinguishes between flows. Before QoS is implemented in the network, the ToS value is 0 for all traffic between a specific source and destination pair. There is one traffic flow between this pair.

Srclf	SrcIPadd	Dstlf	DstIPadd	ToS	Pkts	Src Port	Dst Port	NextHop	Bytes/ Pkt	Start Time	End Time
Fa1/0	172.16.21.2	Fa0/0	10.0.227.12	EF	3,020	00A2	00A2	10.0.23.2	1,528	..	..
Fa1/0	172.16.21.2	Fa0/0	10.0.227.12	CS5	2,212	00A2	00A2	10.0.23.2	1,528	..	..
Fa1/0	172.16.21.2	Fa0/0	10.0.227.12	AF41	4,000	00A2	00A2	10.0.23.2	501	..	..
Fa1/0	172.16.21.2	Fa0/0	10.0.227.12	CS4	3,333	00A2	00A2	10.0.23.2	93	..	..
Fa1/0	172.16.21.2	Fa0/0	10.0.227.12	CS3	7,474	00A2	00A2	10.0.23.2	82	..	..
Fa1/0	172.16.21.2	Fa0/0	10.0.227.12	AF21	2,828	00A2	00A2	10.0.23.2	111	..	..
Fa1/0	172.16.21.2	Fa0/0	10.0.227.12	CS2	993	00A2	00A2	10.0.23.2	256	..	..
Fa1/0	172.16.21.2	Fa0/0	10.0.227.12	AF11	1,404	00A2	00A2	10.0.23.2	64	..	..
Fa1/0	172.16.21.2	Fa0/0	10.0.227.12	CS1	500	00A2	00A2	10.0.23.2	98	..	..
Fa1/0	172.16.21.2	Fa0/0	10.0.227.12	0	11,000	00A2	00A2	10.0.23.2	98	..	..
Fa1/0	172.16.3.2	Fa0/0	10.0.227.12	0	2,491	0015	0015	10.0.23.2	740	..	..
Fa1/0	172.16.20.2	Fa0/0	10.0.227.12	0	10,000	00A1	00A1	10.0.23.2	1,428	..	..
Fa1/0	172.16.6.2	Fa0/0	10.0.227.12	0	2,210	0019	0019	10.0.23.2	1,040	..	..

Figure 11-7 *NetFlow Data After QoS Deployment*

Figure 11-7 illustrates the NetFlow data after QoS is implemented in the network. The multiple ToS values between a specific source and destination pair lead to multiple flows between the pairs as traffic is distributed per class. The NetFlow analysis now shows each CoS between the source and destination pair.

This data can be useful for verifying that QoS configuration is working and bandwidth levels are set appropriately for the volume of traffic.

NetFlow Cache Management

The NetFlow cache management software contains a highly sophisticated set of algorithms to efficiently determine whether a packet is part of an existing flow or should generate a new flow cache entry. The algorithms can also dynamically update per-flow accounting measurements that are residing in the NetFlow cache and determine cache aging or flow expiration. Figure 11-8 shows the logic in the cache management.

1. Create and Update Flows in NetFlow Cache

Srclf	*SrcIPadd	Dstlf	*DstIPadd	*Protocol	*ToS	Flgs	Pkts	*Src Port	Src Msk	Src AS	*Dst Port	Dst Msk	Dst AS	NextHop	Bytes/ Pkt	Active	Idle
Fa1/0	172.16.21.2	Fa0/0	10.0.227.12	11	80	10	11,000	00A2	/24	5	00A2	/24	15	10.0.23.2	1,528	1,745	4
Fa1/0	172.16.3.2	Fa0/0	10.0.227.12	6	40	0	2,491	0015	/26	196	0015	/24	15	10.0.23.2	740	41.5	1
Fa1/0	172.16.20.2	Fa0/0	10.0.227.12	11	80	10	10,000	00A1	/24	180	00A1	/24	15	10.0.23.2	1,428	1,145.5	3
Fa1/0	172.16.6.2	Fa0/0	10.0.227.12	6	40	0	2,210	0019	/30	180	0019	/24	15	10.0.23.2	1,040	24.5	14

* Key Fields

2. Expire Timers

Srclf	*SrcIPadd	Dstlf	*DstIPadd	*Protocol	*ToS	Flgs	Pkts	*Src Port	Src Msk	Src AS	*Dst Port	Dst Msk	Dst AS	NextHop	Bytes/ Pkt	Active	Idle
Fa1/0	172.16.21.2	Fa0/0	10.0.227.12	11	80	10	11,000	00A2	/24	5	00A2	/24	15	10.0.23.2	1,528	1,800	4

3. Package Flows in Export Packet

Non-Aggregated Flows—Export Version 5 or 9
Aggregated Flows–Export Version 8 or 9

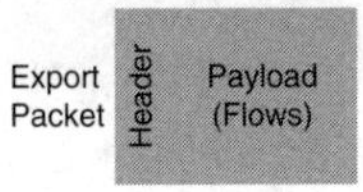

Export Packet | Header | Payload (Flows)

4. Transport Flows to Reporting Server

30 Flows Per 1500-Byte Export Packet for Version 5 or 9

Figure 11-8   *NetFlow Cache Management*

Some rules for expiring NetFlow cache entries are as follows:

- Flows that have been idle for a specified time are expired and removed from the cache.

- Long-lived flows are expired and removed from the cache. (Flows are not allowed to live more than 30 minutes by default; the underlying packet conversation remains undisturbed.)

- As the cache becomes full, a number of heuristics are applied to aggressively age groups of flows simultaneously.

- TCP connections that have reached the end of byte stream (FIN) or that have been reset (RST) are expired.

Figure 11-8 shows an example of the NetFlow cache, aggregation cache, and timers. Expired flows are grouped into NetFlow export datagrams for export from the NetFlow-enabled device. NetFlow export datagrams may consist of up to 30 flow records for NetFlow Version 5 or 9 flow export.

Note NetFlow versions described in next section.

NetFlow Export Versions

Table 11-1 lists the current NetFlow versions. Of note, IPFIX is the IETF standard as defined in RFC 3917.

Table 11-1 *NetFlow Export Versions*

NetFlow Version	Comments
1	Original
5	Standard and most common
7	Supports Cisco Catalyst 6500 series switches with a Multilayer Switch Feature Card (MSFC) on Catalyst operating system
8	Choice of 11 aggregation schemes
Reduces resource usage	
9	Flexible, extensible file export format to enable easier support of additional fields and technologies
IPFIX	IETF working group standard for flow export; based on Cisco NetFlow Version 9

The NetFlow export statically defined fields by version:

■ Version 1 is the original version.

■ Version 5 adds autonomous system data and sequencing information to the NetFlow Data Export (NDE) packets. NetFlow Version 5 is used with traditional NetFlow and is a fixed export format with a limited set of information being exported. Version 5 is commonly found because many devices support only this version.

■ Version 7 supports Cisco Catalyst 6500 series switches with an MSFC on Cisco Catalyst Operating System Version 5.5(7) and later.

■ Version 8 is for on-router aggregation. It includes a choice of 11 aggregation schemes.

The latest generation of NetFlow export supports dynamically defined fields:

■ With NetFlow Version 9, routers send out a template with field IDs and lengths that define the subsequent NDE packets.

■ IPFIX is the IETF standard mechanism for information export. IPFIX is based on NetFlow Version 9.

Although the most commonly used format is NetFlow export Version 5, the latest format, Version 9, has some advantages for key technologies such as security, traffic analysis, and multicast. Some reporting tools may prefer unaggregated Version 5 to Version 9, because Version 9 requires more complicated processing.

NetFlow Version 9 Export Packet

Flexible NetFlow uses the flexible and extensible NetFlow Version 9 format to provide enhanced optimization of the network infrastructure, reduced costs, and improved capacity planning and security detection beyond other flow-based technologies. Figure 11-9 shows what Version 9 includes in the export data and a template to describe what is being exported. The template is periodically sent to the NetFlow collector, notifying which data to expect from the router or switch. The data is then sent for the reporting system to analyze. Matching ID numbers are used to help associate the template to the data records.

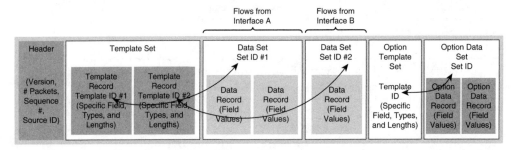

Figure 11-9   *NetFlow Version 9 Export Packet*

The NetFlow Version 9 record format consists of a packet header that is followed by at least one or more templates or data *flow-sets*. A flow-set is a generic term for a collection of records that follow the packet header in an export packet. There are both template and data flow-sets. An export packet contains one or more flow-sets, and both template and data flow-sets can be mixed within the same export packet. A template flow-set provides a description of the fields that will be present in future data flow-sets. Data flow-sets may occur later within the same export packet or in subsequent export packets.

Because NetFlow Version 9 is configurable and customizable, any data that is available in the device can theoretically be sent in NetFlow Version 9 format. The network manager can configure which key and nonkey fields define flows.

Flexible NetFlow Advantages

The current Flexible NetFlow model has several key advantages over traditional NetFlow.

By flexibly targeting specific information, the amount of information is reduced. The number of flows being exported can be reduced, allowing enhanced scalability and aggregation of data beyond traditional NetFlow.

It can monitor a wider range of packet information. Flexible NetFlow enhances the rich feature capabilities of traditional NetFlow by allowing the tracking of information at Layer 2 for switching environments, at Layers 3 and 4 for IP information, and up to Layer 7 with deep packet inspection for application monitoring.

In Flexible NetFlow, nonkey fields are configurable by the user. Flexible NetFlow also allows users to choose which key and nonkey fields define flows. This configuration capability allows users customization and flexibility beyond traditional NetFlow.

The model provides a NetFlow architecture that can track multiple NetFlow applications simultaneously by using different flow monitors. A flow monitor describes the NetFlow cache or information that is stored in the cache and contains the flow records or key and non-key fields within the cache. Part of the flow monitor is the flow exporter, which contains information about the export of NetFlow information including the destination address of the NetFlow collector. The flow monitor includes various cache characteristics, including the timers for exporting, the size of the cache, and if required, the packet sampling rate. The user can create simultaneous separate flow monitors for security analysis and for traffic analysis.

Flexible NetFlow provides enhanced security detection and network troubleshooting by allowing customization of flow information. For example, the user can create a specific flow monitor to focus and analyze a particular network issue or incident. In addition, Flexible NetFlow allows a customizable active timer for the cache that can be set as low as 1 second, compared with the traditional NetFlow minimum value of 60 seconds. This customizable timer aids in tracking security incidents where open or partial flows might be recorded—for example, a synchronization (SYN) flood attack. It provides real-time monitoring with immediate flow cache capabilities and long-term or permanent tracking of flow data.

NetFlow Version 9 is the basis for the IETF standard IPFIX.

Flexible NetFlow is an important technology that is available in Cisco devices to help with visibility into the network behavior and how network assets are being used. Flexible NetFlow is an improved NetFlow, bringing better scalability, aggregation of data, and user customization. Flexible NetFlow enhances the ability to detect security incidents and understand the behavior of traffic in the network beyond what is possible in other flow-based technologies.

NetFlow Deployment

There are many NetFlow collectors, including Cisco, freeware, and third-party commercial products, that report and utilize NetFlow data.

Some reporting systems offer a two-tier architecture, where collectors are placed near key sites in the network. They aggregate and forward the data to a main reporting server. Other solutions use multiple distributed collectors, a central database, a management server, and a reporting server. Smaller deployments may have a single server for reporting and collection.

A number of Cisco NetFlow reporting products are offered. In recent years, many new partners and solutions are available on both Microsoft Windows and Linux operating systems. The typical starting prices for commercial products can range significantly.

Where to Apply NetFlow Monitoring

NetFlow is typically used on a central site, because all traffic from the remote sites is characterized and is available within NetFlow. As shown in Figure 11-10, NetFlow placement has optimal points in the LAN/WAN.

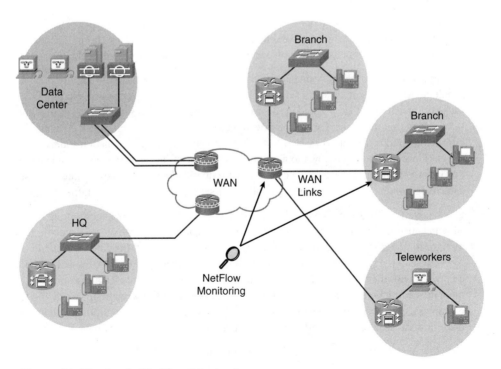

Figure 11-10   *Apply NetFlow Monitoring*

The location where NetFlow is deployed depends on the location of the reporting solution and the topology of the network. If the reporting collection server is centrally located, implementing NetFlow close to the reporting collector server is optimal. NetFlow can also be enabled at remote-branch locations with the understanding that the export data will utilize bandwidth. The two-tier architecture solutions allow remote aggregation of data and can help manage WAN bandwidth.

NetFlow is, in general, an ingress measurement technology that should be deployed on appropriate interfaces on edge, aggregation, or WAN access routers to gain a comprehensive view of originating and terminating traffic to meet customer needs for accounting, monitoring, or network-planning data.

Egress NetFlow accounting is also available in current releases of the Cisco IOS Software. The key mechanism for enhancing NetFlow data volume manageability is careful planning of NetFlow deployment. NetFlow can be deployed incrementally (for example, interface by interface) and strategically (for example, on well-chosen routers) instead of pervasively on every interface on every router in the network. The network designer should determine key routers and key interfaces where NetFlow should be activated based on the customer traffic-flow patterns and network topology and architecture.

The export volume is about 1.5 percent of the total traffic on a NetFlow interface. Cisco recommends careful planning of NetFlow deployment with NetFlow services that are activated on strategically located edge or aggregation routers that capture the data that is required for planning, monitoring, and accounting applications. Careful consideration must be given to determine which interfaces should enable NetFlow collection and export to ensure that flows are not double-counted.

NBAR

Enterprise applications require different levels of service based on business requirements. These requirements can be translated into network policies. Network-Based Application Recognition (NBAR) is an important embedded Cisco IOS Software technology that provides visibility into how network assets are used by applications. This section discusses how NBAR can classify network traffic so that applications can receive the appropriate policy and bandwidth in the network.

NBAR Overview

Traffic classification can help organizations answer many questions about network resources, such as the following:

- Which applications run on the network?

- What is the application resource utilization?

- Are users following application usage policies?

- How much bandwidth should be assigned to different QoS classes?

- How should applications (for example, VoIP) be allocated and deployed most efficiently?

Figure 11-11 introduces NBAR and looks at how it can classify traffic.

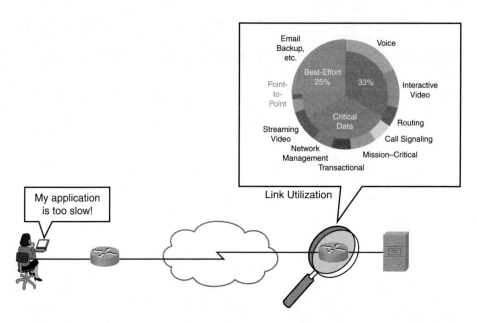

Figure 11-11 *Overview of NBAR*

NBAR is a classification engine that recognizes and classifies a wide variety of protocols and applications. NBAR provides full-packet stateful inspection that identifies applications and even protocols that use dynamic TCP and UDP port assignments.

NBAR includes an optional feature called NBAR Protocol Discovery. NBAR Protocol Discovery analyzes application traffic patterns in real time and discovers which traffic is running on the network. NBAR develops statistics on protocol traffic on interfaces.

NBAR is the foundation for applying QoS policies to traffic flows in the network. NBAR enables network administrators to identify the variety of protocols and the amount of traffic that is generated by each protocol. After gathering this information, NBAR allows the network administrator to organize traffic into classes. These classes can then be used to provide different levels of service for network traffic, allowing better network management by providing the correct level of network resources for network traffic. After NBAR recognizes and classifies a protocol or application, the network can be configured to apply the appropriate QoS for that application or traffic with that protocol.

NBAR Packet Inspection

The NBAR packet classification engine provides full packet inspection that identifies applications and protocols using information from Layer 3 through Layer 7, as shown in Figure 11-12.

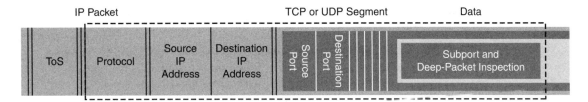

Figure 11-12 *NBAR Packet Inspection*

NBAR uses five elements to identify a flow per incoming interface:

■ Source IP address

■ Destination IP address

■ Source port

■ Destination port

■ Layer 3 protocol type

Note Traditional NetFlow uses these identifiers plus type of service (ToS) for each incoming interface.

NBAR supports several classification methods to identify more than 90 applications and protocols, including the following:

■ **Statically assigned TCP and UDP port numbers:** NBAR can classify application traffic by looking at statically assigned TCP and UDP port numbers. Although access control lists (ACL) can also be used for classifying static port protocols, NBAR is easier to configure and provides classification statistics that are not available when ACLs are used.

■ **Dynamically assigned TCP and UDP port numbers:** NBAR can also classify dynamically assigned TCP and UDP port numbers by using stateful inspection of a protocol across multiple packets during packet classification. NBAR uses approximately 150 bytes of DRAM for each traffic flow that requires stateful inspection.

■ **Subport and deep inspection:** NBAR looks beyond the port numbers of a packet to provide subport and deep packet classification by looking into the Layer 3 payload and classifying packets based on content within the payload, such as the transaction identifier, message type, or other similar data. Deep packet classification provides more granularity. For instance, if a packet is already classified as HTTP traffic, it may be further classified. Classification of HTTP traffic by URL, host, or Multipurpose Internet Mail Extensions (MIME) type is an example of deep packet classification. NBAR classifies HTTP traffic by text within the URL or host fields of a request using regular expression matching. HTTP URL matching in NBAR supports most

HTTP request methods such as GET, PUT, HEAD, POST, DELETE, and TRACE. The NBAR engine then converts the specified match string into a regular expression.

■ **Native and non-native Packet Description Language Modules (PDLM):** NBAR can only monitor applications that it recognizes. However, it does allow adding application-recognition modules known as PDLMs to support additional applications. A non-native PDLM is a separate downloadable file available at http://www.cisco.com that is used to add support for a protocol that is currently not available as part of the native PDLM embedded in the Cisco IOS Software release.

NBAR also provides custom protocol support for static port-based protocols and applications that are not currently supported in NBAR. There are 10 custom applications that can be assigned using NBAR, and each custom application can have up to 16 TCP and 16 UDP ports each mapped to the individual custom protocol. The real-time statistics of each custom protocol can be monitored using NBAR Protocol Discovery.

NBAR Protocol Discovery

NBAR Protocol Discovery discovers any protocol traffic supported by NBAR and gathers real-time statistics associated with that protocol. NBAR Protocol Discovery maintains the following per-protocol statistics for each enabled interface:

■ Total number of input packets and bytes

■ Total number of output packets and bytes

■ Input bit rates

■ Output bit rates

These statistics can be used to define traffic classes and traffic policies for each traffic class. The traffic policies or policy maps are used to apply specific QoS features and functionality to the traffic classes.

> **Note**   NBAR Protocol Discovery is configured with the **ip nbar protocol-discovery** interface configuration command.

NetFlow and NBAR Differentiation

This section contrasts NBAR and NetFlow. Figure 11-13 presents a graphical representation of the overlap and differentiation between NetFlow and NBAR.

The main objective of NetFlow is to provide visibility into network behavior and demonstrate how network assets are being used. In traditional NetFlow, flows are defined by a set of seven key characteristics that document which user is using which part of the network for what purpose at which time. NetFlow is a passive technology that monitors network activity typically from Open Systems Interconnection (OSI) model Layers 2 through 4. NetFlow data export allows trending of network records.

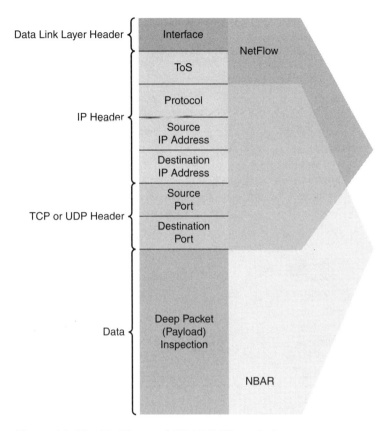

Figure 11-13 *NetFlow and NBAR Differentiation*

The main objective of NBAR is to identify and classify traffic that is based on payload attributes and protocol characteristics. Flows are defined by a set of five key characteristics. NBAR can support static and stateful dynamic inspections. QoS mechanisms work on the classified packets to support optimization of application performance. NBAR is an active technology that can be used to validate or reclassify ToS marking based on packet inspection in OSI Layers 3 through 7. NBAR Protocol Discovery provides an easy way to discover the application protocols that are operating on an interface that can be queried through Simple Network Management Protocol (SNMP).

Reporting NBAR Protocol Discovery Statistics from the Command Line

NBAR Protocol Discovery statistics can be viewed from the Cisco IOS Software CLI or through reporting with third-party vendor applications. Example 11-1 displays output from a Cisco router using the command line to display NetFlow information.

Example 11-1 *NBAR Protocol Discovery Statistics*

```
router# show ip nbar protocol-discovery interface FastEthernet 6/0

FastEthernet6/0
                  Input                         Output
Protocol          Packet Count                  Packet Count
                  Byte Count                    Byte Count
                  5 minute bit rate (bps)       5 minute bit rate (bps)
. . . . . . . .   . . . . . . . . . . . . . .   . . . . . . . . . . . . . .
http              316773                        0
                  26340105                      0
                  3000                          0
pop3              4437                          7367
                  2301891                       339213
                  3000                          0
Snmp              279538                        14644
                  319106191                     673624
                  0                             0
. . .
Total             17203819                      151684936
                  19161397327                   50967034611
                  4179000                       6620000
```

As mentioned earlier, Example 11-1 shows a portion of the output from the **show ip nbar protocol-discovery** command for one Ethernet interface. This command by default displays statistics for all interfaces on which NBAR Protocol Discovery is currently enabled. The default output from this command includes input bit rate (in bits per second), input byte count, input packet count, and protocol name.

An option on this command is to show the **top-n** *number* most active NBAR-supported protocols, where *number* is the number of protocols to be displayed. For instance, if the command **top-n 3** is entered, the three most active NBAR supported protocols will display.

NBAR Protocol Discovery can be used to monitor both input and output traffic and may be applied with or without a service policy enabled. NBAR Protocol Discovery gathers statistics for packets that are switched to output interfaces.

NBAR and Cisco AutoQoS

Cisco IOS Software includes two features to automate the deployment of QoS in the network:

- **Cisco AutoQoS VoIP:** Provides a means for simplifying the implementation and provisioning of QoS for VoIP traffic.

- **Cisco AutoQoS for the Enterprise:** Helps automate the deployment of QoS in a general business environment, particularly for midsize companies and branch offices of larger companies. It expands on the functionality that is available with the Cisco AutoQoS VoIP feature and supports QoS features that are required for voice, video, and data traffic. This feature creates class maps and policy maps that are based on Cisco experience and best-practice methodology after using NBAR Protocol Discovery on lower-speed WAN links.

Both of these Cisco AutoQoS features can take advantage of the traffic-classification functionality of NBAR. When Cisco AutoQoS is configured on an interface with the trust option, the differentiated services code point (DSCP) markings of a packet are relied on for classification of the voice traffic. If the optional **trust** keyword is not specified, the voice traffic is classified using NBAR, and the packets are marked with the appropriate DSCP value.

Cisco AutoQoS for the Enterprise

Implementing Cisco AutoQoS in the Enterprise is a two-phase procedure:

Step 1. Invoke the **auto discovery qos** command on the applicable link.

- Use the **show auto discovery qos** command with traffic running through.

Step 2. Automatically configure the link with the **auto qos** command.

- Use the **show auto qos** command to display the QoS policy settings deployed.

Table 11-2 shows the DSCP values assigned with AutoQoS.

In the first phase, autodiscovery collects data and evaluates traffic in the network. The autodiscovery phase is started by using the **auto discovery qos [trust]** command.

Table 11-2 *Cisco AutoQoS for the Enterprise*

Traffic Class	DSCP
IP Routing	CS6
Interactive Voice	EF
Interactive Video	AF41
Streaming Video	CS4
Telephony Signaling	CS3
Transaction or Interactive	AF21
Network Management	CS2
Bulk Data	AF11
Best Effort	0
Scavenger	CS1

In untrusted mode, the autodiscovery phase uses NBAR Protocol Discovery to detect and classify the applications on the network and perform statistical analysis on the network traffic.

In trusted mode, the autodiscovery phase classifies packets that are based on DSCP values in the IP header, collects the NBAR Protocol Discovery statistics to calculate the bandwidth and average or peak rate, and passes that data to the template module.

The data should be collected for several days to a week as desired. The **show auto discovery qos** command should be used to display the results of the data that is collected during the autodiscovery phase. Example 11-2 shows this, in the next section.

In the second phase, the Cisco AutoQoS template-generation and -installation process generates templates from the data that is collected during the autodiscovery phase and installs the templates on the interface. These templates can be used as the basis for creating the class maps and policy maps for the network. The recommended policy is based on autodiscovery statistics. After the class maps and policy maps have been created with values for bandwidth and scheduling parameters, they are then installed on the interface.

The Cisco AutoQoS template-generation phase is started by using the **auto qos** command. The class maps and policy maps should be reviewed by using the **show auto qos** command.

Example: Cisco AutoQoS Discovery Progress

Example 11-2 shows a sample result from the Cisco AutoQoS discovery process.

Example 11-2 *Cisco AutoQoS Discovery Progress*

```
router# show auto discovery qos
AutoQoS Discovery enabled for applications
 Discovery up time: 2 days, 55 minutes
 AutoQoS Class information:
 Class VoIP:
 Recommended Minimum Bandwidth:    517 Kbps/50% (PeakRate)
 Detected applications and data:
 Application/    AverageRate    PeakRate       Total
 Protocol        (kbps/%)       (kbps/%)       (bytes)
 rtp audio       76/7           517/50 7       703104
Class Interactive Video:
 Recommended Minimum Bandwidth:    24 Kbps/2%    (AverageRate)
 Detected applications and data:
 Application/    AverageRate    PeakRate       Total
 Protocol        (kbps/%)       (kbps/%)       (bytes)
 rtp video       24/2           5337/52        704574
 Class Transactional:
 Recommended Minimum Bandwidth:    0 Kbps/0%     (AverageRate)
```

```
Detected applications and data:
Application/     AverageRate      PeakRate         Total
Protocol         (kbps/%)         (kbps/%)         (bytes)
citrix           36/3             74/7             30212
sqlnet           12/1             7/<1             1540
```

By default, the NBAR mechanisms do not show unclassified traffic. The show ip nbar
unclassified-port-stats command returns the error message shown Example 11-3.

Under carefully controlled circumstances, you can use the **debug ip nbar unclassified-
port-stats** command to configure the router to begin tracking on which ports the packets arrive. Then use the **show ip nbar unclassified-port-stats** command to verify the collected information. The output will then present a histogram of the most commonly
used ports.

Note   Use the **debug** command cautiously in a production environment and enable and
disable it in controlled situations only.

Example 11-3   *Unclassified Traffic Error*

```
router1# show ip nbar unclassified-port-stats
Port statistics for unclassified packets is not turned on.
```

Cisco AutoQoS Suggested Policy

Example 11-4 shows a suggested AutoQoS policy configuration in IOS.

Example 11-4   *Suggested Policy from Cisco AutoQoS*

```
router1# show auto qos
<output omitted>
!
class-map match-any AutoQoS-Voice-Et3/1
match protocol rtp audio
!
class-map match-any AutoQoS-Inter-Video-Et3/1
match protocol rtp video
!
class-map match-any AutoQoS-Signaling-Et3/1
match protocol sip
match protocol rtcp
!
class-map match-any AutoQoS-Transactional-Et3/1
```

```
match protocol citrix
!
class-map match-any AutoQoS-Bulk-Et3/1
match protocol exchange

policy-map AutoQoS-Policy-Et3/1
 class AutoQoS-Voice-Et3/1
 priority percent 1
set dscp ef
class AutoQoS-Inter-Video-Et3/1
bandwidth remaining percent 1
set dscp af41
class AutoQoS-Signaling-Et3/1
bandwidth remaining percent 1
set dscp cs3
```

IP SLA Considerations

Enterprises are under increasing pressure to offer SLAs to their internal customers or other departments or verify and measure outsourced SLAs. The embedded Cisco IOS IP SLA measurement capability allows network managers to validate network performance, proactively identify network issues, and verify service guarantees by using active monitoring to generate probe traffic in a continuous, reliable, and predictable manner. This section discusses the integrated IP SLA measurements that can be used to support network management functions.

IP SLA Overview

The network has become increasingly critical for customers, and any downtime or degradation can adversely impact revenue. Therefore, companies need some form of predictability with IP services.

SLAs

A service-level agreement (SLA) is a contract between a network provider and its customers, or between a network department and internal corporate customers, that specifies connectivity and performance agreements for an end-user service. It provides a form of guarantee to customers about the level of user experience.

An SLA typically outlines the minimum and expected level of service. For example, an IT department can use SLAs to verify that the service provider is meeting its own SLAs or to define service levels for critical business applications. An SLA can also be used as the basis for planning budgets and justifying network expenditures. SLAs also support problem isolation, allowing administrators to reduce the mean time to repair (MTTR).

Table 11-3   *Multimedia Service Requirements*

Traffic Type	Maximum Packet Loss	Maximum One-Way Latency	Maximum Jitter
VoIP	1%	150 ms	30 ms
Interactive video	0.05%	150 ms	10 ms
Streaming video	0.1%	1000 ms	100 ms

Network configurations and other changes can be planned based on optimized performance metrics from SLAs.

Typically, the technical components of an SLA contain a guarantee level for network
availability, performance in terms of round-trip time (RTT), and response in terms of
latency, jitter, and packet loss. The specifics of an SLA vary depending on the applications an organization is supporting in the network. Table 11-3 shows examples of SLA
requirements for voice and video.

For example, converged IP networks must become optimized for performance levels.
Administrators can use various benchmarks, including delay, packet loss, jitter, packet
sequencing, and connectivity to gauge the QoS that is received by the end user.

One-way delay is the difference between the time when the test packet goes out and
when the test packet arrives at the responder. Jitter is the variance of delay. Table 11-3
shows typical multimedia service requirements, which are more stringent than data-only
requirements.

Cisco IOS IP SLA Measurements

Figure 11-14 shows the uses and the theoretical operation of the IP SLA functionality.
The IP SLA measurement functionality in Cisco IOS Software allows configuration of a
router to send synthetic traffic to a host computer or a router that has been configured to
respond. One-way travel times and packet loss data is gathered. Certain measurements
also allow jitter data to be collected.

The several common uses for IP SLA measurements include the following:

- Edge-to-edge network availability monitoring

- Network performance monitoring and network performance visibility

- VoIP, video, and virtual private network (VPN) monitoring

- SLA monitoring

- IP service network health readiness or assessment

- Multiprotocol Label Switching (MPLS) network monitoring

- Troubleshooting of network operation

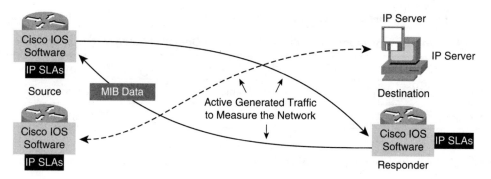

Figure 11-14   *IP SLA Measurements*

IP SLA measurement uses various operations and actively generated traffic probes to gather many types of measurement statistics, including the following:

- Network latency and response time

- Packet-loss statistics

- Network jitter and voice-quality scoring

- Statistical end-to-end matrix of performance information

- End-to-end network connectivity

Multiple IP SLA operations (measurements) can be running in a network at the same time. Reporting tools use SNMP to extract the data into a database and then report on it.

IP SLA measurements allow the network manager to verify service guarantees, which increases network reliability by validating network performance, proactively identifying network issues, and easing the deployment of new IP Services.

IP SLA SNMP Features

Compared with NetFlow, which passively monitors the network, IP SLA measurements actively send data across the network to measure performance between multiple network locations on a hop-by-hop basis or across end-to-end network paths. IP SLA measurements are accessible through SNMP. Figure 11-15 illustrates the logical flow of the IP SLA measurements.

The Cisco Round-Trip Time Monitor (RTTMON) MIB is the MIB that is used with IP SLA measurements. The data from the IP SLA operations is stored within the RTTMON MIB. Network management system applications can retrieve performance statistics from this MIB. Network managers can build custom equations to monitor specific statistics.

The MIB can store measurements over a period of time. IP SLA measurements can be configured to monitor different classes of services over the same link, if the DSCP bits are configured with a **tos** command. This command is supported by all IP SLA measurement operations.

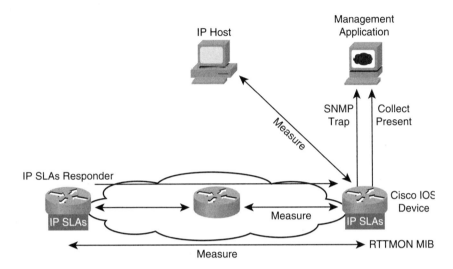

Figure 11-15 *IP SLA SNMP Features*

In addition, IP SLA measurements provide a proactive notification feature with an SNMP trap. Each measurement operation can monitor against a preset performance threshold such as threshold packet loss, latency, and jitter. IP SLA measurements generate an SNMP trap to alert management applications if this threshold is crossed. Available thresholds include RTT average jitter, one-way latency, jitter, packet loss, mean opinion score (MOS), and connectivity tests. Administrators can also configure IP SLA measurements to run a new SNMP operation automatically when the threshold is crossed after a configurable number of times. For instance, if the latency threshold is exceeded three times, a secondary operation measures hop-by-hop latency to isolate the problem area in the network.

Deploying IP SLA Measurements

The first step in IP SLA deployment involves answering the question of what needs to be monitored. A variety of operation types are supported by the IP SLA measurements. The most common operation employed is UDP jitter, which measures IP performance for UDP performance-sensitive applications. Table 11-4 shows the requirements and common IP SLA measurements for several network profiles.

Data-only deployments, for example, typically seek to minimize delay and packet loss. They may obtain the jitter, packet-loss, and latency measurements using the UDP jitter operation.

With the addition of real-time traffic such as VoIP, the focus shifts from just the reliability of the network to also include the delays that are involved in transmitting the data. Real-time traffic is delay sensitive. For VoIP traffic, packet loss is manageable to some extent, but frequent losses impair communication between endpoints. The UDP jitter operation is the most popular because the user can obtain packet-loss, jitter, and latency data from one operation; this also includes unidirectional measurements. VoIP networks may also measure MOS.

Table 11-4   *Deploying IP SLA Measurements*

	Data Traffic	VoIP	SLA Verification	Availability	Streaming Video
Requirement	Minimize delay, packet loss Verify QoS	Minimize delay, packet loss, jitter	Measure delay, packet loss, jitter One-way	Connectivity testing	Minimize delay, packet loss
IP SLA measurement	Jitter Packet loss Latency	Jitter Packet loss Latency MOS voice-quality score	Jitter Packet loss Latency One-way Enhanced accuracy NTP	Connectivity tests to IP devices	Jitter Packet loss Latency

Impact of QoS Deployment on IP SLA Statistics

Table 11-5 illustrates the IP SLA statistics for a particular flow before QoS is deployed in the network. Each row shows a statistical sampling over time that is based on the frequency of measurements.

Table 11-5   *SLA Data Before QoS Deployment*

Srcif	Srcipadd	Dstif	DstIPadd	ToS	Pkts	Src Port	Dst Port	Next Hop	Bytes/Pkt
Fa1/0	173.100.21.2	Fa0/0	10.0.227.12	0	11,000	00A2	00A2	10.0.23.2	1528
Fa1/0	173.100.3.2	Fa0/0	10.0.227.12	0	2491	15	15	10.0.23.2	740
Fa1/0	173.100.20.2	Fa0/0	10.0.227.12	0	10,000	00A1	00A1	10.0.23.2	1428
Fa1/0	173.100.6.2	Fa0/0	10.0.227.12	0	2210	19	19	10.0.23.2	1040

Table 11-6 illustrates the ability for IP SLA to differentiate by QoS markings.

Table 11-6 *IP SLA Data After QoS Deployment*

SrcIf	SrcIPadd	DstIf	DstIPadd	ToS	Pkts	Src Port	Dst Port	Next Hop	Bytes/ Pkt	Start Time	End Time
Fa1/0	173.100.21.2	Fa0/0	10.0.227.12	EF	3020	00A2	00A2	10.0.23.2	1528	..	..
Fa1/0	173.100.21.2	Fa0/0	10.0.227.12	CS6	2212	00A2	00A2	10.0.23.2	1528	..	..
Fa1/0	173.100.21.2	Fa0/0	10.0.227.12	AF41	4000	00A2	00A2	10.0.23.2	501	..	..
Fa1/0	173.100.21.2	Fa0/0	10.0.227.12	CS4	3333	00A2	00A2	10.0.23.2	93	..	..
Fa1/0	173.100.21.2	Fa0/0	10.0.227.12	CS3	7474	00A2	00A2	10.0.23.2	82	..	..
Fa1/0	173.100.21.2	Fa0/0	10.0.227.12	AF21	2828	00A2	00A2	10.0.23.2	111	..	..
Fa1/0	173.100.21.2	Fa0/0	10.0.227.12	CS2	993	00A2	00A2	10.0.23.2	256	..	..
Fa1/0	173.100.21.2	Fa0/0	10.0.227.12	AF11	1404	00A2	00A2	10.0.23.2	64	..	..
Fa1/0	173.100.21.2	Fa0/0	10.0.227.12	CS1	500	00A2	00A2	10.0.23.2	98	..	..
Fa1/0	173.100.21.2	Fa0/0	10.0.227.12	0	11,000	00A2	00A2	10.0.23.2	98	..	..
Fa1/0	173.100.3.2	Fa0/0	10.0.227.12	0	2491	15	15	10.0.23.2	740	..	..
Fa1/0	173.100.20.2	Fa0/0	10.0.227.12	0	10,000	00A1	00A1	10.0.23.2	1428	..	..
Fa1/0	173.100.6.2	Fa0/0	10.0.227.12	0	2210	19	19	10.0.23.2	1040	..	..

Note The abbreviations used in Table 11-5 and 11-6 are as follows:

- **SrcIPadd:** Source IP address
- **DstIPadd:** Destination IP address
- **ToS:** Type of service
- **SD:** Source to destination
- **DS:** Destination to source

In general, QoS is about preferential treatment for certain traffic classes. If all traffic is getting the same treatment, either the network is not congested or the QoS configuration is not working properly at some point in the path.

Scaling IP SLA Deployments

In some cases, it is necessary to cut down on the frequency of the sampling interval or use a dedicated SLA router to perform the IP SLA measurement operations.

The dedicated router (or shadow router) is used when the number of operations is high for an IP SLA source, such as for hundreds or thousands of measurements. A shadow router is simply a router that is dedicated to sourcing IP SLA measurement operations. Dedicated routers are often deployed in large hub-and-spoke networks at the hub site, where spokes respond to IP SLA packers from the shadow router. The advantages of deploying a dedicated router are as follows:

- **Separate memory and CPU from hardware in the switching path:** The dedicated router focuses on IP SLA operations.

- **Easy upgrade of Cisco IOS Software release on the dedicated router:** Upgrades to the shadow router will not affect production traffic.

- **Management and deployment flexibility:** Shadow routers can be deployed at the hub site or at regional aggregation locations.

- **Allows scalability with many endpoints:** A dedicated router provides the benefit of polling a central source location.

Hierarchical Monitoring with IP SLA Measurements

For a large-scale IP SLA enterprise monitoring, a hierarchical strategy may be needed, as shown in Figure 11-16.

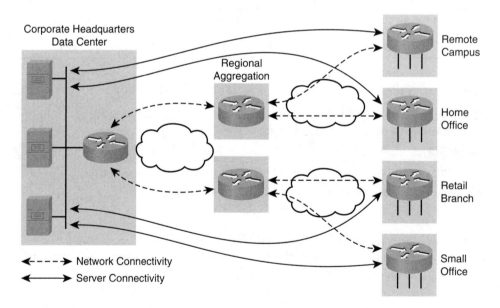

Figure 11-16 *Hierarchical Monitoring with IP SLAs*

If the number of sites is extremely large, the number of measurements for connectivity to every remote site may be prohibitive for even a dedicated router. You can use dedicated routers and a mesh of IP SLA measurements at multiple points in the network. Another way to support large-scale enterprises is to retain a series of measurements in a hierarchical design. Many dedicated routers are also used in large service provider networks for point of presence (POP)-to-POP measurements or from the POP to the customer premises equipment (CPE) routers.

The hierarchical approach allows regional aggregation routers to be the source of IP SLA measurement traffic for access routers in each region. A centralized router is the source of IP SLA traffic to the regional aggregation routers. Potential RTTs can be summed to give an approximate answer for end-to-end measurement. With a hierarchical deployment, the network manager still looks for issues on individual measurements because the reporting tools might not correlate end-to-end times, but threshold violations on single links are all that a collector group usually needs to detect problems.

Network Management Applications Using IP SLA Measurements

IP SLAs are supported by Cisco applications and a wide range of vendor partners that report and use IP SLA data.

Cisco network management solutions include Cisco Unified Service Monitor and CiscoWorks Internetwork Performance Monitor (IPM). Unified Service Monitor is a telephony monitoring system. CiscoWorks is an enterprise performance measuring system.

Note   IPM is end of life but is included to keep parity with the course and exam. See http://www.cisco.com/en/US/products/sw/cscowork/ps1008/index.html.

Third-party SLA monitoring products are available from Hewlett-Packard, IBM, NetQoS, Agilent, and many more. The third-party systems are generally suited for specific monitoring applications and are certified to manage Cisco products..

CiscoWorks IPM Application Example

CiscoWorks IPM is a network response-time and availability troubleshooting application that measures network performance based on the traffic-generation technology within IP SLA. CiscoWorks IPM facilitates performance measurement of differentiated services (for example, voice, video, and data) in an enterprise network.

CiscoWorks IPM helps the network engineer to proactively monitor network response time for problems. CiscoWorks IPM notifies the network engineer when response time degrades or a monitored link becomes unavailable and helps pinpoint the link that is causing the problem.

CiscoWorks IPM enables the network manager to define a collector consisting of one or many IP SLA sources, many IP SLA responders, and many IP SLA operations. Recent versions of the CiscoWorks IPM application have been heavily enhanced in their ability to support IP SLA measurements.

IP SLA Network Management Application Consideration

Several design considerations are involved in selecting a network management application to use with IP SLA measurements.

Network managers should consider how the network management application supports provisioning IP SLA operations by answering the following questions:

1. Does the network management tool provision IP SLA easily, or is manual configuration using a CLI needed for every IP SLA source and responder?

   For large deployments, manual configuration of every device should be avoided. Looking at the details is important, because some applications may emphasize reporting over initial configuration.

2. How much effort is involved in enabling many IP SLA measurements?

   Ease of use promotes use of applications.

Network managers should also consider how the network management application supports reporting on IP SLA operations by answering the following questions:

1. What does the application support for IP SLA data collection and reports?

   A variety of predefined and customizable reports help provide quick views of the results.

2. Is the application easy to set up and maintain?

   Again, ease of use often directly relates to how frequently the application gets used.

The following question about hierarchical reporting should also be considered:

1. Does the tool support aggregation of hierarchical measurements for a more scalable set of measurements?

   At this time, few, if any, products support automated aggregation of hierarchical IP SLA data.

Summary

In this chapter, you learned about the embedded network management tools in the Cisco IOS Software to support application optimization, performance measurement, and SLA verification.

Syslog is a Cisco IOS Software process that enables a device to report and save important error and notification messages. The messages can be saved either locally or to a remote logging server. Syslog messages include both messages in a standardized format and output from **debug** commands. Some issues with syslog include the severity level is not used consistently, the messages can be verbose, the standard UDP communication mechanism is used, and syslog is not a secure mechanism.

The Cisco IOS NetFlow measurement technology measures flows passing through Cisco devices. A NetFlow network flow is a unidirectional sequence of packets between source and destination endpoints and is identified as the combination of seven key fields: source and destination IP address, source and destination port number, Layer 3 protocol field, ToS byte, and input interface.

The NetFlow cache stores IP flow information. The NetFlow export or transport mechanism sends NetFlow data to a network management collector. There are a variety of formats for exporting packets, called export versions. The most common is Version 5, but Version 9 is the latest format.

Fields in a flow record that are not key fields are called nonkey fields. Nonkey fields are added to the flow record in the NetFlow cache and exported. Examples of nonkey fields include flow time stamps, BGP next-hop addresses, and IP address subnet masks. With Cisco IOS Flexible NetFlow, the next-generation in NetFlow technology, these nonkey fields are user configurable. A large number of NetFlow collectors are available—including Cisco, freeware, and third-party commercial products—to report and use NetFlow data.

NBAR is an embedded Cisco IOS Software classification engine that provides full-packet stateful inspection to identify and classify a wide variety of protocols and applications, including those that use dynamic TCP and UDP port assignments. NBAR Protocol Discovery analyzes application traffic patterns in real time to discover which traffic is running on the network. NBAR develops statistics on protocol traffic on interfaces that can be used to apply specific QoS functionality to traffic classes. Application-recognition modules, known as PDLMs, can be added to provide support for additional applications.

An NBAR flow on an interface is identified by five elements: source and destination IP address, source and destination port, and Layer 3 protocol field. NBAR Protocol Discovery statistics can be viewed from the Cisco IOS CLI or through third-party vendor applications.

The Cisco AutoQoS VoIP and AutoQoS for the Enterprise features both use NBAR traffic classification functions to provide a simple, automatic way to enable QoS configurations in conformance with Cisco best-practice recommendations. The two-phase configuration process for the Cisco AutoQoS for the Enterprise feature uses data collected from NBAR to create templates on the configured interface. These templates are used as the basis for creating the class maps and policy maps for the network.

An SLA is a contract between a network provider and its customers, or between a network department and internal corporate customers, that specifies connectivity and performance agreements for an end-user service. The embedded Cisco IOS IP SLA measurement capability provides end-to-end performance measurements by generating and analyzing traffic to measure performance between Cisco IOS Software devices or between a Cisco IOS device and a host, such as a network application server. Jitter, packet loss, and latency are key measurements.

All the IP SLA measurement probe operations are configured on the IP SLA source. The source sends probe packets to the target, the IP SLA measurement accuracy is improved when the target is an IP SLA responder. An IP SLA operation is a measurement that includes protocol, frequency, traps, and thresholds. The most common operation used is the UDP jitter operation, which measures IP performance for UDP performance-sensitive applications.

The IP SLA measurements are accessible through SNMP. Both Cisco and a wide range of vendor partner network management applications report and use IP SLA data.

References

For additional information, refer to the following:

Cisco Systems, Inc. *IOS and IOS-XR System Messages Guide* at
http://www.cisco.com/en/US/docs/ios/system/messages/guide/sm_cnovr.html

Cisco Systems, Inc. *Embedded Syslog Manager (ESM)* at
http://www.cisco.com/en/US/docs/ios/12_3t/12_3t2/feature/guide/gt_esm.html

Cisco Systems, Inc. *NetFlow Services Solutions Guide* at
http://www.cisco.com/en/US/products/sw/netmgtsw/ps1964/products_
implementation_design_guide09186a00800d6a11.html

Cisco Systems, Inc. *Introduction to Cisco IOS NetFlow—A Technical Overview* at
http://www.cisco.com/en/US/prod/collateral/iosswrel/ps6537/ps6555/ps6601/prod_
white_paper0900aecd80406232.html

Cisco Systems, Inc. *Cisco IOS IP Service Level Agreements (SLAs) Introduction* at
http://www.cisco.com/go/ipsla

Cisco Systems, Inc. *Network Based Application Recognition (NBAR) Introduction*
at http://www.cisco.com/go/nbar

Cisco Systems, Inc. *User Guide for Internetwork Performance Monitor 4.2 (With LMS 3.2)* at http://www.cisco.com/en/US/docs/net_mgmt/ciscoworks_internetwork_
performance_monitor/4.2/user/guide/ipmnwf.html

The Internet Engineering Task Force. RFC 3195, *Reliable Delivery for syslog*, at
http://www.ietf.org/rfc/rfc3195.txt

Cisco Systems, Inc. *CiscoWorks Resource Manager Essentials User Guide* at
http://www.cisco.com/en/US/products/sw/cscowork/ps2073/products_user_guide_
list.html

Review Questions

Answer the following questions, and then refer to Appendix A, "Answers to Review Questions," for the answers.

1. Which port does syslog use for sending messages to a syslog server?

    a. UDP 514

    b. UDP 520

    c. UDP 1697

    d. UDP 1967

    e. UDP 2020

    f. Specified in the control message

2. Which four of these key fields are used to identify a flow in traditional NetFlow?

    a. Destination IP address

    b. Destination MAC address

    c. DLCI flag

    d. ifOutput

    e. Layer 3 protocol type

    f. Source IP address

    g. Source MAC address

    h. ToS byte

3. What are three reasons for expiration of NetFlow cache entries?

    a. As the cache becomes full, a number of heuristics are applied to aggressively age groups of flows simultaneously.

    b. Flows in the cache are expired and removed from the cache after the default 20-minute timer.

    c. Flows that have been idle for a specified time are expired and removed from the cache.

    d. TCP connections that have reached the end-of-byte stream (FIN) are expired.

    e. UDP connections that have reached the end-of-byte stream (FIN) are expired.

4. Which NetFlow export record type does Flexible NetFlow use?

   a. Version 1

   b. Version 5

   c. Version 7

   d. Version 8

   e. Version 9

   f. Version 10

5. What are three characteristics of Flexible NetFlow?

   a. It is based on IPFIX.

   b. It is the basis for IPFIX.

   c. It is the most commonly used NetFlow application.

   d. It can monitor a wider range of packet information than traditional NetFlow.

   e. It can track multiple NetFlow applications simultaneously by using different flow-sets.

   f. It can track multiple NetFlow applications simultaneously by using different flow monitors.

6. What are two characteristics of NBAR?

   a. It is based on IPFIX.

   b. It is basis for IPFIX.

   c. It can only monitor applications that are built in or that it recognizes from a PDLM.

   d. It can monitor a wider range of packet or protocol information than traditional NetFlow.

   e. It is enabled with the **ip nbar protocol-discovery** configuration command.

   f. It is enabled with the **ip nbar protocol-match** configuration command.

7. What are two advantages of shadow routers?

   a. They allow scalability with many endpoints.

   b. They cut down on the frequency of the sampling interval.

   c. They are required with hierarchical IP SLA deployments.

   d. They provide separate memory and CPU from hardware in the switching path.

   e. They verify performance per class when QoS is running in the network.

Answers to Review Questions

Chapter 1

1. B, C, F
2. A, C, D
3. B, D, E
4. A, C, D
5. A, B, D

Chapter 2

1. B, E
2. C
3. B, E
4. E
5. E
6. A, D
7. B, C, F
8. A, E
9. A, B
10. E
11. B
12. B, C
13. A, B, D

Chapter 3

1. B, C, F
2. A, B
3. C

4. A, D
5. C
6. A, B, D
7. B
8. A, C, D

Chapter 4

1. D
2. B
3. A, C, D
4. D
5. B, C, D
6. D, E
7. E
8. C
9. A, B, E
10. B, C, D

Chapter 5

1. B, C, E
2. A, C, E
3. C, D
4. A
5. A, C, D
6. B, D, F
7. D

8. E
9. D
10. B
11. D
12. B, D, E
13. A, D

Chapter 6

1. B, D, E
2. D
3. C
4. B, C
5. A, D, E
6. A, D, E
7. B, C
8. B, C, E
9. A, C, D

Chapter 7

1. D
2. B, D, E
3. C, D, E
4. B
5. B, D

Chapter 8

1. A
2. D
3. B, C, E
4. C, F
5. D
6. D, F
7. C, D
8. A, E
9. B, E
10. C
11. A, C, D

Chapter 9

1. E
2. B
3. A, E
4. E
5. C, E
6. C, E
7. A, C
8. B, D, E
9. E
10. B
11. A

Chapter 10

1. B
2. C
3. B
4. D
5. C, D, E
6. C
7. B, C
8. B, C, F
9. D
10. B, D
11. C, D, E
12. A, D, E

Chapter 11

1. A
2. A, E, F, H
3. A, C, D
4. E
5. B, D, F
6. C, D
7. A, D

Appendix C

1. B

2. 802.11A -> 5GHz

   802.11B -> 2.4 GHz

   802.11G -> 2.4 GHz

3. A, E, G

4. Overlapping cells should only be used when there are not enough channels for a specific area. See Figure A-1.

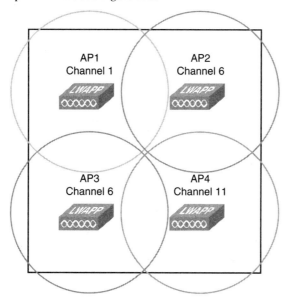

Figure A-1   *Example of Overlapping Cells*

5. B

6. A lightweight AP is controlled and tunneled to a AP controller. An autonomous AP is configured individually and bridges traffic directly to an Ethernet network.

7. Cisco Compatible Extensions—Cisco specific features that optimizes connection to an AP that Cisco has licensed to the industry.

8. SSID—the wireless 'network name'

9. A, B, D

10. The Wireless LAN controller.

11. C

12. Flexibility and mobility of voice services. Advantages over cell phone solutions:

- Some cell phones do not have access to enterprise voice applications such as the corporate directory. However, this is becoming less of an issue with the ubiquity of smart phones.

- Without a single number reach mechanism, using both a cell phone and a VoIP phone results in having multiple phone numbers and multiple voice mailboxes. Productivity could decrease because users must retrieve voice mail from multiple places.

- There are access issues deep inside of some buildings and remote locations.

- There might be security concerns with using mobile phones that are not managed by the organization.

Advantages:

- Enabling access to enterprise unified communications, supporting one phone number and one voice mail per user.

- Helping employees eliminate missed calls by providing mobility within a building or campus.

- Helping organizations gain control over mobile communications costs by leveraging least-cost call routing and providing call detail recording.

- Providing a consistent user experience for improved user satisfaction.

13. RF design cannot be ignored. Implementing an architecture featuring the correct location and density of APs for a WLAN network is the equivalent of correctly installing the cable plant for a wired network. In wired network, problems in the cable plant cannot be completely overcome by advanced features. Similarly, in the WLAN network, Auto-RF is unlikely to overcome a flawed AP deployment.

14.

- **VoWLAN clients:** These clients can be wireless IP phones from Cisco or from vendors supporting CCX. The Cisco IP Communicator software application on a laptop can also function as a VoWLAN client.

- **The voice-ready WLAN:** The WLAN includes APs and antennas to provide optimized packet handling in the RF network.

- **Unified wired or wireless LAN infrastructure:** This infrastructure is used to provide wired and wireless end-to-end prioritization and classification of voice. It includes management tools to control delay, roam time, and packet loss.

- **Cisco Unified Communications and mobility applications:** These applications support increased call capacity, higher network availability, and improved performance for all clients.

15. A, D, E

16. When the wireless client moves its association from one access point to another, the controller simply updates the client database with the newly associated access point. Figure appendix A-2 displays roaming between AP's. If necessary, new security context and associations are established as well. The process becomes more complicated, however, when a client roams from an access point joined to one controller to an access point joined to a different controller. The process also varies based on whether the controllers are operating on the same subnet. Inter-controller roaming occurs when the controllers' wireless LAN interfaces are on the same IP subnet.

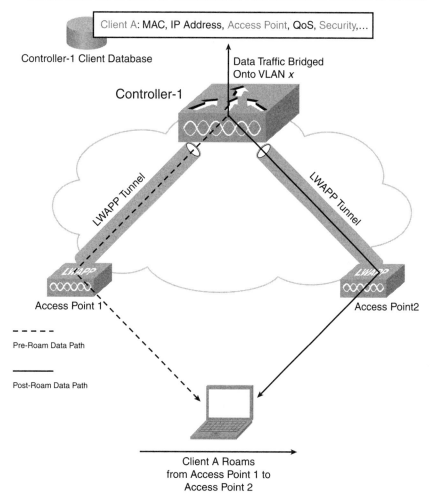

Figure A-2 *AP Roaming*

17. C

18. True

19. CAC—call admission control limits the number of calls on a specific link.

20. A, C

21. C

22. C

23. The maximum number of phones supported per AP depends on the calling patterns of individual users and the AP type. Currently, the recommended call loading for 802.11B and 802.11G is seven active voice calls per AP using the G.711 voice encoding codec or eight active calls using the G.729 codec. These numbers are based on simultaneous requirements for data clients and quality voice calls with current data rates and packet sizes. Beyond the recommended number of active calls, the voice quality of all calls becomes unacceptable if excessive background data is present. In comparison, 802.11A AP radios can support 14 active voice calls using the G.711 codec.

24. C, D

25.

Step 1. Define customer requirements, including the devices to support, the locations of wireless devices, and the service levels expected. Peak requirements such as support for conference rooms should also be defined.

Step 2. Based on the customer requirements, identify planned wireless coverage areas and user density. Obtain a facility diagram to identify the potential RF obstacles. Visually inspect the facility to look for potential barriers to the propagation of RF signals, such as metal racks, elevator shafts, and stairwells. Identify user areas that may be used by many people simultaneously, such as conference rooms, and areas that may only be used for voice, such as stairwells.

Step 3. Determine preliminary AP locations. These locations must include power and wired network access, and must consider cell coverage and overlap, channel selection, antenna, and mounting locations.

Step 4. Perform the actual RF site survey to verify the AP locations. Make sure to use the same AP model for the survey that is in use or that will be used in production. While the survey is being performed, relocate APs as needed and retest.

Step 5. Document the findings, including recording the AP locations and log signal readings and the data rates at outer boundaries.

Appendix B

Acronyms and Abbreviations

This appendix identifies abbreviations, acronyms, and initialisms used in this book and in the internetworking industry.

Many of these acronyms and other terms are also described in the Cisco Internetworking Terms and Acronyms resource, available at http://docwiki.cisco.com/wiki/Category: Internetworking_Terms_and_Acronyms_(ITA).

1RU one-rack unit

2RU two-rack unit

AAA authentication, authorization, and accounting

ABR Area Border Router

ACE Application Control Engine

ACK acknowledgment

ACL access control list

ACS access control server

AD administrative distance

ADU Aironet Desktop Utility

AES Advanced Encryption Standard

AH Authentication Header

ALG application-level gateway

ANSI American National Standards Institute

AP access point

ARCH Designing Cisco Network Service Architectures

ARP Address Resolution Protocol

AS autonomous system

ASA Adaptive Security Appliance

ASBR Autonomous System Boundary Router

ASDM Adaptive Security Device Manager

ASIC application-specific integrated circuit

ASM Any Source Multicast

ASN Abstract Syntax Notation

ASR asymmetric routing

ATA Advanced Technology Attachment

ATM Asynchronous Transport Mode

BASc Bachelor's degree in applied science

BCMSN Building Cisco Multilayer Switched Networks

BDR backup designated router

BEEP Blocks Extensible Exchange Protocol

BFD bidirectional forwarding detection

BGP Border Gateway Protocol

bidir-PIM bidirectional PIM

BPDU bridge protocol data unit

bps bits per second

BR border router

BSCI Building Scalable Cisco Internetworks

BSR bootstrap router

BSS basic service set

BSSID basic service set identifier

CA certificate authority

CAC call admission control

CAM content-addressable memory

CAPEX Capital Expenditure

CatOS Catalyst Operating System

C-BSR candidate BSR

CCDA Cisco Certified Design Associate

CCDE Cisco Certified Design Expert

CCDP Cisco Certified Design Professional

CCIP Cisco Certified Internetworking Professional

CCK Complementary Code Keying

CCKM Cisco Centralized Key Management

CCNA Cisco Certified Network Associate

CCNP Cisco Certified Network Professional

CCNP Cisco Certified Network Professional

CCP Cisco Configuration Professional

CCSI Cisco Certified Systems Instructor

CCX Cisco Compatible Extensions

CDP Cisco Discovery Protocol

CE customer edge

CEF Cisco Express Forwarding

CGMP Cisco Group Management Protocol

CIFS Common Internet File System

CLI command-line interface

CNA Converged Network Adapter

CoS class of service

CPU central processing unit

C-RP candidate RP

CS1 Class Selector 1

CSA Cisco Security Agent

CSM Cisco Security Manager or Content Switching Module

CSMA/CA carrier sense multiple access collision avoidance

CSS Content Services Switch

CST Common Spanning Tree

CWDM coarse wavelength-division multiplexing

DAI Dynamic ARP Inspection

DAS direct-attached storage

dB decibel

dBm dB milliwatt

DCB Data Center Bridging

DDoS distributed denial of service

DES Data Encryption Standard

DESGN Designing for Cisco Internetwork Solutions

DF designated forwarder

DFC distributed forwarding card

DH-CHAP Diffie-Hellman Challenge Handshake Authentication Protocol

DHCP Dynamic Host Configuration Protocol

DLCI data-link connection identifier

DM dense mode

DMA direct memory access

DMVPN Dynamic Multipoint VPN

DMZ demilitarized zone

DNA Do Not Age

DNS Domain Name Service or Domain Name System

DoS denial of service

Dot1q 8021.Q

DR designated router

DSCP differentiated services code point

DSSS direct-sequence spread spectrum

DTCP dynamic transmit power control

DTP Dynamic Trunk Protocol

DVMRP Distance Vector Multicast Routing Protocol

DWDM dense wavelength-division multiplexing

EAP Extensible Authentication Protocol

EAP-FAST Cisco EAP-Flexible Authentication via Secure Tunneling

EAP-GTC EAP-Generic Token Card

EBGP Exterior Border Gateway Protocol

ECMP Equal Cost Multipath

EDCA enhanced distributed channel access

EF expedited forwarding

EHV Ethernet Host Virtualizer

EIGRP Enhanced Interior Gateway Routing Protocol

EMS Ethernet Multipoint Service

EoMPLS Ethernet over MPLS

EOR end-of-row

EOT Enhanced Object Tracking

EPL Ethernet Private Line

ERMS Ethernet Relay Multipoint Service

ERS Ethernet Relay Service

ESA extended service area

ESCON Enterprise System Connection

ESM Embedded Syslog Manager

ESP Encapsulation Security Protocol

EtherIP Ethernet in IP

EVC Ethernet virtual circuit

EWS Ethernet Wire Service

FCIP Fibre Channel over IP

FCP Fibre Channel Protocol

FHRP First Hop Redundancy Protocol

FIB Forwarding Information Base

FICON Fiber Connectivity

FSPF Fabric Shortest Path First

FTP File Transfer Protocol

FWSM Firewall Services Module

GBIC gigabit interface converter

GDOI Group Domain of Interpretation

GE Gigabit Ethernet

GEC Gigabit EtherChannel

GET VPN Group Encrypted Transport VPN

GLBP Gateway Load Balancing Protocol

GRE generic routing encapsulation

GSLB global server load balancing

GSS Global Site Selector

HBA host bus adapter

HCA host channel adapter

HSRP Hot Standby Router Protocol

HTTP Hypertext Transfer Protocol

HVAC heating, ventilation, and air conditioning

H-VPLS Hierarchical VPLS

IANA Internet Assigned Numbers Authority

IBGP Internal Border Gateway Protocol

IBNS Identity-Based Networking Services

ICMP Internet Control Message Protocol

IDE Integrated Drive Electronics

IDS intrusion-detection system

IETF Internet Engineering Task Force

IGMP Internet Group Management Protocol

IGMPv1 IGMP Version 1

IGMPv2 IGMP Version 2

IGMPv3 IGMP Version 3

IGP Interior Gateway Protocol

IKE Internet Key Exchange

IN Intelligent Network

INCITS InterNational Committee for Information Technology Standards

IOS Internetwork Operating System

IP Internet Protocol

IPFIX IP Flow Information Export

IPM Internetwork Performance Monitor

IPS intrusion-prevention system

IPsec IP Security

IP SLA IP service-level agreement

IPv4 IP Version 4

IPv6 IP Version 6

iSCSI Internet Small Computer Systems Interface

IS-IS Intermediate System-to-Intermediate System Protocol

ISL Inter-Switch Link

iSLB iSCSI Server Load Balancing

ISP Internet service provider

iSPF Incremental Shortest Path First

ISR Integrated Services Router

ISR G2 Integrated Services Routers Generation 2

ISSU In-Service Software Update

IVR inter-VSAN routing

JBOD just a bunch of disks

LACP Link Aggregation Control Protocol

LAN local-area network

LANE LAN Emulation

LDAP Lightweight Directory Access Protocol

LEAP Cisco Lightweight Extensible Authentication Protocol

Li-ion lithium-ion

LSA link-state advertisement

LSDB link-state database

LWAPP Lightweight AP Protocol

MAC Media Access Control

MADCAP Multicast Address Dynamic Client Allocation Protocol

MAN metropolitan-area network

MARS Monitoring, Analysis, and Response System

MASc Master's degree in applied science

MBGP Multiprotocol Border Gateway Protocol

MC multipoint controller

MD5 message digest 5 algorithm

MDSP Multicast Source Discovery Protocol

MEC MultiChassis EtherChannel

MED multi-exit discriminator

MIB Management Information Base

MIC message integrity check

MIME Multipurpose Internet Mail Extensions

MISTP Multiple Instances Spanning Tree Protocol

MLS multilayer switching

MPLS Multiprotocol Label Switching

MRTG Multi Router Traffic Grapher

MSFC Multilayer Switch Feature Card

MST Multiple Spanning Tree

MTBF mean time between failure

MTTR mean time to repair

MTU maximum transmission unit

MVPN Multicast Virtual Private Network

MW megawatt

mW milliwatt

NAA NAC Appliance Agent

NAC Network Admission Control

NAM Network Analysis Module

NAM NAC Appliance Manager

NAS NAC Appliance Server or network-attached storage

NAT Network Address Translation

NBAR Network-Based Application Recognition

NBMA nonbroadcast multiaccess

NDE NetFlow data export

NDS Novell Directory Service

NHRP Next Hop Resolution Protocol

NIC network interface card

NIPS network intrusion-prevention system

NSF nonstop forwarding

NSSA not-so-stubby area

NTP Network Time Protocol

OADM optical add/drop multiplexer

OC Optical Carrier

OER Optimized Edge Routing

OFDM orthogonal frequency-division multiplexing

OOB out-of-band

OPEX operating expense

OSA Open Systems Adapters

OSI Open Systems Interconnection

OSPF Open Shortest Path First

OTP one-time password

PAgP Port Aggregation Protocol

PAgP+ Port Aggregation Protocol Plus

PAT Port Address Translation

PBR policy-based routing

PBRST Per-VLAN Rapid Spanning Tree

PDLM Packet Description Language Module

PDM PIX Device Manager

PE provider edge

PEAP Protected Extensible Authentication Protocol

PER packet error rate

PIM Protocol Independent Multicast

PIM-DM PIM dense mode

PIM-SM PIM sparse mode

PIX Private Internet Exchange

PKC Proactive Key Caching

PKI public key infrastructure

PMP Project Management Professional

PoE Power over Ethernet

POP point of presence or Post Office Protocol

POTS plain old telephone service/system

PPDIOO prepare, plan, design, implement, operate, optimize

PSE power sourcing equipment

PVLAN private VLAN

PVS posture validation server

PVST+ Per-VLAN Spanning Tree Plus

QBSS QoS basic service set

QoS quality of service

RAID redundant array of independent/inexpensive disks

RDMA remote direct memory access

RF radio frequency

RFC Request For Comments

RHI Route Health Injection

RIP Routing Information Protocol

RIPv2 Routing Information Protocol Version 2

ROADM reconfigurable OADM

RP rendezvous point

RPF Reverse Path Forwarding

RPR Resilient Packet Ring

RPVST+ Rapid Per-VLAN Spanning-Tree Plus

RRM radio resource management

RSSI received-signal strength indicator

RTP Real-Time Transport Protocol

RTR Response Time Reporter

RTSP Real Time Streaming Protocol

RTT round-trip time

RTTMON Round-Trip Time Monitor

SA security association

SAA service assurance agent

SAN storage-area network

SAP Session Announcement Protocol

SATA Serial ATA

SCCP Skinny Client Control Protocol

SCSI Small Computer Systems Interface

SD Session Directory

SDH Synchronous Digital Hierarchy

SDM Security Device Manager

SDP Session Description Protocol

SFP Small Form-Factor Pluggable

SLA service-level agreement

SLB server load balancer

SM single mode

SMTP Simple Mail Transfer Protocol

SNMP Simple Network Management Protocol

SNR signal-to-noise ratio

SOHO small office/home office

SONA Service-Oriented Network Architecture

SONET Synchronous Optical Network

SPA shared port adapter

SPF shortest path first algorithm

SPT shortest path tree

SRP Spatial Reuse Protocol

SSC Secure Services Client

SSH Secure Shell

SSID service set identifier

SSL VPN IOS Secure Sockets Layer VPN

SSL Secure Sockets Layer

SSLM Secure Sockets Layer Module

SSM source-specific multicast or Storage Services Module

SSO stateful switchover

STP Spanning Tree Protocol

SVF secondary virtual forwarder

TCA target channel adapter

TCO total cost of ownership

TCP Transmission Control Protocol

TDM time-division multiplexing

TFTP Trivial File Transfer Protocol

TKIP Temporal Key Integrity Protocol

TLS Transport Layer Security

TOR top-of-rack

ToS type of service

Tspec traffic specification

TTL Time to Live

UAPSD Unscheduled Automatic Power Save Delivery

UDLD UniDirectional Link Detection

UDP User Datagram Protocol

UNII Unlicensed National Information Infrastructure

URL uniform resource locator

UWN Unified Wireless Network

VACL VLAN ACL

VAM VPN Acceleration Module

VBS Virtual Blade Switch technology

VDC Virtual device context

VIP virtual IP

VLAN virtual local-area network

VLSM variable-length subnet mask

VoD video on demand

VoIP Voice over IP

VoWLAN Voice over WLAN

vPC virtual port channel

VPLS Virtual Private LAN Service

VPN virtual private network

VRF virtual routing and forwarding

VRRP Virtual Router Redundancy Protocol

VSAN virtual storage-area network

VSL virtual switch link

VTI virtual tunnel interface

VTP VLAN Trunking Protocol

vWAAS Virtual Wide Area Application Service

WAN wide-area network

WCS Wireless Control System

Web NS Web Network Services

WEP Wired Equivalent Privacy

WINS Windows Internet Naming Service

WiSM Wireless Services Module

WLAN wireless LAN

WLC WLAN controller

WLCM WLC Module

WLSE Wireless LAN Solutions Engine

WMM Wi-Fi Multimedia

WPA WiFi Protected Access

WPA2 WPA Version 2

WWW World Wide Web

XML Extensible Markup Language

VoWLAN Design

Upon completing this appendix, you will be able to

■ Describe the Cisco voice-ready architecture for supporting VoWLANs

■ Describe VoWLAN infrastructure considerations

■ Discuss VoWLAN coverage concerns and RF survey requirements

IEEE 802.11 wireless local-area networks (WLAN) are rapidly becoming pervasive among enterprises. The availability of wireless voice clients, the introduction of dual-mode (wireless and cellular) smart phones, and the increased productivity realized by enabling a mobile workforce are persuading enterprises to implement Voice over WLANs (VoWLAN).

Note This appendix was a chapter in the previous edition. The content is no longer part of the Designing Cisco Network Service Architectures (ARCH) exam.

This appendix first reviews the Cisco Unified Wireless Network (UWN). The requirements for enterprise VoWLAN are then examined, followed by a discussion of infrastructure considerations for VoWLAN deployment. VoWLAN coverage considerations are examined, and the site-survey process is described. This appendix concludes with a discussion of the Cisco VoWLAN Steps to Success partner program.

Cisco Unified Wireless Network Review

Note Some of the information in this first main section of this appendix is derived from the *Authorized Self-Study Guide: Designing for Cisco Internetwork Solutions (DESGN), Second Edition*, by Diane Teare, Cisco Press, 2007 (ISBN 1-58705-272-5) to provide a detailed review of the Cisco Unified Wireless Network. Some questions related to this material in the "Review Questions" section at the end of this appendix also derive from those in the same DESGN book.

This section first discusses wireless radio frequency communication, antennas, and IEEE 802.11 WLAN operational standards. WLAN components (including clients and access points) are described next, followed by a discussion of WLAN operations. The Cisco UWN architecture is then introduced.

Radio Frequency Communication

A wireless communication system uses radio frequency (RF) energy to transmit data from one point to another, through the air. The term *signal* is used to refer to this RF energy. The data to be transmitted is first modulated onto a carrier and then sent; receivers demodulate the signal and process the data.

WLANs replace the Layer 1 transmission medium of a traditional wired network (usually Category 5 cable) with radio transmission over the air. WLANs can plug into a wired network and function as an overlay to wired LANs, or they can be deployed as a standalone LAN where wired networking is not feasible. A computer with a wireless network interface card (NIC) connects to the wired LAN through an access point (AP). Other wireless endpoint devices supported include wireless phones, such as the Cisco Unified Wireless IP Phone 7921G, and software phones.

WLANs use spread-spectrum RF signals on the three unlicensed bands: 900 MHz, 2.4 GHz, and 5 GHz. The 900-MHz and 2.4-GHz bands are referred to as the industrial, scientific, and medical bands; and the 5-GHz band is commonly referred to as the Unlicensed National Information Infrastructure (UNII) band.

RF *gain* is an increase in the RF signal amplitude or strength. Two common sources of gain are amplifiers and antennas.

RF *loss* is a decrease in the RF signal strength. Losses affect WLAN design and are part of our everyday world. For example, the cables and connections between the AP and the antenna cause loss.

WLANs transmit signals just as radio stations do to reach their listeners. The transmit power levels for WLANs are in milliwatts (mW), and for radio stations the power levels are in megawatts (MW).

Two of the units of measure used in RF are as follows:

- **Decibel (dB):** The difference or ratio between two signal levels. Decibels are used to measure relative gains or losses in an RF system and to describe the effect of system devices on signal strength. The decibel is named after Alexander Graham Bell.

- **dB milliwatt (dBm):** A signal strength or power level. Zero dBm is defined as 1 mW of power into a terminating load such as an antenna or power meter. Small signals, those below 1 mW, are therefore negative numbers (such as –80 dBm); WLAN signals are in the range of –60 dBm to –80 dBm.

Antennas

Antennas used in WLANs come in many shapes and sizes, depending on the differing RF characteristics desired. The physical dimensions of an antenna directly relate to the frequency at which the antenna transmits or receives radio waves. As the gain increases, the coverage area becomes more focused. High-gain antennas provide longer coverage areas than low-gain antennas at the same input power level. As frequency increases, the wavelength and the antennas become smaller.

Omnidirectional antennas are the most widely used today. The radiant energy is shaped like a doughnut. Consequently, the transmitted signal is weak or absent directly under the AP (in the "hole" of the doughnut).

Directional antennas can direct and apply gain to the signal. Semidirectional antennas have radiant energy in a cowbell shape and highly directional antennas have radiant energy in a telescope shape.

IEEE 802.11 Operational Standards

Similar to wired LAN networks, IEEE 802.11 WLANs enable devices to transmit data, voice, and video, at data rates up to 54 Mbps. However, because WLANs are half duplex, the actual maximum throughput is typically 22 Mbps to 26 Mbps.

In September 1999, the IEEE ratified the IEEE 802.11A standard (5 GHz at 54 Mbps) and the IEEE 802.11B standard (2.4 GHz at 11 Mbps). In June 2003, the IEEE ratified the 802.11G standard (2.4 GHz at 54 Mbps); this standard is backward compatible with 802.11b systems, because both use the same 2.4-GHz bandwidth.

The following are the existing IEEE 802.11 standards for wireless communication:

- **802.11A:** 54 Mbps at 5 GHz, ratified in 1999

- **802.11B:** 11 Mbps 2.4 GHz, ratified in 1999

- **802.11D:** World mode, ratified in 2001

- **802.11E:** Quality of service, ratified in 2005

- **802.11F:** Inter-Access Point Protocol, withdrawn in 2006

- **802.11G:** 54 Mbps at 2.4 GHz, ratified in 2003

- **802.11H:** Dynamic frequency selection and transmit power control mechanisms, ratified in 2003

- **802.11I:** Authentication and security, ratified in 2005

- **802.11J:** Additional Japanese frequencies, ratified in 2005

- **802.11K:** Radio resource management draft, ratified in 2008

- **802.11N:** High-throughput draft, ratified in September 2009

IEEE 802.11B/G Standards in the 2.4-GHz Band

The 2.4-GHz band used for 802.11B/G has multiple channels, each 22 MHz wide. In North America, 11 channels are defined, as illustrated in Figure C-1. The top of the figure shows the channel's center frequency (which is the frequency by which the channel is known). The lower numbers show the channel's starting frequency. In North America, the 2.4-GHz band has three nonoverlapping channels: channels 1, 6, and 11.

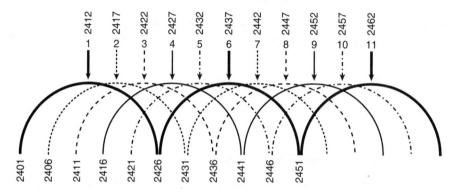

Figure C-1   *2.4-GHz Channels in North America*

Careful channel placement or reuse eliminates overlapping cells on the same channel so that aggregate WLAN throughput is maximized. This concept is similar to the reuse of FM radio stations throughout the country; two radio stations in the same geographic area are never on the same channel.

Therefore, three APs, using the three nonoverlapping channels, could operate in the same area without sharing the medium. For example, an AP on channel 1 does not have any frequencies in common with an AP on channel 6 or with an AP on channel 11. Therefore, no degradation in throughput occurs when three APs are in the same area if they are each on a nonoverlapping channel. Figure C-2 illustrates how 802.11B/G cells can be placed so that no adjacent channels overlap.

Note   802.11G is backward compatible with 802.11B. The 802.11G specification uses orthogonal frequency-division multiplexing (OFDM) modulation for 802.11G data rates and complementary code keying (CCK) modulation for 802.11b data rates. CCK is an extension of direct sequence spread spectrum (DSSS) modulation.

Note   Multipath interference occurs when an RF signal has more than one path between the sender and receiver. The multiple signals at the receiver might result in a distorted, low-quality signal. Multipath interference is more of an issue with 802.11B. Some Cisco APs reduce multipath interference by providing multiple antennas; this feature is called antenna diversity. The device selects the antenna from which the best signal is received. For example, a typical Linksys wireless router has two "rubber duck" antennas. However, only one antenna is used at a time (the one that experiences the least multipath distortion of the signal).

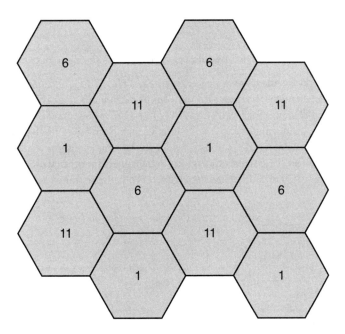

No two adjacent cells use the same channel.

Figure C-2   *2.4-GHz Channel Reuse*

The 802.11G data rates are 54, 48, 36, 24, 18, 12, 9, and 6 Mbps. The 802.11B data rates are 11, 5.5, 2, and 1 Mbps.

IEEE 802.11A Standard in the 5-GHz Band

802.11A and 802.11B/G are incompatible because they use different frequencies. 802.11A requires a different radio and antenna than 802.11B/G.

The 5-GHz UNII band can be divided into multiple channels, depending on the regulations that vary by country. The United States now has three separate 100-MHz-wide bands known as the lower, middle, and upper bands. Within each of these three bands are four nonoverlapping channels. In the United States, the Federal Communications Commission (FCC) specifies that the lower band is for indoor use, the middle band is for indoor and outdoor use, and the upper band is for outdoor use. Figure C-3 illustrates the nonoverlapping 802.11A channels.

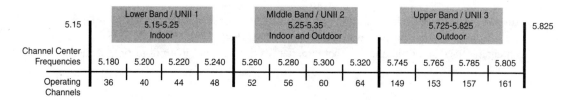

Figure C-3   *5-GHz 802.11A Nonoverlapping Channels*

802.11A uses the same OFDM modulation and supports the same data rates as 802.11G.

802.11A channel placement is easier to deploy than 802.11B/G, because 802.11A has 12 nonoverlapping channels that can provide a simpler channel reuse schema. However, the nonoverlapping channels for 802.11A (as shown in Figure C-3) are close enough to each other that some clients might experience interference from adjacent channels (called side-band or side-channel interference). As a result, the recommendation for 802.11A is that neighboring cells not be placed on neighboring channels (in other words, neighboring channels are skipped) to reduce interference. Figure C-4 illustrates an example of 802.11A channel reuse.

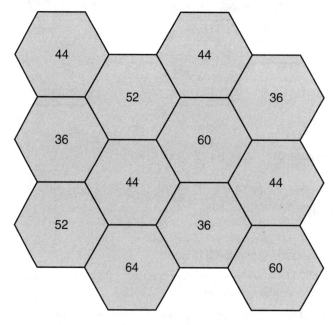

No two adjacent cells use the same channel.

Figure C-4   *5-GHz Channel Reuse*

The 802.11A coverage area is smaller than the 802.11B/G coverage area, requiring more APs on a per-area basis.

WLAN Components

Client devices use wireless NICs or adapters to connect to a wireless network in either ad hoc (peer-to-peer) mode or in infrastructure mode using APs. Cisco APs can be either autonomous or lightweight.

Note   Autonomous APs used to be called thick, fat, or decentralized APs; and lightweight APs were called thin or centralized APs.

Note   Client devices should not be configured in ad hoc mode in the enterprise environment. Apart from the security concerns of ad hoc mode, the data sent in ad hoc mode effectively reduces the bandwidth available for other devices configured for the same channel in infrastructure mode. The remainder of this appendix focuses on infrastructure mode using APs.

These components are described in the following sections.

Cisco-Compatible WLAN Clients

The Cisco Compatible Extensions (CCX) program for WLAN client devices allows vendors of WLAN client devices or adapters to ensure interoperability with the Cisco WLAN infrastructure and take advantage of Cisco innovations. A program participant, such as a maker of a WLAN client adapter or client device, implements support for all features and then submits the product to an independent lab for rigorous testing. Passing this testing process allows the devices to be marketed as Cisco Compatible client devices. There are four versions of the Cisco Compatible specification, versions 1 through 4, as shown in Figure C-5. Each version builds on its predecessors. With a few exceptions, every feature that must be supported in one version must also be supported in each subsequent version.

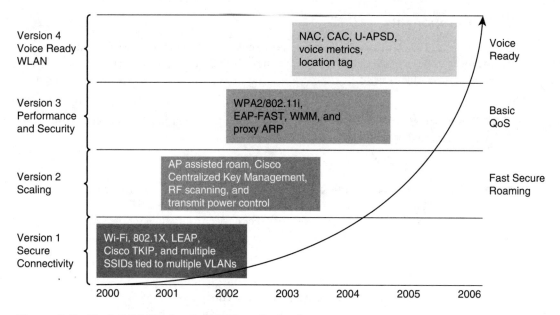

Figure C-5   *Each CCX Version Builds Upon Its Predecessors*

Some features of CCX Version 1 are as follows:

■   Compliance with 802.11A, B, or G and Wi-Fi

■   Support for IEEE 802.1X and Cisco Lightweight Extensible Authentication Protocol (LEAP)

■   Support for Cisco Temporal Key Integrity Protocol (TKIP), a Cisco implementation of TKIP that includes a hashing algorithm and a message integrity check

■   Interoperability with APs that support multiple service set identifiers (SSID) tied to multiple VLANs, providing benefits such as flexible security schemes in a mixed client environment

Some additional features of CCX Version 2 are as follows:

■   Compliance with Wi-Fi Protected Access (WPA), including support for WPA TKIP encryption

■   Support for Protected Extensible Authentication Protocol (PEAP) with Extensible Authentication Protocol (EAP)-Generic Token Card (EAP-GTC)

■   Fast, secure, AP-assisted roaming with Cisco Centralized Key Management (CCKM) support

■   RF scanning, with scanned data sent to the AP and ultimately to CiscoWorks Wireless LAN Solution Engine (WLSE) for analysis and performance of RF management functions such as intrusion detection, assisted site survey, and detection of interference sources

■ Support for AP-specified maximum transmit power

Some additional features of CCX Version 3 are as follows:

■ Compliance with WPA version 2 (WPA2)/802.11i, including support for Advanced Encryption Standard (AES) encryption

■ Support for Extensible Authentication Protocol Flexible Authentication via Secure Tunneling (EAP-FAST)

■ Support for Wi-Fi Multimedia (WMM)

■ Recognition of proxy ARP information elements in beacons to indicate whether proxy ARP is supported in an AP

Some additional features of CCX Version 4 are as follows:

■ Support for Network Admission Control (NAC), to allow network access only to compliant and trusted clients

■ Support for Call Admission Control (CAC), including addressing, VoIP stability, roaming, and other quality of service (QoS)-related issues

■ Support for a power-saving mechanism, Unscheduled Automatic Power Save Delivery (U-APSD), in QoS environments

■ VoIP metrics reporting to optimize WLAN VoIP performance

■ Ability to function as an 802.11 location tag

Note   Many of the protocols mentioned in the CCX version descriptions are described throughout this appendix.

Note   You can find more information about the CCX program at the Cisco Compatible Extensions program website at
http://www.cisco.com/web/partners/pr46/pr147/partners_pgm_concept_home.html.

Autonomous APs

An autonomous AP has a local configuration and requires local management, which might make consistent configurations difficult and add to the cost of network management.

Cisco's core WLAN feature set includes autonomous APs and the CiscoWorks WLSE management appliance.

CiscoWorks WLSE is a turnkey and scalable management platform for managing hundreds to thousands of Cisco Aironet autonomous APs and wireless bridges. Autonomous

APs may also be configured with CiscoWorks WLSE Express, a complete WLAN management solution with an integrated authentication, authorization, and accounting (AAA) server for small to medium-sized enterprise facilities or branch offices using Cisco Aironet autonomous APs and wireless bridges.

Lightweight APs

A lightweight AP receives control and configuration from a WLAN controller (WLC) to which it is associated. This provides a single point of management and reduces the security concern of a stolen AP.

The WLCs and lightweight APs communicate over any Layer 2 (Ethernet) or Layer 3 (IP) infrastructure using the Lightweight AP Protocol (LWAPP) to support automation of numerous WLAN configuration and management functions. WLCs are responsible for centralized system-wide WLAN management functions, such as security policies, intrusion prevention, RF management, QoS, and mobility.

Note   Despite being called a *wireless* LAN controller, a WLC is connected to the *wired* LAN and to the lightweight APs by the wired LAN. The WLC does not have *any* wireless connections.

The Cisco advanced WLAN feature set includes lightweight APs, WLCs, and the Wireless Control System (WCS) management application. These components are the basis for the Cisco UWN.

A Cisco wireless location appliance may be added to track the location of wireless devices.

WLAN Operation

The coverage area of an AP is called the basic service set (BSS); other names for the BSS are *microcell* and *cell*. The identifier of the BSS is called the BSS identifier (BSSID).

If a single cell does not provide enough coverage, any number of cells can be added to extend the range to an extended service area (ESA). It is recommended that the ESA cells have a 10 percent to 15 percent overlap to allow remote users to roam without losing RF connections. If VoIP is implemented in the wireless network, it is recommended that the ESA cells have a 15 percent to 20 percent overlap. As discussed earlier, bordering cells should be set to different nonoverlapping channels for best performance.

An SSID is the identifier (or name) of an ESA, creating a WLAN. An SSID on an AP and on an associated client must match exactly. APs broadcast their SSIDs in a beacon, announcing their available services. Clients associate with a specific SSID or learn the available SSIDs from the beacon and choose one with which to associate.

APs can be configured not to broadcast a particular SSID, but the SSID is still sent in the header of all the packets sent and therefore is discoverable by wireless survey tools.

Therefore, configuring the AP not to broadcast an SSID is not considered a strong security mechanism by itself.

Roaming occurs when a wireless client moves from being associated to one AP to another AP (from one cell to another cell) within the same SSID. Roaming is explored in the "Roaming" section, later in this appendix.

The Cisco UWN Architecture

In a traditional WLAN, each AP operates as a separate autonomous node configured with SSID, RF channel, RF power settings, and so forth. Scaling to large, contiguous, coordinated WLANs and adding higher-level applications is challenging with these autonomous APs. For example, if an autonomous AP hears a nearby AP operating on the same channel, the autonomous AP has no way of determining whether the adjacent AP is part of the same network or a neighboring network. Some form of centralized coordination is needed to allow multiple APs to operate across rooms and floors.

Cisco UWN Elements

The Cisco UWN architectural elements allow a WLAN to operate as an intelligent information network and to support advanced mobility services. The Cisco UWN incorporates advanced features that elevate a wireless deployment from a means of efficient data connectivity to a secure, converged communications network for voice and data applications.

Beginning with a base of client devices, each element provides additional capabilities needed as networks evolve and grow, interconnecting with the elements above and below it to create a unified, secure, end-to-end enterprise-class WLAN solution. The five interconnected elements of the Cisco UWN architecture are as follows:

- **Client devices:** With more than 90 percent of shipping client devices certified as Cisco Compatible under the CCX program, almost any client device that is selected will support the Cisco UWN advanced features, including out-of-the-box wireless client security.

- **Lightweight APs:** Dynamically configured APs provide ubiquitous network access in all environments. Enhanced productivity is supported through "plug-and-play" with LWAPP used between the APs and the Cisco WLCs. Cisco APs are a proven platform with a large installed base and market share leadership. All Cisco lightweight APs support mobility services, such as fast secure roaming for voice, and location services for real-time network visibility.

- **Network unification:** Integration of wired and wireless networks is critical for unified network control, scalability, security, and reliability. Seamless functionality is provided through wireless integration into all major switching and routing platforms, including Cisco WLC appliances, Cisco WLC Modules (WLCM) for Integrated Services Routers (ISR), and Cisco Catalyst 6500 series Wireless Services Modules (WiSM).

- **Network management:** The same level of security, scalability, reliability, ease of deployment, and management for WLANs as wired LANs is provided through network management systems such as the Cisco WCS, which helps visualize and secure the airspace. The Cisco wireless location appliance provides location services.

- **Mobility services:** Unified mobility services include advanced security threat detection and mitigation, voice services, location services, and guest access.

Benefits of the Cisco UWN architecture include ease of deployment and upgrades, reliable connectivity through dynamic RF management, optimized per-user performance through user load balancing, guest networking, Layer 2 and 3 roaming, embedded wireless intrusion-detection system (IDS), location services, VoIP support, lowered total cost of ownership (TCO), and wired and wireless unification.

The Cisco WCS is an optional Windows or Linux server-based network management component that works in conjunction with Cisco lightweight APs and Cisco WLCs. With Cisco WCS, network administrators have a single solution for RF prediction, policy provisioning, network optimization, troubleshooting, user tracking, security monitoring, and WLAN systems management. The Cisco WCS includes tools for WLAN planning and design, RF management, basic location tracking, intrusion prevention systems, and WLAN systems configuration, monitoring, and management.

The Cisco wireless location appliance integrates with Cisco WCS for enhanced physical location tracking of many wireless devices to within a few meters. This appliance also records historical location information that can be used for location trending, rapid problem resolution, and RF capacity management.

An enterprise network can start with client devices, lightweight APs, and WLCs. As the enterprise's wireless networking requirements grow, additional elements, such as the Cisco WCS and the Cisco wireless location appliance, can be incorporated into the network.

Cisco UWN Lightweight AP and WLC Operation

An autonomous AP acts as an 802.1Q translational bridge and is responsible for putting the wireless client RF traffic into the appropriate local VLAN on the wired network.

In contrast, the Cisco UWN architecture centralizes WLAN configuration and control on a WLC; the APs are *lightweight*, meaning that they cannot act independently of a WLC. The lightweight APs and WLCs communicate using LWAPP, and the WLCs are responsible for putting the wireless client traffic into the appropriate VLAN. Figure C-6 shows an example of this architecture.

It is a recommended enterprise practice that the connection between client device and APs be both authenticated and encrypted. When a WLAN client sends a packet as an RF signal, it is received by a lightweight AP, decrypted if necessary, encapsulated with an LWAPP header, and forwarded to the WLC. From the perspective of the AP, the WLC is an LWAPP tunnel endpoint with an IP address. At the WLC, the LWAPP header is stripped off, and the frame is switched from the WLC onto the appropriate VLAN in the campus infrastructure.

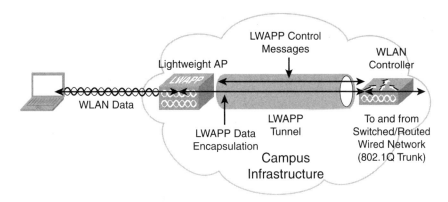

Figure C-6   *Cisco UWN Includes Lightweight APs and WLCs*

In the Cisco UWN architecture, the WLC is an 802.1Q bridge that takes client traffic from the LWAPP tunnel (from the lightweight AP) and puts it on the appropriate VLAN in the wired network. Figure C-7 illustrates this process.

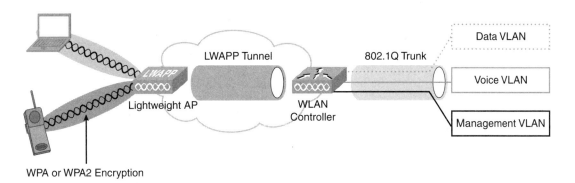

Figure C-7   *In the UWN, the WLC Bridges and Puts Traffic into VLANs*

Note   If you move a statically addressed AP to a different IP subnet, it cannot forward traffic because it cannot form an LWAPP tunnel with the WLC.

When a client on the wired network sends a packet to a WLAN client, the packet first goes into the WLC, which encapsulates it with an LWAPP header and forwards it to the appropriate AP. The AP strips off the LWAPP header, encrypts the frame if necessary, and then bridges the frame onto the RF medium.

Consequently, much of the traditional WLAN functionality has moved from autonomous APs to a centralized WLC under the Cisco UWN architecture. LWAPP splits the MAC functions of an AP between the WLC and the lightweight AP. The lightweight APs handle only real-time MAC functionality, leaving the WLC to process all the non-real-time

MAC functionality. This split-MAC functionality allows the APs to be deployed in a zero-touch fashion such that individual configuration of APs is not required.

Using VoWLAN in an Enterprise Network

This section identifies the drivers for using VoWLAN in the enterprise, provides an overview of the Cisco voice-ready architecture, and describes the impact of voice requirements on WLANs.

VoWLAN Drivers in the Enterprise

Because WLANs are pervasive among enterprises and because VoIP deployments offer a rich set of features, organizations are looking to combine these technologies in VoWLAN to improve productivity and reduce costs. VoWLAN deployments provide multiple benefits, including the following:

- Enabling access to enterprise unified communications, supporting one phone number and one voice mail per user

- Helping employees eliminate missed calls by providing mobility within a building or campus

- Helping organizations gain control over mobile communications costs by leveraging least-cost call routing and providing call detail recording

- Providing a consistent user experience for improved user satisfaction

These factors, coupled with the availability of wireless voice clients and the introduction of dual-mode (wireless and cellular) smart phones, are enticing enterprises to implement VoWLANs.

One alternative to VoWLAN is a cell phone solution. Cell phones can support the mobility requirements of an enterprise similar to VoWLAN. Currently, cell phone solutions have some advantages over VoWLAN solutions because of the good selection of cell phones available and the fact that multiple carriers provide cell phone service.

However, there are some disadvantages to cell phone solutions, including the following:

- Some cell phones do not have access to enterprise voice applications such as the corporate directory. However, this is becoming less of an issue with the ubiquity of smart phones.

- Without a single number reach mechanism, using both a cell phone and a VoIP phone results in having multiple phone numbers and multiple voice mailboxes. Productivity may decrease because users must retrieve voice mail from multiple places.

- There are access issues deep inside of some buildings and remote locations.

- There may be security concerns with using mobile phones that are not managed by the organization.

Note In-building cell phone amplifiers from companies such as Cellphone-Mate Inc, can mitigate some of the access issues mentioned earlier.

Although there is currently no seamless handoff on a dual-mode phone, dual-mode smart phones are starting to replace cell phones.

Therefore, organizations are looking to make WLANs voice ready, for current or future use to protect the upfront investment in infrastructure and services.

Voice-Ready Architecture

Voice services place stringent performance requirements on the entire network. Because digitized voice is a sampling of an analog signal, the transmission of digitized voice is very sensitive to delays during transit. Voice requires a pervasive deployment; the network needs to have continuous coverage everywhere a client may roam to avoid any dead spots or gaps in coverage that may cause a call to drop. This pervasive coverage requirement is not as stringent in data-only networks because data applications are far more tolerant of brief network interruptions.

The end-to-end transit time of a packet is the cumulative delay for the packet to be encoded, to be put on the network by the sending client, to traverse the network, and to be received and decoded at the receiving client. For voice to work correctly over any infrastructure, the end-to-end transmit time must be less than 150 ms.

QoS for a VoIP call must be maintained, whether the call is being delivered to a wired or a wireless endpoint. Issues encountered during transit result in delays and variations in the arrival time of the received signal, known as jitter. It is critically important to minimize end-to-end delay and jitter for VoIP packets to provide optimal audio quality. To maintain QoS, voice must be a priority across the VoWLAN and the packet priority must be translated from the wireless to the wired infrastructure.

The Cisco voice-ready architecture is an end-to-end approach that builds on the highly scalable, low-TCO Cisco UWN and addresses the convergence of VoIP and wireless networks. The voice-ready architecture is designed to support pervasive deployments that are typical of customers with mobile voice applications to flexibly extend the mobility benefits of wireless networks to their voice communications. Additional features, such as end-to-end QoS, and fast, secure roaming, backed by a portfolio of APs with enhanced radios, make the Cisco UWN voice ready.

As illustrated in Figure C-8, the Cisco voice-ready architecture has the following four main components:

- **VoWLAN clients:** These clients can be wireless IP phones from Cisco or from vendors supporting CCX. The Cisco IP Communicator software application on a laptop can also function as a VoWLAN client.

- **The voice-ready WLAN:** The WLAN includes APs and antennas to provide optimized packet handling in the RF network.

- **Unified wired or wireless LAN infrastructure:** This infrastructure is used to provide wired and wireless end-to-end prioritization and classification of voice. It includes management tools to control delay, roam time, and packet loss.

- **Cisco Unified Communications and mobility applications:** These applications support increased call capacity, higher network availability, and improved performance for all clients.

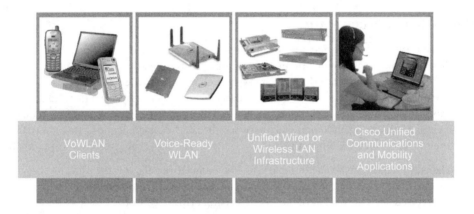

Figure C-8   *Cisco Voice-Ready Architecture*

The architecture supports converged voice and data on wired and wireless networks for an end-to-end intelligent integration.

Voice Impact on WLANs

The WLAN infrastructure is a shared medium among wireless devices. Adding voice services to a WLAN has implications in several design areas, including the following:

- RF coverage requirements and deployment planning

- Network infrastructure and logical subnet design

- Wireless "over-the-air" QoS

- Network security architecture

- VoWLAN client requirements

These topics are discussed throughout the rest of the appendix.

VoWLAN Infrastructure Considerations

There are several voice-specific requirements to consider when you are implementing a VoWLAN, including the following:

- **Roaming:** Voice calls require network connectivity to be maintained while the client is physically moving, changing its association from one AP to another. Voice clients typically move more often than data-only clients.

- **QoS:** QoS is essential to ensure that voice traffic receives timely and reliable treatment with low delay, low jitter, and little or no packet loss on the network. QoS also includes CAC to police the call capacity on a per-AP basis.

- **Security:** Wireless IP telephony networks require a carefully planned security implementation to ensure that the telephony network operates properly and that voice traffic is secure.

- **Intelligent clients:** A voice-ready WLAN requires an intelligent client capable of supporting the voice-ready Cisco infrastructure functions for enterprise roaming, QoS, CAC, and security.

The Cisco UWN supports all these requirements through software capabilities and technological enhancements in both the infrastructure and in Cisco Compatible clients. These capabilities and enhancements are discussed in the following sections.

Roaming

One significant benefit of wireless networks (and a key reason they are deployed) is mobility, or roaming. This is the capability of end devices to move to new locations and remain networked without reassociation and DHCP delays. Roaming occurs when a wireless client moves its association from one AP and reassociates to another AP, within the same SSID.

A WLAN client must be able to maintain its association seamlessly from one AP to another securely and with as little latency as possible. The roaming event is triggered on signal quality, not proximity to an AP. When the signal quality for a client drops as a result of movement, the client device roams to another AP.

Mobility introduces challenges in a network implementation. Roaming must be supported when the wireless client roams from one AP to another, whether both APs are joined to the same WLC (intracontroller) or to different WLCs (intercontroller). Depending on the application, the Cisco UWN might have to support Layer 2 or Layer 3 roaming. These scenarios are described in the following sections.

When WLAN clients roam, they are always reauthenticated by the system in some way, to protect against client spoofing. CCKM is a Cisco standard (supported by Cisco Compatible clients) to provide fast, secure roaming, and is recommended for VoWLANs.

CCKM enables authenticated client devices to roam securely from one AP to another without any perceptible delay during reassociation. During the roaming process, a VoWLAN phone must scan for the nearby APs, determine which AP can provide the best service, and then reassociate with the new AP. If stronger authentication methods, such as WPA and EAP, are used, the number of information exchanges increases and causes more delay during roaming. To avoid these delays, CCKM is recommended for VoWLANs.

Note   Cisco WLCs with software release 4.0.217 or later support CCKM. The Cisco Unified Wireless IP Phone 7921G and Cisco Unified Wireless IP Phone 7920 support CCKM but cannot use Proactive Key Caching (PKC) at this time. The Cisco 7925G does not have this limitation.

Note   This appendix discusses roaming within the enterprise framework. Handoffs or roaming for dual-mode clients between a cellular wireless network and an enterprise WLAN is not covered.

CCKM is further described in the "Security" section, later in this appendix.

Intracontroller Roaming

Intracontroller roaming is roaming between APs joined to the *same* WLC.

When a wireless client associates to an AP and authenticates through a WLC, the WLC places an entry for that client in its client database. This entry includes the MAC and IP addresses of the client, security context and associations, QoS context, WLAN, and associated AP. The WLC uses this information to forward frames and manage traffic to and from the wireless client.

When the wireless client moves its association from one AP to another on the same WLC, as illustrated in Figure C-9, the WLC simply updates the client database with the new associated AP. If necessary, new security context and associations are established, too. With intracontroller roaming, an IP address refresh is not needed.

Intercontroller Roaming at Layer 2

Intercontroller roaming occurs when a client roams from an AP joined to one WLC to an AP joined to a different WLC. Intercontroller roaming can be at Layer 2 or Layer 3.

Figure C-10 illustrates an intercontroller Layer 2 roam.

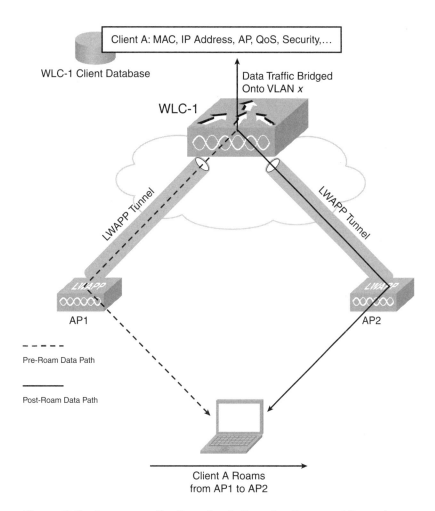

Client A: MAC, IP Address, AP, QoS, Security,...

WLC-1 Client Database

Data Traffic Bridged
Onto VLAN *x*

WLC-1

LWAPP Tunnel

LWAPP Tunnel

AP1

AP2

- - - - -
Pre-Roam Data Path

———
Post-Roam Data Path

Client A Roams
from AP1 to AP2

Figure C-9 *Intracontroller Roaming Is Roaming Between APs on the
Same WLC*

A Layer 2 intercontroller roam occurs when the client traffic is bridged to the same IP
subnet (and therefore the same VLAN) through the LAN interfaces on both WLCs.

When the client reassociates to an AP connected to a new WLC, the new WLC
exchanges mobility messages with the original WLC (using a Mobility Messaging
Exchange protocol), and the client database entry is *moved* to the new WLC. New security context and associations are established if necessary, and the client database entry is
updated for the new AP. With Layer 2 intercontroller roaming, an IP address refresh is not
needed. This process is transparent to the end user.

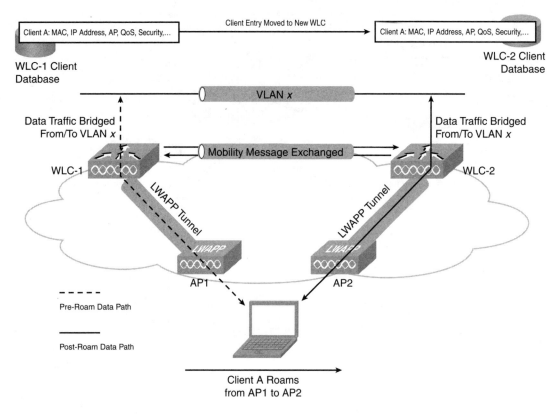

Figure C-10   *Layer 2 Intercontroller Roaming*

> **Note**   Both forms of intercontroller roaming require the WLCs to be in the same mobility group, as described in the upcoming "Mobility Groups" section.

Intercontroller Roaming at Layer 3

Layer 3 intercontroller roaming occurs when the client associates to an AP on a different WLC and the traffic is bridged to a different IP subnet. Layer 3 intercontroller roaming is used when Layer 2 VLANs do not extend across the entire enterprise, and therefore traffic needs to go to a different subnet.

When the client roams at Layer 3 and reassociates to an AP connected to a new WLC, the new WLC exchanges mobility messages with the original WLC, as shown in Figure C-11.

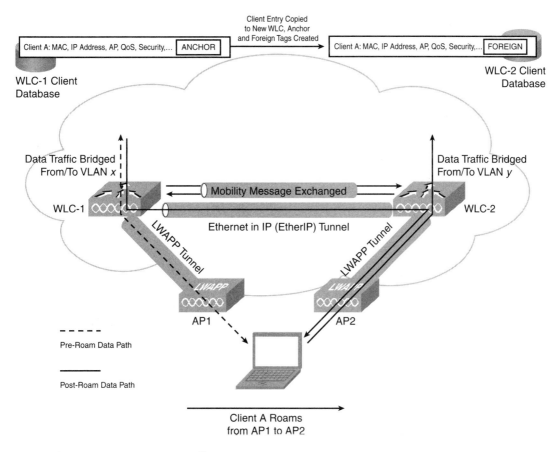

Figure C-11 *Layer 3 Intercontroller Roaming*

With Layer 3 roaming, instead of *moving* the client entry to the new WLC's client database, the original WLC marks the entry for the client in its own client database with an Anchor entry and *copies* the database entry to the new WLC's client database, where it is marked with a Foreign entry.

Security credentials and context are reestablished if necessary. The roam is still transparent to the wireless client, which maintains its original IP address, even though the new WLC uses a different subnet.

After a Layer 3 roam, the data transferred to and from the wireless client might flow in an asymmetric traffic path. The Foreign WLC forwards traffic from the client to the network directly into the network. Traffic to the client arrives at the Anchor WLC, which forwards the traffic to the Foreign WLC in an Ethernet in IP (EtherIP) tunnel. The Foreign WLC then forwards the data to the client.

If a wireless client roams to a new Foreign WLC, the client database entry is moved from the original Foreign WLC to the new Foreign WLC, but the original Anchor WLC is always maintained.

Mobility Groups

A set of WLCs in a network can be configured as a mobility group, which allows them to dynamically share important information among them, including the context and state of client devices and WLC loading information.

With this information, the network can support intercontroller roaming, AP load balancing, and WLC redundancy. A mobility group also supports forwarding of data traffic through EtherIP tunnels for Layer 3 intercontroller roaming. A mobility group does more than just define the RF connectivity of the client; it defines the infrastructure resources and their connectivity to each other. Therefore, if a client needs to seamlessly roam from one location to another across WLCs, the WLCs in those locations need to be in the same defined mobility group.

Each WLC in a mobility group is configured with a list of the other members of the mobility group. Each WLC device builds a neighbor relationship with every other member of the group.

WLCs should be placed in the same mobility group when an intercontroller roam is possible. If no possibility exists of a roaming event occurring, it might make sense to not put WLCs in the same mobility group. For example, suppose that you have deployed two separate WLCs in two buildings, with each WLC managing the APs in its building. If the buildings are separated by a large parking area with no RF coverage, a WLAN client will not roam from an AP in one building to an AP in the other building. These WLCs therefore do not need to be members of the same mobility group. In general, a single mobility group should encompass an area that covers 80 percent to 90 percent of user roaming patterns because clients cannot seamlessly roam across mobility groups. Therefore, the WLAN deployment team must have a good understanding of how users will move throughout the building and incorporate this into the mobility group creation.

A mobility group can include up to 24 WLCs. The number of APs supported in a mobility group is a maximum of 3600 and is bounded by the number of WLCs and WLC types in the mobility group.

Enhanced Neighbor Lists

VoWLAN handsets typically continually scan the APs in the neighbor list to stay associated with the best AP. With the Cisco VoWLAN solution, clients can be classified based on roaming type and participate in the roaming process based on information gathered from the infrastructure.

Examples of roaming classifications are fast roam, slow roam, and 802.11A/B/G only.

The information gathered from the network infrastructure is put in enhanced neighbor lists. The enhanced neighbor lists contain information that helps the client make association decisions between potential APs including a list of neighboring APs that have the ability to service the client based on the client classification.

The enhanced neighbor list includes information such as the following:

- Authorized APs nearby

- RF parameters of nearby APs

- RF measurements at the edge of cells

- Capacity utilization on nearby APs

Based on the information in the neighbor list, the client preemptively decides to associate with an AP that has sufficient capacity and RF parameters. If the AP can service the client, based on the client classification, the AP and the client will successfully associate.

This intelligent roaming process enables the clients to associate to the AP that will provide them the best audio quality and helps minimize or eliminate audio gaps in roams. Overall network capacity is increased through this load balancing.

QoS

QoS is essential to ensure that voice traffic receives timely and reliable treatment with low delay, low jitter, and little or no packet loss on the network.

IEEE 802.11E and Wi-Fi Multimedia

QoS on a pervasive WLAN is much more than simply prioritizing one type of packet over another.

The number of active users in any WLAN location may change dynamically and cannot be addressed through the capacity management tools used in wired networks. WLAN traffic is nondeterministic. Channel access is based on a binary back-off algorithm defined by the 802.11 standard (carrier sense multiple access with collision avoidance [CSMA/CA]) and is variable by nature, based on the number of clients accessing the network. This variability makes maintaining QoS for VoWLAN more difficult.

To improve the reliability of voice transmissions in this nondeterministic environment, the IEEE formed the 802.11E specification that adds QoS features and multimedia support to the existing 802.11G, 802.11G, and 802.11A wireless networks. Before the IEEE 802.11E was ratified, the wireless industry trade association known as the Wi-Fi Alliance accelerated the use of WLAN QoS through an early certification called WMM. The WMM includes some of the 802.11E features for wireless networks to improve the user experience for audio, video, and voice applications. WMM adds prioritization capabilities to wireless networks and optimizes performance when multiple applications, each with different latency and throughput requirements, compete for network resources.

The Cisco Unified Wireless IP Phone 7920 and 7921G devices support the 802.11E standard and are WMM certified. For the 802.11E and WMM differentiated services to provide sufficient QoS for voice packets, only a certain amount of voice bandwidth can be serviced or admitted on a channel at any one time. For example, assume that a network can handle x number of voice calls with its reserved bandwidth; if the number of voice calls is increased beyond this limit (to $x + 1$, for example), the quality of all calls suffer.

Cisco WLANs support four levels of QoS over the air: Platinum (voice), Gold (video), Silver (best effort, the default), and Bronze (background). As a recommended practice, configure the voice traffic WLAN to use Platinum QoS, assign low-bandwidth WLAN traffic to use Bronze QoS, and assign all other traffic between the remaining QoS levels.

The WLAN QoS level defines a specific 802.11E user priority for over-the-air traffic. This user priority is used to derive the over-the-wire priorities for non-WMM traffic, and it also acts as the ceiling when managing WMM traffic with various levels of priorities. APs use this QoS-profile-specific user priority to derive the IP differentiated services code point (DSCP) value that is used on the wired LAN.

Note   WMM requires CCX Version 3 or later.

End-to-End QoS

Separate voice and data VLANs are recommended to support different security features, to support different priorities for voice traffic so that it can be dealt with using minimal delays and to reduce the chance of data clients crowding the voice VLAN and causing unnecessary traffic overhead and delays.

Using separate data and voice VLANs allows specific QoS settings for voice VLAN traffic, enabling end-to-end QoS for this traffic. This separation of client traffic is best continued into separate wireless RF spectrum, such as using IEEE 802.11A (5 GHz) for voice and IEEE 802.11B and IEEE 802.11G (2.4 GHz) for data. The final selection of the RF spectrum used depends on the client hardware capabilities available (for example, if the client supports only 2.4-GHz 802.11B/G or 5-GHz 802.11A, or both radios). Deploying voice in 5 GHz also reduces the RF interference present in the crowded 2.4-GHz RF spectrum.

Note   Using separate VLANs is in addition to the RF recommendation of ensuring nonoverlapping channel frequencies to avoid interference.

As shown in the example in Figure C-12, if the over-the-air packets from the phone or PC to the AP have trust enforced, the QoS marking from the client determines the DSCP value in the LWAPP frame. Because all WLAN traffic that passes between the AP and the WLC is LWAPP encapsulated, the LWAPP encapsulation maintains the Layer 3 marking in the original packet. When the LWAPP packet is de-encapsulated at the WLC, the original Layer 3 marking is again used by QoS mechanisms in the network infrastructure. Therefore, the edge switches of the wired network trust the QoS marking of the packets from the AP. A similar mechanism operates when packets are sent from the wired network to the wireless clients. With this capability enabled in the Cisco UWN infrastructure, the network can achieve end-to-end QoS for the voice traffic both over the air and across the wired network.

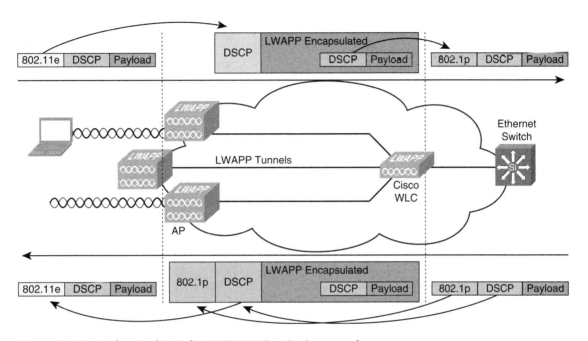

Figure C-12 *End-to-End QoS for VoWLAN Can Be Supported*

Call Admission Control

The Cisco UWN supports call admission control (CAC) to police the call capacity on a per-AP basis. The number of calls on a channel can be limited to a percent of the bandwidth; the remaining bandwidth can be used for data.

The Cisco Unified Communications Manager provides additional CAC features for the wired network, ensuring an end-to-end CAC implementation. Cisco requires the use of Cisco Compatible clients to enable the use of the traffic specification (TSpec) of the traffic flows for the calculation of call limits and proper WLAN load balancing. The TSpec of each voice flow allows the system to allocate bandwidth to client devices on a first-come, first-served basis and maintains a small reserve so that mobile phone clients can roam into a neighboring AP (even though the AP could otherwise be at "full capacity"). When the limit for voice bandwidth is reached, the next call is load balanced to a neighboring AP and the call is completed without affecting the quality of the existing calls on the channel.

Note Earlier names for the Cisco Unified Communications Manager include Cisco CallManager and Cisco Unified CallManager.

With CAC enabled and CCX devices, the Cisco UWN allows the resources to be globally managed by Cisco WLCs across all the adjacent APs. Therefore, APs do not admit the same amount of voice traffic as they could if they were operating in isolation. The number of voice calls on an RF channel is limited to a percentage of the channel bandwidth. A percentage of the bandwidth is reserved to support roaming, and the rest of the bandwidth can be made available for data. APs use measurements from clients and neighboring APs to help determine the amount of traffic on the RF channel and whether a new call should be admitted.

Security

The strict requirements for voice in terms of packet delivery time and predictability, coupled with the ability for clients to roam across APs and subnets (VLANs), presents a challenge to security architectures.

VoWLAN Authentication and Encryption Recommendations

To minimize the delay introduced by authenticating roaming clients, Cisco recommends using EAP-FAST with CCKM.

EAP-FAST is an IEEE 802.1X EAP framework for authentication that encrypts EAP transactions with a Transport Layer Security (TLS) tunnel. The EAP-FAST tunnel is established based upon strong secrets (keys) that are unique to clients. Cisco Unified Wireless IP Phone 7920 clients with firmware release 3.0 or later support EAP-FAST. All Unified Wireless IP Phone 7921G clients support EAP-FAST.

As discussed in the earlier "Roaming" section, CCKM reduces the authentication delay. The alternative is to use an AAA RADIUS server for authentication. With that method, the roaming reauthentication time to the RADIUS server can be 500 ms or more. Cisco recommends using CCKM to achieve AP-to-AP roaming latency of less than 100 ms, allowing the end-to-end latency to be less than 150 ms. CCKM permits the negotiation of a session key from a cached master key and avoids the need to go back to the RADIUS server during a roam. When the client roams, it informs the infrastructure that it has roamed, and the infrastructure forwards the keying information to the new AP.

The efficiency of EAP-FAST with CCKM helps ensure maximum protection with minimum transaction time. CCKM is available with the Unified Wireless IP Phone 7920 and 7921G clients, and any client that is compliant with CCX Version 4.

To ensure that voice traffic is secure, Cisco recommends using TKIP for encryption and using message integrity check (MIC) to ensure that encrypted packets are not being altered. TKIP encrypts both the signaling (Skinny Client Control Protocol [SCCP]) packets and voice (Real-Time Transport Protocol [RTP]) packets between the AP and the wireless IP phone and provides per-packet key ciphering and longer initialization vectors to strengthen encryption. TKIP removes the predictability of the older Wired Equivalent Privacy (WEP) protocol that allows intruders to easily decipher the WEP key.

Other Design Recommendations for VoWLAN Security

For secure voice calls, Cisco recommends creating both separate VLANs and SSIDs for voice. Associating the voice SSID with the voice VLAN creates a single, unified voice network across both the wired and wireless networks with consistent security and QoS profiles; the WLCs bridge the traffic from the voice SSIDs to the voice VLANs. The primary advantage of this physical separation of voice and data traffic is that traffic sent over the voice network is not visible to insiders or outsiders connected to the data network. The converse is also true.

The following are some of the ways that a separate voice VLAN protects the voice system from security threats:

■ **Denial-of-service (DoS) attacks:** Most DoS attacks originate from a PC; PCs cannot affect IP phones and call-processing servers connected to a separate voice VLAN.

■ **Eavesdropping and interception:** Hackers typically eavesdrop on conversations using a PC with special software to connect to the same VLAN as one or more parties in the conversation. If voice participants are logically separated in different VLANs, however, a hacker cannot connect to the voice VLAN with a PC.

■ **Unauthorized access:** Enterprises can apply access control policies to voice VLANs, and authorize employees by their role in the organization to access these VLANs. For example, manufacturing employees may be restricted to accessing only the data segment and not be allowed to access the voice segment.

Note In addition to these voice-specific guidelines, Cisco has published best practices for general wireless security. The paper *Five Steps to Securing Your Wireless LAN and Preventing Wireless Threats* discusses best practices for securing the network from unauthorized use through a WLAN link. These practices should be validated against the risk-management processes of each organization and complemented by a strong security implementation.

This paper is available at available at http://www.cisco.com/en/US/solutions/ns175/networking_solutions_products_genericcontent0900aecd805299d2.html.

Intelligent VoWLAN Clients

To use the voice-ready Cisco infrastructure for enterprise roaming, management, and security features, Cisco recommends the voice clients be either a Unified Wireless IP Phone 7920 or 7921G device or a voice-capable device that supports the advanced voice features through the CCX program.

Note The CCX program is described earlier in this appendix, in the "Cisco-Compatible WLAN Clients" section.

Cisco Unified Wireless IP Phone 7921G

The Unified Wireless IP Phone 7921G, shown in Figure C-13, is a second-generation Cisco wireless IP phone that supports dual-band 802.11A/B/G radios, and has a speaker-phone and a high-resolution color display. It has dedicated volume and mute buttons, and an application button that supports push-to-talk via the Extensible Markup Language (XML). The phone is also compliant with CCX Version 4.

Figure C-13   *The Cisco Unified Wireless IP Phone 7921G*

The 7921G supports a comprehensive list of enterprise wireless security features, including EAP-FAST, TKIP, MIC, and CCKM.

Two types of batteries are available for the phone. The standard lithium-ion (Li-ion) battery provides up to 10 hours of talk time or 80 hours of standby. The extended Li-ion battery provides up to 12 hours of talk time or 100 hours of standby. The actual battery life varies based on environmental factors and the display timeout option selected.

The 7921G supports voice-quality enhancements including 802.11E, TSpec, Enhanced Distributed Channel Access (EDCA), and QoS Basic Service Set (QBSS). Because the

Unified Wireless IP Phone 7921G is designed to grow with system capabilities, features will keep pace with new system enhancements.

The Cisco 7925G Wireless Phone

The Cisco Unified Wireless IP Phone 7925G is built upon the success of the 7921. It is designed for users in rigorous workspaces and general office environments. It supports a wide range of features for enhanced voice communications, QoS), and security. Benefits and highlights include the following:

- IEEE 802.11 A/B/G/ radio

- 2-inch color display

- Bluetooth 2.0 support with Enhanced Data Rate (EDR)

- IP54 rated for protection against dust and splashing water

- MIL-STD-810F standard for shock resistance

- Long battery life (up to 240 hours of standby time or 13 hours of talk time)

- Built-in speakerphone for hands-free operation

- Exceptional voice quality with support for wideband audio

- Support for a wide range of applications through XML

- Hermetically sealed to provide protection against dust and moistureThere is a version of the 7925 (7925 EX) that is certified for deployment in potentially explosive environments such as chemical and manufacturing plants, utilities, and oil refineries. It is certified for use in these environments: Atmospheres Explosibles (ATEX) Zone 2/Class 22 and Canadian Standards Association (CSA) Class I Division II certifications. It includes all of the features above as well.

    For more information on the 7925 EX, go to http://www.cisco.com/en/US/products/ps10649/index.html.

VoWLAN Coverage Considerations

Voice clients are mobile in nature. Users expect that calls will not get dropped as they roam across a building or campus. This expectation means that the network must be deployed pervasively, with continuous coverage in areas where voice services are planned. Areas such as main lobbies; employee entrance areas; parking garages or lots; courtyards; and break, copy, supply, storage, and equipment cage rooms need WLAN coverage when voice clients are deployed on the campus. Additional consideration should be given to providing coverage in stairwells, walkways, and elevators because users have a reasonable expectation of being able to talk on the phone in these areas. Coverage expectations have been established by the cellular network service available. Therefore, WLAN availability and coverage should be significantly more pervasive than the cellular benchmark.

The Cisco UWN provides an extensive product line that satisfies the requirements for pervasive coverage areas, ranging from just one floor of a building to complete campus coverage, for both indoors and outdoors.

A predictable service is also important. Users expect that Wi-Fi phones will, at a minimum, operate with the same quality as a cellular phone and, optimally, with the same quality as a land-line phone. Therefore, the WLAN must minimize interference to optimize call quality. Although many network administrators have already performed RF site surveys for their initial data WLAN deployments, wireless IP phones have somewhat different roaming characteristics and RF coverage requirements than data devices. Therefore, network administrators must perform another site survey for voice to prepare for the performance requirements of wireless IP phones. This additional survey gives network administrators the opportunity to tune the APs to ensure that the wireless IP phones have enough RF coverage and bandwidth to provide proper voice quality. Some of the factors to look at in the survey include signal-to-noise ratio (SNR) and nonoverlapping channel deployment, as described in the following sections.

SNR

Noise is defined as a signal that is not in an IEEE 802.11 format but is in the frequency range of the configured channel for the AP. The noise can originate from devices such as an 802.11 2.4-GHz frequency-hopping radio, a 2.4-GHz or 5-GHz wireless phone, a ham radio, a microwave oven, or a Bluetooth radio. Signals from a distant out-of-network 802.11B/G or 802.11A radio may also be seen as noise. In other words, any signal that the AP cannot decode is considered noise. Noise levels vary from site to site and also within different locations of a site. The noise level affects the ability of a radio to receive data or voice packets.

The SNR is just the ratio of the signal level to the noise level. As illustrated in Figure C-14, because noise levels vary, increasing the signal does not always increase SNR.

If the signal strength of a valid packet is higher than the AP or client radio receiver threshold, the data packet is decoded. The received signal sensitivity value is measured in decibel milliwat (dBm). Most 802.11 radios have a receiver sensitivity value of −94 to −85 dBm at a data rate of 1 Mbps (the lower the dBm value, the better the receiver sensitivity of the radio). Radio receiver sensitivity changes with data rate; for example, an AP radio might have a receiver sensitivity of −94 dBm at 1 Mbps and −84 dBm at 11 Mbps.

The AP discards random traffic, such as valid packets that can be decoded but that are not from clients associated to the AP. Random traffic can originate from shared media or from a client device that is transmitting at a data rate that the AP does not support.

A high data-rate signal needs a larger separation from noise (a larger SNR) than a lower data-rate signal. VoWLANs require higher signal strength and SNR compared to data-only WLANs. Figure C-15 shows recommended SNR values for both data-only cells and VoWLAN cells, for 2.4-GHz WLANs.

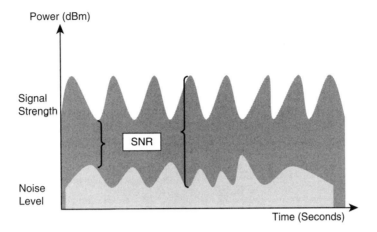

Figure C-14 *Increasing the Signal Does Not Always Increase SNR*

Data Rate (Mbps)	Data Cell		VoWLAN Cell	
	Minimum Signal Strength (dBm)	Minimum SNR (dB)	Minimum Signal Strength (dBm)	Minimum SNR (dB)
54	−71	25	−56	40
36	−73	18	−58	33
24	−77	12	−62	27
11	−82	10	−67	25
6	−89	8	−74	23
2	−91	6	−76	21
1	−94	4	−79	19

Figure C-15 *Recommended SNR Values for 2.4-GHz WLAN Cells*

When designing a VoWLAN deployment, the goal is to target a minimum data rate such as 11 Mbps to improve data throughput, reduce packet delay, and reduce the size of the RF cell. As shown in Figure C-15, the recommended minimum signal strength of −67 dBm and minimum SNR of 25 dB will support a data rate of 11 Mbps.

Figure C-16 shows an example of the signal strength, noise level, and SNR at a specific location within a wireless cell as measured by the Cisco Aironet Desktop Utility (ADU) and a Cisco Aironet IEEE 802.11A/B/G Wireless LAN Client Adapter. The signal strength is −74 dBm, the noise level is −95 dBm, and the SNR is 21 dB. The signal strength value of −74 dBm minus the noise value of −95 dBm equals an SNR of 21 dB as reported by the Cisco ADU.

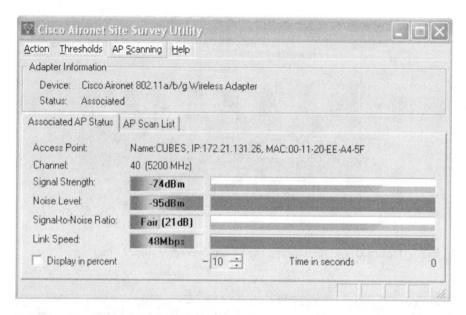

Figure C-16 *Example SNR Display from Cisco Aironet Site Survey Utility*

Because the noise level reported by the Cisco ADU is –95 dBm and the Aironet IEEE 802.11A/B/G Wireless LAN Client Adapter sensitivity at 11 Mbps is –90 dBm, there is a margin of 5 dB at the receiver. The higher the SNR value, the better able the phones are to communicate with the AP.

Nonoverlapping Channels

Because the wireless medium is continuous and shared, all clients that are associated with APs on the same channel share the bandwidth available in that channel, with reception power (and therefore data rates) diminishing with distance.

As mentioned, valid data packets from 802.11b, 802.11G, or 802.11A radios that are not associated to an AP are considered random data traffic. Those packets are decoded by the AP and client devices but are discarded, and therefore increase the channel utilization on the AP and limit the number of voice clients that can associate with the AP. If there are numerous clients in an area, or the supported data applications require significant bandwidth, capacity should be added to the network by using more APs on nonoverlapping channels, to minimize interference.

802.11B/G Channels

As described earlier in the "IEEE 802.11B/G Standards in the 2.4-GHz Band" section, 14 channels are defined for 802.11B/G. Each channel is 22 MHz wide, but the channel separation is only 5 MHz. This leads to channel overlap, and signals from neighboring channels can interfere with each other. In the United States, 11 channels are usable, but only 3 nonoverlapping channels 25 MHz apart are possible: channels 1, 6, and 11. In Europe and Japan, more channels are available, and therefore different nonoverlapping channels can be used (such as 2, 7, and 12, or 1, 7, and 13).

This channel spacing governs the use and allocation of channels in a multi-AP environment, such as an office or campus. As shown earlier, APs are usually deployed in a cellular fashion within an enterprise, with adjacent APs allocated nonoverlapping channels. Alternatively, APs can be collocated using channels 1, 6, and 11; this would for example deliver 33-Mbps bandwidth to a single 802.11B area but only 11 Mbps to a single 802.11B client. A critical issue for voice services is minimizing the co-channel interference (when clients and APs in the same channel interfere with each other) and maximizing coverage and capacity.

Cell Overlap Guidelines

When communicating on one channel, wireless endpoints typically are unaware of traffic and communication occurring on other nonoverlapping channels.

AP coverage should be deployed so that minimal or no overlap occurs between APs configured with the same channel. However, proper AP deployment requires an overlap of 15 percent to 20 percent with adjoining cells (that are on nonoverlapping channels) to ensure smooth roaming for wireless voice endpoints as they move between APs and provide a near-complete redundancy. Overlap of less than 15 percent to 20 percent can result in slower roaming times and poor voice quality, and overlap of more than 15 percent to 20 percent can result in too frequent or constant roaming.

The size of a voice-ready cell is not defined in traditional measurements such as feet or meters; instead, the unit of measurement is the strength or absolute power of the signal. For an ideal voice-ready wireless cell size, the radius or size of each cell should be –67 dBm. This power level can be achieved either in very small physical areas or in cells that are quite large, depending on the RF characteristics of the environment. Separation of 19 dBm for cells on the same channel is recommended. Figure C-17 shows the recommended cell characteristics for a typical 802.11B/G voice deployment.

In a pervasive network, maintaining this policy of nonoverlapping channels requires careful planning to ensure that the network is prepared to support voice services. In general, for office and cubical environments, a convenient guideline to use is that a single cell covers approximately 3000 square feet.

Deploying wireless devices in a multistory building such as an office high-rise or hospital introduces a third dimension to AP and channel reuse planning. As illustrated in Figure C-18, the 802.11B/G 2.4-GHz wave form can pass through floors, ceilings, and walls. For this reason, not only is it important to consider overlapping cells or channels on the same floor, but it is also necessary to consider channel overlap between adjacent floors. With only three channels, proper overlap can be achieved only through careful three-dimensional planning.

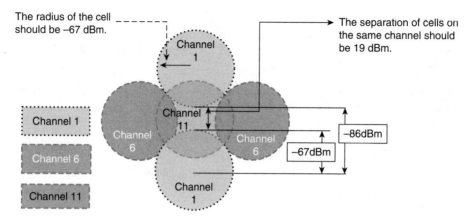

Figure C-17   *802.11B/G Cell Overlap Guidelines*

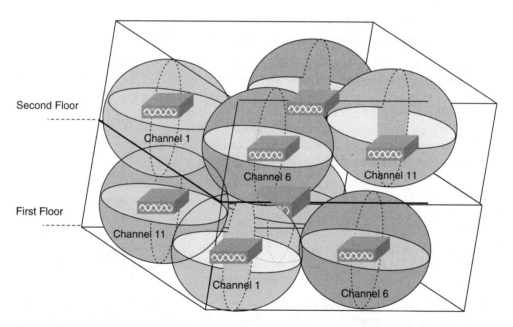

Figure C-18   *802.11B/G Multistory Building Deployments Must Consider Channel Overlap Between Floors*

The RF coverage is mostly dependent on the AP transmitter power and antenna type, and its associated gain and directional beam characteristics. The example in Figure C-18 results from omnidirectional antennas.

802.11A Channels

The majority of enterprises have implemented 802.11B and 802.11G for VoWLAN deployment because of their compatibility and the near ubiquity of those standards in various client devices. More recent deployments are using 802.11A because it can support 12 nonoverlapping channels, significantly more than the 3 nonoverlapping channels that 801.11B/G deployments support. These 12 nonoverlapping channels are described in the earlier "IEEE 802.11A Standard in the 5-GHz Band" section.

An 802.11A WLAN design should provide as much channel separation as possible. Recall that the recommendation is that neighboring cells *not* be placed on neighboring channels (in other words, neighboring channels are skipped) to reduce interference.

As discussed in the earlier "End-to-End QoS" section, separate VLANs for voice and data are recommended, as is keeping the voice and data on separate wireless frequencies if possible. Notable advantages of deploying 802.11A for voice and 802.11B/G for data include the following:

- A significantly greater number of channels are available for higher density deployments. With more channels and a higher approximate throughput, 802.11A AP radios can support up to 14 simultaneous calls.

- The 5-GHz spectrum does not suffer from as much interference from devices such as cordless phones and Bluetooth devices.

- Because the range on the higher frequency radios is generally shorter, the signals do not travel through walls and floors as much as the lower frequency signals do, helping prevent floor-to-floor bleed-through of the signal.

General Recommendations for VoWLANs

This section discusses general recommendations in VoWLAN designs. A site survey is needed to measure these values; site surveys are discussed in the later "VoWLAN Site Surveys" section.

The first step in developing a VoWLAN design is to define and document the coverage areas that will be established and the number of phones to be used in the areas. The design scope should be developed with the target user community so that the appropriate network infrastructure is deployed. The number of phones that will be used in a given area helps determine the transmit power of the clients and AP. The transmit power can be decreased to create smaller coverage cells, which increases the number of APs required and the number of calls supported in a given floor space. 802.11A APs can support more calls than 802.11B and 802.11G APs.

Cisco recommends that a minimum design should use two APs on nonoverlapping channels with 15 percent to 20 percent RF coverage overlap at every location.

The received signal strength indicator (RSSI) will vary with the supported data rate, as follows:

- For data rates of 11 Mbps, the RSSI should be greater than −67 dBm. An AP data rate configuration of 11 Mbps minimum for VoWLAN cells is recommended.

- For data rates of 54 Mbps, the RSSI should be greater than −56 dBm.

The channel utilization QBSS load per AP should be less than 45 percent. The QBSS load represents the percentage of time that the channel is in use by the AP. This channel utilization provides for smoother roaming and a backup AP if one of the APs suddenly becomes unavailable or busy.

The network should maintain a packet error rate (PER) of no higher than 1 percent (which means a success rate of 99 percent). TCP performance and VoIP calls can suffer substantially when the PER increases beyond a value of about 1 percent.

The same transmit power should be used on the AP and on the IP phones so that communication is the same in both directions. If the transmit power of the APs varies, set the transmit power of the phones to the highest transmit power of the APs. If enabled on the AP and supported by the WLAN device, Dynamic Transmit Power Control (DTPC) allows the AP to broadcast its transmit power so that clients can automatically configure themselves to that power while associated with that AP.

All APs should use antenna diversity to provide the best possible throughput by reducing the number of packets that are missed or retried; this is particularly important for voice. With antenna diversity, the AP samples the radio signal from two integrated antenna ports and chooses the preferred antenna. As noted earlier, antenna diversity helps reduce multipath distortion. Some WLAN phones, such as the Cisco Unified Wireless IP Phone 7921G, support antenna diversity.

The maximum number of phones supported per AP depends on the calling patterns of individual users and the AP type. Currently, the recommended call loading for 802.11B and 802.11G is seven active voice calls per AP using the G.711 voice encoding codec or eight active calls using the G.729 codec. These numbers are based on simultaneous requirements for data clients and quality voice calls with current data rates and packet sizes. Beyond the recommended number of active calls, the voice quality of all calls becomes unacceptable if excessive background data is present. In comparison, 802.11A AP radios can support 14 active voice calls using the G.711 codec.

Note A *codec* is a device or software that encodes (and decodes) a signal into digital data stream. The G.711 codec uses the 64-Kbps pulse code modulation (PCM) voice coding technique for standard uncompressed voice. The G.729 codec enables voice to be compressed into 8-Kbps streams, with very good speech quality.

Channel and modulation type determine the number of concurrent calls. If more concurrent phone calls are needed in a high-usage area, more APs must be available. Using overlapping cells (APs sharing the same RF channel) reduces the number of concurrent phone calls per AP.

VoWLAN Site Surveys

An RF site survey is the first step in the design and deployment of a wireless network and is important to ensure desired operation. When building a network designed to support voice services, the site survey and implementation steps are even more important because of the more stringent network and coverage requirements of VoIP. The goal of any site survey should be to gain a total view of the characteristics of the RF environment into which the wireless network will be deployed. Unlicensed frequencies (especially 2.4 GHz, but also 5 GHz,) can be "noisy" environments, with microwave ovens, radar systems, and Bluetooth devices vying for air time. With the advent of emerging RF technologies such as sensor networks, this trend is expected to continue.

Site-Survey Process

Typical steps in an RF site survey include the following:

Step 1.   Define customer requirements, including the devices to support, the locations of wireless devices, and the service levels expected. Peak requirements such as support for conference rooms should also be defined.

Step 2.   Based on the customer requirements, identify planned wireless coverage areas and user density. Obtain a facility diagram to identify the potential RF obstacles. Visually inspect the facility to look for potential barriers to the propagation of RF signals, such as metal racks, elevator shafts, and stairwells. Identify user areas that may be used by many people simultaneously, such as conference rooms, and areas that may only be used for voice, such as stairwells.

Step 3.   Determine preliminary AP locations. These locations must include power and wired network access, and must consider cell coverage and overlap, channel selection, antenna, and mounting locations.

Step 4.   Perform the actual RF site survey to verify the AP locations. Make sure to use the same AP model for the survey that is in use or that will be used in production. While the survey is being performed, relocate APs as needed and retest.

Step 5.   Document the findings, including recording the AP locations and log signal readings and the data rates at outer boundaries.

The site survey should identify areas within the deployment that may require additional capacity because of a concentration of users or the likelihood of co-channel interference.

The site survey should be conducted using the same frequencies as intended for the actual deployment. This provides a more accurate estimate of how a particular channel at a particular location will react to interference and multipath distortion. The site survey should also use the voice client that will be deployed. Each client has a unique RF performance, so different clients will yield different results. The same is true for the radios and external or internal antennas in the infrastructure. In summary, AP and client selection should be finalized before the site survey. As new client devices are added, periodically updating the site survey proactively ensures that the RF network is optimized.

It is also advisable to conduct several site surveys, varying the times and days to ensure that a comprehensive view of the RF domain is obtained. RF activity can vary and depends on many factors, including employee activity. The site survey should identify sources of RF interference and variability in RF patterns due to physical building changes (for example, movement of machinery, and elevators moving in elevator shafts) and employee movements (for example, weekly staff meetings in a conference room).

Spectrum Analysis Tool

The site survey should provide an accurate view of any other RF activity that is present, to help mitigate potential sources of interference. A spectrum analysis tool such as Cognio Spectrum Expert can provide analysis to classify the interference, determine the impact of the interference on the Wi-Fi network, and can enable the administrator to physically locate the source of interference so that appropriate action can be taken. Example output from this tool is provided in Figure C-19.

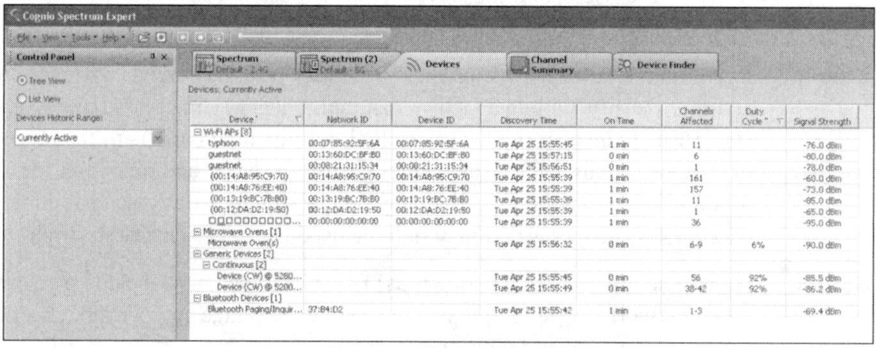

Figure C-19 *Cognio Spectrum Expert Report Regarding 802.11 and Non-802.11 Devices*

WCS Planning Tool

The Cisco UWN integrates Radio Resource Management (RRM) software, which works with the integrated network planning and design features in the Cisco WCS.

Cisco WCS provides integrated RF prediction tools that can be used to create a detailed WLAN design, including AP placement, configuration, and performance or coverage estimates. IT staff can import real floor plans into Cisco WCS and assign RF characteristics to building components to increase the accuracy of the design. The resulting map can help provide a starting point for the location of APs during the site survey and initial estimates on the quantity of APs; an example is provided in Figure C-20. During the final site survey, the actual number and location of APs and associated antennas should be adjusted.

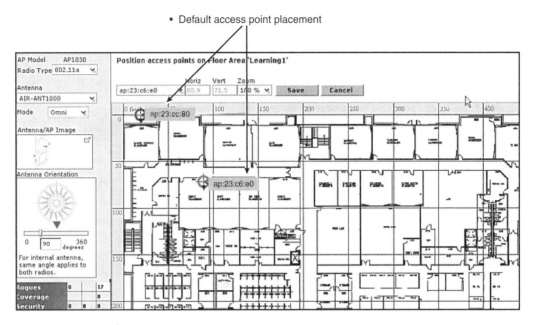

Figure C-20 *Preliminary AP Locations Can Be Predicted Based on the Floor Plan*

The WCS deployment planning tool is ideal for general, open-space office environments. For challenging RF environments, such as those found in hospitals and manufacturing plants, Cisco recommends specialized survey services. In addition, for manual verification of the wireless network, the Cisco Unified Wireless IP Phone 7920 and the Wireless IP Phone 7921G integrate site-survey tools that can display a list of APs that are within range. These tools are useful for validating and troubleshooting specific problem areas.

AP Locations

The location of the APs is the most important characteristic of a voice-ready network.

Traditional Large Cell Deployment

The traditional method of AP deployments recommends deploying APs for greatest range to support data, as illustrated in Figure C-21. However, this approach limits the number of voice calls that can be supported or the data bandwidth per user. Another issue with large cell coverage areas is the lower data rate on VoWLAN clients when users reach the outer edge of a cell. Even though the VoWLAN traffic might have been designed for high data rates, the actual call will receive far less throughput because of the weaker signal, causing a down shift in data rate. An increased cell coverage area also increases the chance of RF interference between the APs and their associated clients.

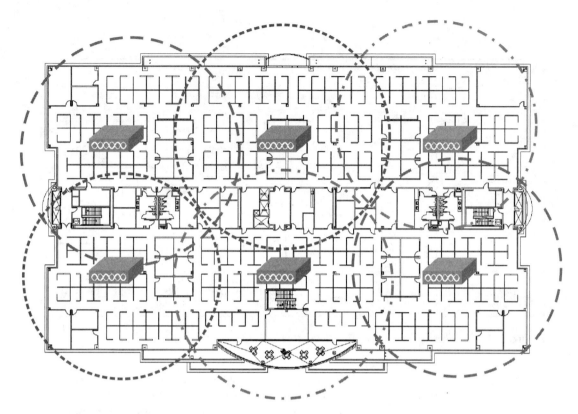

Figure C-21   *Traditional Larger Cells Support Fewer Calls*

Small Cell Deployment for VoWLANs

The voice-services-ready approach to WLANs recommends deploying smaller cell sizes with as many APs as possible to cover a given area without creating excessive interference. Figure C-22 shows an example of such a deployment.

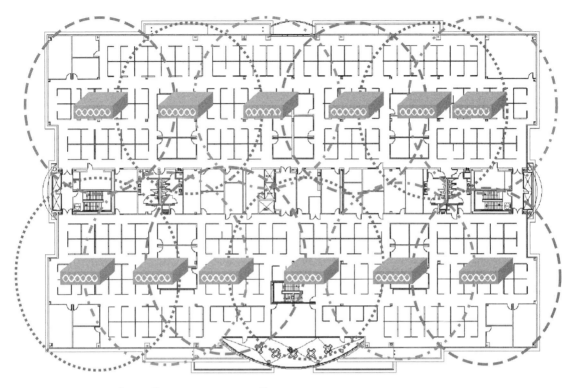

Figure C-22   *Smaller Cells Support More Calls*

Smaller, overlapping cells increase average capacity and provide higher availability in the event of an AP failure. The cell size is estimated based on the requirements for VoWLAN phone call capacities. In dense deployments with many APs, the transmit power of each AP is lowered to limit co-channel interference with neighboring APs. The design should specify the antennas needed and the transmit power required for each of the APs within the site.

Note   It is a good idea to keep the transmit power of the AP and the phone at the same level to avoid one-way audio occurrences, which are a result of a mismatch in the reach of the signal.

As a guideline and starting point for site surveys in a voice-ready WLAN, APs should be deployed approximately every 3000 square feet, versus the recommended AP every 5000 square feet for data-only networks. This AP density helps ensure that voice services have the necessary RF coverage redundancy and throughput required to provide optimal service capacity. The site survey should be conducted to maximize coverage and minimize interference.

Alternative Cell Deployment

An alternative deployment model, shown in Figure C-23, has APs with directional antennas placed around the perimeter of the floor, and APs with omnidirectional antennas staggered in the center of the floor for more complete coverage and greater redundancy, facilitating location tracking and VoWLAN deployment.

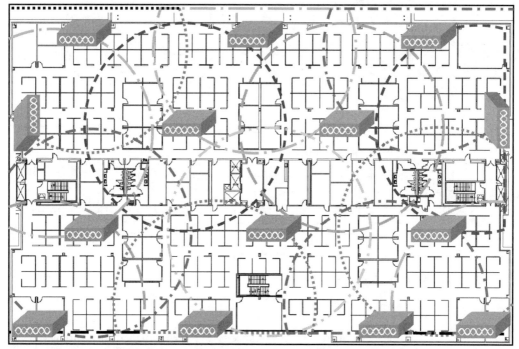

Note: Uses directional antennas at wall. RF extending outside walls is not shown.

Figure C-23 *Alternative Design Includes Perimeter APs with Directional Antennas and Center APs with Omnidirectional Antennas*

This deployment design requires specific placement of APs during the site survey. As a goal, a device at each location on the floor should be able to associate with at least three APs.

This alternative AP deployment facilitates location tracking when combined with the Cisco Wireless Location Appliance along with Cisco WCS for visual maps and reports. The Cisco Wireless Location Appliance performs location computations based on the RSSI information received from the Cisco WLCs. After site floor plans and APs are added to the appliance, RF predictions and heat maps can be generated to graphically display the location of devices on site floor plans. Cisco WCS displays the location information visually, providing an immediate location service for customers who want to enhance their RF capacity management, utilize location-based security, and have asset visibility for WLAN devices.

Conducting a Site Survey

After the requirements are defined, the coverage areas are identified, and the preliminary VoWLAN AP locations are defined, the next step is to conduct the actual RF survey.

When surveying with an existing WLAN or VoWLAN, you should expect that there will be areas to be filled in and changes to be made to existing data rate and transmit power settings and possibly to the antenna types.

At a multifloor site, the coverage survey should also include measurements on the floor above and below the current floor. When doing a manual survey, record the cell edges of the current floor, and then use your survey tool on other floors to measure and record the signal levels. When doing an automated survey, be sure to include the AP on the floors above and below.

When surveying a site without an existing 802.11 network, plan to use two or three APs to measure cell coverage and cell overlap. For example, the cell edge for the Cisco Unified Wireless IP Phone 7920 at an 11-Mbps data rate is −67 dBm. The signal strength at the edge of the cell needs to be 19 dB stronger than the signal from the next cell on the same channel. That means at the −67 dBm edge of the cell, the next cell on the same channel should measure −86 dBm.

Site-Survey Documentation

After completing the RF survey, document the plan for the VoWLAN infrastructure.

The survey documentation should include the following information:

■ Antenna placement and type information for final implementation.

■ Coverage patterns and heat maps for baseline data.

■ Coverage verification information based on at least a two-voice conversation walk-around of all areas. The test should be conducted with known interference sources operational. Document the call results from an analytical tool if available.

■ Coverage area call-capacity test results, for baseline data. For example, you could have seven users make phone calls in a given area and then move apart while placing new calls. Voice quality should be verified during this process.

After conducting an RF site survey and configuring the APs and the phones, it is crucial to conduct verification tests to ensure that everything works as desired. These tests should be performed throughout the VoWLAN coverage area at various times during the day. Tests may include verifying phone association with the appropriate AP and verifying that calls can be placed successfully from the VoWLAN IP phone with acceptable voice quality.

VoWLAN "Steps to Success" Partner Program

VoWLAN coverage and capacity can vary by deployment because of factors such as physical AP placement, building materials, antenna selection, and the type of clients used. In addition, environmental factors such as microwave ovens and cordless phones can also cause interference that may impact VoWLAN performance.

VoWLAN deployments are supported by the Cisco partner Steps to Success program. Cisco partners need both the Cisco Advanced Unified Communications and Advanced Wireless LAN specializations to be authorized to resell Cisco VoWLAN phones. The Steps to Success program provides important templates and tools to assist partners in the proper planning and implementation of WLAN and VoWLAN installations. The following documents are among those accessible with Cisco partner login at the Partner Central Steps to Success home page (at http://www.cisco.com/go/stepstosuccess):

- **Cisco VoWLAN Site Survey Deliverable:** This document provides a template to ensure the proper recording of the survey results of the Cisco VoWLAN site survey. It provides a checklist of all items that need to be considered before a network implementation.

- **VoWLAN Configuration Checklist:** This document provides instructions to help partners apply pertinent configuration information regarding a VoWLAN solution.

- **VoWLAN Design Checklist:** This document provides a checklist template to help partners apply pertinent design information regarding a VoWLAN solution.

- **Voice over Wireless LAN High-Level Design for the Cisco VoWLAN Phone:** This document provides required specifications for availability, capacity, and security that will meet the defined service requirements.

These documents help minimize the chance of an improperly or insufficiently designed VoWLAN. As part of the program, the assessment-to-quality VoWLAN team reviews each order to ensure that the proposed solution and partner meet the published and current Cisco VoWLAN standards. The team may also help identify potential problem areas and suggest solutions as appropriate.

Summary

In this appendix, you learned about the Cisco UWN, and the requirements, infrastructure considerations, and coverage considerations for enterprise VoWLAN deployments.

WLAN signals are in the range of −60 dBm to −80 dBm and are transmitted using antennas. Omnidirectional antennas, with radiant energy shaped like a doughnut, are the most widely used today.

The IEEE 802.11A, B, and G WLAN standards are half-duplex connections, using the CSMA/CA algorithm. 802.11A operates at 5 GHz with a maximum speed of 54 Mbps; 802.11B operates at 2.4 GHz with a maximum speed of 11 Mbps; and 802.11G operates at 2.4 GHz with a maximum speed of 54 Mbps. 802.11E adds QoS to WLANs.

In North America, the 2.4-GHz band has three nonoverlapping channels: channels 1, 6, and 11. Adjacent cells should use nonoverlapping channels.

802.11A has 12 nonoverlapping channels. The recommendation for 802.11A is that neighboring cells not be placed on neighboring channels (in other words, neighboring channels are skipped) to reduce interference.

A computer with a wireless NIC and other wireless devices, such as VoWLAN phones, connect to the wired LAN through an AP. CCX-compliant clients are compatible with Cisco APs. Cisco APs can be either autonomous or lightweight.

An autonomous AP has a local configuration and requires local management.

A lightweight AP receives control and configuration from a WLC to which it is associated. The WLCs and lightweight APs communicate over a wired network using the LWAPP. The WLCs are responsible for putting the wireless client traffic into the appropriate VLAN.

The Cisco UWN elements are CCX WLAN clients, lightweight APs, network unification, network management, and mobility services.

VoWLAN deployment requires a network with continuous coverage, an end-to-end transmit time of less than 150 ms, and QoS to reduce delay and jitter. The Cisco voice-ready architecture includes VoWLAN clients, a voice-ready WLAN, a unified wired or wireless LAN infrastructure, and Cisco Unified Communications and mobility applications.

Voice implications for WLANs include the following:

- RF coverage requirements and deployment planning
- Network infrastructure and logical subnet design, including roaming, QoS, security, and the use of intelligent clients
- Wireless "over-the-air" QoS
- Network security architecture
- VoWLAN client requirements

An SSID is the identifier (or name) of an ESA, creating a WLAN. Roaming occurs when a wireless client moves from being associated to one AP to another AP within the same SSID.

Intracontroller roaming is roaming between APs joined to the *same* WLC. The WLC just updates the client database with the new associated AP.

Intercontroller roaming occurs when a client roams from an AP joined to one WLC to an AP joined to a different WLC. The WLCs must be in the same mobility group. Layer 2 intercontroller roaming occurs when the client traffic is bridged to the same IP subnet. The client database entry is moved to the new WLC. Layer 3 intercontroller roaming occurs when the client associates to an AP on a different WLC and the traffic is bridged to a different IP subnet. The original WLC marks the entry for the client in its own client database with an Anchor entry, and copies the database entry to the new WLC's client database, where it is marked with a Foreign entry.

The Cisco UWN supports CAC to police the call capacity on a per-AP basis.

Recommendations for VoWLAN deployment include the following:

- Use the EAP-FAST with CCKM for authentication.

- Use TKIP for encryption and using MIC to ensure that encrypted packets are not being altered.

- Use separate voice and data VLANs and keep the voice and data on separate wireless frequencies if possible. For secure voice calls, Cisco recommends creating both separate VLANs and SSIDs for voice.

- An overlap of 15 percent to 20 percent between adjoining cells (that are on nonoverlapping channels).

- A cell radius of −67 dBm, with a separation of 19 dBm for cells on the same channel.

- A channel utilization QBSS load per AP of less than 45 percent.

- A PER of no higher than 1 percent on the network.

- Use the same transmit power on the AP and the IP phones.

- Use antenna diversity on all APs.

- Have a maximum of 7 active voice calls per AP using the G.711 voice encoding codec or 8 active calls using the G.729 codec for 802.11B/G, and have a maximum of 14 active voice calls using the G.711 codec for 802.11A.

Typical steps in an RF site survey process include the following:

Step 1.   Define customer requirements.

Step 2.   Identify coverage areas and user density.

Step 3.   Determine preliminary AP locations.

Step 4.   Perform the actual RF site survey.

Step 5.   Document the findings.

A possible deployment model for VoWLANs has APs with directional antennas placed around the perimeter of a floor, and APs with omnidirectional antennas staggered in the center of the floor.

The Cisco partner Steps to Success program provides templates and tools to assist partners in the proper planning and implementation of WLAN and VoWLAN installations.

References

For additional information, refer to the following:

Cisco Systems, Inc. *Design Principles for Voice over WLAN* at http://www.cisco.com/en/US/solutions/collateral/ns340/ns394/ns348/net_implementation_white_paper0900aecd804f1a46.html

Cisco Systems, Inc. *Cisco Unified Wireless IP Phone 7925 Design and Deployment Guide* at http://www.cisco.com/en/US/docs/voice_ip_comm/cuipph/7925g/7_0/english/deployment/guide/7925dply.pdf

Cisco Systems, Inc. *Cisco/Linksys SMB Product Differentiation FAQs* at http://www.cisco.com/web/partners/downloads/765/sell/product_faq.pdf

Cisco Systems, Inc. *Cisco Unified Wireless IP Phone 7920 Design and Deployment Guide* at http://www.cisco.com/en/US/docs/voice_ip_comm/cuipph/7920/5_0/english/design/guide/7920ddg.html

Cisco Systems, Inc. *Five Steps to Securing Your Wireless LAN and Preventing Wireless Threats* at http://www.cisco.com/web/SE/assets/pdfs/smb/cdccont_0900aecd804909a5.pdf

Cisco Systems, Inc. Cisco Compatible Extensions program website at http://www.cisco.com/web/partners/pr46/pr147/partners_pgm_concept_home.html

Cisco Systems, Inc., *Cisco Compatible Client Devices* at http://www.cisco.com/web/partners/pr46/pr147/partners_pgm_partners_0900aecd800a7907.html

Cisco Systems, Inc. Cisco Wireless Control System home page at http://www.cisco.com/en/US/products/ps6305/index.html

Cisco Systems, Inc. *Cisco 7925G Q&A* at http://www.cisco.com/en/US/prod/collateral/voicesw/ps6788/phones/ps379/ps9900/q_a_c67-504099.html

Review Questions

Answer the following questions, and then refer to Appendix A, "Answers to Review Questions," for the answers.

1. Select the device through which a client with a wireless NIC connects to the wired network.

   a. WLC

   b. AP

   c. Switch

   d. WCS

2. Match the standards with the frequency at which they operate.

Standard:

- 802.11A
- 802.11B
- 802.11G

Frequency:

- 2.4 GHz
- 2.4 GHz
- 5 GHz

3. Which of the following are the nonoverlapping 2.4-GHz channels used in North America?

    a. 1

    b. 2

    c. 4

    d. 5

    e. 6

    f. 10

    g. 11

    h. 12

4. What is the recommendation for reuse of 802.11A cells?

5. For a given area, select the true statement regarding the number of APs required by 802.11A versus 802.11B/G to provide the same coverage.

    a. 802.11A requires fewer APs on a per-area basis than 802.11B/G.

    b. 802.11A requires more APs on a per-area basis than 802.11B/G.

    c. 802.11A requires the same number of APs on a per-area basis as 802.11B/G.

6. What is the difference between an autonomous AP and a lightweight AP?

7. What is CCX?

8. What is an SSID?

9. Which of the following are elements of the Cisco UWN?

    a. Client devices

    b. Lightweight APs

    c. Autonomous APs

    d. Network management

    e. Mobility services

10. In the Cisco UWN, which device is responsible for putting the wireless client traffic into the appropriate VLAN?

11. How is a WLC connected to an AP?

    a. Via an 802.11A connection

    b. Via an 802.11B/G connection

    c. Via a wired connection

    d. Via an IPsec tunnel

12. What are some of the advantages of VoWLAN deployments?

13. What are some of the requirements that voice adds to a WLAN deployment?

14. Name the four main components of the Cisco voice-ready architecture.

15. Select the three true statements about roaming.

    a. Roaming occurs when a wireless client re-associates to different AP, within the same SSID.

    b. Roaming occurs when a wireless client re-associates to different AP, using a different SSID.

    c. Intracontroller roaming is roaming between APs associated to different WLCs.

    d. Intracontroller roaming is roaming between APs associated to the same WLC.

    e. Intercontroller roaming is roaming between APs associated to different WLCs.

    f. Intercontroller roaming is roaming between APs associated to the same WLC.

16. What does a WLC do with the client entries in its client database for Layer 3 and Layer 2 intercontroller roaming?

17. Which IEEE standard adds QoS features to WLANs?

    a. 802.11A

    b. 802.11D

    c. 802.11E

    d. 802.11I

    e. 802.11J

18. True or false: Separate voice and data VLANs are recommended when using WLANs.

19. What does CAC do?

20. Which protocols are recommended for authentication and encryption when using VoWLAN? (Choose two.)

    a. EAP-FAST with CCKM

    b. AAA RADIUS

    c. TKIP and MIC

    d. WEP

21. What is the recommended signal strength and SNR for a 2.4-GHz WLAN at 11 Mbps?

    a. Signal strength 40 dB and SNR –56 dBm

    b. Signal strength –56 dBm and SNR 40 dB

    c. Signal strength –67 dBm and SNR 25 dB

    d. Signal strength 25 dB and SNR –67 dBm

    e. Signal strength –79 dBm and SNR 19 dB

    f. Signal strength 19 dB and SNR –79 dBm

22. What is the recommended cell overlap for VoWLAN deployments?

    a. 5 percent to 10 percent

    b. 10 percent to 15 percent

    c. 15 percent to 20 percent

    d. 20 percent to 25 percent

23. What is the recommended size of a voice-ready 802.11B/G wireless cell? What is the recommended separation for cells on the same channel?

24. Select the recommended maximum number of active voice calls per AP on an 802.11B/G WLAN. (Choose two.)

    a. 3 per AP when using G.711

    b. 4 per AP when using G.729

    c. 7 per AP when using G.711

    d. 8 per AP when using G.729

    e. 10 per AP when using G.711

    f. 15 per AP when using G.729

25. List the five typical steps in an RF site-survey process.

Index

Numerics

A

C

Q

W-X-Y-Z

W-X-Y-Z

CISCO

ciscopress.com: Your Cisco Certification and Networking Learning Resource

Subscribe to the monthly Cisco Press newsletter to be the first to learn about new releases and special promotions.

Visit **ciscopress.com/newsletters.**

While you are visiting, check out the offerings available at your finger tips.

–Free Podcasts from experts:
  · OnNetworking
  · OnCertification
  · OnSecurity

Podcasts

View them at **ciscopress.com/podcasts.**

–Read the latest author **articles** and **sample chapters** at ciscopress.com/articles.

–Bookmark the Certification Reference Guide available through our partner site at **informit.com/certguide.**

Connect with Cisco Press authors and editors via Facebook and Twitter, visit informit.com/socialconnect.

Published by Collins
An imprint of HarperCollins Publishers
Westerhill Road
Bishopbriggs
Glasgow G64 2QT

HarperCollins Publishers
1st Floor, Watermarque Building
Ringsend Road, Dublin 4, Ireland

Sixth Edition 2022

10 9 8 7 6 5 4 3 2 1

© HarperCollins Publishers 2004, 2005,
2006, 2007, 2011, 2015, 2019, 2022

ISBN 978-0-00-852388-6

Collins® is a registered trademark of
HarperCollins Publishers Limited

© 2022 Mattel. SCRABBLE™ and
SCRABBLE tiles, including S1 tiles,
are trademarks of Mattel.

www.collins.co.uk/scrabble

Typeset by Davidson Publishing Solutions,
Glasgow

Printed and bound by Replika Press

The contents of this publication are
believed correct at the time of printing.
Nevertheless the Publisher can accept no
responsibility for errors or omissions,
changes in the detail given or for any
expense or loss thereby caused.

HarperCollins does not warrant that any
website mentioned in this title will be
provided uninterrupted, that any website
will be error free, that defects will be
corrected, or that the website or the server
that makes it available are free of viruses or
bugs. For full terms and conditions please
refer to the site terms provided on the
website.

A catalogue record for this book is available
from the British Library.

If you would like to comment on any aspect
of this book, please contact us at the given
address or online.
E-mail: puzzles@harpercollins.co.uk
facebook.com/collinsdictionary
@collinsdict

CW00969736

Collins

OFFICIAL

SCRABBLE™

WORDS

Contents

Editor
Mary O'Neill

Computing Support
Agnieszka Urbanowicz

For the Publisher
Gerry Breslin
Kerry Ferguson

Rules for the Scrabble word list

- Only includes words of between 2 and 15 letters in length

- Does not include proper nouns, place names, and words with an initial capital letter, unless such words can also be spelt with a lower-case initial letter

- Does not include abbreviations, prefixes, suffixes, words requiring apostrophes or hyphens

- Includes foreign words that are considered to have been absorbed into the English language

- Includes inflected forms, such as plurals and verb forms, eg plumb, plumbs, plumbed, plumbing

- Includes words that are old, obsolete, dialectal, historical and/or literary

- Includes World English, including spelling and variants from the US, South Africa, Australia, New Zealand, etc

- Includes words that are denoted contractions, short forms and slang

- Includes words that may be deemed rude or derogatory

Disclaimer
While every effort has been made to exclude words in the category of hate speech, no other word is excluded on the grounds of religion, gender, race, or for any reason other than that it is an invalid word form for the game of Scrabble. The presence or exclusion of any word does not in any way represent the views of the Publisher, HarperCollins.

Other Scrabble resources

Associations

World English-Language Scrabble Players Association (WESPA) –
www.wespa.org

The WESPA website also provides access to resources for national associations, tournament organizers, players and youth players.

Association of British Scrabble Players (ABSP) – www.absp.org.uk

The ABSP website includes details of UK Scrabble clubs and UK tournaments.

North American Scrabble Players Association (NASPA) –
www.scrabbleplayers.org

The NASPA website contains numerous word lists and lists of further Scrabble resources.

Facebook

Several Scrabble groups, including:

World English-Language Scrabble Players Association

Scrabble International

Scrabble Snippetz

Collins Scrabble Players